TAKING SIDES

Clashing Views in

Adolescence

THIRD EDITION

D0060834

TAKING SIDES

Clashing Views in

Adolescence

THIRD EDITION

Selected, Edited, and with Introductions by

Toni Serafini
St. Jerome's University at the University of Waterloo

B.J. Rye
St. Jerome's University at the University of Waterloo

and

Maureen T.B. Drysdale
St. Jerome's University at the University of Waterloo

Higher Education

TAKING SIDES: CLASHING VIEWS IN ADOLESCENCE, THIRD EDITION

Published by McGraw-Hill, a business unit of The McGraw-Hill Companies, Inc., 1221 Avenue of the Americas, New York, NY 10020. Copyright © 2013 by The McGraw-Hill Companies, Inc. All rights reserved. Printed in the United States of America. Previous editions © 2009 and 2007. No part of this publication may be reproduced or distributed in any form or by any means, or stored in a database or retrieval system, without the prior written consent of The McGraw-Hill Companies, Inc., including, but not limited to, in any network or other electronic storage or transmission, or broadcast for distance learning.

Some ancillaries, including electronic and print components, may not be available to customers outside the United States.

This book is printed on acid-free paper.

Taking Sides® is a registered trademark of the McGraw-Hill Companies, Inc.
Taking Sides is published by the **Contemporary Learning Series** group within the McGraw-Hill Higher Education division.

1 2 3 4 5 6 7 8 9 0 DOC/DOC 1 0 9 8 7 6 5 4 3 2

MHID: 0-07-805019-7
ISBN: 978-0-07-805019-0
ISSN: 1933-0499

Managing Editor: *Larry Loeppke*
Marketing Director: *Adam Kloza*
Marketing Manager: *Nathan Edwards*
Senior Developmental Editor: *Jade Benedict*
Senior Content Licensing Specialist: *DeAnna Dausener*
Project Manager: *Erin Melloy*
Cover Designer: *Rick Noel*
Buyer: *Jennifer Pickel*
Media Project Manager: *Sridevi Palani*

Compositor: MPS Limited
Cover Image: © Digital Vision Ltd/Getty Images RF

Editors/Academic Advisory Board

Members of the Academic Advisory Board are instrumental in the final selection of articles for each edition of TAKING SIDES. Their review of articles for content, level, and appropriateness provides critical direction to the editors and staff. We think that you will find their careful consideration well reflected in this volume.

TAKING SIDES: Clashing Views in ADOLESCENCE

Third Edition

EDITORS

Toni Serafini
St. Jerome's University at the University of Waterloo

B.J. Rye
St. Jerome's University at the University of Waterloo

Maureen T.B. Drysdale
St. Jerome's University at the University of Waterloo

Preface

Adolescence is a critical developmental period in everyone's life. In order for us to become adults, we have to "survive" adolescence. For some, this stage of life is characterized by "storm-and-stress," while others glide through the transition unscathed. Most of us have some fond memories of pleasant and exciting experiences coupled with recollections of embarrassing and awkward experiences. Some events that occur during adolescence are universal—such as puberty, physical growth, and psychological maturation—whereas other phenomena are a function of environmental forces—such as cultural context, family structure, school organization, and peer group practices.

How do these different forces and contexts influence the development of adolescents in western society today? The purpose of this book is to examine some of the issues that may have an impact on adolescents in a didactic, dialectic fashion. To this end, *Taking Sides: Clashing Views in Adolescence* has been developed to foster critical and incisive thinking about issues that may have a significant impact on adolescent development in the twenty-first century. We have included interdisciplinary writings (e.g., from psychology, sociology, medicine, law, and religious studies domains) representing issues relevant to the period of adolescence in developed "western" societies (e.g., Australia, Canada, and the United States). *Taking Sides: Clashing Views in Adolescence* presents yes/no perspectives in response to 18 questions. Consequently, 36 lively selections written by opponents who sit on different sides of the various topics under consideration are included. Each issue involves:

- A *question* that attempts to capture the essence of the debate.
- An *introduction* whereby information is presented that can be used by the reader as a background to the issue. Also available is some information about the selection authors of the debate as this may help to explain the perspective from which the writer comes.
- Two *selections* where one supports the yes side of the controversy while the other speaks to the no side of the question.
- An *Exploring the Issue* section that presents additional information, which may help to elucidate the issue further, raises additional and thought-provoking questions, and synthesizes the two authors' perspectives.

It is important to note that no issue is truly binary. There are always "gray" areas that fall in between the yes and the no perspectives. The *Recommended Readings* section provides more references for the interested individual; some readers will wish to delve into particular topics in greater detail. This section was included to give some additional direction for that purpose. At the end of the book, the *Contributors to This Volume* provides information about each selection author. A person's training, career track, and life situation colors her/his perspective on any issue; no one is completely objective. Also, the *Internet References* presents some useful website addresses (URLs) that are relevant to the issues discussed in each part. As you read the different perspectives, you may find that you disagree with one side or both viewpoints. Regardless, it is important to read each selection carefully and critically and respect the opinions of others. The format of this textbook necessarily challenges the reader to face her or his own biases, beliefs, and values about the controversial topics presented. Two of the most important tools that a student can develop in her or his scholarly pursuits are (1) to be able to keep an open mind such that you may consider dissenting views while respecting the opinions of those who disagree with your perspective and (2) to become a critical thinker and evaluate arguments from many different angles and viewpoints. We encourage you to challenge your own perspective so that you can develop these crucial skills.

A word to the instructor An *Instructor's Resource Guide*, with issue synopses, suggestions for classroom discussion, and test questions (multiple choice and essay), is available from McGraw-Hill/Contemporary Learning Series. A general guidebook, *Using Taking Sides in the Classroom*, which discusses methods and techniques for integrating the pro/con approach into any classroom setting, is also available. An online version of *Using Taking Sides in the Classroom* and a correspondence service for *Taking Sides* adopters can be found at www.mhcls.com/usingts.

Taking Sides: Clashing Views in Adolescence is one of the many titles in the Taking Sides series. If you are interested in seeing the table of contents for any of the other titles, please visit the Taking Sides website at www.mhcls.com/takingsides.

Acknowledgments

First, and foremost, we would like to thank our families for their patience (again) with us during this third Taking Sides project. Thanks to Fraser Drysdale, Mallory Drysdale, Adam Drysdale, Megan Drysdale, Bryce Daigle, Judy Helperin, Scott Campbell Rye, Peter Campbell Rye, Barbara Campbell, Donald Campbell, Andrzej Izdebski, Dino Serafini, Rita Serafini, Franca Serafini, and Vicki Baer. Your unconditional support during this third edition is greatly appreciated.

For expert assistance with researching, editing, and fine tuning issues 1, 16, 17, and 18, we wish to express our heart-felt thanks to Adam Drysdale. We also thank Megan Drysdale, Judy Lui, Margaret McBeath, Alisha Pol, and Mackenzie Turow for their assistance and contributions to this book.

Thanks also goes to Jade Benedict at McGraw-Hill for working with us on this project.

In short, thank you to the rich network of colleagues, friends, and family who helped us at various stages of this project. Your support was and is greatly appreciated!

Toni Serafini
St. Jerome's University at the University of Waterloo

B.J. Rye
St. Jerome's University at the University of Waterloo

Maureen T.B. Drysdale
St. Jerome's University at the University of Waterloo

The Educational Experience of Disciplinary Controversy*

BRENT D. SLIFE

Brigham Young University

As a long-time user of the *Taking Sides* books, I have seen first-hand their educational impact on students. A student we will call "Brittany" is a prime example. Until her role in a *Taking Sides'* panel discussion, she had not participated once in class discussions. It is probably fair to say that she was sleepwalking through the course. However, once she was assigned to a "side" of the panel discussion, she vigorously pitched in "to do battle," as she put it, with the opposing team. She described a "kind of energy" as she and the rest of her team prepared for the upcoming debate. In fact, she found herself and her teammates "talking trash" good-naturedly with the opposing team before the actual discussion, despite her usual reserve. Because she wanted to win, she "drilled down" and even did extra research.

The panel discussion itself, she reported, was exhilarating, but what I noticed afterward was probably the most intriguing. Not only did she participate in class more frequently, taking more risks in class discussions because she knew her teammates would support her, she also found herself having a position from which to see other positions in the discipline. Somehow, as she explained, her advocating a particular position on the panel, even though she knew I had arbitrarily assigned it, gave her a stake in other discussions and a perspective from which to contribute to them. Brittany's experience nicely illustrates the unique educational impact of the *Taking Sides* series.

Taking Sides is designed quite intentionally to shore up some of the weaknesses of many contemporary educational settings. The unique energy that Brittany experienced is a result of *Taking Sides'* specific focus on the controversial side of academic disciplines. For several good reasons, instructors and textbooks have traditionally focused almost exclusively on the more factual or settled aspects of their disciplines. This focus has led, in turn, to educational strategies that can rob the subject matter of its vitality.

Taking Sides, on the other hand, is uniquely structured to highlight the more issue-oriented aspects of a discipline, allowing students to care about and even invest in the subject matter as did Brittany. Involvement can spur a deeper understanding of the topic and help students to appreciate how knowledge advancement is sometimes driven by passionate positions.

*The full text of this essay and references are available online at: http://highered.mcgraw-hill.com/sites/0076667771/ information_center_view0/

Including the Controversial

A case could be made that a complete understanding of any discipline includes its controversies. Controversies may not be considered "knowledge" per se, depending on the discipline, but there is surely no doubt that they are part of the process of advancing knowledge. The conflicts generated among disciplinary leaders often produce problem-solving energy, if not disciplinary passions. In fact, they can drive entire disciplinary conferences and whole programs of investigation. In this sense, disciplinary controversies are not just "error" or an indication of the absence of knowledge; they can be viewed as a positive part of the discipline, a generator of disciplinary vigor if not purpose.

If this is true, then de-emphasizing the controversial elements of a discipline is de-emphasizing a vital part of the discipline itself. Students may learn accepted aspects of the discipline, but they may not learn, at least directly, the disputed aspects. This de-emphasis may not only produce an incomplete or inaccurate sense of the discipline, but it may also mislead the student to understand the field as more sterile, less emotional, and less "messy" than it truly is. The more rational, factual side is clearly important, perhaps even more important. The question, however, is: Do these more settled and perhaps rational aspects of the discipline have to monopolize courses for beginning students?

Another way to put the question might be: Couldn't some portion of the course be devoted to the more controversial, thus allowing the student to engage the field in a more emotional manner? In some sense, the more settled and accepted the information is, the less students can feel they are truly participating in the disciplinary enterprise. After all, this information is already decided; there is no room for involvement in developing and "owning" the information. Students may even assume they will be punished for challenging the disciplinary status quo.

Specific Educational Benefits

Engaging the Discipline. When controversy is placed in the foreground of an educational experience, it gives disciplinary novices (students) permission to participate in and perhaps even form their own positions on some of the issues in the field. After all, some issues have not been addressed; some problems have not been solved. As Brittany put it, she was ready to "do battle" with the alternative position, even though she was quite aware of the arbitrariness of her own positional assignment. She was aware that something was at stake; something was to be decided.

In other words, it is the very *lack* of resolution in a controversy that invites students to make sense of the issues themselves and perhaps even venture their own thoughts. Obviously, students should be encouraged to be humble about these positions, understanding that their perspective is fledgling, but even novice positions can facilitate greater engagement with the materials. In a sense, the controversy, and thus a vital part of the discipline, becomes their own, as the example of Brittany illustrates. She not only "owned" a disciplinary position, she used it as a conceptual bridge to engage other settled and unsettled aspects of the discipline.

Appreciating the Messy. Students can also experience the messiness of disciplines using *Taking Sides*. I use the term "messiness" because conventional texts are notorious for representing the field too neatly and too logically, as if there were no human involvement. If disciplines are more than their settled aspects, there are also unsettled elements, including poorly defined terms and inadequately understood concepts, which also need to be appreciated. This messiness is what led Brittany to "drill down" and do "extra research" in her preparation for her panel discussion. She knew that some of the basic terms and understandings were at play.

Good conventional texts may attempt to include these unsettled aspects, but they typically do so in a deceptively logical fashion, as though the controversy is solely rational. This presentation may not only distort these aspects of the discipline but also deliver merely a secondhand report. By contrast, *Taking Sides* books—in pitting two authors against one another—facilitate an *experience* with actual published authorities, who are struggling with the issues from completely different perspectives. In reading both articles, students cannot help but struggle *with* the authors. They do not need to be *told* that the terms of the debate are problematic; the students *experience* these terms as problematic when they attempt to understand what is at stake in the authors' positions.

Preventing Premature Closure. The *Taking Sides* structure also serves to prevent students from prematurely closing controversies. Premature closure can occur by underestimating the controversy's depth or deciding it without a proper appreciation for the issues involved. *Taking Sides* prevents this prematurity by helping the student to experience how two reasonable and highly educated people can so thoroughly disagree. In other words, premature closure is discouraged because real experts are countering each other, sometimes point by point.

A student would almost have to ignore one side of the controversy, one of the experts, to prematurely close the issue. Brittany, for example, reported that she became "absolutely convinced" of the validity of the first authors' position, only to have the second reading put this position into question! Obviously, if the issue could be closed or settled so easily, presumably the experts or leaders of the discipline would have done so already. Controversies are controversies because they are *deeply* problematic, so it is important for the student to appreciate this, and thus have a more profound understanding of the disciplinary meanings involved.

Rehabilitating the Dialectic. One of the truly unique benefits of the *Taking Sides* experience is its rehabilitation of the age-old educational tradition of the dialectic. Since at least the time of Socrates, educators have understood that a *full* understanding of any disciplinary meaning, explanation, or bit of information requires not only knowing what this meaning or information is but also knowing what it isn't. The dialectic, in this sense, is the educational relation of a concept to its alternative (see Rychlak, 2003). As dialectician Joseph Rychlak (1991) explains, all meanings "reach beyond themselves" and are thus clarified and have implications beyond their synonyms. It may be trivial to note, for example, that one cannot fully comprehend what "up" means without understanding what "down" means. However, this dialectic is not trivial when the meanings are disciplinary, such as when the political science student realizes that justice is incomprehensible without some apprehension of the meaning of injustice.

One of the more fascinating educational moments, when using *Taking Sides* books, occurs when students recognize that they cannot properly understand even one side of the controversy without taking into account another side. Brittany described learning very quickly that she clarified and even became aware of important aspects of her own position only after she understood the alternative to her position. This dialectical awareness is also pivotal to truly critical thinking.

Facilitating Critical Thinking. I say "truly" critical thinking because critical thinking has sometimes been confused with rigorous thinking (see Slife et al, 2005). Rigorous thinking is the application of rigorous reasoning or analytical thinking to a particular problem, which is surely an important skill in most any field. Still, it is not truly *critical* thinking until one has an alternative perspective from which to criticize a perspective. Recall that Brittany did not participate in class until she developed a perspective to view other perspectives. In other words, one must have a (critical) perspective "outside of" or alternative to the perspective being critiqued. Otherwise, one is "inside" the perspective being critiqued and cannot "see" it as a whole.

As many recent educational formulations of critical thinking attest, this approach means that critical thinkers should develop at least a dialectic of perspectives (one plus an alternative). That is to say, they should have an awareness of their own perspective as *facilitated by* an understanding of at least one alternative perspective. Without an alternative, students assume either they have no position or their position is the *only* one possible. A point of comparison, on the other hand, prevents the reification of one's perspective and allows students to have a perspective on their perspectives. A clear strength of the *Taking Sides'* juxtaposition of alternative perspectives is that it facilitates this kind of critical thinking.

These five benefits—engaging the discipline, appreciating the messy, preventing premature closure, rehabilitating the dialectic, and facilitating critical thinking—are probably not exclusive to controversy. However, they are, I would contend, a relatively unique *package* of educational advantages that students can gain with the inclusion of a *Taking Sides'* approach in the classroom. Controversy, of course, is rarely helpful on its own; settled information and sound reasoning must buttress and perhaps even ground controversy. Otherwise, it is more heat than light. Even so, an *exclusive* focus on the settled and more cognitive aspects can deprive students of the vitality of a discipline and prevent the ownership of information that is so important to real learning.

Contents In Brief

Contents

UNIT 1 ADOLESCENT HEALTH 1

E. Jane Garland, a clinical professor of psychiatry at the University of British Columbia, Stan Kutcher, a professor of psychiatry at Dalhousie University, and Adil Virani, an assistant professor of pharmaceutical sciences at the University of British Columbia, reviewed numerous randomized double-blind, placebo-controlled trials regarding the role selective serotonin reuptake inhibitors (SSRIs) for the treatment of depression and anxiety in children and youth. They conclude that the risk–benefit balance for fluoxetine is favorable in depression, and the risk–benefit balance for three SSRIs is favorable in anxiety disorders. Tamar D. Wohlfarth, a clinical assessor, and colleagues in the Netherlands assessed antidepressant use in pediatric patients and reported an increased risk for events related to suicidality among those taking antidepressants. They caution the use of all SSRIs and NSRIs (norepinephrine or noradrenergic serotonin reuptake inhibitors) in the pediatric population.

Marita P. McCabe, chair of psychology at Deakin University in Australia, Lina A. Ricciardelli, associate professor, School of Psychology at Deakin University, and Kate Holt, a researcher in psychology at Deakin examined gender differences in overweight and normal-weight adolescents and found that boys and girls were equally dissatisfied with their bodies, but that boys had higher ratings of body importance than did girls. For overweight boys, but not girls, body dissatisfaction (along with peer and parental pressure) predicted weight-loss strategies. This focus on weight loss is consistent with previous research on adolescent girls, but atypical of research with boys. Using data from the National Longitudinal Study of Adolescent Health, Anastasia S. Vogt Yuan, associate professor in the Department of Sociology at Virginia Polytechnic Institute and State University, investigated gender differences in adolescent boys' and girls' psychological well-being (as measured by self-esteem and depressive symptoms) associated with body perceptions and weight over time. Perceptions of being overweight/more developed (for girls) or smaller/less developed (for boys) had greater negative impacts on psychological well-being (lower self-esteem and higher depressive symptoms) for girls than for boys. Similarly, behaviors aimed at changing one's body size/shape were associated with decreases in self-esteem over time for girls, but not for boys. Overall, girls were more negatively affected than boys by body perceptions and body-change behaviors.

Cynthia Dailard, a senior public policy associate at the Guttmacher Institute, argues that making universal vaccination against HPV mandatory for school attendance is a necessary step in preventing cervical cancer and other HPV-related problems. Rebuttals to the issues of the high cost as well as the suitability for the vaccination in schools are presented, and she marks universal vaccination as a key step in future vaccination policy reform. Gail Javitt, Deena Berkowitz, and Lawrence O. Gostin argue that while the risks of contracting HPV are high, and its demonstrated link to cervical cancer has proven strong, it is both unwarranted and unwise to force mandatory vaccination on minor females. They discuss the potential adverse health effects, both long- and short-term risks, the lack of support for the HPV vaccine within the justifications for state-mandated vaccination, the consequences of a vaccination targeted solely at females, as well as the economic impact that would result from making the HPV vaccination mandatory.

In a paper geared at family physicians, Irene Rosen and Douglas Maurer, both family doctors themselves, review treatments for adolescent-smoking cessation; they recommend nicotine replacement therapy (NRT) as well as a variety of other methods to reduce adolescent smoking. K. Heinz Ginzel, a retired medical doctor and professor emeritus of pharmacology and toxicology at the University of Arkansas for Medical Sciences, and his colleagues, argue in a critical review paper that NRT should not be used with adolescents because it simply substitutes one form of nicotine with another, thereby prolonging and/or facilitating nicotine addiction.

Cynthia I. Joiner, MPH, RN and nurse research manager at the University of Alabama, views having body mass index (BMI) report cards in the schools as an extension of what schools are already managing to highlight the important role they play in helping to address childhood obesity. Betsy Di Benedetto Gulledge, an instructor of nursing at Jacksonville State University, highlights what she sees as the disadvantages of having body mass index (BMI) report cards in the schools; she challenges the accuracy of BMI measures and notes the risks of labeling on children's psychological well-being.

UNIT 2   SEX, SEXUALITY, AND GENDER   115

Journalist Sharlene Azam, in a book about teen prostitution, discusses the cavalier attitude toward oral sex that some girls report. As well, she discusses a famous Canadian case of oral sex with under-aged girls that had major press coverage. The Research Coordinator of the Sex Information and Education Council of Canada reviews the academic research regarding oral-sex practices and their associated meaning for youth. Their take-home message is that oral sex among teens is not at "epidemic" levels and that many youth feel that oral sex is an intimate sexual behavior.

Using the ADD Health longitudinal dataset, researchers Justin Jager and Pamela E. Davis-Kean investigated the association of early same-sex attraction on mental health outcomes of depressive affect and self-esteem. Those who had early (12–15 years) same-sex attractions and whose attraction remained stable throughout adolescence had the most negative psychological well-being. However, this group of adolescents gained or "recovered" the most, in terms of psychological well-being, over time. In a longitudinal study, Professor Margaret Rosario and colleagues found that early versus later acknowledgment of one's minority sexual orientation was not related to psychological distress; thus, sexual-minority identity formation was unrelated to psychological distress. Rather, identity integration—how well one accepts and integrates that sexual-minority status into one's life—was predictive of psychological well-being. Those who had a well-integrated sexual-minority identity had the most favorable measure of psychological well-being, while those with lower sexual-minority identity integration had the poorest measures of psychological well-being.

Derek A. Kreager and Jeremy Staff, both associate professors of sociology and crime, law, and justice at Pennsylvania State University, used data from the National Longitudinal Study of Adolescent Health to examine the existence of a contemporary double standard among adolescents. They found significant differences in peer acceptance among sexually experienced males and females, with higher numbers of sexual partners associated with significantly greater peer acceptance for boys than for girls. Heidi Lyons, assistant professor of sociology and anthropology at Oakland University, and her colleagues, Peggy C. Giordano, Wendy D. Manning, and Monica A. Longmore, all of Bowling Green State University's Department of Sociology, examined the sexual double standard in a longitudinal, mixed-method study of adolescent girls' popularity and lifetime number of sexual partners. The results paint a nuanced picture of the contemporary sexual double standard. Number of sexual partners was not associated with negative peer regard, and whereas young women acknowledged the existence of a sexual double standard, violating it did not seem to be associated with significant social costs. In fact, these authors highlight the buffering role of friendships against possible negative outcomes.

Amy Kramer, director of entertainment media and audience strategy at the National Campaign to Prevent Teen and Unplanned Pregnancy, argues that reality television shows engage teens in considering the consequences of pregnancy before they are ready for it and motivate them to want to prevent it. Mary Jo Podgurski, founder of the Academy for Adolescent Health, Inc., argues that although such television shows have potential benefits, they inadequately address the issue and may even have a negative impact on those who participate in them.

Jennifer Brunet and Katherine Sabiston, Department of Kinesiology and Physical Education, McGill University, Montreal, Canada, Kim Dorsch of the University of Regina's Faculty of Kinesiology and Health Studies, and Donald McCreary, a psychologist at Brock University, St. Catharines, Canada, examined the drive for muscularity versus thinness across male and female youth. Consistent with other research, boys in this study reported significantly lower drive for thinness and social physique anxiety than girls, and significantly higher drive for muscularity and self-esteem compared to girls. According to this study, boys focus on being muscular, whereas girls do not. Lauren B. Shomaker, postdoctoral research scientist and adjunct assistant professor in the Department of Medical and Clinical Psychology, Uniformed Services University of the Health Sciences, and Wyndol Furman, professor of psychology at Denver University, examine various interpersonal influences on adolescent girls' and boys' desire for muscularity and thinness. Results highlight unique ways that the drive for muscularity is permeating the developmental experience of adolescent girls: Both boys and girls reported pressure from mothers and friends to be muscular and both were influenced by this pressure. The ideal physique for both genders seems to have evolved over time to include some degree of both thinness and muscularity for both genders—muscularity may not be "just a guy-thing" anymore.

Özgür Erdur-Baker, associate professor in the Department of Educational Sciences, Middle East Technical University, found that males are more likely to engage in bullying behaviors than females, regardless of physical or cyber environment. In fact, she found that males were more likely to experience cyber-victimization and to be cyberbullies than females. Faye Mishna, dean and professor at the Factor Inwentash Faculty of Social Work, University of Toronto, and colleagues Charlene Cook, Tahany Gadalla (associate professor), Joanne Daciuk, and Steven Solomon, all of the University of Toronto, Canada, examined gender differences in the perpetration of cyberbullying among early and mid-adolescents. They found that both middle school and high school boys and girls were equally likely to have engaged in cyberbullying. No gender differences were found in the perpetration of cyberbullying; gender differences in methods of cyberbullying are discussed.

Issue 16.   Does Playing Violent Video Games Harm Adolescents?   348

Cheryl K. Olson and her colleagues from the Center for Mental Health and Media, Massachusetts General Hospital, report a significant positive relationship between playing M-rated video games and both bullying and physical aggression. Christopher J. Ferguson, associate professor of psychology, Department of Behavioral, Applied Sciences and Criminal Justice, Texas A&M International University, argues that the negative effects of violent video games have been inconsistent and exaggerated, while the positive effects—such as social networking and visuospatial cognition—have been ignored. He also states that although video game consumption has steadily increased in the last 10 years, youth violence has decreased.

Issue 17.   Are Social Networking Sites (SNSs), Such as Facebook, a Cause for Concern?   373

Billy Henson, assistant professor of criminal justice at Shippensburg University, Bradford W. Reyns, assistant professor of criminal justice at Weber State University, and Bonnie Fisher, professor of criminal justice at the University of Cincinnati, argue that participation in social networking sites, such as Facebook, exposes many users to interpersonal victimization. Researchers Nicole B. Ellison, Charles Steinfield, and Cliff Lampe from the Department of Telecommunication, Information Studies, and Media, at Michigan State University, argue that SNSs such as Facebook scaffold relationship development, and are positively associated with self-expression, identity formation, and social capital.

Charles D. Stimson, senior legal fellow and Andrew M. Grossman, past senior legal policy analyst, Center for Legal and Justice Studies, The Heritage Foundation, argue that for serious offenses, trying juveniles in adult court and imposing adult sentences—such as life without parole—is effective and appropriate because youth who commit adult crimes should be treated as adults. Laurence Steinberg, Distinguished University Professor, Department of Psychology at Temple University, argues that adolescents often lack the cognitive, social, and emotional maturity to make mature judgments and therefore should not be sanctioned in the same way as adults. He supports a separate juvenile justice system where adolescents should be judged, tried, and sanctioned in ways that do not adversely affect development.

Correlation Guide

The *Taking Sides* series presents current issues in a debate-style format designed to stimulate student interest and develop critical thinking skills. Each issue is thoughtfully framed with an issue summary, an issue introduction, and a postscript. The pro and con essays—selected for their liveliness and substance—represent the arguments of leading scholars and commentators in their fields.

Taking Sides: Clashing Views in Adolescence, 3/e is an easy-to-use reader that presents issues on important topics such as *adolescent health, sex and sexuality,* and *antisocial behavior.* For more information on *Taking Sides* and other *McGraw-Hill Contemporary Learning Series* titles, visit www.mhhe.com/cls.

This convenient guide matches the issues in **Taking Sides: Adolescence, 3/e** with the corresponding chapters in three of our best-selling McGraw-Hill Adolescence textbooks by Santrock and Steinberg.

Taking Sides: Adolescence, 3/e	Adolescence, 14/e by Santrock	Adolescence, 9/e by Steinberg
Issue 1: Should Adolescents Be Taking Selective Serotonin Reuptake Inhibitors (SSRIs) for Mood and/or Anxiety Disorders?	**Chapter 13:** Problems in Adolescence and Emerging Adulthood	**Chapter 13:** Psychosocial Problems in Adolescence
Issue 2: Are Body Dissatisfaction and Its Outcomes of Equal Concern for Boys and Girls?	**Chapter 12:** Culture	**Chapter 5:** Peer Groups **Chapter 8:** Identity
Issue 3: Should the Human Papillomavirus (HPV) Vaccine Be Mandatory for Early Adolescent Girls?	**Chapter 2:** Puberty, Health, and Biological Foundations **Chapter 6:** Sexuality **Chapter 9:** Peers, Romantic Relationships, and Life Styles	**Chapter 11:** Sexuality
Issue 4: Is the Use of Nicotine Replacement Therapy (NRT) an Appropriate Cessation Aid for Adolescents Wishing to Quit Smoking?	**Chapter 2:** Puberty, Health, and Biological Foundations	**Chapter 1:** Biological Transition
Issue 5: Should Schools Be Responsible for Completing Body Mass Index (BMI) Report Cards in the Fight Against Youth Obesity?	**Chapter 10:** Schools	**Chapter 6:** Schools
Issue 6: Is There Cause for Concern About an "Oral-Sex Crisis" for Teens?	**Chapter 6:** Sexuality	**Chapter 9:** Autonomy **Chapter 11:** Sexuality
Issue 7: Is "Coming Out" As a Sexual Minority (Gay/Lesbian/Bisexual) Earlier in Adolescence Detrimental to Psychological Well-Being?	**Chapter 6:** Sexuality **Chapter 9:** Peers, Romantic Relationships, and Life Styles	**Chapter 8:** Identity **Chapter 10:** Intimacy **Chapter 11:** Sexuality

Taking Sides: Adolescence, 3/e	Adolescence, 14/e by Santrock	Adolescence, 9/e by Steinberg
Issue 8: Does a Strong and Costly Sexual Double Standard Still Exist Among Adolescents?	**Chapter 6:** Sexuality **Chapter 9:** Peers, Romantic Relationships, and Life Styles	**Chapter 3:** Social Transitions **Chapter 8:** Identity
Issue 9: Do Reality TV Shows Portray Responsible Messages about Teen Pregnancy?	**Chapter 4:** The Self, Identity, Emotion, and Personality **Chapter 6:** Sexuality **Chapter 9:** Peers, Romantic Relationships, and Life Styles **Chapter 12:** Culture	**Chapter 7:** Work, Leisure, and the Mass Media
Issue 10: Is Having a Muscular Physique in Adolescence Strictly a "Guy Thing"?	**Chapter 4:** The Self, Identity, Emotion, and Personality	**Chapter 2:** Cognitive Transitions **Chapter 8:** Identity
Issue 11: Does Having Same-Sex Parents Negatively Impact Children?	**Chapter 8:** Families	**Chapter 4:** Families **Chapter 8:** Identity
Issue 12: Does Dating in Early Adolescence Impede Developmental Adjustment?	**Chapter 4:** The Self, Identity, Emotion, and Personality **Chapter 9:** Peers, Romantic Relationships, and Life Styles	**Chapter 3:** Social Transitions **Chapter 5:** Peer Groups **Chapter 10:** Intimacy
Issue 13: Should Parents Supervise Alcohol Use by or Provide Alcohol to Adolescents?	**Chapter 8:** Families **Chapter 12:** Culture	**Chapter 4:** Families
Issue 14: Should Parental Consent Be Required for Adolescents Seeking Abortion?	**Chapter 7:** Moral Development, Values, and Religion	**Chapter 4:** Families
Issue 15: Are Boys Bigger Bullies than Girls—In Cyberspace?	**Chapter 5:** Gender	**Chapter 3:** Social Transitions **Chapter 7:** Work, Leisure, and the Mass Media
Issue 16: Does Playing Violent Video Games Harm Adolescents?	**Chapter 4:** The Self, Identity, Emotion, and Personality **Chapter 5:** Gender **Chapter 12:** Culture	**Chapter 2:** Cognitive Transitions **Chapter 7:** Work, Leisure, and the Mass Media
Issue 17: Are Social Networking Sites (SNSs), such as Facebook, a Cause for Concern?	**Chapter 12:** Culture **Chapter 13:** Problems in Adolescence and Emerging Adulthood	**Chapter 7:** Work, Leisure, and the Mass Media
Issue 18: Should Juvenile Offenders Be Tried and Convicted as Adults?	**Chapter 3:** The Brain and Cognitive Development	**Chapter 1:** Biological Transition **Chapter 9:** Autonomy

Topic Guide

T his topic guide suggests how the selections in this book relate to the subjects covered in your course. You may want to use the topics listed on these pages to search the Web more easily. On the following pages a number of websites have been gathered specifically for this book. They are arranged to reflect the units of this *Taking Sides* reader. You can link to these sites by going to www.mhhe.com/cls.

All the issues and their articles that relate to each topic are listed below in the bold-faced term.

Abortion

14. Should Parental Consent Be Required for Adolescents Seeking Abortion?

Anxiety Disorders

1. Should Adolescents Be Taking Selective Serotonin Reuptake Inhibitors (SSRIs) for Mood and/or Anxiety Disorders?

Antidepressants

1. Should Adolescents Be Taking Selective Serotonin Reuptake Inhibitors (SSRIs) for Mood and/or Anxiety Disorders?

Bullying

15. Are Boys Bigger Bullies than Girls—In Cyberspace?
17. Are Social Networking Sites (SNSs), Such as Facebook, a Cause for Concern?

Body Perception

2. Are Body Dissatisfaction and Its Outcomes of Equal Concern for Boys and Girls?
10. Is Having a Muscular Physique in Adolescence Strictly a "Guy Thing"?

Human Papillomavirus Vaccine (HPV)

3. Should the Human Papillomavirus (HPV) Vaccine Be Mandatory for Early Adolescent Girls?

Smoking

4. Is the Use of Nicotine Replacement Therapy (NRT) an Appropriate Cessation Aid for Adolescents Wishing to Quit Smoking?

Body Mass Index

5. Should Schools Be Responsible for Completing Body Mass Index (BMI) Report Cards in the Fight Against Youth Obesity?

Obesity

5. Should Schools Be Responsible for Completing Body Mass Index (BMI) Report Cards in the Fight Against Youth Obesity?

Oral Sex

6. Is There Cause for Concern About an "Oral-Sex Crisis" for Teens?

Sexual Minority

7. Is "Coming Out" As a Sexual Minority (Gay/Lesbian/Bisexual) Earlier in Adolescence Detrimental to Psychological Well-Being?

Sexuality

7. Is "Coming Out" As a Sexual Minority (Gay/Lesbian/Bisexual) Earlier in Adolescence Detrimental to Psychological Well-Being?
8. Does a Strong and Costly Sexual Double Standard Still Exist Among Adolescents?

Parenting

11. Does Having Same-Sex Parents Negatively Impact Children?
13. Should Parents Supervise Alcohol Use by or Provide Alcohol to Adolescents?

Pregnancy

9. Do Reality TV Shows Portray Responsible Messages about Teen Pregnancy?

Introduction

Adolescence is a period of development marked by a transition spanning the second decade of life. Developmentally, adolescence begins at approximately age 10 and lasts into the early twenties, although from 18 or 19 onwards, the period is referred to as "emerging adulthood" (Arnett, 2004). Adolescence is a period of time when individuals leave the security of childhood to meet the demands of the adult world. They pull away from the structure of family in search of independence. This involves finding an identity, making commitments, and carving out a responsible place in society. Although the transition is very individual (i.e., occurring in different ways and at different rates), it involves dealing with three sets of developmental challenges or tasks. The challenges involve the biological, psychological, and social changes occurring during this crucial period of development. The biological changes are the most visible with puberty and hormones driving changes in body appearance. Adolescents must learn to cope and accept these changes. The psychological changes involve advances in cognitions and enhanced emotional development leading to stronger decision making, mature judgment, better planning, and advanced perspective taking. The task here is to cope with these new characteristics and to use them to adapt to the transition and find a place in the world. The third challenge is to find a responsible role in society and commit to a revised sense of self. The social changes (i.e., relationships, newfound independence) taking place during this time permit the adolescent to explore different roles. Taken together, the challenges and changes result in children becoming adults.

History of Adolescence

Historically, the period between childhood and adulthood has always been recognized as distinct; however, it was not researched or given a specific name until the twentieth century. In Ancient Greek times, Plato, Socrates, and Aristotle had specific views of adolescence. Plato, for example, recognizing the advances in thinking and judgment during the second decade of life, believed that formal education should only start at this time. Socrates, also aware of the advances in cognitions, argued that the stronger thinking skills allowed youth to become better at arguing. In addition he recognized the down side to this developmental advancement, arguing that youth were inclined to contradict their parents and tyrannize their teachers. Aristotle argued that the most important aspect of this period of development was the ability to choose. He believed that human beings became capable of making rational choices and good decisions during the second decade. Aristotle also recognized that, although youth exhibited gains in thinking, they were still immature and different from adults. His strong opinion and knowledge about youth is clearly stated in the following passage:

> The young are in character prone to desire and ready to carry any desire they may have formed into action. Of bodily desires it is the sexual to

which they are most disposed to give way, and in regard to sexual desire they exercise no self-restraint. They are changeful, too, and fickle in their desires, which are as transitory as they are vehement; for their wishes are keen without being permanent, like a sick man's fits of hunger and thirst. They are passionate, irascible, and apt to be carried away by their impulses. They are the slaves, too, of their passion, as their ambition prevents their ever brooking a slight and renders them indignant at the mere idea of enduring an injury. They are charitable rather than the reverse, as they have never yet been witnesses of many villainies; and they are trustful, as they have not yet been often deceived. They are sanguine, too, for the young are heated by nature as drunken men by wine, not to say that they have not yet experienced frequent failures. Their lives are lived principally in hope. They have high aspirations; for they have never yet been humiliated by the experience of life, but are unacquainted with the limiting force of circumstances. Youth is the age when people are most devoted to their friends, as they are then extremely fond of social intercourse. If the young commit a fault, it is always on the side of excess and exaggeration, for they carry everything too far, whether it be their love or hatred or anything else. (Aristotle, fourth century B.C.)

The early philosophical views such as those mentioned above went unchallenged for many centuries. However, by the late nineteenth century/early twentieth century, this changed and the age of adolescence was recognized. It was argued that children and youth were not miniature adults and, therefore, should not be treated in the same way as adults, especially with respect to labor and family responsibility. As a result, child labor laws were implemented, followed by mandatory schooling until age 16. Basically, children were being protected and not permitted to work; however, they could not be left unsupervised, aimlessly wandering about, getting into trouble. The solution: "Keep them in school until they can work." With these changes in the early 1900s, the concept of adolescence became more defined. Adolescents were not children and were not yet adults, resulting in the recognition that they were unique in their development and, as such, deserved special attention.

At this time (i.e., circa 1900), G. Stanley Hall began studying adolescence in terms of their behaviors, their emotions, and their relationships. Known as the father of adolescent research, he concluded that children went through turmoil and upheaval during their second decade of life and as such were in a state of constant *storm-and-stress*, a term he coined from the German *"sturm und drang"* movement. Hall identified three key aspects of adolescent storm-and-stress: risky behaviors, mood disruptions, and conflict with parents. Hall argued that the physical changes occurring during this period of the lifespan (e.g., growth spurts, sexual maturation, and hormonal changes) resulted in psychological turbulence. He further argued that the turmoil was both universal and biologically based. In other words, it was inevitable regardless of other factors. To disseminate these arguments, Hall published *Adolescence* (1904), the first text on adolescent development, making the study of adolescence both scientific and scholarly. Since the time of Hall's book, research on adolescence has attracted attention from many disciplines, including psychology, sociology, anthropology, and medicine.

Soon after Hall's view of adolescence, Margaret Mead published *Coming of Age in Samoa* (1928), which challenged Hall's view of universal adolescent storm-and-stress. After conducting observational research in Samoa (a distinctly different culture than western society), Mead explained how Samoan adolescents experienced a gradual and smooth transition to adulthood because of the meaningful connections made between their roles during adolescence and the roles they would perform as adults. She argued that the transition through adolescence was not simply biological, but rather sociocultural, and the turmoil identified by Hall was environmentally and culturally specific and certainly not universal. Some cultures, she stated, provided a smooth, gradual transition that allowed adolescents to experience minimal, if any, storm-and-stress.

For many years, Mead was alone in arguing against Hall's view. Most social scientists based their research on what Richard Lerner (a current and eminent developmental researcher) called Hall's deficit model of adolescence where developmental deficits caused turmoil resulting in problem behaviors such as alcohol and drug use, school failure, teen pregnancy, crime, and depression. Essentially, Hall's deficit model and view of storm-and-stress as universal was not disputed or challenged until the 1960s when it was realized that not all adolescents had a turbulent time during the transition from childhood to adulthood. Research in the 1960s began providing evidence to support Mead's perspective, arguing that many adolescents had good relationships and strong core values with few, if any, problem behaviors. Researchers, in supporting Mead, were not necessarily disputing Hall. They recognized that, while some adolescents did in fact experience an intense period of storm-and-stress, many had a smooth and uneventful transition. This led to the more recent view of a *modified storm-and-stress* period of development. From this perspective, conflict with parents, mood disruptions, and risky behaviors are on a continuum dependent on many psychological, sociological, cultural, and environmental factors.

Theories of Adolescent Development

During the twentieth century, many theories have been proposed to explain human development. A simple overview of a few of the key theories is provided with a particular emphasis on the period of adolescence.

Psychoanalytic theory states that development is unconscious and dependent on early experiences with parents. It is predicated on the premise that personality comprises three mostly unconscious psychological constructs: the Id, where raw desires, urges, and drives are housed (e.g., sexual desires, hunger, thirst); the ego, which "manages" the desires and tries to appease or satisfy the wants of the Id while working within the constraints of the real world (e.g., satisfying unacceptable sexual desires with fantasies or substituted behaviors); and the superego, which is the social conscience of the personality (e.g., where parental and societal values reside). Within the framework of psychoanalytic theory, these three hypothesized constructs must work in harmony in order for the person to be well adjusted and function effectively within society. The development of these structures arises out of different psychosexual stages— which are a series of sexual obstacles the child must overcome in order to proceed to the next stage of development. Sigmund Freud (1938) and daughter Anna Freud (1958) argued that the balance previously achieved between the Id, the ego, and the superego is destroyed during adolescence because of the new pressures on the ego. As a result, the sexual drives brought on by puberty and hormonal changes affect an adolescent's sense of reality and subsequent behavior. From a psychoanalytic point of view, a positive sense of self, prosocial behavior, and overall healthy development can only occur if psychosexual development was not restricted in earlier years. Essentially, the sexual reawakening during adolescence (i.e., the genital stage) leads to healthy adult sexuality and overall well-being if children are not restricted during any of the previous psychosexual stages (i.e., oral, anal, phallic, and latency).

From a *cognitive perspective*, human development is a bidirectional process, explained in terms of an individual's action on the environment and the action of the environment on the individual. As a child matures, he or she becomes more active in his or her environment and more advanced cognitively. Jean Piaget, a pioneer of cognitive developmental theory, proposed that children proceed through a sequence of distinct developmental stages: the sensorimotor stage (birth to age 2), the preoperational stage (ages 2–5), the concrete operational stage (age 6 to early adolescence), and the formal operational stage (early adolescence to adulthood). Piaget argued that, between the ages of 11 and 15, adolescents enter the formal operational stage. Abstract and hypothetical thinking emerges during this stage, and as a result, children attain the ability to see that reality (e.g., how others treat them) and their thoughts about reality (e.g., how others "should" treat them) are different. They gain the ability to generate and recognize hypotheses about reality. The ability to think abstractly also allows adolescents to project themselves into the future, distinguish present reality from possibility, and think about what might be. Once in the formal operational stage, Piaget also argued that adolescents gain competence in formal reasoning, which is marked by a transition from inductive reasoning (e.g., "Jane had unprotected sex and did not get pregnant, therefore if I have unprotected sex, I will not get pregnant") to deductive reasoning (e.g., there are risks involved when having unprotected sex and because Jane did not get pregnant, does not mean that I will not get pregnant"). This transition means that adolescents are not only able to systemize their ideas and critically deal with their own thinking to construct theories, but they are also able to test their theories logically, and scientifically discover truth. They can devise many interpretations of an observed outcome (e.g., pregnancy may be the result of unprotected sex, failed contraception, or in-vitro fertilization), and they can anticipate many possibilities prior to an actual event (e.g., unprotected sex may lead to pregnancy, an STI, or HIV/AIDS).

Currently, there is debate as to whether Piaget was correct in saying that adolescents gain the competencies cited above by age 15. Neuroscientists argue that the adolescent brain may not be fully developed until late adolescence or early adulthood. Neuroimaging indicates that the prefrontal cortex, the "home of the executive functions," is the last part of the human brain to develop, not reaching full maturity until the early twenties or later. This would mean that, until the brain has reached maturity, adolescents would not be competent in planning, setting priorities, organizing thoughts, suppressing impulses, weighing out consequences, and formal reasoning. Without these competencies in place, adolescents may have a difficult time with decision making. Neuroscientists, therefore, tend to attribute bad decisions to an underdeveloped brain (see Steinberg & Scott, Issue 15 for more on this argument).

Social cognitive theory (Bandura, 2005) is another approach to understanding adolescent development and behavior. From this perspective, adolescent development is understood in terms of how adolescents reason about themselves, others, and the social world around them. Theorists such as David Elkind (1967, 1978) describe adolescent reasoning and thinking in terms of the advances in metacognition. With the ability to "think about their own thinking" (metacognition), adolescents spend most of their time focused on themselves. They daydream more and, as they become preoccupied with their own thoughts, they come to believe that others are or should be as preoccupied with them as they are with themselves. As a result, they think everyone notices them. A typical example is the adolescent who cannot possibly go to school because of a facial blemish. To the distraught adolescent, everyone will notice and criticize them. David Elkind uses the term adolescent egocentrism to describe these changes in behavior and thought.

Moving toward a more social perspective is Erik Erikson's (1959) *psychosocial theory* of ego development, which encompasses the entire life span. He describes development from birth to old age as occurring in eight stages with each stage characterized by a crisis, between two opposing forces (e.g., trust versus mistrust), which must be resolved successfully. According to Erikson, the resolution of a crisis is dependent on the successful resolution of all previous crises. For example, the adolescent crisis, of *identity formation* versus *role confusion*, can only be resolved if adolescents were successful in resolving the previous four crises of childhood (i.e., having a sense of trust versus mistrust, autonomy versus shame and doubt, initiative versus guilt, and industry versus inferiority). In addition, the resolution of the adolescent identity crisis will affect the resolution of future crises. Resolving the identity crisis means showing commitment toward a role—personal, sexual, occupational, and ideological (i.e., a concept about human life that involves a set of beliefs and values). Once complete, the established identity is a distinctive combination of personality characteristics and social style by which the adolescent defines himself/herself and by which he or she is recognized by others.

The last theory presented here is Urie Bronfenbrenner's *ecological systems theory* (1979), which examines the role of five different environments in an individual's development and well-being. Imagine the adolescent at the center of a large circle with each system radiating outward. The first system immediately surrounding the adolescent is the microsystem. This is the setting in which a person lives and includes one's family, peers, school, and neighborhood. The second system, called the mesosystem, consists of the relationships between the different microsystems. An example is the relationship between an adolescent's family and school. According to Bronfenbrenner, the relationship between these two microsystems has a different effect on the individual than each microsystem separately. The third system is the exosystem, which comprises the linkages between different settings that indirectly involves the adolescent. An example is the relation between the home and a parent's workplace. Outside the exosystem is the macrosystem. This is essentially the cultural and social influence on an individual, such as belief systems, material resources, customs, and lifestyles, which are embedded in each of the previous inner systems. Finally, there is the chronosystem, which involves environmental events and transitions over time. For example, adolescents who were directly involved in a major trauma such as 911 or hurricane Katrina will have different life experiences affecting their development than adolescents who were not directly involved.

The theories presented above provide only an introduction to understanding human behavior and, in particular, adolescent behavior. Other theories exist and contribute to the interdisciplinary approach currently used to enhance our understanding of adolescence. For a more comprehensive discussion of these theories, refer to the suggested readings list at the end of this introduction.

Adolescence in the Twentieth Century

Adolescence in and of itself is a period of human development marked by many changes, transitions, and both positive and negative behaviors. Adolescents are the individuals going through this particular period of development.

Since the study of adolescence first began in the early twentieth century, researchers have examined how particular events and issues affected adolescent attitudes and behaviors. In this section, we provide an overview of how events shaped the way adolescents behaved and how they dealt with particular issues. For example, in the 1920s, when the period of adolescence was officially recognized, North American youth responded with a sense of newfound freedom. They were essentially given permission to stay young and have fun while they could. The decade became known as the Roaring Twenties, with increased autonomy and freedom. An interesting effect was that many adults responded to the behaviors of the young by adopting a similar appealing lifestyle with more music, dancing, and partying. This was short-lived, however, with the Great Depression of the 1930s followed by World War II in the 1940s. Irresponsibility and the age of adolescence were put on hold during these difficult times. Many young people were forced to seek employment or to serve their country in the war. The exposure to poverty, family struggles, war, violence, and death resulted in a drive for stability and security following the war. The 1950s were a time when adults focused on ensuring this security and stability for their families. During this time, adolescents were considered to be the "silent generation" because life seemed perfect. They had only their futures upon which to focus. In North American society, getting a college degree, finding a good job, getting married, and raising a family were the goals for the adolescents of the fifties.

In the 1960s, there was once again disruption to stability and security with the Vietnam War and the assassinations of North American politicians and leaders. Many adolescents reacted with anger and frustration. They did not trust politicians or decision makers because they were seen as disrupting their perceived ideal world and sense of security. They held political protests to voice their views of idealism. They challenged authority and promoted peace, love, and freedom with drug use, loosening of sexual behavior, and cohabitation. This peace movement of the sixties is remembered with phrases such as "make love not war" and "reject authority." For most, there was no focus on working hard and establishing a stable career. Attending university was as much about fun and freedom from parents as it was about studying.

The sexual revolution of the 1960s lasted into the 1970s, with adolescents becoming more focused on their own needs and goals but not without further struggles. Adolescent girls and young women, aware of the opportunity differential and stereotyped careers for men and women, began the long and difficult fight for equality. The previous argument that women would have babies and be unreliable was no longer valid. Thanks to the contraceptive pill, which was introduced in the 1960s, women gained control over their reproduction and the freedom to choose if and when they would have a family. Gender inequality was no longer an issue of biology. The success of the Women's Movement in the 1970s and 1980s resulted in many more young women attending college and university—eventually bridging the gender gap in many professions such as medicine, law, and engineering. With more women attending to their careers, and postponing childbearing or deciding to be childless, two-income families became more popular. Small families, large homes, travel, and material possessions such as the "best" home computers became the goals. This way of life has had a profound effect on children born since 1980. For example, a carry-over effect from the 1960s and 1970s is the notion that if you want something badly enough, you can get it. Parents have become so involved in their children's lives, providing material possession upon material possession, that kids have come to expect it. Large screen televisions, personal computers, electronic devices, cell phones, and disposable income are common expectations among many of today's youth. The adolescents of the twenty-first century, known as the Millennials, are unique and different from adolescents of the past.

Adolescence in the Twenty-First Century

Today's adolescents have unique experiences and issues not encountered by previous generations. There are many factors contributing to this. For instance, the advances in technology have been influential in shaping the lives of adolescents today. Many carry a cell phone, an iPod, and have their own personal computer, enabling them to communicate with anyone—regardless of where they are. These devices also give them instant access to music, computer games, and information. Essentially, we have technologically savvy adolescents who spend much of their time alone with inanimate objects.

A second factor contributing to the uniqueness of today's adolescents is their perceived sense of entitlement. Parents have protected and given so much to their children that, once they leave home for university or work, they come to expect the same. Having had to fight for rights in the 1960s and

1970s, parents have taught their children "if you want something, it's your right to have it." As university educators, we have seen first-hand the effect this has had. For example, Millennial students are often more persistent in their demands compared to previous cohorts of the 1980s and 1990s. A typical example is demanding an exam be rescheduled because of personal travel plans. Millennials are also more likely to have their parents involved in their postsecondary education, making calls to professors and administrators requesting information or favors for their adolescent.

A third unique factor contributing to the novel experiences of the youth of the Millennial age involves sexual freedom. That is, youth of today experience a more open sexual discourse because of significant social events including the Sexual Revolution and Women's Movement of the 1960s and 1970s, the Gay Rights Movement of the 1970s and 1980s, as well as the HIV/AIDS crisis of the 1980s and onward. Different forms of media have also played a large role in opening up knowledge and discussion about sexuality; for example, the Internet has made many sexually oriented websites accessible to youth despite efforts to provide filters. Some of these websites are informational, while others would be characterized as obscene or pornographic. Television, films, as well as magazines and books tend to involve more overt sexuality as regulations regarding these media have been relaxed over recent decades. These changes have had an impact on social programs including more explicit and precise sexual health education in the school system—although this has involved considerable controversy. All of this cumulates in a more sexually savvy adolescent than perhaps was the case in previous generations.

The Millennial cohort is probably more aware of pregnancy and STI prevention as well as issues surrounding sexual violence—more so than previous generations. According to a recent report published by the Centers for Disease Control and Prevention (Abma et al., 2004), the teenage pregnancy rate has dropped from 1990 to 2000. From 1982 and 1995 to 2002, teen intercourse has decreased (i.e., there has been an increased rate of adolescent "virginity"). Among sexually active teen girls, there has also been increased condom use and decreased "no protection" during intercourse. All of these changes might be positive side-effects of the increased openness and more positive attitudes toward the sexuality of adolescents.

Not only have sexual behaviors of adolescents changed across the generations, but gender roles have also changed significantly. This involves the roles of girls and boys in relation to "feminine" and "masculine" traits. Gender rigidity has declined and greater tolerance for gender variation has increased, although early adolescence is known as a time when youth are less understanding of violations of gender rules. Regardless, this has made the youth of the twenty-first century more accepting of lesbian, gay, bisexual, and transgender people (Ponton & Judice, 2004). In sum, sexual behaviors, attitudes, and roles have changed dramatically for the Millennial Generation and, while always an important aspect of adolescent development, these topics have become more central in adolescent research.

The introduction thus far has provided an overview of adolescence from when the term was first coined to the present. Through the twentieth century, adolescents were faced with many hurdles and issues that affected their development and overall transition from childhood to adulthood. The goal of this book is to present issues facing adolescents in the first decades of the twenty-first century. We address controversies such as adolescent use of antidepressants and smoking-cessation aids, and youth justice. We debate mandatory HPV vaccination, the impact of same-sex parenting on adolescents, as well as consent for abortions and parentally supervised alcohol use by teens. We also cover body image, gender roles, sexuality, dating in early adolescence, cyber-soicalization, obesity, and the impact of reality TV on teenage pregnancy. Finally, we examine behaviors such as cyberbullying, oral sex, and playing violent video games.

These issues will shape the behaviors of tomorrow's adolescents and guide future research. As is evident from the issues listed above, this book presents adolescence as an interdisciplinary topic. We have selected issues that can be used in a variety of disciplines and courses. These issues are addressed and analyzed from multiple perspectives, not limited to psychological analysis. Articles were chosen from a variety of disciplines in order to capture not only the empirical debates around these issues, but also the social spin placed on adolescent concerns. The public discourse around adolescent issues is not necessarily informed by empirical evidence; however, it often holds more power than empiricism in shaping people's views and behaviors. It is in this spirit that the controversies in this book are examined.

References and Suggested Readings

Abma J. C., Martinez, G. M., Mosher, W. D., & Dawson, B. S. (2004). Teenagers in the United States: Sexual activity, contraceptive use, and childbearing, 2002. National Center for Health Statistics. *Vital Health Statistics, 23*(24).

Arnett, J. (2004). *Adolescence and emerging adulthood* (2nd ed.). Upper Saddle River, NJ: Prentice Hall.

Bandura, A. (2005). The evolution of social cognitive theory. In Ken G. Smith & Michael A. Hitt (Eds.), *Great minds in management. The process of theory development* (pp. 9–35). New York: Oxford University Press.

Bronfenbrenner, U. (1979). *The ecology of human development.* Cambridge, MA: Harvard University Press.

Elkind, D. (1967). Egocentrism in adolescence. *Child Development, 38,* 1025–1034.

Elkind, D. (1978). Understanding the young adolescent. *Adolescence, 13,* 127–134.

Erikson, E. (1959). Identity and the life cycle. *Psychological Issues, 1,* 1–171.

Freud, A. (1958). Adolescence. *Psychoanalytic Study of the Child, 13,* 255–278.

Freud, S. (1938). *An outline of psychoanalysis*. London: Hogarth Press.

Hall, G. S. (1904). *Adolescence*. New York: Appleton.

Lerner, R. Brown, J. & Kier, C. (2005). *Adolescence: Development, diversity, context, and application*. Toronto: Prentice Hall.

Mead, M. (1928). *Coming of age in Samoa*. New York: Morrow.

Ponton, L.E., & Judice, S. (2004). Typical adolescent sexual development. *Child & Adolescent Psychiatric Clinics of North America, 13*(3), 497–511.

Santrock, J. (2010). *Adolescence* (13th ed.). New York: McGraw-Hill.

Steinberg, L. (2008). *Adolescence*. Boston, MA: McGraw-Hill.

Internet References . . .

Public Health Agency of Canada

The Public Health Agency of Canada website is a collaboration with provinces and territories in an effort to support a sustainable health care system.

www.phac-aspc.gc.ca/
www.phac-aspc.gc.ca/ch-se-eng.php

Canadian Paediatric Society

This website, from the National Association of Paediatricians, includes several publications regarding adolescent health issues including adolescent dieting, pregnancy, emergency contraception, sexual abuse, and eating disorders among other topics

www.cps.ca/
www.cps.ca/en/issues-questions/adolescent-health-safety

HPVinfo.ca

This site was created by the Society of Obstetricians and Gynaecologists of Canada (SOGC), a group dedicated to promoting optimal women's health.

www.hpvinfo.ca/

Centre for Addiction and Mental Health

The Centre for Addiction and Mental Health (CAMH) is Canada's leading addiction and mental health teaching hospital and a highly respected research institute.

www.camh.ca/en/hospital/care_program_and_services/child_youth_and_
family_program/Pages/child_youth_and_family_program.aspx
www.camh.ca/en/research/research_areas/clinical_research/Pages/child_
youth_research.aspx

Smoke-Free Ontario: Ontario Ministry of Health and Long Term Care

The Ontario Ministry of Health and Long Term Care has put together a vast amount of information about smoking, from Ontario-regulated smoking laws to how to quit smoking.

www.mhp.gov.on.ca/en/smoke-free/smokingTeenager.asp

Caring For Kids

Caring for Kids is designed to provide information about child and adolescent health and well-being. Developed by the Canadian Paediatric Society, the teen and health section includes topics on a range of issues, including adolescent dieting, pregnancy, HPV vaccines, emergency contraception, sexual abuse, and eating disorders.

www.caringforkids.cps.ca/home
www.caringforkids.cps.ca/handouts/teenhealth-index
www.caringforkids.cps.ca/handouts/dieting_information_for_teens

Adolescent Health

*A*dolescent psychical and psychological health has important implications for future well-being. An adolescent who is both mentally and
physically fit has a better chance to develop into a strong, productive, and
happy adult. There are a multitude of adolescent health-related issues
that could have an influence on the healthy development of a teen. In
the following part, five issues that relate to different aspects of adolescent
health are examined.

- Should Adolescents Be Taking Selective Serotonin Reuptake Inhibitors (SSRIs) for Mood and/or Anxiety Disorders?

- Are Body Dissatisfaction and Its Outcomes of Equal Concern for Boys and Girls?

- Should the Human Papillomavirus (HPV) Vaccine Be Mandatory for Early Adolescent Girls?

- Is the Use of Nicotine Replacement Therapy (NRT) an Appropriate Cessation Aid for Adolescents Wishing to Quit Smoking?

- Should Schools Be Responsible for Completing Body Mass Index (BMI) Report Cards in the Fight Against Youth Obesity?

ISSUE 1

Should Adolescents Be Taking Selective Serotonin Reuptake Inhibitors (SSRIs) for Mood and/or Anxiety Disorders?

YES: E. Jane Garland, Stan Kutcher, and Adil Virani, from "2008 Position Paper on Using SSRIs in Children and Adolescents," *Journal of the Canadian Academy of Child and Adolescent Psychiatry* (vol. 18, no. 2, 2009)

NO: Tamar D. Wohlfarth et al., from "Antidepressants Use in Children and Adolescents and the Risk of Suicide," *European Neuropsychopharmacology* (vol. 16, 2006)

Learning Outcomes

After reading this issue, you should be able to:

- Outline and describe the benefits for treating depression and anxiety with SSRIs.
- Outline and describe the risk associated with using SSRIs to treat adolescent depression and anxiety.
- Evaluate the research methodologies from the studies examining SSRI efficacy.

ISSUE SUMMARY

YES: E. Jane Garland, a clinical professor of psychiatry at the University of British Columbia, Stan Kutcher, a professor of psychiatry at Dalhousie University, and Adil Virani, an assistant professor of pharmaceutical sciences at the University of British Columbia, reviewed numerous randomized double-blind, placebo-controlled trials regarding the role of selective serotonin reuptake inhibitors (SSRIs) for the treatment of depression and anxiety in children and youth. They conclude that the risk–benefit balance for fluoxetine is favorable in depression, and the risk–benefit balance for three SSRIs is favorable in anxiety disorders.

NO: Tamar D. Wohlfarth, a clinical assessor, and colleagues in the Netherlands assessed antidepressant use in pediatric patients and reported an increased risk for events related to suicidality among those taking antidepressants. They caution the use of all SSRIs and NSRIs (norepinephrine or noradrenergic serotonin reuptake inhibitors) in the pediatric population.

Researchers have estimated that 2 percent of children and 4–8 percent of adolescents suffer from depression and/or anxiety, and that the lifetime prevalence for a disorder such as major depressive disorder (MDD) by adolescence ranges between 15 and 20 percent (American Academy of Child and Adolescent Psychiatry (AACAP), 1998). Depressive disorders are generally chronic among adolescents with an average episode in a clinical setting lasting 8 months. Unfortunately, children and adolescents with clinical depression and anxiety often go untreated, putting them at risk for substance abuse, school failure, impaired relationships, and personality disorders. Depression is also the strongest predictor of suicidal ideation, attempts, and completions; completions are now the third leading cause of death in 15- to 19-year-olds (Anderson, 2002). Furthermore, depression during adolescence is a major risk for suicide and long-term psychosocial impairment in adulthood.

Given the serious nature of these disorders, along with the fact that the peak onset of depression is in adolescence, early recognition and effective treatment are crucial. Effective treatments for children and adolescents with depressive disorders most often include psychotherapy and antidepressant medications. Studies have indicated that a combination of both treatments is most effective, although studies have also found antidepressants alone to convey almost as much benefit as the combined treatment.

Antidepressants introduced since 1990, especially SSRIs, have become a preferred treatment option for children and adolescents with depression. SSRIs are also used to treat anxiety disorders. Compared to their predecessors, the tricyclic antidepressants (TCAs), SSRIs such as fluoxetine (Prozac), sertraline (Zoloft), paroxetine (Paxil), and citalopram (Celexa) are better tolerated, have a lower frequency of cardiac events and sudden death, fewer anticholonergic effects (dry mouth, somnolence, and constipation), and superior efficacy (Hamrin & Scahill, 2005). SSRIs work by blocking the reuptake of serotonin (5HT), a neurotransmitter in the central nervous system involved in a range of physiological and behavioral functions including sleep, wakefulness, appetite, emotional response, and thought process. Although the etiology of depression and some anxiety disorders is unknown, serotonin is believed to play an important role: for example, depression may be associated with reduced serotoninergic function. Therefore, antidepressants such as SSRIs appear to be effective in treating the disorder. However, the safety of prescribing antidepressants to children and adolescents has been the subject of increasing concern. Specifically, these drugs may be associated with an increased risk of suicidal ideation and behavior (suicidality) in pediatric patients.

The controversy about the safety and efficacy of antidepressants, particularly SSRIs and newer antidepressants such as selective norepinephrine reuptake inhibitors (SNRIs), began in June 2003. At that time, the U.S. Food and Drug Administration (FDA) conducted an investigation of antidepressants, including citalopram, fluoxetine, fluvoxamine (Luvox), nefazodone (Serzone), sertraline, and paroxetine. The meta-analysis of 24 SSRI trials resulted in the FDA issuing a black-box warning describing an increased risk of worsening of depression and suicidality for all current and future antidepressants used in those under the age of 18. The FDA investigation resulted in only fluoxetine receiving approval for major depression and anxiety in children and adolescents. Of note, however, is that of the data reviewed by the FDA, no completed suicides were reported in any of the randomized controlled trials (RCTs) of adolescents taking any of the above medications.

The controversial black-box warning describing the possible link between use of the antidepressants and suicide in adolescents has since led to an active debate regarding the appropriate treatment of depression and anxiety in younger patients. Just how safe and effective are SSRIs in children and adolescents? Do antidepressants, such as SSRIs, increase the risk of suicidal behavior? Ecological studies provide mixed evidence on the risks and benefits of SSRIs. Arguments against their use focus on the increased risk of suicidal behaviors, while those in favor argue that untreated adolescents are at greater risk for long-term psychiatric problems and suicide.

In the YES selection, Garland, Kutcher, and Virani, in a position paper examining current information and data, argue that while studies of SSRI efficacy have been difficult to interpret as a result of problems in their design, implementation, or analysis, there is clear evidence that certain SSRIs have proved efficacious in treating adolescent anxiety and depression. While evidence for SSRI efficacy has proven unsubstantial for adults and pre-pubertal children, one such SSRI, fluoxetine, has been shown to provide benefits that outweigh the risks in depression in adolescent patients, and at least three SSRIs having a favorable risk–benefit balance in treating anxiety in adolescent patients. Garland and colleagues argue that when properly applied and monitored, and when provided for certain patients whose disorder is moderate to severe, SSRIs may provide a substantial benefit.

On the other hand, in the NO selection, Wohlfarth et al. argue that there is evidence to support the position that, far from reducing the risk of completed or attempted suicide, SSRI use may instead increase suicidality in adolescents. They sought to describe the evidence that formed the basis for a recommendation provided by regulatory authorities in 2004 that warned against antidepressants in children and adolescents. Through a meta-analysis of 22 double-blind, placebo-controlled clinical trials, focusing on both SSRI and NSRI (noradrenerge reuptake inhibitors) use spanning two decades, they examined both suicide completion as well as suicide-related events such as self-harm, hostility, or emotional lability. The studies illustrated a higher rate of occurrence of such events in treatment groups compared to placebo groups. They argue that this evidence, and the risks of antidepressant use, far outweighs the potential benefits.

4

YES

E. Jane Garland, Stan Kutcher,
and Adil Virani

2008 Position Paper on Using SSRIs in Children and Adolescents

. . .

Overview of the Evidence

Major Depressive Disorder

At least 16 published and unpublished randomized double-blind, placebo controlled trials (RDBPCTs) in children and adolescents suffering from MDD are now available for review (Bridge et al., [2007]). Currently, fluoxetine is the only SSRI that has evidence outlining that the benefits outweigh the risks and is approved for use in this population (Emslie et al., 1997).

Interestingly, studies in adult populations have not demonstrated substantial differences in efficacy, tolerability or safety of the different SSRIs. Sufficient research designed to address this issue are not available in children or adolescents. Thus it is difficult to assign class general conclusions from currently available information about specific SSRI medications in youth. Given this situation we recommend that class specific generalizations should not be made and that clinical application of SSRI medications be based on available individual SSRI data.

Available studies pertaining to SSRI medications in young people are of variable quality (Bridge et al., [2007]). Some suffer from design, implementation or analytical problems that make results difficult to interpret. . . . Substantial variability in placebo rates across different studies (they range from about 30 percent to about 60 percent) may also confound study interpretation.

These difficulties notwithstanding, available data indicates that fluoxetine, possibly sertraline and citalopram can be considered to have demonstrated efficacy consistent with level 1 evidence for therapeutic effect (Bridge et al., [2007]). If secondary outcome measures are used in the evaluation of paroxetine—one trial can be considered to be positive while two trials, both with substantial methodological difficulties can be considered to be negative. Neither venlafaxine nor mirtazapine have demonstrated potential efficacy in adolescent MDD. No SSRI has consistently demonstrated positive results in prepubertal children. The number needed to treat (NNT) for each SSRI studied has not been well established but literature suggests an approximate number

Garland, Jane; Kutcher, Stan; Virani, Adil. From *Journal of the Canadian Academy of Child and Adolescent Psychiatry*, vol. 18, no. 2, May 2009, pp. 160–165. Copyright © 2009 by Canadian Academy of Child and Adolescent Psychiatry. Reprinted by permission.

of 10 and may be as low as 4 (for fluoxetine in the TADS trial) (Bridge et al., 2007). This means that for every 4–10 adolescents treated with an SSRI (for approximately 12 weeks) instead of a placebo, 1 extra person will achieve significant symptomatic approval.

Furthermore, while many studies have demonstrated reasonable response rates to treatment, rates of remission have been substantially less (Michael & Crowley, 2002). Additionally, there are relatively few continuation studies available. The TADS continuation data demonstrated no significant loss of efficacy over one year of treatment (March et al., 2007). Data from 36 weeks of treatment in the TADS trial confirmed that 86% of youth given the combination of fluoxetine and cognitive behaviour therapy continued to demonstrate noticeably improved symptoms (March et al., 2007). Furthermore, at 36 weeks, improvements in depressive symptoms were seen in approximately 80% of those given only CBT or fluoxetine (March et al., 2007). These data are consistent with another trial that found no difference in depressive symptoms at 28 weeks for youth given an SSRI and CBT vs. those given an SSRI and usual care (Goodyer et al., 2007).

Published maintenance studies of sufficient design to produce meaningful results are very limited. Recently, Emslie and colleagues randomized 102 children and adolescents (7–18 years old) who had improved depressive symptoms to receive fluoxetine or placebo in an open label, six month long maintenance trial (Emslie et al., 2008). In this trial, fluoxetine did demonstrate a benefit in preventing a relapse. The NNT was four, meaning that for every four youth (with improved depressive symptoms) given fluoxetine instead of placebo for six months, one extra person will have a relapse prevented (Emslie et al., 2008).

Unfortunately, restrictive entry criteria in clinical trials make it difficult to generalize their results to real-world populations. For example, severe symptoms, comorbidity, and acute suicidality are often exclusion criteria for participation in an RCT. The more favorable results with fluoxetine may be partially attributable to the fact that these trials included a placebo washout and selected more persistently depressed patients resulting in a lower placebo response. Furthermore, there is a trend in some trials for older adolescents to be responding more robustly than children and young adolescents. However, it should also be noted that in the child and adolescent trials, no antidepressant has been shown to be superior to placebo in achieving remission rates or more traditional measures of response used in adult studies.

Treatment emergent adverse events have included both physical and emotional/behavioural side effects. Physical side effects include headaches, gastric distress, insomnia/hypersomnia and others (Bezchlibnyk-Butler & Virani, 2007). These are variable in their occurrence and are generally only somewhat elevated over placebo. Emotional/behavioural side effect reported include: hyperactivity; irritability; hostility; disinhibition; emotional lability and self-harm (Bezchlibnyk-Butler & Virani, 2007). These adverse events occur in approximately 10–25% of youth (Bezchlibnyk-Butler & Virani, 2007). Discontinuation rates due to severe side effects also vary greatly across studies (from 0 to 9 percent), again making class specific generalizations difficult.

Suicidal behaviour has also been reported in children and adolescents in case reports and clinical trials (Hammad, 2004; Hammad, Laughren, & Racoosin, 2006). The overall statistically significant ($p < 0.05$) relative risk increase is 1.66 in MDD trials and 1.95 when all trials are pooled. This implies that approximately 2 people out of every 100 treated with an SSRI will have a "suicide-related" event (Hammad, 2004). There have been variable methods of reporting and recording "suicide-related" events. These have included: short term suicidal ideation; persistent suicidal ideation; self-harm without suicide intent; self-harm with suicide intent—all of which have been identified as "suicide-related" events. This variability of definitions makes it difficult to evaluate the incidence of actual suicide directed behaviours. There were no reported suicides in the RCT database.

Best available data from controlled trials and health record databases alike show that SSRI treatment significantly decreases suicidal ideation and suicide attempts in young people (Kutcher & Gardner, 2008). Population studies demonstrate an inverse correlation between antidepressant use and youth suicide (Gibbons et al., 2006). In addition, postmortem studies have not demonstrated a relationship between SSRI use and youth suicide (Leon et al., 2006). Given all available data to date it appears far more likely that SSRI use decreases suicide rates rather than increases them. At the individual patient level however, SSRI use can be associated with emotional/behavioral side effects that require appropriate clinical management.

The potential small to moderate effect size for antidepressants for children and adolescents must also be evaluated in the context of the limited evidence base for other treatments. Systematic reviews have identified some evidence to support the efficacy of psychosocial treatments such as cognitive-behavioural therapy (CBT) or interpersonal therapy (IPT) for MDD; however, the effect size is small to moderate, and most of these findings are based on smaller, open or not-well-controlled trials (Compton et al., 2004). The combination of CBT and fluoxetine may be superior to fluoxetine alone according to one controlled study (March et al., 2004b) but not in a natural clinical state study (Goodyer et al., 2007).

> *The bottom line: The risk benefit balance for fluoxetine in child and youth depression is favourable, while it less clear for most other SSRIs, except in older adolescents. Deliberate monitoring for efficacy and adverse effects is critically important.*

Anxiety Disorders

There have been at least 12 published and unpublished well designed RDBPCTs in children and adolescents suffering from various anxiety disorders (Bridge et al., 2007). There have been six trials in OCD, five in mixed anxiety disorders and one trial in social phobia (Bridge et al., 2007). A summary of these trials indicates that the benefits outweigh the risk for most SSRIs (*fluoxetine, fluvoxamine, sertraline and paroxetine*), while there is insufficient data for the remaining SSRIs (*citalopram, escitalopram*) and data is negative for venlafaxine.

The NNT for most SSRIs over placebo, with the endpoint being reduction in anxiety symptoms, can be estimated as being between three—six (Bridge et al., 2007). The moderate to large effect size is attributable both to the fact that placebo response appears to be lower in anxiety than depression for reasons that are not well understood, and the response to medication is also more robust.

As one would expect, the typical emotional and behavioral adverse effects describe above were also seen in the various anxiety disorder trials, with motor hyperactivity being the most common cause of discontinuation (Bezchlibnyk-Butler & Virani, 2007). However, the signal for increased suicidal thoughts and behaviours is less pronounced and more variable relative to the trials for depression (Bridge et al., 2007; Hammad et al., 2006). There appears to be 1 excess case of suicidal ideation or self-harm per 100 treated compared to placebo treated patients (Hammad et al., 2006).

When considering alternatives to pharmacotherapy, it is notable that CBT also has a larger effect size for anxiety disorders than for depression (Compton et al., 2004). Where head to head trials have been carried out, such as in OCD, medication and CBT are of similar efficacy overall with the combination clearly being more beneficial (March et al., 2004a).

The bottom line: The risk benefit balance for at least 3 SSRIs is favourable in anxiety disorders, and it is likely favorable for other SSRIs in the short term. Appropriate monitoring of SSRI treatment is indicated.

A Clinician's Perspective

When faced with a child or adolescent with mild depression or anxiety symptoms the most appropriate initial step would be supportive treatment including psychoeducation, sleep hygiene, practical problem solving including self-help materials, as well as family and school interventions if indicated, while conducting an extended baseline evaluation for persistence of depressive symptoms and functional assessment over several weeks. It is appropriate for clinicians to prescribe an antidepressant for children and adolescents experiencing persistent moderate to severe depressive or anxiety symptoms with clear evidence of functional impairment in addition to supportive treatment or a course of psychotherapy (Cheung et al., 2007). As mentioned above, the likelihood of benefiting from an SSRI is greater for anxiety disorders than depressive disorders. It should be noted that at least 25% of patients with MDD will have a comorbid anxiety disorder, which would strengthen the indication in those patients. . . .

Conclusion

SSRI treatments for young people with MDD and anxiety disorders are neither a panacea nor a contraindication. The best available evidence suggests that fluoxetine may be the medication of choice for use in both MDD and anxiety disorders. In most situations drugs such as venlafaxine and paroxetine would rarely be recommended and would not be used as first line treatments.

When properly applied and monitored, medication treatment may be of substantial benefit to some individuals. Initiation of antidepressant medications should be reserved for those who are moderately to severely depressed and requires careful monitoring. Both patients and caregivers need to be properly informed about both the potential for benefits and risks. We strongly suggest that medications should not be prescribed outside of a comprehensive treatment approach that includes supportive, problem-focused psychotherapeutic interventions, assessment and monitoring of suicide risk and education about the disorder and its treatment.

References

Bezchlibnyk-Butler, K. & Virani, A. S. (2007). *Clinical handbook of psychotropic drugs for children and adolescents,* 2nd ed. Cambridge, MA: Hogrefe & Huber Publishers.

Bridge, J. A., Iyengar, S., Salary, C. B., Barbe, R. P., Birmaher, B., Pincus, H. A., Ren, L. & Brent, D. A. (2007). Clinical response and risk for reported suicidal ideation and suicide attempts in pediatric antidepressant treatment: A meta-analysis of randomized controlled trials. *Journal of the American Medical Association, 297,* 1683–1696.

Cheung, A. H., Zuckerbrot, R. A., Jensen, P. S., Ghalib, K., Laraque, D. & Stein, R. E. (2007). Guidelines for Adolescent Depression in Primary Care (GLAD-PC): II. Treatment and ongoing management. *Pediatrics, 120,* 1313–1326.

Compton, S. N., March, J. S., Brent, D., Albano, A. M., Weersing, R. & Curry, J. (2004). Cognitive behavioral psychotherapy for anxiety and depressive disorders in children and adolescents: An evidence-based medicine review. *Journal of the American Academy of Child and Adolescent Psychiatry, 43,* 930–959.

Emslie, G. J., Kennard, B. D., Mayes, T. L., Nightingale-Teresi, J., Carmody, T., Hughes, C. W. Rush, A. J., Tao, R. & Rintelmann, J. W. (2008). Fluoxetine versus placebo in preventing relapse of major depression in children and adolescents. *The American Journal of Psychiatry, 165,* 459–467.

Emslie, G. J., Rush, A. J., Weinberg, W. A., Kowatch, R. A., Hughes, C. W., Carmody, T. & Rintelmann, J. (1997). A double-blind, randomized, placebo-controlled trial of fluoxetine in children and adolescents with depression. *Archives of General Psychiatry, 54,* 1031–1037.

Gibbons, R. D., Hur, K., Bhaumik, D. K. & Mann, J. J. (2006). The relationship between antidepressant prescription rates and rate of early adolescent suicide. *The American Journal of Psychiatry, 163,* 1898–1904.

Goodyer, I., Dubicka, B., Wilkinson, P., Kelvin, R., Roberts, C., Byford, S., Breen, S., Ford, C., Barrett, B., Leech, A., Rothwell, J., White, L. & Harrington, R. (2007). Selective serotonin reuptake inhibitors (SSRIs) and routine specialist care with and without cognitive behavior therapy in adolescents with major depression: Randomized controlled trial. *BMJ, 335,* 142–149.

Hammad, T. A. (2004). Review and evaluation of clinical data: Relationship between psychotropic drugs and pediatric suicidality. Retrieved November 24, 2008, from http://www.fda.gov/ohrms/dockets/ac/04/briefing/2004-4065b1-10-TAB08-Hammads-Review.pdf.

Hammad, T. A., Laughren, T. & Racoosin, J. (2006). Suicidality in pediatric patients treated with antidepressant drugs. *Archives of General Psychiatry, 63,* 332–339.

Kutcher, S. & Gardner, D. M. (2008). Use of selective serotonin reuptake inhibitors and youth suicide: Making sense from a confusing story. *Current Opinion in Psychiatry, 21,* 65–69.

Leon, A. C., Marzuk, P. M., Tardiff, K., Bucciarelli, A., Markham Piper, T. & Galea, S. (2006). Antidepressants and youth suicide in New York City, 1999–2002. *Journal of the American Academy of Child and Adolescent Psychiatry, 45,* 1054–1058.

March, J. S., Foa, E., Gammon, P., Chrisman, A., Curry, J., Fitzgerald, D., Sullivan, K., Franklin, M., Huppert, J., Rynn, M., Zhao, N., Zwellner, L., Leonard, H., Garcia, A., Freeman, J. & Tu, X. (2004a). Cognitive-behavior therapy, sertraline, and their combination for children and adolescents with obsessive-compulsive disorder: The Pediatric OCD Treatment Study (POTS) randomized controlled trial. *The Journal of the American Medical Association, 292,* 1969–1976.

March, J. S., Silva, S., Petrycki, S., Curry, J., Wells, K., Fairbank, J., Burns, B., Domino, M., McNulty, S., Vitiello, B. & Severe, J. (2007). The Treatment for Adolescents with Depression Study (TADS): Long-term effectiveness and safety outcomes. *Archives of General Psychiatry, 64,* 1132–1143.

Michael, K. D. & Crowley, S. L. (2002). How effective are treatments for child and adolescent depression? A meta-analytic review. *Clinical Psychology Review, 22,* 247–269.

Wagner, K. D., Robb, A. S., Finding, R. L., Jin, J., Gutierrez, M. M. & Heydorn, W. E. (2004), A randomized, placebo-controlled trial of citalopram for the treatment of major depression in children and adolescents. *The American Journal of Psychiatry, 161,* 1079–1083.

Tamar D. Wohlfarth et al.   ➜ **NO**

Antidepressants Use in Children and Adolescents and the Risk of Suicide

1. Introduction

An increasing number of children and adolescents are treated with antidepressants. However, evidence to support such treatment in this age group is lacking. In fact, most pharmacological treatments of paediatric patients in most fields of medicine lack supportive empirical evidence. Regulatory authorities in Europe and the US have undertaken various measures, including guidelines (EMEA, 1999) and legislation (FDA, 1997) in order to try and correct for this situation. These efforts have led to the initiation of numerous randomised clinical studies in paediatric patients, including studies of antidepressants medications.

As the results of these studies have become available, an apparent signal with respect to suicide-related events has begun to emerge, first with respect to paroxetine and later with respect to other antidepressants. These findings have instigated renewed attention to the question whether SSRIs have the potential to induce suicidality. . . . The review of the results of clinical trials in children by Whittington et al. (2004) concluded that the risk involved in the treatment with SSRIs of children with depression outweighs the benefit except for fluoxetine.

Examining a partly overlapping data set, regulatory authorities have concluded that all antidepressants that were examined are associated with a signal of suicidality, and hence recommended issuing a warning against the use of all antidepressants in children and adolescents (EMEA, 2004a; FDA, 2004). The purpose of this paper is to describe the evidence these recommendations were based on. . . .

2. Methods

Altogether 22 short-term randomised double-blind placebo-controlled clinical trials are examined. These studies were conducted and submitted to the registration authorities for the purpose of obtaining a registration for the treatment of depression and anxiety disorders in children and adolescents. . . .

The studies involved eight different pharmaceutical products and included over 4000 paediatric patients. Pharmacodynamically, these products were selective serotonin and/or noradrenerge reuptake inhibitors: SSRIs and NSRIs.

The studies were conducted between 1984 and 2002. Most studies, however, were of recent date. Most trials (15) included patients with major depressive disorders (MDD), four trials were of patients with obsessive–compulsive disorder (OCD), two with generalised anxiety disorder (GAD), and one with social anxiety disorder (SAD).

Diagnoses were made by psychiatrists and were based on DSM-III or DSM-IV criteria, depending on the time period in which the trial was performed. The design of the trials varied with respect to instruments used to measure efficacy. However, most depression trials used the revised version of the Children Depression Rating Scale (CDRS-R) and all OCD studies used the Child Yale-Brown Obsessive Compulsive Scale (CY–BOCS). The mean severity scores at baseline indicated that most patients included in the studies suffered from moderate to severe disorders. Trials varied with respect to the age range of patients, with some including only children, some only adolescents and some both age groups. The duration of the trials varied between 6 and 12 weeks.

The study reports were searched for descriptions of adverse events that could indicate suicide or events related to suicidality. The following strings were searched for: 'suic-', 'self-', 'harm', 'injury', 'injurious', 'intentional', 'non-accidental', 'hostility', 'emotional' and 'lability'. Event descriptions that included the string 'suic-' were defined as adverse events related to suicidality. Events that included any of the other terms but not the term 'suic-' were classified as 'self-harm', 'hostility' or 'emotional lability', unless clearly indicated that these were accidental. Case reports that were identified were counted so that each patient could be counted only once in each category. . . .

2.1. Data Analysis

No tests of significance were performed on event rates in the individual studies, as the studies were not powered in order to detect differences between treatment groups in the rates of these rare events. Instead, for each study, the existence of a signal for suicidality was defined as any rate observed in the treatment group that was higher than that seen in placebo. In addition, where possible, point estimates for the relative risk (RR) were calculated (i.e. if the rate in the placebo group was not zero).

A random effect meta-analysis was conducted over all the studies. The ORs and RDs (with 95% confidence intervals) were calculated based on a random effect model. . . .

3. Results

. . . No completed suicides were reported in any of the studies. . . .

[Events] (including self-harm, hostility and emotional lability), which are thought to have the same underlying mechanism as suicide-related events, occurred more frequently in the treatment groups compared to the placebo groups. . . .

Signals appeared in studies of longer duration (i.e. 10–12 weeks) as well as in studies of shorter duration (i.e. 6–8 weeks) and in studies that included only adolescents as well as in studies that included both children and adolescents. Therefore, it was concluded that there is no association between the appearance of the suicidality signal and the duration of the studies or with the age range of the patients included. Furthermore, an examination of the cases with suicide-related events in studies that included both children and adolescents indicated that an equal number of children and adolescents were involved in these behaviours.

A meta-analysis for the MDD studies showed an overall significant odds ratio (OR) of 1.67 (95% CI: 1.05–2.65, $\chi^2_{(13)\ heterogeneity} = 8.93$, $p = 0.78$) and a significant risk difference (RD) of 1.4% (95% CI: 0.36%–2.46%, $\chi^2_{(14)\ heterogeneity} = 11.25$, $p = 0.66$).

Results for the anxiety disorders studies showed an overall non-significant OR . . . and a non-significant RD. . . .

Meta-analysis of the MDD trials indicated that efficacy results are heterogeneous across trials and hence an overall measure of efficacy could not be meaningfully interpreted. Furthermore, examination of the design of the trials indicated that there were significant differences between the trials in the methods used to select patients into the trials that are likely to lead to differences in the included patient populations. Thus, heterogeneity between the trials with respect to design and with respect to efficacy makes it difficult to derive an overall statement about efficacy with respect to MDD. Because efficacy could be detected in some trials that used more stringent inclusion procedure (e.g. placebo run-in), it may be that some of these compounds are efficacious in a subgroup of children and adolescents who suffer from more severe and more persistent depression.

The trials of the various anxiety disorders were positive in some but not all products. The meta-analysis for the anxiety trials indicated no significant heterogeneity across trials . . . and an overall effect size of 0.39 (95% CI: 0.27–0.51), indicating a small to medium overall effect.

4. Discussion

The review of all trials that were submitted to the European registration authorities has shown that no completed suicide was reported in any of these trials. However, a signal pertaining to suicidality and related behaviours was detected in all products that were examined.

The combined OR for events related to suicidality in all the depression studies (1.67) has reached statistical significance while the OR in the anxiety disorders studies was weaker (1.33) and did not reach statistical significance. However, the existence of a risk for suicidality in patients treated for anxiety cannot be ruled out. Failure to reach statistical significance may be because the studies were not powered to detect differences in this rare event.

The conclusion from the clinical trials data, therefore, is that in children and adolescents, there is an association between the use of all the antidepressants that were examined and suicide-related events.

No relationship to patients' age, gender or duration of the study was detected, although the numbers are too small to allow any definitive conclusions with regard to these factors.

The evidence concerning efficacy seems to suggest that the MDD trials were heterogeneous with respect to both efficacy and methodology, specifically the methods used to recruit patients. Trials that used long and extensive diagnostic procedure and placebo run-in had better efficacy results than trials that did not. These results may indicate that these compounds may be efficacious in a select group of patients who suffer from more severe and more persistent depression. Efficacy results were stronger and more homogeneous in the anxiety trials, indicating that antidepressants may be effective in treating anxiety disorders in children and adolescents. . . .

The FDA has reached similar conclusions to the ones arrived at in this review (FDA, 2004). Two sets of analyses, using different case ascertainment strategies to define suicide-related events, were run by the FDA. The first used cases of suicide-related behaviours that were identified by the sponsors of the studies. The second analysis relied on events that were classified as suicide-related by a group of suicide experts, under the coordination of researchers at Columbia University. Despite this and other differences in the methods, the two analyses arrived at similar results and reached similar conclusions and recommendations. The analyses presented in this paper are similar to the first FDA analysis in the way cases were identified, but differ in that the number of patients rather than the number of person years at risk were used for the denominators. In addition to other technical differences, the analysis in this paper is based on a slightly different set of studies, corresponding to antidepressants that are registered in Europe. In spite of all these differences, similar conclusions were arrived at, namely that all antidepressants are associated with suicide-related events. . . .

Another source of information that may be relevant to the issue at hand is the General Practice Research Database (GPRD), a computerised database of longitudinal clinical records from 777 GP practices covering about 5% of the UK population. Analyses of the GPRD data set (Martinez et al., 2005) have suggested that suicidality in paediatric patients is associated with the use of SSRIs. However, it is known that patients who are at higher risk for suicidality are more commonly prescribed SSRIs as opposed to TCAs. Hence, the observed association might be due to this selection process rather than to a relatively high risk associated with SSRIs compared to TCAs.

Yet another source of evidence outside RCTs are ecological studies investigating co-occurring time trends in the prescription of SSRIs and suicide rates. Several studies have demonstrated that increases in the use of SSRIs are associated with reductions in suicide rates in the total population, among adults (Isacsson, 2000) as well as among male adolescents (Olfson et al., 2003). These findings provide indirect evidence suggesting that, on the group level, SSRIs may be beneficial in their effect on suicidality. However, these findings should be interpreted with caution, as reduction in suicide rates may be due to other trends in risk factors.

In summary, there are grounds for concerns regarding the use of antidepressants in the paediatric population due to the increased risk of suicidality and related behaviours. Although the signal that is detected is weak, the fact that it is consistently found in a large number of studies indicates that this might not be a chance finding. The fact that a signal was detected in studies of all products that were examined suggests that the process responsible for this phenomenon (although the nature of this process is, as of as now, unclear) may be operating in all instances of antidepressants use in paediatrics and not only in those products for which data happened to be available. Hence, the evidence indicates that a warning concerning the use of antidepressants in the paediatric population is called for. While the evidence for efficacy is inconsistent, especially with respect to the treatment of MDD, this does not necessarily indicate that those antidepressants are ineffective in all cases of depression in children or adolescents. Negative results may be due to failures in the design of the studies (e.g. not stringent enough inclusion criteria).

Altogether these results call for caution in the use of all the examined SSRIs and NSRIs in the treatment of paediatric patients. The need for caution also applied to other types of antidepressants (e.g. tricyclic antidepressants). As long as no contradictory information is available, it is safer to assume that the same risks apply to these medications as well. . . .

References

European Agency for the Evaluation of Medicinal products (EMEA), 1999. Committee for Proprietary Medicinal Products: Guidelines for studies in children (CPMP)/(ICH/2711/99), Topic E11 Note for Guidance on Clinical Investigation of Medicinal Products in the Paediatric Population. . . .

European Agency for the Evaluation of Medicinal products (EMEA), 2004a. Press release on Paroxetin. London, 22 April 2004a. Doc. Ref. EMEA/D/11206/04/Final. . . .

Food and Drug Administration (FDA), 1997. Modernization Act, enacted Nov. 21, 1997. . . .

Food and Drug Administration (FDA), 2004. . . .

Isacsson, G., 2000. Suicide prevention: a medical breakthrough? Acta Psychiatr. Scand. 102, 113–117.

Martinez, C., Rietbrock, S., Wise, L., Ashby, D., Chick, J., Moseley, J., Evans, S., Gunnell, D., 2005. Antidepressant treatment and the risk of fatal and non-fatal self harm in first episode depression: nested case-control study. BMJ 330, 373–374.

Olfson, M., Shaffer, D., Marcus S.C., Greenberg, T., 2003. Relationship between antidepressant medication treatment and suicide in adolescents. Arch. Gen. Psychiatry 60, 978–982.

Whittington, C.J., Kendall, T., Fonagy, P., Cottrell, D., Cotgrove, A., Boddington, E., 2004. Selective serotonin reuptake inhibitors in childhood depression: systematic review of published versus unpublished data. Lancet 363, 1341–1345.

EXPLORING THE ISSUE

Should Adolescents Be Taking Selective Serotonin Reuptake Inhibitors (SSRIs) for Mood and/or Anxiety Disorders?

Critical Thinking and Reflection

1. You are sitting in a coffee shop reading a newspaper and notice the headline "Kids and Antidepressants: Why They Are Harmful." Before reading the article, what about this statement pops into your mind? What evidence would you be looking for in the article to support the title?
2. Given the controversy regarding the use of SSRIs for adolescents and children coupled with the need for medications for many mood and anxiety disorders, what health care procedures could be implemented to lessen the risk while maximizing treatment?
3. If you were to design a study examining the efficacy of SSRIs on adolescent depression and/or anxiety, what variables would you measure and what variables would you control for?

Is There Common Ground?

Major depression is a serious illness in children and adolescents and, therefore, it is important to identify safe and effective medications for the treatment of this disorder in our youth. Recent warnings of the potential serious negative effects of antidepressants, especially SSRIs, raise questions about the risk–benefit ratio of these drugs. The YES and NO selections are excellent examples of these opposing views. They also—however—have commonalities. For example, both sides recognize the limitations with respect to research methodologies and how this can impact findings and subsequent conclusions. Garland, Kutcher, and Virani—while advocating SSRI use—point out that many studies indicate that for adolescent depression, antidepressants are no more effective than a placebo. Tamar Wolfarth et al. point out that the negative effects reported may be the result of poorly designed studies. They also conclude that although the evidence of SSRI efficacy is inconsistent, it does not mean they are ineffective. Both groups conclude that children and adolescents should avoid using certain SSRIs such as paroxetine. Both groups also advocate for very close monitoring and follow-up—especially in the first weeks after medication begins. Finally, both groups argue for more research. With future publications of methodologically sound clinical trials, the costs and benefits of SSRIs will become clearer. In the meantime, these selections raise awareness of adolescent depression and anxiety and strengthen the argument that safe and effective treatment is essential.

Additional Resources

American Academy of Child and Adolescent Psychiatry. (1998). Practice parameters for the assessment and treatment of children and adolescents with depressive disorders. *Journal of the American Academy of Child and Adolescent Psychiatry, 37*(suppl.), 63S–83S.

Anderson, R. (2002). Deaths: Leading causes for 2000. *National Vital Statistics Report, 50*, 1–85.

Bailly, D. (2008). Benefits and risks of using antidepressants in children and adolescents. *Expert Opinion Drug Safety, 7*(1), 9–27.

> Bailly offers an expert opinion on the use of antidepressants for treating depression and anxiety. He concludes that all antidepressants may induce suicide-related adverse events and the balance of benefit and risk seems to support fluoxetine as a first choice SSRI.

Hamrin, V., & Scahill, L. (2005). Selective serotonin reuptake inhibitors for children and adolescents with major depression: Current controversies and recommendations. *Issues in Mental Health Nursing, 26*, 433–450.

Masi, G., Liboni, F., & Brovedani, P. (2010). Pharmacotherapy of major depressive disorder in adolescents. *Expert Opinion Pharmacothrepy, 11*(3), 375–386.

> The authors—after an extensive review of the literature—offer an expert opinion regarding the efficacy of pharmacotherapy. They conclude there is evidence that SSRIs can improve adolescent depression better than placebo and that epidemiological studies do not support a relationship between the use of antidepressants and suicide rate.

Lovrin, M. (2009). Treatment of major depression in adolescents: Weighing the evidence of risk and benefit in light of black box warnings. *Journal of Child and Adolescent Psychiatric Nursing, 22*(2), 63–68.

> Lovrin reviews the risks and benefits associated with SSRIs in light of the advisory guidelines of the U.S. FDA and concludes that SSRIs are effective for treating depressive symptoms but should be part of a comprehensive treatment plan.

Taurines, R., Gerlach, M., Warnke, A., Thome, J., & Wewetzer, C. (2011). Pharmacotherapy in depressed children and adolescents. *The World Journal of Biological Psychiatry, 12*(S1), 11–15.

> This short review outlines the role of pharmacotherapy in the treatment of depression in children and adolescents. The authors conclude that nonpharmacological approaches (psychotherapy) play a major role in mild-to-moderate depression but severe symptoms demand a combination with antidepressants. Fluoxetine is recommended as the first choice SSRI because of efficacy and approval.

U.S. Food and Drug Administration. (2004). PDA News. FDA launches a multi-pronged strategy to strengthen safeguards for children treated with antidepressant medication. Retrieved June 05, 2012 from www.fda.gov/NewsEvents/Newsroom/PressAnnouncements/2004/ucm108363.htm

Vitiello, B., Emslie, G., Clarke, G., Wagner, K., Asarnow, J., Keller, M., et al. (2011). Long-term outcome of adolescent depression initially resistant to selective serotonin reuptake inhibitor treatment: A follow-up study of the TORDIA sample. *Journal of Clinical Psychiatry, 71*(3), 388–396.

> This study examined long-term outcomes of participants in the treatment of SSRI resistant depression in adolescents. The researchers concluded that while most adolescents achieved remission, more than one-third did not and one-fourth of remitted patients experienced a relapse. They conclude that more effective interventions are needed for patients who do not show improvement early in treatment.

Wallace, A., Neily, J., Weeks, W., & Friedman, M. (2006). A cumulative meta-analysis of selective serotonin reuptake inhibitors in pediatric depression: Did unpublished studies influence the efficacy/safety debate? *Journal of Child and Adolescent Psychopharmacology, 16*, 37–58.

> The researchers assessed whether unpublished trials of SSRIs in pediatric depression impacted efficacy or safety conclusions. They argue that while simple meta-analysis across all SSRIs in pediatric samples provided general efficacy and safety information, meta-analysis of individual drugs may have expedited the ability to formulate conclusions about safety and efficacy.

ISSUE 2

Are Body Dissatisfaction and Its Outcomes of Equal Concern for Boys and Girls?

YES: Marita P. McCabe, Lina A. Ricciardelli, and Kate Holt, from "Are There Different Sociocultural Influences on Body Image and Body Change Strategies for Overweight Adolescent Boys and Girls?" *Eating Behaviors* (vol. 11, pp. 156–163, 2010)

NO: Anastasia S. Vogt Yuan, from "Body Perceptions, Weight Control Behavior, and Changes in Adolescents' Psychological Well-Being Over Time: A Longitudinal Examination of Gender," *Journal of Youth and Adolescence* (vol. 39, pp. 927–939, 2010), doi: 10.1007/s10964-009-9428-6

Learning Outcomes

After reading this issue, you should be able to:

- Discuss the impact of weight concerns on boys and girls.
- Identify gender differences regarding ideal body type.
- Critically analyze outcomes of body dissatisfaction on girls and boys.
- Evaluate the role of sociocultural messages in adolescents' body satisfaction and body-change behaviors.

ISSUE SUMMARY

YES: Marita P. McCabe, chair of psychology at Deakin University in Australia, Lina A. Ricciardelli, associate professor, School of Psychology at Deakin University, and Kate Holt, a researcher in psychology at Deakin examined gender differences in overweight and normal-weight adolescents and found that boys and girls were equally dissatisfied with their bodies, but that boys had higher ratings of body importance than did girls. For overweight boys, but not girls, body dissatisfaction (along with peer and parental pressure) predicted weight-loss strategies. This focus on weight loss is consistent with previous research on adolescent girls, but atypical of research with boys.

NO: Using data from the National Longitudinal Study of Adolescent Health, Anastasia S. Vogt Yuan, associate professor in the Department of Sociology at Virginia Polytechnic Institute and State University, investigated gender differences in adolescent boys' and girls' psychological well-being (as measured by self-esteem and depressive symptoms) associated with body perceptions and weight over time. Perceptions of being overweight/more developed (for girls) or smaller/less developed (for boys) had greater negative impacts on psychological well-being (lower self-esteem and higher depressive symptoms) for girls than for boys. Similarly, behaviors aimed at changing one's body size/shape were associated with decreases in self-esteem over time for girls, but not for boys. Overall, girls were more negatively affected than boys by body perceptions and body-change behaviors.

Many young adolescents are dissatisfied with their bodies. Research generally maintains that between 50 percent and 70 percent of adolescent girls participate in dieting, and an even higher number feel dissatisfied with their bodies and long to be thinner. This is especially concerning given that body dissatisfaction and affiliated weight-loss strategies may be a precondition for developing an eating disorder (Tomori & Rus-Makovec, 2000). However, body-image concerns are not restricted to females. Research indicates that adolescent boys also have concerns about their bodies. It is estimated that one-third of adolescent boys desire a thinner body, while another one-third desire a larger, more muscular build. McCabe and Ricciardelli (2001) report that as many as 50 percent of boys are trying to lose weight, while just as many are engaged in muscle-building strategies.

These statistics indicate that physical appearance is on the minds of many adolescents. In fact, for both boys and girls, satisfaction with one's body is an important developmental issue during adolescence. It plays a significant role in predicting self-esteem, physical appearance self-concept, emotional distress, depression, eating disorders, and psychological adjustment. Adolescent girls, and women overall, are generally viewed by the public as more concerned about their bodies and their weight than are boys/men. Gender discourses around emotionality and strength suggest that boys are better able to cope with some body dissatisfaction than are females, and some suggest that girls may, in fact, overestimate their negative body perceptions relative to boys. If this is the case, one would expect girls to be more profoundly and negatively impacted by poor body image and high body dissatisfaction than boys. However, social and academic discourses are not always in sync. For this reason, it is important to understand the variables that affect body image and to examine whether they differentially impact boys and girls.

The role of sociocultural pressures regarding the ideal thin body has been researched extensively among adolescent girls and although many factors can contribute to unhealthy and distorted beliefs regarding adolescents' weight and shape, one particularly significant factor is the media. Media play a powerful role in bombarding girls with images of acceptable and unacceptable body shapes and sizes, and the clothing that accompanies those "beautiful bodies." In magazines, television, and film, the ideal female body is tall, thin, and perhaps even prepubescent looking. Research has indicated that as girls progress through adolescence, they become more aware of this sociocultural body ideal, and as a result, increase their attempts to achieve it (McCabe & Ricciardelli, 2005). Essentially, there is a "drive for thinness" among many adolescent girls. In reality, few girls have the genetic makeup to achieve the ideal body type portrayed in the media.

Little research, however, has examined the increasing number of ideal male body images in the media and how they impact male body satisfaction. As with females, there is a clear sociocultural ideal for males, specifically a V-shaped, lean, and muscular build. How are adolescent males impacted by these messages? Are they as dissatisfied as girls are with their bodies when they don't measure up to the media ideal? The drive for thinness has been associated with weight-loss strategies such as excessive dieting and exercise, while the drive for muscularity has been associated with muscle-building strategies such as excessive exercise, bodybuilding, and anabolic steroid use (Ricciardelli & McCabe, 2003). Do these similarities mean that boys and girls worry equally about an ideal body image, or are girls more negatively influenced by the sociocultural pressures regarding an ideal body type? Of equal concern is whether boys and girls are similarly impacted by feelings of body dissatisfaction (e.g., on self-esteem, depression, etc.).

As previously mentioned, the relationship between body image and psychosocial adjustment has been well-documented for girls and women; however, the relationship is less clear for boys and men. The increase in boys' and men's magazines depicting the ideal lean and muscular body has led to a need to examine the effects on male body image. As such, many researchers are including a sample of boys in their research design.

Two such studies examining body-image satisfaction among adolescent boys and girls are presented in this issue. In the YES selection, McCabe, Ricciardelli, and Holt examined differences in body-dissatisfaction and body-image importance between normal-weight and overweight boys and girls. They found that overall, there were no significant differences in body dissatisfaction between boys and girls; however, boys placed greater significance on the importance of body shape and size than did girls. Positive and negative effects were also found to predict body dissatisfaction for overweight boys, but not girls. Contrary to past research, body dissatisfaction and pressure to lose weight (from parents and peers) were not higher for girls than boys. In the NO selection, Yuan investigated the associations between boys' and girls' body perceptions and psychological well-being. She found that girls and boys were more different than similar in body perceptions, especially in terms of the impact of these perceptions on adolescents' psychological well-being.

Girls were more likely to perceive themselves as too large (and overdeveloped), and boys were more apt to consider themselves too small or underdeveloped. Interestingly, when compared to actual Body Mass Index scores, Yuan found that girls tended to overestimate their body size, while boys generally underestimated their size. An additional and concerning difference between boys and girls in this sample was the impact of these self-perceptions. Girls were generally more negatively affected than boys by these body self-perceptions—girls scored lower on self-esteem and higher on depressive symptoms than did boys. Despite shared concerns about body size, girls were more negatively affected over time than were boys.

YES ⤶

Marita P. McCabe, Lina A. Ricciardelli, and Kate Holt

Are There Different Sociocultural Influences on Body Image and Body Change Strategies for Overweight Adolescent Boys and Girls?

1. Introduction

A substantial body of literature has examined the nature of the sociocultural influences on weight loss and strategies to increase muscle bulk among adolescent boys and girls. Most of this research on adolescent girls has focused on losing weight (e.g., Field et al., 2005), and has demonstrated the importance of mothers (e.g., Polivy & Herman, 2002; Shomaker & Furman, 2009), peers (e.g., Jones, 2002; Tremblay & Lariviere, 2009), and the media (e.g., Hargreaves & Tiggemann, 2003; Tiggeman, 2006) in shaping both body dissatisfaction as well as strategies to lose weight. Until recently there has been more limited research among adolescent boys, and the studies that have been conducted have been primarily focused on increasing muscle size (see Ricciardelli & McCabe, 2004 for a review), although they also engage in strategies to lose weight (McCabe & Ricciardelli, 2004; Meesters, Muris, Hoefnagels, & van Gemert, 2007). A limitation of these past studies is that they have not examined the types of messages and subsequent behaviors by adolescents from different body mass index (BMI) groups. Most particularly, it is not clear if adolescent boys and girls who are overweight or obese receive different messages from parents, peers and media regarding weight loss and muscle bulk than those from normal weight adolescents. Although a biopsychosocial model has been developed to explain both disordered eating and strategies to increase muscle bulk among adolescent boys (Ricciardelli & McCabe, 2004), the extent to which this model operates differently for overweight and normal weight boys has not been evaluated. The biopsychosocial model proposed by Ricciardelli and McCabe emphasises the importance of biological (e.g., pubertal development), psychological (e.g., depression, anxiety, and positive affect) and sociocultural (e.g., messages from parents, peers, and media) factors in predicting body image and body change strategies among adolescent boys and girls. The sociocultural aspect of this model is explored in the current study, and the role of this model among overweight adolescents will be investigated.

McCabe, Marita P.; Ricciardelli, Lina A.; Holt, Kate. From *Eating Behaviors,* 2010, pp. 156–163.

. . . Latner and Stunkard (2003) found that there was a high level of stigma associated with being overweight among children. Many overweight adolescents, particularly overweight girls, have been found to adopt unhealthy weight loss behaviors, such as the use of diet pills, laxatives, diuretics or vomiting (Neumark-Sztainer, Story, Hannan, Perry, & Irvine, 2002; Libbey, Story, Neumark-Sztainer & Boutelle, 2008). McCabe, Ricciardelli, and Holt (2005) found that both overweight boys and girls evidenced lower levels of self-esteem and positive affect, as well as higher levels of negative affect when compared to normal weight boys and girls. The remainder of this Introduction reviews the role of sociocultural influences on eating behaviors among adolescents, particularly those who are overweight.

In terms of the sociocultural aspects of Ricciardelli and McCabe's (2004) model, the literature that is available suggests that not only do overweight adolescent girls engage in unhealthy eating behaviors, but they also model on their friends' dietary behaviors (Eisenberg, Neumark-Sztainer, Story, & Perry, 2005). In addition, research has demonstrated that overweight adolescent boys and girls are more likely to be teased by both their peers as well as members of their family about their weight (Neumark-Sztainer, Falkner, Story, Perry, Hannan, & Mulert, 2002). Further, Falkner et al. (2001) demonstrated that both overweight adolescent boys and girls were less likely to spend time with their friends compared to normal weight boys and girls. Although no studies were located that examined the impact of media messages specifically on overweight adolescent boys and girls, it would be expected that the nature and the impact of these messages may be quite different from those among normal weight boys and girls. . . .

The current study was designed to evaluate the differences between overweight and normal weight adolescent boys and girls in their levels of body dissatisfaction and body image importance, as well as their strategies to lose weight and increase muscle bulk. Differences in the types of messages received from the different sociocultural agents (peers, parents, and media) were also investigated. The study also examined the utility of the biopsychosocial model to explain body change strategies for both overweight and normal weight adolescent boys and girls. In particular, the role of pubertal development (biological), positive and negative affect (psychological) and messages from peers, parents and media (sociocultural) for both overweight and normal weight adolescent boys and girls to predict strategies to lose weight and to increase muscle bulk were examined. . . .

2. Method

2.1. Participants

The sample consisted of 590 adolescents. Three hundred and forty-four boys and 246 girls participated in the study from the first year in high school (166 boys and 134 girls) and the third year in high school (178 boys and 112 girls). The age range of the adolescents was 11 to 16 years. Participants were classified as overweight, normal weight or underweight based on international cut off points for gender and age provided by Cole, Bellizzi, Flegal, and Dietz (2000). Of the 344 boys, 268 were classified as within the normal weight range, and 76 boys were classified as overweight. Of the 246 girls, 208 were classified as within the normal weight range, and 38 were classified as overweight. The underweight boys ($n = 12$) and girls ($n = 13$) were excluded from the study.

2.2. Materials

2.2.1. Body Dissatisfaction and Body Importance

Two scales, Body Dissatisfaction and Body Importance from the Body Image and Body Change Questionnaire (McCabe & Ricciardelli, 2004) were included to assess body dissatisfaction and the importance adolescents placed on their body shape and size. Each scale is comprised of five items and rated on a five point Likert scale with responses ranging from "extremely satisfied" (1) to "extremely dissatisfied" (5) or "not at all important" (1) to "extremely important" (5). Scores range from 5 to 25, and higher scores indicated higher levels of each construct.

2.2.2. Body Change Strategies

Two scales, Body Change Strategies to Lose Weight and Body Change Strategies to Increase Muscle Bulk from the Body Image and Body Change Questionnaire (Ricciardelli & McCabe, 2002) were used to assess adolescents' body change strategies. Each scale was comprised of six items. Adolescents were required to indicate the frequency of the attitude or behavior on a five point Likert scale ranging from "never" (1) to "always" (5). Scores range from 6 to 30, and higher scores indicated higher levels of each construct. The Body Image and Body Change Questionnaire has demonstrated excellent reliability and validity with a large adolescent sample (Ricciardelli & McCabe, 2002).

2.2.3. Pubertal Development

The Pubertal Development Scale (Petersen, Crockett, Richards, & Boxer, 1988) was used to assess adolescent's pubertal growth. The scale contains five items regarding pubertal growth and development. Adolescents are asked to indicate pubertal development on a four point scale: "not yet begun" (1), "has barely started" (2), "is definitely underway" (3) and "is completed" (4). Scores range from 5 to 20, and higher scores indicated greater pubertal growth. Table 1 displays Cronbach alpha for the scale. Petersen et al. (1988) reported good reliability and validity data.

2.2.4. Positive and Negative Affect

Positive affect (10 items) and negative affect (10 items) was assessed via the Positive and Negative Affect Schedule (PANAS) (Watson, Clark, & Tellegen, 1988). Items were rated on a five point Likert scale from "very slightly or not at all" (1) to "extremely" (5). Scores range from 5 to 25, and higher scores indicated greater positive or negative affect. Watson et al. reported that the PANAS had high internal consistency ($\alpha = 0.87$) and satisfactory test-retest reliability ($r = 0.71$). Table 1 reports Cronbach alpha for the scales.

Table 1

Differences by Weight and Gender on Body Image, Strategies to Change Weight and Muscle Bulk, Pubertal Development, Affect, and Sociocultural Pressures.

Dependent variables	Normal weight Mean (SE)	Overweight Mean (SE)	F (1,619)	Boys Mean (SE)	Girls Mean (SE)	F (1,619)
Body dissatisfaction	10.73 (0.14)	12.83 (0.29)	41.74***	11.55 (0.19)	12.02 (0.27)	2.15
Body importance	15.31 (0.18)	15.61 (0.37)	0.54	16.44 (0.23)	14.48 (0.33)	23.06***
Strategies to lose weight	11.99 (0.24)	15.12 (0.48)	33.55***	11.94 (0.31)	15.17 (0.44)	35.69***
Strategies to increase muscle bulk	10.19 (0.21)	10.38 (0.43)	0.15	12.13 (0.27)	8.44 (0.39)	59.88***
Pubertal development	12.81 (0.14)	13.13 (0.28)	1.07	12.53 (0.18)	13.41 (0.26)	7.71**
Positive affect	29.41 (0.39)	28.41 (0.79)	1.30	30.01 (0.50)	27.80 (0.72)	6.34**
Negative affect	18.11 (0.32)	18.70 (0.64)	0.69	17.94 (0.41)	18.88 (0.58)	1.75
Messages from media to lose weight	11.10 (0.16)	10.73 (0.31)	1.15	10.38 (0.20)	11.45 (0.29)	9.43**
Messages from media to increase muscle bulk	10.94 (0.15)	11.06 (0.30)	0.12	11.50 (0.19)	10.49 (0.27)	9.33**
Pressure from parents and peers to lose weight	19.20 (0.18)	21.81 (0.36)	42.57***	20.50 (0.23)	20.52 (0.33)	0.00
Pressure from parents and peers to increase muscle bulk	19.79 (0.20)	20.00 (0.41)	0.20	20.92 (0.26)	18.86 (0.37)	20.44***

** $p < .01$, *** $p < .001$.

2.2.5. Sociocultural Influences

The Sociocultural Influences on Body Image and Body Change Questionnaire (McCabe & Ricciardelli, 2001) was completed. There were four items in the Weight Loss (Parents), Weight Loss (Peers), Increase Muscle Bulk (Parents) and Increase Muscle Bulk (Peers) subscales. The Weight Loss (Media) subscale consisted of 3 items and the Increase Muscle Bulk (Media) subscale consisted of 4 items. Adolescents were required to rate each item on a five point Likert scale with responses ranging from "never" (1) to "always" (5) or "strongly disagree" (1) to "strongly agree" (5). Scores range from 4 to 20 for peer and parent influences, and 3 to 15 for media influences. Higher scores indicated higher levels of perceived sociocultural pressure to lose weight or increase muscle bulk.

Whilst separate items assessed perceived pressure from parents and perceived pressure from peers to lose weight and increase muscle bulk, significant moderate to high correlations between these items were observed ($r \geqslant$ 0.43). Therefore, the scales assessing perceived pressure from parents and perceived pressure from peers to lose weight were combined. Similarly, the scales assessing perceived pressure from parents and perceived pressure from peers to increase muscle bulk were combined. Messages from the media were not highly correlated with the other sociocultural messages, and so these were retained as separate scales. McCabe and Ricciardelli (2001) provide evidence for the high levels of internal consistency of the Sociocultural Influences Scales ($r > 0.84$) with adolescent boys and girls. Table 1 displays Cronbach alpha for the scales.

2.3. Procedure

Ethics approval to conduct the study was obtained from the University ethics committee. Principals of 10 secondary schools in Melbourne, Australia, were approached to participate in the study. Once agreement to participate was obtained from six school principals, students were invited to participate in the study via letters sent home to parents. Active written consent was obtained from parents and subsequent verbal consent received from the student. The consent rate from this process was 56%. The study was completed by students in a classroom setting. The questionnaire took approximately 40 min to complete. Students were also asked to report their height and weight in order to calculate their body mass index (BMI). Weight scales and a tape measure were provided for those students who did not know their body dimensions. These scales were only used by a small number of participants. Students were classified as normal weight or overweight according to their BMI (Cole et al., 2000).

3. Results

Mean scores on each of the body image, body change strategies, positive and negative affect, and sociocultural influences for overweight and normal weight boys and girls are summarized in Table [1]. A two-way weight (normal weight and overweight) by gender (boys and girls) multivariate analysis of variance was conducted to examine group differences on all variables. Using Pillai's criterion, the multivariate effect for weight, $F(11, 609) = 8.26$ $p < .001$ was significant. Thirteen percent of the variance in the 11 variables was accounted for by weight. A significant multivariate effect for gender, $F(11, 609) = 17.31$ $p < .001$ was identified. Twenty-four percent of the variance in the 11 variables was accounted for by gender. The interaction between body weight and gender $F(11, 609) = 1.10$ $p > .05$ was not significant.

Overweight adolescents reported greater body dissatisfaction, greater engagement in strategies to lose weight and greater perceived pressure from parents and peers to lose weight than normal weight adolescents (see Table [1]). Boys reported higher scores than girls on body importance, strategies to increase muscle bulk, positive affect, messages from the media to increase muscle bulk and perceived pressure from parents and peers to increase muscle bulk. Girls reported higher scores than boys on strategies to lose weight, pubertal development and messages from the media to lose weight (see Table [1]). . . .

3.1. Strategies to Lose Weight and Increase Muscle Bulk for Boys

. . . [F]or normal weight boys, the only predictor of strategies to lose weight was parent and peer pressure to lose weight . . . For body dissatisfaction, media messages to lose weight and parent and peer pressure to lose weight predicted body dissatisfaction for normal weight boys, whereas positive and negative affect were the predictors for overweight boys.

. . . [For normal weight boys,] the predictors of strategies to increase muscle bulk were parent and peer pressure to increase muscle bulk and body importance. . . . More variables predicted strategies to increase muscle bulk for overweight boys than for normal weight boys. The predictors were pressure from parents and peers to increase muscle bulk, body importance and negative affect. As for strategies to lose weight, media messages to increase muscle bulk predicted body dissatisfaction for normal weight boys, but not for overweight boys.

3.2. Strategies to Lose Weight and Increase Muscle Bulk for Girls

. . . [For] normal weight girls[,] parent and peer pressure to lose weight, body importance, body dissatisfaction, and stage of pubertal development all predicted strategies to lose weight. . . . Overweight girls accounted for 33% of the variance. [M]edia messages to lose weight and pubertal development predicted strategies to lose weight. The predictors of body dissatisfaction for normal weight girls were media messages to lose weight and parent and peer pressures to lose weight. In contrast, there were no significant predictors of body dissatisfaction in the model of strategies to lose weight for overweight girls.

. . . Parent and peer pressure to increase muscle bulk as well as media pressure to increase muscle bulk predicted strategies to increase muscle bulk [for normal weight girls.] [A]mong overweight girls, [t]he only predictor was parent and peer pressure to increase muscle bulk. Negative affect and pubertal timing were significant predictors of body dissatisfaction. There were no significant predictors for body dissatisfaction for overweight girls.

4. Discussion

As expected, overweight adolescents experienced higher levels of body dissatisfaction and were more likely to engage in strategies to lose weight. They also perceived that there were greater pressures from parents and peers to lose weight than normal weight adolescents. These differences according to BMI are consistent with previous research findings (e.g., Neumark-Sztainer, Falkner, et al., 2002). Also consistent with previous research (e.g., Ricciardelli & McCabe, 2004), boys reported higher scores on body importance, strategies to increase muscle bulk, positive affect, and messages from the media, parents and peers to increase muscle bulk. Girls reported higher scores than boys on strategies to lose weight and messages from the media to lose weight. However, contrary to past research, they did not report higher levels of body dissatisfaction or higher perceived pressure from parents and peers to lose weight.

4.1. Strategies to Lose Weight for Boys

The results demonstrated that for normal weight boys, there were a range of factors that predicted body dissatisfaction. These included both positive and negative affect as well as messages from the media, parents and peers. However, consistent with previous research (e.g., McCabe & Ricciardelli, 2004), body dissatisfaction did not predict strategies to lose weight. Only messages from parents and peers predicted weight loss strategies.

As for normal weight boys, positive and negative affect predicted body dissatisfaction among overweight boys. However, in contrast to the results with normal weight boys, body dissatisfaction (together with pressure from parents and peers), was a significant predictor of weight loss strategies among overweight boys. This result is at variance with previous literature with adolescent boys (see Ricciardelli & McCabe, 2004 for a review), but is consistent with findings among adolescent girls, where body dissatisfaction is a predictor of weight lose strategies (e.g., Stice, 2001). This suggests that overweight boys are more focused on weight loss, and their dissatisfaction with their body drives these behaviors. It is interesting to note that, as opposed to normal weight adolescent boys, neither media nor puberty plays a role in predicting either body dissatisfaction or weight loss strategies among overweight boys. Regardless of pubertal development, overweight boys appear to pick up on messages from those closest to them, and these messages appear to shape their general feelings, their feelings about their body, and their body change strategies.

4.2 Strategies to Increase Muscle Bulk for Boys

The factors that predicted strategies to increase muscle bulk for normal weight boys were similar to strategies to lose weight. Although positive and negative affect as well as media messages predicted body dissatisfaction, it was messages from parents and peers and body importance that predicted strategies to increase muscle bulk, and not body dissatisfaction.

The findings in relation to strategies to increase muscle bulk for overweight boys were similar to those obtained for normal weight boys. Both positive and negative affect predicted body dissatisfaction, and body importance as well as messages from parents and peers predicted strategies to increase muscle bulk. However, negative affect also predicted strategies to increase muscle bulk for overweight boys. The results in the current study would suggest that the predictors of increasing muscle bulk are fairly universal for adolescent boys, irrespective of body weight. Body dissatisfaction is not a predictor, but rather the importance boys place on their body and the nature of the messages they received from parents and peers are the major predictors. However, it is interesting to note that for overweight boys, high levels of negative affect predicted high levels of strategies to increase muscle bulk. This suggests that, consistent with the findings of McCabe and Ricciardelli (2006), negative affect is strongly associated with not only how adolescent boys feel about their body, but also with the strategies they use to change their size and shape.

4.3. Strategies to Lose Weight for Girls

The findings in relation to predictors of weight loss strategies for normal weight girls are consistent with previous research findings. All of the sociocultural agents predicted levels of body dissatisfaction, which in turn predicted weight loss strategies. In addition, consistent with past research findings (e.g., McCabe & Ricciardelli, 2004; Polivy & Herman, 2002), messages from parents and peers, body importance and pubertal development independently predicted weight loss strategies. Positive affect provided no significant contribution to the model, but negative affect predicted parent and peer pressure.

The models for overweight girls were very different from those for normal weight girls. Early pubertal development and high levels of media messages predicted weight loss strategies. It may seem surprising that body dissatisfaction and negative affect did not predict strategies to lose weight among this group of respondents, but this is likely to be due to the fact that levels of body dissatisfaction and negative affect were very high among this group, thus limiting their discriminative ability.

The amount of variance explained by both models for adolescent girls was ⩾30%, and modified models provided a good fit to the data. These results would suggest that messages from the main sociocultural agents, as well as the higher adipose tissue that result from early maturation are prime factors predicting weight loss strategies.

4.4. Strategies to Increase Muscle Bulk for Girls

An interesting finding from the current study was that body dissatisfaction did not predict strategies to increase muscle bulk for either normal weight or overweight adolescent girls. Sociocultural pressures from the media, parents and peers were the main factors to predict strategies to increase muscle bulk for normal weight girls. Parent and peer pressure predicted muscle change strategies. Negative affect did not play a role in predicting strategies to increase muscle.

The above results in relation to strategies to increase muscle bulk for both normal weight and overweight girls show the importance of messages from sociocultural agents. There have been limited studies that have examined the predictors of increasing muscle bulk among adolescent girls. However, the research does suggest that sociocultural influences and not body dissatisfaction predict strategies to change muscle bulk among adolescent girls (e.g., Ricciardelli & McCabe, 2001).

4.5. Implications of the Findings

The results of this study demonstrate the central role played by sociocultural pressures from the media, parents and peers in shaping both strategies to lose weight and increase muscle bulk for all groups of adolescent boys and girls. It is clearly important to work with these messages in further shaping body change strategies with these respondents. Affect is also an important variable to address, particularly for weight loss strategies among normal weight girls, and for overweight boys. An interesting finding was that negative affect predicted body change strategies, whereas positive affect only predicted body dissatisfaction, and neither directly nor indirectly predicted body change strategies. Thus prevention programs need to lower levels of negative affect if they are to alter body change strategies that may negatively impact on health.

4.6. Limitations and Future Research

Future research needs to consider more closely the actual health risks associated with the body change strategies investigated in the current study. Some of the SEMs in the current study may be unstable due to the number of respondents being less than 200, and so the relationships among the variables identified in the current study need to be verified with a larger sample size. Larger and more balanced samples, particularly overweight boys and girls, need to be investigated to determine the generalizaiblity of the current findings. Objective measures of BMI also need to be obtained in these studies. Strategies to lose weight, particularly among overweight boys and girls, may be a health enhancing body change strategy. Likewise, strategies to increase muscle bulk may improve the health of adolescent boys and girls. It is only when these strategies are used in excess or lead to an unhealthy BMI that professionals need to become concerned. The current study was a cross-sectional investigation of the relationships between sociocultural pressures and body change strategies. Future research needs to employ a longitudinal study design to explore the nature of these relationships over time.

Intervention programs need to be developed using the information provided about predictor variables in the current study. As demonstrated by this study, different factors need to be targeted for boys and girls, for overweight and normal weight adolescents, and for weight loss and muscle bulk. These programs need to be designed so that they encourage the use of strategies to enhance the health of adolescent boys and girls, and do not lead to an increase in health risk behaviors. Clearly, parents and peers are important agents for weight reduction for adolescent boys, and the media is an important change agent for overweight girls. Appropriate measures to encourage weight reduction are important from these sociocultural agents. Parents and peers also play a major role for messages regarding increasing muscle bulk. Healthy messages regarding muscle bulk from these agents is likely to lead to healthy behaviors. Body image importance is a significant factor predicting muscles bulk for boys. This is an interesting finding, that suggests that boys only act on sociocultural messages if the size and shape of their body is important to them. This finding needs to be explored further in future studies. A limited amount of variance was explained from some of the models in the current study. Further research is necessary to identify other variables that may predict body change strategies. Participants in this study were primarily from Anglo-Saxon backgrounds. Further research also needs to be conducted to determine the generalizability of the models developed in this study for adolescents from other cultural backgrounds.

References

Arbuckle, J. L, & Wothke, W. (2003). AMOS 5.0 user's guide. Chicago; SPSS Inc.

Cole, T, J., Bellizzi, M. C., Flegal, K. M., & Dietz, W. H. (2000). Establishing a standard definition for child overweight and obesity worldwide: International survey. *British Medical Journal, 320,* 1240–1245.

Eisenberg, M. E., Neumark-Sztainer, D., Story, M., & Perry, C. (2005). The role of social norms and friends' influences on unhealthy weight-control among adolescent girls. *Social Sciences & Medicine, 60,* 1165–1173.

Falkner, N. H., Neumark-Stainer, D., Story, M., Jeffery, R. W., Beuhring, T., & Resnick, M. D. (2001). Social, educational, and psychological correlates of weight status in adolescents, *Obesity Research, 9,* 32–42.

Field, A. E., Austin, A. B., Striegel-Moore, R., Taylor, C. B., Camargo, C. A., Laird, N., el al. (2005). Weight concerns and weight control behaviors of adolescents and their mothers. *Archives of Paediatrics & Adolescent Medicine, 159,* 1121–1126.

Hargreaves, D., & Tiggemann, M. (2003). Longer-term implications of responsiveness to 'thin-ideal' television: Support for cumulative hypothesis of body image disturbance? *European Eating Disorders Review, 11,* 465–477.

Jones, D. C. (2002). Social comparison and body image: Attractiveness comparisons to models and peers among adolescent girls and boys. *Sex Roles, 45,* 645–664.

Latner, J. D., & Stunkard, A. J. (2003). Getting worse: The stigmatization of obese children. *Obesity Research, 11,* 452–456.

Libbey, H. P., Story, M. T., Neumark-Sztainer, D. R., & Boutelle, K. N. (2008). Teasing, disordered eating behaviours, and psychological morbidities among overweight adolescents. *Obesity, 16,* S24–S29.

McCabe, M. P., & Ricciardelli, L A. (2001). The structure of the Perceived Sociocultural Influences on Body Image and Body Change Questionnaire. *International Journal of Behavioral Medicine, 8,* 19–41.

McCabe, M. P., & Ricciardelli, L. A. (2004). A longitudinal study of pubertal timing and extreme body change behaviors among adolescent boys and girls. *Adolescence, 39,* 145–166.

McCabe, M. P., & Ricciardelli, L. A. (2006). A prospective study of extreme weight change behaviors among adolescent boys and girls. *Journal of Youth and Adolescence, 35,* 425–434.

McCabe, M. P., Ricciardelli, L. A., & Holt, K. (2005). A longitudinal study to explain strategies to change weight and muscle bulk among normal weight and overweight children. *Appetite, 45,* 225–234.

Meesters, C., Muris, P., Hoefnagels, C., & van Gemert, M. (2007). Social and family correlates of eating problems and muscle preoccupation in young adolescents. *Eating Behaviors, 8,* 83–90.

Neumark-Sztainer. D., Falkner. N., Story, M., Perry, C., Hannan. P. J., & Mulert, S. (2002). Weight-teasing among adolescents: Correlations with weight status and disordered eating behaviors. *International Journal of Obesity, 26,* 123–131.

Neumark-Sztainer. D., Story. M., Hannan, P. J., Perry, C. L., & Irvine, L. M. (2002). Weight-related concerns and behaviors among overweight and nonoverweight adolescents: Implications for preventing weight-related disorders. *Archives of Paediatrics & Adolescent Medicine, 156,* 171–178.

Petersen, A. C., Crockett. L. Richards, M., & Boxer, A. (1988). A self-report measure of pubertal status: Reliability, validity and initial norms. *Journal of Youth and Adolescence, 17,* 117–133.

Polivy, J., & Herman, C. P. (2002). Causes of eating disorders. *Annual Review of Psychology, 53,* 187–213.

Ricciardelli, L. A., & McCabe, M. P. (2001). Dietary restraint and negative affect as mediators of body dissatisfaction and bulimic behavior in adolescent boys and girls. *Behaviour Research and Therapy, 39,* 1317–1328.

Ricciardelli, L. A., & McCabe, M. P. (2002). Psychometric evaluation of the Body Change Inventory: An assessment instrument for adolescent boys and girls. *Eating Behaviors, 2,* 1–15.

Ricciardelli, L. A., & McCabe, M. P. (2004). A biopsychosocial model of disordered eating and the pursuit of muscularity in adolescent boys. *Psychological Bulletin, 130,* 179–205.

Shomaker, L. B., & Furman, W. (2009). Interpersonal influences on late adolescent girls' and boys' disordered eating. *Eating Behaviors, 10,* 97–106.

Stice, E. (2001). A prospective test of the dual-pathway model of bulimic pathology: Mediating effects of dieting and negative affect. *Journal of Abnormal Psychology, 110,* 124–135.

Tiggeman, M. (2006). The role of media exposure in adolescent girls' body dissatisfaction and drive for thinness: Prospective results. *Journal of Social and Clinical Psychology, 25,* 523–541.

Tremblay, L., & Lariviere, M. (2009). The influences of puberty onset. Body Mass Index, and pressure to be think on disordered eating behaviors in children and adolescents. *Eating Behaviors, 10,* 75–83.

Watson, D,. Clark, L. A., & Tellegen, A. (1988). Development and validation of brief measures of positive and negative affect: The PANAS scales. *Journal of Personality and Social Psychology, 54,* 1063–1070.

Anastasia S. Vogt Yuan  NO

Body Perceptions, Weight Control Behavior, and Changes in Adolescents' Psychological Well-Being Over Time: A Longitudinal Examination of Gender

Body perceptions and preferences have been shown to impact adolescents' psychological well-being, with perceptions of being overweight and desires to be thin increasing depressive symptoms and decreasing self-esteem, especially for girls (Ge et al. 2001; Kostanski and Gullone 1998; Pesa et al. 2000; Rierdan and Koff 1997). Interestingly, perceptual measures such as body image or perceptions are more strongly related to psychological well-being (Kostanski and Gullone 1998; Pesa et al. 2000; Rierdan and Koff 1997) than more objective measures such as BMI (Kostanski and Gullone 1998). Additionally, weight control behaviors are also related to adolescents' psychological well-being (Johnson and Wardle 2005; McCabe et al. 2001; Stice and Bearman 2001). Body perceptions and their resultant weight control behavior are consequential for adolescents' psychological well-being regardless of the accuracy of these perceptions.

Gender may influence the association of body perceptions and behavior with adolescents' psychological well-being. Adolescent girls and boys have different body perceptions and behavior, since girls are more likely than boys to perceive that they are overweight and to be trying to lose weight (Kostanski and Gullone 1998; Yates et al. 2004). These differences may be consequential for well-being, as psychological well-being diverges between boys and girls during adolescence while body perceptions and behavior are increasingly emphasized (Stice and Bearman 2001; Wichstrom 1999). Additionally, differences may occur by age (e.g., Jones 2004; Neumark-Sztainer et al. 1999) and race-ethnicity (e.g., Ge et al. 2001; Neumark-Sztainer et al. 1999; Yates et al. 2004) due to differing norms and perceptions. Previous research has not been able to adequately address these issues because it has been predominated by cross-sectional research (e.g., Davison and McCabe 2006; Kostanski and Gullone 1998; Pesa et al. 2000; Rierdan and Koff 1997; Siegel et al. 1999; Yuan 2007; exceptions include Ge et al. 2001 and Stice and Bearman 2001). However, longitudinal data is needed to establish that body perceptions and

Yuan, A.S. V. From *Journal of Youth & Adolescence*, Vol. 39, 2010, pp. 927–939. Copyright © 2010 by Springer Journals (Kluwer Academic). Reprinted by permission via Rightslink.

behavior impact psychological well-being because some previous research has shown that psychological well-being influences body perceptions (Paxton et al. 2006; Ricciardelli and McCabe 2001). Thus, the goal of the current study is to explore whether the influence of body perceptions and behavior on adolescents' psychological well-being is gendered and whether this relationship differs across age or racial-ethnic groups using longitudinal data over a one-year time period.

Gender Differences in Body Perceptions

Feminist scholars have noted that the thinness ideal and society's emphasis on women's appearance is used as a means to control girls and women (Wolf 1991). Objectification theory posits that an aspect of patriarchy is that women are treated as objects whose bodies are evaluated as instruments for men's sexual gratification (Fredrickson and Roberts 1997). Further, women internalize these views, leading them to habitually monitor their bodies and resulting in mental health problems including depression and eating disorders (Fredrickson and Roberts 1997). Although both girls and women are to some extent objectified, girls become fully socialized to the culture of sexual objectification during adolescence (Fredrickson and Roberts 1997). The increasing emphasis for adolescent girls on the validation of others is troubling because dependence on others' perceptions is related to greater volatility in self-worth (Harter and Whitesell 2003; Harter et al. 1996). Thus, the objectification of girls' bodies may result in dramatic decreases in adolescent girls' self-worth and psychological well-being.

Girls are socialized to focus upon appearance with thinness as the goal through the media and peers. For example, images in magazines and advertisements aimed at girls and women imply that thinness will lead to happiness (Kilbourne 1994; Malkin et al. 1999). Television viewing is also associated with a thinner body ideal for postpubescent girls (Harrison and Hefner 2006). Further, adolescent girls' peer groups influence their weight control behaviors (Mackey and La Greca 2008). Additionally, girls' peer activities emphasize appearance, including a focus on cosmetics, hair and clothing style, and body size and development (Eder et al. 1995). Both adolescent boys' and girls' comments concentrate on girls' appearance and negatively sanction girls by teasing or exclusion for violating appearance norms including thinness norms (Eder et al. 1995). Thus, adolescent girls are socialized to view their appearance and bodies as central to their self-image and self-definition.

Adolescent girls and boys have different body ideals and preferences. Most girls desire to be thinner, whereas boys generally prefer to be larger and more developed (Jones 2004; McCabe and Ricciardelli 2003; Yates et al. 2004). However, there is a wider range of acceptable body goals among boys with some wanting to gain weight, some wanting to stay the same weight, and some wanting to lose weight (Grogan and Richards 2002; Yates et al. 2004). The ideal body type for girls does not vary as much[;] . . . most girls want to lose weight and be thinner (Yates et al. 2004). Body ideals are gendered and are more constrained for girls than boys.

Adolescent girls not only have different body ideals but also have different body perceptions than boys do. Girls are more dissatisfied with their weight and body image than boys are (Davison and McCabe 2006; Yates et al. 2004). Further, adolescent girls' body dissatisfaction increases during early adolescence, whereas boys become more satisfied with their bodies (Bearman et al. 2006). The gender differences in body perceptions occur because girls are more likely to value a thin body ideal than boys are and feel that they have less control over their bodies (Klaczynski et al. 2004). Girls are also more likely than boys to perceive themselves to be overweight, even when they are of normal weight (Kostanski and Gullone 1998). Finally, weight more greatly influences girls' body satisfaction than it does for boys (Barker and Galambos 2003). Research on adults supports this finding by indicating that men are more likely to be overweight yet women are more likely to be dissatisfied with their bodies and to engage in both healthy and unhealthy dieting behaviors (Markey and Markey 2005). These findings reveal how body perceptions differ between adolescent girls and boys.

Gender, Body Perceptions, and Psychological Well-Being

In addition to girls and boys having different body ideals, these differences are also consequential for adolescents' well-being. One reason why they are consequential is because the body ideals for women are so thin that they are unattainable to all but a small percentage of women (Kilbourne 1994). Since girls are socialized to view their bodies' appearance as being a central part of their self-identities and normal pubertal changes, such as additional body fat and curviness result in girls diverging farther from the body ideal of thinness, it is understandable that this would lead girls to develop not only a much more negative body image but would also result in lower psychological well-being during adolescence (Freedman 1986; Stice and Bearman 2001; Wichstrom 1999). On the other hand, boys' body image and psychological well-being both become more positive during adolescence compared to childhood (Freedman 1986). Thus, body perceptions play a crucial role in the divergence in psychological well-being between girls and boys during adolescence (Stice and Bearman 2001; Wichstrom 1999).

It is unclear from previous research whether and how gender influences the relationship between body perceptions and psychological well-being. Some research indicates that boys and girls have higher psychological well-being when their body perceptions coincide with the normative expectations for their respective genders. That is, adolescent girls have higher psychological well-being when they are thinner and less developed, whereas boys have higher well-being when they are larger and more developed (e.g., Siegel et al. 1999; Yuan 2007). Alternatively, adolescent girls and boys may both be negatively affected by perceiving that they are overweight. For instance, perceptions of being overweight decrease both girls' and boys' self-esteem and increase their depression and somatization, although it has a stronger association with girls' self-esteem (Ge et al. 2001). Smolak (2004) also notes that body image may be more problematic for girls than boys, especially at moderate levels, possibly because girls are more invested in their body image and perceptions. Thus, even if adolescent girls and boys are influenced by the same body perceptions, body perceptions may affect girls more than boys.

Body perceptions are related to weight control behavior. Body dissatisfaction, although it may lead to healthy weight control behavior, is also associated with unhealthy weight control behavior for adolescent boys and girls (Neumark-Sztainer et al. 2006). Weight control behavior is related to adolescents' psychological well-being as well. For instance, Stice and Bearman (2001) find that dieting increased girls' depressive symptoms over a 5-year time period. Likewise, Johnson and Wardle (2005) find that dietary restraint and body dissatisfaction were related to adolescent girls' self-esteem and depression. Further, weight change strategies are related to adolescent girls' and boys' negative affect (McCabe et al. 2001). Thus, weight control behavior influences adolescents' psychological well-being, and gender differences in these relationships need to be explored further.

Although it is generally thought that greater physical development may improve women's well-being, it appears that perceptions of being more developed than their peers have negative outcomes for adolescent girls. For instance, early-developing girls have lower emotional well-being than girls who develop on-time or late (Ge et al. 2001; Wichstrom 1999). These differences are largely due to body perceptions, such as feeling overweight or perceiving that they are curvier than their peers (Ge et al. 2001; Siegel et al. 1999; Wichstrom 1999). Furthermore, girls who develop early experience more teasing and exclusion by peers (Summers-Effler 2004). Likewise, perceived faster development is associated with increased peer victimization for girls and is even associated with boys' peer victimization but only if they are overweight (Nishina et al. 2006). Alternatively, boys' lower emotional well-being during the transition to puberty appears to be due to perceptions of underdevelopment relative to peers (Yuan 2007). Thus, perceived relative physical development should influence adolescents' psychological well-being.

Hypotheses

The goal of the current study is to determine whether the relationship between body perceptions and behavior and adolescents' psychological well-being varies by gender. [A]re girls and boys influenced by the same or differing body perceptions? Since adolescent girls and boys have differing ideal body types, girls' psychological well-being may be higher when they perceive their bodies are thinner and less developed, whereas boys' psychological well-being may be higher when they perceive their bodies as larger and more developed (e.g., Siegel et al. 1999; Yuan 2007). Alternatively, certain body types (e.g., being overweight) may be generally stigmatizing and decrease both boys' and girls' psychological well-being (e.g., Ge et al. 2001; Wichstrom 1999). This issue is addressed in two stages by exploring first whether adolescent girls' perceptions indicate greater concern with being overweight and more developed while boys' perceptions indicate greater concern with being underweight and less developed, and second, whether these opposite body perceptions and behaviors negatively influence only the psychological well-being of each respective gender.

[A]re adolescent girls more strongly influenced by body perceptions than boys are? Since adolescent girls are socialized to view their bodies and appearance as central to their identity, body perceptions should be more consequential for girls than boys. For example, Ge et al. (2001) find that perceptions of being overweight have a stronger negative relationship with girls' self-esteem than it does for boys. Additionally, Smolak (2004) indicates that girls appear to be more invested in body image than boys are, are more affected by body images in the media, and may face more negative outcomes from moderate-levels of body dissatisfaction. As implied by these previous studies, it is expected that body perceptions and behavior have a stronger influence on adolescent girls' psychological well-being than boys. . . .

Method

Participants

The current study is based on the National Longitudinal Study of Adolescent Health (henceforth, Add Health), which is a nationally representative sample of adolescents in the United States who were in grades 7–11 in the 1994–1995 school year. The current study's sample size was 6,310 boys and 6,504 girls. Weighted sample characteristics for the total sample were similar to other studies using this data set. The average age was 15 years (SD = 1.63). The mean for family income was $45,610 (SD = $43,450). Average father's and mother's education was 13 years (SD = 2.60 and 2.54, respectively), and 11% of the sample received welfare. Fifty-six percent of the adolescents lived in two-parent biological families, 10% lived in stepfamilies, 5% lived with neither parent, and 29% lived in single parent households. Fifteen percent were African American, 12% Hispanic, 4% Asian, 2% other race, and 68% White.

Procedure

For the Add Health study, 80 high schools were selected plus one of their "feeder" junior or middle schools. Detailed information regarding the data design (including information regarding informed consent procedures) is available at Harris et al. (2008). Add Health collected in-school questionnaires from students present on the day of its administration. Add Health also selected a nationally representative sample of students to participate in an in-home interview, which was used in this analysis. The follow-up interviews were done a year later for students who had not yet graduated; thus, the longitudinal results for this study occur over a one-year time period. As graduating twelfth-graders were not re-interviewed, this sample was representative of seventh- through eleventh-graders.

Measures

Psychological Well-being

Psychological well-being was measured by two indexes—self-esteem and depressive symptoms. The two measures indicate positive and negative dimensions of well-being.

Self-esteem was an index constructed from averaging the responses for four items similar to Rosenberg's (1965) self-esteem scale (Cronbach's alpha = .79 in the current study): (1) "You have a lot of good qualities." (2) "You have a lot to be proud of." (3) "You like yourself just the way you are." (4) "You feel like you are doing everything just about right." Responses ranged from (−2) "Strongly disagree" to (0) "Neither agree or disagree" to (2) "Strongly agree."

Depressive symptoms were measured by a 15-item scale of a modified version of the Center for Epidemiological Studies' Depression Scale (CES-D) (Radloff 1977) created by averaging responses to the items. Respondents indicated whether in the past week they experienced symptoms such as feeling depressed, lonely, or sad (Cronbach's alpha = .86 in the current study). Responses ranged from (0) "never or rarely" to (3) "most of the time." Previous studies have indicated that the CES-D seems to have similar psychometric properties for young adolescents as they do for adults (Phillips et al. 2006).

Body Perceptions and Behavior

Body perceptions and behavior included three measures—perceptions of body size, weight control behavior, and perceived relative physical development.

Perceptions of body size were measured by a three-category dummy variable indicating whether adolescents perceived themselves to be overweight, underweight, or the correct weight (reference category).

Weight control behavior was measured by a three-category dummy variable indicating whether adolescents were trying to lose weight, gain weight, or stay the same weight (reference category). A limitation of this measure is that it does not indicate the methods that adolescents are using to try to lose or gain weight and whether these behaviors are healthy or unhealthy. For example, adolescents could use a range of behavior to try to lose weight such as dieting, exercising, taking diet pills, fasting, and/or purging.

Perceived relative physical development was measured by a three-category dummy variable indicating whether adolescents perceived they were more physically developed (i.e., "look older"), were less physically developed (i.e., "look younger"), or were the same compared to their same-age, same-gender peers.

Control Variables

This study controls for body mass index, age, race-ethnicity, family structure, and socioeconomic status (as indicated by family income, mother's and father's education, and welfare status). *Body mass index (BMI)* was calculated from self-reported height and weight and categorized into overweight and underweight BMI compared to normal BMI (reference category). The formula used to calculate BMI was [(weight in pounds/height in inches squared) × 703]. Self-reported and actual height and weight are highly correlated among adolescents

(Crockett et al. 1987). Because body mass differs by gender and age, the Center for Disease Control's (2000a, b) growth charts for children were used to calculate the appropriate cut points for overweight and underweight BMI for each gender and age. *Age* ranged from 11 to 20 years. *Race-ethnicity* compared African Americans, Hispanics, Asians, "other" race, and Whites. *Family structure* compared two-parent biological families, stepfamilies, adolescents living away from parents, and single-parent families. *Socioeconomic status* was indicated by welfare status (received welfare or not), mother's and father's education (in years), and family income (in thousands of dollars). . . .

Results

t-[T]ests and correlations were conducted to determine whether boys and girls significantly differed on the means of the study variables. Adolescent girls had higher depressive symptoms and lower self-esteem. Girls were more likely to perceive that they were overweight, whereas boys were more likely to perceive that they were underweight. Likewise, girls were more likely to be trying to lose weight and boys were more likely to be trying to gain weight Moreover, girls were more likely to think that they were more developed than their same-age, same-gender peers, whereas boys were more likely to think that they were less developed. Contrary to results for perceptions of body size, boys were more likely to have an overweight BMI than girls but did not significantly differ on underweight BMI.

Next, the multivariate results control for BMI and the social characteristics of age, race-ethnicity, family structure, and socioeconomic status. To show changes in psychological well-being over time, prior psychological well-being is controlled in all the multivariate analyses. Thus, in the analyses for self-esteem, the results indicate time 2 self-esteem regressed on time 1 body perceptions with time 1 self-esteem controlled. In the analyses for depressive symptoms, the results indicate time 2 depressive symptoms regressed on time 1 body perceptions with time 1 depressive symptoms controlled. Control variables also are measured at time 1.

Self-Esteem

Model 1 indicates how BMI category influences self-esteem. BMI category did not influence adolescent girls' self-esteem. However, overweight boys had decreasing self-esteem over time compared to boys who had a normal BMI. Underweight boys did not differ from boys with normal BMIs on changes in self-esteem, over time. [P]erceptions of body size influenced the change in self-esteem over time for girls but not boys. For girls, perceiving that they were overweight rather than the correct weight was associated with decreasing self-esteem over time. However, perceiving that they were underweight rather than the correct weight was not significantly associated with changes in girls' self-esteem over time. For boys, neither perceiving that they were overweight nor underweight rather than the correct weight significantly influenced the change in their self-esteem over time.

Weight control behaviors were associated with changes in self-esteem over time for girls but not boys. For girls, trying to lose weight rather than stay the same weight was associated with decreases in self-esteem, whereas trying to gain weight rather than stay the same weight did not significantly influence the change in girls' self-esteem over time. For boys, neither trying to lose weight nor gain weight, rather than stay the same weight, significantly influenced changes in their self-esteem over time. Finally, for both boys and girls, neither perceiving that they were more nor less developed rather than developed the same as peers significantly influenced the change in their self-esteem over time.

Depressive Symptoms

BMI category is not significantly associated with changes in either boys' or girls' depressive symptoms over time. [B]ody perceptions were associated with changes in girls' depressive symptoms over time but not boys'. For girls, perceiving that they were overweight rather than the correct weight was associated with increasing depressive symptoms over time, whereas perceiving that they were underweight rather than the correct weight had no significant influence on the change in their depressive symptoms over time. For boys, neither perceptions of being overweight nor underweight rather than the correct weight significantly influenced changes in their depressive symptoms over time.

. . . [F]or both girls and boys, neither trying to lose nor gain weight rather than stay the same weight significantly influenced changes in their depressive symptoms over time. However, . . . [p]erceiving that they were more developed than their peers was associated with increases in girls' depressive symptoms over time, whereas perceiving that they were less developed than their peers did not significantly influence the change in girls' depressive symptoms over time. The change in boys' depressive symptoms over time did not significantly differ between boys who perceived that they were more or less developed than peers and those who perceived they were developed the same as peers. . . .

Discussion

Although previous research based mainly on cross-sectional data indicated that body perceptions influence both girls' and boys' psychological well-being, gender differences in this relationship may exist, as girls and boys tend to have opposite body ideals and preferences with girls preferring a thin body type and boys preferring a large and physically developed body type. Moreover, few studies have explored the change in psychological well-being over time to eliminate the possibility that poor psychological well-being may lead to worse body perceptions and behavior rather than the reverse. . . .

First, are adolescent boys and girls influenced by differing body perceptions and behavior? Despite gender differences in body perceptions with boys being more likely to perceive that they were too small and not developed enough and girls being more likely to think that they were too large and too developed, opposite body ideals do not appear to influence changes in girls' and boys' psychological well-being over time. Thus, even though perceptions of being overweight and more developed decreased girls' psychological well-being, perceptions of being smaller and less developed did not lower boys' psychological well-being.

Second, are girls more influenced by body perceptions and behavior? Body perceptions and behavior influenced only changes in girls', but not boys', psychological well-being. Perceptions of being overweight and efforts to lose weight decreased girls' self-esteem over time, whereas perceptions of being overweight and more physically developed increased girls' depressive symptoms. Still, body perceptions and behavior seem to have little long-term impact on boys' psychological well-being. These findings support objectification theory (Fredrickson and Roberts 1997) by implying that adolescent girls place more emphasis on their bodies and appearance than boys do. Another implication of these findings is that, although greater equality is occurring in schools, with girls outshining boys for some indicators of academic achievement (Downey and Yuan 2005), adolescent girls are disadvantaged relative to boys through beauty and thinness ideals for girls (Fredrickson and Roberts 1997; Wolf 1991). Despite some improvements, pervasive gender inequalities still exist, especially in regards to body perceptions. . . .

It is noteworthy that perceived relative physical development influenced only girls' depressive symptoms, whereas perceptions of being overweight influenced both girls' self-esteem and depressive symptoms. A possible explanation is that the stigma against being overweight is so pervasive in US society that girls internalize it through socialization resulting in lower self-worth and depression. However, being more developed may not be as stigmatizing but may influence how others respond to girls. For example, being more developed may increase girls' depressive symptoms by exposing them to greater harassment (Summers-Effler 2004). Thus, perceptions of body size may have a more global influence on adolescent girls' psychological well-being than it does for perceived relative physical development. . . .

Conclusions

Body perceptions and behavior only influence the change in psychological well-being over time of girls but not boys. This finding indicates the way that society has unequal effects on the psychological well-being of adolescent girls and boys and how body perceptions and behavior are a means of diminishing adolescent girls' self-worth and well-being. Even though both girls and boys appear to be concerned when they deviate from the body ideals for their respective genders, these body perceptions are only consequential for lowering girls', but not boys', psychological well-being over time. Future research should broaden understanding of this relationship by determining the way that this process unfolds over an even longer time period and including more aspects of body perceptions and behavior.

References

Barker, E. T., & Galambos, N. L. (2003). Body dissatisfaction of adolescent girls and boys: Risk and resource factors. *Journal of Early Adolescence, 23,* 141–165.

Bearman, S. K., Presnell, K., Martinez, E., & Stice, E. (2006). The skinny on body dissatisfaction: A longitudinal study of adolescent girls and boys. *Journal of Youth and Adolescence, 35,* 229–241.

Center for Disease Control. (2000a). *2 to 20 years: Boys, body mass index-for-age percentiles.* Retrieved June 7, 2004, from http://www.cdc.gov/nchs/data/nhanes/growthcharts/setlclinical/cj4l1023.pdf.

Center for Disease Control. (2000b). *2 to 20 years; Girls, body mass index-for-age percentiles.* Retrieved June 7, 2004, from http://www.cdc.gov/nchs/dala/nhanes/growthcharts/setlclinical/cj4l1024.pdf.

Crockett, L. J., Schulenberg, J. E., & Petersen, A. (1987). Congruence between objective and self-reported data in a sample of young adolescents. *Journal of Adolescent Research, 2,* 383–392.

Davison, T. E., & McCabe, Marita. P. (2006). Adolescent body image and psychosocial functioning. *Journal of Social Psychology, 146,* 15–30.

Downey, D. B., & Yuan, A. S. V. (2005). Sex differences in school performance during high school: Puzzling patterns and possible explanations. *Sociological Quarterly, 46,* 299–321.

Eder, D., Evans, C. C., & Parker, S. (1995). *School talk: Gender and adolescent culture.* New Brunswick, NJ: Rutgers University Press.

Fredrickson, B. L., & Roberts, T. (1997). Objectification theory: Toward understanding women's lived experiences and mental health risks. *Psychology of Women Quarterly, 21,* 173–206.

Freedman, R. (1986). *Beauty bound.* Lexington, MA: D. C. Heath and Company.

Ge, X., Elder, G. H., Jr., Regnerus, M., & Cox, C. (2001). Pubertal transitions, perceptions of being overweight, and adolescents' psychological maladjustment: Gender and ethnic differences, *Social Psychology Quarterly, 61,* 363–375.

Grogan, S., & Richards, H. (2002). Body image: Focus groups with boys and men. *Men and Masculinities, 4,* 219–232.

Harris, K. M., Halpern, C. T., Entzel, P., Tabor, J., Bearman, P. S., & Udry, J. R. (2008). *The National Longitudinal Study of Adolescent Health: Research Design.* Retrieved May 4, 2009, from http://www.cpc.unc.edu/projects/addhealth/design.

Harrison, K., & Hefner, V. (2006). Media exposure, current and future body ideals, and disordered eating among preadolescent girls: A longitudinal panel study. *Journal of Youth and Adolescence, 35,* 153–163.

Harter, S., Stocker, C., & Robinson, N. S. (1996). The perceived directionality of the link between approval and self-worth: The liabilities of looking glass self-orientation among young adolescents. *Journal of Research on Adolescence, 6,* 285–308

Harter, S., & Whitesell, N. R. (2003), Beyond the debate: Why some adolescents report stable self-worth over time and situation, whereas others report changes in self-worth. *Journal of Personality, 71,* 1027–1058.

Johnson, F., & Wardle, J. (2005). Dietary restraint, body dissatisfaction, and psychological distress: A prospective analysis. *Journal of Abnormal Psychology, 114,* 119–125.

Jones, D. C. (2004). Body image among adolescent girls and boys: A longitudinal study. *Developmental Psychology, 40,* 823–835.

Kilbourne, J. (1994). Still killing us softly: Advertising and the obsession with thinness. In P. Fallon, M. A. Katzman, & S. C. Wooley (Eds.), *Feminist perspectives on eating disorders* (pp. 395–418). New York, NY: The Guilford Press.

Klaczynski, P. A., Goold, K. W., & Mudry, J. J. (2004). Culture, obesity stereotypes, self-esteem, and the "thin ideal": A social identity perspective." *Journal of Youth and Adolescence, 33,* 307–317.

Kostanski, M., & Gullone, E. (1998), Adolescent body image dissatisfaction: Relationships with self-esteem, anxiety, and depression controlling for body mass. *Journal of Child Psychology and Psychiatry and Allied Disciplines, 39,* 255–262.

Mackey, E. R., & La Greca, A. M. (2008). Does this make me look fat? Peer crowd and peer contributions to adolescent girls' weight control behaviors. *Journal of Youth and Adolescence, 37,* 1097–1110.

Malkin, A. R., Wornian, K., & Chrisler, J. C. (1999). Women and weight: Gendered messages on magazine covers. *Sex Roles, 40,* 647–655.

Markey, C. N., & Markey, P. M. (2005). Relations between body image and dieting behaviors: An examination of gender differences. *Sex Roles, 53,* 519–530.

McCabe, M. P., & Ricciardelli, L. A, (2003). Body image and strategies to lose weight and increase muscle among boys and girls. *Health Psychology, 22,* 39–46.

McCabe, M. P., Ricciardelli, L. A., & Banfield, S. (2001). Body image, strategies to change muscles and weight, and puberty: Do they impact on positive and negative affect among adolescent boys and girls? *Eating Behaviors, 2,* 129–149.

Neumark-Sztainer, D., Paxton, S. J., Hannan, P. J., Haines, J., & Story, M. (2006). Does body satisfaction matter? Five-year longitudinal associations between body satisfaction and health behaviors in adolescent females and males. *Journal of Adolescent Health, 39,* 244–251.

Neumark-Sztainer, D., Story, M., Falkner, N. H., Beuhring, T., & Resnick, M. D. (1999). Sociodemographic and personal characteristics of adolescents engaged in weight loss and weight/muscle gain behaviors: Who is doing what? *Preventive Medicine, 28,* 40–50.

Nishina, A., Ammon, N. Y., Bellmore, A. D., & Graham, S. (2006). Body dissatisfaction and physical development among ethnic minority adolescents. *Journal of Youth and Adolescence, 35,* 189–201.

Paxton, S. J., Eisenberg, M. E., & Neumark-Sztainer, D. (2006). Prospective predictors of body dissatisfaction in adolescent girls and boys: A five-year longitudinal study. *Developmental Psychology, 42,* 888–899.

Pesa, J. A., Syre, T. R., & Jones, E. (2000). Psychosocial differences associated with body weight among girl adolescents: The importance of body image. *Journal of Adolescent Health, 26,* 330–337.

Phillips, G. A., Shadish, W. R., Murray, D. M., Kubik, M., Lytle, L. A., & Birnbaum, A. S. (2006). The Center for Epidemiologic Studies Depression Scale with a young adolescent population: A confirmatory factor analysis, *Multivariate Behavior Research, 41,* 147–163.

Radloff, L. (1977). The CES-D scale: A self-report depression scale for research in the general population. *Applied Psychological Measurement, 1,* 385–401.

Ricciardelli, L. A., & McCabe, M. P. (2001). Self-esteem and negative affect as moderators of sociocultural influences on body dissatisfaction, strategies to decrease weight, and strategies to increase muscles among adolescent boys and girls. *Sex Roles, 44,* 189–207.

Rierdan, J., & Koff, E. (1997). Weight, weight-related aspects of body image, and depression in early adolescent girls. *Adolescence, 32,* 615–625.

Rosenberg, M. (1965). *Society and the Adolescent Self-Image.* Princeton, NJ: Princeton University Press.

Siegel, J. M., Yancey, A. K., Aneshensel, C. S., & Schuler, R. (1999). Body image, perceived pubertal timing, and adolescent mental health. *Journal of Adolescent Health, 25,* 155–165.

Smolak, L. (2004). Body image in children and adolescents: Where do we go from here? *Body Image, 1,* 15–28.

Stice, E., & Bearman, S. K. (2001). Body-image and eating disturbances prospectively predict increases in depressive symptoms in adolescent girls: A growth curve analysis. *Developmental Psychology, 37,* 597–607.

Summers-Effler, E. (2004). Little girls in women's bodies: Social interaction and the strategizing of early breast development. *Sex Roles, 51,* 29–44.

Wichstrom, L. (1999). The emergence of gender differences in depressed mood during adolescence: The role of intensified gender socialization. *Developmental Psychology, 35,* 232–245.

Wolf, N. (1991). *The Beauty Myth: How Images of Beauty Are Used Against Women.* New York: William Morrow and Company.

Yates, A., Edman, J., & Aruguette, M. (2004). Ethnic differences in BMI and body/self-dissatisfaction among whites, Asian subgroups, Pacific Islanders, and African-Americans. *Journal of Adolescent Health, 34,* 300–307.

Yuan, A. S. V. (2007). Gender differences in the relationship of puberty with adolescents' depressive symptoms: Do body perceptions matter? *Sex Roles, 57,* 69–80.

EXPLORING THE ISSUE ↻

Are Body Dissatisfaction and Its Outcomes of Equal Concern for Boys and Girls?

Critical Thinking and Reflection

1. Imagine that you are standing at the check-out line at a grocery store scanning the magazine headlines. What do you notice about the messages directed to boys/men and girls/women about body beauty and body size? Are they the same? Different? How?
2. In the YES selection you read, there were no differences in body dissatisfaction between boys and girls; however, boys rated body importance higher than girls. What was your gut response to this? Were you surprised? Why or why not? Consider your own beliefs about gender differences around body satisfaction and the role that bodies play in defining young people's sense of self (who they are).
3. Body dissatisfaction and negative body self-perceptions have been shown to impact body-change behaviors for both boys and girls. Consider the strategies youth may use to change their bodies to meet a sociocultural ideal. What are the dangers associated with these strategies? Are boys and girls both at risk?

Is There Common Ground?

Both the YES and NO selections point to concerns that adolescent boys and girls share about their body shape and size. While boys and girls have differing body ideals, with girls aiming to be smaller or thinner, and boys desiring to be larger and more muscular, they share dissatisfaction with their actual versus ideal body types. That said, these selections also highlight differences in boys' and girls' self-perceptions, and how they are affected by these perceptions. Contrary to popular belief, McCabe et al. found that boys and girls did not differ in terms of body dissatisfaction; however, boys scored higher than girls on body importance. For overweight boys, body dissatisfaction predicted weight-loss behaviors, a finding that has previously been attributed to girls. Interestingly, media did not play a significant role in predicting such behaviors; rather, messages from parents and peers were more influential in shaping weight-loss and muscle-building strategies among boys. For girls, findings regarding predictors of weight-loss strategies (including body dissatisfaction, body importance, stage of pubertal development, and messages from parents/peers) were consistent with previous research. One interesting difference in this study concerned the significant role of sociocultural messages from media and significant others in overweight girls' weight-loss strategies, and in both normal and overweight girls' strategies to increase muscle bulk. In Yuan's study, both boys and girls held misperceptions about body size/shape; however, these body self-perceptions significantly negatively impacted self-esteem and depressive symptoms for girls, but not for boys.

This research suggests that both boys and girls seem to worry about how they look and that sociocultural messages (from media as well as parents and peers) seem to be implicated in this process; however, these concerns seem to affect girls more deeply on aspects of psychological well-being. What does this mean? What sorts of buffers might be in place to protect boys' self-esteem, despite their concerns about their bodies? Why do these concerns impact girls more negatively than boys? In the YES selection, overweight girls' weight-loss strategies were directly predicted by early pubertal development and high media messages, whereas overweight boys' weight-loss behaviors were moved by a combination of body dissatisfaction and messages from parents and peers, but not media. Regardless of media, boys seemed to pick up on messages from those closest to them, which in turn shaped their behaviors around their bodies. It may be that for boys, media play an indirect role in shaping body-changing behaviors through the perceptions of family/friends. After all, where do parents and peers get their ideas about body ideals? Do media play a role in shaping their beliefs and perceptions about body ideals in some way?

Future research should examine the ways in which sociocultural messages from parents, peers, and media regarding ideal body shape/size impact adolescents' self-perceptions, body-changing behaviors, and a wide array of "well-being" variables. Boys may differ from girls in how self-esteem and depressive symptoms are impacted by negative self-perceptions, but they may be negatively impacted in other psychological or psychosocial domains.

Additional Resources

Delfabbro, P. H., Winefield, A. H., Anderson, S., Hammarstrom, A., & Winefield, H. (2011). Body image and psychological well-being in adolescents: The relationship between gender and school type. *The Journal of Genetic Psychology, 172*(1), 67–83.

Jones, D. C., & Crawford, J. K. (2005). Adolescent boys and body image: Weight and muscularity concerns as dual pathways to body dissatisfaction. *Journal of Youth and Adolescence, 34*, 629–636.

McCabe, M. P., & Ricciardelli, L. A. (2001). Body image and body change techniques among young adolescent boys. *European Eating Disorders Review, 9*, 335–347.

McCabe, M. P., & Ricciardelli, L. A. (2004). A longitudinal study of pubertal timing and extreme body change behaviors among adolescent boys and girls. *Adolescence, 39*, 145–166.

McCabe, M. P., & Ricciardelli, L. A. (2005). A prospective study of pressures from parents, peers, and the media on extreme weight change behaviors among adolescent boys and girls. *Behaviour Research and Therapy, 43*, 653–668.

McCreary, D. P., & Sasse, D. K. (2002). Gender differences in high school students' dieting behavior and their correlates. *International Journal of Men's Health, 1*, 195.

Ricciardelli, L. A., & McCabe, M. P. (2003). Sociocultural and individual influences on muscle gain and weight loss strategies among adolescent boys and girls. *Psychology in the Schools, 40*, 209–224.

Tomori, M., & Rus-Makovec, M. (2000). Eating behaviour, depression, and self-esteem in high school students. *Journal of Adolescent Health, 26*, 361–367.

ISSUE 3

Should the Human Papillomavirus (HPV) Vaccine Be Mandatory for Early Adolescent Girls?

YES: **Cynthia Dailard,** from "Achieving Universal Vaccination Against Cervical Cancer in the United States: The Need and the Means," *Guttmacher Policy Review* (vol. 9, no. 4, 2006)

NO: **Gail Javitt, Deena Berkowitz, and Lawrence O. Gostin,** from "Assessing Mandatory HPV Vaccination: Who Should Call the Shots?" *Journal of Law, Medicine and Ethics* (vol. 36, no. 2, 2008)

Learning Outcomes

After reading this issue, you should be able to:

- Explain what human papillomavirus (HPV) is and how people become infected with it.
- Understand the relationship between HPV and both cervical cancer and genital warts.
- Describe the economics related to mandating an HPV vaccine.
- Understand the gender-equality concerns related to the HPV vaccine.

ISSUE SUMMARY

YES: Cynthia Dailard, a senior public policy associate at the Guttmacher Institute, argues that making universal vaccination against HPV mandatory for school attendance is a necessary step in preventing cervical cancer and other HPV-related problems. Rebuttals to the issues of the high cost as well as the suitability for the vaccination in schools are presented, and she marks universal vaccination as a key step in future vaccination policy reform.

NO: Gail Javitt, Deena Berkowitz, and Lawrence O. Gostin argue that while the risks of contracting HPV are high, and its demonstrated link to cervical cancer has proven strong, it is both unwarranted and unwise to force mandatory vaccination on minor females. They discuss the potential adverse health effects, both long- and short-term risks, the lack of support for the HPV vaccine within the justifications for state-mandated vaccination, the consequences of a vaccination targeted solely at females, as well as the economic impact that would result from making the HPV vaccination mandatory.

Cervical cancer is largely a preventable cancer; it is the second most common cancer among women worldwide. It is generally accepted by the medical community to be caused by HPV, which is the virus that causes genital warts. HPV is considered the most common sexually transmitted infection (STI) in both Canada and the United States with an estimated 75 percent of sexually active people being infected with HPV at some point in their lives, and that percentage is higher for adolescents and young adult women. Rates for adolescent and young men are not as definite and the severe health consequences of HPV infection for males (e.g., penile, anal, and throat cancers) are less common occurrences relative to females. Adolescent and young women—relative to older adults and males—may be more prone to contracting HPV because of biological reasons associated with the developing cervix. The good news is that, in healthy younger individuals, the immune system can "clear" the body of HPV infection in many cases (Moscicki, 2005).

In 2006, Merck & Co., a major pharmaceutical company, introduced the first vaccine for HPV. While there are almost 200 types of HPV, the vaccine has been demonstrated as effective at preventing the strains of HPV that cause 70 percent of cervical cancers. The American Academy of Pediatrics recommends that girls start the vaccine at ages 11 or 12 years (and possibly as young as 9) because to be most effective, the vaccine's three doses must be given to girls before they ever have sex. Besides 11- or 12-year-old girls, other candidates for HPV include females ages 11–26. More recently, a third group—males ages 9–26 years—was approved for the vaccination. HPV vaccine can prevent genital warts in males, and can help decrease the spread of HPV to women.

While some people question the safety of the vaccine, the existing studies warrant global introduction (Agosti & Goldie, 2007) and the Society of Obstetricians and Gynaecologists of Canada calls it ". . . one of the most extensively tested vaccine[s] to ever come [on] the . . . market" (2007). The major safety concern is that the drug has been studied in highly controlled laboratory conditions but needs to demonstrate "real-world" success (Borgmeyer, 2007). The American Association of Family Physicians has characterized mandates for vaccinations as "premature" because of the need for further data on the longer-term effects of the vaccination, yet they have included the HPV vaccination on their recommended schedule of immunizations for adolescents.

Some of the issues associated with the widespread implementation of a mandatory vaccination program include the cost of the drug. Requiring three doses, the total cost in the United States is estimated to be $360 (over €250) per person vaccinated, while the cost in Canada is approximately $450 per person. In some cases, parents would have to pay for the drugs or their daughter would be prohibited from attending school. This is not a concern in Canada where HPV vaccination is voluntary currently. A major concern of conservative groups is that, in recommending a mandatory HPV vaccination, girls will view this as adults condoning teenage sexuality (Sprigg, 2007). This "encouraging sex" worry is not likely to be realized; sexual health education and condom distribution programs, which have been implemented to help reduce the incidence of STIs (e.g., HIV, herpes) or unintended pregnancy, have not been shown to be associated with an increase in sexual activity (Charo, 2007). Also, vaccination for Hepatitis B has not resulted in rampant sexual activity or drug use (Borgmeyer, 2007). Others worry that vaccinated women will no longer value Pap smears and, as a result, will neglect their gyneco-logical health (Zimmerman, 2006). A further concern is that the government may be mandating HPV vaccinations as a result of underlying pressure by and financial weight of the pharmaceutical companies. Thus, the mandating pro-gram is viewed as nefariously financial.

While most people do not debate the value of the HPV vaccination, per se, the controversy lies in the *mandating* of a vaccination for a number of reasons. By creating conditions where children will not be allowed to attend school unless they are vaccinated for HPV creates a lack of parental rights regarding their children's health care (Charo, 2007). The mandatory HPV vac-cination program becomes a question of more complex politics and moral objections rather than simply a public health issue. The YES and NO selections provide evidence to support both sides of this debate.

Dailard presents facts that display the high infection rate of HPV—at an estimated 75 percent among Americans—as well as the strong connection to cervical cancer—HPV is responsible for 70 percent of all cervical cancer cases. These, coupled with the virtual 100-percent efficacy of current HPV vac-cinations, provide, according to Dailard, a clear validation for the need for universal vaccination. She addresses the common argument against universal vaccination, that being the high cost, in a twofold manner. First, she provides evidence for the high cost and impact of medical care related to HPV infec-tions that would be negated by the vaccine and possibly counterbalance some of the cost related to the vaccination. Next, she looks at the policies for private insurance for HPV vaccinations as well as public efforts that could reduce the cost for those who do not have coverage or the ability to afford the vaccina-tion. The issue of school-entry requirements for the vaccination is addressed, wherein she describes the requirements as possibly the most effective way of ensuring widespread immunity. Dailard also brings up the potential future benefits the universal vaccination for HPV could bring for currently under-developed vaccinations for other STIs and diseases.

Javitt, Berkowitz, and Gostin, while not antivaccination, argue that the efforts to mandate HPV vaccination are premature and raise legal, ethical, and social concerns. As the vaccine is still new, there is little evidence to suggest that the vaccine does in fact prevent cervical cancer instead of simply the early symptoms. Additionally, possible long-term adverse reactions are not yet known, neither are the effects of the vaccine on a much wider patient pool. Javitt et al. also bring up the issue of the lack of data for long-term efficacy of the vaccination; the immunity duration has not been defined beyond a few years. Further complications arise from HPV's inability to fulfill the historic requirements for mandated vaccination. It is neither a "public health necessity," nor are children most at risk in school settings. Final issues brought to light by Javitt et al. are the issues of gender inequality from a vaccine targeted primarily at females, a potential public backlash against an aggressive push for mandatory vaccination, and the negative economic impact that could affect government vaccination programs as well as private physicians and the families of patients. As you consider these two viewpoints, is there a compromise between the two positions?

YES ⬅

Achieving Universal Vaccination Against Cervical Cancer in the United States: The Need and the Means

The advent of a vaccine against the types of human papillomavirus (HPV) linked to most cases of cervical cancer is widely considered one of the greatest health care advances for women in recent years. Experts believe that vaccination against HPV has the potential to dramatically reduce cervical cancer incidence and mortality particularly in resource-poor developing countries where cervical cancer is most common and deadly. In the United States, the vaccine's potential is likely to be felt most acutely within low-income communities and communities of color, which disproportionately bear the burden of cervical cancer.

Because HPV is easily transmitted through sexual contact, the vaccine's full promise may only be realized through near-universal vaccination of girls and young women prior to sexual activity—a notion reflected in recently proposed federal guidelines. And history, as supported by a large body of scientific evidence, suggests that the most effective way to achieve universal vaccination is by requiring children to be inoculated prior to attending school. Yet the link between HPV and sexual activity—and the notion that HPV is different than other infectious diseases targeted by vaccine school entry requirements—tests the prevailing justification for such efforts. Meanwhile, any serious effort to achieve universal vaccination among young people with this relatively expensive vaccine will expose holes in the public health safety net that, if left unaddressed, have the potential to exacerbate longstanding disparities in cervical cancer rates among American women.

The Case for Universal Vaccination

Virtually all cases of cervical cancer are linked to HPV, an extremely common sexually transmitted infection (STI) that is typically asymptomatic and harmless; most people never know they are infected, and most cases resolve on their own. It is estimated that approximately three in four Americans contract HPV at some point in their lives, with most cases acquired relatively soon

Dailard, Cynthia. From *Guttmacher Policy Review,* vol. 9, no. 4, Fall 2006, pp. 12–16. Copyright © 2006 by Alan Guttmacher Institute. Reprinted by permission.

after individuals have sex for the first time. Of the approximately 30 known types of HPV that are sexually transmitted, more than 13 are associated with cervical cancer. Yet despite the prevalence of HPV, cervical cancer is relatively rare in the United States; it generally occurs only in the small proportion of cases where a persistent HPV infection goes undetected over many years. This is largely due to the widespread availability of Pap tests, which can detect pre-cancerous changes of the cervix that can be treated before cancer sets in, as well as cervical cancer in its earliest stage, when it is easily treatable.

Still, the American Cancer Society estimates that in 2006, almost 10,000 cases of invasive cervical cancer will occur to American women, resulting in 3,700 deaths. Significantly, more than half of all U.S. women diagnosed with cervical cancer have not had a Pap test in the last three years. These women are disproportionately low income and women of color who lack access to afford-able and culturally competent health services. As a result, the incidence of cer-vical cancer is approximately 1.5 times higher among African American and Latina women than among white women; women of color are considerably more likely than whites to die of the disease as well. Two new HPV vaccines—Gardasil, manufactured by Merck & Company, and Cervarix, manufactured by GlaxoSmithKline—promise to transform this landscape. Both are virtually 100% effective in preventing the two types of HPV responsible for 70% of all cases of cervical cancer; Gardasil also protects against two other HPV types associated with 90% of all cases of genital warts. Gardasil was approved by the federal Food and Drug Administration (FDA) in June; GlaxoSmithKline is expected to apply for FDA approval of Cervarix by year's end.

Following FDA approval, Gardasil was endorsed by the Centers for Disease Control and Prevention's Advisory Committee on Immunization Prac-tices (ACIP), which is responsible for maintaining the nation's schedule of recommended vaccines. ACIP recommended that the vaccine be routinely administered to all girls ages 11–12, and as early as age nine at a doctor's discre-tion. Also, it recommended vaccination of all adolescents and young women ages 13–26 as part of a national "catch-up" campaign for those who have not already been vaccinated.

The ACIP recommendations, which are closely followed by health care professionals, reflect the notion that to eradicate cervical cancer, it will be necessary to achieve near-universal vaccination of girls and young women prior to sexual activity, when the vaccine is most effective. Experts believe that such an approach has the potential to significantly reduce cervical cancer deaths in this country and around the world. Also, high vaccination rates will significantly reduce the approximately 3.5 million abnormal Pap results expe-rienced by American women each year, many of which are caused by transient or persistent HPV infections. These abnormal Pap results require millions of women to seek follow-up care, ranging from additional Pap tests to more invasive procedures such as colposcopies and biopsies. This additional care exacts a substantial emotional and even physical toll on women, and costs an estimated $6 billion in annual health care expenditures. Finally, widespread vaccination fosters "herd immunity," which is achieved when a sufficiently high proportion of individuals within a population are vaccinated that those who go unvaccinated—because the vaccine is contraindicated for them or because they are medically underserved, for example—are essentially protected.

The Role of School Entry Requirements

Achieving high vaccination levels among adolescents, however, can be a difficult proposition. Unlike infants and toddlers, who have frequent contact with health care providers in the context of well-child visits, adolescents often go for long stretches without contact with a health care professional. In addition, the HPV vaccine is likely to pose particular challenges, given that it must be administered three times over a six-month period to achieve maximum effectiveness.

A large body of evidence suggests that the most effective means to ensure rapid and widespread use of childhood or adolescent vaccines is through state laws or policies that require children to be vaccinated prior to enrollment in day care or school. These school-based immunization requirements, which exist in some form in all 50 states, are widely credited for the success of immunization programs in the United States. They have also played a key role in helping to close racial, ethnic and socioeconomic gaps in immunization rates, and have proven to be far more effective than guidelines recommending the vaccine for certain age-groups or high-risk populations. Although each state decides for itself whether a particular vaccine will be required for children to enroll in school, they typically rely on ACIP recommendations in making their decision.

In recent months, some commentators have noted that as a sexually transmitted infection, HPV is "different" from other infectious diseases such as measles, mumps or whooping cough, which are easily transmitted in a school setting or threaten school attendance when an outbreak occurs. Some socially conservative advocacy groups accordingly argue that the HPV vaccine does not meet the historical criteria necessary for it to be required for children attending school; many of them also contend that abstinence outside of marriage is the real answer to HPV. They welcome the advent of the vaccine, they say, but will oppose strenuously any effort to require it for school enrollment.

This position reflects only a limited understanding of school-based vaccination requirements. These requirements do not exist solely to prevent the transmission of disease in school or during childhood. Instead, they further society's strong interest in ensuring that people are protected from disease throughout their lives and are a highly efficient means of eradicating disease in the larger community. For example, states routinely require school-age children to be vaccinated against rubella (commonly known as German measles), a typically mild illness in children, to protect pregnant women in the community from the devastating effects the disease can have on a developing fetus. Similarly, states currently require vaccination against certain diseases, such as tetanus, that are not "contagious" at all, but have very serious consequences for those affected. And almost all states require vaccination against Hepatitis B, a blood borne disease which can be sexually transmitted.

Moreover, according to the National Conference of State Legislatures (NCSL), all 50 states allow parents to refuse to vaccinate their children on medical grounds, such as when a vaccine is contraindicated for a particular child due to allergy, compromised immunity or significant illness. All states except Mississippi and West Virginia allow parents to refuse to vaccinate their children on religious grounds. Additionally, 20 states go so far as to allow parents to refuse to vaccinate their children because of a personal, moral or other belief. Unlike a medical exemption, which requires a parent to provide documentation from a physician, the process for obtaining nonmedical exemptions can vary widely by state.

NCSL notes that, in recent years, almost a dozen states considered expanding their exemption policy. Even absent any significant policy change, the rate of parents seeking exemptions for nonmedical reasons is on the rise. This concerns public health experts. Research shows that in states where exemptions are easier to obtain, a higher proportion of parents refuse to vaccinate their children; research further shows that these states, in turn, are more likely to experience outbreaks of vaccine-preventable diseases, such as measles and whooping cough. Some vaccine program administrators fear that because of the social sensitivities surrounding the HPV vaccine, any effort to require the vaccine for school entry may prompt legislators to amend their laws to create nonmedical exemptions where they do not currently exist or to make existing exemptions easier to obtain. This has the potential not only to thwart the effort to stem the tide of cervical cancer, but to foster the spread of other vaccine-preventable diseases as well.

Financing Challenges Laid Bare

Another barrier to achieving universal vaccination of girls and young women will be the high price of the vaccine. Gardasil is expensive by vaccine standards, costing approximately $360 for the three-part series of injections. Despite this high cost, ACIP's endorsement means that Gardasil will be covered by most private insurers; in fact, a number of large insurers have already announced they will cover the vaccine for girls and young women within the ACIP-recommended age range. Still, the Institute of Medicine estimates that approximately 11% of all American children have private insurance that does not cover immunization, and even those with insurance coverage may have to pay deductibles and copayments that create a barrier to care.

Those who do not have private insurance or who cannot afford the out of pocket costs associated with Gardasil will need to rely on a patchwork system of programs that exist to support the delivery of subsidized vaccines to low-income and uninsured individuals. In June, ACIP voted to include Gardasil in the federal Vaccines for Children program (VFC), which provides free vaccines largely to children and teenagers through age 18 who are uninsured or receive Medicaid. The program's reach is significant: In 2003, 43% of all childhood vaccine doses were distributed by the VFC program.

THE POTENTIAL ROLE OF FAMILY PLANNING CLINICS IN AN HPV VACCINE 'CATCH-UP' CAMPAIGN

Family planning clinics, including those funded under Title X of the Public Health Service Act, have an important role to play in a national "catch-up" campaign to vaccinate young women against HPV. This is particularly true for women ages 19–26, who are too old to receive free vaccines through the federal Vaccines for Children program but still fall within the ACIP-recommended age range for the HPV vaccine.

Almost 4,600 Title X–funded family planning clinics provide subsidized family planning and related preventive health care to just over five million women nationwide. In theory, Title X clinics are well poised to offer the HPV vaccine, because they already are a major provider of STI services and cervical cancer screening, providing approximately six million STI (including HIV) tests and 2.7 million Pap tests in 2004 alone. Because Title X clients are disproportionately low income and women of color, they are at particular risk of developing cervical cancer later in life. Moreover, most Title X clients fall within the ACIP age recommendations of 26 and under for the HPV vaccine (59% are age 24 or younger, and 18% are ages 25–29); many of these women are uninsured and may not have an alternative source of health care.

Title X funds may be used to pay for vaccines linked to improved reproductive health outcomes, and some Title X clinics offer the Hepatitis B vaccine (which can be sexually transmitted). Although many family planning providers are expressing interest in incorporating the HPV vaccine into their package of services, its high cost—even at a discounted government purchase price—is likely to stand in the way. Clinics that receive Title X funds are required by law to charge women based on their ability to pay, with women under 100% of the federal poverty level (representing 68% of Title X clients) receiving services completely free of charge and those with incomes between 100–250% of poverty charged on a sliding scale. While Merck has expressed an interest in extending its patient assistance program to publicly funded family planning clinics, it makes no promises. In fact, a statement on the company's Web site says that "Due to the complexities associated with vaccine funding and distribution in the public sector, as well as the resource constraints that typically exist in public health settings, Merck is currently evaluating whether and how a vaccine assistance program could be implemented in the public sector."

The HPV vaccine, however, is not just recommended for children and teenagers; it is also recommended for young adult women up through age 26. Vaccines are considered an "optional" benefit for adults under Medicaid, meaning that it is up to each individual state to decide whether or not to cover a given vaccine. Also, states can use their own funds and federal grants to support the delivery of subsidized vaccines to low-income or uninsured adults. Many states, however, have opted instead to channel these funds toward childhood-vaccination efforts, particularly as vaccine prices have grown in recent years. As a result, adult vaccination rates remain low and disparities exist across racial, ethnic and socioeconomic groups—mirroring the disparities that exist for cervical cancer.

In response to all this, Merck in May announced it would create a new "patient assistance program," designed to provide all its vaccines free to adults who are uninsured, unable to afford the vaccines and have an annual household income below 200% of the federal poverty level ($19,600 for individuals and $26,400 for couples). To receive free vaccines, patients will need to complete and fax forms from participating doctors' offices for processing by Merck during the patients' visits. Many young uninsured women, however, do not seek their care in private doctors' offices, but instead rely on publicly funded family planning clinics for their care, suggesting the impact of this program may be limited (see box).

Thinking Ahead

Solutions to the various challenges presented by the HPV vaccine are likely to have relevance far beyond cervical cancer. In the coming years, scientific breakthroughs in the areas of immunology, molecular biology and genetics will eventually permit vaccination against a broader range of acute illnesses as well as chronic diseases. Currently, vaccines for other STIs such as chlamydia, herpes and HIV are in various stages of development. Also under study are vaccines for Alzheimer's disease, diabetes and a range of cancers. Vaccines for use among adolescents will also be increasingly common. A key question is, in the future, will individuals across the economic spectrum have access to these breakthrough medical advances or will disadvantaged individuals be left behind?

When viewed in this broader context, the debate over whether the HPV vaccine should be required for school enrollment may prove to be a healthy one. If the HPV vaccine is indeed "the first of its kind," as some have characterized it, it has the potential to prompt communities across the nation to reconsider and perhaps reconceive the philosophical justification for school entry requirements. Because the U.S. health care system is fragmented, people have no guarantee of health insurance coverage or access to affordable care. School entry requirements might therefore provide an important opportunity to deliver public health interventions that, like the HPV vaccine, offer protections to individuals who have the potential to become disconnected from health care services later in life. Similar to the HPV vaccine's promise of cervical cancer prevention, these benefits may not be felt for many years, but nonetheless may be compelling from a societal standpoint. And bearing in mind that school dropout rates begin to climb as early as age 13, middle school might be appropriately viewed as the last public health gate that an entire age-group of individuals pass through together—regardless of race, ethnicity or socioeconomic status.

Meanwhile, the cost and affordability issues raised by the HPV vaccine may help draw attention to the need to reform the vaccine-financing system in this country. In 2003, the Institute of Medicine proposed a series of reforms designed to improve the way vaccines are financed and distributed. They included a national insurance benefit mandate that would apply to all public and private health care plans and vouchers for uninsured children and adults to receive immunizations through the provider of their choice. Legislation introduced by Rep. Henry Waxman (D-CA) and Sen. Edward Kennedy (D-MA), called the Vaccine Access and Supply Act, adopts a different approach. The bill would expand the Vaccines for Children program, create a comparable Vaccines for Adults program, strengthen the vaccine grant program to the states and prohibit Medicaid cost-sharing requirements for ACIP-recommended vaccines for adults.

Whether the HPV vaccine will in fact hasten reforms of any kind remains to be seen. But one thing is clear: If the benefits of this groundbreaking vaccine cannot be enjoyed by girls and women who are disadvantaged by poverty or insurance status, then it will only serve to perpetuate the disparities in cervical cancer rates that have persisted in this country for far too long.

Gail Javitt, Deena Berkowitz, and Lawrence O. Gostin

 **NO**

Assessing Mandatory HPV Vaccination: Who Should Call the Shots?

I. Introduction

The human papillomavirus (HPV) is the most common sexually transmitted infection worldwide. In the United States, more than six million people are infected each year. Although most HPV infections are benign, two strains of HPV cause 70 percent of cervical cancer cases.[1] Two other strains of HPV are associated with 90 percent of genital warts cases.[2]

In June 2006, the Food and Drug Administration (FDA) approved the first vaccine against HPV. Sold as Gardasil, the quadrivalent vaccine is intended to prevent four strains of HPV associated with cervical cancer, precancerous genital lesions, and genital warts.[3] Following FDA approval, the national Advisory Committee on Immunization Practices (ACIP) recommended routine vaccination for girls ages 11–12 with three doses of quadrivalent HPV vaccine.[4] Thereafter, state legislatures around the country engaged in an intense effort to pass laws mandating vaccination of young girls against HPV. This activity was spurred in part by an intense lobbying campaign by Merck, the manufacturer of the vaccine.[5]

The United States has a robust state-based infrastructure for mandatory vaccination that has its roots in the 19th century. Mandating vaccination as a condition for school entry began in the early 1800s and is currently required by all 50 states for several common childhood infectious diseases.[6] Some suggest that mandatory HPV vaccination for minor females fits squarely within this tradition.

Nonetheless, state efforts to mandate HPV vaccination in minors have raised a variety of concerns on legal, ethical, and social grounds. Unlike other diseases for which state legislatures have mandated vaccination for children, HPV is neither transmissible through casual contact nor potentially fatal during childhood. It also would be the first vaccine to be mandated for use exclusively in one gender. As such, HPV vaccine presents a new context for considering vaccine mandates.

In this paper, we review the scientific evidence supporting Gardasil's approval and the legislative actions in the states that followed. We then argue that mandatory HPV vaccination at this time is both unwarranted and unwise.

From *Journal of Law, Medicine and Ethics*, vol. 36, issue 2, Summer 2008, pp. 384–395. Copyright © 2008 by American Society of Law, Medicine & Ethics. Reprinted by permission.

While the emergence of an HPV vaccine refects a potentially significant public health advance, the vaccine raises several concerns. First, the long-term
safety and effectiveness of the vaccine are unclear, and serious adverse events
reported shortly after the vaccine's approval raise questions about its short-
term safety as well. In light of unanswered safety questions, the vaccine should
be rolled out slowly, with risks carefully balanced against benefits in individual
cases. Second, the legal and ethical justifications that have historically supported state-mandated vaccination do not support mandating HPV vaccine.
Specifically, HPV does not threaten an imminent and significant risk to the
health of others. Mandating HPV would therefore constitute an expansion
of the state's authority to interfere with individual and parental autonomy.
Engaging in such expansion in the absence of robust public discussion runs the
risk of creating a public backlash that may undermine the goal of widespread
HPV vaccine coverage and lead to public distrust of established childhood vaccine programs for other diseases. Third, the current sex-based HPV vaccination
mandates present constitutional concerns because they require only girls to
be vaccinated. Such concerns could lead to costly and protracted legal challenges. Finally, vaccination mandates will place economic burdens on federal
and state governments and individual practitioners that may have a negative
impact on the provision of other health services. In light of these potentially
adverse public health, economic, and societal consequences, we believe that it
is premature for states to add HPV to the list of state-mandated vaccines.

II. Background

Before discussing in detail the basis for our opposition to mandated HPV vaccination, it is necessary to review the public health impact of HPV and the data
based on which the FDA approved the vaccine. Additionally, to understand
the potentially widespread uptake of HPV vaccine mandates, we review the
state legislative activities that have occurred since the vaccine's approval.

A. HPV Epidemiology

In the United States, an estimated 20 million people, or 15 percent of the
population, are currently infected with HPV.[7] Modeling studies suggest that
up to 80 percent of sexually active women will have become infected with the
virus at some point in their lives by the time they reach age 50.[8] Prevalence of
HPV is highest among sexually active females ages 14–19.[9]

Human papillomavirus comprises more than 100 different strains of virus,
of which more than 30 infect the genital area.[10] The majority of HPV infections
are transient, asymptomatic, and cause no clinical problems. However,
persistent infection with high risk types of HPV is the most important risk
factor for cervical cancer precursors and invasive cervical cancer. Two strains
in particular, 16 and 18, have been classified as carcinogenic to humans by
the World Health Organization's international agency for research on cancer.[11]
These strains account for 70 percent of cervical cancer cases[12] and are responsible
for a large proportion of anal, vulvar, vaginal, penile, and urethral cancers.[13]

More than 200,000 women die of cervical cancer each year.[14] The majority of these deaths take place in developing countries, which lack the screening programs and infrastructure for diagnosis, treatment, and prevention that exist in the United States. In the U.S., it is estimated that there were about 9,700 cases of invasive cervical cancer and about 3,700 deaths from cervical cancer in 2006, as compared with 500,000 cases and 288,000 deaths worldwide.[15]

Two other HPV types, 6 and 11, are associated with approximately 90 percent of anogenital warts. They are also associated with low grade cervical disease and recurrent respiratory papillomatosis (RRP), a disease consisting of recurrent warty growths in the larynx and respiratory tract. Juvenile onset RRP (JORRP), a rare disorder caused by exposure to HPV during the peripartum period, can cause significant airway obstruction or lead to squamous cell carcinoma with poor prognosis.[16]

Although HPV types 6, 11, 16, and 18 are associated with significant morbidity and mortality, they have a fairly low prevalence in the U.S. population. One study of sexually active women ages 18 to 25 found HPV 16 and 18-prevalence to be 7.8 percent.[17] Another study found overall prevalence of types 6, 11, 16, and 18 to be 1.3 percent, 0.1 percent, 1.5 percent, and 0.8 percent, respectively.[18]

B. Gardasil Safety and Effectiveness

Gardasil was approved based on four randomized, double blind, placebo-controlled studies in 21,000 women ages 16 to 26. Girls as young as nine were included in the safety and immunogenicity studies but not the efficacy studies. The results demonstrated that in women without prior HPV infection, Gardasil was nearly 100 percent effective in preventing precancerous cervical lesions, precancerous vaginal and vulvar lesions, and genital warts caused by vaccine-type HPV. Although the study period was not long enough for cervical cancer to develop, the prevention of these cervical precancerous lesions was considered a valid surrogate marker for cancer prevention. The studies also show that the vaccine is only effective when given prior to infection with high-risk strains.[19]

Gardasil is the second virus-like particle (VLP) vaccine to be approved by the FDA; the first was the Hepatitis B vaccine. VLPs consist of viral protein particles derived from the structural proteins of a virus. These particles are nearly identical to the virus from which they were derived but lack the virus's genetic material required for replication, so they are noninfectious and nononcogenic. VLPs offer advantages over more traditional peptide vaccines as the human body is more highly attuned to particulate antigens, which leads to a stronger immune response since VLP vaccines cannot revert to an infectious form, such as attenuated particles or incompletely killed particles.

No serious Gardasil-related adverse events were observed during clinical trials. The most common adverse events reported were injection site reactions, including pain, redness, and swelling.[20] The most common systemic adverse reactions experienced at the same rate by both vaccine and placebo recipients were headache, fever, and nausea. Five vaccine recipients reported adverse vaccine-related experiences: bronchospasm, gastroenteritis, headache with hypertension, joint movement impairment near injection site, and vaginal hemorrhage. Women with positive pregnancy tests were excluded from the studies, as were some women who became pregnant following receipt of either vaccine or placebo. The incidence of spontaneous pregnancy loss and congenital anomalies were similar in both groups.[21] Gardasil was assigned pregnancy risk category B by the FDA on the basis that animal reproduction studies failed to demonstrate a risk to the fetus.[22]

As of June 2007, the most recent date for which CDC has made data available, there were 1,763 reports of potential side effects following HPV vaccination made to the CDC's Vaccine Adverse Event Reporting System (VAERS). Ninety-four of these were defined as serious, including 13 unconfirmed reports of Guillain-Barre syndrome (GBS), a neurological illness resulting in muscle weakness and sometimes in paralysis. The CDC is investigating these cases. Seven deaths were also reported among females who received the vaccine, but the CDC stated that none of these deaths appeared to be caused by vaccination.[23]

Although the FDA approved the vaccine for females ages 9–26, based on the data collected in those age groups, the ACIP recommendation for vaccination is limited to females ages 11–12. This recommendation was based on several considerations, including age of sexual debut in the United States and the high probability of HPV acquisition within several years of sexual debut, cost-effectiveness evaluations, and the established young adolescent health care visit at ages 11–12 when other vaccines are also recommended.

C. State Legislative Activities

Since the approval of Gardasil, legislators in 41 states and the District of Columbia have introduced legislation addressing the HPV vaccine.[24] Legislative responses to Gardasil have focused on the following recommendations: (1) mandating HPV vaccination of minor girls as a condition for school entrance; (2) mandating insurance coverage for HPV vaccination or providing state funding to defray or eliminate cost of vaccination; (3) educating the public about the HPV vaccine; and/or (4) establishing committees to make recommendations about the vaccine.

In 2007, 24 states and the District of Columbia introduced legislation specifically to mandate the HPV vaccine as a condition for school entry.[25] Of these, only Virginia and Washington, D.C. passed laws requiring HPV vaccination. The Virginia law requires females to receive three properly spaced doses of HPV vaccine, with the first dose to be administered before the child enters sixth grade. A parent or guardian may refuse vaccination for his child after reviewing "materials describing the link between the human papillomavirus and cervical cancer approved for such use by the Board of Health."[26] The law will take effect October 1, 2008.

Additionally, the D.C. City Council passed the HPV Vaccination and Reporting Act of 2007, which directs the mayor to establish an HPV vaccination program "consistent with the standards set forth by the Centers for

Disease Control for all females under the age of 13 who are residents of the District of Columbia."[27] The program includes a "requirement that the parent or legal guardian of a female child enrolling in grade 6 for the first time submit certification that the child has received the HPV vaccine" and a provision that "allows a parent or guardian to opt out of the HPV vaccination requirement." It also directs the mayor to develop reporting requirements "for the collection and analyzation [sic] of HPV vaccination data within the District of Columbia Department of Health," including "annual reporting to the Department of Health as to the immunization status of each female child entering grade 6." The law requires Congressional approval in order to take effect.

In contrast, an Executive Order issued by the Texas governor was thwarted by that state's legislature. Executive Order 4, signed by Governor Rick Perry on February 4, 2007, would have directed the state's health department to adopt rules mandating the "age appropriate vaccination of all female children for HPV prior to admission to the sixth grade."[28] It would have allowed parents to "submit a request for a conscientious objection affidavit form via the Internet." However, H.B. 1098, enacted by the Texas state legislature on April 26, 2007, states that HPV immunization is "not required for a person's admission to any elementary or secondary school," and "preempts any contrary order issued by the governor."[29] The bill was filed without the governor's signature and became effective on May 8, 2007.

Of the 22 other states in which legislation mandating HPV vaccination was introduced in 2007, all would have required girls to be vaccinated somewhere between ages 11 and 13 or before entry into sixth grade. Most would have provided for some sort of parental or guardian exemption, whether for religious, moral, medical, cost, or other reasons. However, vaccine mandate bills in California and Maryland were withdrawn.

Bills requiring insurance companies to cover HPV vaccination or allocating state funds for this purpose were enacted in eight states.[30] Eight states also enacted laws aimed at promoting awareness of the HPV vaccine using various mechanisms, such as school-based distribution of educational materials to parents of early adolescent children.[31] Finally, three states established expert bodies to engage in further study of HPV vaccination either instead of or as an adjunct to other educational efforts.[32]

In total, 41 states and D.C. introduced legislation addressing HPV vaccination in some manner during the 2007 legislative session, and 17 of these states enacted laws relating to HPV vaccination.

III. Why Mandating HPV Is Premature

The approval of a vaccine against cancer-causing HPV strains is a significant public health advance. Particularly in developing countries, which lack the health care resources for routine cervical cancer screening, preventing HPV infection has the potential to save millions of lives. In the face of such a dramatic advance, opposing government-mandated HPV vaccination may seem foolhardy, if not heretical. Yet strong legal, ethical, and policy arguments underlie our position that state-mandated HPV vaccination of minor females is premature.

A. Long-Term Safety and Effectiveness of the Vaccine Is Unknown

Although the aim of clinical trials is to generate safety and effectiveness data that can be extrapolated to the general population, it is widely understood that such trials cannot reveal all possible adverse events related to a product. For this reason, post-market adverse event reporting is required for all manufacturers of FDA-approved products, and post-market surveillance (also called "phase IV studies") may be required in certain circumstances. There have been numerous examples in recent years in which unforeseen adverse reactions following product approval led manufacturers to withdraw their product from the market. For example, in August 1998, the FDA approved Rotashield, the first vaccine for the prevention of rotavirus gastroenteritis in infants. About 7,000 children received the vaccine before the FDA granted the manufacturer a license to market the vaccine. Though a few cases of intussusception, or bowel obstruction, were noted during clinical trials, there was no statistical difference between the overall occurrence of intussusception in vaccine compared with placebo recipients. After administration of approximately 1.5 million doses of vaccine, however, 15 cases of intussusception were reported, and were found to be causally related to the vaccine. The manufacturer subsequently withdrew the vaccine from the market in October 1999.[33]

In the case of HPV vaccine, short-term clinical trials in thousands of young women did not reveal serious adverse effects. However, the adverse events reported since the vaccine's approval are, at the very least, a sobering reminder that rare adverse events may surface as the vaccine is administered to millions of girls and young women. Concerns have also been raised that other carcinogenic HPV types not contained in the vaccines will replace HPV types 16 and 18 in the pathological niche.

The duration of HPV vaccine-induced immunity is unclear. The average follow-up period for Gardasil during clinical trials was 15 months after the third dose of the vaccine. Determining long-term efficacy is complicated by the fact that even during naturally occurring HPV infection, HPV antibodies are not detected in many women. Thus, long-term, follow-up post-licensure studies cannot rely solely upon serologic measurement of HPV-induced antibody titers. One study indicates that protection against persistent HPV 16 infection remained at 94 percent 3.5 years after vaccination with HPV 16.[34] A second study showed similar protection for types 16 and 18 after 4.5 years.[35]

The current ACIP recommendation is based on assumptions about duration of immunity and age of sexual debut, among other factors. As the vaccine is used for a longer time period, it may turn out that a different vaccine schedule is more effective. In addition, the effect on co-administration of other vaccines with regard to safety is unknown, as is the vaccines' efficacy with varying dose intervals. Some have also raised concerns about a negative impact of vaccination on cervical cancer screening programs, which are highly effective at reducing cervical cancer mortality. These unknowns must be studied as the vaccine is introduced in the broader population.

At present, therefore, questions remain about the vaccine's safety and the duration of its immunity, which call into question the wisdom of mandated vaccination. Girls receiving the vaccine face some risk of potential adverse events as well as risk that the vaccine will not be completely protective. These risks must be weighed against the state's interest in protecting the public from the harms associated with HPV. As discussed in the next section, the state's interest in protecting the public health does not support mandating HPV vaccination.

B. Historical Justifications for Mandated Vaccination Are Not Met

HPV is different in several respects from the vaccines that first led to state-mandated vaccination. Compulsory vaccination laws originated in the early 1800s and were driven by fears of the centuries-old scourge of smallpox and the advent of the vaccine developed by Edward Jenner in 1796. By the 1900s, the vast majority of states had enacted compulsory smallpox vaccination laws.[36] While such laws were not initially tied to school attendance, the coincidental rise of smallpox outbreaks, growth in the number of public schools, and compulsory school attendance laws provided a rationale for compulsory vaccination to prevent the spread of smallpox among school children as well as a means to enforce the requirement by barring unvaccinated children from school.[37] In 1827, Boston became the first city to require all children entering public school to provide evidence of vaccination.[38] Similar laws were enacted by several states during the latter half of the 19th century.[39]

The theory of herd immunity, in which the protective effect of vaccines extends beyond the vaccinated individual to others in the population, is the driving force behind mass immunization programs. Herd immunity theory proposes that, in diseases passed from person to person, it is difficult to maintain a chain of infection when large numbers of a population are immune. With the increase in number of immune individuals present in a population, the lower the likelihood that a susceptible person will come into contact with an infected individual. There is no threshold value above which herd immunity exists, but as vaccination rates increase, indirect protection also increases until the infection is eliminated.

Courts were soon called on to adjudicate the constitutionality of mandatory vaccination programs. In 1905, the Supreme Court decided the seminal case, *Jacobson v. Massachusetts*,[40] in which it upheld a population-wide smallpox vaccination ordinance challenged by an adult male who refused the vaccine and was fined five dollars. He argued that a compulsory vaccination law was "hostile to the inherent right of every freeman to care for his own body and health in such way as to him seems best." The Court disagreed, adopting a narrower view of individual liberty and emphasizing the duties that citizens have towards each other and to society as a whole. According to the Court, the "liberty secured by the Constitution of the United States . . . does not import an absolute right in each person to be, at all times and in all circumstances, wholly freed from restraint. There are manifold restraints to which every person is necessarily subject for the common good." With respect to compulsory vaccination, the Court stated that "[u]pon the principle of self-defense, of paramount necessity, a community has the right to protect itself against an epidemic of disease which threatens the safety of its members." In the Court's opinion, compulsory vaccination was consistent with a state's traditional police powers, i.e., its power to regulate matters affecting the health, safety, and general welfare of the public.

In reaching its decision, the Court was influenced both by the significant harm posed by smallpox—using the words "epidemic" and "danger" repeatedly— as well as the available scientific evidence demonstrating the efficacy of the vaccine. However, the Court also emphasized that its ruling was applicable only to the case before it, and articulated principles that must be adhered to for such an exercise of police powers to be constitutional. First, there must be a public health necessity. Second, there must be a reasonable relationship between the intervention and public health objective. Third, the intervention may not be arbitrary or oppressive. Finally, the intervention should not pose a health risk to its subject. Thus, while *Jacobson* "stands firmly for the proposition that police powers authorize states to compel vaccination for the public good," it also indicates that "government power must be exercised reasonably to pass constitutional scrutiny."[41] In the 1922 case *Zucht v. King*,[42] the Court reaffirmed its ruling in *Jacobson* in the context of a school-based smallpox vaccination mandate.

The smallpox laws of the 19th century, which were almost without exception upheld by the courts, helped lay the foundation for modern immunization statutes. Many modern-era laws were enacted in response to the transmission of measles in schools in the 1960s and 1970s. In 1977, the federal government launched the Childhood Immunization Initiative, which stressed the importance of strict enforcement of school immunization laws.[43] Currently, all states mandate vaccination as a condition for school entry, and in deciding whether to mandate vaccines, are guided by ACIP recommendations. At present, ACIP recommends vaccination for diphtheria, tetanus, and acellular pertussis (DTaP), Hepatitis B, polio, measles, mumps, and rubella (MMR), varicella (chicken pox), influenza, rotavirus, haemophilus Influenza B (HiB), pneumococcus, Hepatitis A, meningococcus, and, most recently HPV. State mandates differ; for example, whereas all states require DTaP, polio, and measles in order to enter kindergarten, most do not require Hepatitis A.[44]

HPV is different from the vaccines that have previously been mandated by the states. With the exception of tetanus, all of these vaccines fit comfortably within the "public health necessity" principle articulated in *Jacobson* in that the diseases they prevent are highly contagious and are associated with significant morbidity and mortality occurring shortly after exposure. And, while tetanus is not contagious, exposure to *Clostridium tetani* is both virtually unavoidable (particularly by children, given their propensity to both play in the dirt and get scratches), life threatening, and fully preventable only through vaccination. Thus, the public health necessity argument plausibly extends to tetanus, albeit for different reasons.

Jacobson's "reasonable relationship" principle is also clearly met by vaccine mandates for the other ACIP recommended vaccines. School-aged children are most at risk while in school because they are more likely to be in close proximity to each other in that setting. All children who attend school are equally at risk of both transmitting and contracting the diseases. Thus, a clear relationship exists between conditioning school attendance on vaccination and the avoidance of the spread of infectious disease within the school environment. Tetanus, a non-contagious disease, is somewhat different, but school-based vaccination can nevertheless be justified in that children will foreseeably be exposed within the school environment (e.g., on the playground) and, if exposed, face a high risk of mortality.

HPV vaccination, in contrast, does not satisfy these two principles. HPV infection presents no public health necessity, as that term was used in the context of *Jacobson*. While non-sexual transmission routes are theoretically possible, they have not been demonstrated. Like other sexually transmitted diseases which primarily affect adults, it is not immediately life threatening; as such, cervical cancer, if developed, will not manifest for years if not decades. Many women will never be exposed to the cancer-causing strains of HPV; indeed the prevalence of these strains in the U.S. is quite low. Furthermore, many who are exposed will not go on to develop cervical cancer. Thus, conditioning school attendance on HPV vaccination serves only to coerce compliance in the absence of a public health emergency.[45]

The relationship between the government's objective of preventing cervical cancer in women and the means used to achieve it—that is, vaccination of all girls as a condition of school attendance—lacks sufficient rationality. First, given that HPV is transmitted through sexual activity, exposure to HPV is not directly related to school attendance.[46] Second, not all children who attend school are at equal risk of exposure to or transmission of the virus. Those who abstain from sexual conduct are not at risk for transmitting or contracting HPV. Moreover, because HPV screening tests are available, the risk to those who choose to engage in sexual activity is significantly minimized. Because it is questionable how many school-aged children are actually at risk—and for those who are at risk, the risk is not linked to school attendance—there is not a sufficiently rational reason to tie mandatory vaccination to school attendance.

To be sure, the public health objective that proponents of mandatory HPV vaccination seek to achieve is compelling. Vaccinating girls before sexual debut provides an opportunity to provide protection against an adult onset disease. This opportunity is lost once sexual activity begins and exposure to HPV occurs. However, that HPV vaccination may be both medically justified and a prudent public health measure is an insufficient basis for the state to compel children to receive the vaccine as a condition of school attendance.

C. In the Absence of Historical Justification, the Government Risks Public Backlash by Mandating HPV Vaccination

Childhood vaccination rates in the United States are very high; more than half of the states report meeting the Department of Health and Human Services (HHS) Healthy People 2010 initiative's goal of 95 percent vaccination coverage for childhood vaccination.[47] However, from its inception, state mandated vaccination has been accompanied by a small but vocal antivaccination movement. Opposition has historically been "fueled by general distrust of government, a rugged sense of individualism, and concerns about the efficacy and safety of vaccines."[48] In recent years, vaccination programs also have been a "victim of their tremendous success,"[49] as dreaded diseases such as measles and polio have largely disappeared in the United States, taking with them the fear that motivated past generations. Some have noted with alarm the rise in the number of parents opting out of vaccination and of resurgence in anti-vaccination rhetoric making scientifically unsupported allegations that vaccination causes adverse events such as autism.[50]

The rash of state legislation to mandate HPV has led to significant public concern that the government is overreaching its police powers authority. As one conservative columnist has written, "[F]or the government to mandate the expensive vaccine for children would be for Big Brother to reach past the parents and into the home."[51] While some dismiss sentiments such as this one as simply motivated by right wing moral politics, trivializing these concerns is both inappropriate and unwise as a policy matter. Because sexual behavior is involved in transmission, not all children are equally at risk. Thus, it is a reasonable exercise of a parent's judgment to consider his or her child's specific risk and weigh that against the risk of vaccination.

To remove parental autonomy in this case is not warranted and also risks parental rejection of the vaccine because it is perceived as coercive. In contrast, educating the public about the value of the vaccine may be highly effective without risking public backlash. According to one poll, 61 percent of parents with daughters under 18 prefer vaccination, 72 percent would support the inclusion of information about the vaccine in school health classes, and just 45 percent agreed that the vaccine should be included as part of the vaccination routine for all children and adolescents.[52]

Additionally, Merck's aggressive role in lobbying for the passage of state laws mandating HPV has led to some skepticism about whether profit rather than public health has driven the push for state mandates.[53] Even one proponent of state-mandated HPV vaccination acknowledges that Merck "overplayed its hand" by pushing hard for legislation mandating the vaccine.[54] In the face of such criticisms, the company thus ceased its lobbying efforts but indicated it would continue to educate health officials and legislators about the vaccine.[55]

Some argue that liberal opt-out provisions will take care of the coercion and distrust issues. Whether this is true will depend in part on the reasons for which a parent may opt out and the ease of opting out. For example, a parent may not have a religious objection to vaccination in general, but nevertheless may not feel her 11-year-old daughter is at sufficient risk for HPV to warrant vaccination. This sentiment may or may not be captured in a "religious or philosophical" opt-out provision.

Even if opt-out provisions do reduce public distrust issues for HPV, however, liberal opt outs for one vaccine may have a negative impact on other vaccine programs. Currently, with the exception of those who opt out of all vaccines on religious or philosophical grounds, parents must accept all mandated vaccines because no vaccine-by-vaccine selection process exists, which leads to a high rate of vaccine coverage. Switching to an "a la carte" approach, in which parents can consider the risks and benefits of vaccines on a vaccine-by-vaccine basis, would set a dangerous precedent and may lead them to opt out of other vaccines, causing a rise in the transmission of these diseases. In contrast, an "opt in" approach to HPV vaccine would not require a change in the existing paradigm and would still likely lead to a high coverage rate.

D. Mandating HPV for Girls and Not Boys May Violate Constitutional Principles of Equality and Due Process

1. Vaccination of Males May Protect Them from HPV-Related Morbidity

The HPV vaccine is the first to be mandated for only one gender. This is likely because the vaccine was approved for girls and not boys. Data demonstrating the safety and immunogenicity of the vaccine are available for males aged 9–15 years. Three phase 1 studies demonstrated that safety, tolerance, and immunogenicity of the HPV vaccine were similar to men and women. The first two studies focused on HPV 16 and 11, respectively, while the third study demonstrated high levels of immunogenicity to prophylactic HPV 6/11/16/18 vaccine in 10–15-year-old males.[56] Phase III clinical trials examining the vaccine's efficacy in men and adolescent boys are currently underway, with results available in the next couple of years.[57]

HPV infection is common among men.[58] One percent of the male population aged 15–49 years has genital warts, with peak incidence in the 20–24-year-old age group.[59] A recent cohort study found the 24-month cumulative incidence of HPV infection among 240 men aged 18–20 years to be 62.4 percent, nearly double the incidence of their female counter-parts.[60] This result may have been due to the increased sensitivity of the new HPV-PCR-based testing procedure used in the study. Nonetheless, the results reaffirm that HPV is common and multifocal in males. Males with genital warts have also been shown to carry the genital type specific HPV virus on their fingertips.[61] While HPV on fingertips may be due to autoinoculation, it may also represent another means of transmission.[62] Men are also at risk for HPV-related anogenital cancers. Up to 76 percent of penile cancers are HPV DNA positive.[63] Fifty-eight percent of anal cancers in heterosexual men and 100 percent among homosexual men are positive for HPV DNA.[64] Therefore, assuming vaccine efficacy is confirmed in males, they also could be protected through HPV vaccination.

2. Including Males in HPV Vaccination May Better Protect the Public Than Female Vaccination Alone

As no clinical trial data on vaccine efficacy in men has been published to date, mathematical models have been used to explore the potential benefits and cost effectiveness of vaccinating boys in addition to girls under various clinical scenarios. Even under the most generous assumption about vaccine efficacy in males and females, cost-effective analyses have found contradictory results. Several studies suggest that if vaccine coverage of women reaches 70–90 percent of the population, then vaccinating males would be of limited value and high cost.[65] Ruanne Barnabas and Geoffrey Garnett found that a multivalent HPV vaccine with 100 percent efficacy targeting males and females 15 years of age with vaccine coverage of at least 66 percent was needed to decrease cervical cancer by 80 percent. They concluded that vaccinating men in addition to women had little incremental benefit in reducing cervical cancer,[66] that vaccine acceptability in males is unknown, and that in a setting with limited resources, the first priority in reducing cervical cancer mortality should be to vaccinate females.

Yet several models argue in favor of vaccinating males. Vaccination not only directly protects through vaccine-derived immunity, but also indirectly through herd immunity, meaning a level of population immunity that is sufficient to protect unvaccinated individuals. If naturally acquired immunity is low and coverage of women is low, then vaccinating men will be of significant benefit. James Hughes et al. found that a female-only monovalent vaccine would be only 60–75 percent as efficient as a strategy that targets both genders.[67] Elamin Elbasha and Erik Dasbach found that while vaccinating 70 percent of females before the age of 12 would reduce genital warts by 83 percent and cervical cancer by 78 percent due to HPV 6/11/16/18, including men and boys in the program would further reduce the incidence of genital warts, CIN, and cervical cancer by 97 percent, 91 percent, and 91 percent, respectively.[68] In all mathematical models, lower female coverage made vaccination of men and adolescent boys more cost effective, as did a shortened duration of natural immunity.

All the models include parameters that are highly inferential and lacking in evidence, such as duration of vaccine protection, reactivation of infections, transmission of infection, and health utilities. The scope of the models is limited to cervical cancer, cancer-in-situ, and genital warts. None of the models accounts for HPV-related anal, head, and neck cancers, or recurrent respiratory papillomatosis. As more data become available, the scope of the models will be broadened and might strengthen the argument in favor of vaccinating males. Given that male vaccination may better protect the public than female vaccination alone, female-specific mandates may be constitutionally suspect, as discussed below.

3. The Government Must Adequately Justify Its Decision to Mandate Vaccination in Females Only

While courts have generally been deferential to state mandate laws, this deference has its limits. In 1900, a federal court struck a San Francisco Board of Health resolution requiring all Chinese residents to be vaccinated with a serum against bubonic plague about which there was little evidence of efficacy. Chinese residents were prohibited from leaving the area unless they were vaccinated. The court struck down the resolution as an unconstitutional violation of the Equal Protection and Due Process clauses. The court found that there was not a defensible scientific rationale for the board's approach and that it was discriminatory in targeting "the Asiatic or Mongolian race as a class." Thus, it was "not within the legitimate police power" of the government.[69]

A sex-based mandate for HPV vaccination could be challenged on two grounds: first, under the Equal Protection Clause because it distinguishes based on gender and second, under the Due Process Clause, because it violates a protected interest in refusing medical treatment. In regard to the Equal Protection concerns, courts review laws that make sex-based distinctions with heightened scrutiny: the government must show that the challenged classification serves an important state interest and that the classification is at least substantially related to serving that interest. To be sure, courts would likely view the goal of preventing cervical cancer as an important public health objective. However, courts would also likely demand that the state justify its decision to burden females with the risks of vaccination, and not males, even though males also contribute to HPV transmission, will benefit from an aggressive vaccination program of females, and also may reduce their own risk of disease through vaccination.

With respect to the Due Process Clause, the Supreme Court has, in the context of right-to-die cases, recognized that individuals have a constitutionally protected liberty interest in refusing unwanted medical treatment.[70] This liberty interest must, however, be balanced against several state interests, including its interest in preserving life. Mandated HPV laws interfere with the right of girls to refuse medical treatment, and therefore could be challenged under the Due Process Clause. Whether the government could demonstrate interests strong enough to outweigh a girl's liberty interest in refusing vaccination would depend on the strength of the government's argument that such vaccination is life-saving and the extent to which opt outs are available and easily exercised in practice.

Even if courts upheld government mandates as consistent with the Due Process and Equal Protection clauses, such mandates remain troubling in light of inequalities imposed by sex-based mandates and the liberty interests that would be compromised by HPV mandates, therefore placing deeply cherished national values at risk.

E. Unresolved Economic Concerns

Mandated HPV vaccination may have negative unintended economic consequences for both state health departments and private physicians, and these consequences should be thoroughly considered before HPV vaccination is mandated. In recent years, state health departments have found themselves increasingly strapped by the rising number of mandated vaccines. Some states that once provided free vaccines to all children have abandoned the practice due to rising costs. Adding HPV could drive more states to abandon funding for other vaccinations and could divert funding from other important public health measures. At the federal level, spending by the federal Vaccines for Children program, which pays for immunizations for Medicaid children and some others, has grown to $2.5 billion, up from $500 million in 2000.[71] Such rapid increases in budgetary expenses affect the program's ability to assist future patients. Thus, before HPV vaccination is mandated, a thorough consideration of its economic consequences for existing vaccine programs and other non-vaccine programs should be undertaken.

The increasing number of vaccines has also placed a burden on physicians in private practice. Currently, about 85 percent of the nation's children get all or at least some of their inoculations from private physicians' offices.[72] These offices must purchase vaccines and then wait for reimbursement from either government or private insurers. Some physicians have argued that the rising costs of vaccines and the rising number of new mandatory vaccines make it increasingly difficult for them to purchase vaccinations initially and that they net a loss due to insufficient reimbursement from insurers. Adding HPV to the list of mandated vaccines would place further stress on these practices, and could lead them to reduce the amount of vaccines they purchase or require up-front payment for these vaccines. Either of these steps could reduce access not only to HPV but to all childhood vaccines.

Access to HPV is one reason that some proponents favor state mandates. They argue that in the absence of a state mandate, parents will not know to request the vaccine, or will not be able to afford it because it will not be covered by insurance companies or by federal or state programs that pay for vaccines for the uninsured and underinsured. However, mandates are not the only way to increase parental awareness or achieve insurance coverage. In light of the potentially significant economic consequences of state mandates, policymakers should consider other methods of increasing parental awareness and insurance coverage that do not also threaten to reduce access to those who want vaccination.

IV. Conclusion

Based on the current scientific evidence, vaccinating girls against HPV before they are sexually active appears to provide significant protection against cervical cancer. The vaccine thus represents a significant public health advance. Nevertheless, mandating HPV vaccination at the present time would be premature and ill-advised. The vaccine is relatively new, and long-term safety and effectiveness in the general population is unknown. Vaccination outcomes of those voluntarily vaccinated should be followed for several years before mandates are imposed. Additionally, the HPV vaccine does not represent a public health necessity of the type that has justified previous vaccine mandates. State mandates could therefore lead to a public backlash that will undermine both HPV vaccination efforts and existing vaccination programs. Finally, the economic consequences of mandating HPV are significant and could have a negative impact on financial support for other vaccines as well as other public health programs. These consequences should be considered before HPV is mandated.

The success of childhood vaccination programs makes them a tempting target for the addition of new vaccines that, while beneficial to public health, exceed the original justifications for the development of such programs and impose new financial burdens on both the government, private physicians, and, ultimately, the public. HPV will not be the last disease that state legislatures will attempt to prevent through mandatory vaccination. Thus, legislatures and public health advocates should consider carefully the consequences of altering the current paradigm for mandatory childhood vaccination and should not mandate HPV vaccination in the absence of a new paradigm to justify such an expansion.

Note

The views expressed in this article are those of the author and do not reflect those of the Genetics and Public Policy Center or its staff.

References

1. D. Saslow et al., "American Cancer Society Guideline for Human Papillomavirus (HPV) Vaccine Use to Prevent Cervical Cancer and Its Precursors," *CA: A Cancer Journal for Clinicians 57*, no. 1 (2007): 7–28.

2. Editorial, "Should HPV Vaccination Be Mandatory for All Adolescents?" *The Lancet 368*, no. 9543 (2006): 1212.

3. U.S. Food and Drug Administration, *FDA Licenses New Vaccine for Prevention of Cervical Cancer and Other Diseases in Females Caused by Human Papillomavirus: Rapid Approval Marks Major Advancement in Public Health, Press Release,* June 8, 2006, *available at . . .* (last visited March 5, 2008).

4. Centers for Disease Control and Prevention, *CDC's Advisory Committee Recommends Human Papillomavirus Virus Vaccination*, Press Release, June 29, 2006, *available at . . .* (last visited March 5, 2008).

5. A. Pollack and S. Saul, "Lobbying for Vaccine to Be Halted," *New York Times*, February 21, 2007, *availiable at . . .* (last visited March 14, 2008).

6. Centers for Disease Control and Prevention, *Childcare and School Immunization Requirements, 2005–2006, August 2006, available at . . .* (last visited March 5, 2008).

7. Centers for Disease Control and Prevention, "A Closer Look at Human Papillomavirus (HPV)," 2000, *available at . . .* (last visited March 5, 2008); Centers for Disease Control and Prevention, "Genital HPV Infection—CDC Fact Sheet," May 2004, *available at . . .* (last visited March 5, 2008).

8. See Saslow et al., *supra* note 1.

9. S. D. Datta et al., "Sentinel Surveillance for Human Papillomavirus among Women in the United States, 2003–2004," in Program and Abstracts of the 16th Biennial Meeting of the International Society for Sexually Transmitted Diseases Research, Amsterdam, The Netherlands, July 10–13, 2005.

10. Centers for Disease Control and Prevention, "Human Papillomavirus (HPV) Infection," July 2, 2007, *available at . . .* (last visited March 5, 2008).

11. J. R. Nichols, "Human Papillomavirus Infection: The Role of Vaccination in Pediatric Patients," *Clinical Pharmacology and Therapeutics 81*, no. 4 (2007) 607–610.

12. See Saslow et al., *supra* note 1.

13. J. M. Walboomers et al., "Human Papillomavirus Is a Necessary Cause of Invasive Cervical Cancer Worldwide," *Journal of Pathology 189*, no. 1 (1999) 12–19.

14. J. K. Chan and J. S. Berek, "Impact of the Human Papilloma Vaccine on Cervical Cancer," *Journal of Clinical Oncology 25*, no. 20 (2007): 2975–2982.

15. See Saslow et al., *supra* note 1.

16. B. Simma et al., "Squamous-Cell Carcinoma Arising in a Non-Irradiated Child with Recurrent Respiratory Papillomatosis," *European Journal of Pediatrics* 152, no. 9 (1993): 776–778.

17. E. F. Dunne et al., "Prevalence of HPV Infection among Females in the United States," *JAMA 297*, no. 8 (2007): 813–819.

18. L. E. Markowitz et al., "Quadrivalent Human Papillomavirus Vaccine: Recommendations of the Advisory Committee on Immunization Practices (ACIP)," *Morbidity and Mortality Weekly Report* 55, no. RR-2 (2007): 1–24.

19. L. A. Koutsky et al., "A Controlled Trial of a Human Papillomavirus Type 16 Vaccine," *New England Journal of Medicine* 347, no. 21 (2002): 1645–1651; D. R. Brown et al., "Early Assessment of the Efficacy of a Human Papillomavirus Type 16L1 Virus-Like Particle Vaccine," *Vaccine* 22, nos. 21–22 (2004): 2936–2942; C. M. Wheeler, "Advances in Primary and Secondary Interventions for Cervical Cancer: Human Papillomavirus Prophylactic Vaccines and Testing," *Nature Clinical Practice Oncology* 4, no. 4 (2007): 224–235; L. L. Villa et al., "Prophylactic Quadrivalent Human Papillomavirus (Types 6, 11, 16, and 18) L1 Virus-Like Particle Vaccine in Young Women: A Randomized Double-Blind Placebo-Controlled Multicentre Phase II Efficacy Trial," *The Lancet Oncology* 6, no. 5 (2005): 271–278; see Saslow, *supra* note 1.

20. *Id.* (Villa).

21. See Wheeler, *supra* note 19.

22. N. B. Miller, *Clinical Review of Biologics License Application for Human Papillomavirus 6, 11, 16, 18 L1 Virus Like Particle Vaccine (S. cerevisiae) (STN 125126 GARDASIL), Manufactured by Merck, Inc.,"* Food and Drug Administration, June 8, 2006, *available at* . . . (last visited March 5, 2008).

23. Centers for Disease Control and Prevention, *HPV Vaccine—Questions and Answers for the Public*, June 28, 2007, available at . . . (last visited April 2, 2008).

24. National Conference of State Legislatures, "HPV Vaccine," July 11, 2007, *available at* . . . (last visited March 5, 2008).

25. *Id.*

26. S.B. 1230, 2006 Session, Virginia (2007); H.B. 2035, 2006 Session, Virginia (2007).

27. *HPV Vaccination and Reporting Act of 2007*, B.17–0030, 18th Council, District of Columbia (2007).

28. Governor of the State of Texas, Executive Order RP65, February 2, 2007, *available at* . . . (last visited March 5, 2008).

29. S.B. 438, 80th Legislature, Texas (2007); H.B. 1098, 80th Legislature, Texas (2007).

30. The states are Colorado, Maine, Nevada, New Mexico, New York, North Dakota, Rhode Island, and South Carolina. See National Conference of State Legislatures, *supra* note 24.

31. The states are Colorado, Indiana, Iowa, North Carolina, North Dakota, Texas, Utah, and Washington. *Id.* (National Conference of State Legislatures).

32. The states are Maryland, Minnesota, and New Mexico. *Id.* (National Conference of State Legislatures).

33. Centers for Disease Control and Prevention, *RotaShield (Rotavirus) Vaccine and Intussusception,* 2004, *available at . . .* (last visited March 14, 2008); M. B. Rennels, "The Rotavirus Vaccine Story: A Clinical Investigator's View," *Pediatrics* 106, no. 1 (2000): 123–125.

34. C. Mao et al., "Efficacy of Human Papilomavirus-16 Vaccine to Prevent Cervical Intraepithelial Neoplasia: A Randomized Controlled Trial," *Obstetrics and Gynecology* 107, no. 1 (2006): 18–27.

35. L. L. Villa et al., "Immunologic Responses Following Administration of a Vaccine Targeting Human Papillomavirus Types 6, 11, 16 and 18," *Vaccine* 24, no. 27–28 (2006): 5571–5583; D. M. Harper et al., "Sustained Efficacy Up to 4.5 Years of a Bivalent L1 Virus-Like Particle Vaccine against Human Papillomavirus Types 16 and 18: Follow Up from a Randomized Controlled Trial," *The Lancet* 367, no. 9518 (2006): 1247–1255.

36. J. G. Hodge and L. O. Gostin, "School Vaccination Requirements: Historical, Social, and Legal Perspectives," *Kentucky Law Journal* 90, no. 4 (2001–2002): 831–890.

37. J. Duffy, "School Vaccination: The Precursor to School Medical Inspection," *Journal of the History of Medicine and Allied Sciences* 33, no. 3 (1978): 344–355.

38. See Hodge and Gostin, *supra* note 36.

39. *Id.*

40. *Jacobson v. Commonwealth of Massachusetts,* 197 U.S. 11 (1905).

41. L. O. Gostin and J. G. Hodge, "The Public Health Improvement Process in Alaska: Toward a Model Public Health Law," *Alaska Law Review* 17, no. 1 (2000): 77–125.

42. *Zucht v. King,* 260 U.S. 174 (1922).

43. A. R. Hinman et al., "Childhood Immunization: Laws that Work," *Journal of Law, Medicine & Ethics* 30, no. 3 (2002): 122–127; K. M. Malone and A. R. Hinman, "Vaccination Mandates: The Public Health Imperative and Individual Rights," in R. A. Goodman et al., *Law in Public Health Practice* (New York: Oxford University Press, 2006).

44. See Centers for Disease Control and Prevention, *supra* note 6.

45. B. Lo, "HPV Vaccine and Adolescents' Sexual Activity: It Would Be a Shame If Unresolved Ethical Dilemmas Hampered This Breakthrough," *BMJ* 332, no. 7550 (2006): 1106–1107.

46. R. K. Zimmerman, "Ethical Analysis of HPV Vaccine Policy Options," *Vaccine* 24, no. 22 (2006): 4812–4820.

47. C. Stanwyck et al., "Vaccination Coverage Among Children Entering School—United States, 2005–06 School Year," *JAMA* 296, no. 21 (2006): 2544–2547.

48. See Hodge and Gostin, *supra* note 36.

49. S. P. Calandrillo, "Vanishing Vaccinations: Why Are So Many Americans Opting Out of Vaccinating Their Children?" *University of Michigan Journal of Legal Reform* 37 (2004): 353–440.

50. *Id.*

51. B. Hart, "My Daughter Won't Get HPV Vaccine," *Chicago Sun Times, February* 25, 2007, at B6.

52. J. Cummings, "Seventy Percent of U.S. Adults Support Use of the Human Papillomavirus (HPV) Vaccine: Majority of Parents of Girls under 18 Would Want Daughters to Receive It," *Wall Street Journal Online* 5, no. 13 (2006), *available at* . . . (last visited March 5, 2008).

53. J. Marbella, "Sense of Rush Infects Plan to Require HPV Shots," *Baltimore Sun*, January 30, 2007, *available at* . . . (last visited March 14, 2008).

54. S. Reimer, "Readers Worry about HPV Vaccine: Doctors Say It's Safe," *Baltimore Sun*, April 3, 2007.

55. A. Pollack and S. Saul, "Lobbying for Vaccine to Be Halted," *New York Times*, February 21, 2007, available at . . . (last visited March 14, 2008).

56. J. Partridge and L. Koutsky, "Genital Human Papillomavirus in Men," *The Lancet Infectious Diseases* 6, no. 1 (2006): 21–31.

57. See Markowitz et al., *supra* note 18.

58. *Id.*

59. See Partridge and Koutsky, *supra* note 56.

60. J. Partridge, "Genital Human Papillomavirus Infection in Men: Incidence and Risk Factors in a Cohort of University Students," *Journal of Infectious Diseases* 196, no. 15 (2007): 1128–1136. It should be noted that the higher incidence might be due to the increased sensitivity of the HPV-PCR-based testing procedure used in this recent study.

61. *Id.*

62. J. Kim, "Vaccine Policy Analysis Can Benefit from Natural History Studies of Human Papillomavirus in Men," *Journal of Infectious Diseases* 196, no. 8 (2007): 1117–1119.

63. See Partridge and Koutsky, *supra* note 56.

64. *Id.*

65. R. V. Barnabas, P. Laukkanen, and P. Koskela, "Epidemiology of HPV 16 and Cervical Cancer in Finland and the Potential Impact of Vaccination: Mathematical Modeling Analysis," *PLoS Medicine* 3, no. 5 (2006): 624–632.

66. *Id.*

67. J. P. Hughess, G. P. Garnett, and L. Koutsky, "The Theoretical Population Level Impace of a Prophylactic Human Papillomavirus Vaccine," *Epidemiology* 13, no. 6 (2002): 631–639.

68. D. Elbasha, "Model for Assessing Human Papillomavirus Vaccination Strategies," *Emerging Infectious Diseases* 13, no. 1 (January 2007): 28–41. Please note that these researchers are employed by Merck, the producer of Gardasil vaccine.

69. *Wong Wai v. Williamson*, 103 F. 1 (N.D. Cal. 1900).

70. *Vacco v. Quill*, 521 U.S. 793 (1997); *Washington v. Glucksberg*, 521 U.S. 702 (1997).

71. A. Pollack, "Rising Costs Make Doctors Balk at Giving Vaccines," *New York Times*, March 24, 2007.

72. *Id.*

EXPLORING THE ISSUE

Should the Human Papillomavirus (HPV) Vaccine Be Mandatory for Early Adolescent Girls?

Critical Thinking and Reflection

1. If early adolescent girls (with their parents/caregivers) are to make an informed decision regarding receiving the HPV vaccine, what information should they be given?
2. Are HPV vaccines safe and effective? Do we have enough data (research and clinical trials) to draw a conclusion on safety and effectiveness?
3. Why is the HPV vaccine licensed for use and recommended for pre-adolescent girls as young as 9 years of age?
4. Recently, the HPV vaccine has been approved for adolescent boys. If the vaccine is mandated for girls, should it also be mandated for boys?
5. If an adolescent—who refuses to get the HPV vaccine—is infected with the virus and spreads it to others, should they be held accountable in the same way that someone with HIV "knowingly" spreads HIV?

Is There Common Ground?

An ounce of prevention is worth a pound of cure. . . . Who would disagree that we should prevent cervical cancer in women as opposed to treating it after cancer has occurred? The authors of both YES and NO selections certainly agree on this and other points. They support a vaccine that would eliminate cervical cancer. They agree that the HPV is widespread and is responsible for cervical cancer. Additionally, they agree the HPV vaccine is a significant health advance for women and the medical community. Hence, the debate is not about the vaccine itself but instead about "mandating" it—especially before long-term safety and effectiveness are known. The two authors subscribe to different theoretical frameworks that include social and economic issues in order to make their cases. When reading Dailard's analysis favoring mandatory HPV vaccinations, it appears that she subscribes to a utilitarian theoretical perspective. In this theoretical paradigm, the rightness or wrongness of a particular action is based on a cost–benefit analysis. In this case, the many benefits of universal mandated HPV vaccination (e.g., prevention of cancer with consequent reduced human suffering, long-term health care cost savings, etc.) outweigh the costs in terms of minor side-effects (e.g., pain at the injection site). In contrast, Javitt, Berkowitz, and Gostin's discussion (2008) of the reasons against mandatory HPV vaccinations seems to appeal to the bioethical principles of beneficence (do good), nonmaleficence (do no harm), justice, and autonomy (Zimmerman, 2006). While the principle of beneficence is met with mandatory vaccines (i.e., preventing cervical cancer), the principle of nonmaleficence is not met when one considers possible negative side-effects resulting from the mandatory vaccination. In terms of justice, there may be a "lower class" (financial hardship) that does not have equal access to the vaccine. Finally, mandating HPV vaccination violates the issue of autonomy.

Additional Resources

Agosti, J. M., & Goldie, S. J. (2007). Introducing HPV vaccine in developing countries—Key challenges and issues. *New England Journal of Medicine, 356*(19), 1908–1910.

Borgmeyer, C. (2007). Many states are moving to require HPV vaccination for school entry: AAFP calls such mandates 'premature'. *American Association of Family Physicians News Now*. Retrieved December 10, 2007 from http://www.aafp.org/online/en/home.html

Bryer, J. (2010). Human papillomavirus health policy. *Policy, Politics, and Nursing Practice, 11*(1), 23–28.

> Jennifer Bryer addresses the HPV health policy in this article. She concludes that the HPV vaccine could significantly reduce cervical cancer but to do so would require broad mandated vaccination coverage. She further argues that health care providers are in a position to educate adolescents and their parents about the benefits of the vaccine.

Caseldine-Bracht, J. (2010). The HPV vaccine controversy. *The International Journal of Feminist Approaches to Bioethics, 3*(1), 99–112.

> This article presents an argument for why feminists have reason to be concerned about mandatory HPV vaccinations. The author discusses the potential conflict of interest that could arise given the cost associated with mandating the vaccine, the fact that men can also be infected yet there is no push to mandate a vaccine for them; and finally, that empirical evidence regarding women's safety is lacking.

Charo, R. A. (2007). Politics, parents, and prophylaxis—Mandating HPV vaccination in the United States. *New England Journal of Medicine, 356*(19), 1905–1908.

> Charo offers a perspective.

Gostin, L. O. (2011). Mandatory HPV vaccination and political debate. *The Journal of the American Medical Association, 306*(15), 1699–1700.

> Gostin provides a commentary regarding the attention mandatory HPV vaccination received during recent debates among U.S. republican presidential candidates.

Javitt, G., Berkowitz, D., & Gostin, L. O. (2008). Assessing mandatory HPV vaccination: Who should call the shots? *Journal of Law, Medicine, & Ethics, 36*(2), 384–395.

> The authors review the scientific evidence supporting the approval of the HPV vaccine Gardasil. They also review the legislative actions that followed the approval of Gardasil. Their take home message is that mandatory HPV vaccination is unwarranted and unwise at this time. One reason among several they list is that both short-term and long-term safety is unclear.

Moscicki, A.-B. (2005). Impact of HPV infection in adolescent populations. *Journal of Adolescent Health, 37*, S3–S9.

> Society of Obstetricians and Gynaecologists of Canada (August 14, 2007). Positioning Statements & Guidelines: SOGC Statement on CMAJ Commentary, "Human papillomavirus, vaccines and women's health: questions and cautions." Retrieved December 11, 2007 from www.sogc.org/media/guidelines-hpv-commentary_e.asp

Szarewski, A. (2010). HPV vaccine: Cervarix. *Expert Opinion on Biological Therapy, 10*(3), 477–487.

> Szarewski presents his expert opinion regarding the HPV vaccine. His take-home message is that the vaccine Cervarix has been proven highly effective against diseases associated with HPV. He further states that because the vaccine is not a live virus, it is reassuring in terms of safety.

Vamos, C. A., McDermott, R. J., & Daley, E. M. (2008). The HPV vaccine: Framing the arguments FOR and AGAINST mandatory vaccination of all middle school girls. *Journal of School Health, 78*(6), 302–309.

> This article presents arguments used by advocates who either oppose or endorse routine, mandatory HPV vaccine to school-aged girls. The arguments can assist school health personnel in being effective participants in understanding the debate.

Zimmerman, R. (2006). Ethical analysis of HPV vaccine policy options. *Vaccine, 24*(22), 4812–4820.

ISSUE 4

Is the Use of Nicotine Replacement Therapy (NRT) an Appropriate Cessation Aid for Adolescents Wishing to Quit Smoking?

YES: Irene M. Rosen and Douglas M. Maurer, from "Reducing Tobacco Use in Adolescents," *American Family Physician* (vol. 77, no. 4, pp. 483–490, 2008)

NO: K.H. Ginzel et al., from "Critical Review: Nicotine for the Fetus, the Infant and the Adolescent?" *Journal Health Psychology* (vol. 12, pp. 215–224, 2007)

Learning Outcomes

After reading this issue, you should be able to:

- Articulate and understand the reasons favoring NRT use by adolescents and the rationale for why some are opposed to NRT use by adolescents.
- Form an opinion as to what you think about NRT use by adolescents based on these arguments.
- Frame NRT use pro/con arguments within harm-reduction and zero-tolerance paradigms.

ISSUE SUMMARY

YES: In a paper geared at family physicians, Irene Rosen and Douglas Maurer, both family doctors themselves, review treatments for adolescent-smoking cessation; they recommend nicotine replacement therapy (NRT) as well as a variety of other methods to reduce adolescent smoking.

NO: K. Heinz Ginzel, a retired medical doctor and professor emeritus of pharmacology and toxicology at the University of Arkansas for Medical Sciences, and his colleagues, argue in a critical review paper that NRT should not be used with adolescents because it simply substitutes one form of nicotine with another, thereby prolonging and/or facilitating nicotine addiction.

Tobacco was responsible for 20 percent of deaths at the turn of this century (Koplan, 2007). Cigarette smoking by youth is a major health concern as lifetime complications associated with smoking are severe. In Canada, youth in grades 6–9 report very low rates of smoking (1–3 percent report being smokers). Ten percent of youth in grades 10–12 report being smokers (2010; Health Canada, 2012). Those who characterized themselves as daily smokers (1 percent for grades 6–9 and 5 percent for grades 10–12) indicated that they smoke around nine cigarettes per day. The rates are similar for U.S. youth (i.e., 5 percent and 17 percent, respectively, are smokers; Arrazola et al., 2010). In terms of having *tried* cigarettes, 16 percent in grades 6–9 and 40 percent in grades 10–12 have reported experimentation with cigarettes (Health Canada, 2012). This is particularly alarming because many smokers first start smoking in their teen years (CDCP, 2012) and because there are studies that indicate that adolescents are quite biologically vulnerable to nicotine addiction (DiFranza et al., 2000, 2002a, 2002b). Such experimentation has been found to double the odds of later smoking behavior (Fidler et al., 2006). The good news is that, as opposed to increasing, these rates of smoking and experimentation have remained steady or have been declining (Arrazola et al., 2010; Health Canada, 2012). While primary prevention is ideal, what methods are best for intervening with youth who already smoke?

NRT is a quit-smoking aide where nicotine is delivered to the body through a patch applied to the arm or shoulder (transdermal nicotine). Other means of NRT include nicotine gum (also tablets and lozenges), a nicotine nasal spray, and a nicotine inhaler. NRT methods are accessible to North American youth because they do not require a prescription—unlike smoking cessation drugs—as NRT is sold over-the-counter (with restrictions to the sale of youth in some jurisdictions).

The theory behind NRT is that smoking (cigarettes, cigars) is a "dirty" delivery of nicotine, whereas NRT is a "clean" form of nicotine. It is believed by some that the tobacco is the source of most of the harms associated with smoking, not the nicotine. A cigarette has over 4,000 chemicals in it (Zwar et al., 2006). However, the exogenous chemical addiction to smoking is because of nicotine (see NIDA, 2012). On the *NIDA for Teens* Web site, NRT is characterized as "hav[ing] lower overall nicotine levels than tobacco and they have little abuse potential since they do not produce the pleasurable effects of tobacco products. They also don't contain the carcinogens and gases found in tobacco smoke, making them a good treatment approach for quitting." This suggests that the National Institute for Drug Abuse (2012) endorses the use of NRT for teenagers. The harm reduction model is in effect here—NRT use is better than smoking even if it maintains the addiction to nicotine (also see Zwar et al., 2006).

Those who espouse a zero-tolerance paradigm endorse a "quit all forms of smoking and nicotine" philosophy. They argue that the nicotine itself is a noxious substance and that substituting it for smoking is as bad or can be worse than smoking (Slotkin, 2008). One argument is that NRT is undesirable because it provides a continuous level of nicotine (2 milligrams), whereas cigarettes (while delivering about 1–2 milligrams of nicotine per cigarette over the course of about 7 minutes) provide intermittent nicotine. Further, some fear that youth will use NRT in conjunction with tobacco smoking; supporting this idea, Lane et al. (2011) found that over 20 percent of young Canadian smokers who were using NRT reported having *never* tried to quit smoking. Further, there is a concern that some nonsmoking youth will use NRT as a form of a "drug high" and become addicted to nicotine—one study found that 20 percent of adolescent NRT users were nonsmokers (Klesges et al., 2003). Thus, proponents of zero-tolerance for nicotine fear that even "clean nicotine," in the form of NRT, is too dangerous for adolescents for a variety of reasons.

The efficacy of NRT and other pharmacological treatments for aiding smoking cessation is well established. The typical experimental design is called a randomized control (or placebo-controlled) study; one group of "quitters" is randomly given the active drug/NRT, while a placebo group of "quitters" is randomly assigned to receive inert pills, patches, gum, etc. The participants are "blind," meaning that they do not know whether they are receiving the drug/NRT or placebo. Often the research is blind to which condition the participant is assigned; this is called double-blind. This is done to ensure that quitting efforts are influenced *only* by the drug/NRT. Most studies are conducted with adults and generally find that the participants who receive the active drug/NRT are significantly more successful at quitting smoking relative to the placebo group particularly when NRT is coupled with psychological support (Moore et al., 2009; Zwar et al., 2006). Further, the body of research suggests that drugs/NRT is even more effective when coupled with psychological support (e.g., cognitive therapy, support groups; see Moore et al., 2009). The question is: Do these results with adult smokers translate to adolescent smokers?

Only a few randomized control studies address the use of NRT by adolescents, and none are very recent (Hanson et al., 2003; Hurt et al., 2000; Killen et al., 2004; Moolchan et al., 2005; Rubinstein et al., 2008; Smith et al., 1996; see Karpinski et al., 2010, for an overview). Most of these demonstrate no significant effects of NRT on cessation; however, NRT seems to help adolescents decrease the number of cigarettes they smoke. Given this paucity of research and the relatively weak effect NRT seems to have (relative to the effects for adults), is NRT use warranted in adolescent populations?

Rosen and Maurer clearly endorse the use of NRT with adolescents because of the reduction in cigarette smoking and small-to-no effect on adolescent-smoking cessation rates. In contrast, Ginzel et al. are adamantly opposed to NRT use with adolescents because of the impact on adolescent brain development and the potential to encourage further nicotine dependence. Which set of authors are correct? Is there a middle ground on this issue?

YES ↵

Irene M. Rosen and
Douglas M. Maurer

Reducing Tobacco Use in Adolescents

T obacco is the leading cause of preventable death in the United States, causing more than 440,000 deaths annually.[1] . . .

Of great concern is the large number of adolescents who start smoking early in life and continue throughout adulthood. Currently, 3 million U.S. adolescents younger than 18 years smoke cigarettes.[2] Almost one fourth of adolescents smoke by the time they graduate from high school, and almost 90 percent of adults who smoke began at or before age 18.[2] Each day about 4,400 teenagers try their first cigarette and contribute to the 1.5 million adolescents who begin to smoke each year.[3] A significant number of adolescents who use illicit drugs smoked cigarettes first.[4]

Smoking rates among high school students peaked in 1976, when nearly 40 percent of graduating seniors classified themselves as current smokers. Rates tapered off in the 1980s but then steadily increased, peaking again in 1997.[5] The Tobacco Master Settlement Agreement (MSA) was reached in 1998 between state attorneys general and the major tobacco manufacturers; the settlement banned certain types of tobacco advertising targeted at teenagers, and it launched a national antismoking campaign and several state-level campaigns. At the same time, cigarette prices increased substantially as a result of higher state taxes and the tobacco companies' efforts to recover money lost in the MSA.

All of these factors have contributed to a significant decrease in adolescent smoking rates. Unfortunately, this downward trend has recently stalled and is showing signs of reversal. . . .

Treatment

The ICSI [(Institute for Clinical Systems Improvement)] recommends aggressive intervention for smoking cessation in mature adolescents (i.e., 16 years and older), including community interventions, formal tobacco cessation programs, and pharmacotherapy.[8] The USPSTF [(US Preventive Service Task Force)] found limited evidence to support the effectiveness of counseling children and

Rosen, I. M., Maurer, D. M. From *American Family Physician*, Vol. 77 No. 4, 2008, pp. 483–490. Copyright © 2008 by American Academy of Family Physicians. Reprinted by permission.

Sort: Key Recommendations for Practice

Clinical recommendation	Evidence rating	References
Screening for tobacco use in adolescents is recommended at each physician visit, although the U.S. Preventive Services Task Force has found the evidence insufficient to recommend for or against routine screening in this age group.	B	8, 19, 31
Tobacco cessation should be offered regularly using the 5-A method (ask, advise, assess, assist, and arrange).	C	9
Nicotine replacement therapy is recommended for adolescents who meet criteria for tobacco dependence.	B	15–18, 20

A = consistent, good-quality patient-oriented evidence; B = inconsistent or limited-quality patient-oriented evidence; C = consensus, disease-oriented evidence, usual practice, expert opinion, or case series. For information about the SORT evidence rating system, see page 410 or http://www.aafp.org/afpsort.xml.

adolescents in the primary care setting, but it found that school and classroom smoking cessation programs are more effective than no intervention.[6]

Therapies for adolescents include counseling, nicotine replacement therapy, psychoactive medication (e.g., bupropion [Zyban]), and combination therapy. Pharmacotherapy should be explained and offered to all patients with nicotine dependence *(Table 1*[9–15]*)*.[8] Most studies on smoking cessation have been conducted in adults.[3] The nicotine patch (Nicoderm), nicotine gum (Nicorette), and bupropion [Zyban] are the only therapies that have been studied in adolescents. Most studies in adolescents have shown significant reductions in the number of cigarettes smoked daily, but low overall abstinence rates.[16] Pharmacotherapy of any kind doubles the probability of smoking abstinence in adults.[8]

Counseling

Studies of counseling interventions have been promising. In one retrospective cohort study involving an initial 45-minute consultation and subsequent telephone follow-up with a tobacco treatment counselor, 18 percent of adolescents who previously smoked were abstinent at six months, and 11.5 percent were abstinent after five years.[17] These percentages are significantly higher than those in previous observational studies of adolescent smokers. Several studies have shown increased cessation rates after cognitive behavior therapy.[18] A recent study of more than 2,500 adolescents found that a multipart tobacco intervention increased abstinence rates even up to two years later.[19] Although such labor-intensive interventions may be impractical during a brief office visit, even interventions of five minutes or less can improve smoking cessation rates.[7]

Table 1

Pharmacotherapy for Smoking Cessation

Therapy	Availability	Dosage	Prescribing instructions	Precautions	Side effects	Studied in adolescents?	Cost (generic)*
Bupropion (Zyban)	Rx	150 mg daily for 3 days, then twice daily for 7 to 12 weeks	Stop smoking one week after starting treatment Avoid or minimize alcohol intake Do not cut, crush, or chew tablets Separate doses by at least 8 hours to avoid insomnia; take last dose before 6 p.m.	FDA pregnancy category B Use caution in patients with seizure disorders, eating disorders, alcoholism, or uncontrolled hypertension, and in those who have taken a monoamine oxidase inhibitor within the past 14 days	Seizures, arrhythmias, Stevens-Johnson syndrome, erythema multiforme, hallucinations, mania, suicidality, hypertension, migraines	Yes; safe and mildly effective as monotherapy. Not as effective when used in combination with nicotine replacement therapy[12-14]	$174 ($116) per month
Nicotine gum (Nicorette)	OTC	1 piece every 1 to 2 hours for 6 weeks, then every 2 to 4 hours for 3 weeks, then every 4 to 8 hours for 3 weeks 2-mg gum should be used by patients who smoke ≤ 25 cigarettes per day (maximum, 30 pieces per day) 4-mg gum should be used by patients who smoke > 25 cigarettes per day (maximum, 20 pieces per day)	Chew to activate taste, then hold between mouth and gum for 30 minutes or until taste disappears	FDA pregnancy category D Use caution in patients with cardiovascular disease, arrhythmias, or worsening angina, and in those with a history of myocardial infarction within the past two weeks	Mouth soreness, hiccups, heartburn, jaw pain, tooth disorders, headache, nausea	Yes; effective when combined with counseling[15]	$47 for 110 pieces ($42 to 47)

Agent	Rx/OTC	Dosage	Instructions	Precautions	Adverse effects		Cost
Nicotine inhaler (Nicotrol Inhaler)	Rx	6 to 16 cartridges daily (1 cartridge = 4 mg) After initial therapy for 6 to 12 weeks, taper over 6 to 12 weeks	Stop smoking at onset of treatment Avoid acidic beverages Use frequent, continuous puffing for 20 minutes per cartridge	Same as above Use caution in patients with asthma	Bronchospasm, mouth or throat irritation, cough, headache, rhinitis, dyspepsia, taste changes	No	$133 for 168 cartridges
Nicotine lozenge (Commit)	OTC	1 piece every 1 to 2 hours for 6 weeks, then every 2 to 4 hours for 3 weeks, then every 4 to 8 hours for 3 weeks 2-mg lozenges should be used by patients who smoke their first cigarette > 30 minutes after awakening 4-mg lozenges should be used by patients who smoke their first cigarette ≤ 30 minutes after awakening	Dissolve in mouth over 20 to 30 minutes Do not chew, bite, or swallow Do not eat or drink for 15 minutes before and after use	Same as above	Headache, diarrhea, heartburn, hiccups, flatulence, nausea, sore throat	No	$78 for 192 2-mg lozenges
Nicotine nasal spray (Nicotrol NS)	Rx	1 or 2 sprays in each nostril every hour (maximum, 80 sprays daily for both nostrils) After initial therapy for 8 weeks, taper over 4 to 6 weeks	Stop smoking at onset of treatment Deliver spray with head tilted slightly back Do not sniff, swallow, or inhale spray	Same as above Use caution in patients with asthma, nasal polyps, or allergies	Bronchospasm, nasal or throat irritation, watery eyes, sneezing, cough, headache, rhinitis	No	$148 for four 10-mL bottles
Nicotine patch (Nicoderm, Nicotrol)	OTC	**Nicoderm** Patients who smoke 6 to 10 cigarettes per day: 14 mg daily for 6 weeks, then 7 mg daily for 2 weeks Patients who smoke more than 10 cigarettes per day: 21 mg daily for 6 weeks, then 14 mg daily for 2 weeks, then 7 mg daily for 2 weeks	Stop smoking at onset of treatment Place patch on hairless location of upper body or outer arm; rotate sites Nicoderm CQ or generic: remove after 16 to 24 hours Nicotrol: remove every night	Same as above	Skin irritation, headache, nausea, insomnia	Yes; safe and effective as monotherapy or when combined with counseling; not as effective as in adult smokers[14,16–18]	$63 for 28 14-mg patches ($60)

Continued

Table 1 Continued

Pharmacotherapy for Smoking Cessation

Therapy	Availability	Dosage	Prescribing instructions	Precautions	Side effects	Studied in adolescents?	Cost (generic)*
Nicotrol		Patients who smoke 6 to 10 cigarettes per day: 10 mg daily for 6 weeks, then 5 mg daily for 2 weeks Patients who smoke more than 10 cigarettes per day: 15 mg daily for 6 weeks, then 10 mg daily for 2 weeks, then 5 mg daily for 2 weeks					
Varenicline (Chantix)	Rx	0.5 mg daily for 3 days, then 0.5 mg twice daily for 4 days May continue for an additional 12 weeks if treatment is successful	Stop smoking after 7 days of treatment Take with food	FDA pregnancy category C Adjust dosage in renal-impaired patients Not approved for use in patients younger than 18 years	Nausea, insomnia, headache, abnormal dreams, constipation, flatulence, headache, vomiting	No	$108 for 56 pills

Rx = prescription; FDA = U.S. Food and Drug Administration; OTC = over the counter.

Note: According to product labeling, the safety and effectiveness of smoking cessation drugs in children younger than 18 years have not been established.

*—Estimated cost to the pharmacist based on average wholesale prices (rounded to the nearest dollar) in Red Book. Montvale, N.J.: Medical Economics Data, 2006. Cost to the patient will be higher, depending on prescription filling fee.

Information from references 12 through 18.

Nicotine Replacement Therapy

Trials of nicotine replacement therapy in adolescents have used either the nicotine patch or nicotine gum. Studies using the nicotine patch showed a decrease in the number of cigarettes smoked, but abstinence rates of only 5 percent after six to 12 months.[13,14] Adult trials using the nicotine patch commonly report abstinence rates of up to 30 percent at six to 12 months.[8] The reason for this discrepancy is unclear. Another study demonstrated higher cessation rates when nicotine replacement therapy was combined with intensive cognitive behavior therapy.[12,15] Larger studies are needed to fully examine the potential of nicotine replacement therapy in adolescents.

Most side effects of nicotine replacement therapy are mild and include local skin reactions in patients using the nicotine patch (50 percent); mouth soreness, hiccups, and dyspepsia in those using nicotine gum and lozenges (25 percent); and local throat and nose irritation in those using the nicotine inhaler (40 percent) and nasal spray (90 percent). Caution is advised when using nicotine replacement therapy in pregnant women and in patients with cardiovascular disease.

Other Medications

No psychoactive medications are currently approved by the U.S. Food and Drug Administration for tobacco cessation in adolescents. Recent reports of increased suicidality in adolescents taking antidepressants have further dampened enthusiasm for this approach. Bupropion is one of the most effective treatments for tobacco use in adults, resulting in cessation rates of 23 to 38 percent at 12 months.[8,22,23] Several studies have shown that bupropion is safe and effective in adolescents, resulting in cessation rates of up to 27 percent at six months.[9-11]

Common side effects of bupropion therapy include insomnia (35 to 40 percent) and dry mouth (10 percent). Bupropion should not be prescribed to patients with a history of seizures or eating disorders, or to patients who are taking monoamine oxidase inhibitors.[8]

Selective serotonin reuptake inhibitors (SSRIs), nortriptyline (Pamelor), and clonidine (Catapres) also have been studied for efficacy in smoking cessation. SSRIs have not been proven effective, whereas nortriptyline and clonidine are effective but have more side effects compared with bupropion.[8,22,24,25]

Varenicline (Chantix), a recently approved nicotinic receptor antagonist, is not labeled for use in adolescents.

Combination Therapy

Studies of counseling in combination with pharmacotherapy in adolescent smokers show improved abstinence rates.[8,12,15,17,18] In adults, the combination of nicotine patches with most other forms of nicotine replacement therapy (gum, lozenges, or spray, but not inhalers) is more effective than any replacement method alone.[8,13] Combining bupropion and nicotine replacement therapy results in improved abstinence rates compared with either therapy alone, but the difference is not statistically significant.[23] A study of 211 adolescent smokers randomly assigned to the nicotine patch plus bupropion found no statistically significant treatment effect compared with the nicotine patch plus placebo.[14] . . .

References

1. Centers for Disease Control and Prevention. Annual smoking-attributable mortality, years of potential life lost, and economic costs—United States, 1995–1999. *MMWR Morb Mortal Wkly Rep.* 2002; 51(14):300–303.

2. Centers for Disease Control and Prevention. Cigarette use among high school students—United States. 1991–2005. *MMWR Morb Mortal Wkly Rep.* 2006; 55(26):724–726.

3. Sunday S. R., Folan P. Smoking in adolescence: What a clinician can do to help. *Med Clin North Am.* 2004;88(6):1495–1515, xi.

4. Everett S. A., Giovino G. A., Warren C. W., Crossett L, Kann L. Other substance use among high school students who use tobacco. *J Adolesc Health.* 1998;23(5):289–296.

5. National Institute on Drug Abuse, University of Michigan, Institute for Social Research. The monitoring the future, national results on adolescent drug use. Overview of key findings. Bethesda, Md.: National Institute on Drug Abuse, U.S. Dept. of Health and Human Services, Public Health Service, National Institutes of Health; 1999.

6. U.S. Preventive Services Task Force. Recommendations statement. Counseling to prevent tobacco use and tobacco-caused disease, http://www.ahrq.gov/clinic/3rduspstf/tobacccoun/tobcounrs.htm. Accessed May 4, 2007.

7. Fiore M. Treating tobacco use and dependence. Rockville, Md.: U.S. Dept. of Health and Human Services, Public Health Service, 2000. http://www.ncbi.nlm.nih.gov/books/bv.fcgi?rid=hstat2.chapter.7644. Accessed May 4, 2007.

8. Institute for Clinical Systems Improvement. Health care guideline: tobacco use prevention and cessation for adults and mature adolescents, http://www.icsi.org/tobacco_use_prevention_and_cessation_for_adults/tobacco_use_prevention_and_cessation_for_adults_and_mature_adolescents_2510.html. Accessed May 4, 2007.

9. Upadhyaya H. P., Brady K. T., Wang W. Bupropion S. R. in adolescents with comorbid ADHD and nicotine dependence: A pilot study. *J Am Acad Child Adolesc Psychiatry.* 2004;43(2):199–205.

10. O'Connell M. L., Freeman M, Jennings G, et al. Smoking cessation for high school students. Impact evaluation of a novel program. *Behav Modif.* 2004;28:133–146.

11. Killen J. D., Robinson T. N., Ammerman S, et al. Randomized clinical trial of the efficacy of bupropion combined with nicotine patch in the treatment of adolescent smokers. *J Consult Clin Psychol.* 2004;72(4):729–735.

12. Moolchan E. T., Robinson M. L., Ernst M, et al. Safety and efficacy of the nicotine patch and gum for the treatment of adolescent tobacco addiction. *Pediatrics.* 2005;115(4):e407–414.

13. Smith T. A., House R. F. Jr, Croghan I. T., et al. Nicotine patch therapy in adolescent smokers. *Pediatrics*. 1996;98(4pt 1): 659–667.

14. Hurt R. D., Croghan G. A., Beede S. D., Wolter T. D., Croghan I. T., Patten C. A. Nicotine patch therapy in 101 adolescent smokers: efficacy, withdrawal symptom relief, and carbon monoxide and plasma cotinine levels. *Arch Pediatr Adolesc Med*. 2000;154(1):31–37.

15. Hanson K, Allen S, Jensen S, Hatsukami D. Treatment of adolescent smokers with the nicotine patch. *Nicotine Tob Res*. 2003;5(4):515–526.

16. Sussman S, Lichtman K, Ritt A, Pallonen U. E. Effects of thirty-four adolescent tobacco use cessation and prevention trials on regular users of tobacco products. *Subst Use Misuse*. 1999;34(11):1469–1503.

17. Patten C. A., Ames S. C., Ebbert J. O., Wolter T. D., Hurt R. D., Gauvin T. R. Tobacco use outcomes of adolescents treated clinically for nicotine dependence. *Arch Pediatr Adolesc Med*. 2001;155(7):831–837,

18. McDonald P, Colwell B, Backinger C. L., Husten C, Maule C. O. Better practices for youth tobacco cessation: evidence of review panel. *Am J Health Behav*. 2003;27(suppl 2):Sl44–158.

19. Hollis J. F., Polen M. R., Whitlock E. P., et al. Teen reach: Outcomes from a randomized, controlled trial of a tobacco reduction program for teens seen in primary medical care, *Pediatrics*. 2005;115(4):981–989.

20. Hammad T. A., Laughren T, Racoosin J. Suicidality in pediatric patients treated with antidepressant drugs. *Arch Gen Psychiatry*. 2006;63(3):332–339.

21. Whittington C. J., Kendall T, Fonagy P, Cottrell D, Cotgrove A, Boddington E. Selective serotonin reuptake inhibitors in childhood depression: Systematic review of published versus unpublished data, *Lancet*. 2004; 363(9418): 1341–1345.

22. Hughes J. R., Stead L. F., Lancaster T. Antidepressants for smoking cessation. *Cochrane Database Syst Rev,* 2007;(1):CD000031.

23. Jorenby D. E., Leischow S. J., Hides M. A., et al. A controlled trial of sustained-release bupropion, a nicotine patch, or both for smoking cessation. *N Engl J Med*. 1999;340(9):685–691.

24. Gourlay S. G., Stead LF, Benowitz N. L. Clonidine for smoking cessation. *Cochrane Database Syst Rev*. 2000;(2): CD000058 [Update appears in *Cochrane Database Syst Rev*. 2004;(3):CD000058].

25. da Costa C. L., Younes R. N., Lourenco M. T. Stopping smoking: A prospective, randomized, double-blind study comparing nortriptyline to placebo. *Chest*. 2002;122(2):403–408.

K.H. Ginzel et al.

↪ **NO**

Critical Review: Nicotine for the Fetus, the Infant, and the Adolescent?

Introduction

With the prospect of causing one billion deaths in the 21st century, cigarette smoking has entrapped the planet in a pandemic of tobacco-related morbidity and mortality of unprecedented proportion (Ginzel, 2001). Since addiction to nicotine is at its core, one should expect that efforts be focused on helping smokers to overcome their addiction to nicotine. Instead, nicotine, as in "Nicotine Replacement Therapy" (NRT), is becoming a more and more heavily promoted tool for smoking cessation.

In support of NRT, it is claimed that the main cause of the health damage inflicted by smoking is the cigarette smoke with its contingent of over 4000 substances, many of which are toxic or carcinogenic, but not the nicotine to which the smoker is addicted. Therefore, it is argued, if the addiction to cigarette smoking is too powerful to respond to treatment, providing nicotine via NRT or even smokeless tobacco in place of cigarettes is the correct course of action. This argument is then further strengthened by portraying nicotine as largely innocent, on par with caffeine, thereby ignoring the abundant evidence that nicotine itself can imperil health due to a host of adverse effects independent of its addictiveness.

But even if the toxicity of nicotine were accepted as a given, would medicinal nicotine from NRT not be preferable to nicotine contaminated with the bulk of poisons in cigarette smoke? Although this question may suggest an affirmative answer, it actually hides the need for uncompromised quitting as the only truly lasting solution. There are at least two points to consider. For one, the satisfying experience of a deep inhalation of cigarette smoke correlates with a sudden, steep spike of the blood nicotine level. The generally much gentler and more protracted rise following ingestion of NRT or smokeless tobacco can neutralize the unpleasantness of withdrawal symptoms during quitting attempts but it fails to eliminate the urge to smoke, prompting a relapse to smoking. The unsuccessful quitter then smokes either in alternation or even concurrently with NRT. Despite the inevitable increase in nicotine exposure that this practice entails, it was officially endorsed by the "the new

Ginzel. et. al., From *Journal of Health Psychology*, Vol. 12, Nol. 2, March 2007, pp. 215–224. Copyright © 2007 by Sage Publications—JOURNALS. Reprinted by permission via Rightslink.

rules" (see later). Second, for both the addict and the counselor, the true labor of quitting is comfortably postponed or suspended by resorting to a simple pill or patch. By making "quitting" look so effortless, the health concerns and attitudes toward smoking will have lost their urgency.

When the concept of treating nicotine addiction with nicotine first emerged in the early 1980s, pharmaceutical companies seized upon the opportunity to develop and market several nicotine preparations for this purpose. Available today are nicotine chewing gum, transdermal patch, lozenges, nasal spray and inhaler, which enjoy increasing popularity among cessation specialists and smokers who are trying to quit. However, a critical commentary questions the overall utility and success rate of NRT as an aid to smoking cessation (Polito, 2006). Also, according to a new meta-analysis, the long-term benefit of NRT is modest, while existing treatment guidelines, based on only 6–12 months of follow-up, overestimate the lifetime benefit and cost-efficacy of NRT (Etter & Stapleton, 2006).

Despite the lack of evidence for long-term effectiveness, NRT use continues to grow. . . . [I]n the only two trials conducted in pregnancy, NRT patches had no greater effect on smoking cessation than placebo (Coleman et al., 2004). Neither did NRT prove effective in a study of 120 adolescent smokers (Moolchan et al., 2005).

Whether or not successful in achieving quitting, the recommendation to use NRT in pregnancy and childhood raises the most serious concerns because of potential long-term consequences of nicotine action for this target group. . . .

Nicotine in Adolescence

According to recent human and animal research, adolescents are more susceptible to developing nicotine dependence than adults, because a single drug exposure can lead to lasting neuronal changes associated with learning and memory (Fagen, Mansfelder, Keath, & McGehee, 2003). The earlier the exposure to nicotine, the greater is the impact on the neuronal circuitry of the still developing brain causing irreversible effects on hippocampal structure, function, learning and memory (Slotkin, 2002). This experimental finding was borne out in a study of 5863 students, where a single experience with cigarettes reported at age 11 was found to significantly increase the risk of becoming a smoker as an adolescent even after three intervening years of non-smoking. This dormant vulnerability, termed "sleeper effect" (Fidler, Wardle, Brodersen, Jarvis, & West, 2006), must be made widely known to help prevent preteens from early experimentation with cigarettes or other tobacco products. Early exposure to nicotine can also make children more vulnerable later to stress or depression, prompting them to try some form of nicotine again.

Adolescent smokers have only recently started to receive NRT. Some of them reported simultaneous use of NRT and cigarettes. Nonsmoking teens have also tried NRT and some have even indulged in regular use (Klesges, Johnson, Somes, Zbikowski, & Robinson, 2003). The easy availability of NRT poses a special risk for the curious and adventurous young. Like smoking, NRT has the potential of priming the brain for nicotine addiction and leading to illegal drug use.

A review of teen smoking cessation approaches reveals their complexity and the lack of an effective solution (Mermelstein, 2003). What appears to be missing from the majority of interactions with young people is a totally honest confrontation and a truthful dissection of the tobacco problem in its entirety (Ginzel, 2002).

The New Rules

Against this background, it is with much concern that we confront the recently proposed rules issued by the Committee on Safety of Medicines (CSM) and by the Medicines and Healthcare Regulatory Authority (MHRA) for the use of NRT in the UK (Action on Smoking and Health, 2005), likely to set a precedent for other countries to follow. According to these new rules, all forms of NRT can be used by pregnant smokers; different forms of NRT can be used alternatively or concurrently; NRT can be used while still smoking (!) and can be prescribed for up to nine months if needed; and all forms of NRT can be used by young smokers aged 12 to 17 years as well as by patients with cardiovascular disease if so advised.

These new rules differ fundamentally from past recommendations. Molyneux (2004) states that the effectiveness of NRT in adolescents and children who smoke has not been established, and he also urges smokers not to smoke while using NRT. NRT, especially by transdermal patch, delivers more nicotine to the fetus than smoking does. Nicotine concentrations in fetal rat brain are 2.5 times higher than the mother's blood nicotine level when on continuous nicotine feed; a similar ratio can be expected in pregnant women using the patch (Sarasin et al., 2003). Smokers who use NRT may have nicotine concentrations up to three times higher than the approved dose (Chan, Jeremy, Stansby, & Shukla, 2004). The US Surgeon General's Report of 2001 on Women and Smoking states: 'Because of uncertainties over the safety of nicotine replacement during pregnancy, FDA has assigned a Pregnancy Category C warning to nicotine gum ('Risk cannot be ruled out') and a Pregnancy D warning to transdermal nicotine ('Positive evidence of risk')' (US Department of Health and Human Services, 2001, p. 557). Since many of tobacco smoke's harmful effects on the unborn baby can be attributed to nicotine, NRT or smokeless tobacco products are not a safe alternative to smoking during pregnancy (Cohen et al., 2005). No data are available on long-term effects of NRT use on fetal outcomes (Oncken, Bert, Ockene, Zapka, & Stoddard, 2000). The uncertainty of benefit and the risk of NRT use in pregnancy and by teens are echoed throughout the literature dealing with this topic. The risk of oral NRT use also received new emphasis by the recent finding that nicotine causes concomitant genotoxic and antiapoptotic effects in human gingival fibroblasts, potentially the first step in the neoplastic process (Argentin & Cicchetti, 2004).

It is obvious that the smoker whose body is busy dealing with the nicotine contingent in inhaled smoke ought not to be burdened with additional amounts of nicotine delivered from NRT but should be resolutely supported to overcome the addiction to nicotine altogether. This cannot be achieved by recommending or prescribing nicotine through NRT. The ultimate goal must be total cessation of smoking and nicotine intake in any form. NRT simply substitutes one form of nicotine for another but is neither safe nor as effective as other cessation aids (Hutter, Moshammer, & Neuberger, 2006; Marks, 2005, 2006; Moshammer & Neuberger, 2006). Originally, the tobacco industry opposed the makers of NRT, but now both industrial enterprises seem to be finding common ground as tobacco and NRT have begun reinforcing each other and keeping the addiction to nicotine alive.

Concluding Comments

Prescribing or simply recommending an over-the-counter purchase of one form or another of NRT is unquestionably quicker and less engaging for the health professional than any in depth–one-to-one counsel . . .; it is also easier than a straight talk with a teen or preteen about a future eclipsed by addiction, disease and premature death, exploring the real reasons that made them light up in the first place (Ginzel, 2002). It is easy not only for the counselors to prescribe NRT, it is also easy for the clients to receive it: they may conveniently assume that this is all that needs to be done, and the urge to smoke may go away in due course. . . . Moreover, new evidence reveals that offering a remedy for a risky behavior inadvertently promotes it by suggesting that the risk is manageable (Bolton, Cohen, & Bloom, 2006).

If the new UK rules, which extend and multiply a regimen ill-conceived from the start were followed and also adopted by other countries, they would perpetuate nicotine addiction rather than diminish it. And so would a recently proposed policy of extended, or even indefinitely continuing (!), use of the so-called 'clean nicotine' of NRT (Gray et al., 2005). This could actually set us on a path eventually leading to the end of tobacco control as we know it. Tobacco control must be nicotine control. Without nicotine control, nicotine addiction and nicotine's multifarious and insidious impact on the user would persist and spread at the peril of the unborn, the next generation and public health in general.

Some 4000 years ago the code of Hammurabi decreed the penalty of death for anyone who would harm a child. In an editorial in the *New York Times* in March 1985, William G. Cahan of the Memorial Sloan Kettering Cancer Center identified smoking as the most prevalent form of child abuse. Will nicotine now join this deplorable distinction?

References

Action on Smoking and Health. (2005). Guidance for health professionals on changes in the licensing arrangements for nicotine replacement therapy. Available at http://www.ash.org.uk/html/cessation/Smoking%20reduction/NRT051229.pdf

Argentin, G., & Cicchetti, R. (2004). Genotoxic and antiapoptotic effect of nicotine on human gingival fibroblasts. *Toxicological Sciences, 79*, 75–81.

Bolton, L., Cohen, J., & Bloom, P. (2006). Docs marketing products as remedies create 'Get out of jail free cards'? *Journal of Consumer Research, 33,* 71–81.

Chan, Y., Jeremy, J., Stansby, G., & Shukla, N. (2004). Nicotine replacement therapy is harmful: Rapid responses to Molyneux A. Nicotine replacement therapy. *British Medical Journal, 328,* 454–456.

Cohen, G., Roux, J.-C., Grailhe, R., Malcolm, G., Changeux, J.-P., & Lagercrantz, H. (2005). Perinatal exposure to nicotine causes deficits associated with a loss of nicotinic receptor function. *Proceedings of the National Academy of Sciences, 102,* 3817–3821.

Coleman, T., Antoniak, M,, Britton, J., Thornton, J., Lewis, S., & Watts, K. (2004). Recruiting pregnant smokers for a placebo-randomised controlled trial of nicotine replacement therapy. *BMC Health Services Research, 4,* 29.

Etter, J.-F., & Stapleton, J. (2006). Nicotine replacement therapy for long-term smoking cessation: A meta-analysis. *Tobacco Control, 15,* 280–285.

Fagen, Z., Mansfelder, H., Keath, J., & McGehee, D. (2003). Short- and long-term modulation of synaptic inputs to brain reward areas by nicotine. *Annals of the New York Academy of Sciences, 1003,* 185–195.

Fidler, J., Wardle, J., Brodersen, N., Jarvis, M., & West, R. (2006). Vulnerability to smoking after trying a single cigarette can lie dormant for three years or more. *Tobacco Control, 15,* 205–209.

Ginzel, K. (2001). After some 100 million deaths—what's next? American Council of Science and Health, *Priorities for Health, 13,* 24–39. Available at http://www.gasp.org/HGinzel.html

Ginzel, K. (2002). Can children stop big tobacco? A school project. Testimony presented at the CDC Public Comments Meeting, National Conference on the Healthy People 2010 Tobacco Objectives, San Francisco, CA, 18 November. Available at http://www.gasp.org/ginzelkids.html

Gray, N., Henningfield, J., Benowitz, N., Connolly, G., Dresler, C., Fagerstrom, K, et al. (2005). Toward a comprehensive long term nicotine policy. *Tobacco Control, 14,* 161–165.

Hutter, H., Moshammer, H., & Neuberger, M. (2006). Smoking cessation at the workplace: 1 year success of short seminars. *International Archive of Occupational and Environmental Health, 79,* 42–48.

Klesges, L., Johnson, K., Somes, G., Zbikowski, S., & Robinson, L. (2003). Use of nicotine replacement therapy in adolescent smokers and nonsmokers. *Archives of Pediatrics and Adolescent Medicine, 157,* 517–522.

Marks, D. (2005). *Overcoming your smoking habit.* London: Constable.

Marks, D. (2006). Let's have an independent review of smoking cessation services in the UK. Rapid responses to West R, Sohal T. 'Catastrophic' pathways to smoking cessation: Findings from national survey. *British Medical Journal, 332,* 458–460.

Mermelstein, R. (2003). Teen smoking cessation. *Tobacco Control, 12,* i25.

Molyneux, A. (2004). Nicotine replacement therapy. Clinical review. *British Medical Journal, 328,* 454–456.

Moolchan, E., Robinson, M., Ernst, M., Cadet, J., Pickworth, W., Heishman, S. et al. (2005). Safety and efficacy of the nicotine patch and gum for the treatment of adolescent tobacco addiction. *Pediatrics, 115,* e407–e414.

Moshammer, H., & Neuberger, M. (2006). Long term success of short smoking cessation seminars supported by occupational health care. *Addictive Behaviors* DOI:10.1016/j.addbeh.2006.10.002

Oncken, C., Bert, L., Ockene, J., Zapka, J., & Stoddard, A. (2000). Nicotine replacement prescription practices of obstetric and pediatric clinicians. *Obstetric Gynecology, 96,* 261–265.

Polito, J. (2006). Integrity of NRT studies in serious question. Rapid responses to West R, Sohal T. 'Catastrophic' pathways to smoking cessation: Findings from national survey. *British Medical Journal, 332,* 458–460.

Sarasin, A., Schlumpf, M., Muller, M., Fleischmann, L., Lauber, M., & Lichtensteiger, W. (2003). *Reproductive Toxicology, 17,* 153–162.

Slotkin, T. (2002). Nicotine and the adolescent brain: Insights from an animal model. *Neurotoxicology Teratology, 24,* 369–384.

U.S. Department of Health and Human Services. (2001). *Women and smoking.* A report of the Surgeon General. Rockville, MD: US Department of Health and Human Services.

EXPLORING THE ISSUE

Is the Use of Nicotine Replacement Therapy (NRT) an Appropriate Cessation Aid for Adolescents Wishing to Quit Smoking?

Critical Thinking and Reflection

1. Is the use of "clean nicotine"—such as is provided in the nicotine patch—warranted with adolescents? What are the factors supporting nicotine replacement therapy with adolescents? What are the factors supporting the ban of nicotine replacement therapy with adolescents?

2. What are the harm-reduction arguments for NRT use with adolescents? What are the zero-tolerance arguments regarding adolescent NRT use?

3. Imagine the government gave you a huge grant to investigate NRT use with adolescents; thus, money is no barrier for this research. Design the definitive experimental study of NRT use with adolescents that will address the issues arising from the harm-reduction and the zero-tolerance philosophies.

4. a. A friend has a 13-year-old daughter who started smoking regularly 6 weeks ago. Based on the YES and NO selections, what would you advise your friend to do with regard to NRT and the adolescent's smoking? Would you recommend NRT use or would you advise against it? Justify your answer.

   b. Consider the same question above but imagine the adolescent is 17 years old, male, has been smoking regularly for 2 years, and he wants to quit. Would your advice change? Why or why not?

Is There Common Ground?

Authors of both YES and NO selections would undoubtedly agree that preventing adolescents from beginning to smoke is the best solution to the problem of teenage smoking. Ginzel et al., at the end of their paper, almost suggest that recommending NRT use is a "lazy" health care provider's response to adolescent smoking. However, most of the studies with NRT have examined its use coupled with motivational support (i.e., skills training, psychological counseling). The Rosen and Maurer paper, when discussing treatment alternatives for reducing tobacco use in adolescents, lists counseling first—highlighting its priority. Pharmacotherapies are discussed after counseling, and these authors end by discussing combination therapy—where counseling and NRT are combined. Given that this paper is geared at family physicians, there is an implied expectation that the primary health care provider will assess the review and prescribe the most comprehensive and effective therapy possible.

One perspective that neither paper addresses is the possibility of different types of adolescent smokers. Adelman (2006) asserts that there are theoretically different types of adolescent smokers: (1) the "fixed" smoker—this would be an adolescent whose smoking behavior would be similar to an adult with comparable nicotine dependence, (2) the variable smoker—this would be an adolescent whose smoking behavior is motivated by relationships, activities, emotions, and social support/sanction. These youth would have variable or intermittent patterns of smoking that are influenced by behavioral or social factors. The adult-type smoker would likely respond to NRT, whereas the adolescent-type smoker would be unlikely to be affected in the same way by NRT. There is also an experimental smoker who is in the initiation phase of smoking. This smoker may be more influenced by educational campaigns before the habit is established. These categories are theoretical and based on Adelman's clinical experience, so these hypotheses would have to be tested and verified empirically.

Additional Resources

Arrazola, R. A., Dube, S. R., Kaufmann, R. B., Caraballo, R. S., & Pechacek, T. (2010). Tobacco use among middle and high school students—United States, 2000–2009. *Morbidity and Mortality Weekly Report, 59*(33), 1063–1068.

Bevins, R. A., & Caggiula, A. R. (Eds.). The motivational impact of nicotine and its role in tobacco use. *The Nebraska symposium on motivation, Vol. 55.* New York: Springer 2009.

Centers for Disease Control and Prevention (CDCP). (2012). Fact sheet: Youth and tobacco use. Retrieved from www.cdc.gov/tobacco/data_statistics/fact_sheets/youth_data/tobacco_use/index.htm

DiFranza, J. R., Rigotti, N. A., et al. (2000). Initial symptoms of nicotine dependence in adolescents. *Tobacco Control, 9,* 313–319.

DiFranza, J. R., Savageau, J. A., et al. (2002a). Measuring the loss of autonomy over nicotine use in adolescents: The DANDY (development and assessment of nicotine dependence in youth) study. *Archives of Pediatric Adolescent Medicine, 156,* 397–403.

DiFranza, J. R., Savageau, J. A., et al. (2002b). Development of symptoms of tobacco dependence in youths: 30-month follow-up data from the DANDY study. *Tobacco Control, 11,* 228–235.

Fidler, J., Wardle, J., Brodersen, N., Jarvis, M., & West, R. (2006). Vulnerability to smoking after trying a single cigarette can lie dormant for three years or more. *Tobacco Control, 15,* 205–209.

Frishman, W. H. (2009). Smoking cessation pharmacotherapy. *Therapeutic Advances in Cardiovascular Disease, 3(4),* 287–308.

> A very good summary of different types of medical smoking cessation treatments and associated issues. This paper is factual with little pro or con leanings.

Hanson, K., Allen, S., Jensen, S., & Hatsukami, D. (2003). Treatment of adolescent smokers with the nicotine patch. *Nicotine and Tobacco Research, 5*, 515–526.

A double-blind, randomized, placebo-controlled study was conducted with 100 adolescents. Results for smoking cessation were not significant but there were reductions in craving for cigarettes, fewer withdrawal symptoms, and a reduction in number of cigarettes smoked.

Health Canada. (2012). Summary of results of the 2010–2011 Youth Smoking Survey. Retrieved from www.hc-sc.gc.ca/hc-ps/tobac-tabac/research-recherche/stat/_survey-sondage_2010-2011/result-eng.php

Hurt, R. D., Crogham, G. A., Beede, S. D., et al. (2000). Nicotine patch therapy in 101 adolescent smokers. *Archives of Pediatric Adolescent Medicine, 154*, 31–37.

A study of 101 adolescent smokers using NRT indicated that smoking cessation initially was supported by patch use but not in the long term. However, participants showed reduction in the amount they smoked.

Karpinski, J., Timpe, E. M., & Lubsch, L. (2010). Smoking cessation treatment for adolescents. *Journal of Pediatric Pharmacology Therapy, 15*(4), 249–263.

A very good review of the issues.

Killen, J. D., Robinson, T. N., Ammerman, S., et al. (2004). Randomized clinical trial of the efficacy of bupropion combined with nicotine patch in the treatment of adolescent smokers. *Journal of Consulting and Clinical Psychology, 72*, 729–735.

Authors found that adolescent participants who used NRT had a smoking cessation rate of less than 10 percent at 6-month follow-up.

Klesges, L. M., Johnson, K. C, Somes, G., Zbikowski, S., & Robinson, L. (2003). Use of nicotine replacement therapy in adolescent smokers and nonsmokers. *Archives of Pediatric Adolescent Medicine, 157*, 517–522.

Koplan, J. P. (2007). CDC's 60th anniversary: Director's perspective, 1998–2002. *Morbidity and Mortality Weekly, 56*(33), 846–850.

Lane, N. E., Leatherdale, S. T., & Ahmed, R. (2011). Use of nicotine replacement therapy among Canadian youth: Data from the 2006–2007 National Youth Smoking Survey. *Nicotine & Tobacco Research, 13*(10), 1009–1014.

Moolchan, E. T., Robinson, R. L., Ernst, M., et al. (2005). Safety and efficacy of the nicotine patch and gum for the treatment of adolescent tobacco addiction. *Pediatrics, 115*, e407–e414.

A double-blind, randomized study was conducted with 100 adolescents investigating the impact of NRT patch and gum on smoking rates. There were reductions in smoking although no differences in type of NRT.

Moore, D., Aveyard, P., Connock, M., Wang, D., Fry-Smith, A., & Barton, P. (2009). Effectiveness and safety of nicotine replacement therapy assisted reduction to stop smoking: Systematic review and meta-analysis. *British Medical Journal, 338*, 867–871. doi: 10.1136/bmj.b1024

This is a meta-analysis of studies that supports the efficacy of NRT as an effective smoking cessation aide for smokers who were not ready to quit. Also, they concluded there were no ill effects of smoking while using NRT.

National Institute for Drug Abuse (NIDA). (2012). NIDA for teens, the science behind drug abuse: Facts on drugs–tobacco addiction. Retrieved from http://teens.drugabuse.gov/facts/facts_nicotine1.php#what_is_it

Rubinstein, M. L., Benowitz, N. L., Auerback, G. M., et al. (2008). A randomized trial of nicotine nasal spray in adolescent smokers. *Pediatrics, 122*, e595–e600.

> In a study comparing counseling to counseling plus NRT nasal spray, smoking cessation rates did not change but reduction in cigarettes smoked was observed (from 11 to 5 per day in the NRT group).

Slotkin, T. A. (2008). If nicotine is a developmental neurotoxicant in animal studies, dare we recommend nicotine replacement therapy in pregnant women and adolescents? *Neurotoxicology and Teratology, 30*(1), 1–19.

> An extensive review with supporting arguments against NRT use in these specific groups.

Smith, T. A., House, R. F., Crogham, I. T., et al. (1996). Nicotine patch therapy in adolescent smokers, *Pediatrics, 98*, 659–667.

> A small study of adolescent smokers using NRT in the form of the patch found that smoking cessation was not supported by NRT use but participants showed reduction in the amount they smoked.

Zwar, N., Bell, J., Peters, M., Christie, M., & Mendelsohn, C. (2006). Nicotine and nicotine replacement therapy—the facts. *Australian Pharmacist, 25*(12), 969–973.

> An excellent literature review that addresses myths and facts about NRT. Authors document the research underlying their characterization of myths and facts.

ISSUE 5

Should Schools Be Responsible for Completing Body Mass Index (BMI) Report Cards in the Fight Against Youth Obesity?

YES: Cynthia I. Joiner, from "Writing for the PRO Position—Body Mass Index (BMI) Report Cards: Should Schools Be Responsible for Screening?" *The American Journal of Maternal Child Nursing* (vol. 34, no. 4, 2009)

NO: Betsy Di Benedetto Gulledge, from "Writing for the CON Position," *The American Journal of Maternal Child Nursing* (vol. 34, no. 4, 2009)

Learning Outcomes
After reading this issue, you should be able to: • Gain an understanding of the school's role in children's health. • Assess the role of the school system in the fight against obesity. • Critically consider the research that supports and challenges the usefulness of BMI report cards. • Analyze the benefits and risks of conducting BMI screening in the schools.

ISSUE SUMMARY

YES: Cynthia I. Joiner, MPH, RN and nurse research manager at the University of Alabama, views having body mass index (BMI) report cards in the schools as an extension of what schools are already managing to highlight the important role they play in helping to address childhood obesity.

NO: Betsy Di Benedetto Gulledge, an instructor of nursing at Jacksonville State University, highlights what she sees as the disadvantages of having body mass index (BMI) report cards in the schools; she challenges the accuracy of BMI measures and notes the risks of labeling on children's psychological well-being.

Obesity is a growing concern in North America and around the world. According to the Centre for Disease Control and Prevention (CDC), the obesity rate among children and adolescents has almost tripled in the last 30 years. Using data from the National Health and Nutrition Examination Survey, the CDC reports that about 17 percent of 12–19-year-old Americans are obese. When expanded to include young people who are overweight and at-risk for obesity, the statistic rises to almost 32 percent of American children/youth (Ogden, Carroll, & Flegal, 2008). Overweight and obesity issues are not limited to developed countries; their prevalence is increasing in developing countries, such as the Middle East and Central and Eastern Europe as well (Dehghan et al., 2005). Children who are overweight and obese are at risk for a range health issues and illness, including diabetes, high blood pressure, sleep apnea, cardiovascular disease, joint problems, and gallstones, and a range of psychosocial difficulties such as low self-esteem, poor body image, discrimination, and depression (see CDC; Evans & Sonneville, 2009; Justus et al., 2007). Furthermore, children who are obese and overweight are more likely to become overweight or obese adults, and to suffer from a variety of adult health conditions (CDC; Evans & Sonneville, 2009).

According to the CDC, assessment of overweight and obesity draws on the measure of Body Mass Index (BMI), which is the ratio of a person's weight to height (kg/m^2). Although it is not a direct measure of body fat, the CDC considers BMI "a reasonable indicator of body fatness for most children and teens." Others argue that while BMI may be a useful measure for adults, its use with children may not be appropriate given their changing bodies as they move through the growth cycle and into puberty (Dehghan et al., 2005). Children's and adolescents' weight status is calculated by plotting their BMI scores against a growth chart by gender and age to account for such developmental changes and physical differences across boys and girls (CDC). According to these CDC growth charts, weight status for 2–19-year-olds is defined as follows:

- *Overweight* is defined as a BMI at or above the 85th percentile and lower than the 95th percentile for children of the same age and sex.
- *Obesity* is defined as a BMI at or above the 95th percentile for children of the same age and sex.

However, there are no universal standards currently in place to assess weight status. For example, whereas the United States follows the CDC definitions of weight status, the UK draws on BMI reference curves that classify children with a BMI between the 91st and 97th percentiles as overweight, and those with a BMI at or above the 98th percentile as obese (Whitney & Kendrin, 2009).

Given the prevalence rate of obesity and overweight in young people, it is no surprise that this has become a social concern. How to address this issue and who should be involved are fodder for much debate. At a global level, the World Health Organization held a meeting of experts on childhood obesity in 2005 in order to better understand its contributing factors, assessment, and interventions (Ikeda et al., 2006). In 1998, the U.S. government

103

named childhood obesity as an epidemic, and by 2003 the state of Arkansas passed a law requiring schools to expand their heath monitoring to include BMI assessments and a resulting "Report Card" be sent to families (Evans & Sonneville, 2009; Ikeda et al., 2006). According to Nihiser et al. (2009), at least 13 U.S. states have introduced legislation to implement similar school-based screening initiatives. The use of BMI report cards is grounded in a Health Belief Model whereby behavior changes are preceded by recognitions of vulnerability to illness; for young people who are obese and overweight, the recognition process often rests on parents and caregivers who must first perceive their child as overweight and at risk before behavioral changes can be initiated (Evans & Sonneville, 2009). Herein lies a problem. Research has repeatedly demonstrated that parents are not the best judges of whether their child is overweight or obese. For example, in a study by Chomitz and colleagues, 43 percent of parents inaccurately classified their overweight children as being a healthy weight. Similarly, Newmark-Sztainer et al. (2008) found that over half of parents of overweight adolescents (52.8 percent) did not label them as such. Low parental awareness and inaccurate perceptions are problematic in the fight against obesity; if a child's weight status is not classified correctly, how can behavioral changes to improve health be implemented?

How might BMI screening and subsequent report cards introduce a more objective measure of weight status and marker by which to generate a behavioral change? Many argue that because children and youth spend so much time in school, schools can play an integral role in preventing obesity (Nihiser et al., 2009). In addition to providing healthy foods and promoting physical activity, some schools have expanded their role to include BMI screening and report cards. According to Nihiser et al. (2009), BMI screening programs in schools have the following goals:

- Preventing and reducing obesity in a population;
- Correcting misperceptions of parents and children about the children's weight;
- Motivating parents and their children to make healthy and safe lifestyle changes;
- Motivating parents to take children at risk to medical care providers for further evaluation and, if needed, guidance and treatment; and
- Increasing awareness of school administrators and school staff of the importance of addressing obesity.

(pp. 590–591)

Research on the efficacy of BMI screening programs in schools does not exist; however, issues related to in-school screening programs, such as student perceptions and comfort (Kalich et al., 2008), parental use of information (Chomit et al., 2003; Newmark-Sztainer et al., 2008), and possible harm have been studied (see Ikeda et al., 2006 for a review). It is not clear whether such programs do, indeed, prevent or reduce obesity. What makes this particularly difficult to evaluate is that many schools who have introduced BMI screening have not done so in isolation. They have also implemented changes in physical activity required of students, nutritional contents of foods served, and snack selections in school vending machines.

BMI screening and report cards in schools are becoming a widespread practice in the fight against obesity. Researchers, health practitioners, and the general public seem to endorse the need to reduce overweight and obesity, especially in our young; however, they do not agree on how to do this. Whereas schools can be part of the screening and reporting process, the question on the table is *should* they? Do screening and reporting fall under the responsibility of the school system? Are there measures in place to control for confidentiality of the information gathered and shared? Are parents adequately supported when they do receive BMI report cards from schools? What do they do with this information? Are schools "meddling" where they don't belong—in parents/caregivers parenting practices OR are they "stepping up to the plate" as part of a holistic approach to reducing childhood obesity?

While reading the YES and NO selections, consider the pros and cons of BMI screening in the schools and the role this process plays in helping to address childhood obesity. Weigh the advantages and disadvantages, and decide where you stand on the issue.

YES ↵

Cynthia I. Joiner

Writing for the PRO Position— Body Mass Index (BMI) Report Cards: Should Schools Be Responsible for Screening?

In my opinion, body mass index (BMI) report cards in schools offer an opportunity to help tackle childhood obesity and should be encouraged. Among children 6 to 11 years of age, the prevalence of obesity has increased from 6.5% to 17% over the past three decades, and among adolescents aged 12 to 19 years of age, the rate of obesity has more than tripled, increasing from 5% in 1980 to 17.6% in 2006 (Ogden, 2008). Childhood obesity has reached epidemic proportions.

BMI report cards can provide a means to annually gather detailed data on childhood obesity, and to follow individual and group trends. The data collected can include information on all ages, gender, race, and ethnicity, and can thus provide valuable data necessary to monitor obesity trends at both the state and local level where data often is limited. Information obtained from the report cards can be used to help plan and target public health interventions for specific populations. Although BMI is not a perfect measurement, the BMI report card is intended to be used as a screening tool to help identify potential health risks, identifying the percent of students who are underweight, normal weight, overweight, and obese, detecting those children who are at risk for weight-related health problems (Nihiser, 2007).

Schools are well equipped to take on the responsibility of BMI screening and reporting. They manage other screening programs using standardized protocols (such as those for vision, hearing and scoliosis), and BMI screening is no different. Managing the assessment and findings in a private, sensitive manner, and including education as a key component of the screening and assessment helps to insure that children would not be emotionally harmed or threatened by the process.

BMI screening and reporting programs need to be comprehensive in nature, and should be administered and managed with the assistance of healthcare professionals. School nurses are the appropriate professionals to perform the BMI screening, for accuracy in measurements is essential. Results of the assessment should be individualized and sent to parents in a confidential manner; the findings should include educational information about

Joiner, Cyntha I. From *The American Journal of Maternal Child Nursing*, vol. 34, no. 4, July/August 2009, pp. 208. Copyright © 2009 by Lippincott, Williams & Wilkins/Wolters Kluwer Health—Journals. Reprinted by permission.

healthy diet, physical activity, and referral information for those who might wish additional assistance in managing their child's weight.

The Institute of Medicine (IOM) endorses BMI reporting and recommends that schools measure children's weight, height, and BMI annually. Underscoring the importance of BMI screening in preventing childhood obesity, the Institute of Medicine (2005) has called upon the federal government to develop guidance for measuring BMI in schools, where children spend a majority of their developmental years; 95% of American children ages 5 to 17 are enrolled in school (Institute of Medicine, 2005). Since schools strongly influence a child's health, diet, and physical activity for a greater part of their youth, they are the perfect place for promoting a healthy lifestyle. Schools also have frequent contact with and access to parents, so BMI assessments can be discussed with them along with other health issues they may not have considered to be a problem for their child.

Schools already manage other screening programs using standardized protocols such as those for vision, hearing, and scoliosis. BMI screening is no different.

If school-based BMI screening and report cards are part of a comprehensive program, including other strategies such as limiting access to low-nutrient, high-sugar foods during the school day and increasing the frequency and duration of school-based physical exercise, they can provide important information about the effectiveness of interventions to prevent childhood obesity.

References

Institute of Medicine. (2005). *Preventing childhood obesity: Health in the balance.* Washington, DC: National Academies Press.

Nihiser, A. J., Lee, S. M., Wechsler, H., McKenna, M., Odom, E., Reinhold, C., Thompson, D., & Grummer-Strawn, L. (2007). Body mass index measurement in schools. *Journal of School Health*, 77, 651–671.

Ogden, C. L., Carroll, M. D., Flegal, K. M. (2008). High body mass index for age among US children and adolescents. 2003–2006. *JAMA, 299*, 2401–2405.

Betsy Di Benedetto Gulledge   ➔ **NO**

Writing for the CON Position

The inclusion of body mass index (BMI) report cards as a component of a school's responsibility is disadvantageous on multiple levels. Several states have already implemented BMI report cards as a component of a state-wide initiatives to fight obesity; thus far only Arkansas has demonstrated significant change in BMI among students from 2003 to 2005 (Story, Nanney, & Schwartz, 2009). Does sending home a report of a child's weight classification really contribute to preventing overweight and obese children? Some parents of overweight children who have been a part of BMI report card program have reported that they feel the assessments are counter-productive and perhaps even harmful (Story et al., 2009). Parents of overweight and obese children do not need anyone pointing out the obvious. What they need are real solutions that can be incorporated into real life.

In a society intent on *labeling* every child, such approaches as BMI report card can have disastrous consequences including low self-esteem. In my opinion, the role of the school environment is primarily education, not health assessment. There is also a great irony in the prospect of schools assuming the responsibility of determining body mass index when many school systems have significantly limited the amount of instructional time spent engaged in physical education. Parents who are concerned about their child's weight might desire the school's input, but it would be more appropriately focused on how the school can provide additional educational opportunities about health and wellness, not measuring BMI.

An additional concern is the maintenance of confidentiality. Although schools are accountable to provide privacy for student information, there is the significant concern students may disclose such personal information to one another and then suffer the consequences in the form of bullying, thus being further ostracized from their peer group (Story et al., 2009). Children may also experience feelings of fear and anxiety related to a weight classification associated with serious health issues. These feelings may then lead to the development of psychological distress and associated eating disorders.

Opposition to BMI report cards has also come from healthcare practitioners. BMI has not been shown to be the most accurate measure of body composition in children. When considering body size, stature, and muscle composition, BMI, has questionable validity (Maynard et al., 2001). The use of BMI during childhood, particularly adolescence, can contribute to over-estimations

Gulledge, Betsy Di Benedetto. From *The American Journal of Maternal Child Nursing*, vol. 34, no. 4, July/August 2009, pp. 209. Copyright © 2009 by Lippincott, Williams & Wilkins/ Wolters Kluwer Health—Journals. Reprinted by permission.

in level of body fat (Kimm et al., 2005). Healthcare practitioners also caution against the use of BMI as a definitive measurement tool since there is a distinguishable difference in body mass and body fat. Whereas obesity refers to the amount of body fat, BMI refers to body weight, and the relationship between age and body fat versus body mass may significantly change as the child ages.

Finally, research on childhood overweight and obesity has yet to reach any causal conclusions. Disagreement exists over the classifications of at-risk for overweight, overweight, obese, and severely obese categories. There is, however, consensus that prevalence rates of unhealthy weight among children have increased and there is an immediate need for solutions. However, solutions do not lie in merely the identification and reporting of those children meeting criteria for a high BMI. If the healthcare and education communities are to unite in assisting parents and children achieve a healthy lifestyle, initiatives should be focused on interventions and education, not counterproductive labeling.

References

Kimm, S., Glynn, N., Obarzanek, E., Kriska, A., Daniels, S., Barton, B., & Liu, K. (2005). Relation between the changes in physical activity and body mass index during adolescence: a multicentre longitudinal study. *Lancet, 366*(9482), 301–307.

Maynard, L., Wisemandle, W., Roche, A., Chumlea, W., Guo, S., & Siervogel, R. (2001). Childhood body composition in relation to body mass index. *Pediatrics, 107*(2), 344–350.

Story, M., Nanney, M. S., & Schwartz, M. B. (2009). Schools and obesity prevention: Creating school environments and policies to promote healthy eating and physical activity. *The Milbank Quarterly, 87*(1), 71–100.

EXPLORING THE ISSUE

Should Schools Be Responsible for Completing Body Mass Index (BMI) Report Cards in the Fight Against Youth Obesity?

Critical Thinking and Reflection

1. Given the controversy regarding whether schools should be responsible for BMI screening and report cards, what safeguards need to be put in place to protect young people's privacy and confidentiality surrounding their medical information?

2. If you were to empirically examine the impact of BMI report cards on youth obesity and overweight, how would you design the study? Who would comprise your sample? What variables would you include and why? How would you measure them?

3. Imagine that you are a parent of an early adolescent and that your child brings home a BMI report card, alongside the academic one. This document informs you that your child's BMI is above average for his/her age and labels your child overweight, bordering on obese. Your child reads this and becomes very upset. Take a moment to critically self-reflect on what your response might be: What are your beliefs about the roles of parents and the school system in socializing and caring for our young? Where do your beliefs align with, or diverge from, research data? What actions would you take and why?

4. Consider the role of schools beyond the initial BMI screening process. Should the school's responsibility end at screening? How can schools, parents, and health care practitioners work together beyond the screening process to incorporate prevention and intervention strategies to decrease youth obesity and overweight?

Is There Common Ground?

Childhood and youth obesity and overweight are serious health concerns. Words like "crisis" and "epidemic" have been used to describe the growing concern around the health risks (for both youth and adults) that weight issues in childhood and adolescence pose. Are BMI screening in the schools and subsequent report cards helpful in the fight against obesity? The YES and NO selections hold opposing views. Cynthia Joiner argues that the school system is a logical system to include in this effort, in part, because it is well within the school's ability to conduct BMI screening, and children/youth spend the majority of their time in school. Furthermore, she highlights that the data gathered through such efforts are integral to monitoring obesity trends, and can thus be used to support intervention strategies. Arguing for the CON position, Betsy Di Benedetto Gulledge draws attention to concerns that BMI is a less-than-ideal measuring tool, especially for young people, and that schools are not adept to handle the follow-through of such screening, particularly in terms of ensuring confidentiality of results and preventing the potential negative outcomes of labeling. An additional concern is how the information is used; specifically, how parents are supported in understanding and acting upon the results. Although intuitively reasonable, the efficacy of BMI screening programs and report cards in the schools has not been fully established in the research. Methodological issues are partially at play here—whereas associations between screening programs and decreases in obesity and overweight have been noted, the data do not support inferences regarding causality.

So where does that leave us? Should BMI screening and report cards be standard protocol in all schools? Do the benefits outweigh the risks? Should the responsibility for monitoring and decreasing obesity and overweight concerns in young people move beyond the family to include a more "objective" or "neutral" third party—the school? If so, how should this process be managed (and by whom) in order to protect against the possible negative outcomes, including breach of confidentiality and labeling?

Additional Resources

Centre for Disease Control and Prevention. (CDC, 2012). Basics about childhood obesity. Retrieved from http://www.cdc.gov/obesity/childhood/basics.html

Chomitz, V. R., Collins, J., Kim, J., Kramer, E., & McGowan, R. (2003). Promoting healthy weight among elementary school children via a health report card approach. *Archives of Pediatrics and Adolescent Medicine, 157*(8), 765–772.

Dehghan, M., Akhtar-Danesh, N., & Merchant, A. T. (2005). Childhood obesity, prevalence and prevention. *Nutrition Journal, 4*(24), 1–8. doi:10.1186/1475–2891-4-24

Evans, E. W., & Sonneville, K. R. (2009). BMI report cards: Will they pass or fail in the fight against pediatric obesity? *Current Opinion in Pediatrics, 21*(4), 431–436.

Grimmett, C., Croker, H., Carnell, S., & Wardle, J. (2008). Telling parents their child's weight status: Psychological impact of a weight-screening program. *Pediatrics, 122*(3), 682–688.

Ikeda, J. P., Crawford, P. B., & Woodward-Lopez, G. (2006). BMI screening in schools: Helpful or harmful. *Health Education Research, 21*(6), 761–769.

Justus, M. B., Ryan, K. W., Rockenback, J., Katterapalli, C., & Card-Higginson, P. (2007). Lessons learned while implementing a legislated school policy: Body mass index assessments among Arkansas's public school students. *School of Health Policy, 77*(10), 706–713.

Kalich, K. A., Chomitz, V., Peterson, K. E., McGowan, R., Houser, R. F., et al. (2008). Comfort and utility of school-based weight screening: The student perspective. *BMC Pediatrics, 8:9*, doi:10.1186/1471-2431-8-9.

Newmark-Sztainer, D., Wall, M., Story, M., & van den Berg, P. (2008). Accurate parental classification of overweight adolescents' weight status: Does it matter? *Pediatrics, 121*(6), 1495–1502.

Nihiser, A. J., Lee, S. M., Wechsler, H., McKenna, M., Odom, E., Reinold, C., et al. (2009). BMI measurement in schools. *Pediatrics, 124,* 589-597. doi: 10.1542/peds.2008–3586L.

Ogden, C. L., Carroll, M. D., & Flegal, K. M. (2008). High body mass index for age among US children and adolescents, 2003-2006. *Journal of American Medical Association, 299*(20), 2401–2405.

Internet References . . .

The National Coalition for GLBT Youth

This website provides links to news articles, brochures, and special interests.

www.outproud.org

Youth Resource/Amplify Your Voice

Youth Resource/Amplify Your Voice takes a holistic approach to sexual issues concerning queer youth.

www.amplifyyourvoice.org/youthresource

Sexuality Information and Education Council

SIECUS/SIECCAN have the goals of promoting sexuality education and sexual health, protecting sexual rights by providing information and education, consultations, and aiding in public policy regarding sexuality.

www.siecus.org

www.sieccan.org

National Sexuality Research Center (NSRC)

The NSRC gathers and disseminates the accurate information and research on sexual health, education, and rights (family and youth section).

www.nsrc.sfsu.edu

Guttmacher Institute

The Guttmacher Institute is a think tank that generates social science research, policy analysis, and public education on sexual and reproductive health.

www.guttmacher.org

Resource Center for Adolescent Pregnancy Prevention

This private nonprofit health education promotion website contains practical tools and information designed to help reduce sexual risk-taking behaviors.

www.etr.org/recapp

Canadian Women's Health Network

The Canadian Women's Health Network is a national organization aimed at improving the health and lives of girls and women in Canada.

www.cwhn.ca/en

www.cwhn.ca/node/40776

Sex, Sexuality, and Gender

A very important part of an adolescent's development is sexuality. Unfortunately, many textbooks regarding adolescence will gloss over the topics of sex, sexuality, and sometimes gender issues pertaining to youth because of the controversial nature of these topics. Learning about sex and sexuality is of critical importance to youth. Developing sexual and romantic relationships with peers is considered a critical part of youth development. Adolescence is a time when sexual identity and gender roles are explored and formed. This unit examines five key issues surrounding sexuality and gender in adolescence.

- Is There Cause for Concern About an "Oral-Sex Crisis" for Teens?

- Is "Coming Out" As a Sexual Minority (Gay/Lesbian/Bisexual) Earlier in Adolescence Detrimental to Psychological Well-Being?

- Does a Strong and Costly Sexual Double Standard Still Exist Among Adolescents?

- Do Reality TV Shows Portray Responsible Messages about Teen Pregnancy?

- Is Having a Muscular Physique in Adolescence Strictly a "Guy Thing"?

ISSUE 6

Is There Cause for Concern About an "Oral-Sex Crisis" for Teens?

YES: **Sharlene Azam**, from *Oral Sex Is the New Goodnight Kiss: The Sexual Bullying of Teenage Girls* (Reluctant Hero Publishing Ltd., 2008), ISBN: 978-0-9739711-1-8

NO: **SIECCAN (The Sex Information and Education Council of Canada)**, from "Do You Think 'Oral Sex' Is 'Having Sex'? Does the Answer Matter?" *The Canadian Journal of Human Sexuality* (vol. 20, no. 3, pp. 115–116, 2011)

Learning Outcomes

After reading this issue, you should be able to:

- Summarize the two "case studies" provided by Sharlene Azam that illustrate the "casual attitude" that youth take toward oral sex.
- Describe and evaluate the academic research outlined by the Sex Information and Education Council of Canada with regard to how adolescents view oral sex.
- Compare and contrast the positions of the two different authors.
- Reconcile the two positions and draw conclusions about the state of oral sex and adolescents.
- Explore the role of intimacy and romance in sexual behaviors such as oral sex, intercourse, and anal sex.

ISSUE SUMMARY

YES: Journalist Sharlene Azam, in a book about teen prostitution, discusses the cavalier attitude toward oral sex that some girls report. As well, she discusses a famous Canadian case of oral sex with under-aged girls that had major press coverage.

NO: The Research Coordinator of the Sex Information and Education Council of Canada reviews the academic research regarding oral-sex practices and their associated meaning for youth. Their take-home message is that oral sex among teens is not at "epidemic" levels and that many youth feel that oral sex is an intimate sexual behavior.

For the past decade or so, there has been a surge in media attention given to the "problem" of teen oral sex. Much of this interest started with an *Oprah Winfrey* show (circa, Fall 2003) when she discussed the existence of "Rainbow" clubs—parties for teens where girls wear different colored lipstick and fellate boys. The "goal" is for boys to have many different colors of lipstick on their penis at the end of the party. Oral sex has been called the new "spin the bottle" of teenagers. A book for teens by Paul Ruditis, entitled *Rainbow Party* (Simon & Schuster, 2005), brought with it a flurry of discussion on the topic of teen oral sex. Discussion of these rainbow parties continues on popular television shows (e.g., *Maury Povich*, Fall 2009). Consider this quote from a "psychotherapist" (presumably a reputable source) who appeared on a 2010 episode of *The Doctors* (May 27, 2010; www.thedoctorstv.com/main/show_synopsis/408?section=synopsis):

> Another trend gaining traction among teens is the rainbow party, an oral sex party during which each girl wears a different shade of lipstick and each boy attempts to collect every shade.
>
> "Back in the day, like five years ago, you were hearing about parties where people played spin the bottle and truth or dare, and now it's escalated to a whole other level," says psychotherapist Stacy Kaiser. "There's definitely a competition in how many girls [a boy] can get, how many different colors you can get. I want you all to know this is happening everywhere. It's happening in private schools. It's happening in the suburbs. It's happening in the cities. Kids are doing it everywhere."

Very clearly, the media is keen to keep this issue in the forefront of parents' minds. This "crisis" attracts viewer's/reader's attention and the "sex" sells the show, magazine, book, etc.

But, is there any real cause for concern? When questioned about sex, Michael Learned, a television star of the 1970s, stated in an interview in the 1980s that she thought kids today are doing the same thing that she and her peer group were doing as kids—only the kids of the 1980s talked about their sexual activities more than her cohorts did. Is that the case with oral sex of the "Internet generation" of today's teens? Are they simply talking about oral sex more as opposed to "doing it" more, compared to past generations? And, is oral sex simply an activity that is not considered terribly intimate—akin to a goodnight kiss?

A variety of studies have been conducted recently in North America that have garnered some information about oral sex and adolescents. In a large sample of 12–14-year-olds, De Rosa et al. (2010) found that few (i.e., less than 10 percent) young adolescents have had oral sex. Chandra et al. (2011), in a National Health Statistics Report, found that just under two-thirds of youth and young adults (aged 15–24 years) have had some sort of oral sex. A few points of interest from this study: There were no gender differences in oral-sex incidence: the figures for males and females were essentially the same. A comparison of the national statistics from 2002 to data from 2006–2008 indicated that youth engaged in oral sex (indeed, in all forms of sexual contact) slightly less in more recent years (e.g., oral sex in 2002: 69 percent versus 2006–2008: 63–64 percent). Exploring oral sex further, Chandra et al. found that only 5–7 percent of youth had engaged in oral sex without vaginal sex. About half of youth who have had intercourse have engaged in oral sex. Others have concluded that oral sex and vaginal intercourse tend to occur close together (i.e., within 6 months of each other; Lindberg et al., 2008). Similarly, in a sample comprising mostly older teens, Chambers (2007) found that the majority of youths (95 percent) who had had intercourse had also had oral sex at some point in their lives; however, most (around 60 percent) "virgins" (i.e., those who had not had intercourse) had not had oral sex. Most of these aforementioned studies have been cross-sectional (i.e., at one time point) in nature. Song and Halpern-Felsher (2011) present one of the only studies to date that is longitudinal. Following students from 9th grade through 11th grade, they found that oral sex either preceded or occurred at the same time for youth. Having oral sex during the study time period predicted having vaginal sex later during the study time period. While more longitudinal studies are necessary, it seems that oral sex is part of a sexual repertoire of behaviors as opposed to an alternative to vaginal sex (i.e., it appears that most adolescents are having oral and vaginal sex together rather than using oral sex as a means of maintaining virginity).

In terms of changes over time, there does seem to be somewhat of an increase in oral sex, in recent times. Gindi et al. (2008) compared adolescent and young adult women in 1994 to adolescent and young adult women in 2004 and found that women in 2004 were three times more likely to report performing oral sex than women in 1994. Men in 2004 were twice as likely to report performing oral sex compared to men in 1994. This study, along with others (e.g., Remez, 2000), presents some evidence of a trend for an increase in oral sex for adolescents—but it should be noted that there has been a modest increase in oral sex for adults, too (see McKay, 2004).

An aspect of "concern" regarding oral sex raised by some is that youth view this sexual behavior in a cavalier fashion. Studies of youth attitudes toward oral sex do indicate that adolescents believe having oral sex is more acceptable for their age group than having vaginal sex (Halpern-Felsher et al., 2005). In this study, youth also perceived fewer negative emotional and social consequences of oral sex relative to vaginal sex. Ethically, morally, and religiously, oral sex was rated as more personally acceptable than vaginal sex. In her study of older adolescents, Chambers (2007) found that over half perceived oral sex to be intimate (much lower than the 91 percent who found intercourse to be an intimate behavior). Similarly, a study of Canadian women aged 18–25 years found that about half of women think that oral sex is equally intimate or more intimate than intercourse (Malacad & Hess, 2010). When these women said that they were in love with their partners, they had more positive emotions associated with oral sex and intercourse. Chambers also addressed oral sex and relationship status; a minority of youth reported that they, personally, would be comfortable with having oral sex in a noncommitted or primarily sexually based relationship (i.e., only 12–18 percent; Chambers, 2007). Finally, De Rosa et al. (2010) found that having a boy/girlfriend increased the odds of youth reporting having had oral sex. One implication we might make from this is that oral sex, for these young adolescents (i.e., the sample consisted of middle school students), took place within the context of a relationship. However, this is purely speculative. These studies, collectively, suggest that most youth consider oral sex as an intimate behavior that takes place within the context of romantic relationships.

Given that there is some evidence of a modest increase in oral-sex performance by teens and there are a subset of youth who consider oral sex as a behavior that can take place outside of the context of a committed romantic relationship, should sex educators and those who work with adolescents be concerned about teen oral-sex activity? In the YES selection, journalist Sharlene Azam documents situations in Canada where young girls have been participants in rainbow parties or where girls were "passed around" among group of older, popular boys for fellatio—illustrating the cavalier teen attitude toward oral sex. In the NO selection, the Sex Information and Education Council of Canada reviewed the research on how youth view oral sex (i.e., "is it sex?") and generally concluded that there is no "youth epidemic" of oral sex as the media might lead us to believe.

YES ↵

Sharlene Azam

Oral Sex Is the New Goodnight Kiss: The Sexual Bullying of Teenage Girls

" **A**t one school, students formed a barrier on either side of a narrow hallway to prevent teachers from walking through. In the middle, 12-year-old girls were giving blowjobs to boys," explains Joy Becker, Director of Education for Options for Healthy Sexuality (formerly Planned Parenthood).

12-and 14-year-old campers in Ottawa made headlines when they were found having group oral sex.[1] Counselors assumed the kids were playing cards in a nearby cabin. "Camps reflect what is happening in society," says Dan Offord, executive director of Christie Lake Camp, adding that, "Childcare workers are being caught off guard by the fact that children are engaging in sexual activity. I think parents are also in denial about their children having sex."

It would be easy to believe that these girls and boys are an anomaly, but for this generation, oral sex is like kissing was to their parents.

At Lord Byng in Vancouver, the principal asked Joy Becker and Hannah Varto, a sexual assault nurse, to counsel 4 grade 8 girls who were discovered performing oral sex at school, along with the boys, and the parents.

"The girls were in the boys' bathroom on their knees in a cubicle with urine on the floor," Varto explained. "Or, the boy would stand over them as they sat on the toilet. They described the feeling of being gagged and choked because the boy was on top."

I met Rita and Crystal (names changed), 2 of the Lord Byng students . . .

Why did you do it?

"Everybody does it," Rita says

At school?

"Oral is not even like a question any more: guys want it all the time," says Crystal, . . .

"The girls told us that they loved the attention the boys would give them, which at first was very positive," Varto explained, adding, "The boys would make them feel beautiful, loved, sexy and cared for and that's what they were really needing."

"Was it worth it?"

"After each experience, I think, 'Was that really what I wanted, or was it because I was feeling lonely?' I'll look back on some experiences and think, 'It wasn't worth it. I didn't get anything out of it.' There are a lot of different moments you get caught up in, and a lot happens at parties.[2] I think if you have a spot or hole that needs to be filled, sex can replace it. I'm not saying it's one of the righter choices," Rita says.

Did the boys reciprocate?

"No," Rita says flatly.

Do they ever reciprocate?

"9 times out of 10, if you walk into a room [at a party] you'll see a girl on her knees. But you never see a guy on top of a girl eating her out. It just doesn't usually happen," Crystal explains.

"If it does happen, it's after you leave the party, and only if you're in a relationship. And then, he might do it sometimes really quickly so he can say, 'I ate you out.' But it's not like they're really into it for pleasure. It's just for 2 seconds so they can make you feel like you should give something back," Rita adds.

Why hook up when it is so dissatisfying?

"Oral is a chore. It's not the greatest thing, but you don't have to think about it the way you do with sex," Rita says. . . .

Did you have a boyfriend at the time of the incident in the boys' bathroom?

"No," Rita says softly. . . .

How many boys have you had sex with?

"I've given head to more guys than I've slept with. . . . ," Crystal says.

. . . Through role-playing, Varto and Becker learned that the 8th and 9th grade boys pursued the girls relentlessly. "After 3 hours of being followed around the school being told, 'You're so beautiful why won't you give me a blowjob,' the girls gave in," Becker explained.

Boys have long been taught how to get what they want and to "go for it" when it comes to girls, while girls are expected to be the "gatekeepers." This objectifying mentality speaks to a failure by parents to instill in boys the kind of empathy that would translate into a greater degree of caring in their sexual relationships.

After counseling, Becker and Varto say the boys understood that a girl waving or smiling at them does not mean she wants them, "For them, everything leads to sex," Varto says.

And, the girls realized that they are deserving of respect. "They told us, 'We are better than having our heads pushed down into crotches when we don't want them to be there,'" Becker says.

Although the parents of the boys were surprised their sons were having oral sex at school, they were unwillingly to fault them. "I think a lot of parents think the onus is on the girls because 'boys will be boys,'" Becker says. The girls' parents were upset and embarrassed by their daughters' involvement, but they did not think their behavior was cause for alarm.

"We've counseled girls who give oral sex to a boy leaving a lipstick rainbow on his penis. If it starts out being one blowjob here or there and then it becomes 5 or 10 in a day, it would be natural to eventually think, 'Well, why don't I just get paid for this? Why shouldn't I just take some money for it or something else that I want?' And it can be that innocent and that's where it starts. Yet, parents and schools have a hard time seeing the link between rainbow parties and being recruited into the sex trade," Becker explains.

. . . I am struck by the girls' collusion in what seems like a sexual dystopia; this collusion turns on the idea that oral sex is what girls will do, getting passed around is what girls will endure, and so getting paid is a bonus, rather than an element that further degrades the behavior.

. . . [On Prince Edward Island], a story broke that shone a spotlight on the practice of girls providing sexual favors to older guys. . . . "The girls who testified in the case said that they didn't feel coerced, in fact, there was a willingness on their part."

The case involved Los Angeles Dodgers' draft pick, Cass Rhynes, who testified in 2003 that 12-and 13-year-old girls regularly performed oral sex on him. Rhynes was in the 12th grade, at the time. In his testimony, he described in detail his sexual escapades with the adolescents Sara and Brittney (names changed).

Rhynes was caught when Annie, Sara's mother, overheard a late-night conversation between Rhynes and her daughter. . . .

"I confronted her, and she explained how she had become involved with Cass and his friend, Tyler, over the school year. When I learned their ages, that she had oral sex with 17-and 18-year-old boys, I was outraged," Annie says.

Annie contacted the boys' parents and was told that her daughter must be lying, because their sons would never become sexually involved with such young girls. She called the parents of 15 of the girls Sara claimed were also sexually involved with the boys, but they refused to discuss the issue. She then contacted the school principal. "He told me to keep it 'hush-hush,'" she says That's when I decided to call the police and press charges."

As testimony about the girls' willing participation emerged, the community became increasingly angry that 2 girls would attempt to destroy the reputation of a local hero on his way to the big leagues.

Jamie Ballem, Attorney General . . . spoke . . . about the division in the community. "Some groups are saying, 'Yes, he's guilty, but he's been punished enough by being publicly exposed. He may lose his athletic scholarship.'"

The case garnered a lot of national media attention, but there was never any mention of the negative impact of the extensive coverage on the girls. Although the girls' names were not made public, their identities are known in their city, where the feeling is that girls who "act like boys"—in other words, behave promiscuously—get what they deserve.

Some believe that the girls became sexually involved with Rhynes in a "quest for fame," and so they should not claim to be innocents. Neither of the girls presented themselves as victims. Nor did they want to go to court. Sara's mom pressed charges because the girls are minors.

"There is a lot of discussion about the responsibility of the girls' parents. Where were those girls' parents?" Ballem asks. "A lot of people don't think the courts should be used to decide these issues." Sara, like many of the girls I interviewed, comes from a broken home where her father is absent from her life.

Rhynes was convicted on 2 counts of inciting girls under 14 to touch him for sexual purposes, but the conviction was overturned on appeal. . . .

As a result of our rapidly changing sexual mores, the line between adolescents and adults is blurred. A decade ago, the notion of a 12-year-old giving an 18-year-old, 200-pound, 6-foot athlete oral sex would have enraged most of society and the courts. Today, the girl is vilified and he is back on the field with a lucrative contract. . . .

Reporters described Sara and Brittney as little Lolitas. Rhynes even spoke to reporters about the girls' morality and how much things had changed since he was a kid. "I wasn't even thinking about sex when I was 12," he explained. And yet no one challenged his sexual mores as an 18-year-old. "All the blame is on the girls, as if it's normal for an adult man to want to have sex with 12-year-old girls," Annie says.

Complicating the Cass Rhynes case is the fact that Rhynes falls under the extraordinary protection that is handed out to professional athletes who get caught deviating from the straight and narrow. In *Out of Bounds: Inside the NBA's Culture of Rape, Violence and Crime*, Jeff Benedict explains that when an athlete is accused of sexual assault there are enormous nets that go up around him. "He is a commodity. He's a product. And he's got to be protected.". . .

Increasingly, girls who are victims of sexual exploitation will find there is little incentive to come forward and tell their stories. Girls know that their worth is determined by how they appear to others; they know that fame is more valuable than romance. These are absolutes in our celebrity-obsessed culture. And yet a girl who acts on these messages will be put on the stand and made to feel as though she is in the wrong. The justice system and society, which should protect her, will, in effect, vilify her and the result is that her life will be ruined at the age of 12. . . .

Sara, 12

. . . I met Cass Rhynes through his friend Tyler who I met in September on the school bus. It was the beginning of grade 7. At first I didn't really know who Tyler was. . . . Then a couple times he sat with me and Brittney on the school bus. . . . We'd talk and he was nice to us. I thought we were just friends. I guess he took it a different way.

Tyler added us on his MSN buddy list (Hotmail's chat service) and we would talk online a lot. The fact that I was getting attention from a 17-year-old was big. . . .

Then he got into sex talk. At first I thought it was disgusting, but then he kept on asking. He just kept saying, "Do you think you could give me head?" He was pretty blunt about it. After [a while] it started to click-in that he wasn't joking.

Then I found out that Brittney, my best friend, had done it with him and 2 of his friends. We met him on the school bus at the same time and she was 12 too. She didn't get called names and stuff and she got so much attention from everybody. . . .

When I did it, I didn't necessarily want to do it. It wasn't my main priority to have oral sex with some random guy, but it was like, "Well, my best friend did it, and if she can do it then I can do it." My first time, it was really weird because I hadn't done anything sexual before. I was terrified. I didn't know what to do. I had to ask him what I was supposed to do. I did it, and after that, he just expected it from both of us. I didn't care about doing it. It wasn't like such a big deal, but after we would make fun of him like, "Oh my God, did you see how curly his hair is down there?" and stuff.

I didn't do it for the acceptance. I was already accepted. I wanted to do something that I wasn't supposed to do. I wanted to be a rebel. I thought this would make me greater and better. I got a rush from being with somebody older who has a car. I thought, "They really must have an interest in me, if they're hanging out with a 12-year-old. They can have any girl they want." But I guess we were just easy to get. It didn't really bother me to do It. It was like nothing.

Tyler started to pass us around to his friends after he had been with us, and that's how me and Cass Rhynes got together. Tyler would ask his friends if they wanted us to give them head and stuff. . . .

On October 22, 2003, Cass Rhynes, 18, was convicted of sex crimes involving the underage girls and sentenced to 45 days in jail. Convicted on 2 counts of inciting girls under the age of 14 to touch him for sexual purposes, he was placed on 1 year probation and required to complete 100 hours of community service. . . .

John Mitchell, Cass Rhynes's lawyer, appealed the guilty ruling to the Supreme Court, arguing that Rhynes was a passive participant. The guilty verdict was overturned. Annie, Sara's mother, says, "Most appeals can take up to 2 years to be heard. How did Rhynes get his appeal before the bench in just a few months?" . . .

Notes

1. "Kids have oral sex at summer camp." *Montreal Gazette,* 4 July 2003, P A12.
2. "Grade 9 girls were the group most likely to say, 'They first had sex because they got carried away,'" Council of Ministers of Education. 2003. *Canadian Youth, Sexual Health and HIV/AIDS Study.*

SIECCAN (The Sex Information and
Education Council of Canada)

 **NO**

Do You Think "Oral Sex" Is "Having Sex"? Does the Answer Matter?

In recent years, the topic of oral sex among young people has been frequently discussed in the media. Some media reports have gone as far as to suggest that there is an "epidemic" of oral sex breaking out among teens. In fact, research from both Canada and the United States suggests that less than a third of younger teens (i.e., 17 and under) and about half to two-thirds of older teens (18/19) have participated in oral-genital contact one or more times (Boyce, et al., 2006: Lindberg, Jones, & Santelli, 2008). In other words, among young people, oral-genital contact is about as common as sexual intercourse and the two behaviours typically happen at about the same age (Maticka-Tyndale, 2008).

At the same time, there has also been a lot of discussion as to whether teens and young adults today classify oral-genital contact as "having sex" to the same extent that they would classify intercourse as "having sex." Is oral-genital contact now viewed as an activity that does not carry the same emotional, psychological, social, and health implications as penile-vaginal or penile-anal intercourse and, thus, not considered to be "having sex"?

We examine contemporary research on how people classify oral-genital contact as a behaviour. We will also ask whether classifying oral-genital contact as not "having sex" has implications for our health and well-being that we should be aware of.

Is It Having Sex?

Several studies have examined whether university students classify oral-genital contact as "having sex." Randal and Byers (2003) asked 197 Canadian university students to indicate from a list of 18 behaviours which ones they considered to be "having sex." Here, we will look at how the students classified three different behaviours. As you can see in Table 1, both male and female students were much more likely to classify penile-vaginal and penile-anal intercourse as "having sex" than they were to classify it has "having sex" when a partner performed oral-genital contact.

SIECCAN. From *The Canadian Journal of Human Sexuality,* Vol. 20, No. 3, 2011, pp. 115–116.
Copyright © 2011 by SIECCAN. Reprinted by permission.

Table 1

Percentage of University Students Classifying Behaviours As "Having Sex"*

	Male	Female	Total
Oral contact with genitals	24%	24%	23.2%
Penile-vaginal intercourse	98%	97%	97.6%
Penile-anal intercourse	84%	83%	83.3%

* These results are for the behaviours "with orgasm"; "no orgasm" had similar percentages.
Source: Randall & Byers (2003)

In a similar study, Hans, Gillen, and Akande (2010) asked 477 students at a university in the United States the question "Would you say you 'had sex' with someone if the most intimate behavior you engaged in was," followed by a list of 11 different behaviours. The vast majority of the students said that having penile-vaginal (98%) and penile-anal (78%) intercourse was "having sex" but only about 20% said that oral-genital contact was "having sex." Interestingly, when the researchers compared their results to a very similar study conducted in 1991, they discovered that current university students are about twice as likely than students in the early 1990's to not consider oral-genital contact as "having sex."

Does It Matter That Many Young People Do Not Consider Oral Sex To Be Having Sex?

At first glance we might say that it really doesn't matter whether we label a particular behaviour as "having sex" or not. On the other hand, if saying that oral-genital contact is not "having sex" means that the activity has fewer, if any, implications for our lives, then we may want to examine the issue a little more closely.

First, it is interesting to note that although most of the students in the Randall and Byers (2003) study did not classify oral-genital contact as "having sex," 99% said that if their relationship partner had oral-genital contact with someone else, they would view their partner as having been "unfaithful." For most people, being monogamous means, among other things, that the partners do not have sex with other people. But with so many people not classifying oral-genital contact as "having sex," it might be a good idea for partners at the beginning of a relationship to clarify with each other that they are on the same page on what it means to be monogamous.

Second, some people might assume that if oral-genital contact is not "having sex" then the behaviour has less emotional significance and is less intimate than "having sex" (e.g. intercourse). Malacad and Hess (2010) examined these issues in a study of 181 18 to 25-year-old Canadian women. The authors found that about half (49.7%) indicated that "I think oral sex is a less intimate activity than intercourse," 40.7% said that oral sex and intercourse were equally intimate and about 8% believed that oral sex is more intimate than intercourse. In sum, the women in this study were split about evenly as to whether oral-genital contact is a less intimate behaviour than intercourse.

Malacad and Hess (2010) also found that, overall, the women expressed positive emotions (e.g., excited) about their most recent experiences of both intercourse and oral-genital contact (especially if they were on the receiving end). As might be expected, the women reported more positive emotions about having intercourse if they were "in love" with their partner. However this was also the case for oral-genital contact: those who said they were "in love" with their partner were more likely to express positive emotions about the activity. Similarly, women who were not "in love" with their partner were more likely to express negative emotions (e.g., disappointment, guilt) for both oral-genital contact and intercourse. These findings indicate that, for these women, some considered oral-genital contact less intimate than intercourse, and some didn't, but, overall, the emotional implications of the two activities were similar.

Third, we might assume that if oral-genital contact is not "having sex" then there is no risk of transmitting a sexually transmitted infection (STI) through oral-genital contact. There is, in fact, some risk. According to the U.S. Centers for Disease Control and Prevention (2009), the risk of transmitting HIV through oral-genital contact is "much less" than for penis-vagina or penis-anus intercourse but there have been cases where it has occurred through oral-genital contact and there is some risk of transmission for other STI (herpes, syphilis, gonorrhea, HPV, hepatitis A, intestinal parasites) through oral-genital contact.

What's The Take Home Message?

Oral-genital contact is about as common as penile-vaginal intercourse among young people. Increasingly, young people do not consider oral-genital contact as "having sex." However, we need to be aware that even if we do not classify oral-genital contact as "having sex" this does not mean that we should ignore the potential emotional, relationship, and health implications of the behaviour.

References

Boyce, W. et al. (2006). Sexual health of Canadian youth: Findings from the *Canadian Youth, Sexual Health and HIV/AIDS Study. The Canadian Journal of Human Sexuality*. 15, (2), 59–68. http://www.sieccan.org/pdf/boyce_cjhs2006_sexualhealth.pdf

Centers for Disease Control and Prevention. (2009). *Oral Sex and HIV Risk.* http://www.cdc.gov/hiv/resources/factsheets/PDF/oralsex.pdf

Hans, J. D., Gillen, M., & Akande, K. (2010). Sex redefined: The reclassification of oral-genital contact. *Perspectives on Sexual and Reproductive Health*, 42, (2), 74–78.

Lindberg, L. D., Jones, R., & Santelli, J. S. (2008). Noncoital sexual activities among adolescents. *Journal of Adolescent Health*, 43, 231–238.

Malacad, B. L. & Hess, G. C. (2010). Oral sex: Behaviours and feelings of Canadian young women and implications for sex education. *The European Journal of Contraception and Reproductive Health Care*, 15, 177–185.

Maticka-Tyndale, E. (2008). Sexuality and sexual health of Canadian adolescents. *The Canadian Journal of Human Sexuality*, 17, (3), 85–95. http://www.sieccan.org/pdf/maticka-tyndale_cjhs2008_commentary.pdf

Randall, H. & Byers, E. S. (2003). What is sex? Students' definitions of having sex, sexual partner, and unfaithful sexual behaviour. *The Canadian Journal of Human Sexuality*, 12, (2), 87–96.

EXPLORING THE ISSUE

Is There Cause for Concern About an "Oral-Sex Crisis" for Teens?

Critical Thinking and Reflection

1. Do youth today have a "casual" attitude about oral sex? Is oral sex the new "goodnight kiss" as Sharlene Azam's book title suggests? How does intimacy factor into adolescent sexual behavior?
2. What is the role of morals and ethics in the interpretation of the meaning of sexual behavior? In particular, why is oral sex and youth such an ethically charged, emotionally hot issue? Consider how your own morals, values, ethics, and principles influence your reading and assessment of these two selections. Consider how the morals, values, ethics, and principles of the authors affected their writing. How would different morally inclined audiences interpret these two selections?
3. Sharlene Azam's piece may be taken as evidence of a sexual double standard (i.e., ". . . girls who act like boys, promiscuously, get what they deserve . . ."). Is there a double standard with regard to oral sex? How does the media influence this double standard? Is the double standard different for adolescents versus adults?
4. What is "sex"? If oral sex is not classified as "having sex" by some, then why would many view oral–genital contact outside the primary relationship as "cheating"? Why don't people tend to think of oral sex as "sex"?
5. There is no academic literature that supports the existence of "rainbow parties." Does this mean such parties do not exist? Are "rainbow parties" an urban myth (give a rationale for your answer)?
6. If middle and high school sex educators and teachers were to ask you what should be done (i.e., what they should do) about "the problem of adolescent oral sex," what would your advice be, based on your reading of these two selections? Why is oral sex a topic that is rarely addressed in sex education curricula?

Is There Common Ground?

Is there a teen oral sex crisis? Extreme situations such as the group oral sex that occurred at the Ottawa summer camp and the oral sex that occurred in the bathroom at Lord Byng High School certainly point to some sort of "moral emergency." The Cass Rhynes case, which made national headlines, illustrates that young girls are in danger of being enticed into sexual acts by young men—despite the illegality of these actions under the federal Criminal

Code of Canada. Both Azam and SIECCAN would agree that these situations are extreme, exploitive, and unacceptable. The two diverge on other conclusions: Azam's book goes further into depth by discussing even greater sexual exploitation of girls—that this oral sex phenomenon can lead to, ultimately, prostitution of these girls. Azam would likely view casual attitudes toward oral sex by adolescents as a slippery slope into moral sexual depravity. In contrast, SIECCAN's review of the empirical research suggests that most youth consider oral sex as at least somewhat of an intimate sexual behavior that usually occurs within a romantic relationship. The research does suggest that there is a small subset of youth who view oral sex as a casual behavior (see Chambers, 2007). Perhaps it is this group that needs further study to understand how their perceptions of oral sex differ from their peers who consider oral sex an intimate sexual behavior. Perhaps it is these youth who are the subject of Azam's book; perhaps it is these youth who need to be targeted for differential sex education.

Additional Resources

Barrett, A. (2004). Teens and oral sex: A sexual health educator's perspective. *Canadian Journal of Human Sexuality, 13*, 197–200.

Brady, S. S., & Halpern-Felsher, B. L. (2007). Adolescents' reported consequences of having oral sex versus vaginal sex. *Pediatrics, 119*(2), 229–236.

Brewster, K. L., & Tillman, K. H. (2008). Who's doing it? Patterns and predictors of youths' oral sexual experiences. *Journal of Adolescent Health, 42*, 73–80.

Burns, A., Futch, V. A., & Tolman, D. L. (2011). "It's like doing homework": Academic achievement discourse in adolescent girls' fellatio narratives. *Sexual Research and Social Policy, 8*, 239–251.

> In contrast to many of the articles cited in this section, this piece involved a qualitative, phenomenological investigation of oral sex. That is, the researchers spoke to a large number of girls about their experience of performing oral sex. Many likened performing oral sex to academic tasks such as taking tests and used learning as a framework for explaining their experiences.

Chambers, W. C. (2007). Oral sex: Varied behaviors and perceptions in a college population. *Journal of Sex Research, 44*(1), 28–42.

> This was a survey of youth (late teens, emerging adults) regarding oral sex—assessed was the level of perceived intimacy of oral sex (20 percent viewed oral sex as not intimate), the type of relationship in which oral sex occurred (oral sex tended to occur in committed relationships), and reasons for having oral sex (pleasure rationales were the most frequently endorsed reasons for oral sex).

Chandra, A., Mosher, W. D., Copen, C., & Sionean, C. (2011). Sexual behavior, sexual attraction, and sexual identity in the United States: Data from the 2006–2008 National Survey of Family Growth. *National Health Statistics Reports, 36*. Hyattsville, MD: National Center for Health Statistics.

> Using national data, these researchers describe the sexual behavior of a national representative sample. Embedded in the report is a section on

youth (i.e., 15–24 years of age) sexual behavior. The authors were able to compare data of 2006–2008 with that of 2002.

De Rosa, C. J., Ethier, K. A., Kim, D. H., Cumberland, W. G., Abdelmonem, A. A., Kotlerman, J., et al. (2010). Sexual intercourse and oral sex among public middle school students: Prevalence and correlates. *Perspectives on Sexual and Reproductive Health, 42*(3), 197–205.

This study investigated the oral and vaginal sexual activity of students in grades 6 to 8. They found that the overall prevalence of oral and vaginal sex was low (i.e., less than 10 percent) and that there were differences based on demographic characteristics (e.g., there were large differences between grades 6 and 8, which might indicated that this is a key developmental stage; racial differences were evident, too).

Gindi, R. M., Ghanem, K. G., & Erbelding, E. J. (2008). Increases in oral and anal sexual exposure among youth attending sexually transmitted diseases clinics in Baltimore, Maryland. *Journal of Adolescent Health, 42*, 307–308.

A brief report where the investigators analyzed medical records from youth (12–25 years of age) who had been seen at a reproductive health clinic. Significant increases in receptive oral and anal sex were documented in youth across the decade under study.

Halpern-Felsher, B. L. (2008). Oral sexual behavior: Harm reduction or gateway behavior? *Journal of Adolescent Health, 43*, 207–208.

Halpern-Felsher, B. L., Cornell, J. L., Kropp, R. Y., & Tschann, J. M. (2005). Oral versus vaginal sex among adolescents: Perceptions, attitudes, and behavior. *Pediatrics, 115*(4), 845–851.

Investigators were interested in adolescent perceptions of oral-sex acceptability. Oral sex was more prevalent than vaginal sex with these grade 9 youth. Oral sex attitudes were more liberal relative to perceptions of vaginal sex.

Halpern, C. T., & Haydon, A. A. (2012). Sexual timetables for oral-genital, vaginal, and anal intercourse: Sociodemographic comparisons in a nationally representative sample of adolescents. *American Journal of Public Health*, e1-e8. doi:10.2105/AJPH.2011.300394

An analysis of the prevalence and timing of, among other sexual behaviors, oral sex for a nationally representative sample of 18-year-olds. They found that oral sex rarely was a "sole" sexual behavior—it tended to co-occur with vaginal sex (for 50–55 percent of these youth).

Lindberg, L. D., Jones, R., & Santelli, J. S. (2008). Noncoital sexual activities among adolescents. *Journal of Adolescent Health, 43*, 231–238.

Using nationally representative youth data, these researchers investigated the prevalence of oral sex (among other behaviors). They found that slightly over half had had oral sex. When comparing those who had had vaginal sex, 87 percent had had oral sex, too. Only 23 percent of virgins, on the other hand, had experienced oral sex. Other demographic variables and their relation to oral sex were discussed.

McKay, A. (2004). Oral sex among teens: Research, discourse and education. SIECCAN Newsletter, 39(12) in The Canadian Journal of Human Sexuality, 13, 201–203.

Malacad, B. L., & Hess, G. C. (2010). Oral sex: Behaviours and feelings of Canadian young women and implications for sex education. *European Journal of Contraception and Reproductive Health Care, 15*, 177–185.

> This was a study of female youth (late teens, emerging adults) assessing prevalence of oral sex (75 percent of young women reported having engaged in oral sex), casual attitudes toward/casual performance of oral sex (25 percent had not engaged in either oral or vaginal sex, while those who had engaged in oral sex within serious relationships), and the emotions associated with oral sex (vaginal intercourse and cunnilingus were associated with positive emotions, while fellatio tended to be associate with more negative emotions and fewer positive emotions, relatively speaking).

Remez, L. (2000) Oral Sex Among Adolescents: Is It Sex or Is It Abstinence? Family Planning Perspectives, 43(6).

Ruditis, P. (2005). *Rainbow party*. New York: Simon & Schuster.

> A fictional account of a "rainbow party" marketed toward adolescents. This book has created a great deal of controversy.

Song, A. V., & Halpern-Felsher, B. L. (2011). Predictive relationship between adolescent oral and vaginal sex: Results from a prospective, longitudinal study. *Archives of Pediatric Adolescent Medicine, 165*(3), 243–249.

> The first study to follow the sexual behavior of the same adolescents across three grades (i.e., for about 2.5 years). The researchers were able to document when many of the adolescents first had oral sex and vaginal sex. Three key findings from the study were: (1) having oral sex in grades 9 and 10 increased the likelihood that youth would have vaginal sex; (2) adolescents usually had vaginal and oral sex for the first time within the same 6-month period; and (3) oral sex usually occurred first.

ISSUE 7

Is "Coming Out" As a Sexual Minority (Gay/Lesbian/Bisexual) Earlier in Adolescence Detrimental to Psychological Well-Being?

YES: **Justin Jager and Pamela E. Davis-Kean**, from "Same-Sex Sexuality and Adolescent Psychological Well-Being: The Influence of Sexual Orientation, Early Reports of Same-Sex Attraction, and Gender," *Self and Identity* (vol. 10, pp. 417–444, 2011)

NO: **Margaret Rosario, Eric W. Schrimshaw, and Joyce Hunter**, from "Different Patterns of Sexual Identity Development over Time: Implications for the Psychological Adjustment of Lesbian, Gay, and Bisexual Youths," *Journal of Sex Research* (vol. 48, no. 1, pp. 3–15, 2010)

Learning Outcomes

After reading this issue, you should be able to:

- Describe and deconstruct different ways of defining the "coming out" process in research.
- Compare the similarities and differences between the two studies and their findings.
- Critique the studies such that you are able to form an opinion on which piece most adequately addresses the question posed in this issue.

ISSUE SUMMARY

YES: Using the ADD Health longitudinal dataset, researchers Justin Jager and Pamela E. Davis-Kean investigated the association of early same-sex attraction on mental health outcomes of depressive affect and self-esteem. Those who had early (12–15 years) same-sex attractions and whose attraction remained stable throughout adolescence had the most negative psychological well-being. However, this group of adolescents gained or "recovered" the most, in terms of psychological well-being, over time.

NO: In a longitudinal study, Professor Margaret Rosario and colleagues found that early versus later acknowledgment of one's minority sexual orientation was not related to psychological distress; thus, sexual-minority identity formation was unrelated to psychological distress. Rather, identity integration—how well one accepts and integrates that sexual-minority status into one's life—was predictive of psychological well-being. Those who had a well-integrated sexual-minority identity had the most favorable measure of psychological well-being, while those with lower sexual-minority identity integration had the poorest measures of psychological well-being.

Coming out is the term used to describe a process of self-identification as a lesbian, gay, bisexual, or transgender person. Coming out typically involves forming an LGBT identity and integrating this into one's sense of self. Stage theorists describe the coming out process as a set of stages through which a person progresses. While coming out is not necessarily linear or a stage process, psychosexual stage-theorist psychologists generally agree that there are a series of steps that a person typically goes through when self-identifying as LGBT (Clarke et al., 2010). People who come out with a queer identity experience self-discovery whereby they come to realize that they may be or are LGBT (i.e., awareness). Upon this realization, people can go on to develop a sense of self as LGBT, investigating what this identity means for them (i.e., exploration). Adopting the identity is another step in the process (i.e., acceptance). Finally, this identity becomes a solid, permanent part of the definition of self (i.e., integration). This process can be "shut down" by the person; when this happens, the identity is said to be foreclosed (i.e., rejected and developed no further; Clarke et al., 2010). This identity formation process is probably less stage-like and more dynamic (Shapiro et al., 2010). Regardless of theoretical stance, successful sexual-minority identity development is thought to be marked by such milestones as having successful romantic relationships with people of the same sex, developing a positive sense of self (i.e., deal at least somewhat successfully with internalized homophobia), and integrating one's homosexual self-identity into the overall or more general identity (e.g., Floyd & Stein, 2002). The process may have different content for transgender people but is somewhat parallel to the coming out of GLB people (Bockting & Coleman, 2007). Coming out is an internal process involving the synthesis of being gay, lesbian, bisexual, or transgender into one's sense of self. The person who has come out tends to feel authenticated; typically, most adolescents who come out feel good about their sexual orientation (Savin-Williams, 2005).

Coming out also has a public aspect. However, people have different levels of being "out." That is, some people have only told a few close friends (maybe queer friends) and no one else knows. These people are often referred to as being "in the closet" or "closeted." There are a whole host of stressors associated with being in the closet (Cox et al., 2011; LaSala, 2010). Typically, public disclosure of sexual orientation to others proceeds in a particular order with close friends and family being told first, and then more peripheral friends, workmates/classmates, and/or acquaintances being told next. Telling parents of one's sexual-minority status is often a seminal event in an LGBT person's life (Floyd & Stein, 2002; LaSala, 2010). Finally, complete outness would entail being out to strangers or upon meeting people. An out person might also be involved in LGBT community events or organizations (e.g., online groups, pride celebrations; Clarke et al., 2010). Generally, this kind of disclosure to social sources is viewed as a positive aspect of sexual-minority identity development (LaSala, 2010; Savin-Williams, 2005).

Many LGBT individuals begin this identity process as youth or young adults (Calzo et al., 2011). Retrospective research suggests that LGB people typically come out at a variety of ages; Calzo et al. conducted a study that investigated "groupings" of when people came out in a large sample of Californians aged 18–84 years. They found that three developmental "groups" of people were evident: those who came out early in life (i.e., first same-sex attraction at 12.5 years and identifying as queer at 16.5 years, on average), those who came out in later adolescence or early adulthood (i.e., first same-sex attraction at 18 years and identifying as queer at 25.5 years, on average), and the "older" group, who came out, on average, at 40 years of age. The early group constituted over 75 percent of the sample. The group who came out in late adolescence/early adulthood made up 19 percent of the sample. Many queer individuals report feeling "different" as young as 5 or 6 years of age (D'Augelli & Hershberger, 1993). In short, coming out is a process that primarily affects youth with 9 out of 10 people beginning the coming-out process in the teen years.

Coming out or disclosing one's sexual orientation to significant others is thought to have beneficial effects, while concealing one's sexual orientation is thought to have many negative effects (see Legate et al., 2012). Harvey Milk, a 1970s' gay icon/political leader who was assassinated, encouraged people to "come out . . . and once you do, you will feel so much better." Being public about one's sexual-minority status or even being perceived as a sexual minority often has a dark side: being on the recipient of prejudice toward and discrimination based on sexual-minority status. This seems particularly true when adolescents come out in school settings; this sets the stage for potential bullying based on sexual orientation (Clarke et al., 2010). The supportive context of the situation in which a person comes out interacts with levels of sexual orientation disclosure to have a differential impact on emotional and health-related outcomes. Legate et al. (2012) found that being out was only really beneficial to a person when a social environment was supportive of the individual. The school climate is not known for being a positive atmosphere for LGBT students (Clarke et al., 2010; Taylor et al., 2011).

The YES and NO selections address timing of coming out as beneficial or detrimental to the mental health outcomes of youth. Using a longitudinal design, Rosario et al. (2011) investigated the impact of coming out earlier—defined by both identity formation and identity integration—on depression, anxiety, and self-esteem relative to coming out later. Rosario et al. found that identity formation was not an issue, per se, in terms of psychological distress.

Rather, they found that how well-integrated one's sexual orientation was into one's sense of self was the key predictor of psychological well-being. In fact, having a well-integrated sexual-minority sense of self as early as possible is probably a protective factor for youth's psychological adjustment, based on Rosario et al.'s findings. In contrast, Jager and Davis-Kean (2011) compared sexual-minority youth to sexual-majority youth in terms of the psychological outcomes of depression and self-esteem at different points during adolescence. They found that sexual-minority youth had significantly higher levels of depression and lower self-esteem than sexual-majority youth at the earliest time point in the study. Also, the younger the person was when coming out, the greater the level of depression the person exhibited. The sexual-minority youth "gained" or "recovered" a lot over time in terms of having reduced depression and increased self-esteem relative to the sexual-majority control group. As you are reading the two selections, consider the role of how "coming out" is defined by the two sets of authors and how differences in the research design might contribute to what seem like contradictory results.

Terminology

LGBT is an umbrella term representing lesbian, gay, bisexual, transsexual, and transgender. Sometimes, this is written as LGBTQ and also can include two-spirited, queer, and/or questioning. While being transgender or transsexual involves gender identity and biological disparity—more so than sexual orientation—trans people have communalities with LGB people in that all are sexual minorities. All LGBT people experience a coming-out process—a process of self-discovery of their sexual-minority status. In some instances, this is written as GLBT.

Queer has often been used as a pejorative insult to refer to LGBTQ people. Many LGBT people have "taken back the word"—adopted its use in a positive fashion so that it may lose its pejorative meaning.

Questioning describes those who are in the exploration stage of coming out, those who are unsure, those who have not adopted a sexual-minority status label, or those who eschew such labels.

Homophobia is a bit of a misnomer as it implies an irrational fear of homosexuality. However, this is the term that is common vernacular. **Homonegativity** would be a better term to describe negative attitudes and feelings toward homosexuals. **Internalized homophobia** refers to internalizing negative feels and attitudes toward oneself as a result of one's sexual-minority status. This is often a reflection of negative attitudes toward homosexuality of significant others and of wider societal attitudes.

YES ↵

Justin Jager and
Pamela E. Davis-Kean

Same-Sex Sexuality and Adolescent Psychological Well-Being: The Influence of Sexual Orientation, Early Reports of Same-Sex Attraction, and Gender

Developmental research suggests that the period between late childhood and early adolescence is a time when disparities across race, gender, socio-economic status (SES), and overweight status have a profound influence on psychological well-being. . . . [M]iddle childhood and early adolescence are vulnerable times for youth, when being different from those around them can cause anxiety and stress.

An emerging area of particular concern for psychological well-being is the issue of same-sex sexuality or what is termed sexual minority status (SM). The majority status is exclusive heterosexual attraction or attraction to the opposite sex, and the minority status refers to those who are attracted to the same sex either in combination with an attraction to the opposite sex or solely to the same sex. Emerging research suggests that, on average, SM report somewhat lower levels of psychological well-being than do sexual majorities (Cochran, [et al.], 2003; Fergusson, [et al.], 2005; Galliher, [et al.], 2004; Russell, 2006; Sandford et al., 2003). However, researchers have yet to examine how the relation between SM status and psychological well-being varies across middle childhood and adolescence. Since this particular period proves formative for these other social statuses, perhaps this pattern generalizes to all social statuses, including SM status. Thus, the goal of this study was to examine how, if at all, the relation between SM status and psychological well-being varies across middle childhood and adolescence, with a particular focus on the adolescent years. . . .

Why Are Middle Childhood and Early Adolescence So Important?

While there may be many reasons why middle childhood is an important developmental period with respect to the relation between social status and psychological well-being, two likely reasons for its importance are: (1) advances

Jager, Justin; Davis-Kean, Pamela E. From *Self and Identity*, Vol. 10, Issue 4, October 1, 2011, pp. 417–444. Copyright © 2011 by Taylor & Francis Journals. Reprinted by permission via Rightslink.

in cognitive development during this period that render one's social status(es) more personally relevant to one's sense of self; and (2) increases in the size and instability of the peer network. . . .

Sexual-Minority Status

In terms of the emergence of disparities in psychological well-being, it is not clear whether middle childhood is an important time period for SM as it is for race, gender, overweight status, and SES. An important question regarding SM status is as follows: When does one's awareness of one's SM status emerge? Is it early on in development like one's awareness of race and gender, or is it later on in development like one's awareness of being a college student or a parent? Retrospective reports indicate that SM individuals recall being treated differently by others, often as early as age 8, before they develop or are even aware of their attractions to the same sex (Bell, [et al.], 1981; Zucker, [et al.], 1993). They recall feeling different from their peers, and often this sense of feeling different has a negative valence and is centered around atypical, gender-related traits (Savin-Williams, 2005; Troiden, 1989). Retrospective reports also indicate that around the age of 10 or 11, many SM individuals recall their first awareness of attraction to the same sex (D'Augelli & Hershberger, 1993; Floyd & Stein, 2002; Friedman, [et al.], 2008; Rosario, [et al.], 1996; Savin-Williams & Diamond, 2000). Thus, there is some evidence to suggest that awareness of one's SM status may emerge during the middle-childhood years. . . .

Though one may acquire a vague sense of SM status during middle childhood (i.e., a sense of difference or initial awareness of feelings of same-sex attraction), coming to grips with one's own sexuality does not end there. A subset of youth go on to realize during early adolescence that this attraction to the same sex is what society deems as homosexual, and then an even smaller subset go on to actually identify themselves (as opposed to just their sexual attractions) as homosexual or bisexual (D'Augelli & Hershberger; 1993; Rosario et al., 1996; Savin-Williams & Diamond, 2000). Awareness of SM status is a prerequisite for others' messages regarding sexual minorities to be internalized as personally meaningful, and the period when one's awareness of one's SM status appears to form extends into late adolescence or even early adulthood. Thus, the relation between SM status and psychological well-being may itself be in flux through late adolescence/early adulthood.

Complicating things further is the possibility that growing awareness of one's SM status during adolescence will be accompanied by social isolation as well as victimization and stigmatization. . . . [At] a time when SM adolescents are coming to grips with their status, they are typically doing so alone, perhaps in the face of heightened harassment and aggression. As a consequence, the influence of SM status on psychological well-being may prove stronger between mid- to late-adolescence than between middle childhood and early adolescence.

Moderators of Sexual-Minority Status and Psychological Well-Being

Available cross-sectional research has identified three factors that moderate the relation between SM status and psychological well-being: (1) sexual identification or orientation; (2) age of first awareness/disclosure; and (3) gender status. Importantly, to date the extent to which, if at all, these factors moderate the relation between SM status and growth in psychological well-being is unknown.

Sexual Identification

While all those that exhibit same-sex sexuality share the *status* of SM, they vary dramatically as to whether or not they hold an SM *identity* as well as the nature of that identity, if any. Among those exhibiting same-sex sexuality, some identify as heterosexual, some as homosexual, and others as bisexual (Diamond, 2006). This heterogeneity in identification among those who exhibit same-sex sexuality could have implications for the relation between SM status and psychological well-being. . . .

Age of First Awareness/Disclosure

[R]esearch . . . indicates that coming to terms with one's sexual orientation and integrating it within one's sense of self is associated with higher psychological well-being. However, the extent to which this is the case may vary with age. There are risks associated with disclosing your sexual orientation to others. . . .

Hypotheses and Key Questions

. . . [T]he following hypotheses guided our examination, (1a) By early adolescence, we expected SM youth to report lower levels of psychological well-being than those of sexual-majority status; (1b) Disparities in psychological well-being among SM and sexual-majority individuals were predicted to increase during adolescence. By comparing the size of disparities at early adolescence (i.e., Hypothesis 1a) to the extent, if any, that those disparities increase over adolescence (i.e., Hypothesis 1b), we evaluated the relative influence of middle childhood and adolescence on the relation between SM status and psychological well-being. (2) Among those of SM status, we expected those of bisexual status to report lower psychological well-being at the onset of adolescence as well as lower growth in well-being across adolescence. (3a) In terms of initial status differences and growth differences, we expected earlier awareness of same-sex attractions to be associated with lower psychological well-being; and (3b) we expected that the disparities in psychological well-being between SM and non-SM would be larger among those SM reporting earlier awareness of same-sex attractions. (4) In terms of both intercept differences and growth differences, we expected psychological well-being disparities between SM and non-SM to be more pronounced among males.

Methods

Sample

The data for this study came from the National Longitudinal study of Adolescent Health (Add Health), a multi-wave, nationally representative sample of American adolescents. . . . [After] initial assessment (Wave 1), . . . [t]wo additional waves of data are available, each taking place approximately one (Wave 2) and six years later (Wave 3). . . . For the present study, only those respondents who completed a sexual-orientation measure at Wave 3, completed same-sex attraction measures at Waves 1, 2, and 3, [and] had data for age . . . were included in the study ($N = 7733$). . . .

Measures

Psychological Well-Being

We focused on two indices of psychological well-being: depressive affect and self-esteem. . . .

Sexual Orientation and Sexual-Minority Status

Based on the distinction between SM status (those exhibiting versus those not exhibiting same-sex sexuality) and sexual orientation (those identifying versus those not identifying as an SM), we classified individuals into one of four groups. Classification was based on a single question that was asked at Wave 3 only. . . . All who identified themselves as 100% heterosexual . . . were classified as *Heterosexual identified/non-SM* ($n = 6889$). All who indicated some level of same-sex sexuality . . . qualified as an SM ($n = 844$). Of these individuals, those who identified as gay . . . were classified as *Homosexual-identified/SM* ($n = 129$), those who identified as bisexual . . . were classified as *Bisexual-identified/SM* ($n = 140$), and those who identified as straight but indicated an attraction to the same sex . . . were classified as *Heterosexual-identified/SM* ($n = 575$).

Instability of Reported Same-Sex Attractions

At Wave 1 respondents were asked two yes/no questions: (1) "Have you ever had a romantic attraction to a female?" and (2) "Have you ever had a romantic attraction to a male?" For Waves 2 and 3 respondents were asked the same questions but were asked to indicate if they experienced these attractions since the last time they were interviewed. Using the reported same-sex attraction (or lack thereof) associated with one's Wave 3 sexual orientation as the reference point, we created three variables to assess instability in same-sex attraction— one for each wave. . . .

In concrete terms, relative to the reported same-sex attraction (or lack thereof) associated with one's Wave 3 sexual orientation, these . . . variables were an indication of inconsistency in reported same-sex attraction . . . [T]he Wave 1 and 2 instability [variables] may have reflected developmental changes or instability in awareness of and/or willingness to report same-sex attractions. For example, among those reporting a sexual orientation at Wave 3 that includes same-sex attractions, those who also reported same-sex attractions at Waves 1 and/or 2 may have become aware of their same-sex attractions at an earlier age than those who did not report same-sex attractions at Waves 1 and 2. . . .

Cohort

Although age at Wave 1 ranged between 12 and 20 years of age, over 95% of the sample ranged between 13 and 18 (M = 15.60, SD = 1.73). We dichotomized the sample so that we could more closely examine how the relation between SM status and psychological well-being varied across adolescence. A dichotomous cohort variable was created: Those between the ages of 12 and 15 (51% of the sample) were classified as young, whereas those between the ages of 16 and 20 (49% of the sample) were classified as old. . . .

Results

. . .

Sexual Orientation at Wave 3 and Adolescent Trajectories of Psychological Well-Being

. . .

Depressive Affect

. . . Among the entire sample, intercept levels of depressive affect were low . . . and growth in depressive affect was negative. . . . Intercept levels of depressive affect were equivalent across the three SM groups. . . . However, collectively the three SM groups reported higher intercept levels of depressive affect . . . than Heterosexual-identified/non-SM. . . . Among the three SM groups, growth of depressive affect was more negative among the Bisexual-identified/SM . . . and Homosexual-identified/SM . . . groups than it was among the Heterosexual-identified/SM group. . . . Also, only the Heterosexual-identified/SM group differed from the Heterosexual-identified/non-SM group. . . . In sum, at intercept the three SM groups did not differ from one another, but they collectively reported higher levels than Heterosexual-identified/non-SM. For Heterosexual-identified/SM these initial differences increased over time, but for Homosexual-identified/SM and Bisexual-identified/SM these differences remained stable over time. [Intercept level merely means depressive affect at the beginning of the study i.e., at wave 1 Negative growth in depressive affect means youth become less depressed over time]

Self-Esteem

In the sample as a whole, intercept levels of self-esteem were high . . . , and growth in self-esteem was positive but moderate. Intercept levels of self-esteem were equivalent across the three SM groups. . . . However, collectively the three SM groups reported lower intercept levels of self-esteem . . . than did Heterosexual-identified/non-SM. . . . With respect to growth in self-esteem, none of the four sexuality groups differed from one another.

The Influence of Instability in Reported Same-Sex Attractions

The above analyses suggested that reported sexual orientation during early adulthood (i.e., Wave 3) was associated with psychological well-being during adolescence. Next we examined (1) whether instability in reported same-sex attractions was related to adolescent patterns of psychological well-being, and (2) whether that instability influenced the relation between declared sexual orientation at Wave 3 and psychological well-being during adolescence, We did so by repeating the analyses above but including . . . instability . . . variables . . .: (1) unstable at Waves 1 and 2; (2) unstable at Wave 1 or 2, but not both; and (3) unstable at Wave 3. . . .

[T]he relation between the instability . . . variables and depressive affect did not differ across the three SM groups. However, the relation did differ between the SM groups and Heterosexual-identified, non-SM. The same was true for self-esteem. . . . Focusing first on SM, in reference to those who persistently reported same-sex attractions at all three waves, those who reported no same-sex attractions at Waves 1 and 2 reported higher psychological well-being at intercept (i.e., lower depressive affect and higher self-esteem). However, they reported smaller increases in psychological well-being over time. Among Heterosexual-identified/non-SM the relation between instability in reported same-sex attractions was much more muted, with those reporting same-sex attractions at both Waves 1 and 2 reporting lower depressive affect at intercept.

Controlling for instability in reported same-sex attractions did alter the relation between reported sexual orientation at Wave 3 and adolescent psychological well-being. . . . Concerning depressive affect, intercept levels among the Heterosexual-identified/ SM group and the Bisexual-identified/ SM group were equivalent. . . . Collectively, however, they were higher than levels of depressive affect among both the Homosexual-identified/SM group . . . and the Heterosexual-identified/non-SM group. . . . In addition, the Homosexual-identified/SM group reported higher intercept levels than the Heterosexual-identified/non-SM group. . . . Taken together, at intercept the Heterosexual-identified/non-SM group reported the lowest depressive affect, followed by the Homosexual-identified/SM group, followed by the Heterosexual-identified/SM and Bisexual-identified/SM groups, who reported equivalent levels to one another as well as the highest levels overall. Growth in depressive affect was equivalent across the three SM groups. . . . However, declines in depressive affect over time were more evident among the SM groups . . . than among the Heterosexual-identified/non-SM group. . . . There were fewer group differences in self-esteem. At intercept the three SM groups reported equivalent levels of self-esteem, . . . but collectively they reported lower levels of self-esteem than the Heterosexual-identified/non-SM group. . . . There were no group differences in the growth of self-esteem.

Summary

Wave 3 sexual orientation was associated with psychological well-being. It appeared to have a stronger relation with intercept levels than with growth, with SM reporting lower psychological well-being at intercept. Among the SM groups, early and stable reporting of same-sex attractions was associated with lower initial levels of psychological well-being but greater increases in psychological well-being over time. Within the Heterosexual-identified/non-SM group, early and stable reporting of no same-sex attractions was associated with lower initial levels of depressive affect. Relative to cases of unstable same-sex attractions, the relation between Wave 3 sexual orientation and adolescent depressive affect was different among those who reported stable same-sex attractions. Specifically, after controlling for instability in reported same-sex attractions, the discrepancy between SM and Heterosexual-identified/non-SM was larger at the intercept; however, SM also reported greater increases in psychological well-being over time relative to Heterosexual-identified/non-SM. Thus, relative to those reporting unstable sexual attractions over time, among those reporting stable sexual attractions over time, the initial gap in psychological well-being between SM and Heterosexual-identified/non-SM was larger; however, that gap also closed at a faster rate over time.

Sexual-Minority Status and Psychological Well-Being: Cohort and Gender Differences

. . . The relation between SM status and psychological well-being varied across both cohort and gender. In the case of depressive affect, patterns evident among the entire sample when instability controls were not included (i.e., greater increases in depressive affect over time among SM—Heterosexual-identified/ SM in particular) were more evident among those in the young cohort and females. However, in the case of self-esteem, patterns found among the entire sample (i.e., intercept differences across SM and Heterosexual-identified/ non-SM) were more evident among the young cohort. A pattern that was not evident among the entire sample emerged as well: Among the entire sample there was no instance when growth in self-esteem varied across any of the sexual orientation groups. However, among the young cohort, growth in self-esteem was more positive among SM. Growth in self-esteem was equivalent across SM status among the old cohort. This differential growth pattern across cohort only emerged when controls for instability in reported same-sex attractions were included. Finally, the relation between early and stable reports of same-sex attractions and psychological well-being (i.e., lower initial levels but greater increases over time) was more pronounced among males.

Discussion

Overall, four main conclusions can be drawn from this study: (1) Psychological well-being disparities between SM and non-SM are in place by early adolescence, and then for many the remainder of adolescence is a recovery period when the disparities narrow over time. (2) Early and stable reporting of same-sex attractions is associated with a greater initial deficit in psychological well-being, but because it is also associated with a quicker recovery over time, the effects are often not long lasting. (3) Though the relation between sexual orientation during early adulthood (i.e., Wave 3) and adolescent psychological well-being was quite similar across gender, the negative relation between psychological well-being and early, stable awareness of same-sex attractions was more pronounced among males. (4) Relative to Bisexual- and Homosexual-identified/SM, the understudied yet relatively sizable group of Heterosexual-identified/SM appeared to be at equal risk for deficits in psychological well-being. . . .

The Emergence of the Negative Relation between SM Status and Psychological Well-Being

The driving motivation for this study was to examine whether the negative relation between SM status and psychological well-being (1) is similar to that of other social statuses where differences are primarily in place by early adolescence; or (2) continues to emerge through the adolescent years when SM are thought to encounter unique developmental challenges. The findings suggest that the negative relation between SM status (based on the declaration of a sexual orientation that includes same-sex attractions during early adulthood) and psychological well-being is largely in place by early adolescence. This is evidenced by the fact that among both the young and old cohorts, and regardless of adolescent patterns of reported same-sex attractions, the discrepancies in psychological well-being were largest at the study's onset (when those among the young and old cohorts ranged between 12 and 15, and 16 and 19 respectively). Moreover, middle childhood and early adolescence appear to be more of a struggle for those who report early and stable same-sex attractions, since by early adolescence these individuals report the greatest deficits in psychological well-being relative to Heterosexual-identified/non-SM.

Across adolescence the negative relation between SM status (again based on declared sexual orientation during early adulthood) and psychological well-being either remained stable or decreased. Among those who reported early and stable same-sex attractions, the negative relation between SM status and psychological well-being decreased across time. Importantly, among the young cohort (12–15 years of age at Wave 1), this pattern held true for both depressive affect and self-esteem. This finding suggests that for those who reported early, stable same-sex attractions, the negative relation between SM status and psychological well-being decreased across time, even among those who were early adolescents at the onset of the study. . . .

Why Is the Negative Relation in Place by Early Adolescence?

Most of the challenges associated with being a sexual minority (e.g., dealing with homophobia and bullying, trying to find other SM peers, navigating romantic relationships, coming out) are confronted over the course of adolescence, not prior to it. The relation between declared sexual orientation during early adulthood and psychological well-being seems to manifest by early adolescence and does not increase thereafter, which speaks to the deleterious effects of feeling different from others during middle childhood and early adolescence. Though individuals must deal throughout the lifespan with being members of devalued groups and the sense of difference that accompanies those memberships, middle childhood is the first time individuals are confronted with this sense of difference. After all, it is not until middle childhood that youth are cognitively capable of internalizing this sense of difference as meaningful to their own personal sense of value (Harter, 2006). Consequently, they likely have not yet acquired the tools for dealing with this sense of difference. As a result those in middle childhood may be more likely to have their sense of well-being negatively influenced by that sense of difference.

Potentially compounding the deleterious effects of this sense of difference during middle childhood is the fact that unlike individuals of other stigmatized groups, SM often deal with this sense of difference in isolation, since those around them are predominantly, if not completely, of the sexual majority (D'Augelli & Hershberger, 1993). Contrast this to other youth of at-risk social status, such as females or members of racial minorities, who (1) are likely to have role models in the home or at school as well as peers and friends who share their status; and (2) are likely to have parents or extended family members actively socializing them to deal with the challenges associated with their social status (Bowman & Howard, 1985; Cross, 1991; Thornton, 1997). Finally, the initial deficits may be larger among those SM reporting early and stable same-sex attractions because they are more likely to be dealing with this novel sense of difference at an even earlier age, an age at which they are even more likely to be isolated from others in the SM community (D'Augelli, 1996; Friedman et al., 2008).

Who "Recovers" and Why?

The negative relation between a declared sexual orientation during early adulthood that includes same-sex attractions and adolescent psychological well-being did decrease across adolescence, but only for a select group. The "recovery" or narrowing of psychological well-being deficits between SM and Heterosexual-identified/non-SM was limited to those who reported early and stable same-sex attractions. In the case of self-esteem, the recovery was limited to the young cohort, those who ranged between 12 and 15 at the onset and between 18 and 23 at the conclusion of the study. Why the recovery was limited to those who reported early, stable same-sex attractions requires further examination, but we offer two possible explanations. First, SM who reported early, stable same-sex attractions had farther to recover. That is, relative to Heterosexual-identified/non-SM, SM who reported early and stable same-sex attractions reported far lower initial levels of psychological well-being than did SM who did not report early and stable same-sex attractions. Second, SM who reported early and stable same-sex attractions may have benefited from having longer to adjust to their status and incorporate it into their sense of self (Floyd & Bakeman, 2006; Savin-Williams, 1995). Regardless of the reason, it seems that the earlier the awareness of same-sex attractions, the greater the initial deficit in psychological well-being, but also the steeper the recovery. This pattern of recovery among those reporting early, stable same-sex attraction is inconsistent with Friedman et al.'s (2008) findings that those progressing through gay-related developmental milestones at earlier ages tended to report lower functioning during adulthood. Respondents included in the Friedman et al. (2008) study were teenagers in the early to mid 1980s, whereas respondents in Add Health were teenagers in the mid to late 1990s. Perhaps historical increases in the acceptance of homosexuality (Savin-Williams, 2005) have contributed to reductions in the long-term consequences of an early awareness of same-sex sexuality.

In cases where there was a recovery, such recovery was generally not complete. SM still reported deficits in psychological well-being during early adulthood; those deficits were simply smaller than they were during early adolescence. . . .

Overall Lack of Gender Differences

The relation between sexual orientation during early adulthood (i.e., Wave 3) and adolescent psychological well-being was largely equivalent across gender. . . .

Conclusions and Next Steps

Sexual minorities or those exhibiting same-sex sexuality are a heterogeneous group who vary not only in sexual orientation but also in the developmental course they follow in terms of their awareness and acceptance of their sexual orientation. Among those exhibiting same-sex sexuality, there also is heterogeneity in terms of developmental patterns of psychological well-being. Across adolescence, trajectories of psychological well-being converge, such that by early adulthood those exhibiting same-sex sexuality look more similar to both one another and those not exhibiting same-sex sexuality. In developmental science this phenomenon is termed *equifinality* (Bertalanffy, 1968)—multiple pathways to the same (or similar) end point. This pattern of findings highlights the important contributions that developmental theory and longitudinal data can make to our understanding of same-sex sexuality, sexual orientation, and psychological well-being.

More specifically, the pattern of results suggests that: (1) the negative relation between SM status and psychological well-being is in place by early adolescence; and (2) the exact pathway or trajectory that one follows across adolescence is more a function of the timing of awareness of same-sex attractions than it is of actual sexual orientation (as declared during early adulthood). These results raise the possibility that community resources and social support groups geared towards SM youth, now available in many high-schools, may benefit students in grade school and middle school as well. . . .

References

Bell, A., Weimberg, M., & Hammersmith, K. (1981). *Sexual preference: Its development in men and women.* Bloomington, IN: Indiana University Press.

Bertalanffy, L. V. (1968). *General systems theory: Foundations, development, applications*. New York: George Braziller.

Bowman, P., & Howard, C. (1985). Race-related socialization, motivation, and academic achievement: A study of Black youths in three-generation families. *Journal of the American Academy of Child Psychiatry, 24*(2), 134–141.

Cross, W. (1991). *Shades of Black diversity in ethnic-minority identity*. Philadelphia: Temple University Press.

D'Augelli, A. (1996). Enhancing the development of lesbian, gay, and bisexual youths. In E. Rothblum & L. A. Bond (Eds.), *Preventing heterosexism and homophobia*. Thousand Oaks, CA: Sage.

D'Augelli, A., & Hershberger, S. (1993). Lesbian, gay, and bisexual youth in community settings: Personal challenges and mental health problems. *American Journal of Community Psychology, 21*(4), 421–448.

Diamond, L. (2006). What we got wrong about sexual identity development: Unexpected findings from a longitudinal study of women. In A. Omoto & H. Kurtzman (Eds.), *Recent research on sexual orientation, mental health, and substance use*. Washington, DC: American Psychological Association.

Fergusson, D., Horwood, L., Ridder, E., & Beautrais, A. (2005). Sexual orientation and mental health in a birth cohort of young adults. *Psychological Medicine, 35,* 971–981.

Floyd, F., & Bakeman, R. (2006). Coming-out across the life course: Implications of age and historical context. *Archives of Sexual Behavior, 35*(3), 287–296.

Floyd, F., & Stein, T. (2002). Sexual orientation identity formation among gay, lesbian, and bisexual youths: Multiple patterns of milestone experiences: *Journal of Research on Adolescence, 12*(2), 167–191.

Friedman, M., Marshal, M., Stall, R., Cheong, J., & Wright, E. (2008). Gay-related development, early abuse and adult health outcomes among gay males. *AIDS and Behavior, 12*(6), 891–902.

Galliher, R., Rostosky, S., & Hughes, H. (2004). School belonging, self-esteem, and depressive symptoms in adolescents: An examination of sex, sexual attraction status, and urbanicity. *Journal of Youth and Adolescence, 33*(3), 235–245.

Harter, S. (2006). The self. In N. Eisenberg, W. Damon, & R. Lerner (Eds.), *Handbook of child psychology*. (Vol. III). Hoboken, NJ: Wiley.

Rosario, M., Meyey-Bahlburg, H., Hunter, J., & Exner, T. (1996). The psychosocial development of urban lesbian, gay, and bisexual youths. *Journal of Sex Research, 33*(2), 113–126.

Russell, S. (2006). Substance use and abuse and mental health among sexual minority youth: Evidence from Add Health. In A. Omoto & H. Kurtzman (Eds.), *Recent research on sexual orientation, mental health, and substance use*. Washington, DC: American Psychological Association.

Sandfort, T., de Graaf, R., & Bijl, R. (2003). Same-sex sexuality and quality of life: Findings from the Netherlands mental health survey and incidence study. *Archives of Sexual Behavior, 32*(1), 15–22.

Savin-Williams, R. (1995). Lesbian, gay male, and bisexual adolescents. In A. D'Augelli & C. Patterson (Eds.), *Lesbian, gay, and bisexual identities over the lifespan: Psychological perspectives* (pp. 165–189). New York: Oxford University Press.

Savin-Williams, R. (2005). *The new gay teenager.* Cambridge, MA: Harvard University Press.

Savin-Williams, R., & Diamond, L. (2000). Sexual identity trajectories among SM youths: Gender comparisons. *Archives of Sexual Behavior, 29*(6), 607–627.

Thornton, M. (1997). Strategies of racial socialization among Black parents: Mainstream, minority, and cultural messages. In R. Taylor (Ed.), *Family life in Black America* (pp. 201–215). Thousand Oaks, CA: Sage.

Troiden, R. (1989). The formation of homosexual identities. In G. Herdt (Ed.), *Gay and lesbian youth.* New York: Hayworth Press.

Zucker, K., Wild, J., Bradley, S., & Lowry, C. (1993). Physical attractiveness of boys with gender identity disorder. *Archives of Sexual Behavior, 22*(1), 23–26.

Margaret Rosario, Eric W.
Schrimshaw, and Joyce Hunter

 **NO**

Different Patterns of Sexual Identity Development over Time: Implications for the Psychological Adjustment of Lesbian, Gay, and Bisexual Youths

. . . This report examines whether differences in the formation and integration of an LGB identity are associated with the subsequent psychological adjustment of LGB youths.

We base our conceptualization of sexual identity development on the work of Erik Erikson. The process of identity development consists of identity formation in which the internal reality of the individual begins to assert and demand its expression as earlier identifications are discarded or reconfigured (Erikson, 1968, 1956/1980). Identity development also consists of identity integration, in which a commitment to and integration of the evolving identity with the totality of the self are expected, although not guaranteed (e.g., Kroger, 2007; Marcia, 1966). Identity integration involves an acceptance of the unfolding identity, its continuity over time and settings, and a desire to be known by others as such, none of which is surprising given identity integration concerns an inner commitment and solidarity with who one is (Erikson, 1968, 1946/1980). The antithesis of identity integration is diffusion or confusion; a sense of self as other or inauthentic either because an invalid identity has been assumed or foisted upon one, or because one is searching for a meaningful identity (Erikson, 1968, 1946/1980, 1956/1980). Although most theories of LGB identity development do not explicitly reference Erikson's more general theory of identity development, the general notions of identity formation and integration are implicit in the models (Cass, 1979; Chapman & Brannock, 1987; Fassinger & Miller, 1996; Troiden, 1989).

In keeping with Erikson, sexual identity development is conceived as having two related developmental processes (Morris, 1997; Rosario, [et al.], 2006). The first, identity formation, is the initiation of a process of self-discovery and exploration of one's LGB identity, including becoming aware of one's sexual orientation, questioning whether one may be LGB, and having sex with members of the same sex (e.g., Chapman & Brannock, 1987;

Rosario, Margaret; Schrimshaw, Eric; Hunter, Joyce. From *Journal of Sex Research*, Vol. 48, No. 1, December 21, 2010, pp. 3–15. Copyright © 2010 by Society for the Scientific Study of Sexuality. Reprinted by permission of Taylor & Francis via Rightslink.

Fassinger & Miller, 1996; Troiden, 1989). The second, identity integration, is a continuation of sexual identity development as individuals integrate and incorporate the identity into their sense of self and thereby increase their commitment to the new LGB identity (Morris, 1997; Rosario, [et al.], 2001, Rosario et al., 2006). Specifically, identity integration is composed of engaging in LGB-related social activities, working through negative attitudes toward homosexuality, feeling more comfortable with other individuals knowing about their LGB identity, and disclosing that identity to others (Morris, 1997; Rosario et al., 2001, 2006). . . .

Several studies of LGB youths and adults have examined the relations between sexual identity development and psychological adjustment. . . . Despite the lack of research identifying an association between identity formation and adjustment, the broader literature on identity development of other groups (e.g., adolescent identity, ethnic identity, and general sexual identity) has demonstrated that a stagnated identity development is associated with poorer adjustment (Adams et al., 2001; Archer & Grey, 2009; Kiang, Yip, & Fuligni, 2008; Marcia, 1966; Muise, [et al.] in press). . . .

In contrast to identity formation, aspects of identity integration have been linked to psychological adjustment among both LGB youths and adults. More positive attitudes toward homosexuality (e.g., Balsam & Mohr, 2007; Morris, Waldo, & Rothblum, 2001; Rosario et al., 2001; Wright & Perry, 2006), greater openness and disclosure of one's sexuality (D'Augelli, 2002; Jordan & Deluty, 1998; Morris et al., 2001), and greater involvement in the LGB community (Morris et al., 2001) have each been found to be associated with greater psychological adjustment. Relatedly, LGB individuals who are further along in integrating their sexual identity have been found to have higher self-esteem (Halpin & Allen, 2004; Swann & Spivey, 2004). . . .

[T]his report investigates the heretofore unexamined roles of identity formation and changes in identity integration on the subsequent psychological adaptation of LGB youths. Specifically, we hypothesized that LGB youths who begin identify formation more recently than other youths may be at risk for poorer psychological adjustment. Further, we hypothesized that greater identity integration and increases in identity integration over time will be associated with higher subsequent psychological adjustment. We also examine whether and how different patterns of sexual identity development are associated with psychological adjustment after accounting for other important social-context factors known to be critical for the psychological adjustment of LGB youths (i.e., family and friend support, negative social relationships, and experiences of gay-related stress). Similarly, we control for sociodemographic characteristics (e.g., sex) that covary with sexual identity development or adjustment.

Method

Participants [were] 156 youths (49% female), with a mean age of 18. 30 years (SD =1.65 years). . . .

A two- to three-hour structured interview was conducted at recruitment, with follow-up interviews occurring . . . 12 months later. . . .

Measures of Sexual Identity Formation

Milestones of sexual identity formation were assessed by . . . ask[ing] the ages when they were first erotically attracted to, fantasized about, and were aroused by erotica focusing on the same sex. The mean age of these three milestones was computed to obtain the age of first awareness of same-sex sexual orientation. . . . In addition, youths were asked about the age when they first thought they "might be" lesbian, gay, or bisexual and when they first thought they "really were" lesbian, gay, or bisexual. Finally, they were asked about the age when they first experienced any of several sexual activities with the same sex, with the earliest age in which they engaged in any of these sexual activities used as the age of their first same-sex sexual encounter. . . . [F]or all four developmental milestones, we computed the number of years since the youth first experienced the various milestones by subtracting the age at each milestone from the youth's age at Time 1.

Measures of Sexual Identity Integration

Involvement in LGB-Related Activities
A 28-item checklist assessed lifetime involvement in gay-related social and recreational activities at all assessments (Rosario et al., 2001). At follow-up assessments, youths were asked about their activity involvement . . . since their last assessment. . . .

Positive Attitudes Toward Homosexuality or Bisexuality
. . . 11 items assessed attitudes toward homosexuality (e.g., "My [homosexuality/bisexuality] does not make me unhappy"). . . .

Comfort with Others Knowing About Your Homosexuality or Bisexuality
. . . 12 items assessed comfort with other individuals knowing about the youth's sexuality (e.g., "If my straight friends knew of my [homosexuality/bisexuality], I would feel uncomfortable"). . . .

Disclosure of Homosexuality or Bisexuality to Others
Youths were asked at Time 1 to enumerate "all the people in your life who are important or were important to you and whom you told that you are (lesbian/gay/bisexual)." . . . Subsequently, youths were asked about the number of new individuals to whom the youth had disclosed . . . since their last assessment. . . .

Measures of Psychological Adjustment

Psychological Distress
Depressive and anxious symptoms during the past week were assessed by means of the Brief Symptom Inventory (BSI; Derogatis, 1993). . . .

As the BSI assesses only internalized distress, conduct problems were included as indicators of externalized psychological distress. A 13-item index . . . was created to assess the number of conduct problems experienced by the youths such as skipping school, vandalism, stealing, fighting, and running away. . . .

Self-Esteem
Rosenberg's (1965) 10-item scale was administered at all assessments. . . .

Measures of Social Context and Other Potential Covariates

Social Support from Family and Friends
Procidano and Heller's (1983) measures of perceived social support from family and from friends were adapted, deleting items that might be confounded with psychological health. . . .

Negative Social Relationships
The 12-item Social Obstruction Scale (Gurley, 1990) was administered at Time 1 to assess the presence of negative social relationships with others, including being treated poorly, being ignored, and being manipulated by others (e.g., "Somebody treats me as if I were nobody"). . . .

Gay-Related Stressful Life Events
A 12-item checklist of stressful events related to homosexuality was administered at Time 1 (e.g., "Losing a close friend because of your [homosexuality/bisexuality];" Rosario, [et al.], 2002). . . .

Social Desirability
The tendency to provide" socially desirable responses was assessed at Time 1 by means of the Marlowe–Crowne Social Desirability Scale (Crowne & Marlowe, 1964). . . .

Data Analysis

Cluster analysis was used to identify naturally occurring subgroups of LGB youths on sexual identity formation and integration. Cluster analysis is a . . . procedure to determine whether groups exist. . . . Rather than imposing *a priori* categories on the data, cluster analysis allows for the identification of potentially heretofore unidentified groups based on the data themselves. . . .

Results

To examine potential patterns of LGB identity formation and identity integration, indicators of sexual identity development were cluster analyzed. . . . In summary, three sets of cluster analysis were conducted. First, an analysis of length of time since achieving each of four identity formation milestones (i.e., years since first being attracted to the same sex, years since first thinking one might be LGB, years since first thinking one really was LGB, and years since first same-sex sexual encounter) generated two clusters: one composed of youths whose identity developed earlier (33%) and a second of youths whose identity formation was more recent (67%). . . .

Second, four aspects of identity integration at Time 1 (i.e., involvement in gay-related social activities, positive attitudes toward homosexuality or bisexuality, comfort with other individuals learning about one's homosexuality or bisexuality, and disclosing that sexuality to others) were cluster analyzed. Three clusters emerged: high, middling, and low integration. . . .

Third, the cluster analysis of identity integration at Time 2 (one year later) was conducted relative to . . . Time 1 clusters. Thus, this analysis took into account potential change in clusters from Time 1 to Time 2. Three clusters were found at Time 2, consisting of youths low, middling, or high on identity integration. . . .

Identity Groups and Psychological Adjustment

. . . A comparison of youths whose LGB identity formation had occurred earlier vs. more recently found that the two groups did not differ significantly on any indicator of psychological adjustment at Time 1 or Time 2.

Significant differences were found in psychological adjustment by identity integration groups. The three integration groups at Time 1 differed on their concurrent (Time 1) and subsequent (Time 2) distress and self-esteem. [C]omparison found that highly integrated youths reported significantly less anxious and depressive symptoms, fewer conduct problems, and higher self-esteem, especially at Time 2, than did youths with low integration. Youths with middling integration sometimes differed significantly from youths with high integration, reporting more distress or lower self-esteem than highly integrated peers.

Identity integration groups at Time 2 also differed on psychological distress and self-esteem at Time 2. By Time 2, psychological distress, with the exception of anxiety, did not differ significantly between the high and middling integrated youths, but both groups of youths differed from youths low in integration. All groups differed on self-esteem, with the highly integrated group reporting the highest self-esteem and the low-integrated group reporting the lowest self-esteem.

Individual Change in Identity Integration and Psychological Adjustment

Close examination of the integration data at the individual level indicated that youths followed a number of different patterns of change over time in identity integration, including a large number who remained consistent over time (see Rosario et al., 2008, for details). . . .

A comparison of . . . five integration-change groups on subsequent psychological distress and self-esteem at Time 2 was conducted . . . indica[ting] that youths who were consistently high in integration generally reported lower psychological distress than other youths, with the exception of youths who decreased from high to middling, who often did not differ from consistently high youths. Youths who were consistently high, those who increased from low or middling to high, or those who decreased from high to middling reported higher self-esteem at Time 2 than youths who were consistently middling or low in integration over time.

Social-Context Factors

Social relationships and gay-related stress at Time 1 were related significantly to psychological adjustment at Time 2. Youths with more family and friend support experienced less depressive symptoms. . . . Friend support was related to fewer conduct problems . . . and family support was related to higher self-esteem. . . . Conversely, youths with more negative social relationships reported more anxious and depressive symptoms, more conduct problems, and lower self-esteem. . . . Youths who experienced gay-related stress reported more anxious symptoms ($r = .17$). . . .

Multivariate Analyses Predicting Psychological Adjustment

To examine whether individual-level changes in identity integration over time were associated with youths' psychological adjustment at Time 2, over and above that already accounted for by social-context factors and other potential covariates, multiple linear regression analyses were conducted. First, we controlled for sex, sexual identity, social desirability, and the social-context factors. We then entered the identity–integration–change groups. . . .

[I]mportantly changes in identity integration over time were consistently associated with psychological adjustment, even after controlling for the social-context factors. . . . Specifically, LGB youths who were consistently high in identity integration over time reported less anxious symptoms and higher self-esteem than youths who were consistently low in integration. There was also a . . . trend for consistently high-integration youths to report less depressive symptoms and fewer conduct problems than consistently low-integration youths. This pattern was not restricted to just the consistently high youths. Youths who increased from low or middling to high integration, youths who decreased from high to middling integration, and youths who were consistently middling in their integration were also found to report significantly less anxious symptoms and higher self-esteem than consistently low youths. In addition, consistently middling youths reported fewer conduct problems than consistently low youths.

Discussion

There has been increasing recognition that the sexual identity development of LGB youths may follow multiple paths. . . . [T]his report examined the associations of LGB identity development with psychological distress (i.e., symptoms of anxiety, depression, and conduct problems) and self-esteem. Given that LGB youths followed different developmental patterns, we hypothesized that psychological adjustment would differ by the developmental patterns.

Identity Development and Psychological Adjustment

Consistent with some past research (e.g., D'Augelli, 2002; Floyd & Stein, 2002), we found that patterns of identity formation (early vs. recent development) were not significantly related to psychological distress and self-esteem. This may be because too much time had elapsed since experiencing even "recent" identity formation and subsequent psychological adjustment, resulting in a dilution of the relations between formation and adaptation. . . .

In contrast to the formation findings, different identity integration groups were found to significantly differ on all four indicators of psychological adjustment, both cross-sectionally and over time. Thus, identity integration has short-term and long-term implications for the psychological adjustment of LGB youths.

The relation of identity integration to adjustment also was evident when individual changes in identity integration over time were examined. These findings indicated that youths who were consistently high in integration or had previously been high in integration experienced greater psychological adjustment than other youths. The finding suggests that the latter youths were protected by the immunity afforded by being highly integrated at one point. By comparison, youths who were consistently low in integration reported the highest levels of distress and the lowest self-esteem. The totality of these findings underscores both the benefits of achieving and maintaining identity integration and the costs associated with low identity integration. Such findings are supported by similar findings on heterosexual youths with respect to other identities including ethnic, family, and religious identities (e.g., Adams et al., 2001; Kiang et al., 2008). . . .

Covariates of Adjustment and Changes in Individual-Level Identity Integration

Despite the strong associations found between identity integration and psychological adjustment, we also recognize that the social contexts in which LGB youths live can have important implications for their psychological adjustment. Indeed, we found that supportive relationships were related to better psychological adjustment and that negative social relationships were related to poorer adjustment. In addition, supportive and negative social relationships were related to change in individual-level identity integration. Therefore, it was possible that the association between sexual identity integration and adjustment might be due to social relationships.

. . . As valuable as supportive relationships are for the individual's mental and physical well-being our findings suggest that identity integration captures much more than can be explained solely by social relationships. LGB identity integration, as stated at the beginning of this report, involves both acceptance and commitment to one's sexuality. Social relationships may affect the individual's identity integration (e.g., retarding it for some time), . . . but they do not exclusively determine it.

. . . [I]t was hardly surprising that youths who were consistently high on integration reported higher psychological adjustment than youths who were consistently low in integration, after controlling for social relationships, gay-related stress, and other covariates. . . . [T]here are psychological taxes to be paid for stagnation at low levels of identity integration. As such, the findings suggest that LGB youths who are consistently low in integration should be identified and targeted for interventions. . . .

Conclusion

Our findings underscore the importance of sexual identity development for understanding the adjustment of LGB youths. They suggest that the poor psychological adjustment that has been found among LGB youths relative to heterosexual peers may be attributed to a subset of youths whose identity integration has stagnated, especially at low levels. Indeed, a comparison of our youths' anxious and depressive symptoms with adolescent norms for these symptoms indicates that consistently low and middling youths were more symptomatic than normative peers. By comparison, consistently high youths reported lower levels of anxious and depressive symptoms than normative peers. Moreover, the findings held even when the means were adjusted for social context and other [variables]. . . .

References

Adams, G. R., Munro, B., Doherty-Poirer, M., Munro, G., Petersen, A.-M. R., & Edwards, J. (2001). Diffuse-avoidance, normative, and informational identity styles: Use of identity theory to predict maladjustment. *Identity, 1,* 307–320.

Archer, S. L., & Grey, J. A. (2009). The sexual domain of identity: Sexual statuses of identity in relation to psychosocial sexual health. *Identity, 9,* 33–62.

Balsam, K. F., & Mohr, J. J. (2007). Adaptation to sexual orientation stigma: A comparison of bisexual and lesbian/gay adults. *Journal of Counseling Psychology, 54,* 306–319.

Cass, V. C. (1979). Homosexual identity formation: A theoretical model. *Journal of Homosexuality, 4,* 219–235.

Chapman, B. E., & Brannock, J. C. (1987). Proposed model of lesbian identity development: An empirical examination. *Journal of Homosexuality, 14,* 69–80.

Crowne, D. P., & Marlowe, D. (1964). *The approval motive: Studies in evaluative dependence.* Westport, CT: Greenwood.

D'Augelli, A. R. (2002). Mental health problems among lesbian, gay, and bisexual youths ages 14 to 21. *Clinical Child Psychology and Psychiatry, 7,* 433–456.

Derogatis, L. R. (1993). *BSI, Brief Symptom Inventory: Administration, scoring, and procedures manual.* Minneapolis, MN: National Computer Systems.

Erikson, E. H. (1968). *Identity: Youth and crisis.* New York: Norton.

Erikson, E. H. (1980). Ego development and historical change. In *Identity and the life cycle* (pp. 17–50). New York: Norton. (Original work published 1946).

Erikson, E. H. (1980). The problem of ego identity. In *Identity and the life cycle* (pp. 107–175). New York: Norton. (Original work published 1956).

Fassinger, R. E., & Miller, B. A. (1996). Validation of an inclusive model of sexual minority identity formation on a sample of gay men. *Journal of Homosexuality, 32,* 53–78.

Floyd, F. J., & Stein, T. S. (2002). Sexual orientation identity formation among gay, lesbian, and bisexual youths: Multiple patterns of milestone experiences. *Journal of Research on Adolescence, 12,* 167–191.

Gurley, D. N. (1990). *The context of well-being after significant life stress: Measuring social support and obstruction.* Unpublished doctoral dissertation, University of Kentucky, Lexington.

Halpin, S. A., & Allen, M. W. (2004). Changes in psychosocial well-being during stages of gay identity development. *Journal of Homosexuality, 47,* 109–126.

Jordan, K. M., & Deluty, R. H. (1998). Coming out for lesbian women: Its relation to anxiety, positive affectivity, self-esteem, and social support. *Journal of Homosexuality, 35,* 41–63.

Kiang, L., Yip, T., & Fuligni, A. J. (2008). Multiple social identities and adjustment in young adults from ethnically diverse backgrounds. *Journal of Research on Adolescence, 18,* 643–670.

Kroger, J. (2007). *Identity development: Adolescence through adulthood* (2nd ed.). Thousand Oaks, CA: Sage.

Marcia, J. E. (1966). Development and validation of ego-identity status. *Journal of Personality and Social Psychology, 3,* 551–558.

Morris, J. F. (1997). Lesbian coming out as a multidimentional process. *Journal of Homosexuality, 33,* 1–22.

Morris, J. F., Waldo, C. R., & Rothblum, E. D. (2001). A model of predictors and outcomes of outness among lesbian and bisexual women. *American Journal of Orthopsychiatry, 71,* 61–71.

Muise, A., Preyde, M., Maitland, S. B., & Milhausen, R. R. (in press). Sexual identity and sexual well-being in female heterosexual university students. *Archives of Sexual Behavior.*

Procidano, M. E., & Heller, K. (1983). Measures of perceived social support from friends and from family: Three validation studies. *American Journal of Community Psychology, 11,* 1–24.

Rosario, M., Hunter, J., Maguen, S., Gwadz, M., & Smith, R. (2001). The coming-out process and its adaptational and health-related associations among gay, lesbian, and bisexual youths: Stipulation and exploration of a model. *American Journal of Community Psychology, 29,* 133–160.

Rosario, M., Schrimshaw, E. W., & Hunter, J. (2008). Predicting different patterns of sexual identity development over time among lesbian, gay, and bisexual youths: A cluster analytic approach. *American Journal of Community Psychology, 42,* 266–282.

Rosario, M., Schrimshaw, E. W., Hunter, J., & Braun, L. (2006). Sexual identity development among lesbian, gay, and bisexual youths: Consistency and change over time. *Journal of Sex Research, 43,* 46–58.

Rosario, M., Schrimshaw, E. W., Hunter, J., & Gwadz, M. (2002). Gay-related stress and emotional distress among gay, lesbian, and bisexual youths: A longitudinal examination. *Journal of Consulting and Clinical Psychology, 70,* 967–975.

Rosenberg, M. (1965). *Society and adolescent self-image.* Princeton, NJ: Princeton University Press.

Swann, S. K., & Spivey, C. A. (2004). The relationship between self-esteem and lesbian identity during adolescence. *Child and Adolescent Social Work Journal, 21,* 629–646.

Troiden, R. R. (1989). The formation of homosexual identities. In G. Herdt (Ed.), *Gay and lesbian youth* (pp. 43–73). New York: Haworth.

Wright, E. R., & Perry, B. L. (2006). Sexual identity distress, social support, and health of gay, lesbian, and bisexual youth. *Journal of Homosexuality, 51,* 81–110.

EXPLORING THE ISSUE

Is "Coming Out" As a Sexual Minority (Gay/Lesbian/Bisexual) Earlier in Adolescence Detrimental to Psychological Well-Being?

Critical Thinking and Reflection

1. Consider how Jager and Davis-Kean would define "coming out" at least from their research perspective. What is the role of sexual-minority status in this definition? What is the role of "questioning" individuals in this research? Are Jager and Davis-Kean participants who are labeled as heterosexual-identified/SM really just "questioning" sexual minorities? How might excluding this group (heterosexual-identified/SM) from the study impact Jager and Davis-Kean's findings?

2. Consider how Rosario et al. would define "coming out"—at least from their research perspective. Compare and contrast sexual-identity formation to sexual-identity integration. Why would identity formation (early versus later) show no differences in psychological adjustment but identity integration would? Are less integrated individuals "questioning" sexual minorities? What about low-integration individuals? Are they "questioning" or "closeted"?

3. Are the YES and NO selections really addressing the same issue? Are these two studies comparable with each other? Why or why not? Compare and contrast the two studies in terms of their similarities and their differences.

4. Based on Jager and Davis-Kean's study, what queer teen would have the greatest need for intervention? Based on their findings, what form should that intervention take? What might the unique barriers be for alleviating depression in the different sexual orientation groupings? At what point should intervention occur? Should interventions at different time points take different forms?

5. Based on Rosario et al.'s study, what queer teen would have the greatest need for intervention? Based on their findings, what form should that intervention take? What might the barriers be to further identity integration? How might these be addressed?

Is There Common Ground?

Both sets of authors would likely agree that it is in a person's best interest to come out, and that foreclosing on a sexual-minority self-identity is detrimental to the psychological well-being of the individual. They would agree that

159

coming out is a very important process in the identity development of sexual-minority youth. They would want their research used to better the adolescent experience for sexual-minority youth.

Both studies used longitudinal designs: Both sets of authors would agree that this is an advantageous way of assessing the impact of maturation on psychological adjustment outcomes. It is critically important to view coming out as a developmental process rather than a discrete moment in time.

Jager and Davis-Kean found that there was a subset of their sample who had unstable sexual attractions to the same sex across the three time points. Rosario et al. found that there was variability in integration of sexual identity. These two findings seem very congruent with each other: Both studies found that the instable or the less integrated individuals had poorer mental health outcomes.

Finally, both sets of authors would agree that it is insufficient to simply look at "the age of coming out" (as implied by the question addressing the issue herein). Rather, both sets of authors would agree that there are different developmental trajectories to coming out and multiple factors must be taken into consideration to address the impact of coming out on mental health outcomes of youths. Social context, such as having friend and familial support, is one such factor that may impact mental health outcomes during the coming-out process (see Legate et al., 2012).

Additional Resources

Bockting, W. O., & Coleman, E. (2007). Developmental stages of the transgender coming-out process: Toward an integrated identity. In R. Ettner, S. Monstrey, & E. Evan (Eds.), *Principles of transgender medicine and surgery* (pp. 185–208). New York: Haworth Press.

Calzo, J. P., Antonucci, T. C., Mays, V. M., & Cochran, S. D. (2011). Retrospective recall of sexual orientation identity development among gay, lesbian, and bisexual adults. *Developmental Psychology*, 47(6), 1658–1673.

A study of age of coming-out milestones in a large sample of lesbian, gay, and bisexual Californians. Results indicated the majority began the coming-out process in their childhood or adolescent years. Authors also investigated generational effects (Great Generation, Boomers, Gen X, and Y) and concluded early development is common regardless of age cohort.

Clarke, V., Ellis, S. J., Peel, E., & Riggs, D. W. (2010). *Lesbian, gay, bisexual, trans, and queer psychology: An introduction*. New York: Cambridge University Press.

Cox, N., Dewaele, A., Van Houtte, M., & Vincke, J. (2011). Stress-related growth, coming out, and internalized homonegativity in lesbian, gay, and bisexual youth. An examination of stress-related growth within the minority stress model. *Journal of Homosexuality*, 58, 117–137.

D'Augelli, A. R., & Hershberger, S. L. (1993). Lesbian, gay, and bisexual youth in community settings: Personal challenges and mental health problems. *American Journal of Community Psychology*, 21, 421–448.

D'Augelli, A. R., & Patterson, C. J. (Eds.). (2001). *Lesbian, gay, and bisexual identities and youth: Psychological perspectives*. New York: Oxford University Press.

Drasin, H., Beals, K. P., Elliot, M. N., Lever, J., Klein, D. J., & Schuster, M. A. (2008). Age cohort differences in the developmental milestones of gay men. *Journal of Homosexuality*, 54(4), 381–399.

This study concluded that younger gay men are reaching coming-out developmental milestones at earlier ages relative to older cohorts, particularly in the area of social milestones (e.g., went to a gay bar, came out to a family member).

Floyd, F. J., & Stein, T. S. (2002). Sexual orientation identity formation among gay, lesbian and bisexual youths: Multiple patterns of milestone experiences. *Journal of Research on Adolescence, 12*, 167–191.

These researchers investigate 10 different coming-out events. Analyses identified five unique "clusters" of individuals, which suggest that there are different experiences of the milestones of coming out.

Graham, G., et al. (2011). *The health of lesbian, gay, bisexual, and transgender people: Building a foundation for better understanding.* Washington, DC: National Academies Press.

A very thorough book addressing issues of health, which has chapters relevant to sexual-minority development during different stages in life—including childhood and adolescence.

Halverson, E. R. (2005). InsideOut: Facilitating gay youth identity development through a performance-based youth organization. *Identity: An International Journal of Theory and Research, 5*(1), 67–90.

A very interesting study about a performance art program and how it facilitated identity development in sexual-minority youth. This is an example of a unique form of identity-integration intervention.

Jager, J. & Davis-Kean, P. E. (2011). Same-sex sexuality and adolescent psychological well-being: The influence of sexual orientation, early reports of same-sex attraction, and gender. *Self identity, 10*(4), 417–444.

LaSala, M. C. (2010). *Coming out, coming home: Helping families adjust to a gay or lesbian child.* New York: Columbia University Press.

Legate, N., Ryan, R. M, & Weinstein, N. (2012). Is coming out always a "good thing"? Exploring the relations of autonomy support, outness, and wellness for lesbian, gay, and bisexual individuals. *Social Psychological and Personality Science, 3*(2), 145–152.

This research investigated the impact of coming out in different (e.g., more versus less supportive) social contexts. They found social context of coming out was very important.

Rosario, M., Schrimshaw, E. W., & Hunter, J. (2011). Different patterns of sexual identity development over time: Implications for the psychological adjustment of lesbian, gay, and bisexual youths. *Journal of Sexual Research, 48*(1), 3–15.

Savin-Williams, R. (2005). *The new gay teenager.* Cambridge, MA: Harvard University Press.

Shapiro, D. N., Rios, D., & Stewart, A. J. (2010). Conceptualizing lesbian sexual identity development: Narrative accounts of socializing structures and individual decisions and actions. *Feminism & Psychology, 20*(4), 491–510.

Using qualitative research methodology, these researchers argue in favor of more dynamic models of coming out.

Taylor, C., Peter, T., McMinn, T. L., Elliott, T., Beldom, S., Ferry, A., et al. (2011). *Every class in every school: The first national climate survey on homophobia, biphobia, and transphobia in Canadian schools.* Final report. Toronto, ON: Egale Canada Human Rights Trust.

ISSUE 8

Does a Strong and Costly Sexual Double Standard Still Exist Among Adolescents?

YES: Derek A. Kreager and Jeremy Staff, from "The Sexual Double Standard and Adolescent Peer Acceptance," *Social Psychology Quarterly* (vol. 72, no. 2, pp. 143–164, 2009)

NO: Heidi Lyons et al., from "Identity, Peer Relationships, and Adolescent Girls' Sexual Behavior: An Exploration of the Contemporary Double Standard," *Journal of Sex Research* (vol. 48, no. 5, pp. 437–449, 2011)

Learning Outcomes

After reading this issue, you should be able to:

- Identify the key components involved in the sexual double standard.
- Critically analyze the gendered nature of this double standard.
- Interpret and assess the research on the contemporary double standard and its origins.
- Explain the impact of the sexual double standard on contemporary youth.

ISSUE SUMMARY

YES: Derek A. Kreager and Jeremy Staff, both associate professors of sociology and crime, law, and justice at Pennsylvania State University, used data from the National Longitudinal Study of Adolescent Health to examine the existence of a contemporary double standard among adolescents. They found significant differences in peer acceptance among sexually experienced males and females, with higher numbers of sexual partners associated with significantly greater peer acceptance for boys than for girls.

NO: Heidi Lyons, assistant professor of sociology and anthropology at Oakland University, and her colleagues, Peggy C. Giordano, Wendy D. Manning, and Monica A. Longmore, all of Bowling Green State University's Department of Sociology, examined the sexual double standard in a longitudinal, mixed-method study of adolescent girls' popularity and lifetime number of sexual partners. The results paint a nuanced picture of the contemporary sexual double standard. Number of sexual partners was not associated with negative peer regard, and whereas young women acknowledged the existence of a sexual double standard, violating it did not seem to be associated with significant social costs. In fact, these authors highlight the buffering role of friendships against possible negative outcomes.

"**W**hat do you call a girl with many sexual partners? A slut. What do you call a guy with many sexual partners? A stud." This quote, taken directly from students in a psychology of gender class, illustrates how easily young people can identify the key constructs involved in the sexual double standard. The sexual double standard, put simply, is that the same heterosexual behavior is judged differently depending on whether a male or a female is engaging in the behavior. That is, boys who are sexual are celebrated or rewarded for their behavior, whereas girls who are similarly sexual are censured or punished for their behavior. While the "line" is arguable for what sexual behaviors by girls is acceptable across history and social groups, girls and boys can readily identify what is and is not permissible regarding girls' sexual activity. For example, in the 1950s, a Catholic school girl whose skirt was too short and showed "too much leg" would have been branded "loose." In contrast, sexual intercourse may be permissible for a girl of the 2000s, *if* she is in a romantic relationship with a boy; otherwise, she might also be labeled as "loose" (i.e., in today's language, a slut, whore, etc.). Today's language may be different (e.g., a sexually experienced boy who has had many partners, most of them in noncommitted relationships, may be called a "player"), but the concepts remain the same. That said, it is important to highlight that the English words used to describe similarly promiscuous girls and boys are qualitatively different. Words like "player" and "stud" are far less negative and pejorative than their female-oriented counterparts, such as "whore" and "slut."

Sociologist Ira Reiss was one of the first people to write about the sexual double standard from an academic viewpoint. In his classic 1967 work, *The Social Context of Premarital Sexual Permissiveness*, Reiss discussed the double standard in relation to premarital intercourse and divided the double standard into "orthodox" and "transitional" categories. The orthodox standard viewed premarital intercourse as permissible for males but not for females under *any* circumstance, while the transitional double standard viewed premarital intercourse as permissible for males under any circumstance, and permissible for females *only* if they were engaged or deeply in love. In the 1960s, Reiss optimistically predicted that North American society would move toward increasing sex-role equality and decreasing sexual double standards.

Research on the double standard continued into the 1970s and beyond. A meta-analysis by Oliver and Hyde (1993) found a gender difference in the endorsement of the sexual double standard. Reiss's 1960 studies found that men were more likely than women to endorse the double standard (while women were more likely to endorse total abstinence for all). In contrast, Oliver and Hyde found that women were more likely to endorse the double standard than men. This gender effect became stronger across the years. Thus, both men and women were becoming more permissive in their sexual attitudes, *but* men were dropping their endorsement of the double standard, while women were moving from an abstinence-only attitude to a more double-standard–based attitude. It is noteworthy that this gender difference in double-standard endorsement was only moderate to small, which is not surprising as there is strong and consistent research that men are more sexually liberal than women (i.e., if we consider the double standard as a form of sexist sexual conservatism). Many different types of studies today seem to suggest that the sexual double standard was and is alive and well in the 1980s, 1990s, and 2000s.

In contrast, other researchers maintain that, while lay people believe that the sexual double standard exists and are able to articulate the double standard easily, a sexual double standard does not exist in terms of its application to the evaluation of others. For example, Marks and Fraley (2005) interpret the existing research as failing to support the sexual double standard. Even in considering Reiss's 1967 data, students did not endorse the double standard to any great extent. In fact, only 25 percent endorsed a double standard (either orthodox or transitional; almost half [42 percent] endorsed abstinence from sexual intercourse for all). While reading the YES and NO selections, consider whether the evidence presented can be interpreted as supporting or refuting the existence of the sexual double standard.

In the YES selection Derek Kreager and Jeremy Staff examined the existence of a contemporary double standard among adolescents and the relationship between a double standard and peer acceptance. They found significant differences in peer acceptance among sexually experienced males and females, with higher numbers of sexual partners associated with significantly greater peer acceptance for boys than for girls. Heidi Lyons and colleagues examined the sexual double standard in relation to adolescent girls' popularity and number of sexual partners. In this study, girls with a greater number of sexual partners were not regarded negatively by peers. Whereas girls in this study acknowledged the existence of a sexual double standard, they did not punish one another for violating it.

YES ⬅ Derek A. Kreager and Jeremy Staff

The Sexual Double Standard and Adolescent Peer Acceptance

In contemporary American society, it is a commonly held belief that sexual behaviors are judged differently depending on the gender of a sexual actor (Milhausen and Herold 2001). Boys and men are thought to receive praise and positive attributions from others for nonmarital sexual contacts, while girls and women are believed to be derogated and stigmatized for similar behaviors. The relevance of this double standard for sexual development and gender inequality has prompted substantial research on the topic (see Crawford and Popp 2003 for a review) along with the publication of several popular trade books with titles such as *Slut!*, *Fast Girls*, and *Promiscuities* (Tanenbaum 1999; White 2002; Wolf 1997). Although public perceptions generally support the sexual double standard, scientific evidence remains equivocal and contested. Ethnographies of secondary schools and early attitudinal studies found evidence of the double standard (Eder, Evans, and Parker 1995; Oliver and Sedikides 1992; Sprecher, McKinney, and Orbuch 1987), whereas more recent experimental vignette studies generally fail to find similar results (Gentry 1998; Milhausen and Herold 1999; Marks and Fraley 2005, 2006). The existence of a modern sexual double standard thus remains in doubt, opening the door for further research and innovative study designs.

Quantitative tests of the sexual double standard typically rely on survey instruments to directly measure respondents' judgments of male and female sexual conduct (Crawford and Popp 2003). These studies correctly locate the roots of the double standard in individuals beliefs and attitudes about "gender appropriate" sexual behaviors. However, . . . the attitudes captured in survey designs may not translate to the enactment of gendered behaviors in social situations, leading to a disjuncture between motives and outcomes (Reskin 2003). School-based ethnographies and individual case studies address this issue by focusing on the expression and consequences of gendered sexual attitudes in specific social contexts. Through participant observation, communication analyses, and retrospective interviews (Eder et al. 1995; Tanenbaum 1999), qualitative studies document the application of deleterious labels for sexual norm violations and individuals' responses to discredited sexual identities (Goffman 1963). These studies therefore link psychological concepts with their socially constructed meanings and outcomes, bringing us closer to

Kreager, Derek A., and Jeremy Staff. From *Social Psychology Quarterly*, Vol. 72, No. 2, June 1, 2009, pp. 143–164. Copyright © 2009 by American Sociological Association. Reprinted by permission.

understanding how sexuality is regulated in a given social context and who potentially benefits or is stigmatized by these processes. . . .

In this study, we build on the strengths of both survey and ethnographic research by quantitatively measuring the expected social consequences of sexual behavior in a national sample of adolescent youth. Specifically, we rely on network data collected from the National Longitudinal Study of Adolescent Health (Add Health) to test whether the association between adolescent peer acceptance and the number of self-reported sexual partners varies significantly by gender. Our use of peer-network data allows us to statistically compare the peer-status levels of sexually permissive boys and girls and their nonpermissive peers. . . .

Sex and Adolescent Peer Acceptance

The importance of peer status for adolescent development and informal school organization has prompted generations of researchers to identify the criteria underlying teenage popularity. Coleman (1961), in his seminal work *Adolescent Society*, found that social class background, athletics, physical attractiveness, and material possessions (e.g., cars, expensive clothes) were important symbols for teenage peer acceptance, providing their possessors with valued access to the leading crowds. Developmental research also suggests that prosocial behaviors and individual characteristics—such as cooperativeness, kindness, honesty, leadership, intelligence, and self-confidence—are positively associated with children's popularity across a wide variety of social settings (Coie, Dodge, and Kupersmidt 1990; Newcomb, Bukowski, and Pattee 1993). For the most part, the criteria for adolescent popularity operate in the same directions for both girls and boys, even if some characteristics or activities— such as attractiveness, athletics, or physical aggression—may have stronger associations with peer status for one gender than the other (Coleman 1961; LaFontana and Cillessen 2002; Steffensmeier and Allan 1996). Sexual behaviors may provide an exception to this pattern. According to the sexual double standard, the social consequences of early romantic and sexual experiences differ substantially by gender. Gender-specific norms govern the appropriate number of sex partners, the conditions under which it is acceptable to engage in sexual activity (e.g., on a "first-date," prior to marriage, in a non-committal relationship, etc.), and the appropriate motives for sexual behavior (e.g., a man may have sex without affection, whereas a women can only have sex when she is in love). If women and men are evaluated differently for engaging in the same sexual behaviors, then male sexual permissiveness would be tolerated, or even praised, while female permissiveness would lead to damaged reputations and "spoiled" identities (Goffman 1963).

Although gendered norms of appropriate sexual conduct have existed for centuries (e.g., the harsh penalties historically associated with female infidelity [see Wolf 1997]), it is a debatable claim that strong sexual double standards persist in contemporary, post-sexual revolution, U.S. society (Risman and Schwartz 2002). Shifts in sexual norms may result in a single standard of sexual conduct that is applied to both men and women (Marks and Fraley

2005). Accordingly, negative perceptions of sexual permissiveness may lower the social desirability of a sexual actor regardless of his or her gender.

Tests of a modern sexual double standard remain inconclusive and contested. We first review this research, paying particular attention to modern adolescent peer contexts and potential gender differences in sexual norm enforcement. We also consider sociodemographic variations in the double standard, such that gender and socioeconomic background may combine nonadditively with sexual experiences to affect adolescent peer acceptance. Finally, we discuss those individual and social characteristics that may moderate or make spurious any link between sexual behavior and peer status.

Documenting the Sexual Double Standard

Attitudinal surveys and ethnographic studies have generally found evidence of contemporary sexual double standards. In perhaps the earliest study of sexual attitudes, Reiss (1964) asked student respondents to directly comment on normative sexual behavior, finding that a majority of the respondents who did not endorse sexual abstinence agreed that it was acceptable for a male, but not a female, to have premarital intercourse. Similarly, more recent survey research suggests that respondents perceive women to be judged significantly more harshly than men for having higher numbers of sex partners (Milhausen and Herold 1999; Sheeran et al. 1996). These findings are commonly confirmed in school-based ethnographies. [For example,] Eder, Evans, and Parker (1995) found that "what was considered acceptable behavior in boys—making sexual passes at other boy's girlfriends as well as at their own girlfriends—was definitely not considered acceptable in girls. Those girls who did initiate sexual actions were labeled 'bitches' and 'sluts'" (130). By contrast, "boys tend to perceive girls as objects for sexual conquest as they compete with other boys for sexual achievements" (128). Additional qualitative studies by Orenstein (1994), Moffat (1989), and Tolman (2002) also suggest that young women's fears of the "slut" label curbs their sexual expressions, while young men are encouraged to demonstrate their masculinity through sexually permissive behavior.

Results from experimental vignette designs have been much less consistent. In these studies, subjects are provided with sexual information (e.g., number of intercourse partners, age at first coitus, etc.) for a hypothetical actor and asked to evaluate his or her desirability or popularity. The sexual information and gender of the target are then randomly varied to test for the existence of a double standard. . . .

Although early studies with this method tended to find evidence of the double standard, recent studies fail to find similar results. As an example of the latter, Marks and Fraley (2005) asked a sample of undergraduates and internet-based respondents to evaluate whether a target was popular and likeable based upon the target's gender and number of sexual partners. They found that respondents generally evaluated male and female targets with higher numbers of sexual partners as unpopular and unlikable, suggesting that sexual permissiveness holds a negative connotation regardless of a sexual actor's gender. . . .

A Network Approach

In this study, we extend prior research by testing the sexual double standard using a measure of peer status derived from social network data (see also New-comer, Udry, and Cameron 1983). A *social network* consists of a set of interde-pendent nodes (e.g., individuals, firms, countries, etc.) and ties (e.g., friendships, communications, treaties, etc.) that combine to form a social structure. When applied to the study of school-based peer relations, a social network is created by asking each adolescent to nominate a specified number of friends from a school's attendance roster. These ties are then mapped or tallied . . . to provide an overhead view of the school's friendship system. At the level of the indi-vidual (i.e., ego), the total number of ties *received* from other students captures the extent to which that individual is socially accepted, or well-liked, within the informal organization of the school. Incoming friendship nominations thus provide a measure of peer status for each individual in the network. To test the sexual double standard, we may relate this egocentric measure of peer status with students' self-reported sexual partnerships. If a "strong" double standard exists, then increased numbers of sexual partners should be positively associated with male peer status and negatively associated with female peer status. . . .

Variations by Gender of the Evaluator

. . . If sexual standards do differ by gender, then sexually permissive women may not be accepted by female peers, but be well liked by male peers. Simi-larly, permissive men may be accepted by other men, but be disfavored by women. Assessing whether the gender of the evaluator conditions the associa-tion between sexual partnerships and adolescent peer status is an advantage of a network approach over prior research in the area.

Variations by Socioeconomic Background

The large-scaled Add Health survey also allows us to examine whether vari-ables beyond gender, such as socioeconomic background, potentially moder-ate the link between peer status and sexual behavior. . . .

Alternative Explanations

A final benefit of our study is that it allows us to control for variables that may attenuate any association between sexual permissiveness and peer acceptance. Thus far, we have presented hypotheses stating that sexual behaviors affect peer status and that this association may be conditioned by gender and socio-economic origins. However, other scholars have argued that these correlations are explained by stable individual traits or characteristics of the sexual contacts. For example, Risman and Schwartz (2002) assert that the sexual revolution of the 1960s and 1970s altered young women's attitudes toward premarital sex, such that premarital coitus is now normative behavior for young women as long as it takes place in socially defined "*steady relationships.*" Girls and women who have sex in exclusive relationships may then avoid the "slut" label and maintain high-status positions in the peer structure regardless of their number of sexual partnerships. Likewise, girls and women who have sex in an uncommitted relationship may lose peer status. If this argument is accurate, then relationship exclusivity should attenuate any association between number of sexual partnerships and adolescent peer acceptance. . . .

Data

We test our hypotheses using data from the National Longitudinal Study of Adolescent Health (Add Health). Add Health is a nationally representative longitudinal study of adolescents in grades 7 to 12. From 1994 to 2001, the study collected four waves of student data, with additional surveys administered to parents, siblings, and school administrators. In the current analyses, we rely on data from the first two student surveys (e.g. the in-school and first in-home interviews), collected in 1994 and 1995.

In one class period during the fall of 1994, Add Health administered in-school surveys to all available students in each of 145 sampled schools. Approximately 80 percent of enrolled students (N = 90,118) were surveyed. The questionnaire asked respondents about basic demographic and behavioral characteristics. Students also nominated their five best male and five best female friends. . . . [O]ur analysis sample included 6,613 girls and 6,160 boys. . . .

Measures

Outcome Variable: Peer Acceptance

During the in-school survey conducted in 1994, students in the sampled schools nominated their five best male and five best female friends from a roster of all students enrolled in the respondent's school and in a sister middle or high school. Peer acceptance is measured as the total number of friendship nominations that each Add Health respondent *received* from other students in their high school or associated middle school (Wasserman and Faust 1994). . . . We also create gender-specific measures of our dependent variable. Peer status from female peers is captured by multiplying the number of received friendship nominations by the percentage of the nominations that were female. This value was then subtracted from the total number of received friendship nominations to assess peer status from males.

Predictor Variables

Our key predictor variable is student-reported numbers of lifetime sexual partners. Students were first asked to nominate up to three "special romantic partners" from the 18-month period prior to the . . . survey. If they answered affirmatively to this question, they were asked a series of relationship questions about each romantic relationship, including whether they had sexual intercourse. Following those questions, all respondents were asked if they had sexual relationships with anyone other than the three "special romantic relationships." . . . Those who answered "yes" were asked to provide the total number of lifetime sexual partnerships, including the three "special romantic relationships" and any non-romantic sexual partners. . . . [W]e recoded the number of lifetime partners into four dummy variables (i.e., none, 1 to 2, 3 to 8, and more than 8. Additionally, due to likely mis-reporting, we deleted from our analyses those outlying respondents who reported 100 or more lifetime sexual partners. Less than one percent of the sample (all males) fell into this category, dropping the final sample of boys to 5,522. [A]pproximately two-thirds of youth reported no sexual partnerships, while two percent of girls and five percent of boys fell into the highly permissive category of 8 or more partnerships. . . .

Nonromantic sexual involvement was defined as having had sexual intercourse with someone outside of a "special romantic relationship" during the past year. Respondents who reported having had a nonromantic sexual relationship were asked if they (1) held hands with the nonromantic sexual partner, (2) kissed the partner on the mouth, and (3) said "I love you" to the partner. If the respondent answered no to at least one of these items, we coded him or her as having had a nonromantic relationship (which could be ongoing). If a respondent answered yes to the three items, the relationship was coded as a "special romantic relationship" and the corresponding sexual questions were asked. Approximately 12 percent of boys and 7 percent of girls reported at least one prior or current nonromantic sexual encounter. . . .

Research finds that athletic participation is positively associated with peer status (Holland and Andre 1994) and these activities may also increase sexual opportunities, particularly for males (Miller et al. 2005). We include a self-reported indicator for whether or not respondents participated in any of 12 sports during the prior year (e.g., baseball/softball, basketball, field hockey, football, ice hockey, soccer, swimming, tennis, track, volleyball, wrestling, and other sports). We also measure participation in other nonathletic extracurricular clubs or activities, as these may provide avenues for peer acceptance (Kreager 2007). Peer acceptance is also positively associated with academic achievement and adjustment (Parker and Asher 1987). Academic aptitude was captured by a vocabulary test. . . . Grades indicate the average of student-reported GPAs in four subjects—math, English, social studies, and science. . . .

Attractiveness and early physical maturity may also confound the association between number of sex partners and peer status. Physical attractiveness is based upon an interviewer-rated measure of "how physically attractive is the respondent?" . . . Our measure of female physical development is an additive scale based on three items: (1) "How advanced is your physical development compared to other girls your age?" (five-point scale from 1 = I look younger than most to 5 = I look older than most); (2) "As a girl grows up, her breasts develop and get bigger. Which sentence best describes you?" (five-point scale from 1 = my breasts are about the same size as when I was in grade school to 5 = my breasts are a whole lot bigger than when I was in grade school, they are as developed as a grown woman's breasts); and (3) "As a girl grows up, her body becomes more curved. Which sentence best describes you?" (five-point scale ranging from 1 = my body is about as curvy as when I was in grade school to 5 = my body is a whole lot more curvy than when I was in grade school) . . . . For males, physical development is an additive scale based upon four items: (1) "How much hair is under your arms now" (coded on a five-point scale from 1 = I have no hair at all to 5 = I have a whole lot of hair that is very thick, as much hair as a grown man; (2) "How thick is the hair on your face?" (four-point scale ranging from 1 = I have a few scattered hairs, but the growth is not thick to 4 = the hair is very thick, like a grown man's facial hair); (3) "Is your voice lower now than it was when you were in grade school?" (five-point scale ranging from 1 = no to 5 = yes, it is as low as an adult man's voice); and (4) "how advanced is your physical development compared to other boys your age?" (five-point scale from 1 = I look younger than most to 5 = I look older than most). . . . Finally, we include a measure of body mass index (BMI), which we calculated based upon the respondent's self-reported height and weight. . . .

Results

. . . Our first goal is to document gender differences in the association between number of sex partners and peer acceptance. . . . [S]tatistics for the gender differences between lifetime sexual partners were statistically significant for all partner categories . . ., suggesting that sexual behaviors are one of the few areas where peers evaluate girls and boys differently.

[W]e find evidence that sexually permissive girls (i.e., greater than eight lifetime partners) have fewer friendship nominations than girls who report no sexual partners. This provides some evidence that permissive girls are marginalized within peer groups. In addition, we find no evidence that girls with 1 to 8 sexual partners have fewer friendship nominations than their sexually inexperienced peers.

Girls with greater than eight sexual partners are predicted to have .8 fewer peer nominations than sexually inexperienced girls, holding all other variables constant. . . . Indeed, sexual involvement outside of a romantic relationship during the past year has no direct effect on peer acceptance, failing to support the idea that intercourse outside of a committed relationship results in lowered female peer status. Looking at the remaining effects, we see . . . [f]emale adolescents receive higher numbers of peer nominations if they participate in athletics or club activities, if they are doing well in school, or if they reside with both biological parents. Body mass is inversely related to female peer acceptance, so that girls with higher weight/height ratios have fewer peer nominations. Peer status is also higher among females who perceive that they are more physically mature than other females their age and who are rated as physically attractive by interviewers. Whereas violence has a negative effect on acceptance, alcohol use in the past year is positively associated with popularity. Hispanic and Asian females have significantly fewer friendship nominations than white females.

Supporting the hypothesis that boys are rewarded for sexually permissive behavior, we find that the number of lifetime sexual partners has a positive . . . effect on male peer acceptance. Unlike the results for girls, we find that sexually inexperienced boys have significantly less peer nominations than boys with one or more sexual partners, and more partners are associated with greater numbers of peer nominations. . . . [A]mong youth who report more than 8 lifetime sexual partners, boys have approximately 1.3 additional friendship nominations than girls. By contrast, among the majority of youth who report no current or prior sexual partners, boys report 0.7 fewer friendship nominations than girls.

We next turn our attention to the question, "Which peers provide (or fail to provide) status to sexually permissive youth?" . . . [P]ermissive boys are more likely to gain status from female peers than from male peers, while permissive girls only have lower peer acceptance among other girls. These results suggest that female reactions to sexual behavior simultaneously escalate the status of permissive boys and decrease the status of permissive girls.

[S]ome research suggests that boys from disadvantaged backgrounds are the most likely to derive peer status from numerous lifetime sexual partners, in part because of the heterogeneity of gender frames and relational scripts in poor neighborhoods and urban schools (Anderson 1999; Harding 2007). Moreover, we expect that girls from advantaged backgrounds should receive more consistent messages than disadvantaged girls regarding the negative consequences of sexual permissiveness for life chances and "good" reputations. . . .

[A]mong girls from low educated families, the effect of sexual partners on peer acceptance is statistically nonsignificant. By contrast, girls from high socioeconomic backgrounds who report eight or more lifetime sexual partners have significantly lower peer status than high SES girls who report no sexual partners even after we control for relationship status, school success, physical characteristics, and adjustment.

The positive effect of more than eight lifetime sexual partners on male peer acceptance significantly varies by socioeconomic background. Boys from disadvantaged backgrounds who report eight or more sexual partners have higher peer status than disadvantaged boys who report no partners, and this effect is significantly larger for low versus high SES boys. Thus, even though the association between lifetime sexual partners and peer status differs significantly by gender, the positive effects of sexual contacts are strongest among low SES boys.

Discussion

In this study, we used social network data to explore the association between adolescent sexuality and peer acceptance at school. Our primary interest was to provide an innovative test of the sexual double standard in a nationally representative adolescent sample. Though most covariates of peer acceptance were similar for boys and girls (e.g., sports and club memberships, fighting, attractiveness, physical development, school performance, body mass index, and social background), we found strong gender differences with regard to sexual behavior, such that increased numbers of sexual partnerships were positively associated with boys' peer acceptance but negatively associated with girls' peer acceptance. Boys with many sexual "conquests" are thus expected to be well-liked at schools, while permissive girls are predicted to have low status in school-based networks, regardless of whether or not their sexual behaviors occur within "romantic" relationships. Moreover, the positive association between male sexual permissiveness and peer acceptance was strongest among disadvantaged boys. Together, these findings suggest that gendered and social class-specific perceptions of normative sexual behaviors remain alive in contemporary adolescent peer contexts. . . .

We should also make clear that we do not provide a direct test of whether permissive girls are stigmatized (i.e., rejected) for their sexual behavior. To do so, we would need nominations of peer dislike rather than peer friendships. Female stigmatization would then be apparent when disliked nominations increase with greater numbers of sexual partners. Such nominations . . . were not part of the Add Health study. . . .

Another interesting, and perhaps counterintuitive, finding is that nonromantic sexual partnerships have no net correlation with school-based peer nominations. Several scholars point to nonromantic sexual liaisons as the clearest means for adolescent girls to be rejected by peers and earn "slut" labels (Risman and Schwartz 2002; Tolman 2002). To further explore this expectation . . . [f]or boys, we found a significant positive association between nonromantic sex and peer acceptance, but for girls this estimate was nonsignificant. . . . One possible explanation for this pattern is that boys understand that positive peer attributions follow sexual activity of any sort, and volunteer information about recent nonromantic sexual contacts, whereas girls fear public knowledge of such liaisons and therefore do not disclose the existence of nonromantic sex. Potential gender differences in sexual disclosure also emphasize the importance of social contexts for sexual double-standard research. If female actors are successful at keeping their sexual contacts secret, then they may avoid any stigma associated with permissive behaviors. Clearly, increased frequencies of sexual partners and behaviors raise the risks of public disclosure and social reaction, perhaps explaining why only the most permissive girls have significantly fewer friendship nominations than other girls. . . .

References

Anderson, Elijah. 1999. *Code of the Street; Decency, Violence, and the Moral Life of the Inner City.* New York: Norton.

Networks." *American Journal of Sociology* 11(1):44–91.

Coie, John D., Kenneth A. Dodge and J. B. Kupersmidt. 1990. "Peer Group Behavior and Social Status." pp. 17–59 in *Peer Rejection in Childhood,* edited by Steven R. Asher and John D. Coie. New York: Cambridge University Press.

Cohen, Albert K. 1955. *Delinquent Boys: The Culture of the Gang.* Glencoe, IL: Free Press.

Crawford, Mary and Danielle Popp. 2003. "Sexual Double Standards: A Review and Methodological Critique of Two Decades of Research," *The Journal of Sex Research* 40(1):13–26.

Eder, Donna, Catherine C. Evans, and Stephen Parker. 1995. *School Talk: Gender and Adolescent Culture.* New Brunswick, NJ: Rutgers University Press.

Edin, Kathryn and Maria Kefalas. 2005. *Promises I Can Keep: Why Poor Women Put Motherhood Before Marriage*. Berkeley, CA: University of California Press.

Gentry, Margaret. 1998. "The Sexual Double Standard: The Influence of Number of Relationships and Level of Sexual Activity on Judgments of Women and Men." *Psychology of Women Quarterly* 22(3):505–11 .

Goffman, Erving. 1963. *Stigma: Notes on the Management of Spoiled Identity*. Englewood Cliffs, NJ: Prentice-Hall.

Harding, David J. 2007. "Cultural Context, Sexual Behavior, and Romantic Relationships in Disadvantaged Neighborhoods." *American Sociological Review* 72(3):341–64.

Holland, Alyce and Thomas Andre. 1994. "Athletic Participation and the Social Status of Adolescent Males and Females." *Youth and Society* 25:388–407.

Kreager, Derek A. 2007. "When It's Good to be "Bad": Violence and Adolescent Peer Acceptance." *Criminology* 45(4):893–923.

LaFontana, Kathryn M. and Antonius Cillessen. 2002. "Children's Perceptions of Popular and Unpopular Peers: A Multimethod Assessment." *Developmental Psychology* 38(5):635–47.

Marks, Michael J. and R. Chris Fraley. 2005. "The Sexual Double Standard: Fact or Fiction?" *Sex Roles* 52:175–86.

——. 2006. "Confirmation Bias and the Sexual Double Standard." *Sex Roles* 54:19–26.

Milhausen, Robin R. and Edward S. Herold. 2001. "Reconceptualizing the Sexual Double Standard." *Journal of Psychology and Human Sexuality* 13(2):63–83.

——. 1999. "Does the Sexual Double Standard Still Exist? Perceptions of University Women." *Journal of Sex Research* 36:361–8.

Miller, Kathleen E., Michael P. Farrell, Grace M. Barnes, Merrill J. Melnick, and Don Sabo. 2005. "Gender/Racial Differences in Jock Identity, Dating, and Adolescent Sexual Risk." *Journal of Youth and Adolescence* 34(2):123–36.

Moffat, Michael. 1989. *Coming of Age in New Jersey*. New Brunswick, NJ: Rutgers University Press.

National Longitudinal Study of Adolescent Health. 2001. *Network Variables Codebook*. Chapel Hill, NC: University of North Carolina.

Newcomb, Andrew F., William M. Bukowski, and Linda Pattee. 1993. "Children's Peer Relations: A Meta-Analytic Review of Popular, Rejected, Neglected, Controversial, and Average Sociometric Status." *Psychological Bulletin* 113:99–128.

Newcomer, Susan, J. Richard Udry, and Freda Cameron. 1983. "Adolescent Sexual Behavior and Popularity." *Adolescence* 18(71):515–22.

Oliver, Mary B. and Constantine Sedikides. 1992. "Effects of Sexual Permissiveness on Desirability of Partner as a Function of Low and High Commitment to Relationship." *Social Psychology Quarterly* 55:321–33.

Orenstein, Peggy. 1994. *Schoolgirls: Young Women, Self-Esteem, and the Confidence Gap*. New York: Doubleday.

Parker, Jeffrey G. and Steven R. Asher. 1987. "Peer Relations and Later Personal Adjustment: Are Low-Accepted Children at Risk?" *Psychological Bulletin* 102(3):357–89.

Reiss, Ira L. 1964. "The Scaling of Premarital Sexual Permissiveness." *Journal of Marriage and the Family* 26(2):188–98.

Reskin Barbara F. 2003. "Including Mechanisms in our Models of Ascriptive Inequality: 2002 Presidential Address." *American Sociological Review* 68(1):1–21.

Risman, Barbara and Pepper Schwartz. 2002. "After the Sexual Revolution: Gender Politics in Teen Dating." *Contexts* 1(1):16–24.

Sheeran, Paschal, Russell Spears, Charles S. Abraham, and Dominic Abrams. 1996. "Religiosity, Gender, and the Double Standard." *Journal of Psychology* 130:23–33.

Steffensmeier, Darrell and Emilie Allan. 1996. "Gender and Crime: Toward a Gendered Theory of Female Offending." *Annual Review of Sociology* 22(1):459–88.

Wasserman, Stanley and Katherine Faust. 1994. *Social Network Analysis*. Cambridge, UK: Cambridge University Press.

White, Emily. 2002. *Fast Girls: Teenage Tribes and the Myth of the Slut*. New York: Scribner.

Willis, Paul. 1977. *Learning to Labor: How Working Class Kids Get Working Class Jobs*, Farnborough, UK: Saxon House.

Wolf, Naomi. 1997. *Promiscuities: The Secret Struggle for Womanhood*. New York: Faucet Books.

Heidi Lyons et al.   ➔ **NO**

Identity, Peer Relationships, and Adolescent Girls' Sexual Behavior: An Exploration of the Contemporary Double Standard

The double standard is a well-recognized cultural phenomenon. However, some researchers have suggested that gendered sexual standards of behavior may be undergoing change and increasing in complexity (Marks & Fraley, 2006; Milhausen & Herold, 2001; Moore & Rosenthal, 1994; Risman & Schwartz, 2002; Tolman, 1996). The classic definition of the sexual double standard focuses on the ways in which young men are socialized to value sexual experience and young women learn to emphasize committed relationships (Reiss, 1960). It is believed that, in general, this inhibits young women's sexual behavior, particularly "promiscuous" behavior, by making it socially costly. Accordingly, women who do not fit the conservative ideal are subjected to negative social sanctions or censures. Some research has suggested that this classic pattern may be eroding (Crawford, 2003; Gentry, 1998; Marks & Fraley, 2005, 2006), but more research is needed that investigates not simply whether the sexual double standard exists, but also the social and identity implications of departing from its basic tenets.

In this study, we focused on young women who report a higher number of sexual partners relative to their similarly aged counterparts. . . . [and] investigated two related research questions regarding the social and identity statuses of young women who represented a range of sexual experiences. First, . . . do young women who report a high number of sexual partners report lower popularity or other peer deficits as a result of the double standard? Further, and consistent with this idea of negative "reflected appraisals" from others, do these young women report lower self-esteem than their more sexually conservative counterparts? We tested these associations both cross-sectionally and longitudinally. The cross-sectional assessment documents whether there is a significant association between number of sex partners and perceived popularity with peers, dissatisfaction with number of friends, and level of self-esteem. A longitudinal analysis adds to the portrait by investigating whether the number of sex partners is associated with lower peer popularity as reported one year later.

Lyons, Heidi, Peggy C. Giordano, Wendy D. Manning, and Monica A. Longmore. From *Journal of Sex Research*, Vol. 48, No. 5, September 1, 2011, pp. 437–449. Copyright © 2011 by Society for the Scientific Study of Sexuality. Reprinted by permission of Taylor & Francis via Rightslink.

We also focused the analysis on the attitudes and behaviors of the adolescent's more immediate circle of friends. This *social network* emphasis suggests that young women who report a higher number of sexual partners may not experience the kinds of social costs or deficits described earlier (perceptions of being unpopular or low self-esteem) in large part because they receive support and reinforcement from their friends, whose attitudes about sexuality are similar to their own. This notion is more consistent with the tenets of symbolic interaction, which emphasizes the localized or "situated" nature of action (Mead, 1934), and more general social learning theories (Sutherland, 1934), which stress the role of intimate others in fostering particular patterns of behavior—even those that may be considered "deviant" by the wider society. . . . Thus, it is possible that . . . friends provide a buffer against negative attributions from the wider peer group, as well as actively fostering and reinforcing these behaviors.

Prior Research on the Double Standard

The sexual double standard has evolved over time. Early on, it was considered inappropriate for women to engage in sexual activity outside of marriage (Crawford, 2003; Reiss, 1960). Some researchers have argued that the sexual double standard has changed somewhat, but it is still in place (Milhausen & Herold, 1999; Risman & Schwartz, 2002). Maccoby (1998), for example, suggested that teenage boys who gain considerable sexual experience do not run the same risk of being labeled deviant as do their female counterparts. More specifically, young women who had a high number of sex partners were socially reprimanded for their behaviors, and young men were rewarded (Milhausen & Herold, 1999).

Some research has examined the prevalence of the sexual double standard among samples of American youth. Moore and Rosenthal (1994) focused on the attitudes of 16-year-olds and found that over one half of their sample judged girls and boys similarly regarding the issue of having many sex partners (respondents were asked the general question, "What do you think about girls/boys who sleep around?") Although this suggests some movement away from a clear double standard, nevertheless, a relatively large percentage of teenagers do evaluate males and females differently, with girls most often viewed or judged in a negative manner. One limitation of their study is that it asked respondents to reflect on a hypothetical individual, rather than on one's own behavior or that of friends and classmates.

Another study by Jackson and Cram (2003) relied on focus groups of late adolescent girls. The young women in their sample noted that women are typically labeled "sluts" for the same sexual behavior that would earn boys the label "stud." Although this reflects a continued double standard, as in the Moore and Rosenthal (1994) study, these respondents rarely used experiences from their own lives to explain how the double standard affects them personally; and, although the aforementioned studies find support for the survival of the double standard, other research suggests that this gendered normative system may be eroding. Oliver and Hyde (1993) compiled research conducted between 1966 and 1990 relating to this issue and determined that attitudes toward premarital sexual behaviors are becoming more similar across gender in more recent studies. Further, using a sample of college students and patrons at a bar, Milhausen and Herold (2001) reported that, although men were significantly more likely to endorse the sexual double standard, this nevertheless reflected only a minority of men. The authors stated that most men and women endorsed a single standard that judged men and women's sexual behavior equally.

Some of the variability in results of prior research may be related to variations in methodological approaches across the various studies. Crawford (2003) conducted a meta-analysis of research on the double standard and reported that experimentally designed studies were more likely to indicate less support for the existence of the double standard. In contrast, qualitative approaches, such as interviews and focus groups, tended to reveal that it survives. Marks and Fraley (2006) examined the possible role of confirmation bias in studying the sexual double standard. The researchers concluded that their participants recalled information from a given vignette that confirmed the sexual double standard more often than any other details. This suggests that studies which only focus on the abstract concept of the double standard do not tap into the actual ways individuals understand the sexual behavior of male and female teens and what sexual activities mean within the context of their own lives.

Recently, Kreager and Staff (2009), drawing on data from the National Longitudinal Study of Adolescent Health (Add Health), focused on adolescents' own sexual behaviors and found that those women with many sex partners do report fewer friends, whereas this association was not found for male respondents. This tends to support the idea of the survival of the double standard, particularly the notion of social costs levied against girls whose sexual behavior exceeds normative levels. However, this association with number of friends was found only for those female respondents who reported more than eight partners, a subgroup that comprises about 2% of the sample. In addition, the friends' nominations were limited to those in schools participating in the survey, which may not provide a comprehensive portrait of the adolescent's complete social network. This study contributes beyond this prior work by considering the broader implications of girls' sexual behaviors for peer status and regard as measured by perceived *popularity*, as well as girls' own reports of the adequacy of their friendship networks (*desire for more friends*). The analysis also examines the role of friends' attitudes and behaviors (*friends' liberal sexual attitudes* and *friends' number of sexual partners*), as well as the identity implications (*levels of self-esteem*) of reporting a larger number of sexual partners. . . .

This Study

In this analysis, we explored the variability in number of sex partners girls report to determine whether those who report a greater number of partners also report lower popularity with friends and experience perceived deficits in the number of friends or lower self-esteem. These relationships would be consistent with the basic notion of a double standard and the perspective that there are social costs levied against young women who violate these conservative stand-ards. We concentrated on the perspectives and behaviors of young women in this analysis because (a) the double standard notion emphasizes costs to young women rather than men and (b) we have focused specifically on young men's sexual attitudes and behaviors in prior analyses (Giordano, Longmore, & Manning, 2006; Giordano, Longmore, Manning, & Northcutt, 2009).

Because cross-sectional analyses undoubtedly capture reciprocal proc-esses (less popular girls may have more partners and then experience even more decline in popularity), we also examined these associations longitudi-nally. Our models show how sexual behavior and popularity at Wave 1 influ-ence popularity one year later (Wave 2). This analysis provides an indication of a decline in popularity that is more readily theorized as a consequence, rather than a cause, of the behavior of interest.

Our analysis also evaluated variability across the sample in peer norma-tive climates, consistent with the idea of variability in friends' support for and encouragement of these sexual behaviors. A symbolic interactionist approach leads us to expect that those who report a higher number of sex partners will have friends with more liberal sexual attitudes and a higher level of sexual experience themselves. The symbolic interactionist approach also highlights the importance of identity formation processes, as self-views reflect an inter-nalizalion of prior social experiences. Thus, rather than conceptualizing the self only in positive or negative terms (the self-esteem notion), theories of symbolic interaction stress that the self is comprised of multiple content areas (Matsueda, 1992), including one's sexual self (Giordano et al., 2009). These sexual self-views need not be viewed from a negative lens, but simply as self-definitions that reference the heterosexual realm. For example, young women who believe that they are "sexy" or "hot" may carry a level of confidence about their interactions with young men and engage in more activities (flirting or attending parties) that provide greater opportunities for sexual involvement. Thus, we expect that endorsement of such identities will be associated with a higher number of sex partners, controlling for traditional correlates. Thus, the analysis focuses on different aspects of the adolescent's social world and distinct features of identity. Although we have suggested that the social defi-cit approach focuses on different dynamics than the social learning perspec-tive (e.g., perceived popularity with peers vs. the attitudes and behaviors of close friends), support for one set of relationships does not automatically rule-out support for the other. For example, it is possible that young women who report a larger number of sexual partners score lower on perceived popularity, but also are more likely to have close friends with more liberal attitudes and behavioral repertoires. Such a finding would be consistent with some research on early peer deficits and attachment processes, where it is argued that those who rank low in prestige or popularity with peers may gravitate toward others who tend to reinforce antisocial norms and behaviors (Asher & Coie, 1990).

The in-depth qualitative data we also elicited from a subset of the respond-ents provided a more multilayered view of young women's perspectives on the double standard. The qualitative data allowed us to further explore the impli-cations of the quantitative findings as a whole, including dynamics linked to the idea of social deficits and costs, as well as those typically associated with a social learning framework. Specifically, we contrast general understandings about the double standard as a social phenomenon that exists at the societal or school level, with girls' perspectives on the acceptability of their own behaviors and that of their immediate circle of friends.

Data and Method

This article draws on the TARS. The original sample collected quantitative information on a stratified, random sample of seventh-, ninth-, and eleventh-grade adolescent boys and girls in Lucas County, Ohio, with an over sampling of the African American and Hispanic populations and with a final sample size of 1,316 total youths from the Toledo area, which included 678 girls. . . . The data collection of Wave 1 was June 2001 through February 2002. Wave 2 was collected about one year later . . . [(]August 2002 through June 2003[)]. At Wave 2, 603 girls (89% of the Wave-1 respondents) were interviewed, and our analysis is based on 600 girls with valid data on the dependent and independent indicators.

Forty-six female respondents were interviewed to provide an in-depth portrait of each respondent's romantic relationships and sexual behavior history. These young women were randomly selected from those within the larger quantitative survey sample, who reported at least some dating experience. . . .

TARS is an appropriate dataset for these analyses because the interview protocol includes respondents' subjective views of broader social concerns such as popularity, measures of friends' attitudes and behaviors, as well as several indexes tapping identity domains (self-esteem, as well as sexual identities). Further, unlike the Add Health, the TARS is not a school-based sample. This is of value because young people who do not attend school may report a larger number of sexual partners, and all respondents are able to nominate friends, regardless of whether they attend the same school.

The quantitative analysis focused on two dependent variables. The first is a continuous variable of *number of lifetime sex partners* at Wave 1. The second is a binary variable measuring perceived *unpopularity with females* as reported at Wave 2. This was constructed from responses to the following item: "Others would describe you as popular with females." . . .

There were three measures of social deficits and costs associated with having a larger number of sexual partners: perceived lack of popularity, desire for more friends, and self-esteem. For the longitudinal analysis, self-perceived *unpopularity with females* at Wave 1 was based on the following item: "Others would describe you as popular with females." . . . *Perceived lack of friends* was based on the item, "I wish I had more friends." . . . A six-item scale was used to measure *self-esteem* with items like, "I can do things as well as other people." . . .

We use four items to measure the norms and behaviors of friends and identity content that we argue may be associated with a greater number of sexual partners. *Friends' liberal attitudes* . . . is a three-item scale that taps friends' liberal attitudes toward sex with items like, "My friends think it's okay to have sex with someone you are not actually dating." *Friends' sexual behavior* was measured by the question, "How many of your friends do you think have had sex?," . . . and *sexualized identity* was measured with two items ("I am flirty" and "I am sexy or hot"). . . .

Results

The mean number of *lifetime sex partners* was less than one . . . for the full sample. . . . The majority of girls perceived themselves as popular both at Time I (85%) and Time 2 (82%). At Time 1, the mean of the self-esteem measure was 23.51 (range = 9–30), and the mean for the item indexing a desire for more friends was 2.59 (range = 1–5). The sample had a mean of 7.33 for friends' liberal attitudes, suggesting a trend toward more liberal peers. The mean for number of friends having sex was 2.85 (range = 1–6). Respondents reported a mean of 3.14 for the self-identity of flirty and 3.29 for sexy (range = 1–5). The mean number of partners was 0.90 (SD = 2.40). We first focused on the social deficit indicators, perceived popularity, desire for more friends, and self-esteem. . . . [P]erceived popularity and desire for number of friends were not significantly related to girls' reports about their number of lifetime sex partners. Further, results showed that self-esteem was not associated with the number of lifetime sex partners. This is not consistent with the notion of high social costs or a devalued or stigmatized identity, at least as measured by the idea of lower self-esteem.

The indicators associated with the social networks hypothesis are friends' liberal sexual attitudes, sexual behavior of friends, and the sexualized identity indicator. Friends' liberal sexual attitudes and sexual behavior of friends were significantly and positively related to the number of lifetime sex partners. . . . In addition, "sexy" was no longer significant . . . with the addition of friends' liberal sexual attitudes. We found that respondents' endorsement of the flirty identity was not significantly tied to the number of sex partners. . . .

Longitudinal Assessments

To determine whether the number of lifetime sex partners reported at Wave 1 is associated with a reduction in popularity at Wave 2, we relied on the former as a predictor of the latter. Net of perceived popularity with females as reported at Wave 1, the number of lifetime sex partners also reported at Wave 1 was not significantly related to subsequent popularity, as measured at Wave 2. This finding suggests that within this sample of adolescents, whether we examine the issue cross-sectionally or longitudinally, the number of lifetime sex partners does not seem to be associated with self-perceived lower peer regard, as would be predicted by the basic logic of the sexual double standard and the idea of social costs levied against young women who violate such norms. . . .

Although not a primary focus of this investigation, we also attempted to replicate Kreager and Staff's (2009) finding regarding the relationship between sexual behavior and number of friends reported. Supplemental analyses of the TARS data indicated that girls with a high number of sex partners at Wave 1 are less likely to report five or more friends at Wave 2. However, there was not a significant relationship between number of sex partners and the likelihood of reporting having a few friends compared to reporting five or more friends. It is also interesting to note that across several dimensions of relationship quality (e.g., time spent with friends or levels of intimate self-disclosure to friends), girls who reported a larger number of sexual partners did not score significantly lower on frequency of interaction with friends or intimacy of communication relative to their more sexually conservative counterparts (analyses available upon request).

The Meanings of the Double Standard

Our analyses of the qualitative data provide a more nuanced picture of the double standard—one that generally accords with the quantitative results, but shows distinctions between girls' knowledge and even acceptance of these broader normative prescriptions, on the one hand, and the behaviors of friends and their own sexual experiences, on the other. Sections of the narratives focusing on the double standard suggest that these gendered normative standards survive on many levels, and even those young women who reported a relatively large number of sexual partners do not fully reject its basic tenets. Yet, differences across various reference points are important to consider. Thus, although young women spoke eloquently about the general existence of two standards of sexual comportment, they reserved more harsh attributions for unknown or little-known others who casually violate these standards. As discussions turned to the behavior of intimate friends, and particularly respondents' own behavior, a more measured and complex set of meanings and explanations or "disclaimers" (Scott & Lyman, 1968) often emerged. The qualitative findings complement the quantitative findings in that young women who reported a high number of sex partners did not typically develop a narrative about being unpopular or stigmatized, a desire for more friends, feelings of loneliness, or low self-worth. However, they often referenced the behavior of friends within their own networks. Thus, it is likely that adolescents focus most heavily on this immediate network as a source of reference and influence, which then serves as a form of social support and as a buffer against negative attributions associated with their own behavior.

The Double Standard as a Cultural Reality

During the in-depth interviews, respondents were asked a straightforward question regarding the double standard and whether they thought it still exists. Results of the qualitative data showed that many adolescents in the sample did recognize the survival of the sexual double standard. However, when the girls discussed the meaning of the sexual double standard, it was often viewed as a known, taken-for-granted societal reality or social dynamic that occurs in the larger school environment. . . .

Across a range of different levels of sexual experience, . . . most young women reflected a keen awareness of the core elements of the double standard in pointing out that women are held to different normative standards compared to men. They also reflect on social labeling processes, in that men are subject to social rewards for engaging in behavior that is likely to garner a bad reputation or even labels such as "whore" when enacted by women.

When girls were asked to provide specific examples that related to their school environment, however, these statements are often vague or abstract, not referencing particular girls—especially the respondent's friends or their own behaviors. Kimberly. . . . [a] senior female[,] did harshly judge the younger girls who "put themselves out there" in ways that are too overtly sexual. The narrative also suggests that she has a different orientation. Thus, it is interesting to note that Kimberly is currently dating a boy who started out as a "friends with benefits" relationship, suggesting the idea that multiple—and sometimes contradictory—meanings can be associated with the double standard concept.

This notion is also illustrated by Marie, a 17-year-old who castigated other girls who gain a negative reputation linked to their sexual behaviors[,] . . . [but has herself] had four sex partners. Thus, although castigating other girls, Marie herself scored . . . above the mean in sexual experience relative to other young women who participated in the . . . study. [T]he sexual double standard may exist on a societal or school level but often erodes, or gains a layer of complication, when the referent is one's own behavior or that of intimate friends.

The Meaning of the Sexual Double Standard on the Peer Level

Numerous scholars have pointed out that a key benefit of friendships during the adolescent period is the level of support they provide (Mortimer & Call, 2001); and, as Youniss and Smollar (1985), as well as others, have pointed out, peers, relative to one's parents or other adults, are less likely to be judgmental—a social dynamic that creates many opportunities for frank dialogue and exploration of issues, including issues of sexuality. When asked how she felt about girlfriends who want to participate in sexual behavior as much as boys do, Stephanie, a 17-year-old with six lifetime sex partners . . . did not view her friend negatively because she had engaged in such behaviors; and, . . . Stephanie's own sexual experience level coordinates well with that of her friend, providing an additional motivation to avoid levying any sort of negative social sanction or disapproval of her friend's behavior. This fits well with the quantitative results [of this study]. Along similar lines, Alexis, a 17-year-old with one lifetime sex partner, described how her peer group does not talk about or judge their female friends for the sexual activities in which they participate.

Alexis . . . did not judge her friend for the sexual behavior in which she may be involved. Even more important, she felt the need to uphold certain rules of friendship, which do not include giving the friend a derogatory name or spreading rumors about her. Another participant, Amber, a 17-year-old with two lifetime sex partners, reported that her peer group . . . offers a safe place to discuss romantic and sexual activity[;] . . . She can look to her peer group as an opportunity to discuss issues around sexuality with-out running the risk of getting a negative reputation. Since the peer group is often a safe haven relative to the "wider circle" of peer associations, this is a place for girls to explore their own and others' sexual feelings and experi-ences in ways that, to an extent, "suspend or 'bracket-off'" double standard concerns. This idea is consistent with the quantitative findings demonstrat-ing concordance between adolescent respondents' own behaviors and those of their friends, and results that do not dovetail with the "social costs and deficits" hypothesis. . . .

Discussion

Excerpts from the qualitative narratives revealed that across a range of levels of sexual experience, young women did recognize the survival of a double standard of sexual behavior. Further, whereas some noted that it was "unfair" for others to judge young women according to a different standard, others seemed to accept the inevitability of this gendered pattern, and often provided negative descriptions of young women whose behavior veered from what was considered acceptable within their school or neighborhood (e.g., using terms such as "slut" or describing such behavior as "nasty"). Yet, both the quantita-tive and qualitative data we analyzed suggest a more complex portrait: Girls who reported a relatively large number of sexual partners did not, in turn, perceive lower levels of popularity with other girls, deficits in the number of friends they had, or lower self-esteem relative to their less experienced coun-terparts. These findings are consistent whether we examine such relationships cross-sectionally or longitudinally. . . .

Yet, the quantitative results also show that it is important to take into account the diversity of peer climates, as friends' liberal attitudes and sexual behavior emerged as significant predictors of variations in the number of sexual partners adolescent respondents reported. . . . [T]he qualitative results highlighted that, although these young women may show disdain or other-wise negatively label others in the wider circle of peers (e.g., "those sopho-more girls"), they are reluctant to do this where the referent is their friend or their own behavior. This suggests that similarly situated friends may serve as a source of support or buffer against negative attributions that may take the form of gossip or other labeling that occurs within the context of the broader school normative climate. . . .

These findings are largely based on the adolescent's own perceptions or understandings, as contrasted with objective information, such as the number of friend nominations used by Kreager and Staff (2009). They found that female respondents who reported having a large number of sexual partners received fewer school-based friend nominations relative to respondents with fewer partners. . . . Yet, the perceptual data we described earlier add to this emphasis on objective information, as the youths themselves did not perceive that they would like more friends or that they were unpopular with other girls. Similarly, such girls did not score lower than their more sexually conservative counterparts on various indexes of relationship quality. Future research should explore both objective characteristics and subjectively experienced aspects of girls' friendships and other peer relationships. . . .

References

Asher, S. R., & Coie, J. D. (1990). *Peer rejection in childhood*. New York, NY: Cambridge University Press.

Crawford, M. (2003). Sexual double standards: A review and methodological critique of two decades of research. *Journal of Sex Research, 40*, 13–26.

Giordano, P. C., Longmore, M. A., & Manning, W. D. (2006). Gender and the meaning of adolescent romantic relationship: A focus on boys. *American Sociological Review, 71*, 260–287.

Giordano, P. C., Longmore, M. A., Manning, W. D., & Northcutt, M. J. (2009). Adolescent identities and sexual behavior: An examination of Anderson's "player" hypothesis. *Social Forces, 87*(4), 1813–1844.

Kreager, D., & Staff, J. (2009). The sexual double standard and adolescent peer acceptance. *Social Psychology Quarterly, 72*, 143–164.

Maccoby, E. E. (1998). *The two sexes: Growing up apart, coming together*. Cambridge, MA: Belknap.

Marks, M., & Fraley, R. C. (2005). The sexual double standard: Fact or fiction? *Sex Roles, 52*, 175–186.

Marks, M., & Fraley, R. C. (2006). Confirmation bias and the sexual double standard. *Sex Roles, 54*, 19–26.

Milhausen, R., & Herold, E. (1999). Does the sexual double standard still exist? Perceptions of university women. *Journal of Sex Research, 36*, 361–368.

Milhausen, R., & Herold, E. (2001). Reconceptualizing the sexual double standard. *Journal of Psychology and Human Sexuality, 13*, 63–83.

Mortimer, J., & Call, D. (2001). *Arenas of comfort in adolescence: A study of adjustment in context*. Mahwah, NJ: Lawrence Erlbaum Associates, Inc.

Oliver, M., & Hyde, J. (1993). Gender differences in sexuality: A meta-analysis. *Psychological Bulletin, 114*, 29–51.

Reiss, I. (1960). *Premarital sexual standards in America*. Glencoe, IL: Free Press.

Risman, B., & Schwartz, P. (2002). After the sexual revolution: Gender politics in teen dating. *Context, 1*, 16–24.

Scott, M., & Lyman, S. M. (1968). Accounts. *American Sociological Review, 33*, 46–62.

Younis, J., & Smollar, J. (1985). *Adolescents' relationships with mothers, fathers, and friends*. Chicago: University of Chicago Press.

EXPLORING THE ISSUE

Does a Strong and Costly Sexual Double Standard Still Exist Among Adolescents?

Critical Thinking and Reflection

1. Take a moment to think about the words you would use to describe sexually promiscuous boys and girls. Now critically examine your lists—are they equal in number, tone, and judgment? Now reflect back on the nature of this exercise. What does it illuminate for you about your own perceptions, beliefs, and biases when it comes to the sexual double standard?

2. Consider your experiences (personal or witnessing others) of how boys and girls in your peer group are/have been evaluated differently for the same behaviors. What examples come to mind of instances where a sexual double standard was operating? What were the outcomes for boys versus girls who violated sexual standards?

3. How are boys and girls socialized differently with respect to their development as sexual beings? What are the messages that girls receive about how to be sexual? Are desire and pleasure part of the sexual scripts for both boys and girls? If so, how are they communicated? If not, why not?

Is There Common Ground?

In the YES selection, Kreager and Staff presented evidence for a contemporary double standard among adolescents. They found significant gender differences in the relationship between the number of sexual partners and acceptance by peers whereby boys and girls were evaluated differently (girls more negatively) for the same behaviors. Girls who were considered sexually permissive (with more than eight sexual partners) received fewer friendship endorsements from peers than did girls with no sexual partners. The authors explained this finding to mean that girls who are sexually permissive are marginalized within their peer groups. In contrast, sexually experienced boys were rewarded with peer acceptance, and less experienced boys suffered in terms of friendship ratings from peers. Interestingly, they also found that female peers viewed sexually permissive girls more negatively than they did sexually permissive boys.

In the NO selection, Lyons and colleagues examined the association between adolescent girls' popularity and lifetime number of sexual partners. Contrary to the results of Kreager and Staff's study, in this issue, number of sexual partners was not associated with popularity among peers. They also found no differences in the quality of friendships (i.e., intimacy, time spent together) for girls with higher number of sexual partners compared to those with fewer or no sexual partners, and no differences in self-esteem. Because this was a longitudinal study, the researchers were able to examine the variables cross-sectionally and over time. They found no changes in friendship status over time for sexually permissive girls. They also included a qualitative component to their study and found that these young women acknowledged the existence of a sexual double standard (in interviews), but they did not view themselves as less popular than other girls, or marginalized for their sexual experiences. The authors suggest that one's close network of friends provides a buffer against any possible negative outcomes.

One of the main differences between these two studies is that the second measured friends' liberal attitudes toward sexuality. Perhaps the social costs of the double standard are less and they are less severe when friendship circles consist of people with more liberal attitudes toward sex. Girls in the No selection acknowledged the existence of a normative sexual double standard, but seemed to evaluate themselves and their sexually experienced peers less negatively than the sexual double standard would suggest. That said, the results suggested that they did not apply the same sensitivity or acceptance to "unknown" girls (girls outside their peer group) who violated sexual prescriptions and standards.

Additional Resources

Aubrey, J. S. (2004). Sex and punishment: An examination of sexual consequences and the sexual double standard in teen programming. *Sex Roles, 50,* 505–514.

Double Standard (DVD). (2002). CTV. Product information. Retrieved from www.mcintyre.ca/cgi-bin/search/mmiview.asp?ID=4736

Greene, K., & Faulkner, S. L. (2005). Gender, belief in the sexual double standard, and sexual talk in heterosexual dating relationships. *Sex Roles, 53*(3/4), 239–251.

Marks, M., & Fraley, R. C. (2005). The sexual double standard: Fact or fiction? *Sex Roles, 52*(3/4), 175–186. doi: 10.1007/s11199-005-1293-5

Marks, M., & Fraley, R. C. (2006). Confirmation bias and the sexual double standard. *Sex Roles, 54*(1/2), 19–26.

Milhausen, R. R., & Herold, E. S. (1999). Does the sexual double standard still exist? Perceptions of university women. *The Journal of Sex Research, 36,* 361–368.

Muehlenhard, C. L., & Quackenbush, D. M. (1998). Sexual Double Standard Scale. In C. M. Davis, W. L. Yarber, R. Bauserman, G. Scherer, & S. L. Davis (Eds.), *Handbook of sexuality-related measures* (pp. 186–188). Thousand Oaks, CA: Sage.

Oliver, M. B., & Hyde, J. S. (1993). Gender differences in sexuality: A meta-analysis. *Psychological Bulletin, 114,* 29–51.

Reiss, I. (1967). *The social context of premartial sexual permissiveness*. New York: Holt, Rinehart, and Winston.

Schleicher, S. S., & Gilbert, L. A. (2005). Heterosexual dating discourses among college students: Is there still a double standard? *Journal of College Student Psychotherapy, 19*(3), 7–23.

Sexualityandu.ca. (February 2011). The sexual double standard: Has it disappeared? Retrieved from http://sexualityandu.ca/uploads/files/DoubleStandardfebruary2011.pdf

Welles, C. E. (2005). Breaking the silence surrounding female adolescent sexual desire. *Women & Therapy, 28*(2), 31–45.

White, E. (2001). *Fast girls: Teenage tribes and the myth of the slut*. New York: Scribner.

ISSUE 9

Do Reality TV Shows Portray Responsible Messages about Teen Pregnancy?

YES: Amy Kramer, from "The REAL Real World: How MTV's *16 and Pregnant* and *Teen Mom* Motivate Young People to Prevent Teen Pregnancy," an original essay for this edition (2011)

NO: Mary Jo Podgurski, from "Till Human Voices Wake Us: The High Personal Cost of Reality Teen Pregnancy Shows," an original essay for this edition (2011)

Learning Outcomes

After reading this issue, you should be able to:

- Explain the role of reality TV shows in educating young people about the "reality" of teenage parenthood.
- Critically analyze the possible negative outcomes associated with a "televised" picture of adolescent pregnancy and parenthood.
- Critique the ethical issues associated with "real teens" participating in reality television shows.

ISSUE SUMMARY

YES: Amy Kramer, director of entertainment media and audience strategy at the National Campaign to Prevent Teen and Unplanned Pregnancy, argues that reality television shows engage teens in considering the consequences of pregnancy before they are ready for it and motivate them to want to prevent it.

NO: Mary Jo Podgurski, founder of the Academy for Adolescent Health, Inc., argues that although such television shows have potential benefits, they inadequately address the issue and may even have a negative impact on those who participate in them.

Television (TV) has evolved during the past five decades. Just 50 years ago, families could gather around one immovable set with a limited number of channels and observe Desi Arnaz and Lucille Ball occupy different beds in the wildly popular sitcom *I Love Lucy*. Considered prudent for TV standards at the time, it would strike many today as an odd family life arrangement for the famous couple—who were married both off the air and in character! Fast forward two decades, and we see Mike and Carol Brady sharing the same bed on *The Brady Bunch*, but neither one apparently very interested in sex (and Mike peculiarly and persistently absorbed in reading *Jonathan Livingston Seagull* in bed).

Today's TV has a much more substantial representation of sexual relationships and themes. Leaps and bounds from then-landmark events such as William Shatner and Nichelle Nichol's "first interracial kiss" on TV's *Star Trek*, Ellen DeGeneres coming out on the air in the mid-1990s, and Kerr Smith and Adam Kaufman's "first gay male kiss" on primetime TV in 2000, many of today's TV programs include overtly sexual messages and a greater range of sexual identities and orientations. Indeed, many shows rely and bank on sexual innuendo, humor, and steamy scenes. Although the representation is greater, the *accuracy* of the portrayals is questionable. Is the infrequent gay character actually a *caricature* manifesting common stereotypes? Is sex so closely and frequently tied to crime as portrayed in various crime dramas? Does the constant use of sexual humor mirror and reinforce society's discomfort with sex? Do sexual scenes in prime time dramas make sex appear seamless—and only for the young and beautiful? (Note the hilarious response to 90-year-old Betty White discussing her "Dusty Muffin" on *Saturday Night Live*.)

Another way in which TV has changed is with the emergence of the so-called "reality TV show" genre. Popularized with the success of MTV's *The Real World* and CBS's *Survivor*, many reality TV shows have followed, so much so that there is even a reality TV show network! Perhaps it was inevitable that the worlds of reality TV and sexuality would collide; new shows addressing specific sexual themes emerged in the last few years. Some shows address issues of pregnancy and family life. In 2007, we were introduced to the family life of parents of octuplets on Discovery Health's *Jon and Kate Plus 8*. Later, MTV introduced the real-life teen-focused pregnancy dramas *16 and Pregnant* and *Teen Mom*, which follow the lives of real young people dealing with teen pregnancy. VH-1 also airs *Dad Camp*, a show in which young men go through "boot camp-style group therapy" in preparing them to take responsibility for fatherhood.

Some sexuality educators, looking for ways to connect with students in authentic, meaningful ways, have embraced the popularity of these shows for their potential as teachable moments. Educators can show a clip to build discussion questions themed around the premise, "What would you do if . . .?"

Other sexuality educators express concern over the reality and impact of the shows. Do the networks do an adequate job of portraying all the hardships of teen pregnancy, or will students perceive the characters as TV stars to be admired and emulated?

In the YES and NO selections, Amy Kramer, the director of entertainment media and audience strategy at The National Campaign to Prevent Teen and Unplanned Pregnancy, describes the positive potential these shows can have as allies in sexuality education. She explains how the shows help motivate young people to want to prevent pregnancy before they are ready to be parents. Mary Jo Podgurski, founder of the Academy for Adolescent Health, Inc., who routinely works with pregnant and parenting teens, explains her reasons for declining the opportunity to work with *16 and Pregnant* when producers approached her. Although noting the potential benefits of such shows, she expresses reservations about the impact the shows might have on the teens who appear on a national stage.

YES ↵

Amy Kramer

The REAL Real World: How MTV's *"16 and Pregnant"* and *"Teen Mom"* Motivate Young People to Prevent Teen Pregnancy

Like it or not, media is a huge influence in the lives of young people. Teens spend more hours each week in front of a screen than they do in a classroom.[1] Many teens know a lot more about their favorite shows than they do about any academic subject, and characters on television are often more familiar than neighbors. What young people learn in sex ed, if they have sex ed at all, is a fraction of what pop culture serves up on a daily basis. Which is why parents and educators alike should be thankful that MTV has emerged as a sort of accidental hero in the campaign against teen pregnancy.

Thanks to the reality shows *16 and Pregnant* and *Teen Mom*, millions of young people are now thinking and talking about teen pregnancy. These shows were developed as nothing more than good entertainment but they have succeeded in ways public health initiatives have not—that is getting young people to stop, pay attention, consider, and discuss what happens when someone becomes a parent before they're ready.

Although we know how to avoid teen pregnancy—get teens to avoid having sex at all or to use contraception carefully and consistently when they do have sex—prevention isn't always as easy as it looks. Getting young people to commit to waiting or protecting themselves is tough. After all, they're kids. The consequences of their actions might not seem as likely as the benefit of the risks. Nearly half of teens admit they've never thought about how a pregnancy would change their lives,[2] and most girls who get pregnant say they never thought it would happen to them. It's no wonder young people don't always take precautions to prevent pregnancy—if you never consider that something might happen to you, or what life would be like if it did, why would you consider taking steps to prevent it?

But *16 and Pregnant* and *Teen Mom* seem to be changing that. These shows are bringing the reality of too-early pregnancy and parenthood smack into the middle of the lives and minds of young people in powerful and important ways. Teens come to these shows on their own and they say they come away with a new appreciation for some of the consequences of unprotected sex. In fact, in a nationally representative poll conducted by The National Campaign to Prevent Teen and Unplanned Pregnancy in 2010, 82% of teens who had seen *16 and Pregnant* said that watching the show "helps teens better understand the challenges of pregnancy and parenthood." Only 17% said the show makes teen pregnancy look glamorous.[3] Already, the fact that young people are tuning in week after week makes what MTV is doing more successful than many PSA campaigns could ever hope to be.

* * *

Rates of teen pregnancy and birth are higher in the United States than in any other industrialized nation. The teen birth rate in the United States is more than three times higher than the rate in Canada, and nearly twice that of the United Kingdom (which has the highest rate in Europe). One out of every ten babies born in the United States is born to a teen mother. Three out of every ten girls in the United States get pregnant before their 20th birthday—750,000 girls each year. That's 2,000 girls getting pregnant *every day*. These numbers—as shocking as they are—actually represent dramatic improvements. In the past two decades, rates of teen pregnancy and childbearing in the United States have dropped by more than one-third.[4]

According to the National Center for Health Statistics, in early-1990s America, 117 out of every 1,000 girls ages 15–19 got pregnant, and 62 out of every 1,000 girls ages 15–19 gave birth. Not even twenty years later those rates are down to 72 per 1,000 teens getting pregnant and 39 per 1,000 teens giving birth. Put another way, teen pregnancy has declined by 38% and teen births are down by one-third. Still too high, but a remarkable improvement on an issue once thought to be intractable.

To what do we owe this astonishing decline in teen pregnancy and teen births? Quite simply and perhaps not surprisingly, it's a combination of less sex and more contraception. According to the National Survey of Family Growth (NSFG), a household-based nationally representative survey conducted periodically by the Centers for Disease Control and Prevention to study families, fertility, and health in the United States, in 1988, 51% of girls and 60% of boys ages 15–19 had ever had sex. In 2006–2008 those numbers had declined to 42% of girls and 43% of boys. Condom use increased during that time as well: In 1988, 31% of girls and 55% of boys who had sex in the past 90 days said they used a condom the last time they had sex. In 2006–2008, those numbers had grown to 53% for girls and 79% for boys. So, for a complicated array of reasons, teens have been doing the only two things you can do to prevent pregnancy: delaying sex and being better about contraception when they do have sex.

It's also important to note that abortions to teens declined as well over that same time period. In 1988, 39% of pregnancies to teens ended in abortion, in 2006, it was 27%, meaning that the decline in teen births was not due to an increase in terminations.[5]

* * *

Consider the following: While rates of sexual activity, pregnancy, birth, and abortion among teens were declining enormously, the media were growing exponentially and becoming coarser and more sexualized. There are hundreds

of channels now and an infinite number of websites. Finding sexually sugges-
tive content on television and explicit content online—or it finding you—is
a fact of life for many young people. If media influence on teens' decisions
about sex is so direct and so negative, why might it be that teen sexual behavior has gotten more responsible at exactly the same time the media and popular culture have become more sexualized? Simply put, the media can't be
solely to blame for teens having sex, or having babies. However, the media can
help write the social script and contribute to viewers' sense of what's normal
and acceptable—and can make sex seem casual, inconsequential, or serious.
In fact, polling for The National Campaign to Prevent Teen and Unplanned
Pregnancy shows that year after year, 8 in 10 teens say they wish the media
showed more consequences of sex (not less sex).[6]

So television alone doesn't cause teen pregnancy, but could it actually
help prevent it? Teens themselves suggest that it can. Most teens (79% of girls,
67% of boys,) say that "when a TV show or character I like deals with teen
pregnancy, it makes me think more about my own risk of becoming pregnant/
causing a pregnancy, and how to avoid it," according to the National Campaign to Prevent Teen and Unplanned Pregnancy.[7] "Thinking about my own
risk" is an important piece of the prevention puzzle.

In that same study from The National Campaign, three-quarters of teens
(76%) and adults (75%) say that what they see in the media about sex, love,
and relationships can be a good way to start conversations about these topics.
Communication between parents and teens about their own views and values
regarding these issues is critical. Children whose parents are clear about the
value of delaying sex are less likely to have intercourse at an early age. Parents
who discuss contraception are also more likely to have children who use contraception when they become sexually active.[8] These conversations can be awkward and intimidating (on both sides), but they are important. So anything that
encourages such talk, or makes it easier to start the conversation, is valuable.

MTV's *16 and Pregnant* is a conversation starter, certainly among teens,
but also within families. In a 2010 study of more than 150 teenagers involved
with Boys & Girls Clubs' after-school programs in a southern state, 40% of
teens who watched *16 and Pregnant* with their group at the Club and then
talked about it in a facilitator-led discussion also talked about it again afterward with a parent. One-third discussed it with a boyfriend/girlfriend. More
than half discussed it with a friend.[9] That 40% went home and talked about
with mom or dad is particularly exciting—because the more opportunities parents have to discuss their own ideas and expectations about pregnancy and
parenting, the better. Teens talking about these shows—articulating their own
thoughts about a teen parent on MTV or a situation depicted in an episode—
brings them one step closer to personalizing it, which is an important step
along the behavior change continuum and the path to prevention.

Educators and leaders in youth-serving organizations are using the MTV
shows as teaching tools. A social worker in the Midwest, who frequently speaks
at schools in both urban and rural areas, has used episodes of *16 and Pregnant*
in her work: "With the boys, we had great discussion about what makes a
man a 'father'." Boys were a little defensive about the portrayal of the teen

dads, but after talking it through, began to empathize more with the young women." A teacher in the South incorporated the series into high school lesson plans: "I use it as part of a unit on teen parenting and parenting readiness to discourage teen pregnancies and to encourage students to wait until they are older and 'ready' before having children. . . . Students enjoy watching the 'real-life' stories of teens and are able to really identify with them." A private special education teacher who works with a teen population especially vulnerable to abusive relationships and pregnancy has also watched the series with students: "The kids were very much engaged because it was something they would watch at home. Some of them had seen the episodes already but looked at them differently once viewed in a group, clinical setting. The conversations were often very serious and enlightening for the students. They were able to put themselves into the girls' shoes and talk about how they would feel, react, respond in each of the situations that came up." Staff at a county juvenile detention center in the Southwest includes the show in teen pregnancy prevention programs and calls it "heavy-hitting and impactful": "They cater to the very media-driven nature of teens today—they aren't dry book material, but rather a great combination of reality and entertainment in a condensed format. . . . A whole year in the life of these teen parents in just an hour of viewing."[10]

* * *

Television shows like MTV's *16 and Pregnant* and *Teen Mom* are created for entertainment purposes with the hope of attracting viewers and keeping them engaged. By that measure, these shows are indisputably successful. Millions of people tune in to each new episode—and the ratings are among the highest on the cable network. Recent episodes have drawn more viewers than even the major broadcast network competition. Public attention to the storylines extends beyond the episodes themselves and into Internet discussion forums, where theories and speculation about the lives depicted on the shows are rampant.

Thanks to these very real reality programs, teen pregnancy is no longer a mysterious topic to millions of young people. Viewers have seen in the most vivid way possible what happens when contraception fails, when babies arrive, when boyfriends leave, when money is tight, when parents are disappointed, and when graduating from high school is impossible. Conversations are happening around dinner tables and in carpools, allowing parents and teens to explore their own opinions and behavior. Parents now have an opportunity to discuss their own values and expectations as they pertain to family formation and romantic responsibility. Friends, siblings, and partners are talking to each other about what happens when young people become parents before they're ready. Maybe they're even talking about how to prevent it from happening in the first place.

Every episode of *16 and Pregnant* includes a scene in which the expectant teenager talks about how she got pregnant. Many weren't using any protection at all, others had problems remembering to take their pills every day, some found out that prescribed antibiotics can interfere with the effectiveness of birth control pills, a few missed their Depo shot appointments, others stopped using a method after a break-up and then never returned to its use after reconciliation, etc. This information is presented honestly and in peer-to-peer terms, inviting viewers to listen and learn, and perhaps explore a type of contraception they hadn't previously known about. On *Teen Mom* viewers see the young parents taking steps to prevent subsequent pregnancies: Cameras have captured the girls' discussions with their doctors about the vaginal ring, IUDs, and other long-acting methods of contraception. Even the "reunion" episodes devote time to discussion about birth control between updates on the babies and the relationship drama.

Watching what happens to girls who "never thought it would happen to them" encourages viewers to assess their own risk. When teenage fans of the shows see time and again that having a baby as an adolescent often means educational goals are abandoned, family relationships erode, financial challenges become insurmountable, and romantic fantasies are dashed, the prospect of early parenthood in their own lives becomes far less attractive. Rosier depictions of teen pregnancy and its consequences from movies, scripted television shows, and daydreams start to look silly in comparison. Seeing that teen pregnancy happens in the lives of girls from every sort of background (even a familiar one) reminds viewers that it could happen to them and it pushes them to figure out how to avoid a similar fate.

Separate from the shows themselves is the tabloid coverage they receive, though it is so pervasive right now it deserves mention here. That the tabloid media have decided to treat these struggling young mothers like celebrities is certainly unfortunate. That the real-life people around the teen mothers have obviously decided to cooperate with the tabloids (in the form of photos, tips, and other information) is sadder still. However, the bulk of even that coverage focuses on the turmoil in their lives. These are young mothers agonizing over money, men, family drama, health issues, the law, and the unending responsibility of parenthood. Followers of this often repugnant news stream may know even more about the chaos that swirls around young parents than do mere viewers of the show. Coverage does not necessarily equal glamorization. Bottom line: If you sit through a full episode, any episode, of *16 and Pregnant* or *Teen Mom*, glamour is totally absent.

* * *

MTV's *16 and Pregnant* and *Teen Mom* are not evidence-based teen pregnancy prevention programs. They aren't a substitute for talented teachers or comprehensive sex ed curricula. These shows aren't more meaningful than traditions of faith. They aren't more important than access to quality healthcare or relevant health information. They aren't more powerful than engaged parents willing to talk openly about tough topics. But teen pregnancy prevention needs to happen everywhere, including in the popular media teenagers love to consume. Everyone who cares about teens, babies, and the next generation of Americans needs to do their part to keep rates of teen pregnancy on a downward trajectory. Families, schools, health care professionals, businesses big and small, religious communities, and yes, the media, all have a role to play. Teen pregnancy prevention requires sustained effort over time by all sectors. This isn't an issue where a vaccine or a cure will lead to a drop in incidence. Even new and better methods of contraception won't do the trick if young people aren't motivated to use them. Making headway on this complex topic requires young people to make better choices over and over again. Any way they can get the message that the teen years are not the appropriate time for parenthood matters.

MTV is doing more than most—even if inadvertently—with *16 and Pregnant* and *Teen Mom*. Millions of young people tune in each week and four out of five viewers say that doing so "helps teens better understand the challenges of pregnancy and parenthood." Anyone who cares about reducing rates of teen pregnancy and teen birth should listen to what teens themselves are saying and tune out the rest.

Footnotes/Sources

1. Kaiser Family Foundation, (2010). *Generation M2: Media in the Lives of 8- to 18-Year-Olds.* http://www.kff.org/entmedia/upload/8010.pdf

2. National Campaign to Prevent Teen and Unplanned Pregnancy, (2007). *With One Voice 2007: America's Adults and Teens Sound Off About Teen Pregnancy.* http://www.thenationalcampaign.org/resources/pdf/pubs/WOV2007_fulltext. pdf

3. National Campaign to Prevent Teen and Unplanned Pregnancy, (2010). *With One Voice 2010: America's Adults and Teens Sound Off About Teen Pregnancy.* http://www.thenationalcampaign.org/resources/pdf/pubs/WOV_2010.pdf

4. National Campaign to Prevent Teen and Unplanned Pregnancy, various fact sheets. http://www.thenationalcampaign.org/resources/fact-sheets.aspx

5. Guttmacher Institute, (2010) *U.S. Teenage Pregnancies, Births and Abortions: National and State Trends and Trends by Race and Ethnicity.* http://www.guttmacher .org/pubs/USTPtrends.pdf

6. National Campaign to Prevent Teen and Unplanned Pregnancy, (2007, 2004, 2002). *With One Voice 2007/2004/2002: America's Adults and Teens Sound Off About Teen Pregnancy.* http://www.thenationalcampaign.org/resources/ pdf/pubs/WOV2007_fulltext.pdf http://www.thenationalcampaign.org/resources/ pdf/pubs/WOV_2004.pdf   http://www.thenationalcampaign.org/resources/pdf/pubs/ WOV_2002.pdf

7. National Campaign to Prevent Teen and Unplanned Pregnancy, (2010). *With One Voice 2010: America's Adults and Teens Sound Off About Teen Pregnancy.* http://www.thenationalcampaign.org/resources/pdf/pubs/WOV_2010.pdf

8. Blum, R. W., & Rinehard, P. M. (1998). *Reducing the Risk: Connections that make a difference in the lives of youth.* Center for Adolescent Health and Development, University of Minnesota. Minneapolis, MN.

9. Suellentrop, K., Brown, J., Ortiz, R. (2010) *Evaluating the Impact of MTV's '16 and Pregnant' on Teen Viewers' Attitudes about Teen Pregnancy,* The National campaign to Prevent Teen and Unplanned Pregnancy, Washington DC. http://www.thenationalcampaign.org/resources/pdf/SS/SS45_16andPregnant.pdf

10. Telephone interviews and email inquiries by the author.

Mary Jo Podgurski

➔ **NO**

Till Human Voices Wake Us: The High Personal Cost of Reality Teen Pregnancy Shows

Having a baby young took away my childhood and there's no way I'll ever get it back.

—16-year-old mother

I wouldn't be alive today if I hadn't had her. She's the reason I'm still alive.

—15-year-old mother

The "voices" above are direct quotes from the video I produced in 1998 entitled *Voices: The Reality of Early Childbearing—Transcending the Myths*. The video was marketed nationally by Injoy Productions until 2009 and is still used in the Lamaze teen program Creativity, Connection and Commitment: Supporting Teens During the Childbearing Year (Lamaze International, 2010). Over the course of a year my team interviewed and videotaped young parents with the intent of using their voices and wisdom as a catalyst for teen pregnancy prevention. I share these voices to underscore a acute need to protect teens. When editing the film, I discovered that the teen mothers consistently wanted to reveal very intimate aspects of their lives. Data including early drinking, number of sexual partners, an incestuous relationship, nonconsensual sex, and sexual experimentation were all freely revealed. I cautioned them to think of the future. Would their children relish such revelations a decade later? Were these details pertinent to their messages? I persisted, and only information that was truly educational and not sensationalized remained in the film. I believed then that 16-year-old parents could provide a priceless service to other teens as peer educators; I continue to believe such teaching is effective and significant. I simply refused to expose the truly personal details of their lives to scrutiny. I was interested in education, not drama.

My staff and I remain in contact with many of the teen parents in *Voices*. More than ten years after its production, they are in 100% agreement: Our careful screening spared their children (now young teens) embarrassment. The young parents I've served have taught me to put a face on the statistics surrounding teen pregnancy; while I will always strive to educate all young people about the risks associated with bearing children young, I am deeply cognizant of the price a teen parent pays when offering his or her life as a lesson plan.

The last 30 years of my life have been dedicated to providing comprehensive sexuality education to young people; our programs reach over 18,000 youth a year in all 14 Washington County school districts. Concurrently I've mentored young parents. I served as a doula (providing labor support) for my first adolescent in the '70s; that young mother became one of many. My staff and I provide educational services and support for nearly 100 pregnant and parenting teens annually. When the MTV program *16 and Pregnant* was in its planning stages, I was approached by the producers and asked to provide teens for the show. I declined after much soul searching. This article explores my rationale for that decision.

Why Rethink Reality TV Using Teen Parents?

As an educator I seek teachable moments in everyday life. I am thrilled to have the opportunity to teach; I consider the field of sexuality education a vocation and am blessed to be in a role where life-affirming information is at my disposal and I am free to convey it to teens. I don't deny the impact reality shows like *16 and Pregnant* and *Teen Mom* (now *Teen Mom 2*) can have on teens. The April 10, 2011, edition of *The New York Times* reports anecdotes of teachers using the shows as a part of curriculum in life skills and parenting classes (Hoffman, 2011, April 10). The National Campaign to Prevent Teen and Unplanned Pregnancy has distributed DVDs and teacher guides on *16 and Pregnant* and these materials seem to be well received by educators. I also am not deterred by fears that these reality shows glamorize teen pregnancy. The Campaign conducted a national telephone poll of young people ages 12 to 19; 82% said that the shows aided their understanding of the reality of teen pregnancy. Only 17% stated that the shows gave pregnancy a glamorous spin (Albert, 2010). In the hands of a skilled educator, the shows' influence can be directed away from glamour to empathic awareness. There is no doubt that there are lessons to be learned from these shows, but at what price?

My primary concern with reality TV shows like *16 and Pregnant* and *Teen Mom* deals with the human cost of these lessons. Young parents, like most young people, are not immune to the appeal of fame. I question a teen's ability to give full permission to a life-changing activity that will reframe his or her identity on a national stage. I am concerned that these young people cannot developmentally grasp the far-reaching implications of their decision to participate. Exploitation is a strong word and I use it with a caveat: I do not believe the shows aim to exploit. I believe that their intentions are good; it is society that removes all boundaries and exposes tender lives to the scrutiny of tabloids and the manipulation of the media. When I filmed *Voices,* I stressed the need for discretion; in 10 or 20 years, I said, would your baby want to be known for the things you now reveal? In a decade and more, how will the babies in

16 and Pregnant view their lives? How will they react to their parents, their families, and their infancy and toddler years exposed for posterity?

I am also troubled by a nagging sense that these shows hope to provide a simple solution to the problems associated with adolescent sexuality in America. There are no Band-aids that can be applied to the multi-faceted, complicated situations that arise when teens are sexually involved, yet our culture consistently seeks an easy fix. I was afforded the privilege of attending an Advocates for Youth European Study Tour in 2001. As part of that experience, I was exposed to European approaches to sexuality education. In contrast to American culture, European culture does not deny the fact that teens need education that helps them achieve sexual health; comprehensive sexuality education is the norm. Are reality TV shows that focus on the lives of young parents yet another simplistic answer that distracts from the need to mandate comprehensive sexuality education to all of our children?

No Band-Aids

Research points to antecedents to early pregnancy and risky behavior; I question whether the teen parents in reality TV shows reflect those antecedents or are selected for their "camera" quality and the appeal of their families' dramas. I also ponder the use of dollars to develop these TV shows instead of creating programs that would target youth that evidence-based data show are at risk.

Dr. Doug Kirby's work (2002, 2007) alone and with colleagues (Kirby, Lepore, & Ryan, 2006) is considered seminal in the areas of comprehensive sexuality education and teen pregnancy antecedents. Research into the role of siblings in early childbearing from East and associates (1996 through 2007) is pivotal to understanding generational teen pregnancy (East, Reyes, & Horn, 2007; Raneri & Constance, 2007). Kristen Luker (1999, 2006) is considered a founding theorist of the sociological and political theories surrounding early childbearing and linked poverty to teen pregnancy as an antecedent, not a consequence of the pregnancy. Young people who are survivors of sexual and physical abuse (Boyer & Fine, 1992) are at risk for early childbearing, as are children in placement or foster care (Kirby, Lepore, & Ryan, 2006) and children living with domestic violence, drug/alcohol abuse or incarcerated parents (Coyle, 2005; Goode & Smith, 2005; East & Khoo, 2005; Jekielek, Moore, Hair, & Scarupa, 2002). Do the teens in reality TV reflect these antecedents?

Research at the University of Arkansas showed that girls are more likely to experience teen pregnancy if they live with internal poverty (measured as a low locus of control and future expectations) as well as external poverty (Young, Turner, Denny, Young, 2004). Internal poverty "describes a person's lack of internal resources, such as attitudes and beliefs that attribute outcomes to individual effort, high future expectations, and few perceived limitations for life options" (Coles, 2005, 10). Certainly internal and external poverty are antecedents in the pregnancies of some reality TV participants; at any time are those teens given guidance that will help them develop the skills and self-efficacy they need to succeed?

Antecedents to teen pregnancy in the United States lead dedicated sexuality educators to explore the need for education that affects behavioral change. Dr. Michael A. Carrera's Children's Aid Society is a well-respected and researched youth development approach that targets the whole child through early intervention (Children's Aid Society, 2010). On a much smaller scale, my team and I have tried to emulate his efforts. Although we remain committed to comprehensive sexuality education, we first approached teen pregnancy prevention through pro-active education in 1999 with the initiation of an early intervention educational mentoring program entitled Educate Children for Healthy Outcomes (ECHO). ECHO provides one-on-one mentoring to young people who have been identified as at risk for engaging in high-risk behavior. Specifically, we target girls in grades 2–12 who have experienced sexual abuse, abandonment issues, placement problems, truancy, early sexual acting out, and/or familial teen pregnancy and provide them with a supportive, consistent, empowering educator and role model. Our advisors educate participants on youth development topics that guide them in making healthy life choices. Our program topics include: decision making, refusal, communication, and problem-solving skills, assertiveness training, anger management, conflict resolution, puberty education, socialization skills, life skills, and prevention education. We strive to empower families to communicate well with each other, help children avoid risky behavior during their adolescent years, and strengthen the family unit as a whole. Only three of the 511 high-risk girls we've mentored since 1999 experienced a pregnancy, and all three of those young women were older than 18 when they gave birth.

Reality shows target all teens without the capacity to address the real and complicated issues that may lead to actual teen pregnancy. Focusing on sexual health for all young people is vital; providing personalized instruction to teens at highest risk, while costly, could maximize positive outcomes.

Voices to Break the Cycle: A Phenomenological Inquiry into Generational Teen Pregnancy

I completed my doctoral work late in life; my dissertation was not only informative but also humbling. I looked at the lived experiences of women who gave birth as adolescents to investigate how these adults might help their pubertal-aged children avoid teenage pregnancy. Research participants gave birth as teens (defined as under 19 years of age) and were parenting their biologic children ages 10–15. A key criteria for selection in the study was generational teen pregnancy; participants in the study came from families with a history of teen pregnancy through at least one generation prior to the former teen mother's birth. The study reinforced the antecedents of poverty, foster placement, sexual abuse, and familial patterns of early childbearing (Podgurski, 2009).

Stigmatizing women who conceive and bear children during adolescence is common in American culture and can lead to social inequalities (McDermott & Graham, 2005). Data reinforces young mothers' continuing need for support while teens (Pai-Espinosa, 2010) and as their lives move forward beyond adolescence (Jutte et al., 2010). The voices of former teen mothers in my study also revealed lives deeply affected by their adolescent pregnancies. Many women expressed a desire to move away from the community in which they gave birth; 30% of the former teen mothers in the study did relocate. One participant in the study stated: "When I got married I left the area. I found it easier to reinvent myself than deal with people who had labeled me as that pregnant girl. My life here is better than it would have been if I'd stayed where I was." Where can a teen parent whose life has been exposed on a national reality TV show relocate?

Adult empathic understanding and compassion for the lives of teen parents was not common among the participants in my study; over 80% described self-reported disrespectful treatment during their births, upon their return to school, or while seeking employment. If, as the National Campaign for Teen and Unplanned Pregnancy reports, 41% of adults report the show *16 and Pregnant* glorifies teen pregnancy (Albert, 2010), will that compassion diminish?

Till Human Voices Wake Us

What is the effect of fame on the young parents made into instant celebrities by reality TV? What do they and their children sacrifice to the altar of TV ratings?

To examine the possible long-term effects of fame and celebrity status on young parents, it is illustrative to look at fame as it is perceived in youth culture. Halpern (2007) surveyed 5th to 8th grade students in Rochester, New York, and found 29% of males and 37% of females selected fame over intelligence as a desired trait. The study participants viewed at least five hours of TV daily; that figure is consistent with other studies of youth screen time (defined as TV and computer time). For example, Burnett and her research team (2008) found that 60% of teens spent an average of 20 hours in screen time, a full third spent closer to 40 hours per week and 7 percent were exposed to greater than 50 hours of viewing time weekly. Perhaps most significantly, Halbern's work showed that 17% of the students felt that celebrities owed their fame to luck, and believed that TV shows had the power to make people famous. If fame is valued over intelligence and luck is perceived as a better indicator of future well-being than industry among average children, would pregnant and parenting teens buy into that delusion as well?

An intense desire for fame can lead reality TV participants to believe that "every reality show is an audition tape for future work" (Wolk, 2010, p. 32). If adults are affected by fame hunger that directs their actions and choices, how can adolescents avoid influence from reality TV fame? The sad drama of Amber, violence, and child custody revealed on the show *Teen Mom* was popular among tabloids, magazines, and advertisers. As an educator I am troubled. Did Amber receive guidance or were her actions considered fodder for higher ratings? One need go no further than the cover story of a current *OK! Magazine* to read that "More Teen Mom Babies!" are planned, including one baby that is being conceived to save a relationship (2011, April 18). The same issue proclaims that Amber and Gary will reunite. What type, if any, relationship skill education do these young "reality celebrities" receive as their lives are broadcast nationally?

Putting a Face on the Numbers

The names of the young parents in the following anecdotes are fiction but their stories are not. Any of these young people would produce high ratings on a reality TV show. Protecting their anonymity is a fundamental educational task. Ethical treatment of pregnant and parenting youth demands that respect is rendered at all times.

Picture Tracy: This lively young woman was a National Honor Society student when she found she was pregnant at the age of 16. Articulate, empathetic, and soft-spoken, she is now a caring social worker completing her master's degree in counseling. Tracy did not disclose her history of sexual assault until the baby she birthed as a teen was four years old; she now uses her life experiences to help her connect with young women at risk for early childbearing.

Nina is a bright, intelligent 27-year-old. Her hair color and body piercings change often but her striking hazel eyes and determined expressions remain constant. She is perceptive, a hard worker, and one of the most resilient young people I've ever known. Nina is also the parent of a 12-year-old. She lived in a series of foster homes while pregnant and parenting; her mother gave birth to her as a 15-year-old and her grandmother had her first pregnancy as a 16-year-old. Nina was born into poverty and continues to struggle to make ends meet. She left school at 17 and hasn't completed the GED (General Equivalency Diploma) she frequently talks about. She often bemoans the fact that her daughter "does without" things she too was denied as a teen. She is proud that she has been her child's only parent and that her daughter has never been in foster care. Like her own parents, Nina fights addiction to alcohol and drugs and has been in and out of rehab several times.

Meet Samantha: Sammy planned her baby to prove that she was heterosexual. Her first kiss at 11 was with a girl; she reacted violently to the fear that she was lesbian in a homophobic family and made a conscious decision to conceive a baby to a man ten years her senior. She was only 12 when her pregnancy was discovered; she didn't tell anyone until she was in her third trimester. She came out when her son was two years old and is currently in a five-year relationship with her female partner.

Jodi gave birth as a tenth grader but only disclosed her step father as her baby's daddy when he starting hitting on her younger sister. Her baby was two years old at the time. Disclosure led to her stepfather's arrest and incarceration for over four years of sexual abuse. Her five siblings were divided and sent to three different foster homes. While Jodi is intermittently proud of her disclosure, she blames herself for the dissolution of her family. She is in a new school district where few know her family's history and is starting to shine academically.

Trevor's father reacted to his girlfriend **Amy's** pregnancy by denying his parentage; within an hour he was homeless at 18. Too old for children and youth services, he wandered from one friend's sofa to another until the single mother of his girlfriend allowed him to move in with her family. The baby is due this spring. Trevor is determined to remain with his partner and states firmly that he will not "be a statistic." His girlfriend's mother, while kind and supportive, is skeptical. She sees Amy's father in Trevor. Although she hopes for the best, she expects him to leave before the baby is two.

It's Not about United States

Those of United States who have committed our lives to supporting, empowering, and educating young people approach this charge in unique ways. I humbly acknowledge that there are many paths to reaching youth. I have learned more from listening to the young people I serve than from any other resource. When I train new staff, I reinforce a common theme: Our work is not about us, it's about the young people. I am reminded of the old admonition: First, Do No Harm. As adults, we are responsible for the needs of all youth, regardless of sexual orientation, gender and gender identity, race, ethnicity, socio-economic status, religion, or level of sexual involvement. I challenge all who serve pregnant and parenting teens to examine the effects adult interventions have upon the lives of these young people and their children, bearing in mind that we do not yet have full knowledge of the long-term implications of national exposure at a time of great vulnerability. When in doubt, protect.

References

Albert, B. (2010). *With one voice 2010: Teens and adults sound off about teen pregnancy*. National Campaign to Prevent Teen and Unplanned Pregnancy. Retrieved from http://www.thenationalcampaign.org/resources/pdf/pubs/WOV_2010 .pdf

Barnett, T., O'Loughlin, J., Sabiston, C., Karp, I., Belanger, M., Van Hulst, A., & Lambert., M. (2008). Teens and screens: The influence of screen time on adiposity in adolescents. *American Journal of Epidemiology, 172*(3), 255–262.

Boyer, D. & Fine, D. (1992). Sexual abuse as a factor in adolescent pregnancy and child maltreatment. *Family Planning Perspectives, 24*(1), 4–11.

Children's Aid Society. (2010). Dr. Michael A. Carrera, Retrieved from http://www .childrensaidsociety.org/carrera-pregnancy-prevention/dr-michael-carrera

Coles, C. (2005). Teen pregnancy and "internal poverty." *Futurist, 38*(7), 10.

Coyle, J. (2005, September). Preventing and reducing violence by at-risk adolescents common elements of empirically researched programs. *Journal of Evidence-Based Social Work, 2*(3/4), 125.

Goode, W. W. & Smith, T. J. (2005). *Building from the ground up: Creating effective programs to mentor children of prisoners*. Philadelphia, PA: Public/Private Ventures.

East, P. L., & Khoo, S. (2005, December). Longitudinal pathways linking family factors and sibling relationship qualities to adolescent substance use and sexual risk behaviors. *Journal of Family Psychology, 19*(4), 571–580.

East, P. L., Reyes, B. T., & Horn, E. J. (2007, June). Association between adolescent pregnancy and a family history of teenage births. *Perspectives on sexual and reproductive health, 39*(2), 108–115.

Halpern, J. (2007). *Fame junkies: The hidden truth behind America's favorite addiction*. New York: Houghton Mifflin Company.

Hoffman, J. (2011, April 10). Fighting teen pregnancy with MTV stars as Exhibit A. *The New York Times,* p. ST 1, 11.

Jekielek, S. M., Moore, K. A., Hair, E. C., & Scarupa, H. J. (2002, February). Mentoring: A promising strategy for youth development. *Child Trends Research Brief.* Retrieved from www.mentoring.ca.gov/pdf/MentoringBrief2002.pdf

Jutte, D., Roos, N., Brownell, M., Briggs, G., MacWilliam, L., & Roos, L. (2010). The ripples of adolescent motherhood: social, educational, and medical outcomes for children of teen and prior teen mothers. *Academic Pediatrics, 10*(5), 293–301.

Karcher, M. (2005). The effects of developmental mentoring and high school mentors' attendance on their younger mentees' self-esteem, social skills and connectedness. *Psychology in the Schools, 42*(1), 65–77. Retrieved from www.adolescentconnectedness.com/media/KarcherPITS_mentoring&conn.pdf

Kirby, D. (2002). Antecedents of adolescent initiation of sex, contraceptive use, and pregnancy. *American Journal of Health Behavior, 26*(6), 473.

Kirby, D. (2007). *Emerging answers: Research findings on programs to reduce teen pregnancy and sexually transmitted diseases.* Washington, DC: National Campaign to Prevent Teen Pregnancy.

Kirby, D., Lepore, G., & Ryan, J. (2006). *Sexual risk and protective factors—Factors affecting teen sexual behavior, pregnancy, childbearing and sexually transmitted disease: Which are important? Which can you change?* Scotts Valley, CA: ETR Associates.

Lamaze International. (2010). *Creativity, connection and commitment: Supporting teens during the childbearing year.* Retrieved from http://www.lamaze.org/ChildbirthEducators/WorkshopsConference/SpecialtyWorkshops/SupportingTeens-DuringtheChildbearingYear/tabid/494/Default.aspx

Luker, K. (1997). *Dubious conceptions: The politics of teen pregnancy.* Boston: Harvard University Press.

Luker, K. (2006). When sex goes to school: Warring views on sex—and sex education since the Sixties. New York: W. W. Norton & Company.

McDermott, E. & Graham, H. (2005). Resilient young mothering: Social inequalities, late modernity and the 'problem' of 'teenage' motherhood. *Journal of Youth Studies, 8,* 59–79.

(2011, April 18) More teen mom babies. *OK! Magazine, 16,* 32–35.

Pai-Espinosa, J. (2010). Young mothers at the margin: Why pregnant teens need support. *Children's Voice, 19*(3), 14–16.

Podgurski, MJ. (2009). *Voices to break the Cycle: A phenomenological inquiry into generational teen pregnancy.* (Doctoral dissertation). University of Phoenix, Phoenix, AZ. Raneri, L., & Constance, M. (2007, March). Social ecological predictors of repeat adolescent pregnancy. *Perspectives on Sexual & Reproductive Health, 39*(1), 39–47.

Young, T., Turner, J., Denny, G., Young, M. (2004, July). Examining external and internal poverty as antecedents of teen pregnancy. *American Journal of Health Behavior, 28*(4), 361–373.

Wolk, J. (2002). Fame factor. *Entertainment Weekly,* (665), 32.

EXPLORING THE ISSUE

Do Reality TV Shows Portray Responsible Messages about Teen Pregnancy?

Critical Thinking and Reflection

1. Reality television shows are growing in popularity among teenage and adult audience. How do issues around informed consent differ for adolescent versus adult participants in these shows?
2. Reality TV shows, such as *Teen Mom* and *16 and Pregnant*, feature the real-life struggles associated with becoming a parent in adolescence. The perspective featured is mainly that of the adolescent parent. What are the possible long-term implications for the children of these parents when they grow up with the legacy of having been a child reality-TV star? How might constructions of private and public life be different for these children?
3. Have you viewed a teen pregnancy reality TV show (or has someone you know viewed one)? What kind of discussion did you have about how realistic or unrealistic the show was? How might such a show impact a young person's sexual decision making?
4. Consider the "copy-cat" effect that may occur when adolescents witness other "real-life teens" becoming "famous" for their participation in reality TV shows. How might young people, with various levels of cognitive reasoning abilities, see these teenage parents as playing glamorous roles and desire to emulate them?

Is There Common Ground?

In the YES selection, Amy Kramer highlights the importance of teen-pregnancy reality TV shows in teen-pregnancy prevention efforts. She comments on the popularity of these shows, and the way they engage teenage viewers. As the MTV programs both entertain and educate, Kramer describes how they spark conversation among young people, how parents can utilize the shows as a starting point for discussion about their values, expectations, and how to prevent an unplanned pregnancy. She notes that the shows depict realistic consequences of sexual activity and teen pregnancy without glamorizing these outcomes.

Mary Jo Podgurski does not dispute the potential benefit that reality TV shows about teen pregnancy can have. She notes their merits and their good intentions. However, she is concerned about the potential for teens who appear on the show to be exploited. She says that, developmentally, teens can't fully "grasp the far-reaching implications of their decision to participate." Noting that young people may be blinded by fame, Podgurski also commented on how participants on the show may be selected for their "camera quality." She also expressed concern about society applying a "band-aid" solution to a complex, multifaceted issue, and that perhaps money would be better invested in programs that actually address the variety of antecedents to early pregnancy and risky behavior.

Is there room for *both* evidence-based, teen-pregnancy prevention programs *and* media-driven shows that open the door for discussion between parents and children? Are teen viewers able to differentiate between the "entertainment" and "education" components of these shows? What are the cautions or concerns associated with the media attention devoted to reality-TV "stars"—especially when they are adolescents?

Additional Resources

Chang, J., & Hopper, J. (2011, February 11). Pregnancy pressure: Is MTV's 'Teen Mom' encouraging pregnancy for fame?" *ABC News*.

Dolgen, L. (2011, May 4). Why I created MTV's '16 and Pregnant,' *CNN.com*.

Stanley, A. (2011, January 21). Motherhood's rough edges fray in reality TV . . . and baby makes reality TV," *The New York Times*.

ISSUE 10

Is Having a Muscular Physique in Adolescence Strictly a "Guy Thing"?

YES: Jennifer Brunet et al., from "Exploring a Model Linking Social Physique Anxiety, Drive for Muscularity, Drive for Thinness and Self-Esteem among Adolescent Boys and Girls," *Body Image* (vol. 7, pp. 137–142, 2010)

NO: Lauren B. Shomaker and Wyndol Furman, from "A Prospective Investigation of Interpersonal Influences on the Pursuit of Muscularity in Late Adolescent Boys and Girls," *Journal of Health Psychology* (vol. 15, no. 3, pp. 391–404, 2010), doi:10.1177/1359105309350514

Learning Outcomes

After reading this issue, you should be able to:

- Demonstrate an understanding of the drives for thinness and muscularity in adolescents.
- Distinguish between the traditional drive for muscularity and a focus on a "fit" or "tone" physical body.
- Identify the role of significant others in creating and perpetuating the drives for thinness and/or muscularity.
- Discuss the research that documents a drive for thinness in females and a drive for muscularity in boys.
- Critically analyze the suggestion that a drive for muscularity has infiltrated the female body-ideal domain.

ISSUE SUMMARY

YES: Jennifer Brunet and Katherine Sabiston, Department of Kinesiology and Physical Education, McGill University, Montreal, Canada, Kim Dorsch of the University of Regina's Faculty of Kinesiology and Health Studies, and Donald McCreary, a psychologist at Brock University, St. Catharines, Canada, examined the drive for muscularity versus thinness across male and female youth.

Consistent with other research, boys in this study reported significantly lower drive for thinness and social physique anxiety than girls, and significantly higher drive for muscularity and self-esteem compared to girls. According to this study, boys focus on being muscular, whereas girls do not.

NO: Lauren B. Shomaker, postdoctoral research scientist and adjunct assistant professor in the Department of Medical and Clinical Psychology, Uniformed Services University of the Health Sciences, and Wyndol Furman, professor of psychology at Denver University, examine various interpersonal influences on adolescent girls' and boys' desire for muscularity and thinness. Results highlight unique ways that the drive for muscularity is permeating the developmental experience of adolescent girls: Both boys and girls reported pressure from mothers and friends to be muscular and both were influenced by this pressure. The ideal physique for both genders seems to have evolved over time to include some degree of both thinness and muscularity for both genders—muscularity may not be "just a guy-thing" anymore.

It is well documented in the literature that many young adolescents are dissatisfied with their bodies. Both adolescent boys and girls participate in dieting and exercise, along with other weight-control behaviors, to achieve their beauty ideal—an ideal that is constructed socially, enforced by the media, and has changed over time. As reviewed in Issue 2, statistics indicate that physical appearance is on the minds of many adolescents and satisfaction with one's body plays a significant role in predicting self-esteem, physical appearance, self-concept, emotional distress, depression, eating disorders, and over psychological adjustment. It has been argued that the media play a powerful role in bombarding girls with images of acceptable and unacceptable body shapes. In magazines, on television, and in film, the ideal female body is tall, thin, and perhaps even prepubescent looking. Research has indicated that as girls progress through adolescence, they become more aware of the sociocultural beauty ideal and as a result, increase their attempts to achieve it (McCabe & Ricciardelli, 2005). Essentially, there is a "drive for thinness" among many adolescent girls. In reality, few girls have the genetic makeup for the ideal body type portrayed in the media. For boys, sociocuulutral and media messages present muscularity as central to manliness (Leit et al., 2001), and research demonstrates that boys have bought into this ideal, with boys reporting muscularity as a common concern in adolescence and beyond (Hargreaves & Tiggermann, 2006). In fact, just as young women engage in both healthy and risky strategies to achieve weight-loss and thinness, so do boys engage in strategies specific to increasing muscle mass and the appearance of muscularity, including the use of supplements, anabolic steroids, and body-building activities, sometimes to their detriment (Cafri et al., 2005; Riccardelli & McCabe,

2003). In fact, research on boys in the United States, Canada, and Australia has found that boys as young as 11 and 12 years old engage in muscle-building behaviors (Ricciardelli & McCabe, 2003; Smolak et al., 2005).

For boys, the ideal male body images in the media present a V-shaped, lean, and muscular build as the body-ideal. Where there is a drive for thinness for females, one could say there is a drive for muscularity among males. However, are these truly mutually exclusive drives or do body image ideals for boys and girls actually converge somewhat? Has muscularity become a shared ideal across genders? The term "muscularity" brings to mind images of a muscle-bound, vein-popping, weight lifter with protruding biceps, large defined pecs, and a washboard stomach; however, when we substitute the word "muscular" with words such as "lean," "fit," and "toned," a different picture emerges. In fact, "lean," "fit," and "toned" are often part of the headlines we see in many magazine articles aimed at both men and women—and adolescent boys and girls! Just a short wait in the check-out line at any grocery store, or a perusal of the magazine racks at any variety store or Chapter's/Indigo highlights the diverse line of magazines that tote these phrases—many of them are magazines geared specifically to females. Even the celebrity magazines such as "In Touch," "Star," and "People" feature headlines and articles that celebrate and critique actors, models, and various performers for their tone and fit bodies, or lack thereof.

If the media are known to have a profound impact on how young people construct their body ideals and evaluate their existing bodies, is it safe to say that "muscularity" (or a tone, fit physique) isn't just a guy-thing anymore? Are adolescent girls as focused on appearing fit and tone and perhaps somewhat muscular as are adolescent boys? Do adolescent boys and girls in fact have more in common regarding shared drives for thinness and for muscularity than was once believed?

In the YES and NO selections, gender differences in body ideals among adolescents are examined. Brunet and colleagues found that their data support previous research—boys endorse a significantly greater drive for muscularity than do girls. They also have a lower drive for thinness and experience less anxiety about their physique than do girls. Although Shomaker and Furman also found evidence that boys endorsed a greater drive for muscularity than girls in their sample, boys and girls did not differ significantly on reported pressure to be muscular. Messages about muscularity as a body-ideal seem to no longer be directed solely at boys.

YES

Jennifer Brunet et al.

Exploring a Model Linking Social Physique Anxiety, Drive for Muscularity, Drive for Thinness and Self-Esteem among Adolescent Boys and Girls

Introduction

Adolescents are faced with a multitude of stressors that impact their mental and physical health (Harter, 1999). One of the main sources of distress during this developmental period is body image, in part due to physical developments associated with puberty, increased social comparisons, and the increased importance of social conformity (Harter, 1999; Levine & Smolak, 2002). Although a great deal of research has been conducted on body image during this developmental period, the focus has primarily been on intrapersonal evaluation. Therefore, less is known regarding the effects of interpersonal appearance evaluation (Cash, 2002). Given that youth are generally concerned with how their body appears to others, it is important to understand the emotional experiences that arise when adolescents are concerned with how others view their physique. The concept of social physique anxiety (SPA) appears well suited to address this need because of its focus on interpersonal evaluation (Hart, Leary, & Rejeski, 1989). Specifically, SPA arises when an individual anticipates that others are or could negatively evaluate his/her physical appearance (Hart et al., 1989). As such, SPA reflects an affective dimension of body image (Bane & McAuley, 1998), and has been consistently related to manifestations of eating disorders within adolescent populations (Crocker, Sabiston, Forrester, Kowalski, Kowalski, & McDonough, 2003; Diehl, Johnson, Rogers, & Petrie, 1998; Hausenblas & Mack, 1999). Since the onset of eating disorder symptoms during adolescence is linked to an increased risk for physical and mental health problems during adulthood (Johnson, Cohen, Kasen, & Brook, 2002), studying SPA among adolescents

Brunet, Jennifer; Sabiston, Catherine M.; Dorsch, Kim D; McCreary, Donald R. From *Body Image*, Vol. 7, No. 2, March 2010, pp. 137–142. Copyright © 2010 by Elsevier Health Sciences. Reprinted by permission.

is particularly important to promote future psychological and physical well-being.

Two outcomes that may be important in the experience of SPA for adolescents include the *drive for muscularity* (McCreary & Sasse, 2000) and the *drive for thinness* (Garner, Olmsted, & Polivy, 1983). These drives reflect the pursuit of cultural and gender explicit body shape ideals whereby males in Western cultures tend to desire a more muscular physique, whereas females desire a thinner physique (Martin, Kliber, Hodges Kulinna, & Fahlman, 2006; McCreary & Sasse, 2000; Smolak & Murnen, 2008). Accordingly, when boys and girls become distressed that others will evaluate them negatively, because their body falls short of the idealized physique, their attitudes and behaviours associated with a desire to become more muscular or thin may increase in order to reach this standard.

A number of cross-sectional studies have provided evidence that the drives for thinness and muscularity have similar relationships with SPA. For example, McCreary and colleagues (Duggan & McCreary, 2004; McCreary & Saucier, 2009) and Martin et al. (2006) found a significant positive relationship between SPA and drive for muscularity for boys and girls, Thompson and Chad (2002) and Diehl et al. (1998) found that girls with higher SPA reported higher levels of drive for thinness. While these findings suggest the relationships between SPA and both drives may be similar for adolescent boys and girls, the drive for muscularity and the drive for thinness have rarely been studied concurrently in adolescent boys and girls. Thus, the main purpose of the current study focused on addressing this gap in the literature by examining whether SPA influences adolescents' drive for muscularity and drive for thinness in both genders.

In addition to investigating potential outcomes of SPA, it is important to consider factors that may influence body-related affective experiences. Researchers have demonstrated that individuals who report lower levels of self-esteem are generally more concerned with being evaluated negatively than individuals reporting higher levels of self-esteem (Davison & McCabe, 2006; Diehl et al., 1998). These findings suggest that lower self-esteem may lead to increased experiences of SPA. From this perspective, the hypothesized sequence proposed in the current study was that self-esteem would influence SPA, which in turn would influence adolescents' drive for thinness and/or drive for muscularity. . . .

A second objective of this study was to examine mean level gender differences in self-esteem, SPA, drive for thinness and drive for muscularity, as well as gender differences in the relationships between these constructs. This was deemed important since previous research has found that girls and boys may face different levels of specific body image affect and outcomes. In particular, researchers have documented that females experience greater levels of SPA (Brunet & Sabiston, 2009; Hart et al., 1989; Kowalski, Mack, Crocker, Niefer, & Fleming, 2006), higher drive for thinness (Anderson & Bulik, 2004; McCreary, Sasse, Saucier, & Dorsch, 2004), and lower drive for muscularity (McCreary & Sasse, 2000; Smolak & Murnen, 2008) compared to males. . . .

Method

Participants and Procedures

. . . [P]articipants were recruited into a convenience sample from four high schools in Regina, Saskatchewan, Canada. These schools were located in small semi-rural towns and a suburb of a major metropolis. Participants were recruited by random selection of classes. During regular classes, an initial information session was held where the purposes and procedures of the study were explained. Parental (for those under 18 years old) and participant consent forms were distributed at this time. One week later, participants returned the consent forms and completed the questionnaires. A total of 329 (n_{male} = 190; n_{female} = 139) high school students (99% response rate) were included in the analyses. The average age of the participants was 15.4 years (SD = 1.11), and they ranged between 13 and 19 years.

Measures

. . . *Self-Esteem.* The Rosenberg Self-Esteem Scale (SE; Rosenberg, 1965) was used to assess self-esteem. It is a measure of global self-esteem that consists of 10 statements [e.g., "I feel . . ."] . . .

Social Physique Anxiety. The 9-item truncated Social Physique Anxiety Scale (SPAS; Martin, Rejeski, Leary, McAuley, & Bane, 1997) was used to measure SPA. The SPAS measures the anxiety an individual experiences as a result of interpersonal judgments and evaluations focused on their physiques. . . . An example item from this scale is "In the presence of others, I feel apprehensive about my physique/figure." . . .

Drive for Muscularity. To assess adolescents' attitudes and behaviours associated with a desire to become more muscular, the Drive for Muscularity Scale (DMS; McCreary & Sasse, 2000) was used. The DMS is a 15-item questionnaire that asks respondents to rate the extent to which each item applies to them . . . [(e.g.,] "I think that I would look better if I gained 10 pounds in bulk."[)] . . .

Drive for thinness. The Eating Attitudes Test (EAT; Garner, Olmsted, Bohr, & Garfinkel, 1982) was used as a proxy for drive for thinness. Although the EAT assesses individual's attitudes and behaviours associated with a desire to become thinner, rather than drive for thinness per se, . . . researchers have previously used the EAT as an indication of the degree to which participants experienced a drive for thinness (Duggan & McCreary, 2004; Garfinkel, Coldbloom, Davis, Olmsted, Garner, & Halmi, 1992). As such, the EAT was used in the current study as a proxy measure to assess adolescents' attitudes and behaviours associated with a desire to become thinner.

Respondents were asked to rate the extent to which each of the 26 items applied to them. . . . The EAT can be divided into three factors: dieting (13 items; e.g., "I am preoccupied with a desire to be thinner"), food preoccupation (6 items; e.g., "I feel that food controls my life"), and oral control (7 items; e.g., "Other people think I am too thin"). . . .

Results

. . . On average, the [data] suggest that both boys and girls reported low to moderate levels of SPA, low levels of the drive for muscularity and drive for thinness, and moderate levels of self-esteem.

. . . [I]t was observed that boys reported significantly lower drive for thinness . . . and SPA . . . and higher drive for muscularity and self-esteem compared to girls. . . .

Structural model. The hypothesized model was a good fitting model for the total sample and gender sub-samples (see Fig. 1) . . .

Discussion

The objectives of this study were to (1) examine mean level and relationship gender differences in self-esteem, SPA, drive for thinness and drive for muscularity, and (2) test a model where self-esteem influences SPA, which in turn influences drive for muscularity and drive for thinness in a sample of adolescent boys and girls. Overall, this study provided partial support for [differences] . . . across gender. This is essential in light of the importance placed on gender comparisons in the field of body image. Specifically, the relationship between SPA and the drive for thinness differed significantly for boys and girls, and there were differences in the amount of variance accounted for in the models for boys and girls. In addition, findings provided adequate support for the proposed sequence, where SPA was a significant correlate of the drive for muscularity and thinness in adolescent boys and girls. This adds to the literature since the majority of existing studies have focused on these two factors separately.

Although gender has received a great deal of attention in the body image literature, the focus has primarily been on examining mean level differences. There has been little regard to the assessment of gender differences at the

Figure 1

Structural Equation Model Representing the Relationships Between Self-Esteem, Social Physique Anxiety, Drive for Thinness, and Drive for Muscularity. . . . SPA = Social Physique Anxiety; DMS = Drive for Muscularity; DT = Drive for Thinness. . . .

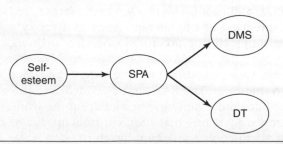

measurement level, which ultimately ensures reliable comparisons between boys and girls (Byrne et al., 1989). The current study found that the factor structure and parameter estimates of the scales assessing SPA, self-esteem, drive for muscularity, and drive for thinness were invariant across gender. [This basically means that the scales work the same way across genders, so we can make meaningful comparisons across males and females using data from these scales.] The findings herein suggest that mean comparisons across gender were feasible in the current study. Subsequently, in examining mean level differences, results revealed several significant gender differences, and this was consistent with the hypothesis. In particular, adolescent boys reported higher drive for muscularity, whereas girls reported higher drive for thinness. The findings compare favorably to past research (McCabe & Ricciardelli, 2001; McCreary et al., 2004; Smolak & Murnen, 2008), demonstrating that females wish to be thinner and males wish to be more muscular. The results also support previous findings showing that adolescent girls experience higher levels of SPA (Brunet & Sabiston, 2009; Kowalski et al., 2006) and have lower self-esteem (see Kling, Hyde, Showers, & Buswell, 1999) than boys. In line with general sociocultural theoretical perspectives (Levine & Smolak, 2002; Muth & Cash, 1997; Smolak & Thompson, 2008; Thompson, Heinberg, Altabe, & Tantleff-Dunn, 1999; Tiggemann, 2002), these differences may reflect: (a) heightened societal pressures for females to be thin and males to be muscular, (b) a greater importance placed on appearance by women, and/or (c) girls gain body fat during puberty which counters the societal thin female ideal figure. The widespread findings that boys have notably lower SPA and higher self-esteem compared to girls does not mean that males are unaffected by the negative affective and behavioural consequences of body image. In fact, existing findings (Martin et al., 2006; Olivardia, Pope, Borowiecki, & Cohane, 2004), coupled with the current results, suggest that adolescent boys report body image concerns and related outcomes. Thus, it is important to continue to study the unique body image issues in both genders, and develop strategies aimed at increasing self-esteem and decreasing SPA since adolescence is a key period for the formation of self-esteem (Kling et al., 1999) and body image dissatisfaction in girls and boys (Levine & Smolak, 2002).

. . . [T]he hypothesized model was an appropriate conceptualization of the relationships among self-esteem, SPA, drive for muscularity, and drive for thinness. As hypothesized, and consistent with past research (Davison & McCabe, 2006; Diehl et al., 1998), adolescents who reported higher levels of self-esteem reported lower levels of SPA. In support of empirical research (Diehl et al., 1998; McCreary & Saucier, 2009; Thompson & Chad, 2002), there was also a positive relationship between SPA and both drives (i.e., muscularity and thinness). Interestingly, the effect of SPA on drive for thinness and the variance explained in drive for thinness was much greater for girls than it was for boys. While this reflects the pattern of gender differences in the body image literature, additional work is warranted to identify what factors may explain the drive for thinness in boys. . . .

In spite of the limitations, this study provides an important initial understanding of the relationships among self-esteem, SPA, drive for muscularity, and drive for thinness in a sample of adolescent boys and girls. The findings of the current study suggest there are similarities in the antecedents of the drives. This highlights the value of including both muscularity and thinness in future research directed at adolescents. Researchers are encouraged to make this line of research a main agenda for youth health given the links between the constructs studied here and unhealthy behaviours (e.g., dieting, fasting, binging, purging, use of anabolic steroids; McCreary & Sasse, 2000), which often develop during adolescence (Reijonen, Pratt, Patel, & Greydanus, 2003). From a practical perspective, key steps can be taken for the consideration of intervention strategies for adolescent body image. As the results have indicated, the focus should be primarily on decreasing SPA given the direct link to drives for muscularity and thinness, which may be targeted by promoting self-esteem.

References

Anderson, C. B., & Bulik, C. M. (2004). Gender differences in compensatory behaviors, weight and shape salience, and drive for thinness. *Eating Behaviors, 5,* 1–11.

Bane, S., & McAuley, E. (1998). Body image and exercise. In J. L. Duda (Ed.), *Advances in sport and exercise psychology measurement* (pp. 311–324). Morgantown, WV: Fitness Information Technology.

Cash, T. F. (2002). Beyond traits: Assessing body image states. In T. F. Cash & T. Pruzinsky (Eds.), *Body image: A handbook of theory, research, and clinical practice* (pp. 163–170). New York, NY: Guilford Press.

Crocker, P. R. E., Sabiston, C. M., Forrester, N. C., Kowalski, N. C., Kowalski, K. C., & McDonough, M. (2003). Predicting change in physical activity, dietary restraint, and physique anxiety in adolescent girls: Examining covariance in physical self-perceptions. *Canadian Journal of Public Health, 94,* 332–337.

Davison, T. E., & McCabe, M. P. (2006). Adolescent body image and psychosocial functioning. *The Journal of Social Psychology, 146,* 15–30.

Duggan, S. L., & McCreary, D. R. (2004). Body image, eating disorders and drive for muscularity in gay and heterosexual men: The influence of media images. *Journal of Homosexuality, 47,* 45–58.

Garfinkel, P. E. Coldbloom, D., Davis, R., Olmsted, M. P., Garner, D. M., & Halmi, K. A. (1992). Body dissatisfaction in bulimia nervosa: Relationship to weight and shape concerns and psychological functioning. *International Journal of Eating Disorders, 11,* 151–161.

Garner, D. M., Olmsted, M. P., Bohr, Y., & Garfinkel, P. (1982). The Eating Attitudes Test: Psychometric features and clinical correlates. *Psychological Medicine, 12,* 871–878.

Harter, S. (1999). *The construction of the self: A developmental perspective.* New York, NY: Guilford Press.

Hausenblas, H. A., & Mack, D. E. (1999). Social physique anxiety and eating disorder correlates among female athletic and nonathletic. *Journal of Sport Behavior, 22,* 502–513.

Johnson, J. G., Cohen, P., Kasen, S., & Brook, J. S. (2002). Eating disorders during adolescence and the risk for physical and mental disorders during early adulthood. *Archives of General Psychiatry, 59,* 545–552.

Kling, K. C., Hyde, J. S., Showers, C. J., & Buswell, B. N. (1999). Gender differences in self-esteem: A meta-analysis. *Psychological Bulletin, 125,* 470–500.

Kowalski, K. C., Mack, D. E., Crocker, P. R. E., Niefer, C. B., & Fleming, T. (2006). Coping with social physique anxiety. *Journal of Adolescent Health, 39,* 275.e9–275.e16.

Levine, M. P., & Smolak, L. (2002). Body image development in adolescence. In T. F. Cash & T. Pruzinsky (Eds.), *Body image: A handbook of theory, research, and clinical practice* (pp. 74–82). New York, NY: Guilford Press.

Martin, J. J., Kliber, A., Hodges Kulinna, P., & Fahlman, M. (2006). Social physique anxiety and muscularity and appearance cognitions in college men. *Sex Roles, 55,* 151–158.

Martin, K. A., Rejeski, W. J., Leary, M. R., McAuley, E., & Bane, S. (1997). Is Social Physique Anxiety Scale really multidimensional? Conceptual and statistical arguments for a unidimensional model. *Journal of Sport and Exercise Psychology, 19,* 359–367.

McCabe, M. P., & Ricciardelli, L. A. (2001). Parent, peer, and media influences on body image and strategies to both increase and decrease body size among adolescent boys and girls. *Adolescence, 36,* 225–240.

Muth, J. L., & Cash, T. F. (1997). Body-image attitudes: What difference does gender make? *Journal of Applied Social Psychology, 27,* 1438–1452.

Olivardia, R., Pope, H. G., Borowiecki, J., & Cohane, G. H. (2004). Biceps and body image: The relationship between muscularity and self-esteem, depression, and eating disorder symptoms. *Psychology of Men and Masculinity, 5,* 112–120.

Reijonen, J. H., Pratt, H. D., Patel, D. R., & Greydanus, D. E. (2003). Eating disorders in adolescent population: An overview. *Journal of Adolescent Research, 18,* 209–222.

Rosenberg, M. (1965). *Society and the adolescent self-image.* Princetown, NJ: Princetown University Press.

Smolak, L., & Murnen, S. K. (2008). Drive for leanness: Assessment and relationship to gender, gender role and objectification. *Body Image, 5,* 251–260.

Thompson, A. M., & Chad, K. E. (2002). The relationship of social physique anxiety to risk for developing an eating disorder in young females. *Journal of Adolescent Health, 31,* 183–189.

Thompson, J. K., Heinberg, L. J., Altabe, M., & Tantieff-Dunn, S. (1999). *Exacting beauty: Theory, assessment, and treatment of body image disturbance.* Washington, DC: American Psychological Association.

Tiggemann, M. (2002). Media influences on body image development. In T. F. Cash & T. Pruzinsky (Eds.), *Body image: A handbook of theory, research, and clinical practice* (pp. 91–98). New York, NY: Guilford Press.

Lauren B. Shomaker
and Wyndol Furman

→ **NO**

A Prospective Investigation of Interpersonal Influences on the Pursuit of Muscularity in Late Adolescent Boys and Girls

The impact of sociocultural pressure to be thin on girls' and women's body image dissatisfaction and disordered eating is well documented (Thompson, Heinberg, Altabe, & Tantleff-Dunn, 1999). In the last decade, growing attention has been paid to what may be parallel sociocultural pressure to be muscular among adolescent boys (Thompson & Cafri, 2007). The ideal masculine body has been described as an Adonis, V-shape physique characterized by a muscular and lean build (Pope et al. 2000), which has become progressively more muscular over the last several decades (Pope, Olivardia, Gruber, & Borowiecki, 1999). Moreover, although the feminine ideal is primarily centered on thinness, a substantial number of adolescent girls also desire a more muscular, toned, and athletic physique (Lenart, Goldberg, Bailey, Dallal, & Koff, 1995; Olivardia, 2004). Such developments have ushered in a wave of descriptive research on the pursuit of muscularity.

Pursuit of muscularity incorporates a wide range of attitudes and behaviors pertaining to increasing muscle mass and size (Ricciardelli & McCabe, 2004). Pursuit of muscularity has been posited to include weight lifting or strength training in moderation, as well as excessive bodybuilding and steroid use in the extreme. In its excessive forms, pursuit of muscularity is associated with negative health consequences (Cafri, van den Berg, & Thompson, 2006). For instance, compared to other athletic activities (e.g., running or martial arts), competitive body building among adult males is associated with lower self-esteem, poorer body image satisfaction, greater symptoms of disordered eating, and more frequent steroid use (Blouin & Goldfield, 1995). The use of steroids or dietary supplements, in and of itself, is associated with many harmful physical health consequences, especially for adolescents (Cafri et al. 2005). An extreme manifestation of the pursuit of muscularity is muscle dysmorphia, which is characterized by a pathological concern with building muscle that interferes with physical health and socio-emotional functioning (Cafri, Olivardia, & Thompson, 2008; Pope, Gruber, Choi, Olivardia, & Phillips, 1997).

For the purpose of the current paper, the term pursuit of muscularity is used to encompass the entire range of behaviors driven at pursuing muscularity as well as concerns or preoccupation with muscularity.

An estimated 21–47 percent of boys in adolescence report pursuing greater muscularity (Krowchuck, Kreiter, Woods, Sinal, & DuRant, 1998; Middleman, Vazquez, & DuRant, 1998; Neumark-Sztainer, Story, Falkner, Beuhring, & Resnick, 1999; Ricciardelli & McCabe, 2003). As many as 91% of late adolescent college males reportedly desire a more muscular build, whereas few to none want to be less muscular (Jacobi & Cash, 1994). Adolescent boys report pursuing muscularity more commonly than adolescent girls, whereas girls more frequently desire weight loss and endorse greater symptoms of disordered eating than boys (McCabe, Ricciardelli, & Finemore, 2002; Vartanian, Giant, & Passino, 2001). Nonetheless, adolescent girls perceive sociocultural pressure to increase body muscle tone (McCabe et al. 2002; Vartanian et al. 2001), and at least 6–9 percent of adolescent girls report pursuing greater muscularity (Krowchuck et al. 1998; Middleman et al. 1998; Neumark-Sztainer et al. 1999; Ricciardelli & McCabe, 2003). Further, adolescent girls' and boys' use of behavioral strategies to gain muscle and to lose weight may be modestly interrelated (Ricciardelli & McCabe, 2001, 2002). For instance, adolescent boys may cycle between unhealthy dieting to lose adiposity and behaviors intended to build muscle mass and size (Cafri et al. 2005). Likewise, adolescent girls engaged in disordered eating behaviors may simultaneously pursue weight loss and increased muscle tone (McCabe et al. 2002; Ricciardelli & McCabe, 2001; Vartanian et al. 2001).

From an interpersonal theoretical perspective, messages relayed from mothers, fathers, friends, and romantic partners about appearance are hypothesized to play an important role in body image attitudes and behaviors aimed at changing appearance (Tantleff-Dunn & Gokee, 2004; Thompson & Cafri, 2007). Perceived interpersonal pressure to be thin from parents, friends, and romantic partners has been demonstrated to be a risk factor for early to late adolescent girls' and boys' disordered eating (Field et al. 2001; Shomaker & Furman, 2009; Stice, 1998, 2002; Stice & Agras, 1998; Stice, Mazotti, Krebs, & Martin, 1998; McKnight Investigators, 2003). Interpersonal factors are expected to affect pursuit of muscularity among adolescent boys and girls as well (Ricciardelli & McCabe, 2004; Thompson & Cafri, 2007), but as of yet, such effects have not been extensively documented.

Perceived pressure to be muscular from mothers, fathers, and friends has been associated cross-sectionally with early and middle adolescent boys' and girls' pursuit of muscularity (McCabe & Ricciardelli, 2003; Smolak, Murnen, & Thompson, 2005). Also, perceptions of both positive and negative comments about appearance are related to late adolescent college males' pursuit of muscularity (Nowell & Ricciardelli, 2008; Vartanian et al. 2001). With regard to associations over time, early and middle adolescent boys' perceptions of pressure to gain muscle from parents and peers predicted increases in strategies to gain muscle over an 8-month period (Ricciardelli & McCabe, 2003). Over a 16-month period, perceived pressure from parents and friends to increase muscle predicted changes in strategies to increase muscle among early to middle adolescent boys as well as among girls (McCabe & Ricciardelli, 2005). Additional prospective investigations of interpersonal influences on adolescents' pursuit of muscularity are warranted. In particular, no longitudinal work to date has examined interpersonal influences on late adolescents, an age-span during which pursuit of muscularity may become increasingly pronounced (McCabe & Ricciardelli, 2001). During the developmental period of late adolescence, relationships with romantic partners and with friends are very salient (Furman & Buhrmester, 1992), although parents remain important relationships as well (Furman & Buhrmester, 1992).

Furthermore, existing findings have almost exclusively been based on assessments of adolescents' perceptions of interpersonal pressures. Yet, it is key that assessments of interpersonal pressures begin to incorporate others' as well as adolescents' reports of these pressures (Ricciardelli & McCabe, 2007). The use of any single reporter's perspective is not as strong psychometrically and presents potential problems of bias and method variance (Schwarz, Barton-Henry, & Pruzinsky, 1985). Adolescents' as well as their mothers' and friends' reports of criticism or pressure to be thin correlate cross-sectionally and prospectively with adolescents' disordered eating symptoms (Baker, Whisman, & Brownell, 2000; Pike & Rodin, 1991; Shomaker & Furman, 2009). To our knowledge, no study has incorporated adolescents' and others' reports of pressure to be muscular.

Although there has been increased attention in recent years to the pursuit of muscularity, there has been limited research on the sociocultural factors that may shape these behaviors and attitudes (Thompson & Cafri, 2007). The current project aimed to expand prior literature on the pursuit of muscularity in a number of important directions. Foremost, our understanding of interpersonal influences on the pursuit of muscularity in adolescence is limited by a paucity of longitudinal data. Thus, the primary objective of the current study was to examine the influence of interpersonal pressure to be muscular on changes over the course of one year. We extended prior longitudinal work by examining such relations in late adolescence (ages 16–19 years). This period has received relatively little attention, yet it is a period during which the pursuit of muscularity may be most pronounced (McCabe & Ricciardelli, 2001; Ricciardelli & McCabe, 2004). We hypothesized that interpersonal pressure to be muscular from mothers, fathers, friends, and romantic partners would predict changes in the pursuit of muscularity over the course of a year. Most of the descriptions of the pursuit of muscularity focus on boys. We included both girls and boys in the present study. We expected that boys would report greater pursuit of muscularity than girls, but we predicted that interpersonal pressure to he muscular would relate to pursuit of muscularity similarly for both genders. We also extended prior research by including mothers' and friends' reports of pressure to be muscular toward the focal adolescent so as to incorporate multiple perspectives on interpersonal pressures. Finally, we tested whether interpersonal pressure to be muscular predicted changes in the pursuit of muscularity after accounting for a number of variables potentially associated with the pursuit of muscularity (i.e., body mass index, pubertal timing, disordered eating symptoms, and physical appearance satisfaction)

(Ricciardelli & McCabe, 2004). By controlling for such factors, we were able to rule out a number of possible alternative explanations of the findings we obtained.

Methods

Participants

Participants were drawn from a community sample of 200 adolescents (50% female) involved in an ongoing longitudinal study of interpersonal relationship influences on adolescent psychosocial adjustment and psycho-pathology. The sample was originally recruited when adolescents were in the 10th grade. The participants were recruited from a diverse range of neighbor-hoods and schools in a large Western metropolitan area. They were selected such that the sample was representative of the ethnic distribution of the United States. . . .

The present paper used two time points of data spaced 12 months apart. At the first time point used in the present study almost all participants were in the 12th grade. . . . One hundred ninety-nine of the 200 originally recruited adolescents participated (99 boys, 100 girls). At the second time point twelve months later, 196 of the original 200 adolescents participated (98 boys, 98 girls).

Mothers and a close friend nominated by the focal adolescent also were asked to participate in the study. One-hundred seventy-four mothers partici-pated at the first time point of the present study; 168 mothers participated at the second time point. . . .

Additionally, 159 close friends . . . participated in the study at the first time point; 141 friends participated in the study at the second time point. Most were same-sex friends (65.5%) rather than other-sex friends (34.5%). . . .

Procedure

Letters and brochures describing the project were sent to families residing in a diverse range of neighborhoods . . . in a large Western metropolitan area. . . . Adolescents who were interested in the project were scheduled for a lab visit. At this assessment, adolescents were administered interviews and participated in videotaped discussions with mothers or peers as part of the larger project. Parti-cipants completed multiple questionnaires at home at their convenience. . . .

Measures

Demographics—Adolescents reported their height and weight, which were used to compute body mass index (BMI = kg/m^2). Self-reports of these varia-bles have been demonstrated to highly correlate with objective measurements (Elgar & Stewart, 2008; Goodman, Hinden, & Khandelwal, 2000). Mothers' reports of adolescents' pubertal timing were used to assess when participants had gone through puberty. Specifically, mothers were asked what grade her daughter experienced her first menstrual period, or what grade her son went through a growth spurt when he increased rapidly in height. Mothers' reports of their children's pubertal status have been shown to highly correlate with physician ratings (Brooks-Gunn, Warren, Rosso, & Gargiulo, 1987). . . .

Interpersonal pressure to be muscular—Adolescents completed the pressure to be muscular scales of the Pressure to be Physically Attractive Questionnaire (PPAQ) (Shomaker & Furman, 2009). This questionnaire assessed interpersonal pressures about physical appearance from a mother, father, close friend, or romantic partner. The pressure to be muscular scales tapped adolescents' perceptions of how often each person compliments and encourages being more muscular. There were three items for each of the four relationship scales (9 items total). . . . An example of an item was, "This person compliments me when I look built and toned." Items were averaged for each relationship. . . . There was good temporal stability over one year for adolescents' reports of mother pressure to be muscular . . . , father pressure to be muscular . . . , friend pressure to be muscular . . . , and romantic partner pressure to be muscular. . . .

Mothers and close friends completed parallel versions of the PPAQ in which they reported on how often they pressured the focal adolescent to be more muscular. An example of an item was, "I compliment my daughter (or friend) when she or he looks built and toned." In order to make use of both sources, mothers' and adolescents' reports were averaged to create a cross-informant mother pressure to be muscular composite; adolescents' and friends' reports were averaged to create a cross-informant friend pressure to be muscular composite. Reports of father pressure to be muscular and romantic partner pressure to be muscular were based on the participants' reports alone.

Physical appearance satisfaction—Adolescents reported how dissatisfied or satisfied they were with their physical appearance on the physical appearance scale of the Adolescent Self-Perception Profile (Harter, 1988). This scale contained five items that assessed participants' feelings of dissatisfaction or satisfaction with their overall physical appearance. . . .

Additionally, mothers and friends completed parallel versions of the physical appearance scale (Harter, 1988) to assess their perceptions of the target adolescent's satisfaction with her or his physical appearance. . . .

Disordered eating—Adolescents completed the Eating Attitudes Test-26 (EAT-26) to assess their symptoms of disordered eating. . . . [T]hey reported how often 26 statements about disordered eating attitudes and behaviors were true for themselves. The dieting scale measured dieting behaviors and drive for thinness (13 items), [t]he bulimia and food preoccupation scale tapped binge eating and vomiting (6 items), [and] [t]he oral control scale assessed perceived social pressure to gain weight (7 items). . . .

Pursuit of muscularity—Pursuit of muscularity was measured with a questionnaire developed by the authors to assess both behavioral and attitudinal components of muscularity. Designed to be consistent with the format of the EAT-26, the measure contained 8 items. . . .

Questions on the drive for muscularity scale (4 items) assessed behaviors and cognitions pertaining to becoming more muscular: a) "I exercise and lift weights to gain muscle mass;" b) "I take dietary supplements to build muscle;" c) "I think about my weight-lifting and training routine;" and d) "I am concerned about not being muscular enough." Questions on the preoccupation with muscularity scale (3 items) assessed excessive concerns about wanting to become more muscular: a) "I feel that my weight-lifting and training routine controls my life;" b) "I find myself preoccupied with building muscle;" and c) "I read bodybuilding magazines." One item ("I take steroids to help build muscle") . . . was not considered in the present paper. . . .

Results

Descriptive Information and Correlations

Boys perceived more pressure to be muscular from romantic partners than girls. In contrast, boys and girls did not differ on self- or other-reports of pressure to be muscular in relationships with mothers or friends. Compared to boys, girls scored higher on all disordered eating symptoms, whereas boys had higher scores than girls on drive for muscularity and preoccupation with muscularity at both Time 1 and Time 2.

Measures of interpersonal pressure to be muscular from mothers, fathers, friends, and romantic partners were moderately interrelated. Interpersonal pressures were correlated with adolescents' pursuit of muscularity at both time points. These associations were generally consistent across the different reporters. Both drive for muscularity and preoccupation with muscularity were moderately consistent over the course of the year.

Confirmatory Factor Analysis and Structural Equation Modeling

. . . [We] investigate[d] whether Time 1 interpersonal pressure to be muscular predicted pursuit of muscularity at Time 2 after controlling for Time 1 pursuit of muscularity, physical appearance satisfaction, disordered eating, BMI, and puberty. . . . [G]ender did not significantly moderate the primary effects of interest in the model. . . . Within Time 1, interpersonal pressure to be muscular was associated with the pursuit of muscularity. . . . Time 1 BMI, appearance satisfaction, pubertal timing, and disordered eating were not significantly related to Time 1 pursuit of muscularity. After accounting for Time 1 pursuit of muscularity and the other variables in the model, Time 1 interpersonal pressure to be muscular predicted significant variations in adolescents' pursuit of muscularity at Time 2. . . . Pursuit of muscularity at Time 1 was also predictive of pursuit of muscularity at Time 2. . . . No other variable significantly predicted changes in the pursuit of muscularity over time. . . .

Adolescents' own reports of interpersonal pressure to be muscular from mothers . . . , fathers . . . , friends . . . , and romantic partners . . . were associated with pursuit of muscularity within Time 1. Further, adolescents' reports of pressure to be muscular from mothers . . . and romantic partners . . . , but not fathers or friends, predicted pursuit of muscularity at Time 2. Mothers' reports of pressure to be muscular toward their children at Time 1 were associated with pursuit of muscularity at both Time 1 . . . and at Time 2. . . . Friends' reports of pressure to be muscular toward focal adolescents were associated with pursuit of muscularity at Time 1 . . . , but did not predict pursuit of muscularity at Time 2.

Discussion

Few prospective studies have examined interpersonal risk factors for the pursuit of muscularity. Thus, the current study aimed to investigate whether interpersonal pressure to be muscular predicted changes in late adolescent boys' and girls' pursuit of muscularity over the course of one year. As hypothesized, interpersonal pressure to be muscular was not only associated concurrently with pursuit of muscularity, but predicted changes in the pursuit of muscularity over time. The current findings are consistent with prior cross-sectional (McCabe & Ricciardelli, 2003; Smolak et al. 2005) and longitudinal (McCabe & Ricciardelli, 2005; Ricciardelli & McCabe, 2003) studies of early to middle adolescents. The results suggest that interpersonal influences play an important role in the pursuit of muscularity even as adolescents approach emerging adulthood. In concert with theoretical perspectives on social pressure to be thin and disordered eating (Stice, 2002; Thompson et al. 1999), close relationships such as those with parents, friends, and romantic partners appear to have significant influences on adolescents' attitudes and behaviors related to gaining muscle as well.

Compared to girls, boys reported more pursuit of muscularity and also perceived greater pressure to be muscular from romantic relationships. Yet, it was interesting that late adolescent boys and girls appeared to receive similar pressure to be muscular from relationships with mothers, fathers, and friends. Moreover, gender did not moderate the effect of interpersonal pressure on the pursuit of muscularity, indicating that interpersonal pressure to be muscular affected changes in late adolescent girls' as well as boys' pursuit of muscularity. This pattern of results underscores that adolescent boys and girls both may be affected by interpersonal messages that encourage gaining muscularity. Indeed, a significant number of adolescent girls as well as boys desire a more muscular and toned body, and in contemporary culture, girls as well as boys are encouraged to be athletic and fit (Lenart et al. 1995; Olivardia, 2004). In a large community sample of adolescents, as many as 12% of boys and 8% of girls reported using products to improve appearance, muscle mass, and strength (Field et al. 2005). Hence, as other researchers have proposed (McCabe & Ricciardelli, 2005), although there are important gender differences in the extent of muscularity or leanness desired, both may be components of the sociocultural ideal physiques for both genders. Indeed, according to contemporary perspectives on the female ideal physique, the rise in adolescent girls' involvement in athletics over the last several decades has been accompanied by girls' greater desire to be lean and toned, with visible muscle (Gruber, 2007). In the current sample, disordered eating symptoms and preoccupation with muscularity showed some overlap, supporting the import of considering both behaviors in understanding adolescent girls' and boys' body image and attempts to change their appearance. . . .

References

Baker C. W., Whisman M. A., Brownell K. D. Studying intergenerational transmission of eating attitudes and behaviors: methodological and conceptual questions. *Health Psychology* 2000;19:376–381. [PubMed: 10907656]

Blouin A. G., Goldfield G. S. Body image and steroid use in male bodybuilders. *International Journal of Eating Disorders* 1995;18:159–165. [PubMed: 7581418]

Brooks-Gunn J., Warren M. P., Rosso J., Gargiulo J. Validity of self-report measures of girls' pubertal status. *Child Development* 1987;58:829–841. [PubMed: 3608653]

Cafri G., Olivardia R., Thompson J. K. Symptom characteristics and psychiatric comorbidity among males with muscle dysmorphia. *Comprehensive Psychiatry* 2008;49:374–379. [PubMed: 18555058]

Cafri G., Thompson J. K., Ricciardelli L., McCabe M., Smolak L., Yesalis C. Pursuit of the muscular ideal: Physical and psychological consequences and putative risk factors. *Clinical Psychology Review* 2005;25:215–239. [PubMed: 15642647]

Cafri G., van den Berg P., Thompson J. K. Pursuit of muscularity in adolescent boys: Relations among biopsychosocial variables and clinical outcomes. *Journal of Clinical Child and Adolescent Psychology* 2006;35:283–291. [PubMed: 16597224]

Elgar F. J., Stewart J. M. Validity of self-report screening for overweight and obesity. Evidence from the Canadian Community Health Survey. *Canadian Journal of Public Health* 2008;99:423–427.

Field A. E., Austin S. B., Camargo C. A. J.r., Taylor C. B., Striegel-Moore R. H., Loud K. J., et al. Exposure to the mass media, body shape concerns, and use of supplements to improve weight and shape among male and female adolescents. *Pediatrics* 2005;116:214–220.

Field A. E., Camargo C. A. Jr, Taylor C. B., Berkey C. S., Roberts S. B., Colditz, G. A. Peer, parent, and media influences on the development of weight concerns and frequent dieting among preadolescent and adolescent girls and boys. *Pediatrics* 2001;107:54–60. [PubMed: 11134434]

Furman W., Burhmester D. Age and sex differences in perceptions of networks of personal relationships. *Child Development* 1992;63:103–115. [PubMed: 1551320]

Goodman E, Hinden B. R., Khandelwal S. Accuracy of teen and parental reports of obesity and body mass index. *Pediatrics* 2000;106:52–58. [PubMed: 10878149]

Gruber, A. J. A more muscular female body ideal. In: Thompson, J. K.; Cafri, G., editors. *The muscular ideal: Psychological, social, and medical perspectives.* Washington, DC: American Psychological Association; 2007. p. 217–234.

Harter, S. *Manual for the Adolescent Self-Perception Profile.* University of Denver; 1988.

Jacobi L., Cash T. F. In pursuit of the perfect appearance: Discrepancies among self-ideal percepts of multiple physical attributes. *Journal of Applied Social Psychology* 1994;24:379–396.

Krowchuck D. P., Kreiter S. R., Woods C. R., Sinal S. H., DuRant R. H. *Disordered eating. Archives of Pediatrics & Adolescent Medicine* 1998;152:884–889. [PubMed: 9743034]

Lenart E. B., Goldberg J. P., Bailey S. M., Dallal G. E., Koff E. Current and ideal physique choices in exercising and nonexercising college women from a pilot athletic image scale. *Perceptual and Motor Skills* 1995;81:831–848. [PubMed: 8668441]

McCabe M. P., Ricciardelli L. A. Parent, peer, and media influences on body image and strategies to both increase and decrease body size among adolescent boys and girls. *Adolescence* 2001;36:225–240. [PubMed: 11572302]

McCabe M. P., Ricciardelli L. A. Sociocultural influences on body image and body changes among adolescent boys and girls. *Journal of Social Psychology* 2003;143:5–26. [PubMed: 12617344]

McCabe M. P., Ricciardelli L. A. A prospective study of pressures from parents, peers, and the media on extreme weight change behaviors among adolescent boys and girls. *Behaviour Research and Therapy* 2005;43:653–668. [PubMed: 15865919]

McCabe M. P., Ricciardelli L. A., Finemore J. The role of puberty, media and popularity with peers on strategies to increase weight, decrease weight and increase muscle tone among adolescent boys and girls. *Journal of Psychosomatic Research* 2002;52:145–153. [PubMed: 11897233]

McKnight Investigators. Risk factors for the onset of eating disorders in adolescent girls: results of the McKnight longitudinal risk factor study. *American Journal of Psychiatry* 2003;160:248–254. [PubMed: 12562570]

Middleman A. B., Vazquez l, DuRant R. H. Eating patterns, physical activity, and attempts to change weight among adolescents. *Journal of Adolescent Health* 1998;22:37–42 [PubMed: 9436065]

Neumark-Sztainer D., Story M., Falkner N. H., Beuhring T., Resnick M. D. Sociodemographic and personal characteristics of adolescents engaged in weight loss and weight/muscle gain behaviors: Who is doing what? *Preventive Medicine: An International Journal Devoted to Practice and Theory* 1999;28:40–50.

Nowell C., Ricciardelli L. A. Appearance-based comments, body dissatisfaction and drive for muscularity in males. *Body Image* 2008;5:337–345. [PubMed: 18723414]

Olivardia, R. Body image and muscularity. In: Cash, T. F.; Pruzinsky, T., editors. *Body image: A handbook of theory, research, and clinical practice.* New York: Guilford Press; 2004. p. 210–218.

Pike K. M., Rodin J. Mothers, daughters, and disordered eating. *Journal of Abnormal Psychology* 1991;100:198–204. [PubMed: 2040771]

Pope H. G. Jr, Gruber A. J., Choi P, Olivardia R., Phillips K. A. Muscle dysmorphia. An underrecognized form of body dysmorphic disorder. *Psychosomatics* 1997;38:548–557. [PubMed: 9427852]

Pope H. G. Jr, Gruber A. J., Mangweth B., Bureau B., deCol C., Jouvent R., Hudson J. I. Body image perception among men in three countries. *American Journal of Psychiatry* 2000;157:1297–1301. [PubMed: 10910794]

Pope H. G. Jr, Olivardia R., Gruber A., Borowiecki J. Evolving ideals of male body image as seen through action toys. *International Journal of Eating Disorders* 1999;26:65–72. [PubMed: 10349585]

Ricciardelli L. A., McCabe M. P. Self-esteem and negative affect as moderators of sociocultural influences on body dissatisfaction, strategies to decrease weight, and strategies to increase muscles among adolescent boys and girls. *Sex Roles* 2001;44:189–207.

Ricciardelli L. A., McCabe M. P. Psychometric evaluation of the Body Change Inventory: An assessment instrument for adolescent boys and girls. *Eating Behaviors* 2002;3:45–59. [PubMed: 15001019]

Ricciardelli L. A., McCabe M. P. A longitudinal analysis of the role of psychosocial factors in predicting body change strategies among adolescent boys. *Sex Roles* 2003;48:349–360.

Ricciardelli L. A., McCabe M. P. A. biopsychosocial model of disordered eating and the pursuit of muscularity in adolescent boys. *Psychological Bulletin* 2004;130:179–205. [PubMed: 14979769]

Ricciardelli, L. A.; McCabe, M. P. Pursuit of muscularity among adolescents. In: Thompson, J. K.; Cafri, G., editors. *The muscular ideal: Psychological, social, and medical perspectives.* Washington, DC: American Psychological Association; 2007. p. 199–216.

Schwarz J. C., Barton-Henry M. L., Pruzinsky T. Assessing child-rearing behaviors: A comparison of ratings made by mother, father, child, and sibling on the CRPBL. *Child Development* 1985;56:462–479. [PubMed: 3987419]

Shomaker L. B., Furman W. Interpersonal influences on late adolescent girls' and boys' disordered eating. *Eating Behaviors* 2009;10:97–106. [PubMed: 19447351]

Smolak L., Murnen S. K., Thompson J. K. Sociocultural influences and muscle-building in adolescent boys. *Psychology of Men & Masculinity* 2005;6:227–239.

Stice E., Modeling of eating pathology and social reinforcement of the thin-ideal predict onset of bulimic symptoms. *Behaviour Research and Therapy* 1998;36:931–944. [PubMed: 9714944]

Stice E., Risk and maintenance factors for eating pathology: A meta-analytic review. *Psychological Bulletin* 2002;128:825–848. [PubMed: 12206196]

Stice E., Agras W. S. Predicting onset and cessation of bulimic behaviors during adolescence: A. longitudinal grouping analysis. *Behavior Therapy* 1998;29:257–276.

Stice E., Mazotti L., Krebs M., Martin S. Predictors of adolescent dieting behaviors: A. longitudinal study. *Psychology of Addictive Behaviors* 1998;12:195–205.

Tantleff-Dunn, S.; Gokee, J. L. Interpersonal influences on body image development, In: Cash, T.F.; Pruzinsky, T., editors. *Body image: A. handbook of theory, research, and clinical practice.* New York: Guilford Press; 2004. p. 108–116.

Thompson, J. K.; Cafri, G. *The muscular ideal: Psychological, social, and medical perspectives.* Washington, DC: American Psychological Association; 2007.

Thompson, J. K.; Heinberg, L. J.; Altabe, M.; Tantleff-Dunn, S. *Exacting beauty: Theory, assessment, and treatment of body image disturbance.* Washington, D.C: American Psychological Association; 1999.

Vartanian L. R., Giant C. L., Passino R. M. Ally McBeal vs. Arnold Schwarzenegger: Comparing mass media, interpersonal feedback and gender as predictors of satisfaction with body thinness and muscularity. *Social Behavior and Personality* 2001;29:711–724.

EXPLORING THE ISSUE

Is Having a Muscular Physique in Adolescence Strictly a "Guy Thing"?

Critical Thinking and Reflection

1. The YES and NO selections confirm established gender differences in adolescents' focus on muscularity. How can these differences be understood in terms of gender socialization and gender scripts for males and females?
2. The NO selection draws attention to similarities in the pressure boys and girls receive from family and peers to be muscular. What does this study tell us about the impact of "compliments" and "suggestions" related to body shape/size on adolescents' ideal body beliefs? How might one explain the power that messages from friends and family have on shaping adolescents' perceptions and behaviors concerning their bodies?
3. Boys and girls both report feeling pressure from parents and friends to be muscular. Consider your own experiences with muscularity discourses. Was being muscular or toned a topic of conversation among your peer group in high school or in university? What sorts of messages did you hear about the importance of muscularity in "beautiful" bodies?
4. The 2012 Olympics in London featured historic accomplishments in women's performance across domains. Given the technological advances of today's society, we were inundated with photos and videos of the Olympic games and athletes' performances.

   a. What did you notice about the visual portrayal of the athletes (action shots, uniforms, interviews, etc.)? Were there differences in how male and female athletes were portrayed?
   b. Given the accessibility of images of male and female athletes' muscular bodies, what impact do you foresee this media frenzy having on society's drive for muscularity in the months and years to come?

Is There Common Ground?

"Men are from Mars and women are from Venus"—are adolescent boys and girls *that* different when it comes to desiring a muscular or fit/toned body? Generally speaking, the YES and NO selections agree that adolescent boys and girls are different in their endorsement of a muscular body ideal. Boys reported a greater desire to be muscular than did girls. This fits well with the sociocultural images of ideal male and female bodies—male bodies are big and muscular; female bodies are tall and thin . . . although, more recently, "beautiful" female bodies are being portrayed as more muscular (or tone/fit) than they have been in the past. These body ideal messages about fit bodies seem to be infiltrating the relationships adolescents have with significant others (such as peers and parents). In the NO selection, when compared to girls, boys reported greater interest in being muscular, and more pressure from romantic partners to be muscular; however, boys and girls were more similar than different in the pressure they felt from parents and peers to be muscular. Muscularity is clearly on adolescent girls' radar.

Future research should examine the role that media play in shaping people's (adolescents, parents, and friends) views of muscularity in relation to the ideal male and female physique. How do teen and women's magazines, with their tips on how to "lose belly fat," get "toned abs," or "Michelle Obama arms," impact this shift in muscularity concerns for young women? Do media play a role in the pressure young girls experience from parents and friends to become more muscular?

Body ideals for men and women have changed over time. Women's bodies have become thinner, and men's bodies have become more muscular. It seems that another sociocultural shift in body ideals is currently underway. The research suggests that the ideal physique for both genders is beginning overlap in the domains of thinness (lean bodies) and muscularity (tone/fit physiques). Muscularity may not be "just a guy-thing" anymore!

Additional Resources

Carlson Jones, D., Bain, N., & King, S. (2008). Weight and muscularity concerns as longitudinal predictors of body image among early adolescent boys: A test of the dual pathways model. *Body Image, 5*, 195–204.

Daniels, E. A. (2012). Sexy versus strong: What girls and women think of female athletes. *Journal of Applied Developmental Psychology, 33*, 79–90.

Jones, D. C., & Crawford, J. K. (2005). Adolescent boys and body image: Weight and muscularity concerns as dual pathways to body dissatisfaction. *Journal of Youth and Adolescence, 34*, 629–636.

Kyrejto, J. W., Mosewich, A. D., Kowalski, K. C., Mack, D. E., & Crocker, P. R. E. (2008). Men's and women's drive for muscularity: Gender differences and cognitive and behavioral correlates. *International Journal of Sport and Exercise Psychology, 6*(1), 69–84. doi: 10.1080/1612197X.2008.9671855

McCabe, M. P., & Ricciardelli, L. A. (2001). Body image and body change techniques among young adolescent boys. *European Eating Disorders Review, 9*, 335–347.

McCabe, M. P., & Ricciardelli, L. A. (2004). A longitudinal study of pubertal timing and extreme body change behaviors among adolescent boys and girls. *Adolescence, 39*, 145–166.

McCabe, M. P., & Ricciardelli, L. A. (2005). A prospective study of pressures from parents, peers, and the media on extreme weight change behaviors among adolescent boys and girls. *Behaviour Research and Therapy, 43*, 653–668.

Ricciardelli, L. A., & McCabe, M. P. (2003). Sociocultural and individual influences on muscle gain and weight loss strategies among adolescent boys and girls. *Psychology in the Schools, 40*, 209–224.

Smolak, L., & Stein, J. A. (2010). A longitudinal investigation of gender role and muscle-building in adolescent boys. *Sex Roles, 63*, 738–746.

Tomori, M., & Rus-Makovec, M. (2000). Eating behaviour, depression, and self-esteem in high school students. *Journal of Adolescent Health, 26*, 361–367.

Internet References . . .

Child Trends: Social Science Research

Child Trends is an independent, nonpartisan research center focusing on children and youth with the goals of improving outcomes for children.

www.childtrends.org

Sexuality and You

As one of North America's oldest national obstetrics and gynecology organizations, they provide credible and current information and education on sexual health. This section focuses on same-sex parenting and family life.

www.sexualityandu.ca/parents/sexual-orientation/same-sex-parenting-and-family-life

eNotAlone

eNotAlone provides information, book reviews, and advice on a variety of relationship issues including cyber relationships, love relationships of teen, the impact of divorce and relationship dissolution on children, and parenting teens.

http://enotalone.com

Kids Help Phone

A well-known and valuable Canadian bilingual telephone service and website resource for youth.

www.kidshelpphone.ca

Focus Adolescent Services

An independent entity, not affiliated with any private, public or governmental organization, nor under the direction of any outside individual or groups, provides comprehensive information and support for teen and family issues.

www.focusas.com

Advocates for Youth

A youth-serving organization that creates programs and advocates for policies that provide information on being productive and sexual health.

www.advocatesforyouth.org

Resource Center for Adolescent Pregnancy Prevention

This private nonprofit health education promotion website contains practical tools and information designed to help reduce sexual risk-taking behaviors.

www.etr.org/recapp

Peer and Family Relationships

*S*ocial relationships are critical in the growth, development, and behavior of adolescents. There are many different types of relationships that are important for teens, including family ties, friendships, and romantic relationships. The following four issues address some aspect of the social relations of youth and the impact that these relationships have on adolescent development.

- Does Having Same-Sex Parents Negatively Impact Children?
- Does Dating in Early Adolescence Impede Developmental Adjustment?
- Should Parents Supervise Alcohol Use by or Provide Alcohol to Adolescents?
- Should Parental Consent Be Required for Adolescents Seeking Abortion?

ISSUE 11

Does Having Same-Sex Parents Negatively Impact Children?

YES: **Michelle Cretella,** from *American College of Pediatricians* (2012), www.acpeds.org/Homosexual-Parenting-Is-It-Time-For-Change.html

NO: **Charlotte J. Patterson,** from "Children of Lesbian and Gay Parents: Psychology, Law, and Policy," *American Psychologist* (vol. 64, pp. 727–736, 2009)

Learning Outcomes

After reading this issue, you should be able to:

- List the areas of contention about same-sex parenting impacts on children.
- Form an opinion on same-sex parenting.
- Consider that and understand how the same research pieces can be used to support diametrically opposite viewpoints.

ISSUE SUMMARY

YES: Michelle Cretella, a physician writing a position statement for The American College of Pediatricians, argues that having biological, heterosexual parents is the best situation for the development of children. She criticizes the same-sex parenting outcome literature as being fraught with design flaws and she argues that homosexual lifestyles pose dangers to children.

NO: Charlotte J. Patterson, a developmental psychologist who is one of the leading scholars in same-sex parenting research, reviews the empirical research regarding the similarities and differences between children reared by homosexual parents and those by heterosexual parents. She concludes that there is no negative impact on children by being raised by a sexual-minority parent.

The issue of same-sex couples, marriage, and relationship rights seems to be integrally linked with same-sex parenting. Often, arguments for marriage move into arguments about same-sex parenting and vice-versa. Same-sex couples' marriage rights set the stage for same-sex parenting. From a worldwide comparative perspective, Canada and the United States are very similar in their culture, practices, and laws. Yet, Canada and the United States diverge greatly with respect to attitudes, policies, and laws regarding people with same-sex sexual orientations and their families.

In 1995, a court decision ruled that sexual orientation was to be considered within the anti-discrimination clause of the Canadian constitution (Canadian Charter of Rights and Freedoms) and sexual orientation was added to the Canadian Human Rights Act. In the late 1990s, Canada recognized that same-sex common-law couples were being treated differently than opposite-sex common-law couples, and this was ruled as unconstitutional. An omnibus bill was passed federally regarding social benefits and obligations of same-sex couples that affected 68 federal statutes. In July 2005, same-sex marriage became legal in all of Canada due to federal legislation. In both 2001 and 2006, Statistics Canada included questions about same-sex families in the census. Same-sex couples represented 0.6 percent of all couples in Canada— which is similar to other countries (e.g., New Zealand, Australia) including the United States (Milan et al., 2007). In Canada in 2006, about 9 percent of same-sex couples had children listed on the census meaning that over 4,000 same-sex households had children living in them. Female same-sex couples (16.3 percent) were more likely than male same-sex couples (2.9 percent) to have children living with them (Milan et al., 2007).

Births and adoption are the purview of the province in Canada. In 1995, an Ontario judge invalidated a portion of the *Child and Family Services Act* that prohibited lesbian couples from legally adopting their partner's children. In 2001, another Ontario law changed, which allowed two partners of the same sex to adopt jointly. In 2007, it became possible to list a same-sex parent on the birth registration form (i.e., birth certificate) of a child in Ontario. Currently, most Canadian provinces have legislation allowing gay and lesbian couples (and singles) to adopt. However, some adoption agencies may have their own policies and regulations surrounding religion, race, age, marital status, and sexual orientation.

In the United States, in contrast, same-sex marriage is not recognized federally, and only six states and the District of Columbia allow same-sex marriage (at the time of this writing). Many states explicitly prohibit same-sex marriage and/or same-sex civil unions. It is a much more contentious rights issue in the United States compared to Canada. Regardless, there are lots of LGBT people in the United States; almost 9 million Americans or 3.8 percent of the U.S. population identify as LGBT, although even more (11 percent) report some same-sex attraction (Gates, 2011a). Different surveys in the United States suggest that many LGB people have children; between one-third and one-half of queer women report having children, while between 17 and 19 percent of queer men report having children (these include couples, single parents, adult children, noncustodial parents). Around 16–19 percent of same-sex couples in the United States have children living with them currently (Gates, 2011b), which is much higher than the 9 percent reported in the Canadian census. These U.S. children are at a distinct legal disadvantage (Baumle & Compton, 2011; Gates, 2011b) compared to the Canadian children where the same-sex parents have legal parental recognition and obligations.

Adoption by same-sex couples is also a contentious and litigious issue in the United States. For example, in 2010, Florida's ban on homosexual people adopting children was overturned in the Florida Appeals court because it was unconstitutional (CNN Wire Staff, 2010). There are states that ban same-sex adoption, restrict same-sex foster care, ban or restrict same-sex second parent adoption or same-sex step-parent adoption, and restrict use of reproductive technology by same-sex couples. The Family Equality Council maintains maps summarizing the state of this legislation (Family Equality Council, 2012; also see Baumle & Compton, 2010). Baumle and Compton (2010) found that certain types of laws had different impacts on same-sex families; they found that in states that had same-sex facilitative laws, same-sex couples were more likely to have children in their home compared to states that did not have favorable same-sex parenting laws. Also, in states that had anti-second parent adoption laws, same-sex couples were less likely to have children in their household. These laws do have some impact on same-sex family formation and parenting.

Societal attitudes become reflected in laws, and laws influence societal attitudes. Those in the United States are markedly less positive toward same-sex marriage compared to Canadians. An Angus Reid poll, conducted in August 2009, found that 61 percent of Canadians agreed with the statement "Same-sex couples should continue to be allowed to legally marry" compared to 33 percent of U.S. respondents who agreed with the statement "Same-sex couples should be allowed to legally marry." The British were in between Canada and the U.S. with 41 percent agreeing with the statement "Same-sex couples should be allowed to legally marry." Canada and the United States are more similar, however, in their attitudes toward same-sex adoption. Miall and March (2005) compared their results of a random sample of Canadians to U.S. poll results; just under half of both samples found same-sex couples acceptable as adoptive parental candidates. There was a gender difference with male respondents being more negative toward same-sex couples' adopting. In reviewing the scientific literature, the research has demonstrated that significant objections exist toward adoption by same-sex couples (McCutcheon, 2011). What are the bases of these objections?

A set of beliefs exist that are used as the rationale for assessing same-sex couples as less acceptable than traditional couples. These beliefs can be loosely grouped into the following: (1) a negative impact on the children including personal psychosexual (e.g., inappropriate gender role, gender identity, homosexual or bisexual sexual orientation), interpersonal (e.g., teasing, rejection from peers), and family relations' difficulties (e.g., lack of attachment to parents) and (2) objections about parenting abilities (e.g., parenting skills, adult relationship quality). People will often admit that same-sex adoption is better than a child being without any parents but that heterosexual couples would be preferable (Dent, 2011). Biological ties are also cited as a factor leading to superiority of heterosexual parents. The preference of one type of parent over another without scientific rationale would be considered an -ism (like sexism or racism); the preference of heterosexual couples over homosexual couples might be best termed heterosexism rather than homophobia or homonegativity, per se (Szymanski & Moffitt, 2012). This preference for heterosexual over homosexual couples as adoptive parents is evident in adoption research (e.g., Miall & March, 2005; Rye & Meaney, 2010).

As you read the YES and NO selections, consider the perspectives and the backgrounds of the authors and their underlying position on the issue of sexual orientation. In 2009, Charlotte Patterson was the recipient of an award for Distinguished Contributions to Research in Public Policy by the American Psychological Association (APA) for her work that supports same-sex parenting. She was a committee member responsible for crafting the APA policies "Marriage of Same-Sex Couples" and "Same-Sex Relationships and Families"; Patterson herself is a member of a same-sex couple who is raising three children (APA, 2009). She clearly has pro-gay leanings.

Michelle Cretella is a pediatrician who is a member of the American College of Pediatricians; she has held executive positions in this organization including vice president and the chair of the sexuality committee. The American College of Pediatricians is a relatively new organization—founded in 2002 with a mission that "recognize[s] the basic father-mother family unit, within the context of marriage, to be the optimal setting for childhood development. . . ." This organization is conservative in relation to sexual issues (e.g., it may be characterized as pro-life/anti-abortion, in favor of parental notification laws (see Issue 14), prefers abstinence-based sex education approaches, is anti–same-sex marriage and anti–same-sex parental adoption). Cretella has written critically about the topic of sexual fisting, gay marriage, and homosexuality, generally (e.g., Cretella & Sutton, 2010; Goldberg & Cretella, 2009). However, her writings are not cited in various scientific databases (e.g., MEDLINE, PsycINFO) but rather tend to be featured on websites that hold negative positions toward LGBT issues such as same-sex marriage or same-sex parenting (e.g., NARTH, The Pro-Family Resource Center of Abiding Truth Ministries). It would be fair to characterize Cretella and the American College of Pediatricians as having anti-gay leanings.

The perspectives of the two authors influence how they interpret studies of same-sex parenting and how the arguments presented in their writing are supported.

Terminology

LGBT is an umbrella term representing lesbian, gay, bisexual, transsexual, and transgender. Sometimes, this is written as LGBTQ and also can include two-spirited, queer, and/or questioning. The word queer has often been used as a pejorative insult to refer to LGBTQ people. Many LGBT people have "taken back the word"—adopted its use in a positive fashion so that it may lose its pejorative meaning.

YES ⤶   Michelle Cretella

Homosexual Parenting: Is it Time for Change?

Biology Matters

Over thirty years of research confirms that children fare best when reared by their two biological parents in a loving low conflict marriage. Children navigate developmental stages more easily, are more solid in their gender identity, perform better academically, have fewer emotional disorders, and become better functioning adults when reared within their natural family.[1,2,3,4,5,6,7] This is, in part, because biology contributes to parent-child bonding.[9]

While single parenthood, adoption, and remarriage are each loving responses to failure of the natural family, children reared in these settings face unique challenges.[8,9] Single parents face greater financial challenges and time constraints. Consequently, children of single mothers often spend significantly less time with both biological parents. Children within stepfamilies can experience difficulties forging a relationship with the stepparent, and be faced with a sense of divided loyalties. Every adopted child must come to terms with a sense of rejection from her biologic parents and a longing to know her roots. While not insurmountable, these challenges can have a negative impact on a child's development. Clearly, apart from rare situations, depriving a child of one or both biologic parents, as same-sex parenting requires in every case, is unhealthy.

Children Need a Mother and a Father

There are significant innate differences between male and female that are mediated by genes and hormones and go well beyond basic anatomy. These biochemical differences are evident in the development of male and female brain anatomy, psyche, and even learning styles.[10] Consequently, mothers and fathers parent differently and make unique contributions to the overall development of the child.[10,11,12] Psychological theory of child development has always recognized the critical role that mothers play in the healthy development of children. More recent research reveals that when fathers are absent, children suffer as well. Girls without fathers perform more poorly in school, are more likely to be sexually active and become pregnant as teenagers. Boys without fathers have higher rates of delinquency, violence, and aggression.[11,12]

Gender-linked differences in child rearing styles between parents are complementary and protective for children. Erik Erikson was among the first to note that mother-love and father-love are qualitatively different. Mothers are nurturing, expressive, and more unconditional in their love for their children. Father-love, by contrast, often comes with certain expectations of achievement.[12] Subsequent research has consistently revealed that parenting is most effective when it is both highly expressive and highly demanding. This approach to parenting "provides children with a kind of communion characterized by inclusiveness and connectedness, as well as the drive for independence and individuality [which is] virtually impossible for a man or woman alone to combine effectively."[12]

Gender differences are also reflected in the way mothers and fathers use touch with their children. Mothers frequently soothe, calm, and comfort with touch. Fathers are more likely to use touch to stimulate or excite their children during play. Mothers tend to engage with children on their level providing opportunities for children to take charge and proceed at their own pace. As fathers engage in rough and tumble play, they take on a teaching role like that of a coach. Roughhousing between fathers and sons is associated with the development of greater self-control in adolescent boys.[12]

Gender-linked diversity is also observed in parental approaches to discipline. "The disciplinary approaches of fathers tend toward firmness, relying on rules and principles. The approach of mothers tends toward more responsiveness, involving more bargaining, more adjustment toward the child's mood and context, and is more often based on an intuitive understanding of the child's needs and emotions of the moment."[12] Consequently, being reared by a mother and a father helps sons and daughters moderate their own gender-linked inclinations. Boys generally embrace reason over emotion, rules over relationships, risk-taking over caution, and standards over compassion. Girls generally place greater emphasis on emotional ties, relationships, caution, and compassion. Over time opposite-sexed parents demonstrate to their children the value of opposing tendencies.

Research on Same-Sex Parenting

Studies that appear to indicate neutral to favorable child outcomes from same-sex parenting have critical design flaws. These include non-longitudinal design, inadequate sample size, biased sample selection, lack of proper controls, failure to account for confounding variables, and perhaps most problematic—all claim to affirm the null hypothesis.[13,14,15] Therefore, it is impossible for these studies to provide any support for the alleged safety or potential benefits to children from same-sex parenting.

Data on the long-term outcomes of children placed in same-sex households is sparse and gives reason for concern.[16] This research has revealed that children reared in same-sex households are more likely to experience sexual confusion, engage in risky sexual experimentation, and later adopt a same-sex identity.[17,18,19,20,21,22] This is concerning since adolescents and young adults who adopt the homosexual lifestyle are at increased risk for mental health problems, including major depression, anxiety disorders, conduct disorders, substance dependence, and especially suicidal ideation and suicide attempts.[23]

Risks of the Homosexual Lifestyle to Children

Finally, research has demonstrated considerable risks to children exposed to the homosexual lifestyle. Violence between same-sex partners is two to three times more common than among married heterosexual couples.[24,25,26,27,28] Same-sex partnerships are significantly more prone to dissolution than heterosexual marriages with the average same-sex relationship lasting only two to three years.[29,30,31,32] Homosexual men and women are reported to be promiscuous, with serial sex partners, even within what are loosely-termed "committed relationships."[33,34,35,36,37] Individuals who practice a homosexual lifestyle are more likely than heterosexuals to experience mental illness,[38,39,40] substance abuse,[41] suicidal tendencies[42,43] and shortened life spans.[44] Although some would claim that these dysfunctions are a result of societal pressures in America, the same dysfunctions exist at inordinately high levels among homosexuals in cultures where the practice is more widely accepted.[45]

Conclusion

In summary, tradition and science agree that biological ties and dual gender parenting are protective for children. The family environment in which children are reared plays a critical role in forming a secure gender identity, positive emotional well-being, and optimal academic achievement. Decades of social science research documents that children develop optimally when reared by their two biological parents in a low conflict marriage. The limited research advocating childrearing by same-sex parents has severe methodological limitations. There is significant risk of harm inherent in exposing a child to the homosexual lifestyle. Given the current body of evidence, the American College of Pediatricians believes it is inappropriate, potentially hazardous to children, and dangerously irresponsible to change the age-old prohibition on same-sex parenting, whether by adoption, foster care, or reproductive manipulation. This position is rooted in the best available science.

References

1. Heuveline, Patrick, et al., Shifting Childrearing to Single Mothers: Results from 17 Western Countries, *Population and Development Review 29*, no. 1 (March 2003) p. 48.

2. Kristen Andersen Moore, et al., *Marriage from a Child's Perspective: How Does Family Structure Affect Children and What Can We Do About It?* (Washington, D.C.: Child Trends, Research Brief, June 2002) pp. 1–2.

3. Sara McLanahan and Gary Sandfeur, *Growing Up with a Single Parent: What Hurts, What Helps* (Cambridge: Harvard University Press, 1994), p. 45.

4. Sotirios Sarantakos, Children in Three Contexts: Family, Education, and Social Development, *Children Australia,* vol. 21 (1996): 23–31.

5. Jeanne M. Hilton and Esther L. Devall, Comparison of Parenting and Children's Behavior in Single-Mother, Single-Father, and Intact Families, *Journal of Divorce and Remarriage* 29 (1998): 23–54.

6. Elizabeth Thomson et al., Family Structure and Child Well-Being: Economic Resources vs. Parental Behaviors, *Social Forces* 73 (1994): 221–42.

7. David Popenoe, *Life Without Father* (Cambridge: Harvard University Press, 1996), pp. 144, 146.

8. Glenn Stanton, *Why Marriage Matters* (Colorado Springs: Pinon Press, 1997) p. 97–153.

9. Schneider B., Atteberry A., Owens A, *Family Matters: Family Structure and Child Outcomes.* Birmingham, AL: Alabama Policy Institute; 2005: 1–42. Available at www.alabamapolicyinstitute.org/PDFs/currentfamilystructure.pdf.

10. Sax, Leonard, *Why Gender Matters: What Parents and Teachers Need to Know About the Emerging Science of Sex Differences* (New York: Doubleday, 2005).

11. Blankenhorn, David, *Fatherless America.* (New York: Basic Books, 1995).

12. Byrd, Dean, Gender Complementarity and Child-Rearing: Where Tradition and Science Agree, *Journal of Law & Family Studies,* University of Utah, Vol. 6 no. 2, 2005. http://narth.com/docs/gendercomplementarity.html.

13. Robert Lerner, Ph.D., Althea Nagai, Ph.D., *No Basis: What the Studies Don't Tell Us About Same Sex Parenting,* Washington DC; Marriage Law Project/Ethics and Public Policy Center, 2001.

14. P. Morgan, *Children as Trophies? Examining the Evidence on Same-Sex Parenting,* Newcastle upon Tyne, UK; Christian Institute, 2002.

15. J. Paul Guiliani and Dwight G. Duncan, *Brief of Amici Curiae Massachusetts Family Institute and National Association for the Research and Therapy of Homosexuality,* Appeal to the Supreme Court of Vermont, Docket No. S1009–97CnC.

16. Perrin, E. C., Technical report: Co parent or Second-Parent Adoption by Same-Sex Parents, *Pediatrics.* 109 (2002): 343. The Academy acknowledges that the "small, non-representative samples . . . and the relatively young age of the children suggest some reserve."

17. F. Tasker and S. Golombok, Adults Raised as Children in Lesbian Families, *American Journal of Orthopsychiatric Association,* 65 (1995): 213.

18. J. Michael Bailey et al., Sexual Orientation of Adult Sons of Gay Fathers, *Developmental Psychology* 31 (1995): 124–129.

19. Ibid., pp. 127, 128.

20. F. Tasker and S. Golombok, Do Parents Influence the Sexual Orientation of Their Children? *Developmental Psychology* 32 (1996): 7.

21. Judith Stacey and Timothy J. Biblarz, (How) Does the Sexual Orientation of Parents Matter, *American Sociological Review* 66 (2001): 174, 179.

22. Nanette K. Gartrell, Henny M. W. Bos, and Naomi G. Goldberg, Adolescents of the U.S. National Longitudinal Lesbian Family Study: Sexual Orientation, Sexual Behavior, and Sexual Risk Exposure, *Archive of Sexual Behavior,* 40 (2011): 1199–1209, p. 1205.

23. Judith Stacey and Timothy J. Biblarz, (How) Does the Sexual Orientation of Parents Matter, *American Sociological Review* 66 (2001): 174, 179.

24. Gwat Yong Lie and Sabrina Gentlewarrier, Intimate Violence in Lesbian Relationships: Discussion of Survey Findings and Practice Implications, *Journal of Social Service Research* 15 (1991): 41–59.

25. D. Island and P. Letellier, *Men Who Beat the Men Who Love Them: Battered Gay Men and Domestic Violence* (New York: Haworth Press, 1991), p. 14.

26. Lettie L. Lockhart et al., *Letting Out the Secret: Violence in Lesbian Relationships, Journal of Interpersonal Violence* 9 (1994): 469–492.

27. *Violence Between Intimates,* Bureau of Justice Statistics Selected Findings, November 1994, p. 2.

28. *Health Implications Associated With Homosexuality* (Austin: The Medical Institute for Sexual Health, 1999), p. 79.

29. David P. McWhirter and Andrew M. Mattison, *The Male Couple: How Relationships Develop* (Englewood Cliffs: Prentice-Hall, 1984), pp. 252–253.

30. M. Saghir and E. Robins, Male and Female Homosexuality (Baltimore: Williams & Wilkins, 1973), p. 225; L.A. Peplau and H. Amaro, Understanding Lesbian Relationships, in *Homosexuality: Social, Psychological, and Biological Issues,* ed. J. Weinrich and W. Paul (Beverly Hills: Sage, 1982).

31. Schumm, Walter R.(2010), Comparative Relationship Stability of Lesbian Mother and Heterosexual Mother Families: A Review of Evidence, *Marriage & Family Review,* 46: 8, 499–509.

32. M. Pollak, Male Homosexuality, in *Western Sexuality: Practice and Precept in Past and Present Times,* ed. P. Aries and A. Bejin, translated by Anthony Forster (New York, NY: B. Blackwell, 1985), pp. 40–61, cited by Joseph Nicolosi in *Reparative Therapy of Male Homosexuality* (Northvale, New Jersey: Jason Aronson Inc., 1991), pp. 124, 125.

33. A. P. Bell and M. S. Weinberg, *Homosexualities: A Study of Diversity Among Men and Women* (New York: Simon and Schuster, 1978), pp. 308, 309; See also A. P. Bell, M. S. Weinberg, and S. K. Hammersmith, *Sexual Preference* (Bloomington: Indiana University Press, 1981).

34. Paul Van de Ven et al., A Comparative Demographic and Sexual Profile of Older Homosexually Active Men, *Journal of Sex Research* 34 (1997): 354.

35. A. A. Deenen, Intimacy and Sexuality in Gay Male Couples, *Archives of Sexual Behavior*, 23 (1994): 421–431.

36. Sex Survey Results, *Genre* (October 1996), quoted in "Survey Finds 40 percent of Gay Men Have Had More Than 40 Sex Partners," *Lambda Report,* January 1998, p. 20.

37. Marie Xiridoui, et al., The Contribution of Steady and Casual Partnerships to the Incidence of HIV infection among Homosexual Men in Amsterdam, *AIDS* 17 (2003): 1029–1038. [Note: one of the findings of this recent study is that those classified as being in "steady relationships" reported an average of 8 casual partners a year in addition to their partner (p. 1032)]

38. J. Bradford et al., National Lesbian Health Care Survey: Implications for Mental Health Care, *Journal of Consulting and Clinical Psychology* 62 (1994): 239, cited in Health Implications Associated with Homosexuality, p. 81.

39. Theo G. M. Sandfort, et al., Same-sex Sexual Behavior and Psychiatric Disorders, *Archives of General Psychiatry* 58 (January 2001): 85–91.

40. Bailey, J. M. Commentary: Homosexuality and mental illness. *Archives of General Psychiatry* 56 (1999): 876–880. Author states, These studies contain arguably the best published data on the association between homosexuality and psychopathology, and both converge on the same unhappy conclusion: homosexual people are at substantially higher risk for some form of emotional problems; including suicidality, major depression, and anxiety disorder, conduct disorder, and nicotine dependence . . .

41. Joanne Hall, Lesbians Recovering from Alcoholic Problems: An Ethnographic Study of Health Care Expectations, *Nursing Research* 43 (1994): 238–244.

42. R. Herrell et al., Sexual Orientation and Suicidality, Co-twin Study in Adult Men, *Archives of General Psychiatry* 56 (1999): 867–874.

43. Vickie M. Mays, et al., Risk of Psychiatric Disorders among Individuals Reporting Same-sex Sexual Partners in the National Comorbidity Survey, *American Journal of Public Health*, vol. 91 (June 2001): 933–939.

44. Robert S. Hogg et al., Modeling the Impact of HIV Disease on Mortality in Gay and Bisexual Men, *International Journal of Epidemiology* 26 (1997): 657.

45. Sandfort, T.G.M.; de Graaf, R.; Bijl, R.V.; Schnabel. Same-sex sexual behavior and psychiatric disorders. *Archives of General Psychiatry* 58 (2001): 85–91.

Charlotte J. Patterson  **NO**

Children of Lesbian and Gay Parents: Psychology, Law, and Policy

. . .

Social Science Research on Lesbian and Gay Parents and Their Children

How do the results of social science research address legal and policy issues raised by child custody, visitation, adoption, and foster care by lesbian and gay parents? . . . I offer an overview of the research literature focused on children of lesbian and gay parents that is relevant to these questions. I summarize research relevant to each of the three main areas of debate about children of lesbian and gay parents—namely, children's gender development, other aspects of children's personal development, and children's social relationships. For other recent overviews of this literature, see Patterson (2006) and Tasker and Patterson (2007).

Children's Gender Development

It has sometimes been suggested that gender development may be compromised among children reared by lesbian or gay parents. Those who express this concern may worry about the development of gender identity (i.e., the fundamental sense of oneself as male or female), about the development of gendered behavior (i.e., the acquisition of behavior that conforms to prevailing norms for masculine or feminine behavior), and/or about the development of sexual orientation (i.e., a person's choice of sexual partners, whether homosexual, heterosexual, or bisexual; see Patterson, 1992). To examine the possibilities in this area, researchers have focused their studies on all three of these aspects of gender development.

The study of gender development and sexual orientation among the offspring of lesbian and gay parents can be criticized on the grounds that atypical gender development and/or nonheterosexuality are neither illnesses nor disabilities. The APA and the American Psychiatric Association, among others, have long disavowed notions of homosexuality or nonnormative gender behavior as representing either disease or disorder (see APA, 2004). Demands for children to embody heterosexuality or demonstrate only gender behavior

Patterson, Charlotte J. From *American Psychologist*, Vol. 64, 2009, pp. 727–736. Copyright © 2009 by American Psychological Association. Reprinted by permission via Rightslink.

that conforms to familiar norms are inappropriate and unwarranted. Nevertheless, such demands are still made in many circles, and they may be especially relevant in child custody cases involving lesbian and gay parents. As a result, researchers have addressed these questions.

It is interesting that research has generally failed to identify important differences in the development of gender identity or gender role behavior as a function of parental sexual orientation (e.g., Golombok, Spencer, & Rutter, 1983; Green, Mandel, Hotvedt, Gray, & Smith, 1986). For example, in interviews with children who had grown up with divorced lesbian mothers and children who had grown up with divorced heterosexual mothers, Green and his colleagues reported no differences with respect to favorite television programs, television characters, games, or toys. Brewaeys, Ponjaert, Van Hall, and Golombok (1997) used the Preschool Activities Inventory—a parental report questionnaire designed to assess children's preferences for gendered games, toys, and activities—to assess gender development among children conceived via donor insemination and reared by lesbian or heterosexual couples and reported no significant differences as a function of parental sexual orientation. Using the same instrument, Patterson, Farr, and Forssell (2009) recently found no significant differences in the gender role behavior of young children adopted by lesbian, gay, and heterosexual couples. No reports of differences in gender identity as a function of parental sexual orientation have emerged.

A number of researchers have also studied the sexual orientation of those reared by lesbian or gay parents. For instance, Huggins (1989) interviewed a group of adolescents, half of whom were the offspring of heterosexual mothers and half of whom were the offspring of lesbian mothers. She found that none of the adolescents with lesbian mothers identified as nonheterosexual, but one child of a heterosexual mother did. Tasker and Golombok (1997) also studied the sexual identities of young adults who had been reared by divorced lesbian or divorced heterosexual mothers and reported no differences. Bailey, Bobrow, Wolfe, and Mikach (1995) interviewed gay fathers about the sexual identities of their adult sons; they found that 7 of 75—9%—of the sons were identified as gay or bisexual.

No information about the daughters of these gay fathers was obtained in this study. Overall, the clearest conclusion from these and related studies is that the great majority of children with lesbian or gay parents grow up to identify as heterosexual (Bailey & Dawood, 1998).

Other Aspects of Children's Personal Development

A general concern about children of lesbian and gay parents that has been mentioned in many legal and policy debates in the United States is the fear that their personal development might be impaired or compromised (see Patterson, 1992, for elaboration of this claim). Research has assessed a broad array of characteristics, including separation-individuation, psychiatric evaluations, behavior problems and competencies, self-concept, locus of control, moral judgment, school adjustment, intelligence, victimization, and substance use (Patterson, 2000, 2006; Stacey & Biblarz, 2001). As was the case for sexual identity, studies of these aspects of personal development have revealed no major differences between the offspring of lesbian or gay parents and those of heterosexual parents. The research findings thus suggest that concern about difficulties in these areas among the offspring of lesbian mothers is unwarranted.

Particular worries have sometimes been voiced for the development of adolescents with lesbian or gay parents, who are seen as possibly experiencing greater difficulties than younger children do (e.g., Baumrind, 1995). In a recent pair of studies, Wainright and colleagues (e.g., Wainright & Patterson, 2006; Wainright, Russell, & Patterson, 2004) have studied adjustment in a national sample of teenagers in the United States. Their data showed that adolescents living with female same-sex couples did not differ significantly from those living with different-sex couples on measures of anxiety, depressive symptoms, self-esteem, delinquency, or victimization or in their use of tobacco, alcohol, or marijuana (Wainright & Patterson, 2006; Wainright et al., 2004). In this nationally representative sample, whether adolescents' parents had same-sex or different-sex partners was unrelated to adolescent adjustment (Patterson, 2006). Overall, the adjustment of children and adolescents does not appear to be related to parental sexual orientation.

Children's Social Relationships

A third type of concern that has been voiced about children and adolescents with lesbian or gay parents is that their social relationships, especially those with peers, may be compromised (see Baumrind, 1995; Patterson & Redding, 1996). To the contrary, however, research has repeatedly found that children and adolescents with nonheterosexual parents report normal social relationships with family members, with peers, and with adults outside their nuclear families. Moreover, observers outside the family agree with these assessments (Tasker & Golombok, 1997; Wainright & Patterson, 2008). In particular, the contacts that children of nonheterosexual parents have with extended family members have not been found to differ significantly from those of other children (e.g., Fulcher, Chan, Raboy, & Patterson, 2002).

Youngsters growing up with lesbian or gay parents have often provided anecdotal reports of teasing or peer harassment that focuses on parental sexual orientation. For instance, Gartrell and her colleagues have reported that a substantial minority of children with lesbian mothers in their longitudinal study reported hearing negative comments from peers (Gartrell, Deck, Rodas, Peyser, & Banks, 2005; see also Bos, Gartrell, Peyser, & van Balen, 2008). In that most children are probably teased about something, an important question has been the degree to which any such teasing or peer harassment may affect overall adjustment or peer relations among the offspring of nonheterosexual parents.

The results of a recent study of peer relations among adolescents living with female same-sex couples are particularly important in addressing this question (Wainright & Patterson, 2008). These authors studied a nationally representative sample of adolescents in the United States and compared peer relations among those who lived with same-sex versus different-sex parenting couples. They studied peer reports as well as adolescents' own self-reports about friendships, activities with friends, and popularity among classmates. They also studied measures of density and centrality in peer networks. Across these and other measures of adolescent peer relations, there were no significant differences as a function of family type (Wainright & Patterson, 2008). In short, claims that youngsters' peer relations suffer when they live with same-sex couples are not supported by the findings of empirical research (see also Vanfraussen, Ponjaert-Kristoffersen, & Brewaeys, 2002).

Summary

More than 25 years of research on the offspring of nonheterosexual parents has yielded results of remarkable clarity. Regardless of whether researchers have studied the offspring of divorced lesbian and gay parents or those born to lesbian or gay parents, their findings have been similar. Regardless of whether researchers have studied children or adolescents, they have reported similar results. Regardless of whether investigators have examined sexual identity, self-esteem, adjustment, or qualities of social relationships, the results have been remarkably consistent. In study after study, the offspring of lesbian and gay parents have been found to be at least as well adjusted overall as those of other parents. . . .

References

American Psychological Association. (2004). *Resolution on sexual orientation, parents, and children* [Policy statement]. (Adopted by the APA Council of Representatives, July 2004).

Bailey, J. M., Bobrow, D., Wolfe, M., & Mikach, S. (1995). Sexual orientation of adult sons of gay fathers. *Developmental Psychology, 31,* 124–129.

Bailey, J. M., & Dawood, K. (1998). Behavior genetics, sexual orientation, and the family. In C. J. Patterson & A. R. D'Augelli (Eds.), *Lesbian, gay and bisexual identities in families: Psychological perspectives* (pp. 3–18). New York: Oxford University Press.

Baumrind, D. (1995). Commentary on sexual orientation: Research and social policy implications. *Developmental Psychology, 31,* 130–136.

Bos, H. M. W., Gartrell, N. K., Peyser, H., & van Balen, F. (2008). The USA National Longitudinal Lesbian Family Study (NLLFS): Homophobia, psychological adjustment, and protective factors. *Journal of Lesbian Studies, 12,* 455–471.

Brewaeys, A., Ponjaert, I., Van Hall, E. V., & Golombok, S. (1997). Donor insemination: Child development and family functioning in lesbian mother families. *Human Reproduction, 12,* 1349–1359.

Fulcher, M., Chan, R. W., Raboy, B., & Patterson, C. J. (2002). Contact with grandparents among children conceived via donor insemination by lesbian and heterosexual mothers. *Parenting: Science and Practice, 2,* 61–76.

Gartrell, N., Deck, A., Rodas, C. Peyser, H., & Banks, A. (2005), The National Lesbian Family Study: 4. Interviews with the 10-year-old children, *American Journal of Orthopsychiatry, 75,* 518–524.

Golombok, S., Spencer, A., & Rutter, M. (1983). Children in lesbian and single-parent households: Psychosexual and psychiatric appraisal. *Journal of Child Psychology and Psychiatry, 24*, 551–572.

Green, R., Mandel, J. B., Hotvedt, M. E., Gray, J., & Smith, L. (1986). Lesbian mothers and their children: A comparison with solo parent heterosexual mothers and their children. *Archives of Sexual Behavior, 15*, 167–184.

Huggins, S. L. (1989). A comparative study of self-esteem of adolescent children of divorced lesbian mothers and divorced heterosexual mothers. In F. W. Bozett (Ed.), *Homosexuality and the family* (pp, 123–135). New York: Harington Park Press.

Patterson, C. J. (1992). Children of lesbian and gay parents. *Child Development, 63*, 1025–1042.

Patterson, C. J. (2000). Family relationships of lesbians and gay men. *Journal of Marriage and Family, 62*, 1052–1069.

Patterson, C. J. (2006). Children of lesbian and gay parents. *Current Directions in Psychological Science, 15*, 241–244.

Patterson, C. J., Farr, R. H., & Forssell, S. L. (2009, April). *Sexual orientation, parenting, and child development in adoptive families.* Paper presented at the biennial meeting of the Society for Research in Child Development, Denver, Colorado.

Patterson, C. J., & Redding, R. (1996). Lesbian and gay families with children: Public policy implications of social science research. *Journal of Social Issues, 52*, 29–50.

Stacey, J., & Biblarz, T. J. (2001). (How) Does sexual orientation of parents matter? *American Sociological Review, 65*, 159–183.

Tasker, F. L., & Golombok, S. (1997). *Growing up in a lesbian family: Effects on child development.* New York: Guilford Press.

Tasker, F., & Patterson, C. J. (2007). Research on gay and lesbian parenting: Retrospect and prospect. *Journal of Gay, Lesbian, Bisexual and Transgender Family Issues, 3*, 9–34.

Wainright, J. L., & Patterson, C. J. (2006). Delinquency, victimization, and substance use among adolescents with female same-sex parents. *Journal of Family Psychology, 20*, 526–530.

Wainright, J. L ., & Patterson, C. J. (2008). Peer relations among adolescents with female same-sex parents. *Developmental Psychology, 44*, 117–126.

Wainright, J. L., Russell, S. T., & Patterson, C. J. (2004). Psychosocial adjustment and school outcomes of adolescents with same-sex parents. *Child Development, 75*, 1886–1898.

EXPLORING THE ISSUE

Does Having Same-Sex Parents Negatively Impact Children?

Critical Thinking and Reflection

1. What constitutes being "a good parent"? What would make a person an unsuitable parent versus a suitable parent? Should there be a hierarchy of desirability in terms of parent constellations (e.g., no. 1 heterosexual, racially and religiously the same; no. 2 heterosexual, bi-religious, and racially the same; no. 3 heterosexual, bi-religious, and bi-racial; no. 4 homosexual, racially, and religiously the same; no. 5 single parent; etc.)?

2. Does biology really matter in terms of family impact? To answer this question, read the academic literature on the impact of adoption on children. Are adult outcomes different for children who were adopted compared to children who were raised in comparable homes by biological families?

3. Is parental gender critical in childrearing? Do children need a father and a mother as parents in order to develop psychosexually "normally"? Do children learn gender roles and rules from sources other than parents (e.g., teachers, extended family)? To address these questions, access the empirical literature on psychosexual development (e.g., gender role development).

4. One argument against same-sex parenting is that same-sex relationships are more turbulent and transient than other-sex relationships. To address this issue, search the psychological and sociological work on relationship quality of same-sex and other-sex relationships. Is this underlying claim valid? Are same-sex relationships quantitatively poorer than other-sex relationships?

5. It is evident that both sets of authors have a bias toward same-sex parenting that influences their writings. Bias often has a negative connotation but we are all bias across most important issues; that is, when a person has a definite opinion, how research is designed, conducted, and interpreted is influenced by that opinion. What an author writes is influenced by his/her perspective on the issue. No human is completely objective. In an attempt to set aside your bias, imagine a nonpartisan group gave you a huge grant to investigate same-sex parenting and asked you to conduct as unbiased a study as possible. Assume that money is no barrier for this research. Design *the* definitive experimental study that will address the questions and concerns about same-sex parents. In creating this study, pay particular attention to various comparison groups. Also, what other

variables need to be taken into account when addressing this question? When considering these two last questions, you will need to review the literature on the factors that influence parents, in general (e.g., socioeconomic status, race, education, relationship duration, relationship status, and relationship quality).

a. Why do discussions and debates about same-sex marriage almost always address the issue of same-sex parenting? How does barring people of the same-sex from marrying impact same-sex parenting as it exists in the U.S. society? Can the reverse argument be made: same-sex marriage must be allowed because of same-sex parenting?

b. Design an anthropological study comparing Canadian same-sex families to U.S. same-sex families. Do the different laws in these two countries with very similar cultural milieus have a differential impact on same-sex parenting?

Is There Common Ground?

Both sets of authors would agree that what is paramount is what is in the best interest of the children. The issue is that the two would disagree on what is "in the best interest." Both would agree that parents and family are critical components in children's health, well-being, and overall development. However, the two differ on their opinions about the form the parents and family are to take. Clearly, Patterson would argue that same-sex parents are equivalent in parenting practices and the children of same-sex parents have equivalent outcomes (e.g., adjustment) to children of other-sex couples. Cretella, outlining the position of her organization, takes a stance against same-sex parenting. In another position paper regarding adoption, the American College of Pediatricians state definitively and succinctly that "adoption agencies should avoid placing children in suboptimal family situations such as with same-sex couples" (Willson, 2008).

Additional Resources

Angus Reid Strategies. (August 2009). Canada more open to same-sex marriage than U.S., UK. Retrieved from www.angus-reid.com/polls/37148/canada_more_open_to_same_sex_marriage_than_us_uk/

APA (American Psychological Association). (2009). Distinguished contributions to the public interest. *American Psychologist, 64*, 724–727.

Baumle, A. K., & Compton, D. R. (2011). Legislating the family: The effect of state family laws on the presence of children in same-sex households. *Law & Policy, 33*(1), 82–115.

Biblarz, T. J., & Stacey, J. (2010). How does the gender of parents matter? *Journal of Marriage and the Family, 72*(1), 3–22.

This thorough review paper addresses the gender-related social science literature with regard to parenting.

Biblarz, T. J., & Savci, E. (2010). Lesbian, gay, bisexual, and transgender families. *Journal of Marriage and the Family, 72*(3), 480–497.

A good review of the empirically published literature on queer families from 2000 on. This paper also identifies areas for future research.

Bos, H. M. W., van Balen, F., & van den Boom, D. C. (2007). Child adjustment and parenting in planned lesbian-parent families. *American Journal of Orthopsychiatry, 77*, 38–48.

CNN Wire Staff. (2010). Florida appeals court strikes down gay adoption ban. Retrieved from www.cnn.com/2010/US/09/22/florida.gay.adoptions/index.html?hpt=T2

Cretella, M. A., & Sutton, P. M. (2010). Health risks: Fisting and other homosexual practices. Retrieved from http://narth.com/docs/healthrisks.html

National Association of Research and Therapy of Homosexuality is an organization with the stated mission of "offer[ing] hope to those who struggle with unwanted homosexuality." This organization's position statement "supports the traditional model of man–woman marriage as the ideal family form for fostering a child's healthy development." As well, Narth characterizes homosexuality as a psychological condition, considers the statements "homosexuality is normal and biologically determined" and *"that homosexuality is as normal and healthy as heterosexuality"* are myths, and asserts that those who are homosexual can change orientations (i.e., can be "healed"). This organization tends to present writings by authors who view homosexuality negatively.

Crowl, A., Ahn, S., & Baker, J. (2008). A meta-analysis of developmental outcomes for children of same-sex and heterosexual parents. *Journal of GLBT Family Studies, 4*(3), 385–407.

Crowl and colleagues conducted a meta-analysis of the studies of the effect of having same-sex parents on outcome measures. Five out of the six outcomes demonstrated no differences between children raised by heterosexual versus those by homosexual parents. Where there was one difference was in parent–child relations: Homosexual parents felt they had a better relationship with their child(ren) relative to heterosexual parents.

Dent, George, Jr. (2011). No difference? An analysis of same-sex parenting. Case Research Paper Series in Legal Studies, Working Paper No. 2011-11. Case Western Reserve University Law School. (To be published in: *Ave Maria Law Review*).

This piece is very similar to Cretella's, although it is more in depth.

Family Equality Council. (2012). Equality maps. Retrieved from www.familyequality.org/get_informed/equality_maps/

Farr, R. H., Forssell, S. L., & Patterson, C. J. (2010). Parenting and child development in adoptive families: Does parental sexual orientation matter? *Applied Developmental Science, 14*(3), 164–178.

Gartrell, N. K., Bos, H. M. W., & Goldberg, N. G. (2011). Adolescents of the U.S. National Longitudinal Lesbian Family Study: Sexual orientation, sexual behavior, and sexual risk exposure. *Archive of Sexual Behavior, 40*, 1199–1209.

Gates, G. J. (2011a). How many people are lesbian, gay, bisexual, and transgender? Report of The Williams Institute, UCLA School of Law.

Gates, G. J. (2011b). Family formation and raising children among same-sex couples. *Family focus on . . . LGBT families* (F1–F4). National Council on Family Relations.

Gates, G. J., & Romero, A. P. (2009). Parenting by gay men and lesbians: Beyond the current research. In H. E. Peters & C. M. Kamp Dush (Eds.), *Marriage and family: Perspectives and complexities* (pp. 227–243). New York: Columbia University Press.

Goldberg, A. E., & Cretella, M. (2009) Gay marriage: Bad science, bad politics. The Jewish State. June 19, 2009.

Goldberg, A. E. (2010). *Lesbian and gay parents and their children: Research on the family life cycle*. Washington, DC: American Psychological Association.

McCutcheon, J. (2011*)*. Attitudes toward adoption by same-sex couples: Do gender roles matter? Unpublished Masters' thesis. Department of Psychology, University of Saskatchewan. Retrieved from http://ecommons.usask
.ca/xmlui/bitstream/handle/10388/ETD-2011-09-143/MCCUTCHEON-THESIS
.pdf?sequence=5

Miall, C. E., & March, K. (2005). Social support for changes in adoption practice: Gay adoption, open adoption, birth reunions, and the release of confidential identifying information. *Families in Society, 86*, 83–92.

These researchers compared a Canada-wide survey to the findings of two American surveys regarding adoption.

Milan, A., Vézin, M., & Wells, C. (2007). *Family portrait: Continuity and change in Canadian families and households in 2006*. Ottawa: Statistics Canada/ Ministry of Industry.

Patterson, C. (2009). In D. Hope (Ed.). *Contemporary perspectives on lesbian, gay, and bisexual identites. The Nebraska symposium on motivation* (Vol. 54 pp. 141–182). New York: Springer.

Powell, B., Bolzendahl, C., Geist, C., & Carr Steelman, L. (2010). *Counted out: Same-sex relations and Americans' definitions of family*. New York: American Sociological Association/Russell Sage Foundation.

Rye, B. J, & Meaney, G. J. (2010). Self-Defense, sexism, and etiological beliefs: Predictors of attitudes toward gay and lesbian adoption. *Journal of GLBT Family Studies, 6*, 1–24.

Szymanski, D. M., & Moffitt, L. B. (2012). Sexism and heterosexism. In D. M., Szymanski & L. B. Moffitt (Eds.), *APA handbook of counseling psychology: Practice, interventions, and applications* (Vol. 2, pp. 361–390). Washington, DC: APA.

Willson, L. (2008). Adoption. Retrieved from www.acpeds.org/adoption.html

ISSUE 12

Does Dating in Early Adolescence Impede Developmental Adjustment?

YES: **Ming Cui et al.**, from "The Association Between Romantic Relationships and Delinquency in Adolescence and Young Adulthood," *Personal Relationships* (vol. 19, pp. 354–366, 2012), doi: 10.1111/j.1475-6811.2011.01366.x

NO: **K. Paige Harden and Jane Mendle**, from "Adolescent Sexual Activity and the Development of Delinquent Behavior: The Role of Relationship Context," *Journal of Youth and Adolescence* (vol. 40, no. 7, pp. 825–838, 2011)

Learning Outcomes

After reading this issue, you should be able to:

- Understand the theoretical perspectives that apply to dating and romantic relationships in adolescence.
- Identify the various types of dating relationships in which adolescents may engage.
- Discriminate the differences in dating outcomes for early and later adolescents.
- Describe the role of genes in adolescent sexual and delinquent behavior.
- Critically analyze the roles that biology and environment play in developmental adjustment for adolescents who date.

ISSUE SUMMARY

YES: Ming Cui, assistant professor in the Department of Family and Child Sciences at Florida State University, and her colleagues found a relationship between delinquency and adolescent romantic relationships, with younger adolescents being at greater risk than older adolescents for engaging in delinquent behavior. Their analyses also pointed to a cumulative effect of relationship history on delinquency and criminal behavior in early adulthood.

No: K. Paige Harden and Jane Mendle, assistant professors of psychology at the University of Texas and the University of Oregon, respectively, examined the associations between adolescent dating, sexual activity, and delinquency, after controlling for genetic influences. They found evidence for genetic influences on sexual behavior and for a link between these genetic predispositions and an increased likelihood to engage in delinquent behavior. They argue that early dating and/or early sexual activity do not cause delinquent behavior; in fact, this study suggests that sex in romantic relationships is related to lower levels of delinquency in both adolescence and later life.

When should teens be allowed to date? What is "too young" and possibly problematic? Are early romantic relationships just inconsequential "puppy love"? Are these relationships good, bad, or even dangerous for adolescents? Does early dating invite early sexual activity? Should adults attempt to dissuade teens from dating? These are just a few questions that capture the debate about adolescent romantic relationships.

Dating is an important developmental process for adolescents. Much of teens' time is spent thinking about dating, talking about dating, attempting to date, actually dating, and recovering from dating relationships. Thus, teen romantic relationships seem like a normal part of adolescent development. Early development theorists in the 1950s, such as Harry Stack Sullivan and Erik Erikson, argued that dating in early and middle adolescence prepares the teen for developing mature, functional adult interpersonal relationships. However, little research has addressed the impact of romantic relationships on adolescent development. Rather, most research in the area of close adolescent relationships has focused on relationships with peers or parents.

Much of the research that does exist seems to focus on adolescent romantic relationships as a negative outcome; that is, romantic relationships are often viewed as part of a constellation of problem behavior such as early initiations of intercourse and other sexual activities, alcohol and substance use, parental defiance, and delinquency. Other research focuses on abuse and violence in teen dating relationships. Indeed, romantic relationships have been linked to stress experiences for adolescents. For example, research suggests that teens sometimes enter into romantic relationships for undesirable motivations such as to elevate their social status, to prove their "maturity," or to help them separate from their family. Teen romance can add to stress levels by interfering with friendships and parental relationships, as well as distracting the adolescent from his/her focus on academic achievement. These romantic relationships have also been investigated as contributing to negative emotions that may lead to depression. Breaking up, in particular, can have a variety of negative effects on youth, including negatively impacting self-image and self-worth, and contributing to feeling undesirable, betrayed, and sad.

Less attention has been placed on the many benefits of teen romantic relationships. For example, romantic partners are a significant source of social support for the adolescent, relationships are a source of strong positive emotions, and dating helps the adolescent to become more autonomous. Romantic relationships can also be a means of developing better interpersonal skills and competencies, gaining status and popularity, and helping to solidify various social identities. Intrapersonally, teens may develop a positive sense of self through dating (i.e., feel desirable, wanted, intimate) and positive self-regard. Research seems to suggest that affiliation, companionship, and friendship are critical components of romantic relationships for adolescent development and that experiencing romantic relationships in adolescence also helps to prepare youth for adult relationships.

Adolescence is a long developmental period marked by increases in physical, emotional, and social maturity, and a developing sense of self or identity. Early and late adolescents differ markedly across these domains; therefore, the dating debate needs to be considered in terms of varying levels of social–emotional maturity. Is it reasonable to assume that the process of dating (and its outcomes) is different for youth in early and late adolescence? The focus of this issue is on the early years—does dating in early adolescence impact youth negatively? Are early adolescents "just too young" to date?

The YES and NO selections investigate delinquency within the context of adolescent dating relationships. Cui and colleagues found that younger adolescents were at greater risk than older adolescents for engaging in delinquent behavior. In fact, they noted a cumulative effect of relationship history on delinquency and criminal behavior in early adulthood. Basically, a negative start-up was related to later difficulties. Harden and Mendle took a different approach to examining these variables by controlling for genetic influences. They found evidence for genetic influences on sexual behavior and the likelihood to engage in delinquent behavior for younger adolescents. The influence of environment, rather than genetics, was stronger for older adolescents in this sample. For early adolescents, sexual activity within the context of romantic or nonromantic relationships was not related to future delinquency. In fact, this study found that after controlling for genetic influences, sex in romantic relationships was related to lower levels of delinquency in both adolescence and later life.

YES ↵

Ming Cui et al.

The Association Between Romantic Relationships and Delinquency in Adolescence and Young Adulthood

As adolescents approach young adulthood, romantic relationships become increasingly central to their social world (Furman & Buhrmester, 1992). However, researchers have only recently begun to focus attention on the developmental significance of romantic relationships during adolescence (e.g., Brown, Feiring, & Furman, 1999; Collins & Steinberg, 2006; Collins & van Dulmen, 2006). Studies have revealed that involvement in romantic relationships is a fairly common adolescent experience but that the associations between romantic relationships and developmental outcomes are complicated. One particularly complicated issue involves the potentially positive association between involvement in romantic relationships and adolescent delinquency (e.g., Meeus, Branje, & Overbeek, 2004; Neeman, Hubbard, & Masten, 1995). This positive association is somewhat different from the finding that involvement in romantic relationships such as marriage is often negatively associated with criminal behavior in adults (see, e.g., Sampson, Laub, & Wimer, 2006). In light of this issue, the goal of this study is to examine the association between romantic relationships and delinquency,[1] both concurrently in adolescence and prospectively to young adulthood. Specifically, we will use a large, longitudinal, and nationally representative sample to examine (a) whether romantic involvement is positively associated with delinquency in adolescence and (b) whether the cumulative number of romantic relationships from adolescence to young adulthood is associated with greater delinquency in young adulthood.

Romantic Involvement and Delinquency in Adolescence

Until recently, it was assumed that romantic relationships among adolescents are trivial and transitory (see Brown et al., 1999; Collins, 2003). However, recent estimates based on the National Longitudinal Study of Adolescent Health (Add Health) project indicate that 25% of 12-year-olds report having a romantic relationship in the past 18 months, and more than 70% of 18-year-olds have been involved in a romantic relationship within the past

18 months, with the median length of romantic relationship for individuals 16 years of age or older being 20.5 months (Carver, Joyner, & Odry, 2003). In addition to the prevalence of romantic relationships in adolescence, involvement in a romantic relationship may be associated with delinquency (Meeus et al., 2004). However, such a topic has been largely ignored until recently (Haynie, Giordano, Manning, & Longmore, 2005). Accordingly, the first focus of this article is to evaluate the connection between involvement in romantic relationships and delinquency in adolescence.

A few studies found that romantic involvement in adolescence was positively associated with alcohol and drug use, and participation in delinquent behavior (e.g., Farrington, 1995; Thomas & Hsiu, 1993; Wong, 2005; Wright, 1982; Zimmer-Gembeck, Siebbenbruner, & Collins, 2001). In particular, Meeus and colleagues (2004) found that for youth aged 12–20, those who had been involved in romantic relationships demonstrated a higher level of delinquency than those who did not have romantic relationships. The results of existing research are, however, not always consistent. For example, van Dulmen, Goncy, Haydon, and Collins (2008) found that there was no association between romantic relationship involvement and delinquent and aggressive behaviors at age 16. To help resolve these inconsistencies, this study will use a large nationally representative sample to evaluate the association between romantic involvement and delinquency in adolescence. There are some general theoretical reasons to expect that involvement in romantic relationships in adolescence might be problematic. For example, psychosocial theory (Erikson, 1959) suggests that romantic involvement may be early for adolescents because their identities are not fully formed; therefore, they are not fully prepared for romantic intimacy. Likewise, a general life-course perspective (Elder, 1985) suggests that early timing of events (e.g., romantic involvement in adolescence) could have negative consequences on subsequent behavior trajectories. Thus, at least two perspectives suggest that involvement in romantic relationships during adolescence might be positively associated with problematic behavior such as delinquency. Based both on the existing findings and the theoretical rationale, we propose our first hypothesis;

> H1: *Romantic involvement is positively associated with delinquency in adolescence.*

Cumulative Number of Romantic Relationships and Delinquency

In addition to evaluating whether involvement in romantic relationships is associated with delinquency in adolescence, we will also evaluate whether the cumulative history of romantic relationships from adolescence to young adulthood is associated with delinquency in young adulthood. Here, we evaluate whether the total number of relationships is a salient developmental consideration for understanding deviant behavior in young adulthood and propose

that the cumulative experiences of romantic involvement in a series of relationships are associated with delinquency in young adulthood.

Several studies have addressed the issue of the cumulative association between romantic relationships and delinquency but only in adolescence. Neemann and colleagues (1995) found that a high degree of romantic
interests and involvement in early adolescence (8–12 years old) predicted a
modest increase in conduct problem behaviors in middle adolescence (14–19
years, $M = 17$). Similarly, Zimmer-Gembeck and colleagues (2001) found that
frequent romantic relationships were associated with increases in externalizing behaviors (e.g., delinquency, aggression) from age 12 to age 16. Likewise,
Davies and Windle (2000) found that, compared to single relationships,
multiple romantic relationships were associated with increasing problem
behaviors (e.g., delinquency, alcohol use) over a 1-year period during middle
adolescence.

Although these studies have consistently demonstrated the negative
effect of cumulative experiences in romantic relationships on delinquency
over time, these findings, with one exception, have not been extended into
young adulthood. Extending the research into young adulthood is particularly
important in that romantic relationships become more central in young
adulthood and that the influence of cumulative experience in romantic
relationships on other aspects of development is more salient in young
adulthood (Fincham & Cui, 2011). Meeus and colleagues (2004) found that
those consistently involved in romantic relationships ("systematic partner
experience" group) during adolescence showed a higher level of delinquency
than those who had a romantic relationship at a later time ("Time 3 partner"
group) or those who never had a romantic relationship ("never partner"
group), but they found no differences in delinquency trajectories from late
adolescence to young adulthood among different groups. However, in Meeus
and colleagues' study, the systematic partner experience group was identified if a participant was involved in a romantic relationship at all three time
points, which reflected to some degree frequent romantic involvement but
did not capture the total number of romantic relationship during the three
time points. By taking into account all romantic relationships between study
time points, this study will be the first to examine the association between
accumulation of romantic relationships and delinquency from adolescence
to young adulthood. This research question again follows from a life-course
perspective (Elder, 1985) that posits that earlier experiences have a cumulative impact on later life trajectories. Based on the life-course perspective and
extending the literature on adolescence, we propose that involvement in a
greater number of romantic relationships over time will be associated with
more delinquent behaviors in young adulthood. This leads to our second
hypothesis:

H2: *The number of romantic relationships from adolescence to young
adulthood is positively associated with delinquency in young
adulthood.*

The Present Study

The goal of this study was to examine (a) whether there is a positive association between romantic involvement and delinquency in adolescence (H1) and (b) whether those who had more romantic relationships report more delinquency in young adulthood than those who had fewer romantic relationships (H2). In addition, several adolescent characteristics will be controlled for because earlier studies have demonstrated their association with delinquency, including adolescent age (Meeus et al., 2004), pubertal timing (e.g., Ge, Brody, Conger, & Simons, 2006), gender (Cauffman, Farruggia, & Gold-weber, 2008), and race and ethnicity (e.g., Paschall, Flewelling, & Ennett, 1998). Furthermore, Collins (2003) suggested that relationship quality is important beyond relationship involvement. Therefore, for a subsample of those currently in a romantic relationship in young adulthood, we also controlled for relationship quality and length. . . . Thus, we attempted to provide a conservative test of our research hypotheses.

Method

Sample and Procedures

[We] draw data from Add Health. Add Health is a school-based longitudinal study of a nationally representative sample of adolescents in Grades 7–12 in the United States during the 1994–1995 school years. Detailed descriptions of the sample and procedures can be found in Harris and colleagues (2008) and at the website http://www. cpc.unc.edu/projects/addhealth/design. . . .

At Wave I, in-home interviews ($N = 20,745$) were administered to students in Grades 7–12 in 1995. The topics included social and demographic characteristics of respondents, household structure, family composition and dynamics, risk behaviors, sexual partnerships, and formation of romantic partnerships. Wave II surveyed students from the original sample (except for those who graduated) 1 year after Wave I. Data were collected from respondents during an in-home interview ($N = 14,738$). In 2001, 15,197 respondents from the original sample, 18- to 27-year-olds, were reinterviewed in Wave III to investigate the influence that adolescence has on young adulthood.

This study used data from Waves I, II, and III. Among respondents in the primary sample, 18,924 participated in Wave I, 13,570 participated in Waves I and II, and 14,322 participated in Waves I and III (Chantala, 2006). In order to address our research questions, which are specific to life stages, we restricted our operational sample to those who were adolescents at Wave I (i.e., between ages 13 and 18). As a result, our final samples included $N = 16,279$ for analyses using Wave I only, $N = 12,243$ for analyses using Waves I and II, and $N = 10,256$ for analyses using Waves I and III for those who had at least one romantic relationship between Waves I and III. Analyses of the missing data suggested that in Wave III, males, African Americans, and those in lower grade levels in earlier waves were more likely to have dropped out from the study. This study will focus on the $N = 16,279$ at Wave I and $N = 12,243$ from Waves I to II for testing H1, and the $N = 10,256$ from Waves I to III for testing H2.

Measures

Delinquency (Waves I, II, and III)

. . . There were seven items asking the target adolescents, during the past 12 months, how often did you deliberately damage property, steal something worth more than $50, go into a house or building to steal something, use or threaten to use a weapon to get something from someone, sell marijuana or other drugs, steal something worth less than $50, and take part in a fight where a group of your friends was against another group. All items ranged from 0 (*never*) to 3 (*5 or more times*). The seven items were then summed together for each wave to serve as the primary variable of interest.

Romantic Involvement (Wave I)

At Wave I, participants were asked "In the last 18 months, have you had a special romantic relationship with any one?" The item was coded as 0 (*no*) and 1 (*yes*). ["Liked"] . . . relationships were defined as relationships that involved hand holding, kissing, and telling the other that the respondent liked or loved him or her, based on respondents' self-report. Because these relationships involved romantic behaviors, we treated them as romantic relationships, following previous Add Health researchers' strategy (see Carver et al., 2003; Cavanagh et al., 2008).

Number of Romantic Relationships (Wave III)

Number of romantic relationships was used to assess the accumulation of romantic relationships between Waves I and III. At Wave III, respondents were asked to list all their romantic relationships since Wave I. . . .

Other Variables

"Adolescent age, pubertal timing, race and ethnicity, parents' education, relationship length, and relationship quality were also assessed." . . .

Results

. . .

Descriptive Statistics

There are several findings worth mentioning. First, the overall mean level of delinquency was highest at Wave I, then decreased over time. Second, 66% of the adolescents reported having had romantic involvement in the past 18 months at Wave I. Third, the average number of relationships during the 6-year study period from Wave I to Wave III was 3.56.

Hypotheses Testing

First, in order to test the association between romantic involvement and delinquency in adolescence (H1), we regressed delinquency at Wave I on romantic involvement at Wave I. Age, puberty, gender, race and ethnicity, and other family demographic variables were included.

Results suggested that there was a significant positive association between romantic involvement and adolescent delinquency at Wave I. . . . [C]ompared to adolescents who had no involvement in romantic relationships during the past 18 months, adolescents who had reported romantic involvement during this period were at increased risks for reporting delinquency. The association between age and delinquency was also significant . . ., suggesting that younger adolescents were at higher risks of engaging in delinquent behavior controlling for all the predictors in the model. Pubertal timing was significantly associated with delinquency, suggesting that early puberty timing is associated with heightened risks of delinquent behavior. Adolescent girls reported lower risks of delinquency than adolescent boys. . . .

Next, we tested whether number of romantic relationships from Wave I to Wave III was associated with delinquency at Wave III (H2). . . .

[D]espite the considerable continuity of delinquency across time, the number of romantic relationships during the period also contributed significantly to higher risks of delinquency in young adulthood. . . . Age was significantly and negatively associated with risks of delinquency, suggesting that younger participants demonstrated higher risks of delinquency at Wave III than older participants. Pubertal timing was slightly negatively associated with risks of delinquency at Wave III in this model. This effect might capture a lagged effect whereby early maturing young people are "faster" to age out of delinquency relative to their later maturing peers. Regarding gender, female participants demonstrated much lower risks of delinquency at Wave III than male participants. . . .

In addition, in order to examine the potential effects of romantic relationship involvement on specific delinquent behaviors, we tested all seven of the individual delinquency item as separate outcomes. Results from the seven models . . . suggested that the number of romantic relationships had a significant effect on five of the seven individual items, including taking part in a fight. . . .

Finally, a subsample of participants was used to test the model adding relationship length and quality. The criteria for inclusion in the model were participants who reported a current relationship at Wave III and had complete data on relationship length and quality of that relationship, as well as other variables of interests included in previous models. At a result, a subsample of N 5 2,789 was used for these analyses. The results . . . showed that even though dissatisfaction with current relationship was positively associated with delinquency, . . . and the number of relationships still remained significant, . . . [The] length of the current relationship was not significantly associated with delinquency in these analyses. . . .

Discussion

The goal of this investigation was to examine the association between romantic relationships and delinquency in adolescence and young adulthood. Based on psychosocial development theory (Erikson, 1959) and the life-course perspective (Elder, 1985), we hypothesized that the association between romantic involvement and delinquency would be positive during adolescence (H1) and that cumulative number of relationships in adolescence and young adulthood was positively associated with delinquency in young adulthood (H2). Findings from negative binomial regressions supported both hypotheses.

Documenting a positive association between romantic involvement and risks of delinquency during adolescence is consistent with findings from earlier studies (e.g., Farrington, 1995; Meeus et al., 2004; Zimmer-Gembeck et at., 2001). Indeed, as we suggested in the Introduction, there are theoretical reasons to argue that involvement in romantic relationships in adolescence might be problematic. From a psychosocial perspective, Erikson (1959) proposed that development of identity is the central task of adolescence. He also suggested that a firm identity should be developed before individuals can meaningfully achieve "real intimacy" (p. 101) with a romantic partner (the central task of early adulthood). Similarly, from a life-course perspective (Elder, 1985), romantic involvements, especially during early adolescence, are "off-timing" events that could pose more challenges and have more negative consequences on subsequent behavioral trajectories than those that are age appropriate. In short, involvement in romantic relationships in adolescence may interfere with normative developmental tasks and otherwise be associated with problematic functioning such as delinquency and depression (Joyner & Udry, 2000; Neemann et al., 1995; Zemmer-Gembeck et al., 2001).

Several potential processes could explain such an association between involvement in relationship and delinquency in adolescence. For example, because adolescents are still trying to figure out who they are (i.e., identity development), premature involvement in a romantic relationship could be a source of distress for adolescents (Davies & Windle, 2000). It might be the case that adolescents become overwhelmed by the demands in romantic relationships and therefore demonstrate more problem behaviors, including delinquency (Neemann et al., 1995; Wright, 1982). Another possibility is that romantic involvement may introduce adolescents to deviant partners who influence adolescent behavior toward additional delinquency. Several studies suggested that romantic involvement with problem partners may exacerbate existing problems, and association with deviant partners are associated with higher level of delinquency (Haynie et al., 2005; Meeus et al., 2004; van Dulmen et al., 2008). Future studies are needed to test these and other explanations of this association.

Extending investigation of the association between romantic involvement and delinquency, we further examined how the cumulative romantic relationships were related to delinquency in young adulthood. . . . [The] findings demonstrated that frequent romantic relationships are associated with greater risks of delinquency in young adulthood, highlighting the potential importance of cumulative romantic relationship history for statistically predicting criminal behaviors in young adulthood. . . .

Note

1. Although the term *delinquency* is usually applied to criminal and other deviant behaviors committed by adolescents, we use the term for both adolescents and young adults for the sake of consistency.

References

Brown, B. B., Feiring, C., & Furman, W. (1999). Missing the love boat: Why researchers have shied away from adolescent romance. In W. Furman, B. B. Brown, & C. Feiring (Eds.), *The development of romantic relationships in adolescence* (pp. 1–18). New York: Cambridge University Press.

Carver, K., Joyner, K., & Udry, J. R. (2003). National estimates of adolescent romantic relationships. In P. Florsheim (Ed.), *Adolescent romantic relations and sexual behavior: Theory, research and practical implications* (pp. 23–56). Mahwah, NJ: Erlbaum.

Cauffman, E., Farruggia, S. P., & Goldweber, A. (2008). Bad boys or poor parents: Relations to female juvenile delinquency. *Journal of Research on Adolescence, 18,* 699–712.

Cavanagh, S. E., Crissey, S. R., & Raley, R. K. (2008). Family structure history and adolescent romance. *Journal of Marriage and Family, 70,* 698–714.

Chantala, K. (2006). *Guidelines for analyzing Add Health data.* Chapel Hill: Carolina Population Center, University of North Carolina at Chapel Hill.

Collins, W. A. (2003). More than myth: The developmental significance of romantic relationships during adolescence. *Journal of Research on Adolescence, 13,* 1–24.

Collins, W. A., & Steinberg, L. (2006). Adolescent development in interpersonal context. In N. Eisenberg (Eds.), *Handbook of child psychology: Vol. 3. Social, emotional, and personality development* (6th ed., pp. 1003–1067). Hoboken, NJ: Wiley.

Collins, W. A., & van Dulmen, M. (2006). The course of true love(s): Origins and pathways in the development of romantic relationships. In A. C. Crouter & A. Booth (Eds.), *Romance and sex in adolescence and emerging adulthood: Risks and opportunities* (pp. 63–86). Mahwah, NJ: Erlbaum.

Davies, P. T., & Windle, M. (2000). Middle adolescents' dating pathways and psychosocial adjustment. *Merrill-Palmer Quarterly, 46,* 90–118.

Elder, G. H., Jr. (1985). *Life course dynamics.* Ithaca, NY: Cornell University Press.

Erikson, E. H. (1959). Growth and crisis of the healthy personality. In E. H. Erikson (Ed.), *Psychological issues: identity and the life cycle* (Vol. 1, pp. 50–100). New York: International Universities Press.

Farrington, D. P. (1995). The development of offending and antisocial behavior from childhood: Key findings from the Cambridge Study in Delinquent Development. *Journal of Child Psychology and Psychiatry and Allied Disciplines, 36,* 929–964.

Fincham, F. D., & Cui, M. (2011). *Romantic relationships in emerging adulthood.* New York: Cambridge University Press.

Furman, W., & Buhrmester, D. (1992). Age and sex differences in perceptions of networks of personal relationships. *Child Development, 63,* 103–115.

Ge, X., Brody, G., Conger, R., & Simmons, R. (2006). Pubertal maturation and African American children's internalizing and externalizing symptoms. *Journal of Youth and Adolescence, 35,* 528–537.

Harris, K. M., Halpern, C. T., Entzel, P., Tabor, J., Bearman, P. S., & Udry, J. R. (2008). *The National Longitudinal Study of Adolescent Health: Research design.* Retrieved January 10, 2010, from http://www.cpc.unc.edu/projects/addhealth/design

Haynie, D., Giordano, P. C., Manning, W. D., & Longmore, M. A. (2005). Adolescent romantic relationships and delinquency involvement. *Criminology, 43*, 177–209.

Meeus, W., Branje, S., & Overbeek, G. J. (2004). Parents and partners in crime: A six-year longitudinal study on changes in supportive relationships and delinquency in adolescence and young adulthood. *Journal of Child Psychology and Psychiatry, 45*, 1288–1298.

Neemann, J., Hubbard, J., & Masten, A. S. (1995). The changing importance of romantic relationship involvement to competence from late childhood to late adolescence. *Development and Psychopathology, 7*, 727–750.

Sampson, R. J., Laub, J. H., & Wimer, C. (2006). Does marriage reduce crime? A counterfactual approach to within-individual causal effects. *Criminology, 44*, 465–507.

Thomas, B. S., & Hsiu, L. T. (1993). The role of selected risk factors in predicting adolescent drug use and its adverse consequences. *International Journal of Addictions, 28*, 1549–1563.

van Dulmen, M. H. M., Goncy. E A., Haydon, K. C., & Collins, W. A. (2008). Distinctiveness of adolescent and emerging adult romantic relationship features in predicting externalizing behavior problems. *Journal of Youth and Adolescence, 37*, 336–345.

Wong, S. K. (2005). The effects of adolescent activities on delinquency: A differential involvement approach. *Journal of Youth and Adolescence, 34*, 321–333.

Wright, L. S. (1982). Parental permission to date and its relationship to drug use and suicidal thoughts among adolescents. *Adolescence, 17*, 409–418.

Zimmer-Gembeck, M. J., Siebbenbruner, J., & Collins, W. A. (2001). Diverse aspects of dating: Associations with psychosocial functioning from early to middle adolescence. *Journal of Adolescence, 24*, 313–336.

K. Paige Harden and
Jane Mendle

 **NO**

Adolescent Sexual Activity and the Development of Delinquent Behavior: The Role of Relationship Context

Introduction

As the number of sexually active American teenagers has increased over the past half-century (Kotchick et al. 2001), both researchers and policymakers have expressed concern about the sequelae of such behavior, particularly whether sexual activity during adolescence might precipitate adverse psychosocial consequences. . . . [A]wide body of research [demonstrates] that teenagers who are sexually active also report a breadth of psychosocial problems, including poor academic achievement, depression, and low self-esteem (Hallfors et al. 2005; Meier 2007; Spriggs and Halpern 2008). Historically, an earlier initiation of sexual activity has been seen as a marker of externalizing problems (Jessor and Jessor 1977). Sexually active adolescents are more likely to engage in delinquent activities (Armour and Haynie 2007; Leitenberg and Saltzman 2000), and adolescents with a history of childhood conduct disorder tend to have earlier ages at first intercourse and higher rates of teenage pregnancy (Emery et al. 1999; Woodward and Fergusson 1999).

While the correlation between adolescent sexual behavior and externalizing problems is well-documented, understanding how adolescent sexual experiences may impact the development of delinquency remains unclear. In the current article, we address two challenges to understanding the mechanisms by which sexual activity and delinquency are associated. First, we consider the diversity of relationship contexts in which adolescent sexual activity occurs. Second, we control for the role of common underlying genetic factors that impact both sexual activity and delinquency in adolescence. By simultaneously considering both the environmental contexts of adolescent sexual experience and the role of genetic predispositions, we hope to advance a more nuanced understanding of the developmental impact of adolescent sexual activity.

Harden, K. Page; Mendle, Jane. From *Journal of Youth and Adolescence*, Vol. 40, No. 7, 2011, pp. 825–838. Copyright © 2011 by Springer Science and Business Media. Reprinted by permission via Rightslink.

Romantic Versus Non-Romantic Relationship Contexts

One challenge in examining the psychosocial sequelae of adolescent sexual behavior is that teenagers are sexually active within different types of relationships, and these relationship contexts may moderate the developmental impact of sexual behaviors. In contrast to the perspective that adolescent sexual activity, in and of itself, is a manifestation of underlying adjustment difficulties, most adolescents first experience sexual intercourse in the course of a romantic relationship (Manning et al. 2000), and romantic relationships are a normative part of adolescent life. . . . Despite the obvious link between romantic relationships and sexual experiences—and the high subjective importance of romantic relationships for adolescents themselves—research on adolescent sexuality has paid little attention to the characteristics of relationships (Collins et al. 2009). In addition, although adolescents most commonly *initiate* sexual intercourse within the context of romantic relationships, they also have sex with people who are not established romantic partners and with whom there are no clear expectations of emotional intimacy, exclusivity, or commitment. . . . These non-romantic sexual experiences may have different developmental sequelae than sex that occurs exclusively within the context of a romantic relationship.

Colloquially, non-romantic sexual experiences are referred to as "hooking up" or "friends with benefits." The popular media broadly denigrates "hooking up" and its negative effects on adolescent well-being (e.g., Blow 2008; Denizet-Lewis 2004; Stepp 2007). However, few empirical studies have directly examined the developmental impact of sexual activity in non-romantic relationships. Of this limited body of research, results reported by McCarthy and Casey (2008) are most relevant for understanding the association between sex and delinquency. [They] found that sexual activity that occurred in the context of non-romantic relationships predicted a 20% increase in delinquency and a 31% increase in substance use, but that sexual activity occurring exclusively in a romantic relationship was not associated with either delinquency or substance use. Similar patterns have been reported for internalizing outcomes, including negative emotions (Donald et al. 1995) and depressive symptoms (Meier 2007). In contrast, other researchers have found negative effects for sex in non-romantic relationships only for girls (Grello et al. 2006; Shulman et al. 2009). Finally, still other studies have failed to find any effects of sex in non-romantic relationships, after controlling for preexisting differences in adolescents' psychosocial functioning (Eisenberg et al. 2009; Grello et al. 2003; Monahan and Lee 2008). It therefore remains unclear whether non-romantic sex can precipitate delinquent behavior, or whether adolescents with pre-existing psychosocial problems are simply more likely to have sex in non-romantic relationship contexts.

The Role of Genes in the Link between Sexual Activity and Delinquency

An additional challenge when examining the psychosocial correlates of adolescent sexual activity is the importance of genetic factors and, specifically, that the association between sexual activity and adolescent delinquency may be partly due to a common set of genes influencing both traits. Developmental research has largely neglected the role of genes in adolescent sexual behavior, but it is certainly clear that adolescents actively shape and select their social environments—including their romantic and sexual experiences. This process is, in part, governed by their own genetically influenced traits and interests, including their personality traits and their levels of physical development. Thus, adolescent sexual activity can be seen as an example of *gene-environment correlation* (rGE), because the likelihood of an adolescent experiencing sexual intercourse within a particular type of relationship is related to his or her genetic propensities.

Three related lines of research support the importance of considering genes in the association between delinquency and adolescent sexual behavior. First, a number of twin studies have demonstrated that a variety of sexual behaviors—including whether a teenager is sexually active, when he or she first becomes sexually active, and his or her number of sexual partners—are all genetically influenced (Bricker et al. 2006; Dunne et al. 1997; Martin et al. 1977; Mustanski et al. 2007). Molecular genetic analyses suggest that genes related to the dopamine system, which is known to be important for sensation-seeking personality traits (Derringer et al. 2010), are also associated with earlier ages at first sex (Guo and Tong 2006; Miller et al. 1999), likelihood of having had sex (Eisenberg et al. 2007), and number of sexual partners (Guo et al. 2007, 2008; Halpern et al. 2007). In addition, genes influence a variety of other fertility-related phenotypes that are positively correlated with age at first sex (Udry and Cliquet 1982), such as age at menarche (Rowe 2002) and age at first birth (Kohler et al. 2002). Second, both twin and molecular genetic studies have shown that genes influence delinquency and antisocial behavior (e.g., Arsenault et al. 2003; D'Onofrio et al. 2007; Scourfield et al. 2004; Slutske et al. 1997; Young et al. 2002; for reviews see Miles and Carey 1997; Raine 2002; Rhee and Waldman 2002; Rowe 2001). Third, and most relevant for the current project, bivariate behavior genetic analyses suggest that the genes influencing sexual behavior overlap with those influencing antisocial behavior. For example, Verweij et al. (2009) found that the correlation between risky sexual behavior (e.g., sex without a condom, multiple partners in 24-h period) and antisocial behavior in adults was primarily attributable to common genetic influences. Similar results have been obtained in a cross-generational analysis: The association between teenage childbearing and children's externalizing problems is due, in part, to the parent-to-child transmission of genes influencing both sexual behavior and externalizing symptomatology (Harden et al. 2007).

Analyses that control for the genetic influences common to adolescent sexual activity and delinquency can yield surprising results. In a previous article using twin data from the National Longitudinal Study of Adolescent Health (Add Health), we reported that earlier age at first sex was actually associated with *lower* involvement in delinquency in early adulthood after controlling genetic influences on both delinquency and age at first intercourse (Harden et al. 2008). This provocative finding suggests that adolescent sexual activity may represent a marker for underlying genetic predispositions for delinquent behavior, while also being a developmental transition that may confer some psychosocial benefits. Our previous study focused on a single dimension of sexual experience—age of first sexual intercourse. As we discussed above, however, sexual activity may occur in a variety of social contexts that may modify the relation between sex and delinquency.

Goals of the Current Article

In the current article, we extend previous behavior genetic analyses of the association between adolescent sexual activity and delinquency by examining differences between sexual activity that occurs in romantic relationships versus non-romantic relationships. . . . Specifically, we address two research questions. First, to what extent do common genetic factors account for the associations between delinquency and sexual activity in romantic and non-romantic relationship contexts? . . . Second, after controlling for these common genetic factors, does the association between sexual activity and the development of delinquent behavior differ between romantic and non-romantic contexts? . . .

Method

Participants: National Longitudinal Study of Adolescent Health

Data are drawn from the National Longitudinal Study of Adolescent Health (Add Health; Udry 2003), a nationally representative study designed to evaluate adolescent health behaviors. . . .

[A]dolescents were asked whether they currently lived with another adolescent in the same household. This information was used to deliberately oversample adolescent sibling pairs. . . . The focus of the current analyses is a subsample of 519 same-sex twin pairs divided into two age cohorts: *younger adolescents* were ages 13–15 at Wave I ($N = 114$ DZ pairs, 126 MZ pairs) and *older adolescents* were ages 16–18 at Wave I ($N = 126$ DZ pairs, 153 MZ pairs). Twin zygosity was determined primarily on the basis of self-report and responses to four questionnaire items concerning similarity of appearance and frequency of being confused for one's twin. . . . Analyses were restricted to same-sex twins, in order to prevent bias in estimates of genetic influence due to MZ twins necessarily being identical for sex. . . .

There have been three follow-up interviews with the Add Health participants: Wave II in 1996, Wave III in August 2001–2002, and Wave IV in 2007–2008. The current study examines the effects of sexual activity on desistance from delinquency from adolescence to early adulthood, thus we use data from the Wave I (adolescent) and Wave III (early adulthood; 6 year follow-up) interviews. At Wave III, the younger cohort was 19–21 years old, while the older cohort was 22–24 years old.

Measures

Delinquency

The current analyses use 6 items from the Wave I and Wave III interviews that measure engagement in the following delinquent activities: painting graffiti, deliberately damaging someone else's property, stealing something worth more than $50, stealing something worth less than $50, taking something from a house or store, and selling marijuana or drugs. . . . Participants rated how often they had engaged in each delinquent act in the past 12 months. . . . As expected, mean levels of delinquency were higher in adolescence . . . than in early adulthood. . . .

Sexual Activity

During the Wave I . . . interview, adolescents reported whether or not they had ever had sexual intercourse. Sexual intercourse was specifically defined as heterosexual vaginal penetration. Adolescents who reported a past history of sexual activity were classified as having had sex in romantic relationships and/or non-romantic relationships. First, adolescents reported whether they had a "special romantic relationship" with anyone in the last 18 months. If an adolescent denied being in a "special romantic relationship," but reported that he or she had told another person (who was not a family member) that he or she "loved or liked them," and had held hands and kissed this person, then the adolescent was classified as being in a "liked relationship." For each romantic or liked relationship in the last 18 months (up to 3 relationships), adolescents reported whether they had sexual intercourse in that relationship. If an adolescent reported intercourse in either a "special romantic" or a "liked" relationship in the last 18 months, then they were classified as Romantic Sex = 1. Adolescents also reported at Wave I whether they had ever had a "sexual relationship" with anyone, "not counting the people you described as romantic relationships." Adolescents who reported sexual activity in the context of a non-romantic relationship were classified as Non-Romantic Sex = 1. Sex in romantic and non-romantic contexts were not mutually exclusive categories: Adolescents who reported both were scored as Romantic Sex = 1, Non-Romantic Sex = 1. . . . Finally, adolescents who reported that they were virgins were classified as not having sex in either romantic or non-romantic relationships [Romantic Sex = 0; Non-Romantic Sex = 0].

. . . As expected, a history of sexual intercourse was more common among older adolescents (approximately 42% of adolescents ages 16–18) than among younger adolescents (approximately 13% of adolescents ages 13–15). . . .

Results

Genetic and Environmental Influences on Sexual Activity in Romantic and Non-Romantic Relationships

. . . First, for both romantic and non-romantic sex in both older and younger adolescents, the MZ twin correlation substantially exceeded the DZ correlation, indicating the existence of genetic influences on adolescent sexual behavior generally. Second, the MZ correlations were higher for younger adolescents than for older adolescents, indicating that nonshared environmental influences were less important in younger adolescents. In fact, the correlation for non-romantic sex approached unity in younger adolescents: There were very few younger adolescent pairs discordant for reporting a history of non-romantic sex. Third, non-romantic sex in older adolescents was the only instance in which the MZ correlation did not exceed twice the value of the DZ correlation, suggesting that the role of shared environment was limited.

. . . Consistent with the observed twin correlations, sexual activity in younger adolescents was very strongly influenced by genetic factors . . . plus small non-shared environmental influences . . . [(shared environmental influences were negligible).]

Among 13–15 years olds, sexual activity, in both romantic and non-romantic contexts, is a relatively rare behavior that is almost entirely attributable to genetic factors.

. . . Among 16–18 year olds, . . ., the etiology of sexual activity differs by relationship context, with sex in romantic relationships more attributable to genes and sex in non-romantic relationships more attributable to environmental factors.

. . . For younger adolescents, the association between romantic and non-romantic sex was due entirely to a genetic path, whereas environmental differences between twins' sexual experiences in romantic relationships did not significantly predict non-romantic sex. Of the total variance in non-romantic sex in younger adolescents, 81% was due to genetic influences shared with romantic sex, 12% was due to genetic influences independent of romantic sex, and the final 7% was due to unique environmental influences.

In contrast, the association between romantic and non-romantic sex in older adolescents was due to both genetic *and* environmental pathways. Of the total variance in non-romantic sex in older adolescents, 29% was due to genetic influences shared with romantic sex, 24% was due to non-shared environmental influences shared with romantic sex, 16% was due to unique shared environmental influences, 30% was due to unique non-shared environmental influences. There were no genetic influences unique to non-romantic sex for older adolescents.

Environmental and Genetic Paths from Sexual Activity to Delinquency

Results from the longitudinal twin model for younger adolescents [indicate a] significant association between genetic influences on sex in romantic relationships and delinquency in adolescence; however, this association did not persist into early adulthood. Moreover, unique genetic influences on sex in non-romantic relationships that were independent of sex in romantic relationships did not predict delinquency at either time point. Finally, twins who differed in their sexual experiences did not show significantly different levels of delinquency in either adolescence or early adulthood. Overall, for younger adolescents (ages 13–15), associations between sexual activity and delinquency were limited to adolescence and were entirely driven by genetic factors.

. . . [F]or older adolescents . . ., [the] results are particularly notable. . . . First, genetic influences on romantic sex predicted higher levels of delinquency in adolescence, as well as increases in delinquency from adolescence to early adulthood. Second, after controlling for these genetic influences, twins who differed in whether they had sex in a romantic relationship showed significantly different levels of delinquency, such that the twin who had experienced sexual intercourse in a romantic relationship showed *lower* levels of delinquency. Moreover, this within-twin pair association persisted into early adulthood, with the twin who had experienced sex in a romantic relationship showing greater decreases in delinquent behavior. Third, there were also significant within-twin pair associations for sex in the context of a non-romantic relationship; however, the direction was reversed, such that the twin who had experienced non-romantic sex showed *higher* levels of delinquency cross-sectionally, and greater increases in delinquent behavior in early adulthood. . . .

Discussion

. . . The current article presents results from analyses of longitudinal, behavioral genetic data on sexual activity in romantic relationships and non-romantic relationships. We compared MZ and DZ twin pairs, in order to control for unmeasured genes that influence both sexual behavior and delinquent behavior. Overall, our results are consistent with the hypothesis that the etiology and developmental impact of adolescent sexual activity depends on the relationship context and the developmental stage in which it occurs. For younger adolescents (ages 13–15), sexual activity was a relatively rare occurrence, and a common set of genetic factors was the predominant influence on sexual activity in both romantic and non-romantic relationship contexts. These genetic influences on sexual activity, in turn, were entirely responsible for the association between sexual activity and delinquency in early adolescents. That is, genetic propensities to engage in sex during early adolescence also increase propensity to engage in delinquent behavior. Notably, there was no evidence for an environmental path between sexual activity and delinquency among younger adolescents. That is, the few young adolescent twin pairs who were discordant for sexual activity did not demonstrate differing levels of involvement in delinquent behavior. Moreover, sexual activity at ages 13–15 was not significantly associated with future levels of delinquency in early adulthood beyond what could be predicted given initial levels of delinquency in adolescence.

A different pattern was evident for older adolescents (ages 16–18). Not only was sexual activity, regardless of context, more common, but it was also more influenced by environmental differences. Genetic influences on sexual activity were not context-specific; a common set of genetic factors influenced sexual activity in both romantic and non-romantic contexts, but there was evidence of shared environmental influences specific to non-romantic sex. Genetic propensities to engage in sexual intercourse predicted higher involvement in delinquent behavior in adolescence, and predicted greater increases in delinquent behavior 6 years later in early adulthood. After controlling for these genetic influences, however, sex in romantic relationships was associated with *lower* levels of delinquency in adolescence and predicted future decreases in delinquency in early adulthood, whereas sex in non-romantic relationships was cross-sectionally associated with *higher* levels of delinquency in adolescence and predicted future increases in delinquency in early adulthood. Thus, the current article adds to a small but growing body of literature suggesting that the psychological correlates of adolescent sexual behavior are complex, and that—particularly for older adolescents—certain negative outcomes are only evident for sex outside the context of a romantic relationship (McCarthy and Casey 2008; Meier 2007). . . .

References

Armour, S., & Haynie, D. L. (2007). Adolescent sexual debut and later delinquency. *Journal of Youth and Adolescence, 36,* 141–152.

Arsenault, L., Moffitt, T. E., Caspi, A., Taylor, A., Rijsdijk, F. V., Jaffee, S. R., et al. (2003). Strong genetic effects on cross-situational antisocial behavior among 5-year old children according to mothers, teachers, examiner-observers, and twins' self-reports. *Journal of Child Psychology and Psychiatry, 44,* 832–848.

Blow, C. M. (2008, December 13). The demise of dating. *New York Times.* Retrieved from http://www.nytimes.com/2008/12/13/opinion/13blow.hfml.

Bricker, J. B., Stallings, M. C., Corley, R. P., Wadsworth, S. J., Bryan, A., Timberlake, D. S., et al. (2006). Genetic and environmental influences on age at sexual initiation in the Colorado Adoption Project. *Behavior Genetics, 36,* 820–832.

Collins, W. C., Welsh, D. P., & Furman, W. (2009). Adolescent romantic relationships. *Annual Review of Psychology, 60,* 631–652.

Denizet-Lewis, B. Friends, Friends With Benefits and the Benefits of the Local Mall. New York Times. May 30, 2004.

Donald, M., Lucke, J., Dunne, M., & Raphael, B. (1995). Gender differences associated with young people's emotional reactions to sexual intercourse. *Journal of Youth and Adolescence, 24,* 453–464.

Dunne, M. P., Martin, N. G., Statham, D. J., Slutske, W. S., Dunwiddie, S. H., Bucholz, K. K., et al. (1997). Genetic and environmental contributions to variance in age at first sexual intercourse. *Psychological Science, 8,* 211–216.

Eisenberg, M. E., Ackard, D. M., Resnick, M. D., & Neumark-Sztainer, D. (2009). Casual sex and psychological health among young adults: Is having "friends with benefits" emotionally damaging? *Perspectives on Sexual and Reproductive Health, 41,* 231–237.

Emery, R. E., Waldron, M., Kitzmann, K. M., & Aaron, J. (1999). Delinquent behavior, future divorce or nonmarital childbearing, and externalizing behavior among offspring: A 14-year prospective study. *Journal of Family Psychology, 13,* 568–579.

Grello, C. M., Welsh, D. P., & Harper, M. S. (2006). No strings attached: The nature of casual sex in college students. *Journal of Sex Research, 43,* 255–267.

Grello, C. M., Welsh, D. P., Harper, M. S., & Dickson, J. W. (2003). Dating and sexual relationship trajectories and adolescent functioning. *Adolescent and Family Health, 3,* 103–112.

Hallfors, D. D., Waller, M. W., Bauer, D., Ford, C. A., & Halpern, C. T. (2005). Which comes first in adolescence—sex and drugs or depression? *American Journal of Preventive Medicine, 29*(3), 163–170.

Jessor, R., & Jessor, S. L. (1977). *Problem behavior and psychosocial development: A longitudinal study of youth.* New York: Academic Press.

Kotchick, B. A., Schaffer, A., Miller, K. S., & Forehand, R. (2001). Adolescent sexual risk behavior: A multi-system perspective. *Clinical Psychology Review, 21*, 493–519.

Leitenberg, H., & Saltzman, H. (2000). A statewide survey of age at first intercourse for adolescent females and age of their male partners: Relation to other risk behaviors and statutory rape implications. *Archives of Sexual Behavior, 29*, 203–215.

Manning, W. D., Longmore, M. A., & Giordano, P. C. (2000). The relationship context of contraceptive use at first intercourse, *Family Planning Perspectives, 32*, 104–110.

Martin, N. G., Eaves, L. J., & Eysenck, H. J. (1977). Genetical, environmental, and personality factors influencing the age of first sexual intercourse in twins, *Journal of Biosocial Science, 9*, 91–97.

McCarthy, B., & Casey, T. (2008). Love, sex and crime: Adolescent romantic relationships and offending. *American Sociological Review, 73*, 944–969.

Meier, A. M. (2007). Adolescent first sex and subsequent mental health. *American Journal of Sociology, 11*, 1811–1847.

Meier, A. M. Adolescent First Sex and Subsequent Mental Health. *American Journal of Sociology,* Vol 112, No. 6 (May 2007).

Monahan, K. C., & Lee, J. M. (2008). Adolescent sexual activity: Links between relational context and depressive symptoms. *Journal of Youth and Adolescence, 37*, 917–927.

Mustanski, B., Viken, R. J., Kaprio, J., Winter, T., & Rose, R. J. (2007). Sexual behavior in young adulthood: A population-based twin study. *Health Psychology, 26*, 610–617.

Shulman, S., Walsh, S. D., Weisman, O., & Schelyer, M. (2009). Romantic contexts, sexual behavior, and depressive symptoms in adolescent males and females. *Sex Roles, 61*, 850–863.

Spitz, E., Moutier, R., Reed, T., Busnel, M. C., Marchaland, C., Roubertoux, P. L., et al. (1996). Comparative diagnoses of twin zygosity by SSLP variant analysis, questionnaire, and dermatoglyphic analysis. *Behavior Genetics, 26*, 55–63.

Spriggs, A. L., & Halpern, C. T. (2008). Timing of sexual debut and initiation of postsecondary education by early adulthood. *Perspectives on Sexual and Reproductive Health, 40*, 152–161.

Stepp, L. S. (2007). *Unhooked: How young women pursue sex, delay love and lose at both.* New York: Riverhead Books.

Stepp, L.S. Unhooked: How Young Women Pursue Sex, Delay Love, and Lose at Both. Penguin Group (New York, 2007).

Udry, J. R., & Cliquet, R. L. (1982). A cross-cultural examination of the relationship between ages at menarche, marriage, and first birth. *Demography, 19*, 53–63.

Woodward, L., & Fergusson, D. (1999). Early conduct problems and later risk of teenage pregnancy in girls. *Development and Psychopathology, 11*, 127–141.

EXPLORING THE ISSUE

Does Dating in Early Adolescence Impede Developmental Adjustment?

Critical Thinking and Reflection

1. All dating relationships involve some form of sexual activity (from holding hands and kissing to sexual intercourse); however, the range of sexual activities in which adolescents engage varies across age and other variables. Is dating in early adolescence less harmful when sexual activity is minimal? Does sex complicate the relationship and set youths up for negative outcomes?
2. According to the study by Harden and Mendle, sexual behavior is genetically programmed—genetics plays a larger role than environment in determining when youth become sexually active. What are the implications of this research for parents of young adolescents? How should they approach sexuality and dating with their teenagers?
3. Cui and colleagues offer several possible explanations for the positive association between dating, especially in early adolescence, and delinquency. How might relationships with romantic partners or the process of starting and ending several relationships during early adolescence negatively impact developing youths?
4. The YES and NO selections offer differing perspectives on the relationship between romantic liaisons and delinquency in youth. How would you construct a study to examine these variables differently? What would you need to do in order to capture both biological and environmental contributions?

Is There Common Ground?

Cui and colleagues would likely argue that younger adolescents are more adversely affected by early romantic relationships than older adolescents. Their research supports an environmental explanation for the association between early dating and delinquent behaviors. Drawing on psychosocial and life course theories, they argue that identity construction, as the central task of adolescence, must precede intimacy formation; therefore, younger adolescents, in particular, are not psychosocially equipped to handle the demands of dating relationships. Dating in early adolescence may also be considered an "off timing" event on the developmental continuum such that youth may not have the resources to manage age-inappropriate relationships. Harden and Mendle examine the biological rather than psychosocial influences on development in adolescence and find evidence that suggests that genetic influences play a greater role in sexual and delinquent behavior than environment, at least in early adolescence. According to this study, the timing of dating and involvement in sexual relationships is not a major determinant of adjustment for adolescents.

What do we make of these results? Are positive and negative outcomes with respect to dating and delinquency predetermined at birth? Are socialization influences, such as parents, friends, and significant others, inconsequential when it comes to the timing of romantic relationships? These selections seem to present a "nature versus nurture" debate on the issue. Is the answer this clear-cut, or do nature and nurture work together in some way? Future research should examine these relationships more closely—how might environmental variables navigate the direction of biological influences with respect to early dating and developmental adjustment? Are the outcomes set in stone, or are there ways to prevent negative outcomes for early-dating youth?

Additional Resources

Adolescent lovers studies. (February 14, 2001). Hypography: Science for everyone. Retrieved from www.hypography.com/article.cfm?id=29888

Bouchey, H. A., & Furman, W. (2003). Dating and romantic experiences in adolescence. In G. R. Adams & M. D. Berzonsky (Eds.). *Blackwell handbook of adolescence* (pp. 313–329). Malden, MA: Blackwell.

Collins, W. A., Welsh, D. P., & Furman, W. (2009). Adolescent romantic relationships. *Annual Review of Psychology, 60*, 631–652. doi:10.1146/annurev.psych.60.110707.163459

Florsheim, P. (Ed.). (2003). *Adolescent romantic relations and sexual behavior: Theory, research, and practical implications*. Mahwah, NJ: Erlbaum.

Furman, W. (2002). The emerging field of adolescent romantic relationships. *Current Directions in Psychological Science, 11*(5), 177–180.

Joyner, K., & Udry, J. R. (2000). You don't bring me anything buy down: Adolescent romance and depression. *Journal of Health and Social Behavior, 41*, 369–391.

McCarthy, B., & Casey, T. (2008). Love, sex, and crime: Adolescent romantic relationships and offending. *American Sociological Review, 73*(6), 944–969.

Monahan, K. C., & Lee, J. M. (2008). Adolescent sexual activity: Links between relational context and depressive symptoms. *Journal of Youth and Adolescence, 37*, 917–927. doi:10.1007/s10964–007–9256–5

Natsuaki, M. N., Biehl, M. C., & Ge, X. (2009). Trajectories of depressed mood from early adolescence to young adulthood: The effects of pubertal timing and adolescent dating. *Journal of Research on Adolescence, 19*(1), 47–74.

ISSUE 13

Should Parents Supervise Alcohol Use by or Provide Alcohol to Adolescents?

YES: Mark A. Bellis et al., from "Teenage Drinking, Alcohol Availability and Pricing: A Cross-Sectional Study of Risk and Protective Factors for Alcohol-Related Harms in School Children," *BMC Public Health* (vol. 9, no. 380, 2009), doi:10.1186/1471-2458-9-380

NO: Barbara J. McMorris et al., from "Influence of Family Factors and Supervised Alcohol Use on Adolescent Alcohol Use and Harms: Similarities Between Youth in Different Alcohol Policy Contexts," *Journal of Studies on Alcohol and Drugs* (vol. 72, no. 3, pp. 418–428, 2011)

Learning Outcomes

After reading this issue, you should be able to:

- Understand the harm-reduction arguments underlying the rationale for parental supervision of teen alcohol consumption.
- Articulate a position on zero-tolerance alcohol policies for youth.
- Understand how adult-supervised alcohol use might be a risk factor for or a protective factor against harms for youth.
- Form an informed opinion about supervised teen alcohol consumption.

ISSUE SUMMARY

YES: Mark A. Bellis, a professor at Liverpool John Moores University in the UK, and colleagues suggest that potential harms to youth can be reduced by having them drink in the safety of their own home where they can be supervised by their parents.

NO: Barbara J. McMorris, a senior research associate in the Healthy Youth Development Prevention Research Center within the medical school at the University of Minnesota, and colleagues argue that early alcohol use coupled with adult supervision of alcohol consumption leads to increased alcohol-related problems.

Alcohol-use prevention may not seem like a controversial issue, and parental supervision of teen alcohol use may seem even less controversial—after all, alcohol use is strictly regulated and illegal for adolescents. Substance abuse can create a host of social, health, and legal problems; therefore, adolescent prohibition is easily justified, and adult supervision of underage drinking can lead to charges against the adult. Organizations such as MADD (Mothers Against Drunk Driving) and AA (Alcoholics Anonymous) attest to the potential harm of alcohol use; this harm is thought to be even more detrimental for adolescents relative to adults. So, what makes the provision of alcohol to minors by parents even a question, let alone a controversial issue? The majority of youth try alcohol at some point during their adolescence. Among youth, the prevalence of current alcohol use increases with age; a national survey found that from 14 percent of 8th graders to 29 percent of 10th graders to 41 percent of 12th graders admitted to drinking alcohol in the last month (Johnston et al., 2011). Further, adolescents often engage in "binge drinking"—heavy, excessive drinking at one time—which is a particularly dangerous drinking behavior. Between 7 percent (grade 8) and 23 percent (grade 12) of youth reported having engaged in binge drinking in the last two weeks (in 2010—Table 8, Johnston et al., 2011). Those who drink at younger ages are also at more risk to develop alcohol dependence relative to those who drink at later ages (Hingson et al., 2006). Some evidence suggests that adolescent use of alcohol is a root cause of later harms (e.g., criminal behavior, sexually transmitted infection, unexpected pregnancy; Odgers et al., 2008). These findings suggest that youth drinking patterns may have a significant negative impact on later life.

Most countries have regulations governing the use and sale of alcohol—called alcohol control measures. One common control measure is an "age of majority." This differs from place to place; for example, in Wisconsin, the age of majority for drinking is 21 years, while in Quebec, it is 18 years. In some European countries (e.g., Belgium, Germany), 16-year-olds can drink wine and beer but not liquor. Interestingly, most of the age-of-majority regulations speak to public consumption and purchase; very little mention of consumption in the home typically occurs within these policies (ICAP, 2012). Regardless of the legislation around age of majority, states tend to have one of two orientations toward alcohol consumption by youth: zero tolerance or harm reduction.

Zero tolerance is an abstinence-only policy. Under this philosophy, policies exist that prohibit the purchase, possession, and consumption of alcohol by youth. Alcohol control laws and ordinances target retailers and bars (i.e., commercial hosts) as well as private adult social sources who may provide adolescents with alcohol (e.g., social-host-liability laws; Coppock, 2009). The effectiveness of these types of laws is somewhat mixed, but these laws generally seem to lead to the reduction of alcohol-related harms (Wagoner, 2010).

The harm-reduction orientation views youth as inevitably going to experiment with alcohol. Youth drinking is considered a normal, if undesirable, part of adolescence. The goals of policies guided by a harm-reduction philosophy are to minimize the harm that can occur from underage drinking and to teach the youth to become responsible adult drinkers. One way to reach these goals would be to have adults—typically parents—supervise the drinking context of the adolescents or have parents provide alcohol to the youth (i.e., limiting the amount and type of alcohol). Parents who provide alcohol to their teens or who supervise underage drinking parties are usually subscribing to a harm-reduction paradigm (Graham et al., 2006). They feel that by providing alcohol or watching their children while they drink, short-term harms (such as impaired driving or binge drinking) will be reduced.

There are cultural or regional differences in relation to the philosophies adopted and the ensuing legislation and policy enacted. The United States and Canada have zero-tolerance policies. Other countries, such as Australia and the Netherlands, have been more supportive of harm-reduction policies when it comes to youth and alcohol consumption. The cultural and policy contexts surrounding drinking may contribute to youth alcohol consumption and parental influence on teen drinking behavior.

In the YES and NO selections, Bellis et al. present findings that suggest that adolescents who drink experience different harm outcomes based on who provides them with alcohol. In particular, having parents provide alcohol acted as a protective factor for youth—as long as they were not binge drinking. In contrast, McMorris et al. conducted a study with youth in both the United States and Australia and found that parental provision of alcohol was related to alcohol-related harms (such as regretted sex and violence). As you read the two selections, consider how these two conflicting results could be reconciled.

YES ↵

Mark A. Bellis et al.

Teenage Drinking, Alcohol Availability and Pricing: A Cross-Sectional Study of Risk and Protective Factors for Alcohol-Related Harms in School Children

Background

In recent decades alcohol has emerged as one of the major international threats to public health,[1] and is now the third largest risk factor for disability and death in Europe[2]. . . . Despite much of the chronic burden of alcohol-related disease falling on adults,[3] the foundations of such damage are often established in childhood. Early alcohol initiation (e.g. before age 15)[4,5] and drinking in larger quantities in childhood and adolescence[6,7] are associated with a wide range of negative outcomes. . . .

Misuse of alcohol by children is an international problem. . . . [I]ncreases in alcohol-related ill health in children are not restricted to the UK (e.g. Germany,[10] Australia[11]).

Despite considerable acute and chronic health and social consequences relating to child alcohol consumption, evidence based guidance on whether children should drink alcohol at all, and how to moderate potential harm, is still being sought.[12] In particular, the effects of moderate or occasional consumption are unclear. Thus, while drinking at early ages (under 15 years) is linked to experiencing a range of health and social problems, the effects of alcohol use at age 15 can depend on amounts consumed, frequency of consumption, types of alcohol consumed and the context in which consumption takes place.[13,14] Alcohol illicitly obtained by children is associated with misuse.[15] However, alcohol provided by parents has been associated with reduced involvement in binge drinking and drinking in public places[15,16] compared with other means of access, and strict alcohol-specific parenting rules have been associated with reduced consumption.[17,19] However, in those aged 12, easy access to alcohol from parents is associated with increased alcohol abuse[20] and parental provision for parties has been linked to increased drinking.[16] With no clear understanding of the relationships between drinking behaviours, environments where alcohol is accessed and consumed, and resultant harms, more research is urgently needed to examine how such factors interact and to inform appropriate interventions.

In this paper we examine the drinking behaviours of alcohol-consuming 15–16 year olds and their relationships with a range of adverse alcohol-related outcomes. Thus, based on previous associations between alcohol consumption and violence[21] we examine experience of violence when drunk and how it relates to current drinking behaviours. With greater alcohol consumption at early ages also being associated with sexual risk-taking,[22,23] we explore relationships between drinking behaviours and having experienced regretted sex following alcohol consumption. As a proxy measure of potential damage to mental health we analyse associations between drinking patterns and reported tendency to forget things after drinking.[24] Finally, to measure effects on others through public nuisance and potentially anti-social behaviour, we examine which drinking patterns are associated with consumption in public places (here; outside in streets, around shops and in parks). Together, analyses are also used to examine potential thresholds for safer drinking and explore factors that may moderate relationships between consumption and immediate harms. . . .

Methods

. . . [A]n anonymous school based survey was undertaken . . . to examine drinking behaviours . . . . [T]he questionnaire consisted of closed, self-completed questions including: demographics (age, sex and postcode of residence); usual frequency of alcohol consumption and bingeing (here, drinking five or more drinks in one session[8]); and how individuals accessed alcohol and types of alcohol products consumed in a typical week (e.g. cans of beer, bottles of wine). . . . Individuals were . . . asked to identify if they drank alcohol in public places and these were described to respondents as outside in streets, parks or shops. The questionnaire asked respondents to identify (by tick box) if they had ever been violent or in a fight whilst drunk; whether they had regretted having had sex with someone after drinking; and whether they tended to forget things when they had been drinking alcohol. . . . For access to alcohol, variables measured were: personal purchase from on- and off-licence settings; access through parents, friends and family; and proxy purchasing through other adults. Access through parents distinguished between deliberate provision of alcohol by parents and alcohol covertly taken by youths.

. . . [T]he sample was . . . restricted to those aged 15 or 16 (n = 9,833). . . . To study drinking behaviour the sample was further limited only to those who identified that they drank alcohol (n = 8,263; 84%). . . .

Results

Regretted sex after drinking (12.5%), having been involved in violence when drunk (28.8%), consuming alcohol in public places (e.g. streets, parks and shops; 35.8%) and forgetting things after drinking (45.3%) had all been experienced by relatively large proportions of respondents. Violence when drunk and alcohol-related regretted sex both increased with age. While violence when drunk and drinking in public places were more common amongst boys, alcohol-related regretted sex and forgetting things after drinking were more commonly reported by girls. . . . Importantly, accessing alcohol through parents was associated with significantly lower levels of having experienced all (negative outcomes (Table 1). . . .

Table [2] presents the relationship between three reported drinking measures (units per week, frequency of drinking, and of bingeing) and proportions reporting each negative outcome overall and separately for those who do and do not have alcohol provided by parents. Overall, all negative outcomes increased in frequency significantly as drinking frequency, bingeing frequency and units of alcohol consumed per week increased. However, provision of alcohol by parents was associated with lower levels of harm at the same drinking and bingeing frequency, and at the same weekly quantities of consumption. Thus, while 19.9% of individuals whose parents provide alcohol and who drink once a week had been involved in violence when drunk, this rises to 35.9% in those whose parents do not provide alcohol (Table [2]). Similarly for those without parental provision of alcohol, 15.2% of those who drink up to five units of alcohol per week reported some alcohol-related regretted sex, while for those with parental provision rates are only 11.7% even at >10–20 units per week (Table [2]). However, such protective effects were not sustained across all adverse outcomes at higher levels of consumption (especially at high levels of binge drinking). . . .

Table 1

Relationships Between Sources of Alcohol and Percentage of Children Aged 15 to 16 Years Having Experienced Negative Alcohol-Related Outcomes

			n	Drink in public places (streets, parks, shops)	Violence when drunk	Alcohol-related regretted sex	Tend to forget things after drinking
Source	Buy my own	No	5923	32.15	22.41	8.86	42.61
		Yes	2340	45.00	44.82	21.39	51.98
		P		<0.001	<0.001	<0.001	<0.001
	Parents provide	No	4182	47.0	37.1	15.3	51.4
		Yes	4081	24.3	20.3	9.6	39.1
		P		<0.001	<0.001	<0.001	<0.001
	Get adults outside shop to buy it	No	7060	27.9	24.7	11.1	42.8
		Yes	1203	82.2	52.4	20.8	59.7
		P		<0.001	<0.001	<0.001	<0.001

Table [2]

Percentage of 15–16 Year Olds Having Experienced Negative Alcohol-Related Outcomes, by Drinking Behaviour and Parental Alcohol Provision.

Percentage Reporting Negative Outcomes Related to Alcohol

| | | Sample Characteristics | | | Drink in public places (streets, parks, shops) | | | | Violence when drunk | | | | Alcohol-related regretted sex | | | | Tend to forget things after drinking | | | |
| | | | Parents Provide | | | | Parents Provide | | | | Parents Provide | | | | Parents Provide | | | | Parents Provide | |
	n	No	Yes	All	No	Yes	P§	All	No	Yes	P§	All	No	Yes	P§	All	No	Yes	P§
Binge Frequency																			
Never	1007	36.4	63.6	11.2	24.0	3.9	***	7.1	13.0	3.7	***	3.8	6.9	2.0	***	21.6	32.4	15.6	***
<1/month	2302	43.1	56.9	21.4	33.1	12.5	***	13.6	21.0	8.1	***	6.1	8.0	4.7	**	36.6	43.7	31.2	***
1–3/month	1894	48.9	51.1	34.2	43.5	25.3	***	24.6	30.9	18.6	***	8.6	9.8	7.4	ns	47.4	51.5	43.7	***
1/week	1533	60.9	39.1	48.9	55.0	39.5	***	40.0	42.9	35.4	**	15.4	16.6	13.5	ns	54.9	55.6	53.8	ns
2/week	1173	62.4	37.6	64.5	69.3	56.7	***	59.8	63.6	53.6	***	28.4	29.0	27.4	ns	61.9	62.4	60.9	ns
3+/week	254	65.0	35.0	63.4	61.8	66.3	ns	72.4	75.5	66.7	ns	39.1	39.5	38.3	ns	63.6	66.7	58.1	ns
P			***	***	***	***		***	***	***		***	***	***		***	***	***	
Drinking Frequency																			
<1/month	1750	44.2	55.8	14.9	24.3	7.5	***	10.6	16.5	6.1	***	4.7	5.4	4.2	ns	31.6	39.6	25.5	***
1–3/month	2097	46.8	53.2	27.2	37.8	17.9	***	17.9	24.3	12.3	***	7.1	8.5	5.9	*	40.8	46.1	36.3	***

	N														
1/week	2041	53.7	46.4	40.7	52.1 ***	27.5 ***	28.4 ***	35.9	19.9 ***	11.0 ***	13.5 ***	8.2 ***	47.5 ***	52.1	42.2 ***
2/week	1791	56.9	43.1	54.3	63.5 ***	42.2 ***	48.4 ***	55.8	38.8 ***	21.7 ***	24.3 ***	18.3 **	57.5 ***	61.0	53.0 ***
3+/week	575	53.0	47.0	55.8	62.3 ***	48.2 ***	61.7 ***	69.9	52.1 ***	30.2 ***	36.3 ***	23.0 ***	56.1 ***	63.1	48.5 ***
P		***	***	***	***	***	***	***	***	***	***	***	***	***	***
Units per week[$]															
<= 5	469	39.9	60.1	27.1	51.3 ***	11.0 ***	18.2 ***	33.7 ***	8.4 ***	9.4 ***	15.2 ***	5.8 **	36.5 **	47.2	29.5 ***
>5–10	700	41.7	58.3	29.7	41.1 ***	21.6 ***	20.4 ***	29.5 ***	13.9 ***	8.8 ***	13.6 ***	5.4 ***	42.7 ***	52.1	35.9 ***
>10–20	1106	51.9	48.1	45.6	54.9 ***	35.5 ***	35.1 ***	40.9 ***	28.8 ***	13.2 ***	14.5 ns	11.7 ns	56.1 ns	57.2	55.0 ns
>20–30	604	59.8	40.2	60.1	67.3 ***	49.4 ***	55.3 ***	57.8 ***	51.5 ns	21.4 ns	19.8 ns	23.8 ns	57.7 ns	58.0	57.2 ns
>30	700	60.4	39.6	68.1	72.1 **	62.1 ***	64.9 ***	69.0 ***	58.8 **	32.7 **	36.3 *	27.4 *	59.5 *	60.8	57.5 ns
P		***	***	***	***	***	***	***	***	***	***	***	***	*	***

P compares those whose parents provide and do not provide any alcohol for proportions having experienced each negative risk behaviour within categories of units per week, drinking and binge drinking frequency. * P < 0.05, ** P < 0.01, *** P < 0,001. [$]Units per week consumed could only be calculated for those reporting a drinking frequency of once per week or greater and for those individuals providing details of types of alcohol products consumed and quantities of each product consumed in a typical week.

Discussion

Consistent with studies in the USA,[7,21] our results show that substantial proportions of even those that drink at relatively low frequencies (e.g. weekly) or never binge have experienced adverse effects. Thus, 10.6% of individuals who drink less than once a month have still experienced violence when drunk and nearly a third report forgetting things after drinking (Table [2]). However, amongst children whose parents provide alcohol, violence when drunk and forgetfulness drop to 6.1% and 25.5% in such lower frequency drinkers. Previous studies suggest that both parental attitudes towards, and their supervision of youth drinking can affect young people's drinking behaviours.[15,20] However, results here suggest that similar drinking patterns are more likely to be related to adverse outcomes when alcohol is accessed outside of parental environments. Thus, as well as drinking frequency, parental provision also appears to have a mediating effect on risks associated with binge drinking and units consumed per week (Table [2]). However, any protective effects are limited. Thus, 35.4% of those bingeing once a week, even with parental provision, have been involved in violence when drunk (Table [2]) and amongst respondents reporting the highest frequency of binge drinking, protective effects of parental provision disappear (Table [2]). However, as we were unable to differentiate types of parental provision (e.g. for unsupervised parties or consumption at family meals), here we cannot identify specifically how context relates to risks. . . .

With our results showing cheaper alcohol products linked most strongly to adverse drinking outcomes and other work identifying underage alcohol consumption being sensitive to price,[25] governments should establish a minimum price for alcohol (per unit). Drinking bottles and cans of beer was also linked to violence, regretted sex and public drinking while alcopops and wine appeared protective against alcohol-related violence and public drinking respectively. Although it is possible to speculate that such effects may relate to the image of each product (e.g. beer may be considered a drink for tougher youths than alcopops) or the location in which such drinks are consumed (e.g. wine may be more likely to be consumed in moderating environments such as at home with parents) understanding such factors requires further investigation.[26]

As with any questionnaire based cross-sectional study this survey has a number of limitations. Both drinking behaviours and negative outcomes were self-reported and relied on the honesty and recollection of respondents.[27] Whilst guaranteed anonymity can encourage the former, . . . recollection of behaviours relating to alcohol consumption may be incomplete because of forgetting things after drinking, especially amongst those who binge. Calculations of units of alcohol consumed per week could only be broad approximations as a wide variety of products are available. . . . [W]hile the survey specifically examined alcohol-related outcomes (e.g. violence when drunk), it did not provide information on the amount individuals had consumed precisely when such outcomes occurred but only measured their current typical drinking patterns. Consequently, we cannot rule out that some adverse drinking behaviours may have developed as a coping mechanism after, for instance, being a victim of alcohol-related violence or regretted sex[28,29]. . . . Adverse effects of alcohol were limited to four measures and did not include correlates with prevalence of injury (e.g. hospital attendance) or other potential consequences (e.g. effects on education, relationship problems).[8,30] However, chosen outcomes did include adverse measures previously associated with males (violence),[21] an adverse sexual outcome linked to alcohol (regretted sex),[22,23] a measure of potential damage to mental health and development (forgetting things after drinking)[24] and a proxy for involvement in public nuisance (drinking in public places). . . .

Conclusion

Our results support those of others that suggest even low levels of consumption can not be considered safe for children.[19] While studies suggest that levels of youth alcohol consumption may be high in England, and especially in the North West region,[31] the reality in many countries is that by the ages of 15 and 16 a higher proportion of children drink alcohol than abstain.[8,9] Any efforts to move more children towards or into abstinence through parental rules and controls may be effective for some individuals,[18,19] but may also result in alcohol consumption moving out of the family environment into parks, streets or other public spaces. Our results suggest that such a move, even if overall consumption did not increase, could exacerbate negative outcomes from alcohol consumption amongst teenagers. More studies and meta-analyses are needed to refine public information on alcohol consumption by children. Our results, nevertheless, do suggest that those parents who allow children aged 15–16 years to drink may limit harms by restricting consumption to lower frequencies (e.g. no more than once a week) and under no circumstances permitting binge drinking. However, parental efforts should be matched by genuine legislative and enforcement activity to reduce independent access to alcohol by children, and examination of costs per unit and bottle sizes to discourage large bottle purchases. While these measures are unlikely to eradicate the negative effects of alcohol on children, they may reduce them substantially while allowing children to prepare themselves for life in an adult environment dominated by this drug. . . .

References

1. World Health Organization: *WHO Expert Committee on Problems Related to Alcohol Consumption. Second report WHO technical report series 944* Geneva: World Health Organization; 2007.

2. Ezzati M, Lopez AD, Rodgers A, Murray CJ, eds: *Comparative quantification of health risks. Global and regional burden of disease attributable to selected major risk factors* Geneva: World Health Organization; 2004.

3. Alcohol-related deaths in the United Kingdom 1991–2006 [http://www.statistics.gov.uk/statbase/Product.asp?ylnk=14496]

4. Gruber E, DiClemente RJ, Anderson MM, Lodico M: Early drinking onset and its association with alcohol use and problem behavior in late adolescence. *Prev Med* 1996, 25:293–300.

5. Swahn M, Bossart R: Gender, early alcohol use and suicide ideation and attempts: finding from the 2005 Youth Risk Factor Behaviour Survey. *J Adolesc Health* 2007, 41:175–181.

6. Best D, Manning V, Gossop M, Gross S, Strang J: Excessive drinking and other problem behaviours among 14–16 year old children. *Addict Behav* 2006, 31:1424–1435.

7. Miller JW, Naimi TS, Brewer RD, Everett Jones S: Binge drinking and associated health risk behaviors among high school students. *Pediatrics* 2007, 119:76–85.

8. Hibell B, Guttormsson U, Ahlström S, Balakireva O, Bjarnason T, Kokkevi A, Kraus L: *The 2007 ESPAD Report: substance use among students in 35 European countries* Stockholm: Swedish Council for Information on Alcohol and Other Drugs; 2009.

9. Fuller E. ed: *Smoking, drinking, and drug use among young people in England in 2008* London: National Centre for Social Research and National Foundation for Educational Research; 2009.

10. Meyer S, Steiner M, Mueller H, Nunold H, Gottschling S, Gortner L: Recent trends in the burden of alcohol intoxication on pediatric in-patient services in Germany. *Klin Padiatr* 2008, 220:6–9.

11. Livingston M: Recent trends in risky alcohol consumption and related harm among young people in Victoria, Australia. *Aust N Z J Public Health* 2008, 32:266–271.

12. HM Government; *Safe Sensible Social. The next steps in the National Alcohol Strategy* London: HM Government; 2007.

13. Andersen A, Due P, Holstein BE, Iversen L: Tracking drinking behaviour from age 15–19 years. *Addiction* 2003, 98:1505–1511.

14. Kuntsche E, Knibbe R, Gmel G, Engels R: 'I drink spirits to get drunk and block out my problems . . .' Beverage preference, drinking motives and alcohol use in adolescence. *Alcohol Alcohol* 2006, 41:566–573.

15. Bellis MA, Hughes K, Morleo M, Tocque K, Hughes S, Allen T, Harrison D, Fe-Rodriguez E: Predictors of risky alcohol consumption in schoolchildren and their implications for preventing alcohol-related harm. *Subst Abuse Treat Prev Policy* 2007, 2:15.

16. Foley KL, Altman D, Durant RH, Wolfson M: Adults approval and adolescent alcohol use. *J Adolesc Health* 2004, 34:345e17–26.

17. O'Donnell L, Stueve A, Duran R, Myint-U A, Agronick G. San Doval A, Wilson-Simmons R: Parenting practices, parents' underestimation of daughters' risks, and alcohol and sexual behaviors of urban girls. *J Adolesc Health* 2008, 42:496–502.

18. Vorst H Van der, Engels RCME, Meeus W, Dekovic M, Van Leeuwe J: The role of alcohol-specific socialization in adolescents' drinking behaviour. *Addiction* 2005, 100:1464–1476.

19. Van Zundert RM, Vorst H Van Der, Vermulst AA, Engels RC; Pathways to alcohol use among Dutch students in regular education and education for adolescents with behavioral problems: the role of parental alcohol use, general parenting practices, and alcohol-specific parenting practices, *J Fam Psychol* 2006, 20:456–467.

20. Komro KA, Maldonado-Molina MM, Tobler AL, Bonds JR, Muller KE: Effects of home access and availability of alcohol on young adolescents alcohol use. *Addiction* 2007, 102:1597–1608.

21. French M, MacLean J: Underage alcohol use, delinquency, and criminal activity. *Health Econ* 2006, 15:1261–1281.

22. Bonomo Y, Coffey C, Wolfe R, Lynskey M, Bowes G, Patton G: Adverse outcomes of alcohol use in adolescents. *Addiction* 2001, 96(10): 1485–1496.

23. Wells JE, Horwood LJ, Fergusson DM: Drinking patterns in mid-adolescence and psychosocial outcomes in late adolescence and early adulthood. *Addiction* 2004, 99(12):1529–1541.

24. Zeigler DW, Wang CC, Yoast RA, Dickinson BD, McCaffree MA, Robinowitz CB, Sterling ML: The neurocognitive effects of alcohol on adolescents and college students. *Prev Med* 2005, 40:23–32.

25. Booth A, Meier P, Stockwell T, Sutton A, Wilkinson A, Wong K: *Independent review of the effects of alcohol pricing and promotion. Part A: systematic reviews* Sheffield; University of Sheffield; 2008.

26. Lintonen TP, Konu AI: Adolescent alcohol beverage type choices reflect their substance use patterns and attitudes. *J Youth Adolescence* 2003, 32:279–289.

27. Greenfield TK, Kerr WC: Alcohol measurement methodology in epidemiology: recent advances and opportunities. *Addiction* 2008, 103:1082–1099.

28. Bellis MA, Hughes K, Hughes S, eds: *World Health Organization. Interpersonal violence and alcohol: WHO Policy Briefing* Geneva: World Health Organization; 2006.

29. Young R, Sweeting H, West P: A longitudinal study of alcohol use and anti-social behaviour in young people. *Alcohol Alcohol* 2008, 43:204–214.

30. Lavikainen HM, Lintonen TP: Alcohol use in adolescence: identifying harms related to teenager's alcohol drinking. *Journal of Substance Use* 2009, 14:39–48.

31. North West Public Health Observatory: *Locol alcohol profiles for England* [http://www.nwph.net/alcohol/lape/].

Influence of Family Factors and Supervised Alcohol Use on Adolescent Alcohol Use and Harms: Similarities Between Youth in Different Alcohol Policy Contexts

Adolescent alcohol use is related to a variety of problem behaviors, including harmful alcohol use, drinking and driving, risky sex, and violence (Sise et al., 2009; World Health Organization, 2008). . . .

[T]he U.S. surgeon general issued a call to action promoting a zero-tolerance position toward youth alcohol use that was characterized by abstinence messages, severe consequences for use, and the illegality of underage drinking (U.S. Department of Health and Human Services, 2007). Despite this orientation, some parents still provide alcohol to their children, as illustrated by a 2005 American Medical Association study in which 25% of teens reported being at a party at which underage drinking was occurring in the presence of parents (American Medical Association, 2006). . . .

In Australia, surveys indicate that 30%–50% of adolescent drinkers obtain alcohol from their parents (Hayes et al., 2004), suggesting that it is more normative for parents to be involved in their children's alcohol use. . . . Harm-minimization advocates contend that exposure to supervised drinking contexts (i.e., drinking with parents or other adults present) may help youth learn responsible drinking (McBride et al., 2000, 2003) and, therefore, encourage responsible drinking in contexts where alcohol is available but adults are not present. . . .

The purpose of the current article is to examine and test hypotheses derived from zero-tolerance and harm-minimization policies regarding how family factors influence use in different policy contexts.

Research Objectives

This study investigates the impact of family factors on early adolescent use and harmful use among youth from Victoria, Australia, and Washington State, United States. Specifically, we explore whether adult-supervised alcohol use is a risk factor, as predicted by zero-tolerance policy, or a protective factor for harmful

McMorris, Barbara J.; et al. From *Journal of Studies on Alcohol and Drugs*, Vol. 72, No. 3, May 2011, pp. 418–428. Copyright © 2011 by Alcohol Research Documentation, Inc., Rutgers University. Reprinted by permission.www.jsad.com

alcohol use, as predicted by harm-minimization policy, and whether the influence of other family risk factors on adolescent alcohol use and harmful use is mediated by adult-supervised alcohol use in different ways, cross-nationally. . . .

The current study has the following research objectives: (a) to examine cross-state variation in levels of seventh-grade family factors, opportunities to use alcohol in supervised settings in eighth grade, and alcohol use and harmful use in ninth grade; (b) to investigate the contribution of family factors to ninth-grade alcohol use and harmful use and whether these relationships are differentiated or moderated by states adopting zero-tolerance or harm minimization policies; and (c) to investigate whether adult supervision of alcohol use in eighth grade mediates the impact of seventh-grade family variables. . . .

Method

[S]ample

. . . The analysis sample (n = 1,888) comprised primarily 13-year-olds . . . (Victoria: M = 13.0, SD = 0.4; Washington: M = 13.1, SD = 0.4). . . .

Measures

. . . Frequency of alcohol use and number of harmful consequences as a result of alcohol use in the past year in Grade 9 were used as the two dependent variables. . . . Eight harmful consequences resulting from alcohol use were examined: . . . loss of control ("not able to stop drinking once you had started") and social conflict "arguments" violent [/], . . . "got injured or had an accident," "had sex with someone, which you later regretted," "got so drunk you were sick or passed out," and. . . .

[O]pportunities to use alcohol under adult supervision was measured on the Grade 8 survey by asking how many times in the past year the student had consumed alcohol: "at dinner, or on a special occasion or holiday, *with* adult supervision?" or "at parties *with* adult supervision?" . . .

[P]ositive family management . . . measu[red] the extent to which students perceive that their parents monitor their activities, that their families establish clear rules, and their likelihood of being caught by parents for drinking, carrying a weapon, or skipping school. . . . Second, parental attitudes favorable toward alcohol use was [measured by] asking how wrong would parents feel it would be for their child to drink beer or wine regularly and to drink distilled spirits regularly. . . . Third, substance use problems in the family was measured by . . . asking "Has anyone in your family ever had a severe alcohol or drug problem?". . . .

Results

Differences in Prevalence of Alcohol Use

Predictably, the prevalence of alcohol use behavior in both states increased over time between seventh and ninth grades. Lifetime alcohol use by seventh grade among Victoria students was significantly higher than among

Washington students (59% vs. 39%). By eighth grade, drinking in adult-supervised settings was reported by two thirds of students in Victoria and 35% of Washington youth. By ninth grade, rates of alcohol use had increased to 71% in Victoria and 45% in Washington. More than a third of Victoria students (36%) also reported having experienced any harmful consequences resulting from their alcohol use, compared with about a fifth of Washington students (21%). . . .

Path Models

. . . Hypothesized relationships between family risk and protective factors generally look similar across the two states, despite policy and cultural differences.

. . . For youth in both states, lifetime alcohol use (Grade 7), family alcohol/drug problems (Grade 7), and adult-supervised alcohol use (Grade 8) were positively related and positive family management practices (Grade 7) were negatively related to later alcohol use and alcohol harms in Grade 9. . . .

Favorable parental attitudes indirectly influenced alcohol use and alcohol harm through the impact of adult-supervised alcohol use at eighth grade for youth in both Washington State and Victoria. . . . [Thus,] adult-supervised alcohol use served as a mediator of the association between parental attitudes and alcohol use and harm for youth in both states.

Lifetime alcohol use in seventh grade was . . . partially mediated by adult-supervised alcohol use at eight-grade . . . on ninth-grade alcohol use and harms. . . .

[F]indings indicated that the overall . . . relationships . . . [are] similar for students in Washington and Victoria.

. . . [U]sing single measures of supervised alcohol use, one at a time, results indicated that supervised alcohol use in either context—"at parties" or "at dinner or a special occasion"—increased the risk of alcohol use and harms for students in both states. . . .

Discussion

The national policy contexts concerning adolescent drinking were strikingly different in Washington and Victoria at the time of this study, reflecting different perspectives on underage drinking. Despite policy differences, results from the multiple-group path analysis demonstrate that relationships between family context variables and alcohol use and harms are remarkably similar between youth in both states; thus, there was no evidence for a moderating effect of state context on these relationships. . . .

Higher levels of early alcohol use seem to set the stage for increased use during middle adolescence regardless of country; however, the impact of frequency of ever using alcohol by seventh grade on adult supervision of alcohol use in eighth grade is 1.5 times larger in Victoria, contributing to increases in alcohol use and harms in ninth grade. Supervised drinking is a response that parents make to adolescent alcohol use in both states but more strongly in Victoria. It appears likely that, in the Australia harm-minimization context, a

Figure 1

Standardized Coefficients from the Unconstrained Path Models for Washington State and Victoria Students. Analysis Sample Sizes: Washington State: *n* = 918; Victoria: *n* = 908. All Estimates Are Standardized. Coefficients for Victoria Are in Parentheses. The Significant Between-State Difference Is Indicated by the Bold Line. G7 = Grade 7; G8 = Grade 8; G9 = Grade 9.

*p < .05 or better.

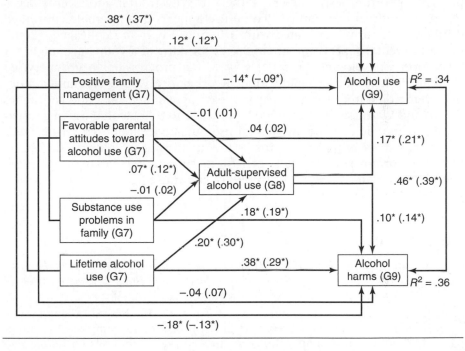

greater number of parents find themselves in the position of having to manage adolescent drinking. Our findings suggest that higher rates of early-age alcohol use and higher levels of adult-supervised use contribute to higher rates of alcohol-related problems in Australia. This clearly contradicts the position that supervised alcohol use or early experience with alcohol will have a reduced impact on the development of adolescent alcohol problems in the harm-minimization setting. Thus, our results run counter to harm-minimization hypotheses, which contend that youth will learn how to use alcohol safely in controlled, supervised settings and apply that knowledge to future opportunities to drink. . . .

In summary, although harm-minimization perspectives contend that youth drinking in adult-supervised settings is protective against future harmful use, we found that adult-supervised drinking in both states resulted in higher levels of harmful alcohol use. This finding has implications for many national contexts that encourage parents to supervise their children's drinking. In addition to Australia, many European countries favor this approach to prevention of alcohol-related harm (Bellis et al., 2007; Pavis et al., 1997; van der Vorst et al., 2010). However, evidence from the current study and previous studies (van der Vorst et al., 2010) provides little support for parental supervision of alcohol use as a protective factor for adolescent drinking.

Providing opportunities for drinking in supervised contexts did not inhibit alcohol use or harmful use in either state. These results, coupled with recent evidence from van der Vorst and colleagues (2010), lead us to suggest that policies should not encourage parents to drink with their children nor provide opportunities to supervise their use. Even after adolescents begin to drink, adult supervision of alcohol use appears to exacerbate continued drinking and harms associated with drinking. Kypri and colleagues (2007) suggest parental supervision of children's drinking at a young age might set in motion a developmental process by which progression to unsupervised drinking is made more rapidly than it otherwise would be. Similar findings were noted in differing policy contexts by van der Vorst and colleagues (2010) and Warner and White (2003), who found that alcohol use in a supervised setting and subsequent alcohol use outside a supervised setting both influenced the likelihood of progression to misuse in adulthood. Results from the current study provide consistent support for parents adopting a "no-use" standard if they want to reduce harmful alcohol use among their adolescents.

References

American Medical Association. (2006). *Teenage drinking: Key findings of the Teenage Research Unlimited (TRU) survey of teenagers and Harris Interactive survey of parents.* Chicago. IL; Office of Alcohol and Other Drug Abuse.

Bellis, M. A., Hughes, K., Morleo, M., Tocque, K., Hughes, S., Allen, T., . . . Fe-Rodriguez, E. (2007). Predictors of risky alcohol consumption in schoolchildren and their implications for preventing alcohol-related harm. *Substance Abuse Treatment, Prevention, and Policy, 2,* 15. Retrieved from http://www .substanceabusepolicy.com/content/2/1/15

Hayes, L., Smart, D., Toumbourou, J. W., & Sanson, A. (2004). *Parenting influences on adolescent alcohol use* (Research report No. 10). Melbourne, Australia: Australian Institute of Family Studies. Retrieved from http://www.aifs.gov .au/institute/pubs/resreport10/main.html

Kypri, K., Dean, J. I., & Stojanovski, E. (2007). Parent attitudes on the supply of alcohol to minors. *Drug and Alcohol Review. 26,* 41–47.

McBride, N., Farringdon, F., Midford, R., Meuleners, L., & Phillips, M. (2003). Early unsupervised drinking—reducing the risks: The School Health and Alcohol Harm Reduction Project. *Drug and Alcohol Review, 22,* 263–276.

McBride, N., Midford, R., Farringdon, F., & Phillips, M. (2000). Early results from a school alcohol harm minimization study: The School Health and Alcohol Harm Reduction Project. *Addiction, 95,* 1021–1042.

Pavis, S., Cunningham-Burley, S., & Amos, A. (1997). Alcohol consumption and young people: exploring meaning and social context. *Health Education Research. 12,* 311–322.

Sise, C. B., Sack, D. I., Sise, M. J., Riccoboni, S. T., Osler, T. M., Swanson, S. M., & Martinez, M. D. (2009). Alcohol and high-risk behavior among young first-time offenders. *The Journal of Trauma: Injury, Infection, and Critical Care, 67,* 498–502.

U.S. Department of Health and Human Services, (2007). *The Surgeon General's call to action to prevent and reduce underage drinking.* Rockville, MD: Office of the Surgeon General.

van der Vorst, H., Engels, R. C. M. E., & Burk, W. J. (2010). Do parents and best friends influence the normative increase in adolescents' alcohol use at home and outside the home? *Journal of Studies on Alcohol and Drugs, 71,* 105–114.

Warner, L. A., & White, H. R. (2003). Longitudinal effects of age at onset and first drinking situations on problem drinking. *Substance Use & Misuse, 38,* 1983–2016.

World Health Organization. (2008). *Strategies to reduce the harmful use of alcohol.* Retrieved from http://apps.who.int/gb/ebwha/pdf_files/A61/A61_13-en.pdf

EXPLORING THE ISSUE

Should Parents Supervise Alcohol Use by or Provide Alcohol to Adolescents?

Critical Thinking and Reflection

1. How does harm reduction work as a philosophy in relation to adolescent drinking? Are there other harm-reduction strategies that would work to facilitate safer adolescent drinking aside from parental provision/supervision of alcohol consumption? Does the culture or locale have any implication for harm-reduction strategies?
2. How does zero-tolerance work as a philosophy in relation to adolescent drinking? How does zero-tolerance for alcohol consumption by youth compare to other zero-tolerance strategies for other areas of contention (such as substance use or teenage sexuality)? What is the impact of zero-tolerance policies within different cultural milieu?
3. What role does binge drinking play in policy development, implementation, and enforcement? What is the role of moderate drinking? What might the role of differing types of alcohol (e.g., spirits versus wine versus beer) be in adolescent drinking?
4. Consider your local environment; which policy (i.e., zero-tolerance or harm reduction) would likely be most effective and why?
5. If a parent were to ask you, "What should I do in relation to my child's drinking?" what would your recommendation be based on your reading of the empirical literature?

Is There Common Ground?

The authors of the YES and NO selections seem to be in direct conflict with each other. Bellis et al. state that parental provision of alcohol is a protective factor—provides protection against harms such as regretted sex, violence, and blacking out. In contrast, McMorris et al. state explicitly that adult supervision and provision of alcohol to teens resulted in increased risk of alcohol use and associated harms. One major difference between the two studies was the age of the youth involved. Bellis et al. were studying 15–16-year-olds whereas McMorris et al. were studying 13–15-year-olds. Both authors would likely agree that drinking at younger ages (i.e., before 15 years) is associated with a greater risk of alcohol-related harms for the youth.

Both authors would likely agree that binge drinking (i.e., usually defined as drinking five or more alcoholic beverages on one drinking occasion) is a particularly risky behavior. In the literature, binge drinking has been found to be a particularly noxious drinking behavior; it is a very common drinking behavior in youth (64 percent of those who reported drinking in the past month), and it is associated with a large variety of harms to these youth (academic problems, involvement with drinking and driving, being sexually active, smoking, dating violence, suicide attempts, and illicit drug use; Miller et al., 2007). Bellis et al. found that the protective effects of parental supervision tended to disappear for those youth who had high levels of binge drinking.

Both sets of authors would agree that family (i.e., parents) is really important in relation to adolescent drinking; just what role family takes in reducing teen alcohol use or how family acts as a protective or risk factor is not entirely clear. Part of the problem for both of these studies is that the context in which parental alcohol provision/supervision occurred was not well defined. For example, neither study compared alcohol provision for "parties" versus family functions. The results of these types of supervision/provision may be very different. Further, the role that parental supervision/provision plays in teen harms may not be a simple one. This may interact with or be mediated through some other variable (e.g., the parents own drinking behavior or drinking attitudes).

In sum, there is research to support both perspectives. A person who says that it is bad for parents to provide alcohol to their drinking teens is correct (McMorris et al. support this). A person who says that it is good for parents to provide alcohol to their drinking teens is correct (Bellis et al. support this). Regardless of which approach we take, programs aimed at reducing alcohol consumption should be part of a broader societal response. Youth attitudes about alcohol likely reflect the modeling of adult attitudes and behavior.

Additional Resources

Bellis, M., Hughes, K., Morleo, M., Tocque, K., Hughes, S., Allen, T., et al. (2007). Predictors of risky alcohol consumption in schoolchildren and their implications for preventing alcohol-related harm. *Substance Abuse Treatment, Prevention, and Policy* 2007, *2*(15) [page numbers unknown]. Retrieved from doi:10.1186/1747-597X-2-15

> An additional study by the Bellis lab that also argues that parental provision of alcohol to youth may be warranted.

Coppock, L. A. (2009). Social host immunity: A new paradigm to foster responsibility. *Capital University Law Review*, *38*(1), 19–40.

> This article reviews the history of social host responsibility (e.g., people who host a party where alcohol is present or bars where alcohol is served) for the actions of people who are drunk and describes the current state of social host laws in the United States. Finally, the author presents arguments for and against holding social liability. The author concludes in favor of social host liability laws. Retrieved February 2012 from http://law.capital.edu/Inside_Capital_Law/Current_Students/Law_Review/ Articles/Volume_38_Issue_1/Volume_38_Issue_1_—_Back_Issues.aspx

Foley, K. L., Altman, D., Durant, R. H., & Wolfson, M. (2004). Adults' approval and adolescents' alcohol use. *Journal of Adolescent Health, 35*(4), 345 e17–e26.

> This classic citation has caused much controversy. "Parents who provided alcohol to their adolescent children or drank with them were more likely to have children who neither regularly used nor abused alcohol" (p. e25) caused many to conclude that parental provision of alcohol to youth might be a protective factor for teens.

Graham, M. L., Ward, B., Munro, G., Snow, P., & Ellis, J. (2006). Rural parents, teenagers, and alcohol: What are parents thinking? *Rural and Remote Health*, 6(383). Retrieved from http://www.rrh.org.au/publishedarticles/article_print_383.pdf

> This was a qualitative focus-group study where the investigators interviewed parents in an attempt to understand why parents would provide alcohol to their adolescent children. The interviews indicated that parents were using a number of harm-reduction strategies to ward off short-term harms (e.g., youth drinking and driving, aspiration of vomit) and were not as concerned about longer-term risks. However, parents felt ill-prepared to apply harm-reduction strategies and struggled with how to deal with youth alcohol consumption.

Hingson R. W., Heeren T, & Winter M. R. (2006). Age at drinking onset and alcohol dependence: age at onset, duration, and severity. *Archives of Pediatric Medicine, 160*, 739–746.

> A large, cross-sectional sample of adults were surveyed about their current and adolescent drinking. Results suggested that clinical alcohol dependence was associated with age; those who drank at younger ages were more likely to have some experience with alcohol dependence in their lifetime.

International Center for Alcohol Policies (ICAP). (2012). *Young people's drinking: Key facts and issues*. Washington, DC. Retrieved from www.icap.org/PolicyIssues/YoungPeoplesDrinking/KeyFactsandIssues/tabid/119/Default.aspx

> The International Center for Alcohol Policies (ICAP) is a not-for-profit organization, *supported* by major producers of alcoholic beverages with the stated mission to understand alcohol's role in the U.S. society and reduce the abuse of alcohol. The organization publishes scholarly books and many other papers are available on the ICAP Web page. The Web site is well sourced. This fact sheet is from the Policy section of the ICAP Web site dedicated to "Young People's Drinking."

Johnston, L. D., O'Malley, P. M., Bachman, J. G., & Schulenberg, J. E. (2011). *Monitoring the Future national results on adolescent drug use: Overview of key findings, 2010*. Ann Arbor, MI: Institute for Social Research, The University of Michigan.

> This document is one of many overviews of a long-running study of youth. Each year, a large, representative sample of grade-12 students (and, since 1991, grades 8 and 10 students) are surveyed about their drug use—this includes alcohol. This type of long-term investigation, with reliable and valid data, allows researchers, educators, and politicians to monitor the trends in adolescent alcohol and other substance use.

Kliewer, W. (2010). Family processes in drug use etiology. In L. M. Scheier (Ed.), *Handbook of drug use etiology: Theory, methods, and empirical findings* (pp. 365–381). Washington, DC: American Psychological Association.

This chapter presents an overarching socialization model of adolescent substance use behavior—the majority of which involves familial influences. Three family influence areas are parental coaching (messages relayed from parents to their adolescent children), parental modeling (parental use of substances), and family context (all areas of family climate such as family structure, parent–child relations, and parenting). These are thought to influence coping processes, which, in turn, is thought to impact adolescent substance abuse.

Komro, K. A., Maldonado-Molina, M. M., Tobler, A. L., Bonds, J. R., & Muller, K. E. (2007). Effects of home access and availability of alcohol on young adolescents' alcohol use. *Addiction, 102*, 1597–1608.

A longitudinal study of the impact of provision of alcohol by parents at age 12 on alcohol-related outcomes at age 14. Parental provision of alcohol was associated with greater use of alcohol and greater intentions to use alcohol in the future by the youth. The authors concluded that it is risky for parents to provide alcohol to their children.

Logan, D. E., & Marlatt, G. A. (2010). Harm reduction therapy: A practice-friendly review of the research. *Journal of Clinical Psychology: In Session, 66*(2), 201–214.

A review paper of harm-reduction theory and clinical research applied to cigarettes and substance use in addition to alcohol. Aimed at practitioners and therapists, this paper focuses on research involving the individual as opposed to more general policies.

Maloney, E., Hutchinson, D., Vogl, L., Essau, C., & Mattick, R. (2010). Adolescent drinking: The social influence of the family. In K. T. Everly & E. M., Cosell (Eds.), *Social drinking: Uses, abuses, and psychological factors* (pp. 141–175). New York: Nova Science Publishers.

This chapter is an excellent review of the family characteristics that are associated with adolescent alcohol use and abuse. Three key areas reviewed include parental provision of alcohol, parental alcohol attitudes, and modeling. Recommendations for parents based on the academic literature are made.

Miller, J. W., Naimi, T. S., Brewer, R. D., & Jones, S. E. (2007). Binge drinking and associated health risk behaviors among high school students. *Pediatrics, 119*, 76–85.

A population-based study of binge drinking by U.S. adolescents; a variety of harms had a much greater likelihood (called odds ratio) for binge drinkers compared to drinkers who did not report binge drinking or compared to non-drinkers.

Nakaya, A. C. (2008). *Alcohol*. Farmington Hills, MI: Greenhaven Press.

This book addresses a number of alcohol-related issues from an "opposing sides" perspective—which is much like the current *Taking Sides* series. In particular, Chapter 2 of this book has two pieces that address the seriousness of underage drinking. Chapter 4 of this book has two pieces that speak to parental supervision of teenage drinking (one being "beneficial" and the other being "encourages dangerous behavior"). These latter two pieces are excerpts from news sources.

Nelson, D. E. (2011). *Teen drug abuse*. Farmington Hills, MI: Greenhaven Press.

This book addresses a number of drug-related issues from an "opposing sides" perspective—which is much like the current *Taking Sides* series. In particular, Chapter 2 of this book addresses the threat that alcohol may pose to teens. Two pieces, in particular, speak to parental supervision of teenage drinking; one is titled "It is healthy for teens to drink moderately in the home," while the other is called "The dangers of allowing children to drink in the home." The first piece is an excerpt from a newspaper, while the second is an excerpt from a self-help book aimed at parents.

Odgers, C. L., Caspi, A., Nagin, D. S., Piquero, A. R., Slutske, W. S., Milne, B. J., et al. (2008). Is it important to prevent early exposure to drugs and alcohol among adolescents? *Psychological Science, 19*(10), 1037–1044.

This is a research article describing a 30-year longitudinal study that investigated the impact of early alcohol exposure on adult outcomes. The findings suggested two key things: (1) early exposure to alcohol (before 15 years of age) resulted in negative adult outcomes and (2) children who were "normal" (i.e., no pre-existing conduct problems) demonstrated negative adult outcomes of early alcohol exposure. This last finding is particularly poignant because, prior to these findings, people argued it was youth who had "problems" that led them to drink and this led to adult problems. This well-designed study speaks to that idea—and disconfirms it. Age when drinking begins is the key, not who the child is.

Toomey, T. L, Lenk, K. M. & Wagenaar, A. C. (2007). Environmental policies to reduce college drinking: An update of research findings. *Journal of Studies on Alcohol and Drugs, 68*(2), 208–219.

This paper reviews the published literature on the effects of campus policies on drinking by university students. The authors conclude that policies can make a difference in drinking behavior but a multi-strategy policy (i.e., combining different policies such as required server intervention training plus increasing roadside checks) would probably be the most effective. However, the authors caution that more research is needed regarding the impact of policies.

Wagoner, K. G. (2010). *An Examination of Social Host Policies: Relationship with Social Drinking Context and Alcohol Use among Adolescents*. Dissertation, The University of North Carolina at Greensboro (UNCG). Retrieved from http://libres.uncg.edu/ir/uncg/f/Wagoner_uncg_0154D_10351.pdf

This is a dissertation where the author investigated the impact of social host laws, specifically aimed at private adults who serve alcohol to adolescents or allow alcohol to be consumed by adolescents at their home. Her findings suggest that these policies are not immediately effective at achieving the ultimate goal of reducing youth drinking.

ISSUE 14

Should Parental Consent Be Required for Adolescents Seeking Abortion?

YES: Teresa Stanton Collett, from Testimony Before the United States House of Representatives Committee on the Judiciary, Subcommittee on the Constitution. H.R. 2299 the "Child Interstate Abortion Notification Act" (March 8, 2012)

NO: Laurence Steinberg et al., from "Are Adolescents Less Mature Than Adults?" *American Psychologist* (vol. 64, no. 7, pp. 583–594, 2009)

Learning Outcomes

After reading this issue, you should be able to:

- Understand some of the reasons for and against the existence of parental involvement laws and policies; specifically,
  - Articulate why the American Psychological Association supports the minor's right to obtain an abortion without parental consent or knowledge.
  - Articulate why some stakeholders support the value of having legislation requiring parental consent or notification of their child's abortion.
- Define the role of *judicial bypass* in adolescent abortion—from a legal standpoint and a *Loco Parentis*—"in place of parents or instead of a parent"—perspective.
- Examine the concept of "maturity" in abortion decisions from psychological, legal, and moral perspectives.

ISSUE SUMMARY

YES: Teresa Stanton Collett, law professor at the University of St. Thomas School of Law in Minnesota, testified about the "Child Interstate Abortion Notification Act" before a U.S. House of Representatives subcommittee that minors would benefit greatly from parental involvement in youth abortion decisions. She argues a federal law is needed to protect girls from exploitation and improve medical care.

NO: Laurence Steinberg, a psychology professor at Temple University, and his colleagues conclude that adolescent girls have the cognitive maturity to make abortion decisions independently, without parental input. They base their conclusions on their own research studies and their reading of the developmental psychology literature.

In 1973, the U.S. Supreme Court decision *Roe v. Wade* guaranteed a woman's right to access to abortion without restriction during the first trimester. The decision did not mention, however, the age of the woman seeking the abortion. One of the most contentious controversies surrounding adolescent abortion involves consultation: A majority of individual states have introduced requirements that a girl under the age of 18 have one or both parents' or legal guardians' consent in order to obtain an abortion. Alternatively, states may require that parents/guardians be notified prior to their daughter's abortion.

Since two key legal decisions in 1969 and 1988, abortion has been legal in Canada and it is treated like any other medical procedure. Canada has no age restrictions, and nothing similar to the U.S. state parental notifications/consent laws is required when adolescents seek abortions. However, some Canadian provinces have general consent-to-treatment law age limits, which would apply to abortion, and some hospitals have policies requiring youth to obtain parental consent for abortions, specifically (Downie & Nassar, 2007). Because the Canadian legal situation is quite different than that of the United States, parental notification/consent is not as contentious issue.

Discussion about abortion rights are rooted in the fundamental support or opposition to abortion itself. It can be quite challenging, then, to separate out one's opinion about abortion, per se, from a minor's ability to make an informed decision about abortion. People who hold opinions that abortion is morally wrong would argue that, at minimum, parental notification/consent for a minor's abortion is mandatory. Even some adults who are pro-choice would advocate for parental notification/consent requirements. And still others believe that any girl or woman, regardless of age, is able and has the right to make this personal decision for herself. Ultimately, the question of consultation with parents implies that some people think that adolescents are competent, while others think that adolescents are not competent to make this decision.

Scholars in favor of parental involvement legislation and policies argue that parental involvement laws reduce abortion rates through various mechanisms: For example, parents will intervene and prevent a teen from having an abortion, such laws will deter teens from becoming pregnant (e.g., encourage greater/more consistent contraceptive use or encourage less sexual activity), and abortion providers may be more cautious about performing abortions on teens. As well, those in favor of parental notification/consent requirements also argue that parental involvement is a protective factor for their children: The parents know the unique medical history of their child (of which, she herself may be unaware), sexual abuse or coercion may have resulted in the pregnancy and the parents may take action, and family communication may be enhanced.

Scholars who are opposed to parental involvement legislation and policies argue that family communication is not enhanced, that when girls do not communicate with their parents about their pregnancies, it is because they fear family discord, harm to the parent–child relationship, or physical reactions from parents. Medical associations support the involvement of parents in adolescent abortion decisions but do not support such involvement when it compromises the girl's medical privacy/confidentiality (Webster et al., 2010). Opponents also argue that these laws result in greater travel for out-of-state abortions (which may account for the decrease in abortion rates/ratios), delays in obtaining abortion (later abortions being a greater health hazard), and potentially create a high-risk living environment for the resultant child of the unexpected pregnancy (e.g., Sen et al., 2012). Opponents are unconvinced that evidence exists that the parental consent/information laws result in greater practice of birth control or reductions in teen pregnancy (Dennis et al., 2009).

In the United States, girls who want an abortion, who do not want, or who are unable to obtain parental consent can access a process called "judicial bypass." A judge can decide if a youth is mature enough to make her own decision regarding abortion or, even if she is not mature enough, an abortion would be in her best interest. The existence of judicial bypass allows states to have parental consent laws and not be in violation of the constitutional rights of the pregnant teen (Bonny, 2007). Thirty-six states have some form of judicial bypass available as of April 2012. Based on the writings around judicial bypass of parental involvement (e.g., Bonny, 2007; Rebouché, 2011), it is clear that adolescent maturity and competence is the key question and purpose underlying parental consent/notification laws and policies.

Steinberg and colleagues present a study that demonstrates that cognitive capacity—defined by information-processing abilities—peaks after age 15. They argue that, insofar as cognitive capacity reflects decision-making skills, adolescents 16 and over are mature enough to weigh all available evidence and facts, and make their own decisions regarding abortions. Stanton Collett argues that parental involvement benefits teens because parents are more capable of obtaining information and better equipped to deal with the medical aspects of abortion relative to a panicky teen. She also argues that parents should be involved in abortion decisions in order to reduce coercion—either leading to the pregnancy or leading to the abortion decision.

YES ↵

Teresa Stanton Collett

Testimony Before the United States House of Representatives Committee on the Judiciary, Subcommittee on the Constitution. H.R. 2299 the "Child Interstate Abortion Notification Act"

... [T]he "Child Interstate Abortion Notification Act" ("CIANA") ... bill is the culmination of a decade of Congressional effort to insure that young girls are not coerced or deceived into crossing state lines to obtain secret abortions. ... [It is] premised on what Justice O'Connor has called "the quite reasonable assumption that [pregnant] minors will benefit from consultation with their parents and that children will often not realize that their parents have their best interests at heart."

Sizable bipartisan majorities of both Congressional houses voted to enact this common sense legislation during the last legislative session, only to have those votes nullified by opponents' last-minute procedural maneuvering. House leadership refused to even allow a hearing on CIANA during the 2008 legislative session. This outcome is particularly troubling in light of the public's strong support for parental involvement.[1]

My testimony today is based on my scholarly study of parental involvement laws, and my practical experience in assisting state legislators across the country evaluate parental involvement laws during the legislative process. It also represents my experience in assisting the attorneys general of Florida, New Hampshire, and Oklahoma in defending their parental involvement laws. [Recently] I testified as an expert witness in an Alaska District Court regarding judicial bypass of parental notification laws.

... I ... discuss [how] minors benefit from parental involvement when deciding whether to continue or terminate a pregnancy. ...

Minors Benefit from Parental Involvement

There is widespread agreement that as a general rule, parents should be involved in their minor daughter's decision to terminate an unplanned pregnancy. The national consensus in favor of this position is illustrated by the fact

U.S. House of Representatives, March 8, 2012.

that there are parental involvement laws on the books in forty-five of the fifty states although only thirty-seven are in force due primarily to judicial actions Only five states in the nation have not attempted to legislatively insure some level of parental involvement in a minor's decision to obtain an abortion.[2]

This agreement even extends to young people, ages 18 to 29.[3] To my knowledge, no organizations or individuals, whether abortion rights activists or pro-life advocates, dispute this point. On an issue as contentious and divisive as abortion, it is both remarkable and instructive that there is such firm and long-standing support for laws requiring parental involvement.

Various reasons underlie this broad and consistent support. As Justices O'Connor, Kennedy, and Souter observed in *Planned Parenthood v. Casey* [1992], parental consent and notification laws related to abortions "are based on the quite reasonable assumption that minors will benefit from consultation with their parents and that children will often not realize that their parents have their best interests at heart." Writing for a unanimous court in 2005, Justice O'Connor noted "States unquestionably have the right to require parental involvement when a minor considers terminating her pregnancy, because of their 'strong and legitimate interest in the welfare of [their] young citizens, whose immaturity, inexperience, and lack of judgment may sometimes impair their ability to exercise their rights wisely'."[4]

. . . I will limit my remarks to examining two of the benefits that are achieved by parental involvement statutes: improved medical care for young girls seeking abortions and increased protection against sexual exploitation by adult men.

Improved Medical Care of Minor Girls

Medical care for minors seeking abortions is improved by parental involvement in three ways. First, parental involvement laws allow parents to assist their daughter in the selection of the abortion provider.

As with all medical procedures, one of the most important guarantees of patient safety is the professional competence of those who perform the medical procedure. In *Bellotti v. Baird,* the United States Supreme Court acknowledged the superior ability of parents to evaluate and select appropriate healthcare providers [1979].

> In this case, however, we are concerned only with minors who according to the record range in age from children of twelve years to 17-year-old teenagers. Even the latter are less likely than adults to know or be able to recognize ethical, qualified physicians, or to have the means to engage such professionals. Many minors who bypass their parents probably will resort to an abortion clinic, without being able to distinguish the competent and ethical from those that are incompetent or unethical.

Historically, the National Abortion Federation has recommended that patients seeking an abortion confirm that the abortion will be performed by a licensed physician in good standing with the state Board of Medical Examiners and that the doctor have admitting privileges at a local hospital not more than twenty minutes away from the location where the abortion is to occur in order to insure adequate care should complications arise.[5] These recommendations were deleted after they were introduced into evidence in malpractice cases against abortion providers. Notwithstanding this change in the NAF recommendations, a well-informed parent seeking to guide her child is more likely to inquire regarding these matters than a panicky teen who just wants to no longer be pregnant.

Second, parental involvement laws insure that parents have the opportunity to provide additional medical history and information to abortion providers prior to performance of the abortion.

In *Edison v. Reproductive Health Services,* 863 S.W.2d 621 (Mo. App. E.D. 1993), the court confronted the question of whether an abortion provider could be held liable for the suicide of Sandra, a fourteen-year-old girl, due to depression following an abortion. Learning of the abortion only after her daughter's death, the girl's mother sued the abortion provider, alleging that her daughter's death was due to the failure to obtain a psychiatric history or monitor Sandra's mental health. *Id.* at 624. An eyewitness to Sandra's death "testified that he saw Sandra holding on to a fence on a bridge over Arsenal Street and then jumped in front of a car traveling below on Arsenal. She appeared to have been rocking back and forth while holding onto the fence, then deliberately let go and jumped far out to the driver's side of the car that struck her. A second car hit her while she was on the ground. Sandra was taken to a hospital and died the next day of multiple injuries." *Id.* at 622.

The court ultimately determined that Sandra was not insane at the time she committed suicide. Therefore her actions broke the chain of causation required for recovery. Yet evidence was presented that the daughter had a history of psychological illness, and that her behavior was noticeably different after the abortion. *Id.* at 628. If Sandra's mother had known that her daughter had obtained an abortion, it is possible that this tragedy would have been avoided.

> The medical, emotional, and psychological consequences of an abortion are serious and can be lasting; this is particularly so when the patient is immature. An adequate medical and psychological case history is important to the physician. Parents can provide medical and psychological data, refer the physician to other sources of medical history, such as family physicians, and authorize family physicians to give relevant data.[6]

Abortion providers, in turn, have the opportunity to disclose the medical risks of the procedure to the adult who can advise the girl in giving her informed consent to the surgical procedure. Parental notification insures that the abortion providers inform a mature adult of the risks and benefits of the proposed treatment, after having received a more complete and thus more accurate medical history of the patient.

The third way in which parental notification will improve medical treatment of pregnant minors is by insuring that parents have adequate knowledge to recognize and respond to any post-abortion complication that may develop. While it is often claimed that abortion is one of the safest surgical procedures performed today, the actual rate of many complications is simply unknown because there is no coordinated national effort to collect and maintain this information. . . .

Many minors may ignore or deny the seriousness of post-abortion symptoms or may lack the financial resources to respond to those symptoms. This is because some of the most serious complications are delayed and only detected during the follow-up visit; yet, only about one-third of all abortion patients actually keep their appointments for post-operative checkups. Absent parental notification, hemorrhaging may be mistaken for a heavy period and severe depression as typical teenage angst.

Effectiveness of Judicial Bypass

In those few cases where it is not in the girl's best interest to disclose her pregnancy to her parents, state laws generally provide the pregnant minor the option of seeking a court determination that either involvement of the girl's parent is not in her best interest, or that she is sufficiently mature to make decisions regarding the continuation of her pregnancy. This is a requirement for parental consent laws under existing United States Supreme Court cases, and courts have been quick to overturn laws omitting adequate bypass.

In the past, opponents to the predecessor of this Act, the Child Custody Protection Act, have argued that passage of federal legislation in this area would endanger teens since parents may be abusive and many teens would seek illegal abortions. This is a phantom fear. Parental involvement laws are on the books in over two-thirds of the states, some for over thirty years, and there is no case where it has been established that these laws led to parental abuse or to self-inflicted injury.[7] Similarly, there is no evidence that these laws have led to an increase in illegal abortions or attempted self-induced abortions.

It often asserted that parental involvement laws do not increase the number of parents notified of their daughters' intentions to obtain abortions, since minors will commonly seek judicial bypass of the parental involvement requirement. Assessing the accuracy of this claim is difficult since parental notification or consent laws rarely impose reporting requirements regarding the use of judicial bypass. Alabama, Idaho, South Dakota and Wisconsin are four of the few states that report the number of minors who obtain judicial bypass orders related to abortion. Data regarding the number of bypasses granted in those states from 2005 to 2010 reveals that the judicial bypass is relatively rare and its use varies significantly among states. . . .

CIANA Addresses a Real Problem

It is beyond dispute that young girls are being taken to out-of-state clinics in order to procure secret abortions. In 2005, the House Subcommittee on the Constitution heard the testimony of Marsha Carroll, the mother of a fourteen year-old-girl, who was secretly taken out-of-state by her boyfriend's parents to obtain an abortion. Upon arriving at the abortion clinic, Mrs. Carroll's daughter began to cry and tried to refuse the abortion. The boy's parents told her they would leave her in New Jersey if she resisted. She gave in to their pressure, had the abortion, and now suffers from depression and guilt.[8]

A recent study of the literature documenting the impact of parental involvement laws concluded, "Some minors travel to other states with no, or at least less restrictive, parental involvement laws in order to obtain an abortion. To travel out of state, a minor must have access to transportation and must be within a reasonable distance of a state with less restrictive laws. The degree to which minors exercise this option varies by age, socioeconomic status and access to public transportation." "In general, the impact of these laws on minors' travel appears to vary widely, depending on the specifics of the requirements, the abortion regulations of surrounding states and the state's geography."[9]

Statutory Rape

Some teens who obtain abortions are pregnant as the result of statutory rape. National studies reveal "[a]lmost two thirds of adolescent mothers have partners older than 20 years of age."[10] "Younger teenagers are especially vulnerable to coercive and nonconsensual sex. Involuntary sexual activity has been reported by 74% of sexually active girls younger than 14 years and 60% of those younger than 15 years."[11] In a study of over 46,000 pregnancies by school-age girls in California, researchers found that "71%, or over 33,000, were fathered by adult post-high-school men whose mean age was 22.6 years, an average of 5 years older than the mothers. . . . Even among junior high school mothers aged 15 or younger, most births are fathered by adult men 6–7 years their senior. *Men aged 25 or older father more births among California school-age girls than do boys under age 18.*"[12] Other studies have found that most teenage pregnancies are the result of predatory practices by men who are substantially older.[13]

Failure to Report by Abortion Providers

Abortion providers are reluctant to report information indicating a minor is the victim of statutory rape.[14] The clearest example of this reluctance is the arguments presented in the lawsuit filed by a Kansas abortion provider to prohibit enforcement of that state's reporting requirement related to sexual abuse of minors. Claiming that children under the age of sixteen were sufficiently mature to engage in non-abusive sexual intercourse, Aid for Women, a Kansas City abortion provider, sued to enjoin the state's mandatory reporting law on the basis that it violated minors' constitutional right to informational privacy. The district court, adopting the arguments of the abortion provider, ruled that minors between the ages of twelve and fifteen had a constitutional right to engage in non-coercive sexual activity, including but not limited to "penile-vaginal intercourse, oral sex, anal sex, and touching of another's genitalia by either sex." On appeal from a preliminary injunction in the case, the Court . . . rejected such a constitutional right, but the district continued to assert the unconstitutionality of the reporting law at the conclusion of trial. Unfortunately the appeal to the Tenth Circuit was rendered moot by unrelated legislative changes in the law.[15]

Failure to report the sexual abuse of minor may result in the minor returning to an abusive relationship. In Ohio, a thirteen-year-old girl was impregnated by her twenty-one-year old soccer coach, John Haller. In order to conceal the illegal relationship, Mr. Haller arranged for the girl to obtain an abortion by first impersonating her father during a telephone call with the clinic, and then pretending to be her brother while accompanying the girl to the clinic to obtain an abortion. The sexual abuse was only discovered after another teacher overheard the girl arguing with Haller about their relationship, and reported the conversation to law enforcement. Subsequently the girl and her parents sued the abortion provider, Planned Parenthood of Southwest Ohio Region, for failure to comply with the Ohio sexual abuse reporting statute. "Planned Parenthood did not deny that it had not filed an abuse report."[16]

In 2001 an Arizona Planned Parenthood affiliate was found civilly liable for failing to report the fact that the clinic had performed an abortion on a twelve-year-old girl who had been impregnated by her foster brother. The abortion provider did not report the crime as required by law and the girl returned to the foster home where she was raped and impregnated a second time.[17] In 2003 two Connecticut doctors were prosecuted for failing to report to public officials that an eleven-year old girl had been impregnated by a seventy-five year old man.[18]

By failing to report, abortion providers reduce the chances that rapes will be discovered, and by failing to preserve fetal tissue, they may make it impossible to effective prosecute those rapes that are discovered. . . .

Conclusion

In balancing the minor's right to privacy and her need for parental involvement, the majority of states have determined that parents should know before abortions are performed on minors. This is a reasonable conclusion and well within the states' police powers. However, the political authority of each state stops at its geographic boundaries. States need the assistance of the federal government to insure that the protection they wish to afford their children is not easily circumvented by strangers taking minors across state lines.

By passage of the Act before this Committee, Congress will protect the ability of the parents to be involved in the decisions of their minor daughters facing an unplanned pregnancy.

Experience in states having parental involvement laws has shown that, when notified, parents and their daughters unite in a desire to resolve issues surrounding an unplanned pregnancy. If the minor chooses to terminate the pregnancy, parents can assist their daughters in selecting competent abortion providers, and abortion providers may receive more comprehensive medical histories of their patients. In these cases, the minors will more likely be encouraged to obtain post-operative check-ups, and parents will be prepared to respond to any complications that arise.

If the minor chooses to continue her pregnancy, involvement of her parents serves many of the same goals. Parents can provide or help obtain the necessary resources for early and comprehensive prenatal care. They can assist their daughters in evaluating the options of single parenthood, adoption, or early marriage. Perhaps most importantly, they can provide the love and support that is found in the many healthy families of the United States.

Regardless of whether the girl chooses to continue or terminate her pregnancy, parental involvement laws have proven desirable because they afford greater protection for the many girls who are pregnant due to sexual assault. By insuring that parents know of the pregnancy, it becomes much more likely that they will intervene to insure the protection of their daughters from future assaults.

In balancing the minor's right to privacy and her need for parental involvement, the majority of states have determined that parents should know before abortions are performed on minors. This is a reasonable conclusion and well within the states' police powers. However, the political authority of each state stops at its geographic boundaries. States need the assistance of the federal government to insure that the protection they wish to afford their children is not easily circumvented by strangers taking minors across state lines.

The Child Interstate Parental Notification Act has the unique virtue of building upon two of the few points of agreement in the national debate over abortion: the desirability of parental involvement in a minor's decisions about an unplanned pregnancy, and the need to protect the physical health and safety of the pregnant girl. . . .

Notes

[1]. "Even among those who say abortion should be legal in most or all cases, 71% favor requiring parental consent." Pew Research Center for The People and The Press, *Support for Abortion Slips* at 9 (conducted August, 2009).

[2]. Hawaii etc.

[3]. A 2011 Poll by the Public Religion Research Institute found that 71% of millennial youth (18–29) supported parental consent laws. *Committed to Availability, Conflicted about Morality* at 17 available at http://publicreligion.org/site/wp-content/uploads/2011/06/Millenials-Abortion-and-Religion-Survey-Report.pdf (conduct May 2011).

[4]. *Ayotte v. Planned Parenthood,* 546 U.S. 320, 326 (2006).

[5]. National Abortion Federation, *Having an Abortion? Your Guide to Good Care* (2000) which was available at <http://www.prochoice.org/pregnant/goodcare.htm> (visited Jan. 1, 2000).

[6]. *H.L. v. Matheson,* 450 U.S. 398 at 411 (1981). Accord *Ohio v. Akron Ctr. for Reproductive Health,* 497 U.S. 502, 518–19 (1990).

[7]. A 1989 memo prepared by the Minnesota Attorney General regarding Minnesota's experience with its parental involvement law states that "after some five years of the statute's operation, the evidence does not disclose a single instance of abuse or forceful obstruction of abortion for any Minnesota minor." Testimony before the Texas House of Representatives on the Massachusetts' experience with its parental consent law revealed a similar absence of unintended, but harmful, consequences. Ms. Jamie Sabino, chair of the Massachusetts Judicial Consent for Minors Lawyer Referral

Panel, could identify no case of a Massachusetts' minor being abused or abandoned as a result of the law. *See Hearing on Tex. H.B. 1073 Before the House State Affairs Comm.*, 76th Leg., R.S. 21 (Apr. 19, 1999) (statement by Jamie Sabino, JD).

[8]. *Child Interstate Abortion Notification Act: Hearing on HR 748 before the Subcomm. on the Constitution, H. Comm. on the Judiciary,* 109th Cong. (2005) (testimony of Marsha Carroll in support of HR 748).

In 1998, Joyce Farley testified before the House Subcommittee on the Constitution about the complications her daughter, Crystal, suffered as a result of a secret abortion. Crystal became pregnant at the age of twelve when Michael Kilmer, an eighteen-year-old neighbor, got her drunk and then raped her. Mr. Kilmer's mother, Rosa Hartford, took the young girl to a New York abortion clinic to avoid Pennsylvania's parental consent law. Crystal's mother, a registered nurse, learned of her daughter's abortion when Crystal began experiencing severe pain and hemorrhaging at home following the abortion. The abortion was incomplete, and additional surgery was required. Ms. Hartford was convicted for interfering with the custody of the child's parent. *Commonwealth v. Hartford,* No. 95–98 (Ct. Com. Pl. Sullivan County, Pa. Dec. 5, 1996). Ms. Hartford's conviction was reversed for failure to provide proper jury instructions on the elements of interference with custody. *Commonwealth v. Hartford,* No. 00088PHL97 (Pa. Super. Ct. Oct. 28, 1997).

[9]. Dennis A *et al., The Impact of Laws Requiring Parental Involvement for Abortion: A Literature Review* at 4, New York: Guttmacher Institute, 2009.

[10]. American Academy of Pediatrics Committee on Adolescence, *Adolescent Pregnancy—Current Trends and Issues: 1998,* 103 PEDIATRICS 516, 519 (1999).

[11]. American Academy of Pediatrics Committee on Adolescence, *Adolescent Pregnancy—Current Trends and Issues,* 116 PEDIATRICS 281, 281 (2005).

[12]. Mike A. Males, *Adult Involvement in Teenage Childbearing and STD,* LANCET 64 (July 8, 1995) (emphasis added).

[13]. *Id.* citing [others].

[14]. *See* Chinué Turner Richardson and Cynthia Dailard, *Politicizing Statutory Rape Reporting Requirements: A Mounting Campaign?,* THE GUTTMACHER REPORT ON PUBLIC POLICY 1 (Aug. 2005) and Patricia Donovan, *Caught Between Teens and the Law: Family Planning Programs and Statutory Rape Reporting,* 3 FAM. PLAN. PERSPECTIVES 5 (1998).

[15]. *Aid to Women v. Foulston,* [2004–2007].

[16]. *Roe v. Planned Parenthood Southwest Ohio Region,* [2007–2009].

[17]. See *Glendale Teen Files Lawsuit Against Planned Parenthood,* THE ARIZONA REPUBLIC, Sept. 2, 2001 and *Judge Rules Against Planned Parenthood* at www.12news.com/headline/PlannedParenthood122602.html

[18]. *See* Charlotte Allen, *Planned Parenthood's Unseemly Empire,* 13 Weekly Standard (2007).

Laurence Steinberg et al.   ➡ **NO**

Are Adolescents Less Mature Than Adults?

[**I**]n a U.S. Supreme Court case, *Hodgson v. Minnesota* (1990), which concerned a minor's right to obtain an abortion without parental notification, APA had argued that because adolescents had decision-making skills comparable to those of adults, there was no reason to require teenagers to notify their parents before terminating a pregnancy (APA. 1987, 1989). . . .

Opponents of adolescents' autonomous abortion rights had taken the Court's characterization of adolescent immaturity in the juvenile death penalty case and used it to argue in favor of parental involvement requirements. . . . [T]hey argued.

> Parental involvement is critical to ensure not only that the adolescent's choice is informed, but that it is freely made and not the result of coercion or duress. . . . These concerns are heightened for adolescents who, as this Court has recently observed, are more susceptible than adults to "outside pressure" and other "negative influences," and more likely than adults to make decisions that are "impetuous and ill-considered." *Roper v. Simmons*, 125 S.Ct. 1183, 1195 (2005). (*Ayotte v. Planned Parenthood of Northern New England*, 2006, p. 15)

. . . In its amicus brief arguing for adolescents' abortion rights, . . . APA stated.

> [*B*]*y age 14 most adolescents have developed adult-like intellectual and social capacities* [italics added] including specific abilities outlined in the law as necessary for understanding treatment alternatives, considering risks and benefits, and giving legally competent consent. (APA, 1989, p. 20). . . .

The abortion rights case was a 14th Amendment case involving the amendment's due process clause. The central question considered in *Hodgson* was whether the state had a compelling interest in mandating that an adolescent seeking an abortion be required to first notify both her parents. Several legal issues were relevant, including whether the notification requirement

Steinberg, L.; Cauffman, E.; Woolard, J.; Graham, S.; Banich, M. From *American Psychologist,* Vol. 64, No. 7, October 1, 2009, pp. 583–594. Copyright © 2009 by American Psychological Association. Reprinted by permission via Rightslink.

placed an undue burden on adolescents (especially those whose parents were divorced or estranged) and whether providing for a judicial hearing as an alternative to parental notification (known as a "judicial bypass") was acceptable, but the most relevant for the present discussion concerned the competence of adolescents to make informed and sound health care decisions on their own. If it could be concluded that adolescents were sufficiently competent to make an informed decision about whether to terminate a pregnancy, the state's interest in requiring parental notification would be rendered less compelling. Ultimately, the Court ruled that requiring parental notification *was* constitutional so long as a bypass provision was part of the law. . . .

. . . [W]e have been studying age differences in many of the cognitive and psychosocial capacities that have been at issue. . . . We have been studying basic intellectual abilities, such as working memory and verbal fluency, but also aspects of psychosocial development, including impulse control (Steinberg et al., 2008), future orientation (Steinberg et al., 2009), reward sensitivity, sensation seeking (Steinberg et al., 2008), and susceptibility to peer influence (Steinberg & Monahan, 2007). To our knowledge, ours is the first study to include both cognitive and psychosocial measures administered to the same sample, to include an ethnically and socioeconomically diverse group of individuals, and to span the period from preadolescence through young adulthood.

. . . [O]ur findings, as well as those of other researchers, suggest that whereas adolescents and adults perform comparably on cognitive tests measuring the sorts of cognitive abilities that were referred to in the *Hodgson* brief—abilities that permit logical reasoning about moral, social, and interpersonal matters—adolescents and adults are not of equal maturity with respect to the psychosocial capacities . . . —capacities such as impulse control and resistance to peer influence. . . . Unlike adolescents' decisions to commit crimes, which are usually rash and made in the presence of peers, adolescents' decisions about terminating a pregnancy can be made in an unhurried fashion and in consultation with adults.

We recognize that not all abortion decisions are deliberative, rational, and autonomous. . . . After all, any decision about whether to abort a pregnancy or carry it to term has an emotional component, involves both immediate and long-term consequences, and may be influenced by the opinions of family and friends. . . . In general, though, when contemplating an abortion, an adolescent has time to deliberate before making a final choice and has an opportunity to consult with an adult expert. . . .

For example, studies indicate that about half of all pregnant adolescents contemplating an abortion whose parents are unaware of the situation consult with a nonparental adult other than medical staff (e.g., a teacher, school counselor, clergyperson, older relative, or adult friend of the family); this figure is the same among younger (under age 16) and older adolescents (Henshaw & Kost, 1992). Moreover, 35 states require all women seeking an abortion to receive some type of counseling from the abortion provider before the procedure is performed, usually including information about the specific procedure as well as the health risks of abortion and pregnancy (Guttmacher Institute, 2009). Twenty-four states mandate a waiting period of at least 24 hours between the counseling and the medical procedure (Guttmacher Institute, 2009). Thus, it does not appear as if a high proportion of pregnant teenagers decide to terminate a pregnancy under circumstances that are rushed or in the absence of adult advice. . . .

The importance of maintaining a distinction between cognitive and psychosocial maturity in discussions of the legal status of adolescents is supported by other research that has examined age differences in each of these domains. Studies that have examined logical reasoning abilities in structured situations and basic information-processing skills, for instance, have found no appreciable differences between adolescents age 16 and older and adults; any gains that take place in these domains during adolescence occur very early in the adolescent decade, and improvements after this age are very small (Hale, 1990; Kail, 1997; Keating, 2004; Overton, 1990). The results of [an] earlier study of age differences in competence to stand trial, which depends on individuals' ability to understand facts about a court proceeding and to reason with those facts in a rational fashion, also were consistent with these findings. We found significant differences between the competence-related abilities of adults and those of adolescents who were 15 and younger, but no differences between the abilities of adults and those of adolescents who were 16 and older (Grisso et al., 2003). This general pattern, indicating that adolescents attain adult levels of competence to stand trial somewhere around age 15, has been reported in similar studies of decision making across a wide variety of domains (e.g., Grisso, 1980; Jacobs-Quadrel, Fischhoff, & Davis, 1993) and in many studies of age differences in individuals' competence to provide informed consent (Belter & Grisso, 1984; Grisso & Vierling, 1978; Gustafson & McNamara, 1987; Weithorn & Campbell, 1982).

In contrast, the literature on age differences in psychosocial characteristics such as impulsivity, sensation seeking, future orientation, and susceptibility to peer pressure shows continued development well beyond middle adolescence and even into young adulthood (Scott, Reppucci, & Woolard, 1995; Steinberg & Cauffman, 1996), although few studies have gone much beyond adolescence. Consistent with this literature, and in contrast to the pattern of age differences seen in the information-processing, logical reasoning, and informed consent literatures, studies of age differences in the sorts of risky behavior likely to be influenced by the psychosocial factors listed above— such as reckless driving, binge drinking, crime, and spontaneous unprotected sex—indicate that risky behavior is significantly more common during late adolescence and early adulthood than after (Steinberg, 2007). In other words, although adolescents may demonstrate adult-like levels of maturity in some respects by the time they reach 15 or 16, in other respects they show continued immaturity well beyond this point in development.

Participants

The [current] [s]tudy was designed to examine age differences in a variety of cognitive and psychosocial capacities that are relevant to debates about the relative maturity of adolescents and adults . . . 935 individuals ranging in age from 10 to 30 years (M = 17.84 years). Participants were recruited via newspaper advertisements and flyers. . . .

Procedure

. . . Participants took part in a two- to two-and-one-half-hour interview that included . . . a series of questionnaires designed to measure a variety of psychosocial capacities relevant to discussions of how adolescents should be treated by the legal system; and . . . tests of basic intellectual functioning. . . .

Measures

Of interest in the present report are the demographic measures and IQ (which were used to ensure that the various age groups had comparable social and intellectual backgrounds), the measures of psychosocial capacities, and the tests of basic intellectual functioning.

Demographic Variables

. . . [F]or purposes of data analysis, we created age groups as follows: 10–11, 12–13, 14–15, 16–17, 18–21, 22–25, and 26–30 years. . . .

IQ

The Wechsler Abbreviated Scale of Intelligence (WASI) Full-Scale IQ Two-Subtest (FSIQ-2) . . . was used to produce an estimate of general intellectual ability based on two . . . of the four subtests. . . . [M]ean IQ . . . was controlled for in all subsequent analyses.

Psychosocial Maturity

. . . Three instruments were used to assess *risk perception* (the extent to which one perceives a potentially dangerous or harmful activity as risky), *sensation seeking* (the extent to which one actively seeks experiences that provide thrills), and *impulsivity* (the extent to which one acts without thinking or has difficulty controlling impulses). . . .

Two additional psychosocial capacities, *resistance to peer influence* and *future orientation,* were assessed using new self-report measures developed for this program of work. . . . Resistance to peer influence was . . . designed to measure the extent to which individuals change their behavior or opinions in order to follow the crowd. . . . Future orientation was . . . the anticipation of future consequences, planning ahead, and thinking about the future. . . .

A composite measure of *psychosocial maturity* was formed by . . . standardizing all five measures, and averaging the standardized scores. Thus, individuals who score relatively lower on the composite characterize themselves as less likely to perceive dangerous situations as risky, more impulsive, more thrill seeking, more oriented to the immediate, and more susceptible to peer influence. . . .

Cognitive Capacity

The test battery included several widely used tests of basic cognitive skills, including a test of resistance to interference in working memory, a digit-span memory test, and a test of verbal fluency. . . .

. . . [The] standard scores were averaged to create an index of *general cognitive capacity*. Not surprisingly, our composite measure of general cognitive capacity is significantly correlated with IQ ($r = .46$, $p < .001$). Unlike IQ scores, however, which are adjusted for chronological age, the measure of cognitive capacity is not. More important, because we controlled for IQ in all analyses, any observed age differences in general cognitive capacity are not due to age differences in intelligence.

In its original amicus brief in *Hodgson,* the APA (1987) made reference to the "cognitive capacity" (p. 6) of adolescents and cited sources that referred to both information-processing abilities (Keating, 1980) and logical reasoning (Inhelder & Piaget, 1958) in support of its argument that adolescents are as cognitively competent as adults. We acknowledge that our index, which tilts heavily toward measuring how many pieces of information an individual can process or produce, does not measure logical or moral reasoning and as such is an incomplete measure of cognitive capacity as conceptualized in the APA *Hodgson* brief. Our measure assesses cognitive ability in a highly structured manner and as such does not tap aspects of executive function that may be important in novel situations. It is also important to note that our measure of general cognitive capacity does not include tests of higher order executive functioning, such as comparing short- versus long-term consequences, coordinating affect and cognition, or balancing risk and reward. Many such executive functions have both cognitive and psychosocial aspects to them, however, and given that our interest was in maintaining a distinction between general cognitive and psychosocial capacities so as to better examine their distinct developmental timetables, it was important not to conflate the two. The measures of psychosocial maturity and cognitive capacity are very modestly correlated once age is controlled, $r(922) = .15$, $p < .001$. Although our operationalization of general cognitive capacity is not identical to that used by APA in its argument, it is very clear that the authors of the *Hodgson* brief (APA, 1987) were referring to cognitive abilities and not psychosocial maturity. . . .

Results

. . . As Figure 1 indicates, age differences in psychosocial maturity, as assessed in this study, did not emerge until mid-adolescence but were present throughout late adolescence and early adulthood. [There were] no significant differences in psychosocial maturity among the first four age groups (10–11, 12–13, 14–15, and 16–17 years) but significant differences between the 16–17-year-olds and those 22 and older, and between the 18–21-year-olds and those 26 and older . . . and . . . the patterns were the same among males and females.

Figure 1

Psychosocial Maturity (Standardized Composite Scores) as a Function of Age (in Years)

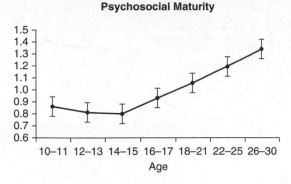

Figure 2

General Cognitive Capacity (Standardized Composite Scores) as a Function of Age (in Years)

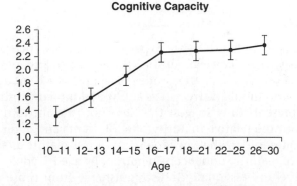

The analysis of age differences in cognitive capacity shows a very different pattern. [A]s Figure 2 indicates, age differences in cognitive capacity were evident during the first part of adolescence but not after age 16—just the opposite from the pattern seen with respect to psychosocial maturity. [There were] significant differences in general cognitive capacity between each of the first four age groups but no age differences after age 16.

Figure 3 presents these data in a somewhat different way. Here we show the proportion of individuals in each age group who scored at or above the mean level of the 26- to 30-year-olds in our sample on the psychosocial and cognitive composites, graphed in the same figure. As the figure indicates,

Figure 3

Proportion of Individuals in Each Age Group Scoring at or Above the Mean for 26- to 30-Year-Olds on Indices of Cognitive Capacity and Psychosocial Maturity

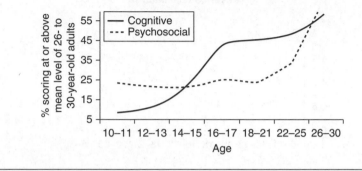

general cognitive capacity reaches adult levels long before the process of psychosocial maturation is complete.

. . . [In other words,] data supports the argument that adolescents reach adult levels of cognitive maturity several years before they reach adult levels of psychosocial maturity.

Discussion

Developmental psychologists with expertise in adolescence are frequently called on to provide guidance about the appropriate treatment of young people under the law and about the proper placement of legal age boundaries between those who should be treated as adults and those who should not. The results of the present study suggest that it is not prudent to make sweeping statements about the relative maturity of adolescents and adults, because the answer to the question of whether adolescents are as mature as adults depends on the aspects of maturity under consideration. By age 16, adolescents' general cognitive abilities are essentially indistinguishable from those of adults, but adolescents' psychosocial functioning, even at the age of 18, is significantly less mature than that of individuals in their mid-20s. . . .

Whether and how these findings should inform decisions about adolescents' treatment under the law depends on the specific legal issue under consideration. To varying degrees, such decisions rely on value judgments (e.g., about what aspects of maturity are relevant to a particular decision or about what is mature "enough" to warrant autonomy and/or culpability), which science alone cannot dictate. Nevertheless, the legal treatment of adolescents should at the very least be informed by the most accurate and timely scientific evidence on the nature and course of psychological development. On the basis of the present study, as well as previous research, it seems reasonable to distinguish between two very different decision-making contexts in this regard: those that allow for unhurried, logical reflection and those that do not. This distinction is also in keeping with our emerging understanding of adolescent brain maturation, which suggests that brain systems responsible for logical reasoning and basic information processing mature earlier than those that undergird more advanced executive functions and the coordination of affect and cognition necessary for psychosocial maturity (Steinberg, 2008).

When it comes to decisions that permit more deliberative, reasoned decision making, where emotional and social influences on judgment are minimized or can be mitigated, and where there are consultants who can provide objective information about the costs and benefits of alternative courses of action, adolescents are likely to be just as capable of mature decision making as adults, at least by the time they are 16. Three domains of decision making that would seem to fit into this category are medical decision making (where health care practitioners can provide information and encourage adolescents to think through their decisions before acting), legal decision making (where legal practitioners, such as defense attorneys, can play a comparable role), and decisions about participating in research studies (where research investigators, guided by institutional review boards, can function similarly). Although adults in these positions cannot and should not make the decision for the adolescent, they surely can take steps to create a context in which adolescents' decision-making competence will be maximized. The position taken by APA in *Hodgson v. Minnesota* (1990), in favor of granting adolescents' access to abortion without the necessity of parental involvement, therefore seems to us to be consistent with the available scientific evidence, so long as youngsters under the age of 16 have the opportunity to consult with other, informed adults (e.g., health care practitioners, counselors).

. . . The skills and abilities necessary to make an informed decision about a medical procedure are likely in place several years before the capacities necessary to regulate one's behavior under conditions of emotional arousal or coercive pressure from peers.

Science alone cannot dictate public policy, although it can, and should, inform it. Our data can neither "prove" nor "disprove" the appropriateness of requiring parental involvement before a teenager can obtain an abortion, but they do inform the debate. . . .

Developmental science can and should contribute to debates about the drawing of legal age boundaries, but research evidence cannot be applied to this sort of policy analysis without a careful and nuanced consideration of the particular demands placed on the individual for "adult-like" maturity in different domains of functioning. . . .

References

American Psychological Association. (1987, March 16). [Amicus curiae brief filed in the U.S. Court of Appeals for the Eighth Circuit in *Hodgson v. Minnesota*, 497 U.S. 417 (1990)]. Retrieved February 11, 2009, from http://www.apa.org/psyclaw/hodgson.pdf

American Psychological Association. (1989, September 1). [Amicus curiae brief filed in U.S. Supreme Court in *Ohio v. Akron Center for Reproductive Health, Inc.,* 497 U.S. 502 (1990) and Hodgson v. Minnesota, 497 U.S. 417 (1990)]. Retrieved February 11, 2009, from http://www.apa.org/psyclaw/reproductivehealth.pdf

Ayotte v. Planned Parenthood of Northern New England, 546 U.S. 320 (2006).

Belter, R., & Grisso, T. (1984). Children's recognition of rights violations in counseling. *Professional Psychology: Research and Practice, 15,* 899–910.

Grisso, T. (1980). Juveniles' capacities to waive *Miranda* rights: An empirical analysis. *California Law Review, 68,* 1134–1166.

Grisso, T., Steinberg, L., Woolard, J., Cauffman, E., Scott, E., Graham, S., et al. (2003). Juveniles' competence to stand trial: A comparison of adolescents' and adults' capacities as trial defendants. *Law and Human Behavior, 27,* 333–363.

Grisso, T., & Vierling, L. (1978). Minors' consent to treatment: A developmental perspective. *Professional Psychology, 9,* 412–426.

Gustafson, K., & McNamara, J. (1987). Confidentiality with minor clients: Issues and guidelines for therapists. *Professional Psychology: Research and Practice, 18,* 503–508.

Guttmacher Institute. (2009, February). Counseling and waiting periods for abortion. In *State policies in brief.* Retrieved February 11, 2009, from http://www.guttmacher.org/statecenter/spibs/spib_MWPA.pdf

Hale, S. (1990). A global developmental trend in cognitive processing speed. *Child Development, 61,* 653–663.

Henshaw, S., & Kost, K. (1992). Parental involvement in minors' abortion decisions. *Family Planning Perspectives, 24,* 196–207, 213.

Hodgson v. Minnesota, 497 U.S. 417 (1990).

Inhelder, B., & Piaget, J. (1958). *The growth of logical thinking from childhood to adolescence.* New York: Basic Books.

Jacobs-Quadrel, M., Fischhoff, B., & Davis, W. (1993). Adolescent (in)vulnerability. *American Psychologist, 48,* 102–116.

Kail, R. (1997). Processing time, imagery, and spatial memory. *Journal of Experimental Child Psychology, 64,* 67–78.

Keating, D. (1980). Thinking processes in adolescence. In J. Adelson (Ed.), *Handbook of adolescent psychology* (pp. 211–246). New York: Wiley.

Keating, D. (2004). Cognitive and brain development. In R. Lerner & L. Steinberg (Eds.), *Handbook of adolescent psychology* (2nd ed.). New York: Wiley.

Overton, W. (1990). Competence and procedures: Constraints on the development of logical reasoning. In W. Overton (Ed.), *Reasoning, necessity, and logic: Developmental perspectives* (pp. 1–32). Hillsdale, NJ: Erlbaum.

Roper v. Simmons, 543 U.S. 551 (2005).

Scott, E., Reppucci, N., & Woolard, J. (1995). Evaluating adolescent decision making in legal contexts. *Law and Human Behavior, 19,* 221–244.

Steinberg, L. (2007). Risk taking in adolescence: New perspectives from brain and behavioral science. *Current Directions in Psychological Science, 16,* 55–59.

Steinberg, L. (2008). A social neuroscience perspective on adolescent risk taking. *Developmental Review, 28,* 78–106.

Steinberg, L., Albert, D., Cauffman, E., Banich, M., Graham, S., & Woolard, J. (2008). Age differences in sensation seeking and impulsivity as indexed by behavior and self-report: Evidence for a dual systems model. *Developmental Psychology, 44,* 1764–1778.

Steinberg, L., & Cauffman, E. (1996). Maturity of judgment in adolescence: Psychosocial factors in adolescent decision-making. *Law and Human Behavior, 20,* 249–272.

Steinberg, L., Graham, S., O'Brien, L., Woolard, J., Cauffman, E., & Banich, M. (2009). Age differences in future orientation and delay discounting. *Child Development, 80,* 28–44.

Steinberg, L., & Monahan, K. (2007). Age differences in resistance to peer influence. *Developmental Psychology, 43,* 1531–1543.

Weithorn, L., & Campbell, S. (1982). The competency of children and adolescents to make informed treatment decisions. *Child Development, 53,* 1589–1598.

EXPLORING THE ISSUE

Should Parental Consent Be Required for Adolescents Seeking Abortion?

Critical Thinking and Reflection

1. What constitutes "mature" enough to make a decision about having an abortion? Who should decide a person's level of maturity? Is maturity a psychological concept—is it about decision-making abilities or is it about morality, executive functions (i.e., supervisory cognitive skills), logical reasoning, or psychosocial capacities (e.g., ability to delay gratification, not be impulsive, etc.)? Or, is maturity a legal term?

2. Do these parental consent and parental notification laws violate the constitutional right of girls to have authority over their own body? While *judicial bypass* is meant to provide an alternative to parental consent/notification, it is not an ideal process (see Bonny, 2007; Rebouché, 2011). Given the problems identified with judicial bypass (e.g., it's inaccessibility, delay in decision due to the court petition process, potential judicial bias), are these laws fair to girls?

3. Given the fact that many young pregnant women discuss their decision to have an abortion with their parents or a trusted adult before they seek an abortion (Webster et al., 2010), are these laws and policies necessary? Are we simply legislating common practice?

4. How might a pro-parental involvement law scholar discount the findings of Steinberg and colleagues? In contrast, how might Steinberg et al.'s findings affect or change the opinions of a pro-parental involvement law individual?

5. How might an anti-parental involvement law scholar discount the arguments of Stanton Collett? In contrast, how might Stanton Collett's arguments impact or change the opinions of an anti-parental involvement law individual?

6. Consider the differences in laws between Canada and the United States with regard to parental involvement in teen abortion. What differences exist in abortion trends between the two countries? Do similarities exist? Could a cross-country examination help inform the issue?

Is There Common Ground?

Steinberg and colleagues would probably support the statement that youth under 15 years of age are not as cognitively mature as their older teen counterparts, and thus, they would likely benefit from the more advanced decision-making skills of a parent when making an abortion decision. Stanton Collett would likely agree with this, as well. Steinberg and colleagues maintain that, for the purposes of cognitively assessing the pros and cons of having an abortion, a 16-year-old is as capable as an adult at thinking the issue through. In her testimony, Stanton Collett does not directly address the issue of cognitive maturity, per se. However, her writing implies a "parents know best" leaning. Steinberg and colleagues' study does not address the arguments made by Stanton Collett that parental involvement improves medical care of the girl or may help prevent coercion of the girl. In these respects, the YES and NO selections address different components of the parental involvement laws issue. Ultimately, the issue of parental involvement laws must consider many different factors and various moral perspectives.

Additional Resources

Bonny, A. C. (2007). Parental consent and notification laws in the abortion context: Rejecting the "maturity" standard in judicial bypass proceedings. *UC Davis Journal of Juvenile Law & Policy, 11*(2), 311–333.

> The author discusses the problems inherent in the judicial bypass process.

Dennis, A., Henshaw, S. K., Joyce, T. J., Finer, L. B., & Blanchard, K. (2009). *The impact of laws requiring parental involvement for abortion: A literature review*. New York: Guttmacher Institute.

> These authors review the empirical research regarding the impact of parental consent/notification laws on various teen pregnancy outcomes. They critique the literature with respect to methodological bias and flaws. They conclude that the most compelling evidence is that parental involvement laws result in increased out-of-state abortions.

Downie, J., & Nassar, C. (2007). Barriers to access to abortion through a legal lens. *Health Law Journal, 15*, 143–174.

Finken, L. L. (2005). The role of consultants in adolescents' decision making: A focus on abortion decisions. In J. E. Jacobs & P. A. Klaczynski (Eds.), *The development of judgement and decision making in children and adolescents* (pp. 255–278). Mahwah, NJ: Erlbaum.

> In this chapter, the role of romantic partners, peers, and family in consultation to decision-making is described. A review of published studies suggests that romantic partners, then best friends, and then family (mother, then father, then sister) would be consulted about pregnancy resolution.

Haugen, D., Musser, S., & Lovelace, K. (2010). *Abortion*. Farmington Hills, MI: Greenhaven Press.

> This book addresses a number of abortion-related issues from an "opposing sides" perspective—which is much like the current *Taking Sides* series. In particular, Chapter 2 of this book addresses the issue of restricting abortion rights. Within this chapter, two topics are addressed—late-term abortion bans and parental consent laws.

Holder, A. R. (2010). From chattel to consenter: Adolescents and informed consent. 2009 Grover Powers Lecture. *Yale Journal of Biology and Medicine, 83*(1), 35–41. Retrieved from www.ncbi.nlm.nih.gov/pmc/articles/PMC2844691/

> The author discusses the reasons why laws requiring others to give permission for abortion in lieu of the adolescent giving permission are unfair and problematic.

New, M. (2011). Analyzing the effect of anti-abortion U.S. state legislation in the post-*Casey* era. *State Politics & Policy Quarterly, 11*(1) 28–47.

> This article is an analysis of abortion rates and ratios as a function of abortion laws across states. The findings suggest that different laws affect women differently. Logically, parental involvement laws had an effect on the abortion rates and ratios of women under 18 years but no impact on the rates/ratios for older women. States with these laws had lower abortion rates/ratios for women under 18 years of age. In general, informed consent laws and funding restriction laws had an effect on abortion rates and ratios such that states with these laws had lower abortion rates and ratios.

Rebouché, R. (2011). Parental involvement laws and new governance. *Harvard Journal of Law & Gender, 34*, 175–223.

> This article addresses the discord between parental involvement laws judicial bypass procedure as it is meant to exist in theory and the practice of judicial bypass. Of particular interest in this article is the documentation of problems a minor who is seeking judicial bypass faces such as the fact that minors often do not know that the judicial bypass procedure exists, costs to petition a court and travel to court which may be difficult for a minor, delays (e.g., some judges refuse to hear judicial bypass petitions), and lack of available, qualified lawyers.

Sen, B., Wingate, M. S., & Kirby, R. (2012). The relationship between state abortion-restrictions and homicide deaths among children under 5 years of age: A longitudinal study. *Social Science & Medicine*, 1–9 [uncorrected proofs]. doi:10.1016/j.socscimed.2012.01.037

> Using an ecological analysis, with state-level data (as opposed to individual-level information), these researchers found an association between child mortality and parental involvement laws. That is, states that had greater restrictions to abortion for teens (e.g., parental consent laws) had higher childhood mortality. The authors speculated that these abortion restrictions might lead to children being born into higher-risk life situations (e.g., younger mothers, more poverty) that are risk factors for childhood homicide. It is very important to note that association (correlation) does not mean causation (i.e., one caused the other). More research would need to be conducted to flesh out this supposition.

Watkins, C. (2009). *Teens at risk*. Farmington Hills, MI: Greenhaven Press.

> This book addresses a number of teen risk-related issues from an "opposing sides" perspective—which is much like the current *Taking Sides* series. In particular, Chapter 2 of this book addresses the adverse consequences of teenage sex and pregnancy and can these be reduced. Two pieces within this chapter speak of parental consent for teen abortion.

Webster, R. D., Neustadt, A. N., Whitaker, A. K., & Gilliam, M. L. (2010). Parental involvement laws and parent–daughter communication: Policy without proof. *Contraception, 10*, 310–313.

This editorial reviews parent–daughter communication in the context of parental involvement laws. The authors consider the implications for medical practitioners.

Internet References . . .

Bullying.org

Created by W. Belsey in response to school shootings in Colorado and Alberta in 1999, this website was designed to raise awareness about bullying, support individuals who have been bullied, and help organizations respond to bullying.

www.bullying.org

Cyberbullying.org

This website is a collection of valuable resources, facts about cyberbullying, and examples of cyberbullying.

www.cyberbullying.org

Entertainment Software Rating Board

This website was created by the Entertainment Software Rating Board, a non-profit, self-regulatory body that independently assigns ratings, enforces guidelines, and helps ensure responsible online privacy practices for the interactive entertainment software industry.

www.esrb.org

Parents' Choice

The Parent's Choice Foundation bills itself as the nation's oldest nonprofit guide to quality children's media and toys (1978).

www.parents-choice.org

Caring for Kids

Developed by the Canadian Paediatric Society, the *Behaviour and Parenting* section of this web site includes topics on a large range of issues.

www.caringforkids.cps.ca/home

www.caringforkids.cps.ca/handouts/social_media/

American Academy of Child and Adolescent Psychiatry: Facts for Families

The American Academy of Child and Adolescent Psychiatry has a subpage titled *Facts for Families* that has a number of research-based fact sheets regarding the impact of media on children and youth.

www.aacap.org/cs/root/facts_for_families/facts_for_families

Technology, Mass Media, and Criminal Justice

*T*here are many areas where adolescent behavior can cause problems for the developing teen. This area of study is sometimes called abnormal adolescent psychology or the sociology of juvenile delinquency. By studying these behaviors, we can attempt to prevent problems before they occur and intervene when problems do occur. What is defined as a "problem" or an antisocial behavior can change depending on the social, political, and economic climate of the time. The following unit deals with four contemporary problem issues, most of them specifically connected to the technological climate in which our contemporary youths reside.

- Are Boys Bigger Bullies than Girls—In Cyberspace?
- Does Playing Violent Video Games Harm Adolescents?
- Are Social Networking Sites (SNSs), such as Facebook, a Cause for Concern?
- Should Juvenile Offenders Be Tried and Convicted as Adults?

ISSUE 15

Are Boys Bigger Bullies than Girls—In Cyberspace?

YES: Özgür Erdur-Baker, from "Cyberbullying and Its Correlation to Traditional Bullying, Gender and Frequent and Risky Usage of Internet-Mediated Communication Tools," *New Media & Society* (vol. 12, no. 1, pp. 109–125, 2010), doi:10.1177/1461444809341260

NO: Faye Mishna et al., from (2010). "Cyber Bullying Behaviors Among Middle and High School Students," *American Journal of Orthopsychiatry* (vol. 80, no. 3, pp. 362–374, 2010), doi:10.1111/j.1939-0025.2010.01040.x

---

Learning Outcomes

After reading this issue, you should be able to:

- Identify the differences between traditional bullying and cyberbullying.
- Critically consider the role of gender in aggressive behaviors.
- Evaluate the evidence on who cyberbullies and the contextual factors associated with cyberbullying.
- Assess the role of technology in young people's covert aggressive behaviors.

ISSUE SUMMARY

YES: Özgür Erdur-Baker, associate professor in the Department of Educational Sciences, Middle East Technical University, found that males are more likely to engage in bullying behaviors than females, regardless of physical or cyber environment. In fact, she found that males were more likely to experience cyber-victimization and to be cyberbullies than females.

NO: Faye Mishna, dean and professor at the Factor Inwentash Faculty of Social Work, University of Toronto, and colleagues Charlene Cook, Tahany Gadalla (associate professor), Joanne Daciuk, and Steven Solomon, all of the University of Toronto, Canada, examined gender differences in the perpetration of cyberbullying among early and mid-adolescents. They found that both middle school and high school boys and girls were equally likely to have engaged in cyberbullying. No gender differences were found in the perpetration of cyberbullying; gender differences in methods of cyberbullying are discussed.

Bullying has become increasingly more serious among today's youth. Conflict and misunderstandings are part of normal development; as cognitive capacities become more sophisticated, adolescents learn to argue. This is a part of gaining independence and learning to think for themselves. Bullying, however, introduces risks to normal development. There is evidence that physical and verbal aggressions decline in early adolescence, at the same time as the more covert types of aggression escalate. Research has indicated that between the ages of 8 and 18, physical aggression declines in both males and females, whereas indirect aggression increases significantly between 8 and 11 years of age, and then starts to decline. Some argue that with the development of social intelligence, direct physical and verbal aggressions are replaced with indirect, relational, or social aggression (Björkqvist et al., 1992). The decline in physical and verbal aggression after age 11 can also be linked to adolescent moral and cognitive development. Essentially, with advanced cognitions and moral reasoning, adolescents make better choices (e.g., aggression is unacceptable), have enhanced perspective-taking skills, and more mature conflict resolution strategies (i.e., talking it through versus using aggression). Development is gradual and individual; therefore, the decline in physical aggression and the initial increase followed by a decrease in relational aggression will be different for each individual and dependent on a number of factors.

Traditional bullying has been defined as a subset of aggression occurring when one or more individuals verbally, physically, and/or psychologically harass another person (Olweus, 1997). According to Olweus, there are three core characteristics of bullying: It is aggressive behavior, it occurs over time, and it involves a power imbalance. Regarding the aggressive behavior, bullying may involve physical aggression (e.g., hitting, punching, pushing), verbal aggression (e.g., name-calling, insulting, yelling obscenities), and the more psychological form of aggression often referred to as indirect, relational, or social aggression. Indirect, relational, or social aggression each can be defined differently, but are similar in terms of the types of manipulations involved.

Indirect aggression is defined as a "type of behavior in which the perpetrator attempts to inflict pain in such a manner that he or she makes it seem as though there is no intention to hurt at all" (Björkqvis et al., 1992, p. 118). Essentially, this is "behind-the-back" or "stabbing-in-the-back" type of aggression. Relational aggression is defined as behaviors that hurt others by damaging relationships or feelings (Crick & Grotpeter, 1995). This type of mainly covert aggression is about the endpoint, where the goal is to disrupt friendships. Social aggression is also focused on the endpoint and involves damaging another's self-esteem and/or social status, usually through tactics used to alienate or ostracize a person from the group. Indirect, relational, and social aggression have the following characteristics in common: gossiping, spreading rumors, ignoring, deliberately throwing someone out of a group, turning others against others, embarrassing others in public, performing practical jokes, and sending abusive phone calls (Archer & Coyne, 2005).

With increasing access to technology, cyberbullying has emerged as a contemporary bullying problem (Li, 2006). Cyberbullying falls within the domain of indirect aggression and can involve "flaming, harassment, cyberstalking, denigration (put-downs), masquerade, outing and trickery, exclusion . . . and death threats and can be very serious" (Li, 2006, p. 158). Contemporary adolescents' computer proficiency and more time spent on the Internet are directly related to cyberbullying (Hinduja & Patchin, 2008). With the use of electronic communication devices, such as mobile phones, e-mail, social networking sites, blogs, and chatrooms, this type of psychological aggression can be carried out anonymously, which may make it even more common, or easily performed, than traditional bullying. Unlike traditional bullying, researchers agree that cyberbullying is unique in that it affords the perpetrator this safety (or protection) of anonymity (DeHue et al., 2008; Li, 2006; Rivers & Noret, 2010). As a result, bullies are not confronted with their victims' reactions. This type of "depersonalization" makes it easier to engage in cyberbullying because bullies are not directly confronted with the consequences of their actions (DeHue et al., 2008). Moreover, technology now allows for bullying to transcend the safety of the home environment because cyberbullying can occur anywhere and anytime the youth is "logged on." According to Hinduja and Patchin (2008), cyberbullying is "the unfortunate by-product of the union of adolescent aggression and electronic communication" (p. 131).

Research suggests that there are gender differences with respect to bullying, but have not yet reached a consensus on bullying and gender-related issues. Some suggest that males are more likely to bully and be bullied both physically and online (Li, 2006). Others deny gender differences and state that boys and girls participate equally in cyberbullying, but participation depends on a variety of contextual factors (Hinduja & Patchin, 2008; Rivers & Noret, 2010). One point of general agreement is that that boys and girls bully differently (Wang et al., 2009). Whereas, generally speaking, girls are found to be relational bullies, boys are more likely to be physical bullies. In fact, findings indicate that while girls engage in fewer acts of physical aggression than boys, they engage in equal if not higher levels of indirect, relational, or social aggression (Morett et al., 2005). Based on evidence that girls tend to be relational bullies (Crapanzano et al., 2011), advances in technology seem to provide girls with an additional vehicle through which to bully in ways consistent with their gender (i.e., relationally). The research on gender differences and cyberbullying, however, is somewhat mixed. While one would expect girls to be bigger cyberbullies than boys, given the multitude of opportunities to execute relational aggression, some have found no real differences in the prevalence of cyberbullying among boys and girls (Hinduja & Patchin, 2008).

During the transition into adulthood, are girls as aggressive as boys? Given the advances in and accessibility to technological tools, such as computers and smart phones, do adolescent boys continue to engage in more physically aggressive acts than girls, or are they just as likely to engage in indirect aggression via these new communication tools? Is cyberbullying a "new problem" or merely a new guise of an old problem? Does this new medium for aggression tip the scales, making girls as aggressive as boys, especially in the cyber domain?

In the YES selection, Erdur-Baker found that males are more likely to engage in bullying behaviors than females, regardless of physical or cyber environment. In fact, she found that males were more likely to experience cyber-victimization and to be cyberbullies than females. In the NO selection, Mishna and colleagues found that middle school and high school boys and girls were equally likely to have engaged in cyberbullying. No gender differences were found in the perpetration of cyberbullying; gender differences in methods of cyberbullying are discussed.

YES ↵

Özgür Erdur-Baker

Cyberbullying and Its Correlation to Traditional Bullying, Gender and Frequent and Risky Usage of Internet-Mediated Communication Tools

Bullying, defined as a deliberate and repeated aggression among peers (Olweus, 1993), is now changing its form as information and communication technologies (ICT) progress. Aggression using ICT is referred to as cyberbullying (also called electronic bullying or online bullying) when it is identified as intentional and repeated aggression. More specifically, cyberbullying is defined as hurtful and intended communication activity using any form of technological device such as the internet or mobile phones (e.g. Belsey, 2006; Patchin and Hinduja, 2006).

Due to their unique characteristics, online environments might be perceived by youngsters as a very liberating platform on which to express themselves. As several researchers have identified, such platforms result in positive consequences such as establishing social ties (Henderson and Gilding, 2004; Mesch and Talmud, 2006), which are perhaps more difficult for some adolescents to have offline (Amichai-Hamburger and Ben-Artzi, 2003). At the same time, online environments are a place where children and adolescents are less likely to inhibit their emotions, including negative ones such as anger (Erdur-Baker and Yurdugül, under review). As Ybarra and Mitchell (2004) point out, the anonymity of the internet allows children and adolescents to adopt a more aggressive persona than they may express in real life. Also, since people can hide behind fake screen names and/or use someone else's screen name, the cyber-environment might be a more appealing environment for bullies (Kowalski and Limber, 2007) and a safer environment for victims of traditional bullying to seek revenge (King et al., 2007). Therefore, peer bullying now goes beyond school borders to become a larger concern that must be dealt with not only by school and mental health professionals, but also by parents, policymakers, professionals working in the area of new media and the community at large. . . .

Erdur-Baker, Özgür. From *New Media & Society*, Vol. 12, No. 1, February 1, 2010, pp. 109–125.

Given that cyberbullying is a relatively new issue, the literature on the traditional form of bullying is typically taken as a framework to elucidate the nature of cyberbullying in terms of its specific characteristics and contributing factors. However, despite some efforts, the relationship between traditional bullying and cyberbullying has not yet been substantiated.

. . . Gender seems to be an important factor in understanding the experiences of both cyber and traditional bullying. Previous studies report inconsistent results regarding gender differences. Several authors claim that girls are more likely to engage in cyberbullying due to the fact that it is a form of relational or verbal aggression (Keith and Martin, 2005; Nelson, 2003). However, other research has failed to find gender differences (e.g. Patchin and Hinduja, 2006). Finally, Li (2006) reports that no gender difference was observed for being a victim of either traditional or cyberbullying; however, more male students report being a traditional bully and cyberbully. Therefore, the main goal of the present study is to explore adolescents' cyberbullying experiences by clarifying their links to traditional bullying with respect to gender.

. . . In sum, there has been growing concern regarding the cyberbullying experiences of children and adolescents (Strom and Strom, 2004; Ybarra et al., 2007b). Survey results regarding the prevalence of cyberbullying provide support for this concern. Given the fact that ICT tools are a vital part of youngsters' lives, youths may be having negative online experiences in increasing numbers. Since cyberbullying is a relatively new issue, the literature on the traditional form of bullying is often taken as a framework to understand and deal with the issue. However, the relationship between traditional bullying and cyberbullying has not been fully substantiated yet. As a result, the related literature lacks conceptual clarity (Schrock and boyd, 2008). Therefore, the main goal of the study is to shed light on whether cyberbullying is indeed associated with traditional bullying, and on what role gender plays in the relationship between traditional and cyberbullying. In addition, this study aims to elucidate the contributions of risky internet usage and usage frequency of ICT to cyberbullying and cyber-victimization.

Method

Data Collection

The data collection took place in the north-west part of Turkey. This area is one of the most industrialized and populated areas and has attracted migrants from all parts of Turkey. The participants were recruited from three high schools through a sampling of convenience procedure. . . . In the presence of school counselors, questionnaires were distributed to classes that the school administration had suggested, based on availability. Approximately 290 questionnaires were given to the students. No students declined to participate in the study. However, a total of 14 questionnaires were excluded from the analyses due to too many unanswered questions (six questionnaires) or the same answer for more than one page (four questionnaires) and four outliers in terms of age (older than 18).

Participants

The participants were 276 adolescents (123 females, 151 males and 2 unknown) ranging in age from 14 to 18. Of the participants, 14 (5.1%) were 14 years old, 91 (33%) were 15, 114 (41.3%) were 16, 49 (17.8%) were 17 and 7 (2.6%) were 18 (one participant's age is unknown). The participants were students in the 9th (70.7%), 10th (15.2%) and 11th (14.1%) grades. There was found to be no statistical differences among the grades or schools in terms of their bullying and cyberbullying scores, and therefore data from different grades and schools were collapsed. . . .

Measures

Traditional Form of Bullying

This was measured by the Turkish version of Olweus's bullying questionnaire . . . [with] 49 items measuring several aspects of bullying. For the purpose of this study, only the part that measured victimization (six items) and bullying (six items) was used. This part consists of five-point Likert-type items providing scores for being a bully and a victim in a given semester. . . .

For this study, . . . participants were divided into four groups based on their traditional bullying experiences: bully (44 students), victim (66 students), bully and victim (59 students) and not involved (99 students). Those students who bullied others and/or were victimized at least two to three times per month were considered as a 'bully,' 'victim' or 'bully and victim' accordingly. The 'not involved' group answered all the questions as 'never happened' in this semester. . . .

Cyberbullying Scale

This was constructed for a previous study by Erdur-Baker and Kavşut (2007) to measure the nature and severity of cyberbullying among Turkish adolescents. The scale has two very similar parallel forms: one form measures cyber-victimization and the other measures cyberbullying. . . . Sample items from the cyberbully form were 'I have insulted people in the chatroom,' and from the cybervictim form, 'I have been slandered by fake photos of me on the internet'. . . .

Additionally, the participants' usage frequency of the internet, SMS, MSN, forums and chatrooms were asked by a question for each one. Note that for the purposes of this study, internet usage is defined as all internet activities except MSN, forums and chatrooms and includes activities such as blogging, emailing, reading or creating webpages, surfing, downloading music or videos, etc.

Risky usage of internet-mediated communication tools were measured by three common questions utilized by previous studies (e.g. Liau et al., 2005; Ybarra et al., 2007b): (1) Have you ever asked someone you met on the internet to meet face to face? ('Inviting to meet in person'); (2) Have you ever disclosed your personal information to unknown people over the internet, including password and username? ('Sharing personal information'); and (3) have you ever accepted an invitation to meet in person someone you met over the internet? ('Accepting to meet in person'). . . .

Results

Data Analysis

Usage Frequency of Internet-Mediated Communication Tools

[P]articipants use internet-mediated communication tools quite frequently. Only 7 percent of the participants reported that they never use the internet, while 24 percent indicated that they use the internet everyday. Chatrooms seemed to be the least used whereas MSN was the most frequently used communication tool. Mobile phone text messaging was also reported to be used by 84.8 percent of the participants at least one to two times a month.

Descriptive Analyses of Cyberbullying Experiences Regarding Gender and Traditional Bullying Experiences

. . . Overall, male students with traditional bullying experiences scored relatively higher than female students [(on measures of cyberbullying and cyber-victimization).] Correlation coefficients displayed that cyber-victimization and cyberbullying were significantly correlated. Also, being a bully in cyber and physical environments was correlated for both male and female students, but not for being a victim.

Examination of how much overlap existed between cyber and traditional bullying showed that 32 percent (89) of the students reported being victims of both traditional and cyberbullying, and 26 percent (73) of the students reported being bullies in both the physical and cyber-environments.

Relationships of Gender and Traditional Bullying to Cyberbullying

. . . [Analyses were] conducted to examine the effect of the four levels of traditional bullying experiences (bully, victim, bully and victim and no bullying experiences) and gender on two dependent variables (cyberbullying and cyber-victimization). . . .

Multiple comparisons results revealed that differences in cyberbullying experiences among the four groups of students with traditional bullying experiences are not consistent between male and female students. Female students' scores on cyberbullying and cyber-victimization were not found to be different across the levels of traditional bullying experiences. . . . However, male students' cyberbullying and cyber-victimization scores were found to vary based on their four levels of traditional bullying experiences. In terms of cyberbullying, male students who reported being a traditional bully scored significantly higher than students who reported being a traditional victim, bully and victim[,] and not involved. Also, male students who reported being a traditional bully and victim scored significantly higher on cyberbullying than male students who reported not being involved in traditional bullying. [Regarding] cyber-victimization among male students, male students who reported being a traditional bully and traditional victim scored significantly higher on the cyber-victimization scale than students who reported not being involved in traditional bullying.

Moreover, the results of the comparisons by gender across levels of traditional bullying show that within some levels of traditional bullying experiences there were statistically significant gender differences in being a cybervictim and cyberbully. For cyber-victimization, these significant gender differences were found in the levels of being a traditional bully and being a traditional victim. For cyberbullying, the only significant gender difference was found in the level of being a traditional bully. Male students demonstrated higher levels of cyber-victimization and cyberbullying than female students. . . .

Discussion and Conclusion

This study investigated whether traditional and cyberbullying experiences indeed overlap and whether the usage frequency and risky use of internet-based communication tools contributes to the cyberbullying experiences of Turkish students. Before discussing the results of the relationship between cyber and traditional bullying, the relation of cyber-victimization to cyberbullying should be noted. Regardless of gender differences, the relationships between being a cybervictim and cyberbully are significant and much stronger than the relationships between cyber and traditional bullying. This result suggests that the same adolescents who are victims are also bullies in cyber-environments, and is consistent with previous studies (e.g. Kowalski and Limber, 2007; Ybarra and Mitchell, 2004). . . .

The results of this study provide some support for previous studies that have pointed out the relationship between cyber and traditional forms of bullying (e.g. Li, 2005, 2006; Raskauskas and Stoltz, 2007; Ybarra et al., 2007a). However, it should be noted that, as Ybarra et al. (2007a) conclude, the amount of the overlap between traditional and cyberbullying (32% of overlap for cyber and traditional bullying victimization, and 26% of overlap for bullying) is not too large. The conclusion may be drawn from this result is that although cyber and traditional bullying share some common ground, cyberbullying seems to be composed of its own unique characteristics. According to previous studies, anonymity (Greene, 2006; Ybarra et al., 2007b), impersonation, decreased fear of being caught (Kowalski et al., 2008) and being more aggressive than they are offline are the most essential factors that distinguish cyberbullies from traditional bullies. Thus, despite the fact that the literature on traditional bullying is helpful to understand cyberbullying, the results of this study suggest a need for more research to establish the theoretical background required to shed light on cyberbullying.

A further contribution of this study is the finding that the nature of the relationship between cyber and traditional bullying may differ for male and female adolescents. For both male and female students the results showed that being a bully in cyber and physical environments were correlated, but being a victim in cyber and traditional environments were not. [M]ale students demonstrated higher levels of cyber-victimization and cyberbullying experiences across all levels of traditional bullying except one. The exception is for the case of being a traditional bully and victim, in which male students scored lower than female students in the level of cyber-victimization, but this gender difference was not significant. The largest gender differences for both cyber-victimization and cyberbullying were found for traditional bullies. For female students, there are no significant differences in cyberbullying or victimization among the four levels of traditional bullying. However, male students who reported being a traditional bully are more likely to report experiences of cyberbullying. Thus, the gender of students should be considered when examining the relationship between traditional bullying and cyberbullying. . . .

The result of this study on gender differences is parallel to previous studies conducted in Turkey: as compared to boys, girls are less likely to engage in cyberbullying either as a cybervictim or bully (Erdur-Baker and Kavşut, 2007; Topçu et al., 2008). . . . [S]uch results . . . challenge the claim that girls are more likely to engage in cyberbullying because cyberbullying is a form of relational or verbal aggression (Keith and Martin, 2005; Nelson, 2003). . . .

References

Amichai-Hamburger, Y. and E. Ben-Artzi (2003) 'Loneliness and Internet Use,' *Computers in Human Behavior 19*(1): 71– 80.

Belsey, B. (2006) 'Cyberbullying: An Emerging Threat to the Always On Generation,' URL (consulted October 2006): http://www.cyberbullying.ca/pdf/Cyberbullying_Article_by_Bill_Belsey.pdf

Erdur-Baker, Ö. and F. Kavşut (2007) 'Cyberbullying: A New Face of Peer Bullying,' *Eurasian Journal of Educational Research 27*(7): 31–42.

Erdur-Baker, Ö. and H. Yurdugül (under review) 'The Nomological Network of Cyberbullying: The Relations of Cyberbullying to Traditional Bullying, Anger and Loneliness.'

Greene, M. B. (2006) 'Bullying in School: A Plea for Measure of Human Rights,' *Journal of Social Issues 62*(1): 63–79.

Henderson, S. and M. Gilding (2004) 'I've Never Clicked This Much with Anyone in My Life: Trust and Hyperpersonal Communication in Online Friendships,' *New Media & Society 6*(4): 487–506.

Keith, S. and M. E. Martin (2005) 'Cyber-bullying: Creating a Culture of Respect in a Cyber World,' *Reclaiming Children and Youth 13*(4): 224–8.

King, J., C, Walpole and K. Lamou (2007) 'Surf and Turf Wars Online: Growing Implications of Internet Gang Violence,' *Journal of Adolescent Health 41*(6): 66–8.

Kowalski, R. M. and S. P. Limber (2007) 'Electronic Bullying among Middle School Students,' *Journal of Adolescent Health 4*(6): 22–30.

Kowalski, R. M., S. P. Limber and P.W. Agatston (2008) *Cyberbullying: Bullying in the Digital Age.* Malden, MA: Blackwell.

Li, Q. (2005) 'New Bottle but Old Wine: A Research of Cyberbullying in Schools,' *Computers in Human Behavior 23*: 1777–91.

Li, Q. (2006) 'Cyberbullying in Schools: A Research of Gender Differences,' *School Psychology International* 27: 157–70.

Liau, A. K., A. Khoo and P. Hwaang (2005) 'Factors Influencing Adolescents' Engagement in Risky Internet Behavior,' *Cyberpsychology and Behavior* 8(6): 513–20.

Mesch, G. and I. Talmud (2006) 'Online Friendship Formation, Communication Channels and Social Closeness,' *International Journal of Internet Science* 1(1): 29–44.

Nelson, M. (2003) 'School Bullies Going High Tech,' URL (consulted November 2005): http://canoe.ca/NewsStand/LondonFreePress/2003/09/02/174030

Olweus, D. (1993) *Bullying at School: What We Know and What We Can Do.* Cambridge, MA: Blackwell.

Patchin, J. W. and S. Hinduja (2006) 'Bullies Move Beyond the Schoolyard: A Preliminary Look at Cyberbullying,' *Youth Violence and Juvenile Justice* 4(2): 148–69.

Raskauskas, J. and A. D. Stoltz (2007) 'Involvement in Traditional and Electronic Bullying among Adolescents,' *Developmental Psychology* 43(3): 564–73.

Schrock, A. and Boyd, d. (2008) 'Online Threats to Youth: Solicitation, Harassment and Problematic Content. Literature Review by the Research Advisory Board of the Internet Safety Technical Task Force,' URL (consulted January 2009): http://cyber.law.harward.edu/research/isttf/RAB

Strom, P. and R. Strom (2004) 'Bullied by Mouse,' URL (consulted June 2006): http://www.childresearch.net/RESOURCE/RESEARCH/2004/MEMBER35.HTM

Topçu, Ç., Ö. Erdur-Baker and Y. Çapa-Aydin (2008) 'Examination of Cyber Bullying Experiences among Turkish Students from Different School Types,' *Cyberpsychology and Behavior* 11(6): 643–8.

Ybarra, M. and K. Mitchell (2004) 'Online Aggressor/Targets, Aggressors and Targets: A Comparison of Associated Youth Characteristics,' *Journal of Child Psychology and Psychiatry* 45(7): 1308–16.

Ybarra, M. L., M. Diener-West and P. J. Leaf (2007a) 'Examining the Overlap in Internet Harassment and School Bullying: Implications for School Intervention,' *Journal of Adolescent Health* 41(6): 42–50.

Ybarra, M., K. J. Mitchell, D. Finkelhor and J. Wolak (2007b) 'Internet Prevention Messages: Targeting the Right Online Behaviors,' *Archives of Pediatric Adolescence Medicine* 161(4): 138–45.

Fayc Mishna et al. ➔ **NO**

Cyber Bullying Behaviors Among Middle and High School Students

The exponential growth of electronic and computer-based communication and information sharing during the last decade has radically changed individuals' social interactions, learning strategies, and choice of entertainment. Most notably, technology has created new communication tools. The tools are particularly influential among young people, who extensively utilize websites, instant messaging, web cams, e-mails, chat rooms, social networking sites, and text messaging (Boyd, 2008; Bryant, Sanders-Jackson, & Smallwood, 2006; Palfrey & Gasser, 2008). Youth spend an average of 2–4 hr online each day (Media Awareness Network, 2005), and it has been suggested that the majority of youth view electronic communication tools as essential for their social interactions (Kowalski, Limber, & Agatston, 2008).

The Internet provides innumerable possibilities for growth among children and youth, including benefits such as social support, identity exploration, and development of interpersonal and critical thinking skills, as well as educational benefits generated from expansive access to knowledge, academic support, and worldwide cross-cultural interactions (Jackson el al., 2006; Tynes, 2007; Valken-burg & Peter, 2007). The Internet is, however, concurrently a potential site for abuse and victimization (Mitchell, Finkelhor, & Wolak, 2003a, 2003b).

The Internet and other forms of communication technology place children and youth at risk of being bullied online. Cyber bullying comprises "willful and repeated harm" inflicted toward another and includes the use of e-mail, cell phones, text messages, and Internet sites to threaten, harass embarrass, or socially exclude (Patchin & Hinduja, 2006; Williams & Guerra, 2007). Cyber bullying further encompasses the use of electronic media to sexually harass (Shariff & Johnny, 2007), including distributing unsolicited text or photos of a sexual nature or requesting sexual acts either online or offline (Schrock & Boyd. 2008). The nature of what constitutes repetition with respect to cyber bullying is complex. Occurring in the public domain (W. Craig, personal communication, February 25, 2009), cyber bullying by its very nature involves repetition, because material such as e-mail, text, or pictures can be viewed far and wide, and can be distributed not only by the perpetrator but also by anyone with access (Campbell, 2005; Slonje & Smith, 2008), and can be difficult or impossible for the victimized child or youth to eliminate (Wolak. Mitchell, & Finkelhor, 2007).

Mishna, Faye; et al. From *American Journal of Orthopsychiatry*, Vol. 80, No. 3, July 16, 2010, pp. 362–374. Copyright © 2010 by American Orthopsychiatric Association. Reprinted by permission of John Wiley via Rightslink.

Recent large scale cross-sectional studies demonstrate that cyber bullying is a significant problem (Berson, Berson, & Ferron, 2002; Mitchell et al., 2003a; Ybarra & Mitchell, 2004a, 2004b). Current evidence indicates that the prevalence of cyber bullying ranges from 9% to 25% (Kowalski & Limber, 2007; Li, 2007; Williams & Guerra, 2007). Given such vast potential exposure to cyber bullying, research in this field is imperative to understand and reduce the risks associated with the online world. Reducing online risks for children and youth is especially vital to support the positive elements associated with online activity, particularly the accessibility of information and social support.

The pervasiveness of bullying among children and adolescents is well documented. The effects may be far-reaching for children who bully and for those who are victimized, both of whom are at risk of emotional, social, and psychiatric problems that may persist into adulthood (Nansel, Overpeck, Haynie, et al., 2003). Recognition of the seriousness of bullying has led to the accumulation of a large body of research and numerous school-wide interventions throughout the world (Olweus, 1994; Roland, 2000).

Although the research on cyber bullying is sparse, largely because of the relative newness of the phenomenon, efforts to document the impact of cyber bullying provide a picture of the significant psychosocial and academic repercussions of cyber bullying as well as the vulnerability of targeted children and youth. Students who were cyber bullied reported feelings of sadness, anxiety, and fear, and an inability to concentrate which affected their grades (Beran & Li, 2005). Youth who were bullied online were more likely to have skipped school, to have had detentions or suspensions, or to have carried a weapon to school (Ybarra, Diener-West, & Leaf, 2007). Research has also shown that depression, substance use, and delinquency are significantly higher among youth who report experiencing cyber bullying or online sexual solicitation.

Youth who cyber bully others online are also at high risk. Research suggests that children and youth who were both victimized online and perpetrators of online sexual solicitation and harassment were far more likely to experience high substance use, offline victimization, delinquency, and aggression (Ybarra, Espelage, & Mitchell, 2007). Additional evidence reveals that youth who perpetrate cyber bullying are more likely to concurrently engage in rule breaking and to have problems with aggression (Ybarra & Mitchell, 2007).

Much of the current literature on cyber bullying has been conducted with small samples (Li, 2007) or samples that were quite homogenous regarding participant ethnicity (Kowalski & Limber, 2007). It is vital that this phenomenon be thoroughly explored with a diverse sample, to gain a greater understanding of the prevalence and impact of cyber bullying. To date, the few larger studies have not focused on cyber bullying exclusively and therefore have not examined this phenomenon in depth (Finkelhor, Mitchell, & Wolak, 2000; Williams & Guerra, 2007). In this article, we report on a survey on cyber bullying with a large and diverse sample of students in Grades 6, 7, 10, and 11, in a large urban setting. The study reported in this article addresses the gap in the literature and is among the first to examine cyber bullying with a large and diverse sample of middle and high school students.

Method

This study employed an exploratory, cross-sectional survey design to examine cyber bullying as experienced by students in Grades 6, 7, 10 and 11, attending schools in a large Canadian city. These grades were chosen to reflect middle or junior and high school students, respectively, as the school boards felt sampling from Grades 5 to 12 would prove too unwieldy and involve too many disruptions for participating schools. The study received approval from the University of Toronto Research Ethics Board and the External Research Review Committee of Board 1. Board 2 did not require further ethics approval.

Sample

. . . Thirty-three schools (20 secondary and 13 elementary/middle) participated. All students in the targeted grades of the selected schools were invited to participate but only those who received parental consent participated. . . .

Procedure

The questions in the survey were informed by various sources including information gathered in focus groups that had been conducted by the research team with students in the targeted grades. . . . An identical questionnaire was administered to all students, with the exception of the wording and terminology of two questions related to online sexual content and online contact of a sexual nature. The wording for Grades 6 and 7 slightly differed from the wording for Grades 10 and 11 to ensure age-appropriate language.

. . . The pencil and paper questionnaire was administered to students by research assistants during class hours. The questionnaire took approximately 30 min to complete. . . .

Measures

The questionnaires included general questions about the socio-demographic characteristics of students and their families, technology use, and experience of cyber bullying.

Socio-Demographic Characteristics

Questions related to individual and family characteristics included grade, gender, age, ownership, or rental status of the family residence, typical academic achievement in school, and years at current school. Questions related to possible racial and/or cultural marginalization included language spoken at home, country of birth or years in Canada, and parents' country of birth.

Technology Use

Technology use was measured using items including: how many hours spent on a computer daily; the frequency with which computers were used for activities such as homework, communicating with friends, playing games, and sending pictures; which websites were visited most frequently; if passwords were shared among friends; and how often cell phones were used to talk to friends, text message, and send photographs.

Experience of Cyber Bullying

To gain a more comprehensive understanding of online behavior, the questionnaire involved a series of questions aboul perpetrating or being the victim of various online behaviors, without explicitly defining the behaviors as bullying. Participants were asked to indicate if they had experienced or perpetuated any of the following in the 3 months prior to the administration of the survey; calling someone names, threatening, spreading rumors, sending a private picture without consent, pretending to be someone else, receiving or sending unwanted sexual text or photos, or being asked to do something sexual. Following these sections, a general question was asked to see if respondents felt that online they bullied or were bullied, with the following definition of cyber bullying: Cyber bullying includes the use of e-mail, cell phones, text messages, and Internet sites to be mean to, make fun of, or scare people.

Participants were asked who they bullied or were bullied by, how their experience as a perpetrator and/or victim made them feel, if they had ever witnessed cyber bullying, and, for those who had been victimized, if they told someone about the bullying or confronted the perpetrator. The questionnaire also included questions asking participants to identify the characteristics (such as sexuality, race, appearance, family, etc.) that they believed resulted in their bullying or that were the reason they bullied others. Additionally, participants were asked if they experienced traditional bullying as a perpetrator and/or victim.

Results

Demographics

Slightly more than half the sample (55%) were female. More than three fourth of participants (76.4%) lived with both biological parents, followed by a single parent (16.8%), a biological and stepparent (3.6%), and other (3.4%). Participants were drawn from a diverse range of ethnic and cultural groups, as only two thirds of the sample (66%) had been born in Canada and almost half of the sample (44%) spoke a language other than English at home, most notably languages from China or South East Asia (20%), the Middle East or India (8%), Eastern Europe (5%), and Western Europe (2%). . . .

Technology Use and Internet Safety Knowledge

Almost all participants (99%) had a computer in their home, and 98% of all participants used the computer for at least 1 hr daily. Approximately two thirds of participants (65%) indicated they communicated with friends online every day, and over half (55%) of participants revealed that they used their cell phones daily to speak to friends. One third of participants (32%) have given their online passwords to friends, and only one fourth (25%) of participants were aware that content uploaded online cannot be completely deleted. Additionally, over half of participants (53%) had cell phones. Of those participants with cell phones, two fifths (38.5%) reported using their phone daily to send text messages.

Experience of Being Cyber Bullied

Across bullying behaviors, half of the students (49.5%) indicated that they had been bullied online in the previous 3 months. Being called names was the most common form, accounting for over one fourth (27%) of cyber bullying incidents. This was followed by having rumors spread about the participant (22%), having someone pretend to be the participant (18%), being threatened (11%), receiving unwelcome sexual photos or text (10%), being asked to do something sexual (9%), and having had private pictures of themselves distributed without their consent (7%). Two fifths of bullying took place through instant messages, one fourth occurred by e-mail, and the remainder took place during Internet games (12%) or on social networking sites (10%). Over one third of online bullying (36%) was perpetrated by friends, followed by a student at their school (22%), a stranger (13%), a student from another school (11%), and unknown (11%).

Although 21% of students indicated that being bullied online did not bother them, others reported feeling angry (16%), embarrassed (8%), sad (7%), or scared (5%). More than half of the participants who were cyber bullied (52%) indicated that they did not do anything in response, while others confronted the person (20%), told a friend (13%), told a parent (8%), or told a teacher (3%). It is striking that in the majority of the cyber bullying incidents (89%) the students reported knowing the identity of the perpetrator and most participants indicated that the perpetrator was someone they considered a friend or a student at the respondent's school or at another school. Additionally, one fourth of students indicated they had witnessed an act of cyber bullying online.

More than one tenth of participants (11%) believed they were bullied online because of their appearance, followed by race (6%), school performance (5%), other (4%), gender (3%), sexuality (2%), family (2%), and disability (2%).

Cyber Bullying Others

In the previous 3 months, just over one third (33.7%) of participants indicated that they had bullied others online. Almost one fourth (22%) of these incidents involved calling someone names. Other acts of cyber bullying constituted pretending to be someone else (14%), spreading rumors about someone (11%), threatening someone (5%), sending someone's private pictures to someone else (3%), or sending unwelcome sexual pictures or text to someone (2%). Over half (60%) of the bullying behavior took place through instant messages, followed by social networking sites (15%), e-mail (10%), Internet games (10%), and other websites (5%). Friends were the most common targets of the participants' cyber bullying behavior, with 52% of bullying aimed at friends. This was followed by another student at school (21%), a stranger (11%), a student in another school (9%), and unknown (6%). While 41% of those who cyber bullied indicated that they did not feel anything in response, other participants who bullied others online relayed feeling guilty (16%), powerful (9%), popular (6%), or better than other students (4%). One fourth of participants (25%) reported that cyber bullying another person made them feel that they were funny, suggesting the bullying had been entertaining for themselves or others.

Participants were most likely to indicate that they bullied online because of the target's appearance (6%), other (5%), race (3%), school performance (3%), sexuality (2%), family (2%), disability (1%), and gender (1%).

. . .

Relationship Between Gender, Grade, and Cyber Bullying

While there was no difference in having been cyber bullied among girls and boys in Grades 6 and 7 . . . , older girls (Grades 10 and 1 1) were more likely to be cyber bullied than older boys. . . . Notably, boys and girls were equally likely to have cyber bullied others in both Grades 6 and 7 . . . and Grades 10 and 11. . . .

In addition to these overall findings, it emerged that the type of cyber bullying participants experienced and perpetuated was influenced by gender. Girls in all grades were more likely to have been called names than boys. Older boys were more likely than older girls to have been threatened online. Girls in both grade levels were more likely than boys to have had rumors spread about them online. Older girls were more likely than older boys to have had someone send them unwelcome sexual pictures or text, to be asked to do something sexual online, and to have had their private photos distributed online without their consent. Younger boys, however, were more likely than younger girls to have been asked to do something sexual online. . . .

Older boys were more likely than older girls to have called someone names or to have threatened someone online. Younger boys were more likely than younger girls to have sent unwelcome sexual words or photos to someone else online. Girls were more likely than boys to have spread rumors about someone in both grade levels. . . .

Older boys were more likely than older girls to believe they were cyber bullied due to their race . . . or disability. . . . Older girls were more likely to believe they were cyber bullied due to their sexuality . . . , gender . . . or appearance. . . .

Boys in both grade levels were more likely to indicate that they cyber bullied someone because of their race. . . . Younger boys were more likely to indicate that they cyber bullied someone because of their sexuality . . . , whereas older boys were more likely to indicate that they cyber bullied someone because of their family. . . .

. . .

Discussion

This research is among the first in-depth investigations of cyber bullying among middle and high-school students in a large city, with a large and diverse sample. According to our results, cyber bullying is a significant problem among middle and high school students.

Analyses reveal that students are clearly proficient with and regularly use technology, which corresponds with the literature (Agatson, Kowalski, & Limber, 2007; Nie & Hillygus, 2002). The vast majority of respondents appear highly dependent on communication technology for interaction and connection as well as for activities such as homework and games. The findings are supported by evidence which suggests that most youth use the Internet to communicate with others they already know (Gross, 2004; Valkenburg & Peter, 2007) and that this online communication with others who the students know has a positive effect on the quality of their friendships and romantic relationships (Blais et al., 2008; Valkenburg & Peter, 2007). Respondents in this study were not always knowledgeable, however, about the best ways to remain safe while online. This was made evident by the one third of participants who had given their online passwords to friends and the three fourths of participants who did not realize that text or images uploaded to the Internet could remain online indefinitely, even after deletion.

A sizable number of the respondents reported being involved in cyber bullying. Almost half of all participants identified as having been bullied online. This rate is higher than that reported in other studies on cyber bullying (Beran & Li, 2005; Li, 2007; Patchin & Hinduja, 2006; Ybarra & Mitchell, 2004a). Additionally, one in three respondents admitted to bullying others online, also greater than the rates reported by previous studies (Beran & Li, 2005; Li, 2007; O'Connell et al., 2004; Patchin & Hinduja, 2006; Williams & Guerra, 2007). There is some research, however, in which findings approach or exceed the prevalence of online bullying or harassment of others found in this study (Beran & Li, 2007; Juvonen & Gross, 2008; Raskauskas & Stotlz, 2007; Ybarra & Mitchell, 2004b, 2007).

The high rate of reported cyber bullying victimization and perpetration in this study may be due in part to the nature of the survey. A review of questions employed by several other surveys (Kowalski & Limber, 2007; Li, 2007; Raskauskas & Stotlz, 2007; Williams & Guerra, 2007; Ybarra & Mitchell, 2004a, 2007), revealed that after being provided a definition of online bullying or harassment, students in these studies were asked to identify whether they thought they were "bullied" or "harassed" by others or whether they thought they "bullied" or "harassed" others online based on the definition provided. In contrast, in this study we asked students whether they engaged in or were the target of distinct cyber bullying behaviors without labeling these behaviors as bullying. When explicitly asked about their experience with "bullying" and "being bullied" online, the results were very different: 85.8% of respondents indicated that they do not bully or get bullied online, 6.4% indicated that they bully and get bullied online, 5.1% indicated that they are bullied online, and only 2.6% indicated that they bully others online. Although students admitted to engaging in specific behaviors online, they may not have considered these behaviors as constituting bullying. Exploring cyber bullying in this manner provided an opportunity to examine the prevalence of bullying behavior without classifying it as such. Therefore, it appears that the scope of cyber bullying behavior experienced and perpetuated by this sample far exceeds what participants explicitly identified as bullying, which is itself a notable finding.

No gender differences were found in the overall perpetration of cyber bullying in our study, which corresponds to the literature (Kowalski & Limber, 2007; Williams & Guerra, 2007; Ybarra & Mitchell, 2004b). However, gender differences were evident in this analysis regarding the form of cyber bullying in which participants were involved. The nature of these differences is consistent with the well-documented gender differences evident in traditional bullying, whereby boys are more involved in direct or overt and physical forms of aggression and girls are more involved in indirect, and relational forms (Cullerton-Sen & Click, 2005; Prinstein et al., 2001). According to our findings, even in the online environment, there is evidence that boys are more likely to be victims or perpetrators of direct bullying such as threatening and that girls are more likely to be victims or perpetrators of indirect bullying such as rumors or pretending to be someone else. . . .

References

Agatson, P., Kowalski, R., & Limber, S. (2007). Students' perspectives on cyber bullying. *Journal of Adolescent Health, 41*, S59–S60.

Beran, T., & Li. Q. (2007). The relationship between cyberbullying and school bullying. *Journal of Student Wellbeing, 1*, 15–33.

Berson, L R., Berson, M. J., & Ferron, J. M. (2002). Emerging risks of violence in the digital age: Lessons for educators from an online study of adolescent girls in the United States. *Meridian: A Middle School Technologies Journal, 5*, 1–32.

Boyd, D. (2008). Why youth heart social network sites: The role of networked publics in teenage social life. In D. Buckingham (Ed.), *Youth, identity, and digital media* (pp. 199–142). Cambridge. MA: MIT Press.

Bryant, J. A., Sanders-Jackson, A., & Smallwood, A. (2006). IMing, text messaging, and adolescent social networks. *Journal of Computer-Mediated Communications, 11*, 577–592.

Campbell, M. (2005), *The impact of the mobile phone on young people's social life.* Presented at the Social Change in the 21st Century Conference, Queensland University of Technology.

Finkelhor, D., Mitchell, K., & Wolak. J. (2000). *Online victimization: A report on the nation's youth.* National Center for Missing & Exploited Children. Retrieved April 11, 2009, from http://www.unh.edu/ccrc/ YouthInternetinfopage.html

Gross, E. F. (2004). Adolescent Internet use: What we expect, what teens report. *Journal of Applied Developmental Psychology, 25*, 633–649.

Jackson, L., von Eye, F., Biocca, F., Barbatsis, G., Zhao, Y., & Fitzgerald, H. (2006). Does home Internet use influence the academic performance of low-income children? *Developmental Psychology, 42*, 429–435.

Juvonen, J., & Gross, E. F. (2008). Extending the school grounds? Bullying experiences in cyberspace. *Journal of School Health, 78*, 496–505.

Kowalski. R., & Limber, S. (2007). Electronic bullying among middle school students. *Journal of Adolescent Health, 41*, S22–S30.

Kowalski, R., Limber, S., & Agatston, P. W. (2008). *Cyber bullying.* Malden, MA: Blackwell.

Li, Q. (2007). New bottle but old wine: A research of cyberbullying in schools. *Computers in Human Behavior, 23*, 1777–1791.

Media Awareness Network. (2005). *Young Canadians in a wired world.* Retrieved April 11, 2009, from http://www.media-awareness.ca/english/research/ycww/ phaseII/key_findings.cfm

Mitchell, K. J., Finkelhor. D., & Wolak, J. (2003a). Victimization of youth on the internet. *Journal of Aggression, Maltreatment & Trawna, 8*, 1–39.

Mitchell, K. J., Finkelhor, D., & Wolak, J. (2003b). The exposure of youth to unwanted sexual material on the Internet: A national survey of risk, impact, and prevention. *Youth & Society, 34*, 330–358.

Nansel, T., Overpeck, M., Haynie, D., Ruan, J., Scheidt, P. (2003). Relationships between bullying and violence among U.S. youth. *Archives of Pediatric and Adolescent Midicine, 157,* 348–353.

Olweus, D. (1994). Annotation: Bullying at school: Basic facts and effects of a school based intervention program. *Journal of Child Psychology and Psychiatry and Allied Disciplines, 35,* 1171–1190.

Palfrey, J., & Gasser, U. (2008). *Born digital: Understanding the first generation of digital natives.* New York, NY: Basic Books.

Patchin, J., & Hinduja, S. (2006). Bullies move beyond the school yard: A preliminary look at cyberbullying. *Youth Violence and Juvenile Justice, 4,* 148–169.

Roland, E. (2000). Bullying in school: Three national innovations in Norwegian schools in 15 years. *Aggressive Behavior, 26,* 135–143.

Schrock, A., & Boyd, D. (2008). *Online threats to youth: Solicitation, harassment, and problematic content: Literature review prepared for the Internet Safety Technical Task Force.* Retrieved March 25, 2009, from http://cyber.law.harvard.edu/sites/cyber.law.harvard.edu/files/RAB_Lit_Review_121800.pdf

Shariff, S., & Johnny, L. (2007). Cyber-libel and cyber bullying: Can schools protect student reputations and free expression in virtual environments? *McGill Journal of Education, 16,* 307–342.

Slonje, R., & Smith, P. K. (2008). Cyberbullying: Another main type of bullying? *Scandinavian Journal of Psychology, 49,* 147–154.

Tynes, B. (2007). Role taking in online "classrooms": What adolescents are learning about race and ethnicity. *Developmental Psychology, 43,* 1312–1320.

Williams, K., & Guerra, N. (2007). Prevalence and predictors of Internet bullying. *Journal of Adolescent Health, 41*(6). S14–S21.

Wolak, J., Mitchell, K. J., & Finkelhor, D. (2007). Does online harassment constitute bullying? An exploration of online harassment by known peers and online-only contacts. *Journal of Adolescent Health, 41,* S51–S58.

Ybarra, M., Diener-West, M., & Leaf, P. (2007). Examining the overlap in Internet harassment and school bullying: Implications for school intervention. *Journal of Adolescent Health, 41,* S42–S50.

Ybarra, M. L., Espelage. D., & Mitchell, K. J. (2007). The co-occurrence of internet harassment and unwanted sexual solicitation victimization and perpetration: Associations with psychosocial indicators. *Journal of Adolescent Health, 41,* S31–S41.

Ybarra, M., & Mitchell, K. J. (2004a). Online aggressor/targets, aggressors and targets: A comparison of associated youth characteristics. *Journal of Child Psychology and Psychiatry, 45,* 1308–1316.

Ybarra, M., & Mitchell, K. J. (2004b). Youth engaging in online harassment: Associations with caregiver-child relationships, internet use, and personal characteristics. *Journal of Adolescence, 27,* 319–336.

Ybarra, M., & Mitchell. K. J. (2007). Prevalence and frequency of Internet harassment instigation: Implications for adolescent health. *Journal of Adolescent Health, 41,* 189–195.

EXPLORING THE ISSUE

Are Boys Bigger Bullies than Girls—In Cyberspace?

Critical Thinking and Reflection

1. The movie "Mean Girls" illustrates some of the ways that girls engage in indirect, relational, or social aggression. If the movie was remade today, how might the bullying tactics look different? How would technology be used to achieve the same results?
2. Consider the public discourse on traditional overt bullying (physical) versus covert/indirect bullying (relational/social and cyberbullying). Do traditional bullying and cyberbullying carry the same weight socially, or is one considered more "severe" than another? Is there a prevailing gender assumption around bullying (e.g., male bullies cause more harm—physical—than do female bullies)? What are the implications for prevention and intervention programs aimed at stopping bullying in all its forms?
3. What role might gender socialization play in the bullying preferences and options of male and female adolescents?
4. Take a moment to review your technological exchanges with peers and classmates over the last 5–7 years. Can you identify instances where you either engaged in, or were a recipient of, cyberbullying? When did you realize this was a form of bullying? How did you react? Would you have reacted similarly or differently if the bullying had been overt (i.e., physical)? If you disclosed your experiences to others, what were their reactions?

Additional Resources

Archer, J. (2004). Sex differences in aggression in real-world settings: A meta-analytic review. *Review of General Psychology, 4,* 291–322.

Archer, J., & Côté, S. (2005). Sex differences in aggressive behavior: A developmental and evolutionary perspective. In R. E., Tremblay, W. W. Hartup, & J. Archer (Eds.), *Developmental Origins of Aggression* (pp. 425–443). New York: Guilford.

Archer, J., & Coyne, S. M. (2005). An integrated review of indirect, relational, and social aggression. *Personality and Social Psychology Review, 9,* 212–230.

Björkqvist, K., Österman, K., & Kaukiainen, A. (1992). The development of direct and indirect aggressive strategies in males and females. In K. Björkqvist & P. Niemelä (Eds.), *Of Mice and Women. Aspects of Female Aggression* (pp. 51–64). San Diego, CA: Academic Press.

Crapanzano, A. M., Frick, P. J. Childs, K., & Terranova, A. M. (2011). Gender differences in the assessment, stability, and correlates to bullying roles in middle school children. *Behavioral Sciences and the Law, 29*, 677–694. doi: 10.1002/bsl.1000

Crick, N. R., & Grotpeter, J. (1995). Relational aggression, gender, and social-psychological adjustment. *Child Development, 66*, 710–722.

DeHue, F., Bolman, C., & Völlink, T. (2008). Cyberbullying: Youngsters' experiences and parental perception. *Cyberpsychology & Behavior, 11*(2), 217–223. doi:10.1089/cpb.2007.0008

Hinduja, S., & Patchin, J. W. (2008). Cyberbullying: An exploratory analysis of factors related to offending and victimization. *Deviant Behavior, 29*, 129–156.

Li, Q. (2006). Cyberbullying in schools: A research of gender differences. *School of Psychology International, 27*(2), 157–170.

Moretti, M. M., Catchpole, R. E. H., & Odgers, C. (2005). The dark side of girlhood: Recent trends, risk factors and trajectories to aggression and violence. *The Canadian Child and Adolescent Psychiatry Review, 14*, 21–25.

Olweus, D. (1997). Bullying/victim problems in school: Facts and intervention. *European Journal of Psychology of Education, 12*, 495–510.

Rivers, I., & Noret, N. (2010). "I h8 u": Findings from a five-year study of text and email bullying. *British Educational Research Journal, 36*(4), 643–671. doi:10.1080/01411920903071918

Wang, J., Iannotti, R. J., & Nansel, T. R. (2009). School bullying among adolescents in the United States: Physical, verbal, relational, and cyber. *Journal of Adolescent Health, 45*, 368–375.

ISSUE 16

Does Playing Violent Video Games Harm Adolescents?

YES: Cheryl K. Olson et al., from "M-Rated Video Games and Aggressive or Problem Behavior Among Young Adolescents," *Applied Developmental Science* (vol. 13, no. 4, 2009)

NO: Christopher J. Ferguson, from "Blazing Angels or Resident Evil? Can Violent Video Games Be a Force for Good?" *Review of General Psychology* (vol. 14, no. 2, 2010)

Learning Outcomes

After reading this issue, you should be able to:

- Compare and contrast M-rated violent video games with other video games.
- Explain the methodological problems with violent video games' research.
- Explain the theoretical problems with violent video games' research.
- Describe the relationship between M-rated violent video games and bullying.
- Describe the relationship between M-rated violent video games and physical aggression.

ISSUE SUMMARY

YES: Cheryl K. Olson and her colleagues from the Center for Mental Health and Media, Massachusetts General Hospital, report a significant positive relationship between playing M-rated video games and both bullying and physical aggression.

NO: Christopher J. Ferguson, associate professor of psychology, Department of Behavioral, Applied Sciences and Criminal Justice, Texas A&M International University, argues that the negative effects of violent video games have been inconsistent and exaggerated, while the positive effects—such as social networking and visuospatial cognition—have been ignored. He also states that although video game consumption has steadily increased in the last 10 years, youth violence has decreased.

Understanding adolescent behavior (both prosocial and antisocial) requires an understanding of the way adolescents think. Not surprising, research on adolescent cognition and behavior focuses on the many variables in their lives that could have an impact on their developing brains. A variable that has received much attention is the media. It has been documented in many studies how the media influence adolescent thinking and hence behavior. A recent focus in the research is on the form and impact of the deleterious effects of violent video game play on adolescents, such as the potential for increased antisocial behavior—such as aggression—as well as examining whether or not positive effects of violent video game exposure exist.

Video games were first introduced in 1958 with Tennis for Two, followed by Spacewar in 1961. The more popular Pong was released in 1972. This was the first generation of this new form of entertainment. Soon after, adventure games were introduced, followed by role-playing games. Although the first games appeared mainly in video arcades, the home computer and smaller consoles brought them into people's homes. By the 1980s, online gaming and handheld LCD games were introduced, and when the successful Nintendo Entertainment System emerged in 1985, gaming became a very popular form of entertainment. The gamepad took over the joysticks, keypads, and paddles. Games such as the Legend of Zelda, Super Mario Bros., Final Fantasy, and Metal Gear took over sports games and Pac-Man. The 1990s saw the beginning of Internet gaming with real-time strategy (RTS) games such as Warcraft, where players were able to compete against each other online. First-person shooter (FPS) games also became popular during the 1990s. FPS is defined as a type of game with a first-person view, where the player maneuvers through a 3-D world, using the computer or television screen to see through the eyes of their character. The character's weapon and part of his/her hand are shown, almost always centered around the act of aiming and shooting at objects and/or the enemy (Schneider et al., 2004; Wikipedia, 2012). Examples of FPS games are GoldenEye 007 and Medal of Honor.

By the end of the 1990s, Sony introduced the PlayStation, and became a strong contender against Nintendo in the game industry. The twenty-first century continues to see advancements in technology and game sophistication, leading to more realistic and immersive games. This contributes to a more capturing and addictive form of entertainment. In fact, the video game industry has become so popular in recent years that it now rivals the film industry as the most profitable entertainment industry. Such success is due in part to the increasing number of people playing video games. It, therefore, comes as no surprise that research on the effects of playing video games has increased substantially in the last decade.

Most research has focused on the negative effects that video games have on social and emotional development, such as the relationship between violent video game play (e.g., Mortal Kombat and the Grand Theft Auto series) and aggressive and violent behaviors. For example, Barlett et al. (2007) reported a significant increase in hostility and aggression with increased play of a violent FPS video game. Uhlman and Swanson (2004) reported similar findings where individuals playing a FPS for 10 minutes attributed more aggressive actions and traits to themselves. Contrary to these negative findings, Ferguson (2007) in a meta-analysis of the research on video game violence effects found no support for either a correlational or a causal relationship between violent game play and actual aggressive behavior. These mixed findings have led to the current debate regarding the effects of violent video games on all aspects of adolescent development (i.e., social, emotional, cognitive).

In the YES and NO selections, Olson, Kutner, Baer, Beresin, Warner, and Nicholi II provide evidence to support the negative effects of playing violent video games on social development. They argue that playing violent—or M-rated—video games predicted a greater risk for adolescents engaging in bullying and physical fights. Their study, examining data collected from adolescents who had been exposed to violent electronic games, found a significant positive relationship between M-rated video game play and both bullying behavior and physical aggression—a connection that appears stronger in girls than boys. Olson and colleagues conclude that each relative "dose" of violent video game exposure increases the odds of aggressive and bullying behavior in adolescents.

On the other hand, Ferguson argues that the negative effects of violent video game play have been greatly exaggerated as a result of media panic, and that the potential positive effects have been largely ignored. He examined the current state of research, revealing inconsistencies in the results as well as methodological and theoretical problems inherent to the studies that create a biased and false understanding of violent video games' relation to aggression. Next he argues that violent video games may instead have positive effects on adolescents. He points out benefits to visuospatial cognition, social involvement, and use in education that have been largely ignored in the discussion on violent video games and adolescents.

YES ↵

Cheryl K. Olson et al.

M-Rated Video Games and Aggressive or Problem Behavior Among Young Adolescents

Video and computer games have become a fixture of 21st century childhood. A Kaiser Family Foundation (KFF) survey (Roberts, Foehr, & Rideout, 2005) found that on an average day, half (52%) of children aged 8 to 18 played games on a console or handheld player, and one-third (35%) played games on a computer. In 2006, just over half of games designed for sale at retail outlets were rated "E" (deemed suitable for "Everyone") by the industry-sponsored Entertainment Software Rating Board (ESRB, 2006). However, a substantial minority were rated as not appropriate for children under 13: 23% were rated "T" (Teen—may be suitable for ages 13+) and 8% were rated "M" (Mature—may be suitable for ages 17+), most often due, at least in part, to violent content. The KFF study asked children in grades 7 to 12 whether they had ever played four popular video games. The top choice, by 65% of respondents, was the M-rated *Grand Theft Auto* series.

With advances in game technology, the depiction of violence and blood can be increasingly realistic. Researchers and policymakers have raised concerns that exposure to game violence could be a risk factor or trigger for aggressive or violent behavior (Funk, 2005). Some hypothesize that violent games could be more influential than savage television content, by increasing identification with aggressors through active participation, and rewarding the repetition of violent behavioral sequences (Gentile & Anderson, 2003). . . .

Utility of Video Game Violence Research for Youth Policy

. . . [T]he body of violent game research (experimental and correlational studies) merits a closer look. Since 2001, a series of research reviews and meta-analyses have appeared in peer-reviewed journals and academic books (e.g., Anderson, 2004; Sherry, 2006). Some reported clear evidence that exposure to violent games increases aggression in terms of behavior, cognition, and affect, including serious real-world aggression and violence. Others found support only for small, short-term increases in aggression, or equivocal findings, and insufficient evidence to support a link between violent games and real-life violence. A new meta-analysis by Ferguson (2007a) examined the possibility of a "file drawer effect" in video game research, where nonsignificant or negative results go unreported. When publication bias was factored in, results did not support an effect of violent game play on aggressive behavior, though there was some support for an effect on aggressive thoughts. . . .

Violent Electronic Game Content and Aggression

. . . .

Violent Game Content and Criminal/Delinquent Behavior

. . . . As yet, there are no studies linking violent video games to real-world crime. In Savage's 2004 review of studies on television and movie violence and criminal aggression, the researcher found that evidence for such a link was "practically nonexistent." There is also no indication that juvenile crime increased during the past decade, as games with increasingly realistic violence became more widely available in homes. . . .

Instead, juvenile arrests declined in each of the next seven years. Between 1994 and 2001, arrests for murder, forcible rape, robbery, and aggravated assaults fell 44%, resulting in the lowest juvenile arrest rate for violent crimes since 1983. Juvenile murder arrests reached a high of 3,790 in 1993. By 2004, arrests were down 71%, to 1,110 (Snyder, 2006). According to the latest available data, juvenile violent crime arrests were up slightly in 2005 and 2006, although the number of 2006 arrests was still lower than any year in the 1990s. Arrests for property crimes have continued to decline (Snyder, 2008).

Potential Effects of Violent Games on Fighting, Delinquency, and School Problems

However, the pattern is different for less visible aggressive acts. For reasons not yet understood, arrests for simple assault (actual or attempted attack, without a weapon) increased by 106% for boys and 290% for girls between 1980 and 2004 (Snyder, 2006).

A related concern, bullying, creates misery for a substantial proportion of American youths. In the 2005 School Crime Supplement to the National Crime Victimization Survey, about 28% of students aged 12 to 18 said they had been bullied at school (from being made fun of or excluded, to being pushed, tripped or spat on) at least once in the past six months. About 9 percent of students had been physically bullied in some way; a quarter of that group sustained cuts or bruises, chipped teeth, or worse. Young teens were most likely to be victimized (Dinkes, Cataldi, Lin-Kelly, & Snyder, 2007). . . .

Factors That May Mediate the Relationship Between Video Games and Behavior

In recent years, researchers have begun to look at traits that might mediate any relationship between violent video games and aggressive feelings or behaviors. Some studies found greater effects of violent content in video games among subjects high in trait hostility, while others did not (Kirsh, 2003). . . . Giumetti & Markey (2007) gave college undergraduates a written test of trait anger, and then randomly assigned them to play one of several violent or nonviolent Xbox games. After play, subjects were asked to expand on written "story stems" that involved negative outcomes such as a car accident; their responses were coded as aggressive (e.g., "punch them in the face") or nonaggressive ("ask for their insurance information"). Violent game play was linked to a higher number of aggressive responses for high anger and (to a lesser extent) moderate anger subjects, but did not significantly affect low anger subjects. As is typical for laboratory studies, both of these experiments looked at short-term effects of brief play sessions (15 to 20 minutes).

Goals and Hypotheses

The goal of the present study is to fill a gap in the literature and inform public policy by looking for evidence of a link between children's violent video game exposure and everyday aggressive or delinquent behaviors. Taking note of previous studies' limitations, we developed a more specific and policy-relevant measure of exposure to violent media. . . . [W]e chose to focus on young adolescents' use of Mature-rated (age 17+) games. Early adolescence is also a time when adult oversight decreases, and bullying behavior peaks. To increase the generalizability of our findings, we sought a larger, more diverse sample, and a higher survey response rate.

Based on research cited previously, we hypothesized that children who frequently played violent (Mature-rated) games were more likely to be involved in fights, and more likely to be bullies as well as victims of bullies. Because Mature-rated games often feature socially undesirable or criminal activities, we expected to find some association between heavy use of such games and delinquent behavior. We also hypothesized that these relationships might be reduced or eliminated when controlling for trait anger, aggressive temperament, and school performance. Finally, we expected that aggressive children might be more likely to seek out violent media, and thus be heavier users of M-rated games (Lancet, 2008).

Method

Sample and Procedures

In the fall of 2004, 1,254 7th and 8th grade students completed self-administered surveys during English/Language Arts class periods at two middle schools in Pennsylvania and South Carolina. At the suburban Pennsylvania school, the student population was 90% white, 4% black, 4% Asian, and 1% Hispanic; median household income in that county for 2003 was $60,700. At the urban South Carolina school, the student body was 50% white, 43% black, 5% Hispanic, and 2% Asian; 2003 median household income in that city was $40,600. . . .

Measures

The instrument created for this study included questions on amount of time typically spent playing electronic games, game preferences, and context of and motivations for game use. We defined electronic games as "computer games, video games (Xbox, PlayStation, GameCube, etc.) and handheld games (Game Boy, etc.)." Other questions addressed non-media activities, including attitudes, beliefs and experiences related to aggression and conflict, and school performance. To facilitate comparison with other studies, some questions or subscales not directly related to media use were drawn from existing validated instruments, including the Olweus Bully/Victim Questionnaire (Solbert & Olweus, 2003). Questions on delinquent behaviors (damaging property for fun, stealing from a store, skipping school, or getting in trouble with the police) and physical aggression (hitting or beating up someone, or getting in physical fights) were adapted from the Profiles of Student Life: Attitudes and Behaviors survey (Leffert et al., 1998) and the Youth Risk Behavior Survey (Brener et al., 2002).

We used the Attitude Toward Conflict scale as a measure of aggressive personality (Dahlberg, Toal, & Behrens, 1998). The scale was designed to measure attitudes toward the use of violence in response to disagreements or conflicts. . . . To assess trait anger, we created a new three-item measure to briefly capture key aspects of this trait, i.e., greater frequency of angry feelings and outward expression of anger (Deffenbacher et at., 1996) and an attentional bias for angry faces (van Honk, Tuiten & de Haan, 2001). Children were asked, "How often do you feel angry?" "How often do other people say you seem angry?" and "How often do other people seem angry at you?" with response options offered on a five-point scale from "never" to "always." . . .

To estimate exposure to various types of game content, we asked children to list five games they had "played a lot in the past six months." This allowed us to focus on the types of content children had been exposed to most recently and frequently, and to reliably and independently assess the level of violence in those games (rather than relying on children's definitions and estimates). We also asked children to estimate the number of days each week they usually played any electronic games, choosing from six response options (none, 1, 2, 3, 4–5, and 6–7 days). . . .

Results

Study Population

A total of 1,254 students completed the survey; participation was considered evidence of assent. Virtually all eligible students in attendance on the day of the survey (including 78 children in special-needs classrooms) took part; 88% of enrolled students in Pennsylvania and 79% of enrolled students in South Carolina completed surveys. . . .

Exposure to M-Rated Electronic Games

Eighty children had not played any games in the previous six months; 1,126 children wrote down at least one game. The 5,030 titles identified as commercially available games or game series were entered into a database, and matched with age-based ratings assigned by the ESRB (2006). Other listings (e.g., "driving game") were treated as missing data. In cases where a game title's rating varied across play platforms (e.g., handheld vs. console version), or only a series title was listed, we assigned a rating based on the least violent version available during the previous two years. Collapsing titles from series with similar content and mode of play into single categories resulted in a list of roughly 500 unique titles of games or game series.

Among children who were current game players, 48.8% had at least one M-rated game on their "five most played" list (67.9% of boys, and 29.2% of girls), with no apparent pattern by age. By far the most popular M-rated game series was *Grand Theft Auto* (played by 44% of boys and 20% of girls). To ensure adequate exposure to game content, the analyses . . . were limited to children who typically played electronic games at least one day per week, ...

We computed children's approximate "dose" of violent content exposure by multiplying days played per week by the percentage of their five most-played games that were rated Mature. Dose of exposure to nonviolent/less violent video games (i.e., those rated Teen or younger) was computed as days per week played multiplied by the percentage of nonviolent/less violent video games played. We statistically controlled for these potential confounding variables: 1) gender; 2) school attended; 3) grade level (7th or 8th grade); 4) school grades earned (self-reported on an eight-point scale from "mostly A's" to "mostly D's, F's and Incompletes"); 5) trait anger; 6) aggressive personality; and 7) dose of exposure to nonviolent/less violent games. . . .

Problem behaviors were analyzed based on five response categories, from "never" to "5+ times" during the past 12 months, with the exception of bullying. In line with previous research (Solbert & Olweus, 2003), children were classified as bullies or victims if they reported involvement in these behaviors on a regular basis (at least two or three times a month).

. . . [E]ven after controlling for a variety of possible confounding variables, exposure to M-rated games remained a strongly significant predictor of engaging in bullying and physical aggression. Further, this relationship was dose-related: each additional day-per-week category of exposure to M-rated games increased the probability of bullying behavior by 45%. Similarly, each additional day per week of exposure to M-rated games was related to an increase of 24% in the physical aggression score. However, we found no significant relationship between playing M-rated games and being a victim of bullies, or engaging in delinquent behaviors. . . .

[D]ose of exposure to games with lesser amounts of violence (rated Everyone to Teen) had the same pattern of relations to the four outcome measures as did dose of exposure to M-rated games. . . . Trait anger was highly predictive of all four outcome measures, while aggressive personality was not significantly predictive of any of the four. Contrary to expectations, preference for M-rated games was significantly predicted neither by trait anger (OR = 1.07) nor aggressive personality (OR = 1.00).

Finally, given that boys and girls differ significantly in use of M-rated games, time spent with games overall, and self-reported motivations for game play (Olson et al., 2007), we re-ran our analyses by gender. For boys,

M-rated game play no longer predicted bullying; instead, aggressive personality emerged as the strongest predictor. Violent games still predicted greater risk of physical fights, although E- and T-rated game "dose" did not.

When girls were analyzed separately, frequent M-rated game use became an even stronger predictor of bullying and fighting. Amount of time spent on younger-rated games was a weak significant predictor for physical aggression only.

Discussion

As hypothesized, this study found significant relationships between M-rated electronic game play and routine engagement in bullying behaviors and physical aggression in a diverse sample of young adolescent game players. The odds of engaging in these behaviors increased with the relative "dose" of M-rated game exposure (i.e., the percentage of M-rated games on children's lists of "five games played a lot in the past six months"). No relationship was found between violent game play and delinquency or victimization.

For the total sample, dose of exposure to M-rated games was only slightly more predictive of problems than was dose of exposure to younger-rated games. In the case of girls, however, heavy use of M-rated games in particular was linked to a higher risk of bullying and fighting. Parents of young adolescent girls should be mindful of this increased risk and limit or monitor M-game use.

When boys were analyzed separately, dose of M-rated game exposure ceased to be a significant predictor of bullying, and aggressive personality . . . became a strong predictor. (Note, the odds ratio was less than one on this control variable, so this may be a spurious result; it should not be taken out of context.) M-rated game play was still a significant, though weaker, predictor of fighting for boys, whereas use of younger-rated games was not. Overall, our hypothesis that heavy play of Mature-rated, violent games would predict a greater risk for common problem behaviors, even when controlling for potential confounders suggested by previous research, was partially supported. . . .

Limitations

It is important to note that most young adolescents who play M-rated games are neither bullies nor victims, and that not all children who engage in bullying or aggressive behaviors are frequent players of M-rated games. Involvement in problem behaviors is common among adolescents; for example, over half of boys and one-third of girls in our sample had hit or beaten up someone at least once during the previous year.

This study used a conservative estimate of Mature-rated game exposure: asking children to list five games they had "played a lot" in the past six months, not *all* games they had recently played. This should therefore be considered a minimum estimate of exposure.

We were not able to independently verify the accuracy of their responses. In the Kaiser Family Foundation survey (Roberts et al., 2005) over three quarters of boys in grades 7 to 12 reported playing an M-rated *Grand Theft Auto* game at least once; this suggests that our results are consistent with previous self-report data. However, "played a lot" likely encompasses a range of actual time spent playing across children. We also cannot determine how much total play time was spent on any particular game. This would be virtually impossible to accurately assess solely through children's self-reports.

This study had a larger, more diverse sample and higher response rate than previous correlational studies. However, as with all cross-sectional studies, it cannot demonstrate causality. We cannot say that M-rated game play causes bullying or physical aggression. It is likely that any influence of violent games is mediated by a child's individual characteristics, experiences, and environment, including discipline, supervision and affection from parents; affiliation with antisocial peers; and family or community violence (Ferguson et al., 2008). Although, in our sample, children with high trait anger and aggressive personality were not more likely to play M-rated games; other research suggests that such children are drawn to violent activities, whether contact sports such as football or wrestling, or more aggressive schoolyard play (Steinberg, 2000). For some, playing football or a violent video game might reinforce and worsen their aggressive behavior; for others, these activities might be socially acceptable ways to work through and get rid of hostile feelings (Sherry, 2006). . . .

This paper did not address potential positive aspects of video game use. Some research suggests that video game play is compatible with, and perhaps supportive of, school engagement, family closeness, improved cognitive abilities, and other positive aspects of adolescent development . . . (Feng, Spence, & Pratt, 2007). . . . As with most research on adolescents (Steinberg & Morris, 2001), studies of media effects have focused much more on potential harms than on potential benefits. We must also consider adolescents' strengths and how electronic games might support them (Levesque, 2007).

Policy Implications

Although we found that frequent use of M-rated games statistically predicts a greater risk of some problem behaviors, especially for girls, policymakers must pay careful attention to the limits on interpreting this type of study, especially with respect to causality. Given that nearly all children play electronic games, and nearly half of those regularly play at least one M-rated title (Olson et al., 2007), a limited amount of M-rated game use is not automatic cause for concern. A Mature rating cannot encompass all of the factors that might make violent content harmful to youth. . . .

Perhaps the best advice to parents is to play video games with their child, or at least observe the play by keeping the game console or computer in a common area of the home. This gives parents an opportunity to understand the types of games that appeal to their child, why their child is attracted to them, and the positive or negative effects those games may have for that child (Villani, Olson, & Jellinek, 2005). Studies on television violence suggest that asking questions is more effective in mediating preteens' and teens' perceptions of media content; judgmental statements may backfire and increase the appeal of game violence (Nathanson & Yang, 2003).

References

Anderson, C. A. (2004). An update on the effects of playing violent video games. *Journal of Adolescence, 27,* 113–122.

Brener, N. D., Kann, L., McManus, T., Kinchen, S. A., Sundberg, E. C., & Ross, J. G. (2002). Reliability of the 1999 Youth Risk Behavior Survey Questionnaire. *Journal of Adolescent Health, 31,* 336–342.

Dahlberg, L. L., Toal, S. B., & Behrens, C. B. (Eds.). (1998). *Measuring Violence-Related Attitudes, Beliefs and Behaviors Among Youths: A Compendium of Assessment Tools.* Atlanta, GA: National Center for Injury Prevention and Control, Centers for Disease Control and Prevention.

Deffenbacher, J. L., Oetting, E. R., Thwaites, G. A., Lynch, R. S., Baker, D. A., Stark, R. S., Thacker, S., & Eiswerth-Cox, L. (1996). State-trait anger theory and the utility of the trait anger scale. *Journal of Counseling Psychology, 43*(2), 131–148.

Dinkes, R., Cataldi, E. F., Lin-Kelly, W., & Snyder, T. D. (2007, December). *Indicators of School Crime and Safety: 2007* (NCES 2008–021/NCJ 219553). U.S. Departments of Education and Justice. Washington, DC: U.S. Government Printing Office.

Entertainment Software Rating Board (ESRB). (2006). Rating category breakdown. Retrieved May 8, 2007 from http://www.esrb.org/about/categories.jsp.

Feng, J., Spence, I., & Pratt, J. (2007). Playing an action video game reduces gender differences in spatial cognition. *Psychological Science, 18*(10), 850–855.

Ferguson, C. J., (2007a). Evidence for publication bias in video game violence effects literature: A meta-analytic review. *Aggression and Violent Behavior, 12*(4), 470–482.

Ferguson, C. J., Rueda, S. M., Cruz, A. M., Ferguson, D. E., Fritz, S., & Smith, S. M. (2008). Video games and aggression: Causal relationship or byproduct of family violence and intrinsic violence motivation? *Criminal Justice and Behavior, 35,* 311–332.

Funk, J. B. (2005). Children's exposure to violent video games and desensitization to violence. *Child and Adolescent Psychiatric Clinics of North America, 14*(3), 387–404.

Gentile, D. A., & Anderson, C. A. (2003). Violent video games: The newest media violence hazard. In D. A. Gentile (Ed.), *Media Violence and Children.* Westport, CT: Praeger.

Giumetti, G. W., & Markey, P. M. (2007). Violent video games and anger as predictors of aggression. *Journal of Research in Personality, 41,* 1234–1243.

Kirsh, S. J. (2003). The effects of violent video games on adolescents: The overlooked influence of development. *Aggression and Violent Behavior, 8*(4), 377–389.

Lancet. (2008). Is exposure to media violence a public-health risk? (Editorial). *The Lancet, 371,* 1137.

Leffert, N., Benson, P. L., Scales, P. C., Sharma, A., Drake, D., & Blyth, D. A. (1998). Developmental assets: Measurement and prediction of risk behaviors among adolescents. *Applied Developmental Science, 2*(4), 209–230.

Levesque, R. J. R. (2007). *Adolescents, media and the law: What developmental science reveals and free speech requires.* New York: Oxford University Press.

Nathanson, A. I., & Yang, M. S. (2003). The effects of mediation content and form on children's responses to violent television. *Human Communication Research, 29*(1), 111–134.

Olson, C. K., Kutner, L. A., Warner, D. E., Almerigi, J. B., Baer, L., Nicholi, A. M. II., & Beresin, E. V. (2007). Factors correlated with violent video game use by adolescent boys and girls. *Journal of Adolescent Health, 41*, 77–83.

Roberts, D. F., Foehr, U. G., & Rideout, V. (2005, March). *Generation M: Media in the Lives of 8–18-Year-Olds*. Menlo Park, CA: Kaiser Family Foundation.

Savage, J. (2004). Does viewing violent media really cause criminal violence? A methodological review. *Aggression and Violent Behavior, 10*, 99–128.

Sherry, J. L. (2006). Violent video games and aggression: Why can't we find effects? In R. W. Preiss, B. M. Gayle, N. Burrell, M. Allen, & J. Bryant (Eds.), *Mass Media Effects Research: Advances Through Meta-Analysis*. Mahwah, NJ: Lawrence Erlbaum.

Snyder, H. N. (2006, December). *Juvenile Arrests 2004*. Juvenile Justice Bulletin, U.S. Department of Justice, Washington, D.C.

Snyder, H. N. (2008, November). *Juvenile Arrests 2006*. Juvenile Justice Bulletin, U.S. Department of Justice, Washington, D.C.

Solbert, M. E., & Olweus, D. (2003). Prevalence estimation of school bullying with the Olweus Bully/Victim Questionnaire. *Aggressive Behavior, 29*, 239–268.

Steinberg, L. (2000, April). Youth violence: Do parents and families make a difference? *National Institute of Justice Journal*, 31–38.

Steinberg, L., & Morris, A. S. (2001). Adolescent development. *Annual Review of Psychology, 52*, 83–110.

van Honk, J., Tuiten, A., & de Haan, E.(2001). Attentional biases for angry faces: Relationship to trait anger and anxiety. *Cognition and Emotion, 15*(3), 279–297.

Villani, V. S., Olson, C. K., & Jellinek, M. S. (2005). Media literacy for clinicians and parents. *Child and Adolescent Psychiatric Clinics of North America, 14*, 523–553.

Christopher J. Ferguson  **NO**

Blazing Angels or Resident Evil? Can Violent Video Games Be a Force for Good?

The era of the modern video game began in the 1970s with the advent of arcade features such as *Space Invaders* and *Asteroids* and the quick launch of the Atari 2600 home game console. Debates immediately emerged about the moral and social implications of video games featuring violent content, as well as their potential positive use in education and other settings. Arguably, from *Death Race* to *Grand Theft Auto*, the greater part of the debate has focused on the negative effects of violent content. Such a debate is understandable. Social science has come to understand aggression as primarily socially learned (Bandura, 1965; . . . Fears about video game violence also fit into a sociological and historical context of fears of new media, particularly in United States culture, but also in a broader historical world context (Grimes, Anderson, & Bergen, 2008). However there is a risk that such concerns could move beyond objective scientific examination and into the realm of ideology, dogma and moral panic (Grimes et al., 2008). An overemphasis on the potential deleterious effects of violent games, whether real or imagined, also preempts discussion of the strategic use of violent games as a positive force in cognitive development, education, psychological treatment, and health care. In this article, I attempt to bridge the gaps in the current discussion of violent video game effects, and open a wider discussion of the potential benefits and risks of video game playing among youth. . . .

The Sociological and Historical Context of Violent Video Game Fears

Most psychologists are likely aware that debates and concerns about media—particularly media with violent. sexual, political, or antiauthority content—have raged in the social sciences and public arena across the 20th and 21st centuries. . . .

Exactly what impact such debate has on the perceptions of individual news consumers or parents is unclear. Some research suggests that most parents express some concern that *other* children may be influenced by violent games, but that their own are not (Kutner, Olson, Warner, & Hertzog, 2007).

Ferguson, Christopher. From *Review of General Psychology*, vol. 14, no. 2, 2010, pp. 68–81. Copyright © 2010 by American Psychological Association. Reprinted by permission.

Public fears about violent video games may be further assuaged by a recent study by the Pew Research Center (Lenhart et al., 2008) that found video game playing, including games with violent content, is nearly ubiquitous among youth with 97% of youth playing some form of video games and that negative impact appeared to be negligible. In fact, video game playing was found to offer significant opportunities for social interaction and civic engagement. Similarly, Durkin and Barber (2002) found that frequent video game playing children were better adjusted than nonplaying peers. It is this positive side of video games, violent games included, that receives little attention from either the public or the scientific community. . . .

Violent Video Games and Aggression: State of the Research

. . . A close look at the research on violence in video games reveals that findings are far less consistent than have been reported by some sources. For instance, while some research does find an effect for violent game playing on aggression (Bartholow, Bushman, & Sestir, 2006) others clearly do not (e.g., Durkin & Barber, 2002; Ferguson, San Miguel, & Hartley, 2009). Some find that exposure to violent games is related to *reduced* aggression (e.g., Barnett, Coulson, & Foreman, 2008[)] and others claim to have found effects, but a close examination of their results demonstrates that they have not (Anderson & Dill, 2000; Gentile, Lynch, Linder, & Walsh, 2004). For example, a correlation between video game exposure and aggression all but disappears once gender is controlled in one study (Gentile et al., 2004) and, in a common problem among media violence studies Anderson and Dill (2000) focus on one out of four aggression outcome measures that was significant and ignore the other three that were not in interpreting their results (a Bonferronni correction, if correctly applied, would have rendered all four results nonsignificant). Indeed the Anderson and Dill (2000) paper provides an example of the limitations of the peer-review process that has overseen the violent video games effects literature. The error in interpretation is readily apparent upon reading the results section of their experimental study, but appears to have escaped notice during peer-review and the paper continues to be influential if misleading.

Meta-analyses of video games similarly produce weak and inconsistent results. Two early meta-analyses claimed to find small but significant effects for video game violence on aggression (Anderson & Bushman, 2001; Anderson, 2004), although a subsequent review of these meta-analyses during a court case revealed that the authors may have simply ignored research that didn't fit with their hypotheses (ESA, VSDA and IRMA v. Blagojevich, Madigan, & Devine, 2005). . . .

A contemporary meta-analysis by Sherry (2001) found only weak effects, and Sherry concluded that any effects were weaker than for TV, contradicting concerns that the active nature of video games may produce higher effects on aggression. In a follow-up analysis Sherry (2007) concluded that the video game violence research currently available did not support the social learning view of aggression effects questioning "Further, why do some researchers continue to argue that video games are dangerous despite evidence to the contrary?" (p. 244). This conclusion was supported by two meta-analyses by Ferguson (2007a/2007b) who concluded that video game violence effects research had been deeply affected by publication bias problems which inflated reported effect sizes, and the misuse of unstandardized unreliable measures of aggression, which allowed researchers too much latitude in picking results that supported their hypotheses. . . .

Taken together these meta-analyses range from those which argue against meaningful effects (Sherry, 2001, 2007; Ferguson 2007a; 2007b[)]) to those which find weak effects (e.g., Anderson, 2004; Anderson et al., 2010). Thus the debate on video game violence has been reduced to whether video game violence produces no effects . . . or almost no effects.

Methodological and Theoretical Problems That Limit Our Interpretation of Video Game Violence and Aggression Research

For a research field to have addressed the level of certainty claimed by some researchers (e.g., Huesmann, 2007) it must rest on solid methodology, firm theoretical footing, and highly invariant findings with a high degree of pre-dictability in relation to real-world phenomenon (Uttal, 2007). . . . Other scholars have pointed to vast methodological and theoretical problems with media effects research in general, and violent video game effects specifically (Grimes, Anderson, & Bergent, 2008; Savage, 2004). These issues are described briefly below:

1. Many Aggression Measures Used Are Invalid

Put simply, many measures used in video game studies claiming to represent "aggression" in fact don't correlate well with actual real-life aggressive acts or violent behaviors (Ferguson & Rueda, 2009[)]). . . .

2. The "Third Variable" Effect

This concern is that other variables such as gender, family violence, genet-ics, and so forth, may account for any small relationship between violent video game exposure and aggression (Ferguson, 2007b; Savage, 2004). Uni-variate statistics may be overinterpreted at the expense of multivariate statistics. For example, as noted above Gentile et al., (2004) overinterpret bivariate correlations between violent video games and aggression, and fail to note that controlling for gender alone removes most of the overlapping variance. . . .

3. Citation Bias

Numerous critics have noted that media effects scholars ignore work, even from their own results, which contradicts their hypotheses (Savage, 2004). . . .

4. Publication Bias

Although this is certainly not an issue specific to video game violence, studies of video game violence appear to be deeply influenced by publication bias (Ferguson, 2007a/2007b). Studies with statistically significant effects, no matter how small in practical effect, are more likely to be published than those with null results. . . .

5. Small Effect Sizes

Estimates on the size of effect for violent video games on aggressive behavior range from (using $r^2 \times 100$) effectively zero through 2.5% (Anderson & Bushman, 2001; Anderson, 2004; Anderson et al., 2010; Ferguson 2007a/2007b; Sherry, 2001/2007). Many scholars have argued that these effects, even if assumed to have been produced by methodologically perfect research, are too small to be meaningful (Savage, 2004; Sherry, 2007). Some scholars have countered that these effects are similar to those found in smoking and lung cancer research or other medical effects although these claims appear to be based on faulty statistics which underestimate medical effect sizes (Ferguson, 2009b).

6. Absence of Clinical Cut-Offs

The absence of clinical cut-offs on aggression measures make it impossible to document whether a particular variable influences *pathological* aggression. Instead it is assumed that aggression has no adaptive function and is always pathological and undesirable. This would appear to be naïve, and at best is an assumption. In moderate doses, aggression may very well be adaptive, guiding individuals toward many behaviors approved of by society including standing up for one's beliefs, assertiveness, defending others in need, careers in law enforcement, the military, business, legal affairs, and so forth, sporting activities, political involvement, debate and discourse indeed including scientific debate (Smith, 2007). Particularly as most video game research uses individuals who may be expected to be below average in aggression, such as college students or healthy children, we should be wary of regression to the mean effects. In the absence of clinical cut-offs aggression scores remain difficult to interpret.

7. Unstandardized Use of Aggression Measures

As noted in Ferguson (2007a) one significant concern is that some measures of aggression, such as the modified Taylor Competitive Reaction Time Test have been used in an unstandardized way. . . . Ferguson found that measures used in such an unstandardized way resulted in higher effect sizes, likely as authors were free to choose outcomes that supported their hypotheses and ignore outcomes which did not.

8. The Mismatch Between Violent Video Game Consumption and Violent Crimes

Put simply, this issue notes that both public and scientific concern is not matched by violent crime data, which for both adults and youth (Childstats. gov, 2008; FBI, 1951–2007) has plummeted at the same time as video games have increased in popularity. . . . It should be carefully noted that video game consumption is unlikely to be responsible for this decline (e.g., ecological fallacy), even in part. . . . However, we can be sure that violent video games have not sparked a violent crime epidemic because there is no violent crime epidemic. . . .

9. Low Standards of Evidence

As noted above, one issue that is oftentimes raised (Ferguson, 2007b; Savage, 2004) is that video game violence effects, like those in media violence more broadly, are small, but that some authors exaggerate their significance promoting unnecessary concern. . . .

One other issue that bears mentioning is that some studies do not clearly distinguish violent from non violent video games in making contrasts. For example, Konijn, Nije Bijvank, and Bushman (2007) examined the impact of playing violent video games on young boys. The authors found that boys who played a violent game were more likely to select these supposedly damaging noise levels on the Taylor Competitive Reaction Time Test (TCRTT). However, when a personality variable, namely identification with aggressive role models was controlled, the direct impact of video games became negligible. Of greater concern however, was that several of the "nonviolent" games that the authors test (*The Sims 2, Tony Hawk's Underground 2, Final Fantasy*) have actually received Entertainment Software Ratings Board (ESRB) content descriptors for violence. As such, the authors appear to have unsatisfactorily distinguished nonviolent from violent games. Thus any alleged difference between game conditions cannot be due to violence, since the researchers inadequately controlled for violence in the "nonviolent" game condition. . . .

The Positive Effects of Violent Video Games

To many, the very idea that violent video games can have a positive impact will seem absurd. Yet I'd argue that this is an emotional reaction, not an objective one, particularly if it rises up before even the evidence is fully heard. . . . [I]n the following section, this paper will discuss a different kind of information than that assumed to transfer via aggression. Namely, for the media effects on aggression hypothesis to work, viewers must learn to shape their internal goals, motivation, and core personality as a result of media exposure. As already argued, the evidence that this happens appears to be quite thin. . . . By contrast, other kinds of learning, such as visuospatial cognitions, information about medical diseases, science and math skills, and so forth, don't require internal shifts in a largely stable personality. Put more simply, video games may be effective in communicating raw data or information, but they aren't effective in transmitting moral beliefs, personality traits, and so forth. Information transfers but personality traits such as aggressiveness do not. A few of the most promising positive developments regarding video games, including those with violence, are outlined below. It should be noted at the outset that, like the research on aggression, none of these research fields are without flaws. Indeed the merits of all research, positive or negative, should be subject to more intense scrutiny than has previously been the case. However, an intelligent discussion of violent game effects needs to consider both sides of the coin if it is to escape the realm of moral panic.

Visuospatial Cognition

Broadly defined visuospatial cognition involves intellectual and cognitive processes related to attending, scanning, selecting, processing, and mentally altering visual information (Spence & Feng, 2010). These tasks are oftentimes thought to relate to the performance subtests on common intelligence tests such as the Wechsler scales and may be important for career paths involving visual acuity and processing.

Currently, a number of studies, both experimental and correlational, have found that playing violent video games is associated with higher visuospacial acuity, perception, processing, visual memory, and mental rotation (Feng, Spence, & Pratt, 2007; Ferguson, Cruz, & Rueda, 2008). For reasons that are not well understood, results for nonviolent games such as Tetris are considerably weaker. A recent meta-analysis of studies examining the effects of violent video games on visuospatial cognition (Ferguson, 2007b) found that, after controlling for publication bias effects, video games still had a moderate effect on visuospatial cognition ($r = .36$) where as no effect was found in studies of aggressive behavior ($r = .04$). These results appear to support the earlier suggestion that cognitive information can be transmitted more easily via video games than can moral information or personality traits. It is not clear that the violence, per se, is the primary agent of increased visuospatial cognition. Rather, it may be the type of fast action commonly found in a first-person-shooter game that increases visuospatial cognition rather than violence per se. Nonetheless these game engines may be of practical value. . . .

It should be noted that, in comparison to the research on video games and aggression, research on violent video games and visuospatial cognition is much more consistent, yet at the same time generally smaller regarding the number of studies. . . .

As a side issue it is interesting to note that most publications in this research area prefer the term "action" game rather than "violent" game (notwithstanding that many of the same or similar games are used). Choosing the term "violent" as opposed to "action" (or vice versa) appears to be a clear effort by researchers to frame the debate in prosocial or antisocial terms which once again might be expected in the atmosphere of moral panic. . . .

Social Involvement

One common concern is that video games impair social connections for youth. It is feared that video games may lead to reduced social skills and fewer friendships among youth players. However, beginning in the 1990s, easy access to the Internet expanded games into a new realm for potential social interaction (Olson, 2010). Players could now play first-person-shooter games such as *Medal of Honor* against (or in cooperation with) other players online. Some games allowed for entire social communities to develop online. Collectively called Massively MultiPlayer On-Line Role Playing Games (MMORPG), games such as *Everquest* and *World of Warcraft* allowed for complex social interactions to occur within the game world (Barnett & Coulson, 2010). Current evidence suggests that social connections formed through such online games can be very deep and meaningful to those involved (Murphy, 2007[)].

The Pew Research Center's study on youth and video games (Lenhart et al., 2008) found that video games, far from being an isolationist activity, were highly social activities for most children. Children who engaged in highly social interactions while playing video games were also highly likely to take an interest in civic involvement. Violent and nonviolent games appear to be equally predictive of such involvement. . . .

Use in Education

. . . There has been some evidence to suggest that video games may provide a useful platform for education (Annetta, 2010[)]. Some of the most promising research in this regard has come out of health psychology, where specifically targeted video games have promoted the health of young medical patients. In one remarkable recent study, researchers found that a first-person shooter game *Re-Mission* improved self-efficacy, cancer knowledge, and treatment adherence in teen and young adult cancer patients (Kato, Cole, Bradlyn, & Pollock, 2008). . . . Arguably the game succeeds because it presents a lively action-oriented platform that holds players' attention, allowing the educational components of the game greater opportunity for impact. *Re-Mission* takes advantage of the existing, popular first-person shooter format and applies this format for a prosocial purpose. . . .

The use of video games directly in educational settings faces several practical constraints, including time commitment limitations and teacher prejudices against video games (Rice, 2007[)]. However, the use of violent video games in informal settings may also promote some cognitive development, although this is usually an unintended element of game play. For instance research in this area has typically focused on *World of Warcraft* (WoW) a MMORPG that has enjoyed an unusually long active life. WoW is a fantasy role-playing game with violent content, for which many players actively participate in message boards and blogs related to the game (Barnett & Coulson, 2010). Some early research has suggested that WoW may promote reading and writing achievement, including among boys who previously had little interest in such activities (Steinkuehler & Duncan, 2008). Similarly VanDeventer and White (2002) found that children who displayed expertise at mildly violent games were likely to display higher-ordered thinking skills. . . .

Conclusions

Research regarding the impact of violent video games on aggression is inconsistent and hampered by poor methodologies and the intrusion of ideology and scientific dogma. Particularly in light of increased video game consumption and declining youth violence, at present time, there appears to be little reason for speculation that violent video games are a significant factor in promoting youth violence. Unfortunately, by maintaining a myopic view on negative issues related to video game violence, a broader discussion of the benefits and risks of violent game playing is prohibited. It is argued here that if psychology is serious about understanding violent video games from an objective rather than ideological view, a broader and less activist stance must be taken. . . .

References

Anderson, C. (2004). An update on the effects of playing violent video games. *Journal of Adolescence, 27,* 113–122.

Anderson, C., & Dill, K. (2000). Video games and aggressive thoughts, feelings and behavior in the laboratory and in life. *Journal of Personality and Social Psychology, 78,* 772–790.

Anderson, C. A., & Bushman, B. J. (2001). Effects of violent video games on aggressive behavior, aggressive cognition, aggressive affect, physiological arousal and prosocial behavior: A meta-analysis. *Psychological Science, 12,* 353–359.

Anderson, C. A., Shibuya, N., Ihori, N., Swing, E. L., Bushman, B. J., Sakamoto, A., & Saleem, M. (2010). Violent video game effects on aggression, empathy, and prosocial behavior in Eastern and Western countries. *Psychological Bulletin.* Advance online publication, doi:10.1037/a0018251

Annetta, L. (2010). The "I's" have it: A framework for serious educational game design. *Review of General Psychology, 14,* 105–112.

Bandura, A. (1965). Influence of models' reinforcement contingencies on the acquisition of imitative response. *Journal of Personality and Social Psychology, 1,* 589–595.

Barnett, J., & Coulson, M. (2010). Virtually real: A psychological perspective on massively multiplayer online games. *Review of General Psychology, 14,* 167–179.

Barnett, J., Coulson, M., & Foreman, N. (2008, April). The WoW! factor: Reduced levels of anger after violent on-line play. Poster presented at the British Psychological Society Annual Meeting, Dublin, Ireland.

Bartholow, B., Bushman, B., & Sestir, M. (2006). Chronic violent video game exposure and desensitization to violence: Behavioral and event-related brain potential data. *Journal of Experimental Social Psychology, 42,* 532–539.

Childstats.gov. (2008). *America's children: Key national indicators of well-being, 2007.* Retrieved from: www.childstats.gov/

Durkin, K., & Barber, B. (2002). Not so doomed: Computer game play and positive adolescent development. *Applied Developmental Psychology, 23,* 373–392.

ESA, VSDA, and IRMA v. Blagojevich, Madigan, and Devine. (2005). Case No. 05 C 4265.

Federal Bureau of Investigation. (1951–2009). *Uniform crime reports*. Washington, DC: U.S. Government Printing Office.

Feng, J., Spence, I., & Pratt, J. (2007). Playing an action video game reduces gender differences in spatial cognition. *Psychological Science, 18,* 850–855.

Ferguson, C. J. (2007a). The good, the bad and the ugly: A meta-analytic review of positive and negative effects of violent video games. *Psychiatric Quarterly, 78,* 309–316.

Ferguson, C. J. (2007b). Evidence for publication bias in video game violence effects literature: A meta-analytic review. *Aggression and Violent Behavior, 12,* 470–482.

Ferguson, C. J., Cruz, A., & Rueda, S. (2008). Gender, video game playing habits and visual memory tasks. *Sex Roles: A Journal of Research, 58,* 279–286.

Ferguson, C. J., & Rueda, S. M. (2009). Examining the validity of the Modified Taylor Competitive Reaction Time Test of aggression. *Journal of Experimental Criminology, 5,* 121–137.

Ferguson, C. J., San Miguel, C., & Hartley, R. D. (2009). A multivariate analysis of youth violence and aggression: The influence of family, peers, depression and media violence. *Journal of Pediatrics, 155,* 904–908.

Gentile, D., Lynch, P., Linder, J., & Walsh, D. (2004). The effects of violent video game habits on adolescent hostility, aggressive behaviors and school performance. *Journal of Adolescence, 27,* 5–22.

Grimes, T., Anderson, J., & Bergen, L. (2008). *Media violence and aggression: Science and ideology*. Thousand Oaks, CA: Sage.

Huesmann, L. R. (2007). The impact of electronic media violence: Scientific theory and research. *Journal of Adolescent Health, 41,* S6–S13.

Kato, P., Cole, S., Bradlyn, A., & Pollock, B. (2008). A video game improves behavioral outcomes in adolescents and young adults with cancer: A randomized trial. *Pediatrics, 122,* e305–e317. Retrieved from: http://pediatrics .aappublications.org/cgi/content/full/122/2/e305

Konijn, E. A., Nije Bijvank, M., & Bushman, B. J. (2007). I wish I were a warrior: The role of wishful identification in effects of violent video games on aggression in adolescent boys. *Developmental Psychology, 43,* 1038–1044.

Kutner, L., Olson, C., Warner, D., & Hertzog, S. (2007). Parents' and son's perspectives on video game play: A qualitative study. *Journal of Adolescence Research, 23,* 76–96.

Lenhart, A., Kahne, J., Middaugh, E., MacGill, A., Evans, C., & Mitak, J. (2008). *Teens, video games and civics: Teens gaming experiences are diverse and include significant social interaction and civic engagement*. Retrieved from: www.pewinternet .org/PPF/r/263/report_display.asp

Murphy, S. (2007). A social meaning framework for research on participation in social on-line games. *Journal of Media Psychology, 12,* Retrieved from: www .calstatela.edu/faculty/sfischo/ A_Social_Meaning_Framework_for_Online_Games.html

Olson, C. K. (2010). Children's motivations for video game play in the context of normal development. *Review of General Psychology, 14,* 180–187.

Rice, J. (2007). New media resistance: Barriers to implementation of computer video games in the classroom. *Journal of Educational Multimedia and Hypermedia, 16,* 249–261.

Savage, J. (2004). Does viewing violent media really cause criminal violence? A methodological review. *Aggression and Violent Behavior, 10,* 99–128.

Sherry, J. (2001). The effects of violent video games on aggression: A meta-analysis. *Human Communication Research, 27,* 409–431.

Sherry, J. (2007). Violent video games and aggression: Why can't we find links? In R. Preiss, B. Gayle, N. Burrell, M. Allen, & J. Bryant, (Eds.) *Mass media effects research: Advances through meta-analysis* (pp. 231–248). Mahwah, NJ: L. Erlbaum.

Smith, P. (2007). Why has aggression been thought of as maladaptive? In P. Hawley, T. Little, & P. Rodkin, (Eds.), *Aggression and adaptation: The bright side to bad behavior* (pp. 65–83). Mahwah, NJ: Erlbaum.

Spence, I., & Feng, J. (2010). Video games and spatial cognition. *Review of General Psychology, 14,* 92–104.

Steinkuehler, C., & Duncan, S. (2008). Scientific habits of mind in virtual worlds. *Journal of Scientific Education and Technology.* doi:10.1007/s10956-008-9120-8

Uttal, W. (2007). *The immeasurable mind.* Amherst, NY: Prometheus Books.

VanDeventer, S., & White, J. (2002). Expert behavior in children's video game play. *Simulation & Gaming, 33,* 28–48.

EXPLORING THE ISSUE

Does Playing Violent Video Games Harm Adolescents?

Critical Thinking and Reflection

1. An area of research receiving increasing attention is the relationship between playing video games (including M-rated FPS games) and cognitive development—attention span, executive functioning, and performance at school and work. Do you think playing video games can make you smarter or do you think they turn our youth into inattentive zombies?
2. Given some of the reported positive effects of playing video games, do you see a place for some (or all) of them in the classroom?
3. Do you think there is a difference between the effects of TV and film violence versus video games' violence?
4. We have heard in the media that many school shootings are linked to violent video game playing. We also know that there are thousands of well-adjusted adolescents who play these games and never exhibit any form of antisocial behavior. Do you think there are other variables involved in the relationship that has been reported between violent video games and both bullying and aggression?
5. If you were to design the "perfect" study examining the effects of violent video games, what would it look like? What variables would you measure? What variables would you control for?

Is There Common Ground?

Enhanced prosocial behavior, responsible citizenship, academic performance, and educational success are goals for many youth and certainly goals that parents have for their children. Enhancing cognitive development, therefore, is on the minds of parents and educators. While at school, children are engaged in tasks that contribute to these areas of development. Outside of school, however, there is some concern that children are not engaged in activities that further develop their social and cognitive capacities. An activity receiving much attention is video game playing. While some parents and educators criticize video game playing and especially violent action games, others believe they can benefit children. The YES and NO selections are excellent examples of these opposing views; however, there is also common ground between the two. For example, in the YES selection, although Olson and her colleagues argue that playing violent video games increases the risk for bullying and aggression, they also (in their limitations) point to possible positive aspects of video game use. They acknowledge specific positive outcomes such as school enhancement, family closeness, and improved cognitive abilities. They also state that future research must address adolescents' strengths and how video games might support them. In the NO selection, Ferguson does not dismiss the negative effects reported but argues they have been largely exaggerated by the media because of research methodological and theoretical problems that limit interpretation. He (like Olson and colleagues) states that the potential positive effects of violent video game play have been ignored in the debate. In summary, the authors of both selections recognize the balance between the negative and positive effects of video game play—especially violent M-rated games. Future research is strongly recommended to further our understanding of the debate on the outcomes of playing action video games. In the meantime, these selections raise awareness of the effects (both positive and negative) that these games can have on adolescents.

Additional Resources

Barlett, C. P., Harris, R. J., & Baldassaro, R. (2007). Longer you play, the more hostile you feel: Examination of first-person shooter video games and aggression during video game play. *Aggressive Behaviour, 33,* 486–497.

> This is a study investigating the effects of video games on aggression. The authors report that increased video game play resulted in a significant increase from baseline in hostility and aggression.

Ferguson, C. J. (2007). Evidence for publication bias in video game violence effects literature: A meta-analytic review. *Aggression and Violent Behavior, 12,* 470–482.

> This meta-analysis addresses the publication bias with respect to the research examining the negative effects of video games. Ferguson reports that publication bias does exist for both experimental and non-experimental studies of aggressive behavior.

Schneider, E., Lang, A., Shin, M., & Bradley, S. (2004). Death with a story: How story impacts emotional, motivational, and physiological responses to first-person shooter video games. *Human Communication Research, 30,* 361–375.

Spence, I., & Feng, J. (2010). Video games and spatial cognition. *Review of General Psychology, 14*(2), 92–104.

> Spence and Feng review studies that examined the relationship between video game playing, learning, and spatial cognition. They report that several studies indicate that playing video games enhances several sensory, perceptual, and attentional abilities that are important for spatial cognition. In addition, video games have a beneficial effect on mental rotation—a more complex spatial task. They conclude that researching video games may contribute to a better understanding of learning as well as new strategies for teaching spatial skills.

Uhlmann, E., & Swanson, J. (2004). Exposure to violent video games increases automatic aggressiveness. *Journal of Adolescence, 27*, 41–52.

Whitaker, J. L., & Bushman, B. J. (2009). A review of the effects of violent video games on children and adolescents. *Washington and Lee Law Review, 66*, 1033–1051.

> Whitaker and Bushman offer a comprehensive review of the effects of violent video games and the psychological processes in children and adolescents that are affected. They conclude that although video game playing can be entertaining and produce positive experiences, parents should also be aware of the dangers, such as aggressive thoughts.

ISSUE 17

Are Social Networking Sites (SNSs), Such as Facebook, a Cause for Concern?

YES: Billy Henson, Bradford W. Reyns, and Bonnie S. Fisher, from "Security in the 21st Century: Examining the Link Between Online Social Network Activity, Privacy, and Interpersonal Victimization," *Criminal Justice Review* (vol. 36, no. 3, 2011)

NO: Nicole B. Ellison, Charles Steinfield, and Cliff Lampe, from "Connection Strategies: Social Capital Implications of Facebook-Enabled Communication Practices," *New Media & Society* (vol. 13, no. 6, 2011)

Learning Outcomes

After reading this issue, you should be able to:

- Compare and contrast different types of social networking sites currently being used by adolescents.
- Judge the privacy and security of posting personal information on SNSs.
- Distinguish between online friend and offline friend.
- Describe how SNSs can contribute to social capital.
- Describe how personal information posted on an SNS can become very public and perhaps lead to victimization.

ISSUE SUMMARY

YES: Billy Henson, assistant professor of criminal justice at Shippensburg University, Bradford W. Reyns, assistant professor of criminal justice at Weber State University, and Bonnie Fisher, professor of criminal justice at the University of Cincinnati, argue that participation in social networking sites, such as Facebook, exposes many users to interpersonal victimization.

NO: Researchers Nicole B. Ellison, Charles Steinfield, and Cliff Lampe from the Department of Telecommunication, Information

Studies, and Media, at Michigan State University, argue that SNSs such as Facebook scaffold relationship development, and are positively associated with self-expression, identity formation, and social capital.

The ways in which adolescents communicate with and maintain friends have become more complex in recent years. Gone are the days where face-to-face or phone conversations were the norm. Adolescents today are using modern technology to interact with their friends and acquaintances. In particular, social network sites (SNSs) have become increasingly popular.

SNSs are open or semi-open public systems (Valkenburg et al., 2006) where anyone can join at any time (open) or an individual is invited to join by another member (semi-open). There are numerous SNSs available and although they all have features in common, they vary as a function of purpose. For example, Match.com is a dating site, Bookcrossing.com an interest site, and Friendster, MySpace, or Facebook, friendships sites. The focus of this *Taking Sides* issue is on friendship sites such as Facebook, which started in 2004 as a Harvard-only SNS (Cassidy, 2006). The initial goal of Facebook at Harvard (and later at other universities) was to support college/university networks. It has since spread to the point where users can connect with and keep in touch with all friends, regardless of location, as well as friends they have lost touch with from childhood, high school, university, previous workplaces, and/or previous communities. Not only do users connect and stay in touch with each other but they can also view personal information about each other. With Facebook for example, users create a very detailed unique profile typically containing name, e-mail address, personal address, phone number, school affiliation, major, gender, religion, hometown, birthdate, sexual orientation, relationship status, interests, job/occupation, favorite music, favorite books, favorite movies, friend network, and a photo.

A user's Facebook site with his/her profile is called a homepage or "wall" and they as well as their "friends" can post messages there. The messaging feature can either be private (similar to e-mail) or be public (all who have access to the user's profile can read the posted messages). In addition to the personal information on each homepage, users can add modules ("applications" such as interest groups, travel logs, or photo albums), and/or join networks (organized by city, school, workplace, etc.). The photo album application is very popular because users can share photos from recent events and travels. In addition, users can identify all other people in their photos (called tagging). This permits any user with access to the album to view and share pictures of people who are tagged. All applications and networks added can be viewed by those with access to the user's profile unless the user specifically denies access.

Once a Facebook is set up, a user can add friends or have others add them. This is done with a message such as "Susan has added you as a friend on Facebook. We need to confirm that you are, in fact, friends with Susan." Each new "friend" is added to the user's Friends list. This list is then visible to anyone who has access to the user's profile, resulting in somewhat of a popularity contest. As a result, users will increase their Friends list by adding distant acquaintances and sometimes complete strangers. Regardless of the nature of the relationship, every single individual added is called a "friend."

There is little doubt that Facebook is convenient and effective for keeping in touch with "friends"; however, there are concerns about Facebook as well. First, it is argued that it is addictive. With an increasing number of adolescents using Facebook, a "Friends" list can include as many as several hundred "friends." This equates into many hours reading homepages and writing on walls. Second, there are privacy concerns. There is increasingly more information being displayed on these homepages. Although Facebook includes numerous tools available to protect privacy, many users are not using the tools. While it has been reported that the majority of users feel "safe" displaying personal information, they in fact have "zero privacy" (Regan, 2003). Specifically, Facebook administrators have access to a database about who knows who, and how they know them.

The issues surrounding SNSs has increasingly led to more research examining their impact on adolescent well-being. Are friendships enhanced with Facebook? Are Facebook users at risk for privacy attacks? Are employers using Facebook to check up on employees? Are online social networks healthy? Questions such as these will be addressed in this issue.

Billy Henson, Bradford W. Reyns, and Bonnie S. Fisher provide evidence for the dangers of having and using SNSs. They argue that participation in social networking sites, such as Facebook, exposes users to increased risk of online interpersonal victimization. Henson and colleagues examined the type and frequency of SNS users' online activity and the security of both the SNS as a whole and the security options chosen by the users. They then compared this data to frequency of online victimization among the same users, discovering a link that leads them to argue that riskier SNS use and behavior is directly correlated to an increase in the risk of online victimization. Their findings suggest that the risks inherent to SNS use are high and, while they may be lessened, there is no way to entirely avoid the possibility of online victimization.

On the other hand, Nicole Ellison, Charles Steinfield, and Cliff Lampe present evidence suggesting that Facebook can build and maintain social capital, self-esteem, and life satisfaction. They explore the possibility that users of the SNS Facebook have developed different connection strategies from nonusers. They then examine the relation between these different connection strategies and an increase in social capital. Ellison and colleagues propose that while Facebook may not aid in strengthening existing "close friendships" or creating friendships out of nonexistent connections, it does work to strengthen friendships between acquaintances or to develop new relationships between individuals who share some sort of small connection. They believe that Facebook provides a new venue for converting latent to weak ties and build greater social capital.

YES

Billy Henson, Bradford W. Reyns, and Bonnie S. Fisher

Security in the 21st Century: Examining the Link Between Online Social Network Activity, Privacy, and Interpersonal Victimization

Introduction

In the last decade, online social networking has evolved from an entertaining novelty to a multibillion dollar global industry. Users of these sites range from adolescents to grandparents, and they are spread throughout almost every developed nation in the world. With over 400 million users on Facebook alone, the total number of online social network users worldwide has exceeded the populations of every country except India and China, and the number of users continues to grow every year (Facebook, 2010).

Given the sheer number of users and the ever-looming threat of online victimization, personal privacy has become a major security issue for online social networking sites and users. . . . Recently, a number of studies have been produced examining the use of and behavior on social networking sites, with many specifically focusing on the issues of privacy and security (e.g., Acquisti & Gross, 2006; Dwyer, Hiltz, & Passerini, 2007; Jones & Soltren, 2005). The majority of these studies have only examined user perceptions of privacy and the use of security features with very few studies examining the link between social network privacy and security and online victimization. Utilizing a sample of social network users, the current study adds to this small body of research by examining the relationship between personal and site-provided security and online interpersonal victimization (i.e., repeated unwanted contact, harassment, unwanted sexual advances, and threats of physical violence).

Online Social Networks

Social networking sites such as Facebook, Friendster, and MySpace are web-based "communities" that allow users to create profiles and virtually interact with other members. With an online social network account, individuals can add personal information to their profiles, link with other users (also called "friending"), post photographs and videos, and chat with other users around the world. . . .

Since their initial introduction in the late 1990s, the number and popularity of social networking sites has grown dramatically among all age groups. From the global giants to the school-based networks, there are currently hundreds of social networking sites on the Internet. . . .

Although each social networking site varies in its design, there are certain features that most networks provide, particularly features based on the types of information users post online. Typically, this information includes the user's name, sex, birthday/age, and contact information. Contact information may include the individual's e-mail address, instant messenger screen name, telephone number, and address. Depending on the social networking site, users may also be able to post their sexual orientation, where they work or attend school, their class schedule, religious affiliation, political affiliation, and much more personal information. . . .

Social Network Security

Given the large number of users and vast amount of information shared on online social networking sites, protecting the privacy of users has become a primary point of concern for social network providers. To that end, there are two main types of security features on social network sites. First, there is a privacy option made available to users by the social networking site providers. There is some variation in the extent of options, but all major social networking sites have a privacy setting. With this feature, users can limit who can see their social network profile. . . . While many social networking sites have an all or nothing approach to privacy—meaning the user must make all the information on his or her profile private or public—some, such as Facebook, allow users pick and choose what information is made private. For the purpose of the current study, the use of the privacy setting refers to having the entire profile set to private.

The second major form of security for social networking sites is user control. If a user wants to link his or her account with that of another user, he or she must first send a friend request. That request must be accepted before the two accounts can be linked as friends. If a user has his or her account set to private, then it is only by having a friend request accepted that another user can view that person' profile information. . . .

Security and protection of private information has become a central topic for online social network research. Several researchers have found that while social network users claim that personal privacy is a major concern, their actions directly contradict that claim. One of the first studies to examine privacy on social networking sites reported that a key factor that undermines privacy for Facebook users is the amount of information they disclose on their profiles (Jones & Soltren, 2005). . . . In a similar study, Dwyer et al. (2007) examined both Facebook and MySpace users. They reported that while users of both providers were concerned with privacy, Facebook users were willing to post identifying information, such as their name and contact information, and MySpace users frequently began new online relationships with individuals they did not previously know. While risky online behavior has been linked to online victimization in prior research (Reyns, 2010a; Wolak, Finkelhor, Mitchell, & Ybarra, 2008; Ybarra, Mitchell, Finkelhor, & Wolak, 2007), there have been few studies published to date examining the relationship between users' behavior on social networking sites and online interpersonal victimization.

Online Interpersonal Victimization

While still in its early stages, the body of research examining online or electronic forms of victimization is growing. To date, much of the research related to online forms of interpersonal victimization has been focused upon adolescent populations (Finkelhor, Mitchell, & Wolak, 2000; Noll, Shenk, Barnes, & Putnam, 2010; Ybarra & Mitchell, 2008; Ybarra, Mitchell, et al., 2007). These studies have adopted a limited definition of online interpersonal victimization that includes only harassment or sexual solicitation online. Among the first studies, Finkelhor et al. (2000) examined harassment and sexual solicitation among a nationally representative sample of youths (ages 10 to 17) in the United States and reported that approximately 20% of the sample was approached or sexually solicited in the year prior to the survey. Also, 1 in 17 participants were either harassed or threatened during that time (Finkelhor et al., 2000). Ybarra and Mitchell (2008) have reported that among a national survey of 1,588 youths, 15% of respondents were victims of sexual solicitation and 4% of these transpired on online social networks. Further, 33% of youths were victims of online harassment, 9% of which could be traced to online social network interactions (Ybarra & Mitchell, 2008). The results from these studies point to a growing need for research into the online interpersonal victimization of social network users. . . .

Although researchers have examined a variety of types of online victimization, a large portion of studies have focused specifically on cyberstalking victimization (D'Ovidio & Doyle, 2003; Reyns, 2010a; Sheridan & Grant, 2007). For instance, D'Ovidio and Doyle (2003) analyzed official crime data from the New York City Police Department's (NYPD) cybercrimes investigation unit and reported that 42.8% of cybercrimes investigated by the unit were cyberstalking cases. Sheridan and Grant (2007) examined the extent of cyberstalking victimization experienced by a sample of traditional stalking victims. They estimated that 7.2% of the sample had experienced cyberstalking in addition to stalking. . . .

The Present Study

The purpose of the present study is to address an unexplored area in the online victimization research by examining the link between the use of online social networks, social network security, and online interpersonal victimization. This examination focuses on the various privacy and security aspects of online social networks, including the use of security settings and personal user security behaviors. In doing so, we attempt to answer three key questions:

1. Does the use of privacy settings protect users from online interpersonal victimization?
2. Does allowing strangers access to social network profile information increase the likelihood of users experiencing online interpersonal victimization?
3. Do other security-related behaviors influence one's likelihood of being victimized online?

Description of Data

The data for the current study were collected as part of a larger study of college student online victimization. During the spring quarter of 2009, a web-based survey was administered to a simple random sample of undergraduate college students at a large urban university in the Midwest. Initially, 9,926 invitations were sent via e-mail to students, with follow-up e-mails sent weekly for 4 weeks. Of those who were sent an invitation, 1,951 students followed the web link embedded in the e-mail invitation to the informed consent form and 1,310 students participated in the survey. Based on the initial group of 9,926 students who were invited to participate, the resulting response rate is 13.1%. . . .

Respondents who had a significant number of missing survey item responses were removed, leaving a sample size of 974 respondents. Since the present study seeks to examine experiences with online social networking sites, only those respondents that stated they had an online social network account were included in the analysis. The size of the analytic sample for the current study is 914 respondents. Of the respondents in this sample, 61% were female, 86% were White, and the mean age was 20 years old. At the time the survey was administered, 49% of the undergraduate student population was female, 80% was White, and the mean age was 21 years old. . . .

Respondents reported having accounts with over a dozen different social network providers. Given the low number of users of certain types of social network providers, only those that 50 or more respondents reported using are examined. All other providers are included in an "other" category. As expected, the most popular social network provider is Facebook with 890 users. With 515 users, MySpace is the second most popular service provider among members of the sample. With substantially fewer users, Xanga and Twitter are the third and fourth most popular providers, with 150 and 138 users, respectively. The last provider to be included, LiveJournal, has 95 users. Finally, the "other" category includes 187 users who have accounts with Friendster, Classmates, Bebo, Blogger, Tagged, LinkedIn, and several other social network providers. It should also be noted that many respondents have multiple social network accounts. The 914 participants have a total of 1,975 online social network accounts.

Dependent Measures

In this study, every effort was made to utilize a comprehensive definition of online interpersonal victimization so to create a measure that has better content validity than previously employed measures. The definition used includes any or all of the following behaviors: unwanted contact, harassment, unwanted sexual advances, and/or threats of violence or physical harm. Respondents were asked if they had ever experienced these behaviors on multiple occasions (two or more times) through social networking websites, after asking/telling the person to stop. Each of the four types of behavior was measured as a simple "yes" or "no" dichotomous variable. The "yes" responses were summed across the four types and recoded to create a single dichotomous measure of online interpersonal victimization, indicating whether or not the respondent had ever experienced any of the behaviors.

Independent Measures

The key independent variables are divided into three main categories: (a) demographic information, (b) basic social network information, and (c) social network security information. [T]he demographic information includes measures of gender (male or female), race (White or non-White), age, sexual orientation (heterosexual or nonheterosexual), and relationship status (single or non-single). With the exception of age, which is a continuous variable (18–24 years), each of the demographic measures is a dichotomous variable.

The six social network information and activity measures include (a) number of online social network accounts, (b) how long had accounts, (c) time spent on social network, (d) number of social network updates, (e) number of friends, and (f) number of photos posted online. . . .

Security features are the primary focus of the current study and include four dichotomous variables: (a) set account to private, (b) added strangers as friends, (c) used friend service, and (d) used profile tracker. *Set account to private* measures whether the respondent has his or her social network account set to private access. Next, *added strangers as friends* denotes whether the respondent has added people as friends that they did not previously know. *Used a friend service* identifies respondents who joined an online service that assists individuals with getting large numbers of new friends. With these services, individuals enter their profile ID into an online program, which then sends friend requests to a large number of other users. The main goal is to increase one's number of friends very quickly. Finally, *used profile tracker* indicates whether or not a respondent has used a program designed to track and report the names of individuals who have visited his or her social network profile. . . .

Results

Previous studies of online social network privacy and security issues directly examined the types of information users posted to their accounts, such as Acquisti and Gross's (2006) and Dwyer et al.'s (2007) works. As noted in those studies, social network users often post an array of personal information on their profiles. [T]he types of information users [% of respondents] in the current sample posted to their social network account included full name, [(>70%)] birth date, [(>85%)] relationship status, [(>80%)] sexual "orientation), [(>70%)] home address, e-mail address, cell phone number, instant messenger ID, school name, [(>90%)] school address, academic major, work name, activities, photos, [(>90%)] and videos. Less than 10% of respondents posted their home and/or school address to their social network profile. However, while most respondents did not post information that would allow someone to come into direct physical contact with them, many did post information that makes them easily accessible through electronic means. For example, almost 70% of respondents posted their e-mail address on their social network profile. Further, almost 40% of respondents posted their instant messenger ID and about 25% posted their cell phone numbers.

. . . . With respect to the demographic variables, gender is the only measure significantly related to online victimization. Female students are approximately twice as likely as males to experience online victimization. Regarding the social network activity measures, both the number of social network accounts and the number of weekly profile updates are significantly associated with online victimization, although the odds ratios are only slightly above 1.00. Finally, in terms of social network security, setting one's account to private access is not significantly related to online victimization. This is contrary to expectations, as privacy and/or guardianship are hypothesized to decrease likelihood of victimization. However, both adding strangers as friends and using a profile tracker are positively and significantly associated with online victimization, increasing odds of victimization over two times.

To provide more detailed information about the relationship between online social networks and online victimization, several binary logistic regression models were estimated to examine the links between all measures and online victimization for specific social network providers. [T]he significant relationships discussed above are largely driven by the two most popular social network providers—Facebook and MySpace. With these two providers, significant relationships exist between online victimization and gender, number of social network accounts, number of updates, adding strangers as friends, and the use of a profile tracker. Female users of both Facebook and MySpace are almost twice as likely to experience online victimization as their male counterparts. Further, the number of social network accounts and the number of updates to those accounts are significantly and positively related to online victimization; however, the odds ratios are just over 1.00. Finally, Facebook and MySpace users that added strangers as friends, and those that utilized profile trackers are over twice as likely to experience online victimization.

[T]here are also significant findings across several other social network providers. One of the most significant and consistent measures across providers is whether the respondent added strangers as friends. Adding strangers as friends increases the likelihood of online victimization 3 to almost 4.5 times for users of Xanga, Twitter, LiveJournal, and "other" providers. Further, for Xanga users, there is a significant relationship between the number of account updates and online victimization, though frequently updating one's account only slightly increases the odds of experiencing online victimization. Two additional measures are related to specific social network providers. First, setting one's social network account to private is significantly related to online victimization for LiveJournal users. Interestingly, however, the relationship is positive, indicating that those respondents who have their account set to private are over 5 times more likely to experience online victimization. Second, for individuals who have a social network account with a provider in the "other" category, there is a significant and negative relationship between relationship status and online victimization, with non-single individuals having lower odds of experiencing online victimization than single individuals.

Discussion and Conclusion

In the current study, approximately 42% of social network users experienced some kind of interpersonal victimization while online. For this group, five factors stand out as statistically significant predictors of victimization. First, the gender of the social network user, specifically being female, increases one's chances of experiencing online interpersonal victimization by nearly two times. It could be that females are more attractive targets for online offenders, have social networks comprised of a greater proportion of likely offenders, or there may be a difference in online lifestyles or routine activities between male and female users. . . . Second, the respondent's number of online social networks modestly increases their odds of online victimization. Having and maintaining numerous social networking accounts have the effect of increasing opportunities for online interpersonal victimization, since would-be offenders have more avenues/methods for contacting their targets (Reyns, 2010b). Third and similarly, the number of daily updates to one's online social networks moderately increases the odds of online victimization. It may be that (as was the case with the number of social networks) the number of daily updates not only supplies added opportunities for victimization but increases one's overall exposure to risk by making the user more available to other users and presenting a more attractive or suitable target (Reyns, 2010b). Fourth, allowing strangers to have access to online social networking profiles increases the likelihood of victimization approximately 2.6 times, meaning that those individuals who add strangers as friends to their networks are 2.6 times more likely to be victimized. Fifth, and contrary to expectations, use of an online profile tracker is associated with an increased likelihood of online interpersonal victimization. This may be a reflection of the way this particular survey item was worded rather than a positive causal relationship between using a profile tracker and being victimized. It is possible that respondents adopted such programs as a result of problems that they had experienced online rather than opening themselves up to victimization using these programs.

Perhaps, just as important as the significant predictors of victimization are those online social network features and characteristics that are not statistically significant. For instance, the network privacy feature is designed to act as a buffer against unwanted communications and similar problems that might be experienced by users, but keeping one's online profile private did not impact the likelihood of online victimization in the current study. A plausible explanation for this is simple—these types of privacy settings are only effective as long as the user is selective about whom they allow into their network as a friend. Having one's profile set to private makes little difference if the user is allowing strangers (i.e., likely or motivated offenders) to access their profiles and information. Similarly, the type of information that user's post online (e.g., Instant Messenger ID and photos) does not ultimately affect their odds of victimization. Again, it is whether those who have access to the information are trustworthy rather than what is posted that appears to increase victimization risks. . . .

The variable effects described above appear to be driven by users of the top two online social networking sites—Facebook and MySpace. Few statistically significant effects were uncovered in predicting the victimization of users of other types of social networking sites such as Xanga, Twitter, and LiveJournal. Among those who use Xanga, the number of social network updates, and adding strangers as friends are the only significant predictors of victimization, with adding strangers as friends increasing odds of victimization over 4 times. Among Twitter users, the only variable that improves prediction of online interpersonal victimization is the added stranger measure, which increases victimization risk nearly 4.5 times. Users of LiveJournal are 5.7 times more likely to experience victimization if their profile is set to private access. . . . Finally, among users of other social networking sites (e.g., Friendster and Bebo), adding strangers increases odds of victimization over 4 times, and being single decreases likelihood of victimization. . . .

While the current study makes an overdue contribution to the online victimization literature by addressing the roles of online social networks, privacy, and online security, it is important to recognize that the results should be considered in light of three primary limitations. First, as mentioned previously, attaining high response rates, especially when no financial incentive is given, continues to be a challenge for survey methodologists utilizing web-based surveys. . . . Second, the cross-sectional nature of the research design, coupled with differing time referents among the independent and dependent variables creates some potential temporal ordering issues that could not be fully addressed. . . . Finally, the statistically significant relationships found for some of the social networks necessarily requires further explanation. . . .

References

Acquisti, A., & Gross, R. (2006). Imagined communities: awareness, information sharing, and privacy on the Facebook. In *6th Workshop on privacy enhancing technologies*. UK: Cambridge University.

D'Ovidio, R., & Doyle, J. (2003). A study on cyberstalking: Understanding investigative hurdles. *FBI Law Enforcement Bulletin, 73*, 10–17.

Dwyer, C., Hiltz, S. R., & Passerini, K. (2007). Trust and privacy concern within social networking sites. In *Proceedings of the Thirteenth Americas Conference on Information Systems*.

Facebook. (2010). Press room: Statistics. Retrieved March, 30, 2010, from http://www.facebook.com/press/info.php?statistics

Finkelhor, D., Mitchell, K. J., & Wolak, J. (2000). *Online victimization: A report on the Nation's Youth.* Washington, DC: U.S. Department of Justice.

Jones, H., & Soltren, J. H. (2005). *Facebook: Threats to privacy.* Retrieved March 30, 2010, from http://www.swiss.ai.mit.edu/6095/student-papers/fall05-papers/facebook.pdf

Noll, J. G., Shenk, C. E., Barnes, J. E., & Putnam, F. W. (2010). Child abuse, avatar choices, and other risk factors associated with Internet-initiated victimization of adolescent girls. *Pediatrics, 123,* 1078–1083.

Reyns, B. W. (2010a), Being pursued online: The extent and nature of cyberstalking victimization from a lifestyle/routine activities perspective (Doctoral dissertation, University of Cincinnati, 2010).

Reyns, B. W. (2010b). A situational crime prevention approach to cyberstalking victimization: Preventive tactics for Internet users and online place managers. *Crime Prevention and Community Safety, 12,* 99–118.

Sheridan, L. P., & Grant, T. (2007). Is cyberstalking different? *Psychology, Crime & Law, 13,* 627–640.

Wolak, J., Finkelhor, D., Mitchell, K. J., Ybarra, M. L. (2008). Online "predators" and their victims: Myths, realities, and implications for prevention and treatment. *American Psychologist, 63,* 111–128.

Ybarra, M. L., & Mitchell, K. J. (2008). How risky are social networking sites? A comparison of places online where youth sexual solicitation and harassment occurs. *Pediatrics, 121,* 350–357.

Ybarra, M. L., Mitchell, K. J., Finkelhor, D., & Wolak, J. (2007). Internet prevention messages: Targeting the right online behaviors. *Archives of Pediatrics and Adolescent Medicine, 161,* 138–145.

Nicole B. Ellison, Charles Steinfield, and Cliff Lampe

NO

Connection Strategies: Social Capital Implications of Facebook-Enabled Communication Practices

The concept of social capital describes the benefits individuals derive from their social relationships and interactions: resources such as emotional support, exposure to diverse ideas, and access to non-redundant information. Social capital is embedded in the structure of social networks and the location of individuals within these structures (Burt, 2005). Because social network sites (SNSs) have the potential to reshape social networks and lower the costs of communicating with (and thus contributing to and extracting benefits from) this social network, SNS use may have social capital implications. This study is among the first to explore the relationship between social capital and specific communication practices on the most popular SNS among US undergraduates, Facebook.

Previous scholarship has addressed issues such as the demographic characteristics of SNS users (Hargittai, 2007) and the personal information they reveal on these sites (Acquisti and Gross, 2006), but there is currently little empirical research that describes the specific communication-based relational activities that occur on these sites (who does what and with whom) and how these behaviors affect outcomes of interest. Similarly, while the literature provides a basic understanding of whether Friendships on SNSs represent pre-existing offline connections or new relationships forged online (Ellison et al., 2007), measurement difficulties hamper our ability to provide a clear picture of how online and offline modes of communication replace, complement, and facilitate one another. In the research presented here, we test the proposition that Facebook users will have different 'connection strategies,' a term which describes a suite of Facebook-related relational communication activities, and explore the relationship between these connection strategies and social capital outcomes.

Previous work has established a relationship between Facebook use and social capital levels among undergraduate students (Ellison et al., 2007; Steinfield et al., 2008; Valenzuela et al., 2009). It is not clear, however, whether there are *particular uses of Facebook* that are more likely to result in positive social capital outcomes. In other contexts, scholars have argued that while the

Ellison, Nicole; Steinfield, Charles; Lampe, Cliff. From *New Media & Society,* vol. 13, no. 6, January 27, 2011. Copyright © 2011 by Sage Publications, Ltd. Reprinted by permission.

internet makes vast amounts of information available, only those who have the skills necessary to locate and evaluate this content can take full advantage of it (Hargittai, 2008). Examining SNS use more specifically, Papacharissi and Mendelson (2008) explored the relationship between motivations for using Facebook and social capital outcomes and Burke et al. (2010) found that while Facebook use overall was associated with social capital, there was a stronger association between social capital and active contributions to the site (versus passive consumption of others' information). These studies suggest that users who have the ability and inclination to engage in certain SNS activities may be more likely to reap social capital benefits.

In addition to explicating this relationship between SNS communication behaviors and social capital, this study advances our ability to measure internet-related social behaviors. Currently, SNS researchers use a variety of measures to assess SNS use, such as number of Friends (Joinson, 2008), time on site (Tong et al., 2008), or the number of completed profile fields (Stecher and Counts, 2008). The Facebook Intensity (FBI) scale, developed by Ellison et al. (2007) and used in other Facebook research (e.g., Valenzuela et al., 2009), uses time on site, number of Friends, and a series of Likert-scale attitudinal items such as, 'I feel out of touch when I haven't logged onto Facebook for a while.' Similar to the way in which scholarship on the digital divide has evolved from simple measures of internet access to nuanced assessments of internet activities, SNS researchers need to develop measures of specific SNS-based communication practices, not just generic usage, in order to better discern usage patterns and their effects.

An important component of measuring SNS communication practices entails accurately characterizing the kinds of social relationships that are being formed and maintained via SNSs. One question is whether SNSs are primarily used to form mixed-mode relationships (which form online and then migrate offline) or to support existing relationships. In general terms, there is evidence that SNSs are more often used to articulate previously established relationships. However, measurement difficulties, especially surrounding the concepts of 'offline' and 'online' interaction, point to a need to confirm and unpack this general trend. . . . Assessing the role of SNS use in offline and online interactions will contribute to our understanding of how these tools reshape social networks and the outcomes of these practices.

Social Capital and Relationship Development Online and Offline

. . . Social capital can be understood as a form of capital, like financial or human capital, that is embedded in the relationships between individuals, and can be measured at the individual or group level.

Putnam (2000) delineated two basic forms of social capital: bonding and bridging. Bonding social capital describes benefits from close personal relationships, which might include emotional support, physical succor, or other 'large' benefits (such as willingness to loan a substantial sum of money). Bridging social capital, the benefits derived from casual acquaintances and connections, can also lead to tangible outcomes such as novel information from distant connections and broader world-views. Empirical research confirms the practical importance of bridging social capital. . . .

Social Interactions on SNSs

SNSs are bundles of technological tools that incorporate features of earlier technologies (such as personal websites) but recombine them into a new context that supports users' ability to form and maintain a wide network of social connections. Although precise data regarding usage are not available, survey data suggest that upwards of 90 percent of undergraduates use Facebook (Lampe et al., 2008). After creating a profile on a SNS such as Facebook, users typically invite others into their network, thus giving one another increased access to profile information and more communication options. . . .

The extant literature . . . suggests that Facebook is used more for communication among acquaintances and offline contacts than it is for connecting with strangers (Ellison et al., 2007) and that most Facebook 'Friend' connections represent 'in person' relationships (Subrahmanyam et al., 2008). . . .

In addition to supporting existing social relationships, Facebook contains many features that could be used to create new connections, although this seems to be a less common use. . . . In short, Facebook supports a wide spectrum of possible connections, ranging from those who share an offline connection to complete strangers who find one another through a variety of features such as Groups, networks, fan pages, social games and applications, photographs, interest-based profile fields, status updates, and Friend networks.

The concept of latent ties can help distinguish between these different Friending practices on Facebook. . . . As Ellison et al. (2007) speculated, Facebook's inclusion of a wide range of identifying information, including mutual friends and shared interests, may encourage users to activate latent ties, transforming them into the weak and bridging ties associated with positive bridging social capital outcomes. . . . Our use of the term 'latent tie' thus describes a relationship between two individuals which has not been socially activated. . . .

SNSs are also used by close friends, although little published research focuses on these uses. Close friends who connect through Facebook are likely to find it an efficient and easy way to keep in touch, and the lightweight interactions enabled by the site are likely to benefit these more developed relationships as well. In fact, 20 percent of the SNS users in research by Subrahmanyam et al. (2008) reported that their SNS use brought them closer to friends, and Ellison et al. (2007) found that intensity of Facebook use predicted bonding social capital, which is often associated with strong ties such as close friends. . . .

In summary, although research suggests that Facebook users are more likely to use the site to articulate existing relationships than they are to use the site to meet strangers, there is also some indication that users may use the site to convert latent into weak ties. We are particularly interested in distinguishing among the various uses of Facebook aimed at connecting with diverse types of others, including existing strong ties, casual acquaintances (i.e., latent ties), and strangers who share no prior or offline connection. Given the ambiguity in the literature about these specific behaviors, our first research question asks:

> RQ1: Are there distinct patterns in the online and offline communication behaviors employed by Facebook users in relation to close friends, latent ties, and strangers?

Assuming different connection strategies exist among users, it is important to assess how these strategies relate to outcomes of interest, such as bridging and bonding social capital. Just as Quan-Haase and Wellman (2004: 125) point out that 'not all uses of the Internet are social,' different uses of the site will result in different social capital outcomes. Connecting with latent ties may increase bridging social capital while using the site to maintain existing close friendships may encourage bonding social capital. Thus, we ask whether distinct types of communication behaviors on Facebook lead to different social capital outcomes.

> RQ2: Which Facebook-related communication behaviors, if any, are more likely to predict bridging social capital?
>
> RQ3: Which Facebook-related communication behaviors, if any, are more likely to predict bonding social capital?

We also explore the relationship between number of Friends and social capital. The site's affordances facilitate giving and receiving emotional support through one's Friend network; for instance, a status update complaining about an illness serves to inform one's social network and may generate supportive comments or advice. Friends may be more likely to respond to requests for social support if they see the request was posted recently . . . ; thus, it may be that larger Friend networks are more likely to generate social support messages because someone in the network will see the request immediately and respond. Likewise, the site supports requests for information or perspective-sharing, which can be easily shared with one's entire Friend network; responses are more likely to be useful when contributed by weak ties (Granovetter, 1973) and, therefore, the larger one's Friendship network, the more likely it is to include someone with access to the necessary information. Therefore, we expect Friend counts will be positively correlated with both types of social capital. . . .

Some Friends may be less beneficial than others from a social capital perspective. Although Facebook enables users to broadcast requests, we suspect that information requests are less likely to be answered by Friends who are strangers . . . and that provisions of emotional support will be less meaningful when coming from strangers with little personal knowledge of the recipient. We expect that connection strategies that reflect use of the site to express and develop relationships rooted in some kind of offline connection (operationalized as 'actual friends') are more likely to predict social capital than will using the site to meet strangers, and that social capital is more likely to be generated from latent ties and strong tie Friends as opposed to Friends who start out as complete strangers. . . . Thus:

H1: The greater the number of Facebook Friends, the greater the reported bridging social capital.

H1a: This relationship will be stronger for the number of actual friends on the site than for the total number of all Facebook Friends.

H1b: The relationship between the number of actual friends and bridging social capital will be curvilinear, reaching a point where increases in the number of actual friends is no longer associated with higher social capital.

H2: The greater the number of Facebook Friends, the greater the reported bonding social capital.

H2a: This relationship will be stronger for the number of actual friends on the site than for the total number of all Facebook Friends.

H2b: The relationship between the number of actual friends and bonding social capital will be curvilinear, reaching a point where increases in the number of actual friends is no longer associated with higher social capital.

Methods

In order to address our research questions and hypotheses about the relationship between distinct Facebook connection strategies and social capital, a survey of undergraduate students at a large Midwestern university was fielded in April 2008. A random sample of 2000 undergraduate students, provided by the university registrar, was invited to participate, yielding 450 respondents for a response rate of 22.5 percent. . . .

Measures

Demographics. For descriptive and comparative purposes, we asked a series of questions about the demographics of our sample. Sixty-two percent of respondents were female, with an average age of 20.4. They were primarily white (81%), approximately evenly split between on-campus (49%) and off-campus (51%) residence, and the average year in school was 2.68 (where 1 = first year and 4 = senior). They reported using the internet for a mean of 4.01 hours a day and spent 81.4 minutes on Facebook each day; we capped the total hours of Facebook use at 8, approximately three standard deviations from the mean.

Psychological well-being measures. Self-esteem was found to be an important predictor in previous work exploring Facebook use and social capital (Ellison et al., 2007; Steinfield et al., 2008). Thus, we included a measure of self-esteem as a control variable in our regressions. Self-esteem was measured using seven items from the Rosenberg Self-esteem Scale (Rosenberg, 1989) as reported in Ellison et al. (2007). . . .

Facebook use. Respondents were first asked if they were Facebook members. Those who responded in the affirmative . . . were then asked a series of questions related to their Facebook usage. These included when they first joined the site, how many minutes they spent using it each day in the past week, and how many total Facebook Friends they had. . . .

Friends on Facebook. In order to see if actual friends were more likely to be associated with social capital than the total number of Friends (including those who are not considered actual), we asked about the total number of Facebook Friends reported by participants . . . and what proportion of these Friends were considered 'actual' friends. . . . We intentionally did not specify what 'actual friends' meant in order to tap into individual understandings of friendship. The median number for total Facebook Friends was 300 and the median number of 'actual' Facebook friends was 75. Overall, the percentage of all Facebook Friends who were considered 'actual' friends was 25 percent.

Connection strategies. We created a series of items asking respondents to indicate how likely they were to browse the Facebook profile, contact via Facebook, add as a Facebook friend, and ultimately meet face-to-face with various types of others. . . . We focused on three types of others reflecting distinct sets of behavior: use of the site for connecting with total strangers at the university, with latent ties representing an offline connection, and with close friends. The three relationship prompts, in order of increasing prior offline connection, were:

- *Total stranger:* 'Imagine a MSU student you've never met in real life or had a face-to-face conversation with.'
- *Someone from your residence hall (latent tie):* 'Imagine someone at MSU who lives in your residence hall who you would recognize but have never spoken to.'
- *Close friend:* 'Think about one of your close friends.'

We further assessed respondents' connection practices with several items gauging the extent to which they used Facebook to meet new people and learn more about acquaintances. . . .

Bridging social capital. We adapted the bridging social capital measure constructed by Ellison et al. (2007), which contained five items from Williams' (2006) Bridging Social Capital subscale as well as three additional items intended to place these dimensions of bridging social capital in the specific university context. . . . The final scale (Cronbach's α = .84; M = 3.74; SD = 0.61) consisted of the items: I feel I am part of the MSU community; Interacting with people at MSU makes me want to try new things; Interacting with people at MSU makes me feel like a part of a larger community; I am willing to spend time to support general MSU activities; At MSU, I come into contact with new people all the time; Interacting with people at MSU reminds me that everyone in the world is connected.

Bonding social capital. We used the bonding social capital measure employed by Ellison et al. (2007), comprised of five items from the bonding subscale of the internet social capital scales developed and validated by Williams (2006) and adapted to the university context.

Findings

RQ1 probed whether there exist distinct groupings of specific online and offline communication behaviors employed by Facebook users in relation to close friends, latent ties, and strangers. We conducted an exploratory factor analysis (available from the authors upon request) of the 12 connection strategies items and the items probing other purpose of use behaviors. . . . After removing cross-loading items, the remaining items factored cleanly into three dimensions, each of which represents a distinct set of social behaviors:

- *Initiating:* This dimension represents the use of Facebook to meet strangers or make new friends without any prior offline connection. . . .
- *Maintaining:* This dimension reflects using the site to maintain existing close ties. . . .
- *Social information-seeking:* This dimension reflects use of the site for learning more about people with whom the user has some offline connection. . . .

High loading items on each scale were averaged to create three separate scales representing each connection strategy. All items were measured on 5-point scales, so the connection strategy scales range from a minimum of 1 ('Strongly Disagree') to a maximum of 5 ('Strongly Agree'). Initiating connections with strangers is clearly not a typical usage of Facebook, as evidenced by the low mean ($M = 1.87$), which was significantly lower than the other connection strategies based on matched sample t-tests. . . . Nearly all respondents used Facebook to maintain ties with close friends ($M = 4.68$), which was significantly higher than social information-seeking ($M = 3.40$). . . .

For RQ2 and RQ3, we explored whether any of these communication patterns were predictive of respondents' reported levels of bridging and bonding social capital. We conducted a series of regression analyses predicting social capital in order to isolate the effect of the various communication patterns above and beyond the factors identified in other work. . . . Regressions included both total Friends and actual friends in order to assess H1a and H2a. In order to explore whether the effect of actual friends diminishes at a certain point, we included a squared term for actual friends.

Our first regression model, addressing RQ2 and H1, examined bridging social capital as the dependent variable; control variables, total number of Facebook Friends, actual Facebook Friends, and the squared term for actual Facebook Friends were included as independent variables. This model has an adjusted R^2 of .12. Adding social information-seeking to the model increased the adjusted R^2 to .16. . . . Using the model that included social information-seeking, standardized coefficients reveal that the extent to which students engaged in social information-seeking behaviors did, in fact, contribute significantly . . . to bridging social capital. Year in school . . . , number of actual friends . . . , and self-esteem . . . were also significant predictors. The number of total Facebook Friends was not a significant predictor, thus supporting H1a, which predicted that the number of actual friends would be more predictive of bridging social capital than the number of Facebook Friends. This effect appears to diminish if the number of actual friends is too large, . . . supporting H1b. . . . Social capital benefits appear to diminish after approximately 500 reported actual friends.

In order to address RQ3 and H2, we examined these same variables in a regression predicting bonding social capital. After first controlling for year in school, self-esteem, general internet use and Facebook use, as well as the number of total Friends on Facebook, actual friends on Facebook, and the square of actual friends, the extent to which students engaged in social information-seeking behaviors did contribute significantly . . . to bonding social capital. . . . As with bridging social capital, self-esteem . . . was a significant predictor of bonding social capital. The number of actual friends . . . was significant, although the number of total Facebook Friends was not, supporting H2a. Once again, the squared term for actual friends . . . suggests a diminishing return beyond approximately 500 actual friends, supporting H2b. . . .

Discussion

The overarching goal of this study was to explore how undergraduates use Facebook to initiate and develop social relationships and to assess the impact of these practices on perceived social capital levels. . . .

Our first research question asked about Facebook users' communication practices. . . . Our findings suggest that there are three distinct modes of interaction employed by our participants. 'Initiating' describes behaviors aimed at meeting strangers through Facebook. . . . This suite of behaviors was the least common. On the other end of the spectrum, 'maintaining' behaviors include engaging in all the behaviors we examined—browsing, communicating, Friending, and meeting—with one's close friends, and was by far the most common. Finally, and perhaps most interestingly, 'social information-seeking' describes a suite of behaviors that revolve around using the site to discover more information about someone with whom the user shares some kind of offline connection. . . .

The social information-seeking strategy is intriguing because it encapsulates the organic interplay between offline and online communication found on many SNSs. People who report engaging in information-seeking behaviors are using the site to learn more about people around them. Although our measures do not enable us to claim with certainty what they are doing with this information or whether an offline interaction preceded the online investigation, we speculate that the identity information typically included in Facebook profiles may be used to trigger offline interactions. In this sense, Facebook use can act as a catalyst of, rather than a replacement for, offline interaction, supporting earlier research that suggested that 'highly engaged users are using Facebook to crystallize relationships that might otherwise remain ephemeral' (Ellison et al., 2007: 1162). . . .

For RQ2 and RQ3, we explored whether these strategies were significant predictors of perceptions of social capital. Social information-seeking was significant in both regressions, whereas including the other two strategies did not explain more variance, nor were they significant when included. . . .

Considering the significant influence of social information-seeking behaviors, we believe the social and technical affordances of Facebook support the conversion of latent ties to weak ties, in that the site provides identity information, enables communication between parties, and helps bring together those with shared interests. . . . We believe that the identity information in Facebook serves as a *social lubricant,* providing individuals with social information that is critical for exploiting the technical ability to connect provided by the site. Using Facebook to try to connect with 'total strangers' (initiating) did not have an impact on social capital scores, whereas using the site to 'check out' or 'learn more about' proximate latent or very weak ties (social information-seeking) did. The process by which Facebook can be used to scaffold productive social interactions is complex and is only partially illuminated by our data.

Our analyses suggest 'Friends' who are not considered 'actual' friends are unlikely to provide social capital benefits. For H1 and H2, we examined the role played by the number of total Facebook Friends and actual friends on the site. A simple quantity-centric view of social networks would assume that more Friends (regardless of tie strength) should result in higher levels of bridging social capital because more of these friends are likely to be bridging, or weak, ties and because higher numbers represent more potential sources of information and perspectives. However, this was not the case: the number of Facebook Friends alone did not predict bridging social capital, but the number of actual friends did. Given the high median number of actual friends reported by our subjects (75, out of a median estimate of 300 total Friends), we surmise that not all actual friends are truly close ties or intimate friends, but are likely to be individuals with whom the user has a stronger offline connection. Our findings suggest that these perceived actual Friends are more likely to be productive from a social capital standpoint. . . . The fact that total and 'actual' friends had different effects in our models suggests that future studies should probe self-reported total Friends, which are very highly correlated with Friend counts as extracted from server-level data (Burke et al., 2010), as well as perceptions of 'actual' friends.

Finally, our findings suggest a point of diminishing returns, even for those considered to be actual friends, in terms of the association with social capital once the number of reported actual friends exceeds the 400–500 range. . . .

Conclusion

Emerging adults such as college students, who are experimenting with various identities, may benefit from the larger, more heterogeneous network that Facebook enables. . . . This study sheds light on the processes by which SNSs can scaffold relationship development in both online and offline contexts. Our findings suggest that communication practices on the site impact social capital outcomes and underscore the importance of examining not just whether individuals use a particular site, but what they do with it and, as our findings regarding different 'connection strategies' and their relationship to social capital suggest, who they do it with. . . .

Limitations to this study include the fact that we studied just one social network site, Facebook, and thus our results cannot be generalized to other sites. . . . Additionally, survey data suffer from concerns regarding self-report and social capital is notoriously hard to measure. Our measures of social capital reflect limited dimensions of the concept and should be refined in future studies. . . .

SNSs such as Facebook are well designed to support relational development in that they perform all three of these relationship-supporting tasks. Facebook enables individuals to find those with shared interests (e.g., through Groups or searchable profile fields). It enables self-expression through the profile, which consists of multiple opportunities to share information about one's cultural tastes, friendship networks, political affiliations, and other aspects of the self. Finally, Facebook provides multiple communication opportunities, both public and private, broadcast and targeted, lightweight and more substantive. We believe these social and technical affordances play an important role in helping students maintain and develop social networks and the social capital that is embedded within them.

References

Acquisti A. and Gross R. (2006) Imagined communities: Awareness, information sharing, and privacy on the Facebook, *Lecture Notes in Computer Science* 4258: 36–58.

Burke M, Marlow C. and Lento T. (2010) Social network activity and social well-being. In: *Proceedings of the 2010 ACM Conference on Human Factors in Computing Systems*. New York: ACM, 1909–1912.

Burt R. S. (2005) *Brokerage and Closure: An Introduction to Social Capital*. Oxford: Oxford University Press.

Ellison N. B., Steinfield C. and Lampe C. (2007) The benefits of Facebook 'friends': Exploring the relationship between college students' use of online social networks and social capital. *Journal of Computer-mediated Communication* 12: 1143–1168.

Granovetter M. (1973) The strength of weak ties. *American Journal of Sociology* 78: 1360–1380.

Hargittai E. (2007) Whose space? Differences among users and non-users of social network sites. *Journal of Computer-mediated Communication* 13: 276–297.

Hargittai E. (2008) The digital reproduction of inequality. In: Grusky D (ed.) *Social Stratification*. Boulder, CO: Westview, 936–944.

Joinson A. N. (2008) Looking at, looking up or keeping up with people?: Motives and use of Facebook. In: *Proceedings of the SIGCHI Conference on Human Factors in Computing Systems*. New York: ACM, 1027–1036.

Lampe C, Ellison N. and Steinfield C. (2008) Changes in use and perception of Facebook. In *Proceedings of the 2008 Conference on Computer-supported Cooperative Work*. New York: ACM, 721–730.

Papacharissi Z. and Mendelson A. (2008) Toward a new(er) sociability: Uses, gratifications, and social capital on Facebook. Paper presented at the Internet Research conference, Copenhagen, Denmark, October 2008.

Putnam R. D. (2000) *Bowling Alone: The Collapse and Revival of American Community*. New York: Simon and Schuster.

Quan-Haase A. and Wellman B. (2004) How does the Internet affect social capital? In: Huysman M. and Wulf V. (eds) *Social Capital and Information Technology*. Cambridge, MA: MIT Press, 113–135.

Rosenberg M. (1989) *Society and the Adolescent Self-image* (revised ed). Middletown, CT: Wesleyan University Press.

Stecher K. and Counts S. (2008) Thin slices of online profile attributes. In: *Proceedings of the Second International Conference on Weblogs and Social Media* Seattle, WA: AAAI Press.

Steinfield C, Ellison N. B. and Lampe C. (2008) Social capital, self-esteem, and use of online social network sites: A longitudinal analysis. *Journal of Applied Developmental Psychology* 29: 434–445.

Subrahmanyam K, Reich S. M., Waechter N. and Espinoza G. (2008) Online and offline social networks: Use of social networking sites by emerging adults. *Journal of Applied Developmental Psychology* 29: 420–433.

Tong ST, Van Der Heide B, Langwell L. and Walther J. (2008) Too much of a good thing? The relationship between number of friends and interpersonal impressions on Facebook. *Journal of Computer-mediated Communication* 13: 531–549.

Valenzuela S, Park N. and Kee K. F. (2009) Is there social capital in a social network site?: Facebook use and college students' life satisfaction, trust, and participation. *Journal of Computer-mediated Communication* 14: 875–901.

Williams D. (2006) On and off the 'net: Scales for social capital in an online era. *Journal of Computer-mediated Communication* 11: 593–628.

EXPLORING THE ISSUE

Are Social Networking Sites (SNSs), Such as Facebook, a Cause for Concern?

Critical Thinking and Reflection

1. How has the concept of *friendship* changed as a result of SNSs?
2. Do social networking sites supplant or expand opportunities for daily, meaningful contact with close friends?
3. SNSs are continuously increasing in popularity and becoming more available to younger adolescents and children (under age 13). In fact, Facebook has recently proposed *Social Kids: Social Networking for Young Children.* Is Facebook an appropriate venue for teaching the lessons of digital citizenship to young children? Do the risks outweigh the benefits for this young age group?
4. Many interpersonal qualities (e.g., honesty, patience, kindness) that we value evolved in the context of face-to-face communication. Do you think these qualities are sacrificed with online communication?

Is There Common Ground?

SNSs have rapidly become popular as ways for adolescents to form and maintain relationships. As such, there is increasingly more debate regarding the impact (both positive and negative) of their use on adolescent well-being. While some researchers criticize SNSs, such as Facebook, as being addictive, invasive, and exposing, others believe SNSs can enhance healthy adolescent relationship formation. The YES and NO selections are excellent examples of these opposing views. Despite the opposing arguments, there is some common ground.

Although Henson and colleagues focus on the dangers of SNSs such as online interpersonal victimization, they also acknowledge that the sites allow users to communicate in new ways that were once not possible. More specifically, they state that users can meet new people, establish friendships, and share their thoughts. These statements support the arguments made by Ellison, Steinfield, and Lampe who argue that SNSs not only enhance existing social relationships but also allow for developing new relationships. Ellison and colleagues also report that when it comes to providing social capital, it is "actual" or "close" friends that matter. In that sense, the arguments made in both selections point to an important issue that requires examining in more detail: the relationship between online victimization and quality of the friendships. What is the level of the relationship between bully and victim? Is the bully an "actual" friend or an acquaintance with little invested in the relationship? One of the main arguments against SNSs such as Facebook is the disregard for controlling personal information that the users of Facebook exhibit. Although users have numerous tools available to them to protect their privacy, the majority does not enable the privacy settings—hence allowing all "friends" and perhaps strangers to have access to their information. The lesson for adolescents might be in distinguishing between the different levels of friendships followed by applying privacy settings accordingly. This could capture the arguments made in both selections: enhancing social capital, while protecting against online victimization.

Additional Resources

Boyd, D. M., & Ellison, N. B. (2008). Social network sites: Definition, history, and scholarship. *Journal of Computer-Mediated Communication, 13*, 210–230.

In this special theme section of the *Journal of Computer-Mediated Communication*, the authors propose a comprehensive definition of SNSs and present their perspective on the history of the sites. They conclude with recommendations for future research.

Cassidy, J. (2006). Me media: How hanging out on the internet became big business. *The New Yorker, 82*(13), 50.

Hargittai, E. (2008). Whose space? Differences among users and non-users of social network sites. *Journal of Computer-Mediated Communication, 13*, 276–297.

This article examines the differences between people who use social networking sites and those who do not. Hargittai reports that usage is dependent on gender, race, ethnicity, parental education, and finally experience and autonomy of use.

Livingstone, S. (2008). Taking risky opportunities in youthful content creation: Teenagers' use of social networking sites for intimacy, privacy and self-expression. *New Media and Society, 10*(3), 393–411.

Livingstone examines the practices of social networking and the relationship with online opportunity and risk. Results indicate that younger teenagers like the opportunity to create elaborate highly decorated identities, while older teenagers prefer a simple aesthetic that expresses them in terms of their authentic relationships.

Nosko, A., Wood, E., & Molema, S. (2010). All about me: Disclosure in online social networking profiles: The case of FACEBOOK. *Computers in Human Behavior, 26*, 406–418.

The authors examined disclosure in online social networking profiles and reported that presenting personal information such as gender and age was correlated with disclosure of other personal and sensitive information. As age increased, amount of personal information in profiles decreased and users who indicated their gender had higher rates of disclosure. Finally, the authors report that those seeking a relationship had an increased risk of threat and disclosed the greatest amount of highly sensitive information.

Regan, K. (2003). Online privacy is dead—what now? *E-Commerce Times*, January 2. Retrieved from www.ecommercetimes.com/story/20346.html

Steinfield, C., Ellison, N., & lampe, C. (2008). Social capital, self-esteem, and use of online social network sites: a longitudinal analysis. *Journal of Applied Developmental Psychology, 29*, 434–445.

> This study examined the relationships between Facebook usage, measures of psychological well-being, and social capital. The authors report that Facebook helps "reduce barriers that lower self-esteem students might experience in forming the kinds of large, heterogeneous networks that are sources of bridging social capital" (p. 434).

Valkenburg, P. M., Peter, J., & Shouten, A. P. (2006). Friend networking sites and their relationship to adolescents' well-being and social self-esteem. *CyberPsychology and Behavior, 9*(5), 584–590.

> The aim of this study was to examine the usage of friend networking sites (e.g., MySpace) on self-esteem and well-being. Valkenburg and colleagues report that usage stimulated the number of relationships formed as well as the amount and type (positive versus negative) of feedback received on an adolescent's site. Positive feedback enhanced self-esteem and well-being.

ISSUE 18

Should Juvenile Offenders Be Tried and Convicted as Adults?

YES: Charles D. Stimson and Andrew M. Grossman, from *Adult Time for Adult Crime. Life Without Parole for Juvenile Killers and Violent Teens* (The Heritage Foundation, August 2009)*

NO: Laurence Steinberg, from "Adolescent Development and Juvenile Justice," *Annual Review of Clinical Psychology* (vol. 5, 2009)

Learning Outcomes

After reading this issue, you should be able to:

- Outline the history of the juvenile justice system in Canada and the United States.
- Describe the current juvenile justice system in Canada and the United States.
- Explain why adolescents do not "think" and "behave" in the same way as mature adults.
- Justify why adolescents may not be as culpable as adults.
- Explain why some crimes committed by adolescents may warrant a "get tough" approach.

ISSUE SUMMARY

YES: Charles D. Stimson, senior legal fellow and Andrew M. Grossman, past senior legal policy analyst, Center for Legal and Justice Studies, The Heritage Foundation, argue that for serious offenses, trying juveniles in adult court and imposing adult sentences—such as life without parole—is effective and appropriate because youth who commit adult crimes should be treated as adults.

NO: Laurence Steinberg, Distinguished University Professor, Department of Psychology at Temple University, argues that adolescents often lack the cognitive, social, and emotional maturity to make mature judgments and therefore should not be sanctioned in the same way as adults. He supports a separate juvenile justice system where adolescents should be judged, tried, and sanctioned in ways that do not adversely affect development.

Not much more than a century ago, little distinction was made between how children and adults were tried and convicted. This changed, however, when child development researchers recognized the time between childhood and adulthood as a distinct period of development. As such, child advocacy groups argued that children and adolescents should be removed from adult courts and prisons. This led to the first juvenile court in the United States in 1899 and the Juvenile Delinquent's Act of 1908 in Canada. These changes to the justice system were based on arguments of providing care and custody to vulnerable children with a focus on rehabilitation and reintegration.

For over 50 years, both systems ran smoothly. It was not until the 1960s when the recognition and protection of children's legal rights were questioned. Child welfare groups argued that juveniles within the system were not being rehabilitated and were being given long cruel sentences. By the 1970s, following several class-action lawsuits alleging cruel and unusual punishment, governments reexamined the way youth were tried, convicted, and rehabilitated, resulting in the United States's 1974 Juvenile Justice and Delinquency Prevention Act (JJDPA) and Canada's 1984 Young Offenders Act (YOA). Both acts, focusing on children's rights, rehabilitation and reintegration, mandated that juveniles be protected and cared for and not be placed in adult jails. The JJDPA is still in effect in the United States, while the YOA was replaced in 2003 with the Youth Criminal Justice Act (YCJA). The change in Canada was made to address the escalating incarceration rates that had been higher than other western countries. Custody in Canada now is reserved for violent offenders and serious repeat offenders.

Although the JJDPA and YCJA addressed the rehabilitation of youth, problems continue to exist. As youth violence and crime rates rose through the 1980s and 1990s, there was public demand for a "get tougher" approach to juvenile crime. Public perception was that the JJDPA and YCJA protected youth too much, resulting in higher crime rates and compromised social order. In the United States this "get tougher" approach resulted in government taking action and the majority of states having laws making it easier to try young juveniles in adult criminal court. For example, the youngest in American history was Michigan's Nathaniel Abraham. He was 11 years old when, in 1999, he was charged and prosecuted as an adult for murder (Tuell, 2002). Interestingly, youth crime rates have dropped since the mid-1990s.

If adolescents can be tried and convicted as adults, can they also be executed like adults? In the United States, the answer is yes. Every nation in the world prohibits the execution of juvenile offenders, except for the United States where only 13 U.S. jurisdictions prohibit the execution of juveniles (Tuell, 2002). Between 1973 and 2003, 2.6 percent (22 of 859) of the total executions in the United States were juvenile offenders. How are these decisions made? Who essentially decides which juveniles to transfer to adult court, and what factors do they consider in the decision? In the United States and in Canada, judicial waiver (i.e., one method of transfer to adult court) is initiated by the prosecutor, decided by the judge, and usually based on age, criminal history, seriousness of offense, likelihood to rehabilitate, and threat to the public. Is this the right way to deal with young offenders? Should adolescents who commit serious offenses be tried and convicted as adults? Should the decision be based on public opinion, threat to society, seriousness of the crime, or age and maturity of the defendant? How do we balance the individuals' rights against those of society? These questions will be addressed in the selections that follow.

Charles D. Stimson and Andrew M. Grossman argue that adult sentences for juveniles who commit serious offenses do not violate U.S. law or the Constitution, negating the argument that adult sentences are inhuman, cruel, or a violation of human rights. Reference is also made to the *Roper* case, which prohibits the death penalty in relation to juveniles, and Stimson and Grossman base their arguments on the continued existence of *Roper's* reliance on life without parole. They argue that while most juvenile offenders should not and do not receive adult sentences in an adult criminal justice system, some juvenile crimes evince enough cruelty, wantonness, and disregard of human life that these juveniles have characteristics that put them beyond the discipline abilities of a juvenile court.

Laurence Steinberg, on the other hand, argues that cognitive development is still in process through adolescence and into adulthood, and that the social and emotional capacities of adolescents will continue to develop beyond late adolescence. As a result, adolescents are more impulsive, more susceptible to peer pressure, and less cognizant of potential future consequences. Adolescents are not as able as fully developed adults and thus should be less blameworthy. Steinberg also argues that adult sentencing of juveniles may have a significant negative effect on their future development, putting them at higher risk of repeat offenses and increasing antisocial behavior.

(Note: these selections have been heavily edited due to space restrictions. We recommend the readers access and read the full documents to gain a better understanding of this debate.)

YES ←

**Charles D. Stimson and
Andrew M. Grossman**

Adult Time for Adult Crime. Life Without Parole for Juvenile Killers and Violent Teens

Introduction

The United States leads the Western world in juvenile crime and has done so for decades. Juveniles commit murder, rape, robbery, aggravated assault, and other serious crimes—particularly violent crimes—in numbers that dwarf those of America's international peers.

The plain statistics are shocking. Between 1980 and 2005, 43,621 juveniles were arrested for murder in the United States. The picture is just as bleak with respect to arrests for rape (109,563), robbery (818,278), and aggravated assault (1,240,199).

In response to this flood of juvenile offenders,[1] state legislatures have enacted commonsense measures to protect their citizens and hold these dangerous criminals accountable. The states spend billions of dollars each year on their juvenile justice systems, which handle the vast majority of juvenile offenders. Most states have also enacted laws that allow particularly violent and mature juveniles to be tried as adults. And for the very worst juvenile offenders, 43 state legislatures and the federal government have set the maximum punishment at life without the possibility of parole.[2]

This represents an overwhelming national consensus that life without parole (LWOP) is, for certain types of juvenile offenders, an effective, appropriate, and lawful punishment. Moreover, no state court that has addressed the constitutionality of sentencing juvenile offenders to life without parole has struck the sentence down as unconstitutional. Federal courts have consistently reached the same conclusion.[3]

Nonetheless, the right of the people, acting through their representatives, to impose this punishment is under attack. . . .

A Small but Coordinated Movement

Opponents of tough sentences for serious juvenile offenders have been working for years to abolish the sentence of life without the possibility of parole. . . . Emboldened by the Supreme Court's decision in *Roper*, which relied on the "cruel and unusual punishments" language of the Eighth Amendment to the Constitution to prohibit capital sentences for juveniles, they have set about to extend the result of *Roper* to life without parole.

These groups wrap their reports and other products in the language of *Roper* and employ sympathetic terms like "child" and "children" and *Roper*-like language such as "death sentence" instead of the actual sentence of life without parole. Their reports are adorned with pictures of children, most of whom appear to be five to eight years old, despite the fact that the youngest person serving life without parole in the United States is 14 years old and most are 17 or 18 years old.

A careful reading of these groups' reports, articles, and press releases reveals that their messages and themes have been tightly coordinated. There is a very unsubtle similarity in terminology among organizations in characterizing the sentence of life without parole for juvenile offenders. For example, they consistently decline to label teenage offenders "juveniles" despite the fact that the term is used by the states, lawyers, prosecutors, state statutes, judges, parole officers, and everyone else in the juvenile justice system. Instead, they use "child."

There is nothing wrong, of course, with advocacy groups coordinating their language and message. The problem is that this important public policy debate has been shaped by a carefully crafted campaign of misinformation.

The issue of juvenile offenders and the proper sentence they are due is much too important to be driven by manufactured statistics, a misreading of a Supreme Court case, and fallacious assertions that the United States is in violation of international law. Instead, the debate should be based on real facts and statistics, a proper reading of precedent, an intelligent understanding of federal and state sovereignty, and a proper understanding of our actual international obligations.

The Public Is Disserved by a One-Sided Debate

Regrettably, that has not been the case, as opponents of life without parole for juvenile offenders have monopolized the debate. As a result, legislatures, courts, the media, and the public have been misled on crucial points.

One prominent example is a frequently cited statistic on the number of juvenile offenders currently serving life-without-parole sentences. Nearly all reports published on the subject and dozens of newscasts and articles based on those reports state that there are at least 2,225 juveniles sentenced to life without parole. That number first appeared in a 2005 report by Amnesty International and Human Rights Watch, *The Rest of Their Lives: Life Without Parole for Child Offenders in the United States*.[4]

But a careful look at the data and consultation with primary sources— that is, state criminal-justice officials—reveals that this statistic is seriously flawed. [O]fficials in some states reject as incorrect the figures assigned to their states. Others admit that they have no way of knowing how many juvenile offenders in their states have been sentenced to life without parole—and that, by extension, neither could activist groups.

Nonetheless, this statistic has gone unchallenged even as it has been cited in appellate briefs[5] and oral arguments[6] before state supreme courts and even in a petition to the United States Supreme Court. All of these courts have been asked to make public policy based on factual representations that even cursory research would demonstrate are questionable.

Another example is the unrealistic portrait of the juvenile offenders who are sentenced to life without parole that activist groups have painted. Nearly every report contains sympathetic summaries of juvenile offenders' cases that gloss over the real facts of the crimes, deploying lawyerly language and euphemism to disguise brutality and violence.

For example, consider the case of Ashley Jones [(see case study 6 after the end notes)]. The Equal Justice Initiative's 2007 report describes Ms. Jones's offense as follows: "At 14, Ashley tried to escape the violence and abuse by running away with an older boyfriend who shot and killed her grandfather and aunt. Her grandmother and sister, who were injured during the offense, want Ashley to come home."[7]

The judge's account of the facts, however, presents a somewhat different picture. An excerpt:

When Ashley realized her aunt was still breathing, she hit her in the head with a heater, stabbed her in the chest and attempted to set her room on fire. . . .

As ten-year old Mary Jones [Ashley's sister] attempted to run, Ashley grabbed her and began hitting her. [Ashley's boyfriend] put the gun in young Mary's face and told her that that was how she would die. Ashley intervened and said, "No, let me do it," and proceeded to stab her little sister fourteen times.[8]

In a similar vein, many of the studies feature pictures of children who are far younger than any person actually serving life without parole in the United States.[9] When these reports do include an actual picture of a juvenile offender, the picture is often one taken years before the crime was committed.[10] The public could be forgiven for believing incorrectly that children under 14 are regularly sentenced to life behind bars without the possibility of release.

A final example is the legality of life-without-parole sentences for juvenile offenders. Opponents make the claim, among many others, that these sentences violate the United States' obligations under international law. Yet they usually fail to mention that no court has endorsed this view, and rarely do they explain the implications of the fact that the United States has not ratified the treaty that they most often cite, the Convention on the Rights of the Child, and has carved out legal exceptions (called "reservations") to others.

Further, they often abuse judicial precedent by improperly extending the death penalty–specific logic and language of *Roper* into the non–death penalty arena,[11] an approach that the Supreme Court has repeatedly rejected.[12]

Again, the public could be forgiven for believing incorrectly that the Supreme Court, particularly in *Roper*, has all but declared the imposition of life sentences without parole for juvenile offenders to be unconstitutional. A more honest reading of the precedent, however, compels the opposite conclusion: that the sentence is not constitutionally suspect.

The Whole Story

Public policy should be based on facts, not false statistics and misleading legal claims. For that reason, we undertook the research to identify those states that have authorized life without parole for juvenile offenders and wrote to every major district attorney's office across those 43 states. To understand how prosecutors are using life-without-parole sentences and the types of crimes and criminals for which such sentences are imposed, we asked each office for case digests of juvenile offenders who were prosecuted by their offices and received the specific sentence of life without parole.

The response from prosecutors around the country was overwhelming. Prosecutors from across the United States sent us case digests, including official court documents, police reports, judges' findings, photos of the defendants and victims, motions, newspaper articles, and more. From that collection of case digests, we selected typical cases, all concerning juvenile offenders, and assembled a complete record for each. In sharp contrast to the practices of other reports, these case studies recount all of the relevant facts of the crimes, as found by a jury or judge and recorded in official records, in neutral language. . . .

Based on this research, we conclude that the sentence of life without parole for juvenile offenders is reasonable, constitutional, and (appropriately) rare. Our survey of the cases shows that some juveniles commit horrific crimes with full knowledge of their actions and intent to bring about the results. In constitutional terms, the Supreme Court's own jurisprudence, including *Roper*, draws a clear line between the sentence of death and all others, including life without parole; further, to reach its result, *Roper* actually depends on the availability of life without parole for juvenile offenders. We also find that while most states allow life-without-parole sentences for juvenile offenders, judges generally have broad discretion in sentencing, and most juvenile offenders do not receive that sentence.

We conclude, then, that reports by activist groups on life without parole for juvenile offenders are at best misleading and in some instances simply wrong in their facts, analyses, conclusions, and recommendations. Regrettably, the claims made by these groups have been repeated so frequently that lawmakers, judges, the media, and the public risk losing sight of their significant bias.

To foster informed debate, more facts—particularly, good state-level statistics—are needed about the use of life-without-parole sentences for juvenile offenders. But even on the basis of current data, as insufficient as they are, legislators should take note of how these sentences are actually applied and reject any attempts to repeal life-without-parole sentences for juvenile offenders.

The U.S. Has a Juvenile Crime Problem

Underlying nearly every argument made by opponents of life without parole for juvenile offenders is the premise that, because many other countries have not authorized or have repealed the sentence, the United States should do the same so that it can be in conformance with the international "consensus" on the matter.

In fact, this premise is the cornerstone of the litigation strategy to extend the Eighth Amendment's prohibition on "cruel and unusual punishments" to reach life-without-parole sentences for juveniles. This application of foreign sources of law to determine domestic law, in addition to being legally problematic, too often overlooks the qualitative differences between the United States and other countries.

This has certainly been the case in the debate over life without parole for juvenile offenders. The leading reports on the issue do not grapple seriously with the facts concerning juvenile crime and how those facts differ between nations. Instead, they play a crude counting game, tallying up nations while ignoring the realities of their circumstances and juvenile justice systems.

The Facts on Worldwide Crime and Sentencing

The fact is that the United States faces higher rates of crimes, particularly violent crimes and homicides, than nearly any other country. Adults and juveniles commit crimes in huge numbers, from misdemeanor thefts to premeditated murders. The root causes of this epidemic have been debated, studied, tested, and analyzed for decades, but the fact of its existence is neither controversial nor in doubt.

After a decade of gains in deterring juvenile crime, the trend has turned the other way in recent years. According to the U.S. Department of Justice, there was "substantial growth in juvenile violent crime arrests. . . . in the late 1980s [which] peaked in 1994."[13] Between 1994 and 2004, the arrest rate for juveniles for violent crimes fell 49 percent, only to see a 2 percent uptick in 2005 and then a 4 percent gain in 2006.[14] In 2005 and 2006, arrests of juveniles for murder and robbery also increased.[15]

Despite the progress made through 2004, juvenile violent crime remains much higher in the United States than in other Western nations. Some statistics:

- In 1998 alone, 24,537,600 recorded crimes were committed in the United States.[16]
- Of the 72 countries that reported recorded crimes to the United Nations Seventh Survey of Crime Trends, the United States ranked first in total recorded crimes.[17]
- Worse still, the United States reported more crimes than the next six countries (Germany, England/Wales, France, South Africa, Russia, and Canada) combined. Their total was 23,111,318.[18] . . .

In terms of violent crime rates, the U.S. ranks highly in every category, and the same is true in the realm of juvenile crime. For example:

- In 1998, teenagers in the United States were suspects in 1,609,303 crimes, and 1,000,279 juveniles were prosecuted.[19]
- That is as many juvenile prosecutions as the next seven highest countries combined.[20] Those countries are England/Wales, Thailand, Germany, China, Canada, Turkey, and South Korea.[21]
- According to 2002 World Health Organization statistics, the United States ranks third in murders committed by youths[22] and 14th in murders per capita committed by youths.[23] . . .

Given this domestic crime problem, it should come as no great surprise that the United States tops the lists of total prisoners and prisoners per capita.[24] . . .

These crucial statistics are not mentioned by those who urge abolition of life-without-parole sentences for juvenile offenders. The reason may be that it undercuts their arguments: If the juvenile crime problem in the United States is not comparable to the juvenile crime problems of other Western nations, then combating it may justifiably require different, and stronger, techniques. The fact that some other nations no longer sentence juvenile offenders to life without parole loses a significant degree of its relevance. In addition, the data on sentence length demonstrate that the use of life-without-parole sentences is not a function of excessive sentence lengths in the United States, but rather an anomaly in a criminal justice system that generally imposes shorter sentences than those of other developed nations.

Life Without Parole for Juvenile Offenders Is Constitutional

In 2005, the Supreme Court held in *Roper v. Simmons* that the Eighth and Fourteenth Amendments to the U.S. Constitution bar the application of the death penalty to offenders who were under the age of 18 when their crimes were committed.[25] Since then, the decision's reasoning has become the cornerstone of the efforts of those who oppose life without parole for juvenile offenders and has reinvigorated their legal crusade to put an end to the practice.

The text and history of the Eighth Amendment, however, provide little support for the idea that life without parole for juvenile offenders constitutes prohibited "cruel and unusual" punishment. Even departing from the text and employing a *Roper*-style analysis is unavailing; the factors that the Court considered in that case all mitigate in favor of life without parole's constitutionality, even as applied to juvenile offenders. [For information regarding the Eighth Amendment, please go to the original full document. . . .]

The U.S. Has No International Obligation to Ban Juvenile Life Without Parole

Many opponents of life without parole for juvenile offenders claim that the continued use of this sentence puts the United States in breach of its obligations under international law.[26] Specifically, they name three treaties as barring the administration of this sentence in the United States: the Convention on the Rights of the Child, the International Covenant on Civil and Political Rights, and the Convention Against Torture.

All of these assertions are false. . . .

A careful analysis of the treaties and, crucially, the United States' obligations under them refutes the claim that international law precludes U.S. states from sentencing juvenile offenders to life without parole.

The Constitution Is America's Fundamental Law

The Constitution is America's fundamental law, and it controls how treaties interact with its provisions and other domestic laws.[27] . . .

For the United States to become a party to a treaty, the President first must sign the treaty and send it to the Senate, at least two-thirds of which must give its advice and consent before the treaty can be ratified.[28] After the Senate has voted to give its consent to ratification, the President may then ratify it, if he so chooses, by signing the instrument of ratification.[29] Treaties that have not been approved in this way are generally not binding on the United States.[30] Even in the extremely rare circumstance that treaties or parts of treaties become a part of "customary" international law and thereby binding upon the United States even though unratified, they still cannot by themselves override domestic statutes.[31]

Many treaties, even if ratified, do not themselves preempt existing domestic laws, but must await subsequent legislation to implement their terms.[32] Only "self-executing" treaties—those that do not require implementing legislation—become the type of federal law that can preempt conflicting state and federal laws.[33]

Few modern treaties, however, are self-executing, and often a treaty will provide on its face that it is not self-executing. Whether express or implied, courts will not enforce treaties that are not self-executing until an act of Congress specifies how the rights or privileges are to be enforced. Thus, treaties that are not self-executing and that have not been implemented by Congress (which may include specifying available causes of action, remedies, court jurisdiction, etc.) do not themselves establish domestically binding legal remedies.

Further, the United States often does not agree to be bound by every term of an international convention, and it cannot do so if some terms conflict with the U.S. Constitution. As a matter of national sovereignty, the United States may adopt whatever portion of international conventions it deems appropriates. . . . When nations sign or ratify a treaty, they often enter "reservations" and "understandings" that govern the treaty's domestic and international implementation. . . .

Once a treaty has been properly executed and implementing legislation has been enacted, there is the question of how it interacts with other laws. In general, a federal statute and a properly executed treaty have equal status in law, with the latter in time taking precedence. This is true, though, only to the extent that a conflict actually exists between the two; to the extent possible, courts interpret statutes so as to avoid violation of international obligations.[34] Therefore, if Congress passes a law that clearly contradicts earlier treaty obligations, courts will enforce the law over the treaty.[35] The obligations of properly executed and implemented treaties, being a part of federal law, can be enforced against the states under the Supremacy Clause, but only if they do not violate the U.S. Constitution, including fundamental protections of state sovereignty. . . .

The result of these requirements is that those who would wield vague language in international treaties against state laws have a number of hurdles to clear before a court even considers the substance of their claims, and failure to clear even one of these hurdles will defeat the claim.

Conclusion: A Lawful and Appropriate Punishment

The United States has a juvenile crime problem that far exceeds the juvenile crime problems of other Western countries. Over the years, state legislatures have responded to this increase in the volume and severity of juvenile crime by providing for sentences that effectively punish offenders, incapacitate them, and deter serious offenses. They have determined by an overwhelming majority that fulfilling their duty to protect their citizens requires making available life-without-parole sentences for juvenile offenders.

The sentence stands up to constitutional scrutiny. All state supreme courts and federal courts that have considered the question have concluded that life without parole for juvenile offenders does not violate the Eighth Amendment's prohibition on cruel and unusual punishment. The Supreme Court's proportionality standard—the highest level of scrutiny it has applied to non-capital punishment—does not prohibit states from punishing murder and other serious offenses with lengthy prison terms; the Court has said that judges should second-guess state legislatures' determinations of criminal punishment only in the rarest cases where the punishment is wholly disproportionate to the harm of the offense.

Most juvenile offenders should not and do not have their cases adjudicated in the adult criminal justice system. Every state has a juvenile justice system, and those courts handle the majority of crimes committed by juveniles. But some crimes evince characteristics that push them beyond the leniency otherwise afforded to juveniles: cruelty, wantonness, a complete disregard for the lives of others. Some of these offenders are tried as adults, and a small proportion of those tried as adults are sentenced to life without parole—the strongest sentence available to express society's disapproval—to incapacitate the criminal and deter the most serious offenses. . . .

A fair look at the Constitution, whether from the perspective of original meaning or from the perspective of current interpretation, provides no basis for overruling the democratic processes of 43 states, the District of Columbia, and the U.S. Congress. Neither do international law, even under broad and sweeping interpretations of its terms, or the misleading and sometimes just wrong statistics and stories marshaled in activists' studies.

Used sparingly, as it is, life without parole is an effective and lawful sentence for the worst juvenile offenders. On the merits, it has a place in our laws.

Notes

1. Following the academic literature, this report uses the term "juvenile offender." *See, e.g.,* Joseph Sanborn, *Juveniles' Competency to Stand Trial: Wading Through the Rhetoric and the Evidence,* 99 J. Crim. L. & Criminology 135, 149 (2009). The term "juvenile killer" would be equally appropriate, because almost all juveniles sentenced to life without parole have committed homicides.

2. *See infra* app. III.

3. *See, e.g.,* United States v. Pete, 277 Fed. Appx. 730, 734 (9th Cir. 2008); United States v. Feemster, 483 F.3d 583, 588 (8th Cir. 2007), *vacated on other grounds,* 128 S. Ct. 880 (2008); United States v. Salahuddin, 509 F.3d 858 (7th Cir. 2007); Calderon v. Schribner, No. 2:06-CV-00770-TMB, 2009 WL 89279, *4–6 (E.D. Cal. Jan. 12, 2009); Price v. Cain, No. 07-937, 2008 U.S. Dist. LEXIS 23474, *17–23 (W.D. La. March 4, 2008); Pineda v. Leblanc, No. 07-3598, 2008 WL 294685, *3 (E.D. La. Jan. 31, 2008); Douma v. Workman, No. 06-CV-0462-CVE-FHM, 2007 WL 2331883, *3 (N.D. Okla. Aug 13, 2007).

4. AI/HRW Report, *supra* note, at 1, 25, 35, 52, 124.

5. *See* Appellant's Opening Brief at 8, Torres v. Delaware, No. 504 (Del. Supr. filed Nov. 14, 2008). Brian Stevenson, Executive Director of the Equal Justice Initiative, represented the appellant. *Id.* at cover. The appellant's brief cites the Equal Justice Initiative's report on juvenile life-without-parole sentences. *Id.* at 8 ("While at least 2,225 people in the United States are serving sentences of life without parole for crimes they committed under the age of 18, extensive research found that only 73 people in the United States are serving such sentences for crimes committed when they were fourteen or younger.").

6. Oral Argument, Torres v. Delaware, No. 504 (Del. Supr. held Feb. 4, 2009), *available at* http://courts.delaware.gov/Courts/Supreme%20Court/oral%20arguments/2009-02-04_504,_2008_Torres_v_State.MP3. In this argument, counsel for Donald Torres cited misleading statistics regarding the number of states that had mandatory sentences of life without parole for juveniles and that had discretionary sentences for first-degree murderers. Deputy Attorney General Paul Wallace, who argued on behalf of the State of Delaware, took issue with the numbers asserted by Torres's counsel and provided the court with accurate statistics. He stated that 49 states permit a 14-year-old to be prosecuted as an adult for first-degree murder, 44 states permit juveniles to receive a life-without-parole sentence for first-degree murder, and only 29 states mandate a life-without-parole sentence for a juvenile who is tried as an adult and convicted of first-degree murder.

7. EJI REPORT, *supra* note 9, at 25.
8. Finding of Fact from Guilt Phase of Trial, Alabama v. Jones, No. CC-2000-0151 (Cir. Ct. Jefferson Cty. Ala. May 25, 2001).
9. For an example, see the cover of the University of San Francisco School of Law's report, which depicts a boy no older than eight years old. USF REPORT, *supra* note 9. *See also* EJI REPORT, *supra* note 9 (this report's unnumbered opening pages contain pictures of juveniles who appear to be from eight to 12 years old).
10. *See* AI/HRW REPORT, *supra* note 9, at 4, 19, 29, 43, 59, 68.
11. *See* AI/HRW REPORT, supra note 9, at 86, 115; EJI REPORT, *supra* note 9, at 11; USF REPORT, *supra* note 9, at 16.
12. Jeffrey Abramson, *Death-Is-Different Jurisprudence and the Role of the Capital Jury,* 2 OHIO ST. J. CRIM. L. 117, 117 n.1 (2004); *Roper,* 543 U.S. at 568 ("Because the death penalty is the most severe punishment, the Eighth Amendment applies to it with special force.").
13. Howard Snyder, *Juvenile Arrests 2006,* JUVENILE JUSTICE BULLETIN, Nov. 2008, at 1, *available at* http://www.ncjrs.gov/pdffilesl/ojjdp/221338.pdf [hereinafter *Juvenile Arrests*].
14. *Id.*
15. *Id.*
16. DIVISION FOR POLICY ANALYSIS AND PUBLIC AFFAIRS, UNITED NATIONS OFFICE ON DRUGS AND CRIME, SEVENTH UNITED NATIONS SURVEY OF CRIME TRENDS AND OPERATIONS OF CRIMINAL JUSTICE SYSTEMS (1998–2000) 10–12 (2004), *available at* http://www .unodc.org/pdf/crime/seventh_survey/7pv.pdf [hereinafter SEVENTH SURVEY].
17. *Id.*
18. *Id.*
19. *Id.* at 154–155. The U.N. Report does not indicate whether that statistic includes all juveniles prosecuted in both adult and juvenile courts.
20. *Id.*
21. *Id.*
22. WORLD HEALTH ORGANIZATION, WORLD REPORT ON VIOLENCE AND HEALTH 28–29 (2002), *available at* http://whqlibdoc.who.int/hq/2002/9241545615.pdf.
23. *Id.*
24. ROY WALMSLEY, INTERNATIONAL CENTRE FOR PRISON STUDIES, KING'S COLLEGE LONDON, WORLD PRISON POPULATION LIST, EIGHTH EDITION (2009), *available at* http://www .kcl.ac.uk/depsta/law/research/icps/downloads/wppl-8th_41.pdf.
25. *Roper,* 543 U.S. at 551.
26. AI/HRW REPORT, *supra* note 9, at 94–109; USF REPORT, *supra* note 9, at 14–18; EJI REPORT, *supra* note 9, at 13.
27. Edwin Meese III, *The Meaning of the Constitution, in* THE HERITAGE GUIDE TO THE CONSTITUTION 5 (Edwin Meese III ed. 2005).
28. RESTATEMENT (THIRD) OF FOREIGN RELATIONS LAW OF THE UNITED STATES §§ 303(1), 303 cmt. a (1987).
29. *Id.* at § 305 cmt. d.
30. In some rare cases, treaties may become customary international law, though this is unlikely to bind those who are subject to U.S. law without the consent of the President and the Senate. *See infra* note 188. In other cases, Congress (that is, both the Senate and the House of Representatives) may authorize the President to enter into an international agreement. This arrangement, sometimes controversial, has not been used to accede to the kind of multilateral agreements discussed in this paper.

See generally RESTATEMENT (THIRD) OF FOREIGN RELATIONS LAW OF THE UNITED STATES § 303 cmt. e (1987).

31. Even a concession by an American official that the U.S. is out of compliance with international practice cannot change binding domestic law. It certainly would not empower a court to do anything about the supposed non-compliance with international norms. *See infra* note 188.

32. Medellin v. Texas, 128 S.Ct. 1346, 1356–57 (2008).

33. Foster v. Nelson, 27 U.S. 253, 314–15 (1829) (explaining that, had the treaty at issue "acted directly on the subject" (i.e., been self-executing), it "would have repealed those acts of Congress which were repugnant to it"); Dennis Arrow, *Treaties,* in THE HERITAGE GUIDE TO THE CONSTITUTION 245 (Edwin Meese III ed., 2005).

34. RESTATEMENT (THIRD) OF FOREIGN RELATIONS LAW OF THE UNITED STATES § 114 (1987); Murray v. Schooner Charming Betsy, 6 U.S. 64, 118 (1804) (explaining that "an act of Congress ought never to be construed to violate the law of nations if any other possible construction remains").

35. RESTATEMENT (THIRD) OF FOREIGN RELATIONS LAW OF THE UNITED STATES § 114 (1987) (statutes should be construed so as not to conflict with international obligations only "where fairly possible" to do so) (quoting Ashwander v. Tennessee Valley Authority, 297 U.S. 288, 348 (1936)).

CASE STUDY 6

Defendant:	Ashley Jones
Victims:	Deroy Nalls (grandfather; murdered)
	Millie Nalls (aunt; murdered)
	Mary Elizabeth Nalls (grandmother; attempted murder)
	Mary Elizabeth Jones (sister; attempted murder)
Crimes:	Two counts, first degree capital murder
	Two counts, attempted first degree murder
	First degree robbery
Age:	14
Where:	Birmingham, Alabama
Crime date:	August 30, 1999

Summary

In a span of minutes, Ashley Jones and her boyfriend shot her grandfather twice in the face and then stabbed him until he died; shot her sleeping aunt three times; shot her grandmother in the shoulder and then stabbed her, poured lighter fluid on her, set her on fire, and watched her burn; and stabbed her 10-year old sister 14 times. Jones then took $300 from her grandfather's wallet and the keys to his Cadillac, which she drove away from the crime scene.

Facts

After Ashley Jones stabbed her father and pregnant mother in 1998, killing neither, she and her younger sister were sent to live with her grandparents and maternal aunt. Deroy Nalls, her 78-year-old grandfather, was a retired steelworker and deacon at his church. His wife, Mary Nalls, 73, was a homemaker.

By late August of 1999, the Nallses were growing tired of Jones's bad behavior and grounded her for staying out all night at a party. The Nallses did not approve of Jones's boyfriend, Geramie Hart, and told him not to visit their house. This angered Jones.

NO PHOTOS FOR THIS CASE STUDY AVAILABLE

Jones and Hart decided to kill everyone in the house, set it on fire, and take their money. To prepare, Jones stole two of her grandfather's guns and smuggled them out of the house to Hart. She mixed together rubbing alcohol, nail polish remover, and charcoal fire starter in anticipation of setting the house ablaze.

It took the couple two days to put their plan into action. On the evening of August 30,1999, Jones kept an eye on her relatives until they had settled in for the evening. Then she called Hart. He arrived around 11:15 p.m., and Jones led him into the house. He was carrying the .38 revolver taken from Jones's grandfather.

Jones and Hart sneaked into the den, where her grandfather was watching television. Hart shot him twice in the face; still alive, Deroy stumbled toward the kitchen. Next, they visited the bedroom of Millie Nalls, 30, Ashley's aunt, and shot her three times. Seeing that her aunt was still breathing, Jones hit her in the head with a portable heater, stabbed her in the chest, and attempted to set the room on fire.

The gunshots awakened Jones's grandmother, and she got out of bed. That was when Jones and Hart entered her bedroom and shot her once in the shoulder. It was their last bullet.

Jones and Hart returned to the den to discover that her grandfather was still alive. With knives from the kitchen, they stabbed him over and over again and left one knife embedded in his back. Jones poured charcoal lighter fluid on her grandfather, set him ablaze, and listened to him groan as he burned alive.

The noise attracted Jones's 10-year-old sister, Mary Elizabeth Jones, to the kitchen. From there, she could see her grandfather on the den floor, ablaze. Soon after, the wounded Mary Nalls entered the kitchen and called out to her dying husband. Jones stabbed her grandmother in the face with an ice pick. Jones then poured lighter fluid on her, set her on fire, and watched her burn.

Mary Elizabeth attempted to leave, but Jones grabbed her and began punching. Hart shoved the pistol in Mary's face and said that he was going to shoot her. Jones intervened: '"No, let me do it." She stabbed her sister 14 times and stopped only after Mary curled up in a ball on

Continued

the floor and pretended to be dead. Jones and Hart piled sheets, towels, and paper on the floor and set the pile on fire.

Jones and Hart removed about $300 from her grandparents' mattress and took the keys to their Cadillac, which they drove to a local hotel. Jones spent the night partying at the hotel, with her grandfather's blood on her socks and grandmother's blood on her shirt.

Miraculously, Mary Elizabeth and her grandmother Mary had survived. Mary Elizabeth helped her grandmother out of the house and walked to a neighbor's home for help. They called the police, who quickly responded to the scene. Police officers found Deroy Nalls dead on the living room floor, Millie Nalls dead in her bed, and Mary Nalls heavily wounded. Firefighters were able to extinguish the fire lit by Jones and Hart.

The following morning, news outlets reported the murders, as well as the fact that Jones's sister had survived. The news angered her. "I thought I killed that bitch," she later explained.

Mary Elizabeth received stitches for her numerous stab wounds and was hospitalized with a collapsed lung. Mary was treated for gunshot and stab wounds and the burns that covered a third of her body. She spent a month in the burn unit of a local hospital, undergoing multiple skin grafts, before undergoing treatment at a rehabilitation facility to relearn how to use her arms after the burns.

Hart and Jones were arrested the next morning after police identified the Nallses' vehicle in the parking lot.

Speaking to police, Jones admitted that "we both" stabbed her grandfather. She explained further: "I mean we shot Millie second . . . me and Geramie just started shooting her. And then . . . and then I went back in there and she was still breathing, so . . . I hit her on the head with the heater and stabbed her in her heart. And she just started coughing up blood."

According to the prosecutor, Laura Poston, Ashley Jones displayed no emotion throughout the trial:

> Sociopaths can however be in the form of a 14, now 15 year old petite girl with a pretty face who can sit all week in a courtroom, look at pictures of her dead grandfather and aunt, listen to her sister cry as she recounts the horrors of that night, and not shed a tear. The first time Ashley showed any emotion about what happened that night was when the jury read the verdicts finding her guilty of two counts of capital murder and two counts of attempted murder—she cried her first tears.

Judge Gloria Bahakel noted in her sentencing decision that Jones "did not express genuine remorse of her actions." The judge continued: "Although she apologized, at the prompting of the Court, her words were hollow and insincere. Furthermore, it was brought to the attention of the Court that while awaiting her sentencing, the defendant had threatened older female inmates in the Jefferson County Jail by telling them she would do the same thing to them that she had done to her family."

Sources

Letter from Laura Poston, Deputy District Attorney, Birmingham, AL, to Charles Stimson (Aug. 15, 2008) (on file with author); Letter from Laura Poston, Deputy District Attorney, Birmingham, AL, to Charles Stimson (Mar. 30, 2009) (on file with author); Carol Robinson, *Two Teens Accused of Bloody Rampage*, BIRMINGHAM NEWS, Aug. 31,1999, at 1A; Steve Joynt, *Arrest of Teenager Revives Question of What Can Turn People into Killers*, BIRMINGHAM POST-HERALD, Sept. 18, 1999, at E1; Carol Robinson, *Young Victim of Massacre Received 13 Stab Wounds*, BIRMINGHAM NEWS, Sept. 1, 1999, at 1C; Carol Robinson, *Girl Accused in Family Attack Still in Detention*, BIRMINGHAM NEWS, Sept. 2, 1999, at 4B; Carol Robinson, *Teen Guilty of Stabbing Family*, BIRMINGHAM NEWS, Mar. 3, 2001, at 1A; Alabama v. Jones, No. CC-2000-0151 (Cir. Ct. of Jefferson County, AL. May 25) (finding of fact from guilt phase of trial).

Laurence Steinberg  **NO**

Adolescent Development and Juvenile Justice

Juvenile Justice Issues Informed by Developmental Science

Criminal Culpability of Youth

The adult justice system presumes that defendants who are found guilty are responsible for their own actions, should be held accountable, and should be punished accordingly. Because of the relative immaturity of minors, however, it may not be justified to hold them as accountable as one might hold adults. If, for example, adolescents below a certain age cannot grasp the long-term consequences of their actions or cannot control their impulses, one cannot hold them fully accountable for their actions. In other words, we cannot claim that adolescents "ought to know better" if, in fact, the evidence indicates that they do not know better, or more accurately, cannot know better, because they lack the abilities needed to exercise mature judgment. It is important to note that culpability cannot really be researched directly. Because an individual's culpability is something that is judged by someone else, it is largely in the eye of the beholder. What can be studied, however, are the capabilities and characteristics of individuals that make them potentially blameworthy, such as their ability to behave intentionally or to know right from wrong.

I use the term "culpability" in this review as a shorthand for several interrelated phenomena, including responsibility, accountability, blameworthiness, and punishability. These notions are relevant to the adjudication of an individual's guilt or innocence, because an individual who is not responsible for his or her actions by definition cannot be guilty, and to the determination of a disposition (in juvenile court) or sentence (in criminal court), in that individuals who are found guilty but less than completely blameworthy, owing to any number of mitigating circumstances, merit proportionately less punishment than do guilty individuals who are fully blameworthy.

The starting point in a discussion of criminal culpability is a principle known as penal proportionality. Simply put, penal proportionality holds that criminal punishment should be determined by two criteria: the harm a person causes and his blameworthiness in causing that harm. The law recognizes that different wrongful acts cause different levels of harm through a complex system of offense grading under which more serious crimes (rape, for example) are punished presumptively more severely than less serious crimes (shoplifting, for example). Beyond this, though, two people who engage in the same wrongful conduct may differ in their blameworthiness. A person may be less culpable than other criminals—or not culpable at all—because he inadvertently (rather than purposely) causes the harm, because he is subject to some endogenous deficiency or incapacity that impairs his decision making (such as mental illness), or because he acts in response to an extraordinary external pressure—a gun to the head is the classic example. Less-blameworthy offenders deserve less punishment, and some persons who cause criminal harm deserve no punishment at all (Scott & Steinberg 2008).

The concept of mitigation plays an important role in the law's calculation of blame and punishment, although it gets little attention in the debate about youth crime. Mitigation applies to persons engaging in harmful conduct who are blameworthy enough to meet the minimum threshold of criminal responsibility but who deserve less punishment than a typical offender would receive. Through mitigation, the criminal law calculates culpability and punishment along a continuum and is not limited to the options of full responsibility or complete excuse. Indeed, criminal law incorporates calibrated measures of culpability. For example, the law of homicide operates through a grading scheme under which punishment for killing another person varies dramatically depending on the actor's blameworthiness . . . Under standard homicide doctrine, mitigating circumstances and mental states are translated into lower-grade offenses that warrant less punishment.

Generally, a person who causes criminal harm is a fully responsible moral agent (and deserves full punishment) if, in choosing to engage in the wrongful conduct, he has the capacity to make a rational decision and a "fair opportunity" to choose not to engage in the harmful conduct. . . .

Under American criminal law, two very different kinds of persons can show that their criminal conduct was less culpable than that of the offender who deserves full punishment—those who are very different from ordinary persons due to impairments that contributed to their criminal choices and those who are ordinary persons whose offenses are responses to extraordinary circumstances or are otherwise aberrant conduct (Scott & Steinberg 2008).

Although it seems paradoxical, adolescents, in a real sense, belong to both groups. In the first group are individuals with endogenous traits or conditions that undermine their decision-making capacity, impairing their ability to understand the nature and consequences of their wrongful acts or to control their conduct. In modern times, this category has been reserved mostly for offenders who suffer from mental illness, mental disability, and other neurological impairments. . . .

Individuals in the second group are ordinary persons whose criminal conduct is less culpable because it is a response to extraordinary external circumstances: These cases arise when the actor faces a difficult choice, and his response of engaging in the criminal conduct is reasonable under the circumstances, as measured by the likely response of an ordinary law-abiding person in that situation. . . .

Although youths in mid-adolescence have cognitive capacities for reasoning and understanding that approximate those of adults, even at age 18 adolescents are immature in their psychosocial and emotional development, and this likely affects their decisions about involvement in crime in ways that distinguish them from adults. Teenagers are more susceptible to peer influence than are adults and tend to focus more on rewards and less on risks in making choices. They also tend to focus on short-term rather than long-term consequences and are less capable of anticipating future consequences, and they are more impulsive and volatile in their emotional responses. When we consider these developmental factors within the conventional criminal law framework for assessing blameworthiness, the unsurprising conclusion is that adolescent offenders are less culpable than are adults. The mitigating conditions generally recognized in the criminal law—diminished capacity and coercive circumstances—are relevant to criminal acts of adolescents and often characterize the actions of juvenile offenders. This does not excuse adolescents from criminal responsibility, but it renders them less blameworthy and less deserving of adult punishment.

Although in general lawmakers have paid minimal attention to the mitigating character of adolescents' diminished decision-making capacities, some legislatures and courts have recognized that immature judgment reduces culpability. . . . In *Roper v. Simmons,* the 2005 case that abolished the juvenile death penalty, the Court adopted the developmental argument for mitigation that follows from the research reviewed above. Justice Kennedy, writing for the majority, described three features of adolescence that distinguish young offenders from their adult counterparts in ways that mitigate culpability—features that are familiar to the reader at this point. The first is the diminished decision-making capacity of youths, which may contribute to a criminal choice that is "not as morally reprehensible as that of adults" because of its developmental nature. . . . Second, the Court pointed to the increased vulnerability of youths to external coercion, including peer pressure. Finally, the Court emphasized that the unformed nature of adolescent identity made it "less supportable to conclude that even a heinous crime was evidence of irretrievably depraved character." Adolescents are less blameworthy than are adults, the Court suggested, because the traits that contribute to criminal conduct are transient, and because most adolescents will outgrow their tendency to get involved in crime as they mature. . . . Although most impulsive young risk takers mature into adults with different values, some adult criminals are impulsive, sensation-seeking risk takers who discount future consequences and focus on the here and now. Are these adolescent-like adults also less culpable than other adult offenders and deserving of reduced punishment? I think not. Unlike the typical adolescent, the predispositions, values, and preferences that motivate the adult offenders are not developmental but characterological, and they are unlikely to change merely with the passage of time. Adolescent traits that contribute to criminal conduct are normative of adolescence, but they are not typical in adulthood. In an adult, these traits are often part of the personal identity of an individual who does not respect the values of the criminal law and who deserves punishment when he or she violates its prohibitions (Scott & Steinberg 2008).

Competence of Adolescents to Stand Trial

Before discussing adolescents' competence to stand trial, it is worth underscoring the distinction between competence and culpability. . . . Competence to stand trial refers to the ability of an individual to function effectively as a defendant in a criminal or delinquency proceeding. In contrast, determinations of culpability focus on the defendant's blameworthiness in engaging in the criminal conduct and on whether and to what extent he will be held responsible. Although many of the same incapacities that excuse or mitigate criminal responsibility may also render a defendant incompetent, the two issues are analytically distinct and separate legal inquiries, and they focus on the defendant's mental state at two different points in time (the time of the crime and the time of the court proceeding).

The reason that competence is required of defendants in criminal proceedings is simple: When the state asserts its power against an individual with the goal of taking away his liberty, the accused must be capable of participating in a meaningful way in the proceeding against him. . . .

In 1960, the Supreme Court announced a legal standard for trial competence in *Dusky v. United States* that has since been adopted uniformly by American courts. . . . [T]here are two parts to the competence requirement: The defendant must be able to consult with her attorney about planning and making decisions in her defense, and she must understand the charges, the meaning, and purpose of the proceedings and the consequences of conviction (Scott & Grisso 2005). . . .

The competence requirement is functional at its core, speaking to questions about the impact of cognitive deficiencies on trial participation. Functionally it makes no difference if the defendant cannot understand the proceeding she faces or assist her attorney, whether due to mental illness or to immaturity (Scott & Grisso 2005). In either case, the fairness of the proceeding is undermined. In short, the same concerns that support the prohibition against trying criminal defendants who are incompetent due to mental impairment apply with equal force when immature youths are subject to criminal proceedings. . . .

Three broad types of abilities are implicated under the *Dusky* standard for competence to stand trial: (*a*) a factual understanding of the proceedings, (*b*) a rational understanding of the proceedings, and (*c*) the ability to assist counsel (Scott & Grisso 2005). . . .

Factual understanding focuses on the defendant's knowledge and awareness of the charges and his understanding of available pleas, possible penalties, the general steps in the adjudication process, the roles of various participants in the pretrial and trial process, and his rights as a defendant. Intellectual immaturity in juveniles may undermine factual understanding, especially given that youths generally have less experience and more limited ability to grasp concepts such as rights. . . .

The rational understanding requirement of *Dusky* has been interpreted to mean that defendants must comprehend the implications, relevance, or significance of what they understand factually regarding the trial process. . . . Intellectual, emotional, and psychosocial immaturity may undermine the ability of some adolescents to grasp accurately the meaning and significance of matters that they seem to understand factually.

Finally, the requirement that the defendant in a criminal proceeding must have the capacity to assist counsel encompasses three types of abilities. The first is the ability to receive and communicate information adequately to allow counsel to prepare a defense. This ability may be compromised by impairments in attention, memory, and concentration, deficits that might undermine the defendant's ability to respond to instructions or to provide important information to his attorney. . . . Second, the ability to assist counsel requires a rational perspective regarding the attorney and her role, free of notions or attitudes that could impair the collaborative relationship. . . . Third, defendants must have the capacity to make decisions about pleading and the waiver or assertion of other constitutional rights. These decisions involve not only adequate factual and rational understanding, but also the ability to consider alternatives. . . . Immature youths may lack capacities to process information and exercise reason adequately in making trial decisions. . . .

As juveniles' competence to stand trial began to emerge as an important issue in the mid-1990s, the need for a comprehensive study comparing the abilities of adolescents and adults in this realm became apparent. . . . In response to that need, the MacArthur Foundation Research Network on Adolescent Development and Juvenile Justice sponsored a large-scale study of individuals between the ages of 11 and 24—half of whom were in the custody of the justice system and half of whom had never been detained—designed to examine . . . the relationship between developmental immaturity and the abilities of young defendants to participate in their trials (Grisso et al. 2003). The study also probed age differences in psychosocial influences on decision making in the criminal process.

Based on participants' responses to a structured interview . . . the researchers found that competence-related abilities improve significantly between the ages of 11 and 16 . . . There were no differences between the 16- and 17-year-olds and the young adults. . . . Nearly one-third of 11- to 13-year-olds and about one-fifth of 14- and 15-year-olds, but only 12 % of individuals 16 and older, evidenced impairment at a level comparable to mentally ill adults who had been found incompetent to stand trial with respect to either their ability to reason with facts or understand the trial process. Individual performance did not differ significantly by gender, ethnicity, or, in the detained groups, as a function of the extent of individuals' prior justice system experience. This last finding is important because it indicates that there are components of immaturity independent of a lack of relevant experience that may contribute to elevated rates of incompetence among juveniles.

A different structured interview was used to probe how psychosocial influences affect decision making by assessing participants' choices in three hypothetical legal situations involving a police interrogation, consultation with a defense attorney, and the evaluation of a proffered plea agreement. Significant age differences were found in responses to police interrogation and to the plea agreement. First, youths, including 16- to 17-year-olds, were much more likely to recommend waiving constitutional rights during an interrogation than were adults, with 55% of 11- to 13-year-olds, 40% of 14- to 15-year-olds, and 30% of 16- to 17-year-olds choosing to "talk and admit" involvement in an alleged offense (rather than "remaining silent"), but only 15% of the young adults making this choice. There were also significant age differences in response to the plea agreement. . . . [T]hese results suggest a much stronger tendency for adolescents than for young adults to make choices in compliance with the perceived desires of authority figures (Grisso et al. 2003). . . .

This research provides powerful and tangible evidence that some youths facing criminal charges may function less capably as criminal defendants than do their adult counterparts. This does not mean, of course, that all youths should be automatically deemed incompetent to stand trial any more than would a psychiatric diagnosis or low IQ score. It does mean, however, that the risk of incompetence is substantially elevated in early and mid-adolescence; it also means that policy makers and practitioners must address developmental incompetence as it affects the treatment of juveniles in court (Scott & Grisso 2005). . . .

Impact of Punitive Sanctions on Adolescent Development and Behavior

[T]he increasingly punitive orientation of the justice system toward juvenile offenders has resulted in an increase in the number of juveniles tried and sanctioned as adults and in the use of harsher sanctions in responding to the delinquent behavior of juveniles who have been retained in the juvenile justice system. Research on the impact of adult prosecution and punishment and on the use of punitive sanctions . . . suggests, . . . that these policies and practices may actually increase recidivism and jeopardize the development and mental health of juveniles (Fagan 2008). Consequently, there is a growing consensus among social scientists that policies and practices, such as setting the minimum age of criminal court jurisdiction below 18 (as about one-third of all states currently do), transferring juveniles to the adult system for a wide range of crimes, including nonviolent crimes, relying on incarceration as a primary means of crime control, and exposing juvenile offenders to punitive programs such as boot camps, likely do more harm than good, cost taxpayers much more than they need spend on crime prevention, and ultimately pose a threat to public safety (Greenwood 2006).

In order to understand why this is the case, it is important to begin with a distinction between adolescence-limited and life-course-persistent offenders (Moffitt 1993). Dozens of longitudinal studies have shown that the vast majority of adolescents who commit antisocial acts desist from such activity as they mature into adulthood and that only a small percentage—between five and ten percent, according to most studies—become chronic offenders. . . . This observation is borne out in inspection of what criminologists refer to as the age-crime curve, which shows that the incidence of criminal activity increases between preadolescence and late adolescence, peaks at about age 17 (slightly younger for nonviolent crimes and slightly older for violent ones), and declines thereafter. . . .

In view of the fact that most juvenile offenders mature out of crime . . . one must . . . ask how to best hold delinquent youth responsible for their actions and deter future crime . . . without adversely affecting their mental health, psychological development, and successful transition into adult roles. . . .

Within the juvenile system, of course, there is wide variation in the types and severity of sanctions to which offenders are exposed. Some youths are incarcerated in prison-like training schools, whereas others receive loosely supervised community probation—neither of which is effective at changing antisocial behavior. An important question therefore is, what can the juvenile system offer young offenders that will be effective at reducing recidivism? . . .

In general, successful programs are those that attend to the lessons of developmental psychology, seeking to provide young offenders with supportive social contexts and to assist them in acquiring the skills necessary to change problem behavior and to attain psychosocial maturity. In his comprehensive meta-analysis of 400 juvenile programs, Lipsey (1995) found that among the most effective programs in both community and institutional settings were those that focused on improving social development skills in the areas of interpersonal relations, self-control, academic performance, and job skills. Some effective programs focus directly on developing skills to avoid antisocial behavior, often through cognitive behavioral therapy. Other interventions that have been shown to have a positive effect on crime reduction focus on strengthening family support, including Multisystemic Therapy, Functional Family Therapy, and Multidimensional Treatment Foster Care, all of which are both effective and cost effective (Greenwood 2006). . . . Punishment-oriented approaches, such as "Scared Straight" or military-style boot camps, do not deter future crime and may even inadvertently promote reoffending. . . .

[A]dolescence is a formative period of development. In mid and late adolescence, individuals normally make substantial progress in acquiring and coordinating skills that are essential to filling the conventional roles of adulthood. First, they begin to develop basic educational and vocational skills to enable them to function in the workplace as productive members of society. Second, they also acquire the social skills necessary to establish stable intimate relationships and to cooperate in groups. Finally, they must begin to learn to behave responsibly without external supervision and to set meaningful personal goals for themselves. For most individuals, the process of completing these developmental tasks extends into early adulthood, but making substantial progress during the formative stage of adolescence is important. This process of development toward psychosocial maturity is one of reciprocal interaction between the individual and her social context. Several environmental conditions are particularly important, such as the presence of an authoritative parent or guardian, association with prosocial peers, and participation in educational, extracurricular, or employment activities that facilitate the development of autonomous decision making and critical thinking. For the youth in the justice system, the correctional setting becomes the environment for social development and may affect whether he acquires the skills necessary to function successfully in conventional adult roles (Steinberg et al. 2004).

Normative teenagers who get involved in crime do so, in part, because their choices are driven by developmental influences typical of adolescence. In theory, they should desist from criminal behavior and mature into reasonably responsible adults as they attain psychosocial maturity—and most do, especially as they enter into adult work and family responsibilities. Whether youths successfully make the transition to adulthood, however, depends in part on whether their social context provides opportunity structures for the completion of the developmental tasks described above. The correctional environment may influence the trajectories of normative adolescents in the justice system in important ways. Factors such as the availability (or lack) of good educational, skill building, and rehabilitative programs; the attitudes and roles of adult supervisors; and the identity and behavior of other offenders shape the social context of youths in both the adult and the juvenile systems. These factors may affect the inclination of young offenders to desist or persist in their criminal activities and may facilitate or impede their development into adults who can function adequately in society. . . .

Summary

. . . Although justice system policy and practice cannot, and should not, be dictated solely by studies of adolescent development, the ways in which we respond to juvenile offending should at the very least be informed by the lessons of developmental science. Taken together, the lessons of developmental science offer strong support for the maintenance of a separate juvenile justice system in which adolescents are judged, tried, and sanctioned in developmentally appropriate ways. . . .

Reference

Lipsey M. 1995. What do we learn from 400 research studies on the effectiveness of treatment with juvenile delinquents? In *What Works? Reducing Reoffending,* ed. J McGuire, pp. 63–78. New York: Wiley

Moffitt T. 1993. Adolescence-limited and life-course persistent antisocial behavior: a developmental taxonomy. *Psychol. Rev.* 100:674–701

Roper v. Simmons, 541 U.S. 1040 2005

Scott E, Grisso T. 2005. Developmental incompetence, due process, and juvenile justice policy. *N. C. Law Rev.* 83:793–846

Scott E, Steinberg L. 2008. *Rethinking Juvenile Justice.* Cambridge, MA: Harvard Univ. Press.

Steinberg L, Chung H, Little M. 2004. Reentry of young offenders from the justice system: a developmental perspective. *Youth Violence Juv. Just,* 1:21–38

EXPLORING THE ISSUE

Should Juvenile Offenders Be Tried and Convicted as Adults?

Critical Thinking and Reflection

1. Is there enough evidence in this issue to support a juvenile justice system separate from the adult system?
2. If adolescents are treated less harshly by the criminal justice system, will there be more incidents of crime in the future? Will there be more violent crime?
3. At present, most transfers to adult court are a function of age and seriousness of a crime (e.g., murder). Should the decision to transfer youth to adult court remain as it is? Should brain development be considered? How would "mature" be determined? Is there an upper age where examining brain development is not longer necessary?
4. Imagine you are the parent (or the sibling) of a 15-year-old who was brutally assaulted by a 16-year-old. What penalty would you want for the 16-year-old?
5. Imagine you are the parent (or the sibling) of a 16-year-old who brutally assaulted a 15-year-old. What penalty would you want for your son/daughter/brother/sister?
6. Should policies regarding juvenile justice reflect public sentiment? Are individual rights more important than collective rights or how can we balance the two?

Is There Common Ground?

Steinberg argues that the way we respond to juvenile offending should be somewhat guided by developmental science. He explains the factors that reduce culpability among adolescents, which he argues should reduce the grade of an offense and subsequently the punishment. Steinberg recommends a separate justice system for adolescents with a focus on rehabilitation, more lenient punishments, and laws prohibiting execution. Many brain researchers support Steinberg's argument stating that structurally, the brain is still growing and maturing during adolescence. For example, Jay Giedd (2004) of the National Institute of Mental Health (NIMH) considers 25 the age at which the brain has reached maturity. Because the adolescent brain is not fully developed, adolescents are more prone to erratic behavior driven by emotions and are not as morally culpable as adults.

Stimson and Grossman don't dispute brain development or a separate justice system for youth but they do argue that for *serious* offenses (e.g., murder), trying juveniles in adult court and imposing adult sentences do not violate human rights and do not violate the U.S. law. Their argument (based on their review) is that life without parole is both effective and appropriate because youth who commit adult crimes should be treated as adults. The U.S. law views adolescent decision making much the same as Stimson and Grossman. Essentially, past the age of 14 years, adolescents are competent decision makers under the informed-consent model as long as they are of average or above-average intelligence and can make a knowing, voluntary, intelligent decision (Ambuel & Rappaport, 1992). Steinberg, however, argues that the informed-consent model is inadequate because it overemphasizes the cognitive components at the expense of the noncognitive components (e.g., social factors such as peer influence) that may influence mature judgment and sound decision making. Adolescents at 14 may or may not have the cognitive capacity necessary to make good choices and therefore deciding on an exact age for informed consent or transfer to adult court is impossible. According the Steinberg, the age is more likely to be over 16. He states that adolescents older than 16 are more likely to have adult-like capacities but those under 16 are not. Each case must be examined carefully.

Additional Resources

Ambuel, B., & Rappaport, J. (1992). Developmental trends in adolescents' psychological and legal competence to consent to abortion. *Law and Human Behavior, 16*, 129–154.

> The authors of this article argue that minors are not competent decision makers with respect to consenting to abortion.

Beckman, M. (2004). Crime, culpability, and the adolescent brain. *Science, 305*, 596–599.

Giedd, J. N. (2004). Structural magnetic resonance imaging of the adolescent brain. *Annals of the New York Academy of Science, 1021*, 77–85.

Grisso, T., Steinberg, L., Woolard, J., Cauffman, E., Scott, E., Graham, S., et al. (2003). Juveniles' competence to stand trial: A comparison of adolescents' and adults' capacities as trial defendants. *Law and Human Behavior, 27*, 333–363.

Loughran, T., Mulvey, E., Schubert, C., Chassin, L., Steinberg, L., Piquero, A., et al. (2010). Differential effects of adult court transfer on juvenile offender recidivism. *Law and Human Behavior, 34*, 476–488.

> This research article examines the effect of transfer of adolescents to adult court on later crime. The sample consisted of serious juvenile offenders, 29 percent of whom were transferred. Results indicated no difference in re-arrest between those transferred to adult court and those retained in the juvenile system but there were differences based on offending histories. Transferred adolescents who committed "person" crimes showed lower rates of re-arrest.

Mears, D. P., Hay, C., Gertz, M., & Mancini, C. (2007). Public opinion and the foundation of the juvenile court. *Criminology, 45* (1), 223–257.

> This study examines public views about abolishing juvenile justice and the upper age of original juvenile court jurisdiction. Results suggest, "support for the lingering appeal of juvenile justice among the public and the idea that youth can be 'saved' as well as arguments about the politicization and criminalization of juvenile justice" (p. 223).

Office of Juvenile Justice and Delinquency Prevention. (1999). *Juvenile justice: A century of change.* Washington, DC: Office of Juvenile Justice.

Shook, J. J. (2005). Contesting childhood in the US justice system: The transfer of juveniles to adult criminal court. *Childhood, 12*, 461–478.

Statistics Canada. (1997 through 2000). *Youth court statistics.* Ottawa: Canadian Centre for Justice Statistics.

Streib, V. L. (2003). The juvenile death penalty today: Death sentences and executions for juvenile crimes, January 1, 1973–June 30, 2003. Retrieved from www.law.onu.edu/faculty/streib

Tonry, M. (2007). Treating juveniles as adult criminals. *American Journal of Preventive Medicine, 32*(4S), S3-S4.

> A report from the Task Force on Community Preventive Services examines whether transfers reduce or prevent violent crimes by youth under age 18. They conclude that youth transferred have higher rates of future violent crime compared to younger youth not transferred. The report also determines that there is insufficient evidence to reach conclusions regarding general deterrence.

Tuell, J. A. (2002). *Juvenile offenders and the death penalty.* Washington, DC: Child Welfare League of America. National Center for Program Standards and Development.

Contributors to This Volume

EDITORS

TONI SERAFINI is an assistant professor in the Department of Sexuality, Marriage, and Family Studies at St. Jerome's University in the University of Waterloo. She received her PhD in family relations and human development, and her MSc in couple and family therapy. Serafini teaches courses on parent, child, and family relationships; relationship formation, maintenance, and conflict/crisis; human sexuality; communication and counseling skills; research methods; and introductory psychology. She also has over 15 years of clinical experience; much of this has been with adolescents and their families in both counseling and residential settings, and concerning issues such as violence and abuse, family relationships, child and adolescent behavioral problems, and mental health concerns. Serafini's research interests are related to identity formation across the life span. She developed and validated an instrument to measure identity functions, which has been translated into several languages and is used internationally, and has examined how identity is shaped through transformative experiences. She is also interested in the role of critical self-reflection in teaching and learning, and how self-reflective processes contribute to identity development. Her work has been published in journals such as *Identity: An International Journal of Theory and Research; Testing, Psychometrics, Methodology in Applied Psychology*; and *Child & Family Journal.*

B.J. RYE is an associate professor of psychology and teaches within the Sexuality, Marriage, and Family Studies program at St. Jerome's University at the University of Waterloo in Waterloo, Ontario, Canada. Rye teaches such courses as Introduction to Human Sexuality, The Psychology of Gender, and The Psychology of Sexual Orientation. Her research focuses on attitudes toward sexual-minority groups (e.g., attitudes toward gay and lesbian parenting, persons with HIV/AIDS, transgender individuals, and intersex people) and mental health and prevention approaches (e.g., school dropout, perceptions of teacher, and classmate support). She has also evaluated the efficacy of sexual health education programs and interventions as well as investigated sexual health behavior practices from social psychological perspectives. Her writings have appeared in such journals as *Canadian Journal of the Behavioural Sciences, The Journal of Homosexuality*, and *The Canadian Journal of Human Sexuality.* She received her PhD in social psychology from the University of Western Ontario with a specialization in human sexuality.

MAUREEN DRYSDALE is an associate professor of psychology, and sexuality, marriage, and family studies at St. Jerome's University in the University of Waterloo. She is also an associate with the Waterloo Centre for the Advancement of Co-operative Education (WatCACE; www.watcace.uwaterloo.ca/). Drysdale teaches courses in adolescence, educational psychology, abnormal child psychology, and statistics. Her research primarily examines school-to-work transitions and the many factors that impact learning and achievement at the secondary and postsecondary education levels. This includes examining the learning environments and learning outcomes of students with emotional and behavioral problems; the relationship between adolescent self-concept/self-esteem and educational outcomes; and general adolescent transitions. Of particular interest is the role of experiential education on adolescent transitions. She is currently examining whether work-integrated learning has an effect on self-concept/self-esteem, tacit knowledge, hope, procrastination, study skills, and the overall transition from postsecondary education to the workplace. Maureen has presented her research findings at numerous professional conferences (SRA, CPA, AERA, CEIA, and WACE) and has been published in journals such as *The Journal for Students Placed at Risk*, *Exceptionality Education Canada*, *The Journal of Neurotherapy*, *The Asia Pacific Journal of Cooperative Education*, and the *Journal of Cooperative Education*. She received her PhD in teaching, learning, and human development from the University of Calgary.

AUTHORS

SHARLENE AZAM is a journalist, author, and filmmaker. She was the founder of two youth magazines, a weekly columnist for the Toronto Star, and was named one of the *"100 Canadians to Watch"* by Maclean's Magazine. She is the author of the recently published *Rogue, Rebel, Mischievous Babe: A Survival Guide for Canadian Teen Girls.*

LEE BAER is an associate chief of psychology in the Department of Psychiatry at Massachusetts General Hospital and clinical professor of psychology in the Department of Psychiatry at Harvard Medical School, both in Boston, Massachusetts.

MARIE T. BANICH is a professor of psychology at the University of Colorado Boulder, where she also serves as the director of the Institute of Cognitive Science, a multidisciplinary institute dedicated to exploring the science of the mind.

MARK A. BELLIS is a professor at Liverpool John Moores University in the UK. He is also the director of the Centre for Public Health, the North West Public Health Observatory, and the NICE National Collaborating Centre for Drug Prevention. His research includes alcohol and drug use, sexual behaviour, violence, and public health intelligence.

EUGENE V. BERESIN is a professor of psychology at Harvard University. He is also the director of Child and Adolescent Psychiatry in the Psychiatry Residency at McLean Hospital.

DEENA BERKOWITZ is a pediatric emergency department physician. Her clinical and research interests include laser-assisted penetration of topical anesthesia in children.

BETSY DI BENEDETTO GULLEDGE is an instructor of nursing at Jacksonville State University.

JENNIFER BRUNET is a postdoctoral fellow in the Department of Social and Preventive Medicine at the Université de Montréal and the School of Nursing at McGill University. Her research interest is in health and well-being, and in particular on identifying psychological and social factors that may increase physical activity levels.

RICHARD F. CATALANO is the Bartley Dobb Professor for the study and prevention of violence in the School of Social Work, and the director of the Social Development Research Group at the University of Washington in Seattle, Washington. He is also an adjunct professor of education and sociology.

ELIZABETH CAUFFMAN is a professor of psychology and social behavior and education at University of California, Irvine. She specializes in adolescent development, mental health, juvenile justice, and legal and social policy.

TERESA STANTON COLLETT is a professor at the School of Law, University of St. Thomas. She writes about marriage, abortion, religion, and bioethics.

CHARLENE COOK is the manager of research, public policy, and evaluation at United Way of Toronto, Ontario, Canada.

PENNY A. COOK leads sexual health research on behalf of the Centre for Public Health at the Liverpool John Moores University in the UK. Her research interests include alcohol use, sexual health, HIV, and AIDS.

MICHELLE CRETELLA is a pediatrician and board member of the American College of Pediatricians. Her research interests include preventative medicine, learning disabilities, and adolescent health.

MING CUI is an assistant professor in the Department of Family and Child Sciences at Florida State University. Her research interests include marital and interpersonal relationships, parenting, adolescent and young adult development, and research methods and statistics.

JOANNE DACIUK is a research manager at Factor-Inwentash Faculty of Social Work, University of Toronto.

CYNTHIA DAILARD was a senior public policy associate at the Guttmacher Institute, a nonprofit research and advocacy group on women's sexual and reproductive health issues. Before joining Guttmacher, she was associate director for domestic policy for President Bill Clinton, legislative assistant, and counsel for Senator. Olympia J. Snowe, and a fellow at the National Women's Law Center. Her work focused on issues around family planning, adolescent sexual behavior, and insurance coverage for contraception.

PAMELA E. DAVIS-KEAN is an associate professor in psychology, and research associate professor at the Institute for Social Research and Center for Human Growth and Development at the University of Michigan. Her research interests include parental education and family home environment, the importance of race and culture in family and child development, education and child development, and self-esteem development across the lifespan.

KIM. D. DORSCH is an associate professor in the University of Regina's Faculty of Kinesiology, Centre for Kinesiology, Health and Sport. Her research spans sport psychology, health psychology, athletic performance, officiating performance, and group dynamics in sport.

NICOLE B. ELLISON is an associate professor in the Department of Telecommunication, Information Studies, and Media at Michigan State University. She studies the ways in which new information and communication technologies shape social processes, and vice versa. Some of this work focuses on the social capital implications of social network site use and issues of self-presentation, relationship formation and maintenance, and impression formation in online contexts.

ÖZGÜR ERDUR-BAKER is an associate professor in the Department of Educational Sciences at Middle East Technical University. Her research interests include outcome and process research in counseling, gender and culture sensitive counseling, peer bullying (traditional and cyber bullying), trauma, grief, and disaster psychology.

CHRISTOPHER J. FERGUSON is an assistant professor of psychology at Texas A&M International University. He studies violent behavior, examining the combined impact of genetics, family environment, personality, mental health, and media violence and more recently on the positive and negative effects of playing violent video games.

BONNIE S. FISHER is a professor in the Division of Criminal Justice and research fellow in the Center for Criminal Justice Research at the University of Cincinnati. Her research focuses on issues concerning crimes against and within small businesses, fear of crime, crime prevention and security, and the measurement of victimization and attitudes.

WYNDOL FURMAN is a professor in the University of Denver psychology department. His research interests are centered around the study of close relationships in childhood, adolescence, and early adulthood.

TAHANY M. GADALLA is an associate professor at the Factor-Inwentash Faculty of Social Work, University of Toronto. Her research covers identification of determinants, correlates and risk factors for mental ill-health, as well as the impact of mental ill-health on disability and quality of life.

E. JANE GARLAND is a clinical professor of psychiatry and clinical head of the Mood and Anxiety Disorders Clinic at BC's Children's Hospital at the University of British Columbia. Her work focuses on mood and anxiety disorders in young people.

K.H. GINZEL is a retired medical doctor and professor emeritus of pharmacology and toxicology at the University of Arkansas for Medical Sciences.

PEGGY C. GIORDANO is a sociology professor at Bowling Green State University. Her interests include the nature of peer influence and its specific role in the etiology of problem outcomes.

LAWRENCE O. GOSTIN is a professor at Georgetown Law, Faculty Director of the O'Neill Institute for National and Global Health Law, and Director and Principal Investigator for the Center for Law and the Public's Health. His research areas are constitutional law, health law and policy, bioethics, and human rights law.

SANDRA GRAHAM is a professor in the Department of Education and Information Studies at UCLA (University of California, Los Angeles). Her teaching interests lie in motivation and educational attribution theory, social psychology of education, and educational psychology.

ANDREW M. GROSSMAN is a visiting legal fellow in The Heritage Foundation's Center for Legal and Judicial Studies, where he researches and writes about law and finance, bankruptcy, national security law, and the constitutional issue of separation of powers.

KERIN HANNON is a research associate with the Health Sciences Research Group at the University of Manchester.

K. Paige HARDEN is an assistant professor of psychology at the University of Texas at Austin. Her research is broadly concerned with adolescent developmental psychopathology.

SHERYL A. HEMPHILL is a research professor at the School of Psychology, Australian Catholic University, and an honorary principal research fellow at the Centre for Adolescent Health, Department of Paediatrics, at the University of Melbourne.

BILLY HENSON is an assistant professor of criminal justice at Shippensburg University of Pennsylvania. His research interests include victimology, criminology, policing, and criminal justice in popular culture.

KATE HOLT is a researcher associated with the psychology department at Deakin University, Australia.

KAREN HUGHES is a behavioral epidemiologist and head of Violence and Nightlife Research at Liverpool John Moores University in the UK. Her current research examines violence and risk behaviors among young people, and environmental factors that influence health in nightlife.

SARA HUGHES works at the Centre for Public Health, Faculty of Applied Health and Social Sciences at the Liverpool John Moores University in the UK.

JOYCE HUNTER is a research scientist at the HIV Center and assistant professor of clinical psychiatric social work (in psychiatry) and assistant professor of sociomedical sciences, both at Columbia University. Her work centers on HIV/AIDS prevention for women, youth, and families; combating homophobia for LGBT youth; HIV/STD risk behaviors and best health practices for at-risk and HIV-positive youth; and needs of street, runaway, and homeless youth across racially and culturally diverse populations and families.

JUSTIN JAGER is a post-doctoral research fellow with the *Research Center for Group Dynamics* within the Child and Family Research Section of the National Institute of Child Health and Human Development (NICHD). His research focuses on pathways or models of development and how person–context interactions inform developmental trajectories across adolescence and the transition to adulthood, as well as family systems and family functioning and relationships.

GAIL JAVITT is a research scholar at Johns Hopkins Berman Institute of Bioethics and an adjunct professor at the Georgetown University Law Center. The focus of her work is on developing policy options to guide the development and use of reproductive technologies and she is currently leading an initiative to improve oversight of genetic testing quality

CYNTHIA L. JOINER is a registered nurse and nurse research manager at the University of Alabama.

LISA JONES is the evidence review and research manager in the substance review team at the Centre for Public Health at John Moores University in the UK. She manages a team undertaking evidence review and other research in the field of drug and alcohol prevention and treatment and related public health topics.

MIN JUNG KIM has published work with the Social Development Research Group of Seattle, Washington, and researchers in the psychology department at Deakin University, Australia.

AMY KRAMER is the director of Entertainment Media and Audience Strategy at The National Campaign to Prevent Teen and Unplanned Pregnancy, a private and independent nonprofit organization working to promote values, behavior, and policies that reduce both teen pregnancy and unplanned pregnancy, especially among single, young adults.

DEREK A. KREAGER is an associate professor of sociology and crime, law, and justice at Pennsylvania State University. His research interests include juvenile delinquency and adolescent development, and he examines how adolescent social networks either inhibit or contribute to individual criminal behaviors.

LAWRENCE A. KUTNER is the author of several books about child psychology and parent–child communication. He's a licensed psychologist, a fellow of the American Psychological Association, and co-founder of the Harvard Medical School Center for Mental Health and Media.

STAN KUTCHER is a professor of psychiatry at Dalhousie University, staff psychiatrist at IWK Health Centre, Sunlife financial chair in Adolescent Mental Health, and the director of the WHO Collaborating Centre. His current interests include translating mental health research into clinical care, patient and parent empowerment, health systems/health policy, and optimization of mental health care/mental health clinical research through the training of community-based healthy human resources in primary care.

CLIFF LAMPE is a professor in the School of Information at the University of Michigan. His research includes work on interactions in "social computing" sites, such as Slashdot and Facebook.

MONICA A. LONGMORE is a professor of sociology at Bowling Green State University. She specializes in social psychology and family relations, and her current interests include adolescence, fertility-related outcomes, and social psychological processes.

HEIDI LYONS is an assistant professor of sociology and anthropology at Oakland University. Her research interests include family, population, social demography, sex and gender, quantitative and qualitative methods, intimate dyads, and the life course.

WENDY D. MANNING is a professor of sociology at Bowling Green State University. Her interests include complex family relationships, cohabitation and fertility in cohabiting unions, and adolescent relationships.

DOUGLAS M. MAURER is the program director of the Family Medicine Residency Program at the Carl R. Darnall Army Medical Center at the Uniformed Services University of the Health Sciences, Texas.

MARITA P. MCCABE is an Alfred Deakin professor of psychology and chair of psychology at Deakin University. She is also the director of the Centre for Mental Health and Wellbeing Research. She is the associate editor for *Body Image* and *Journal of Sexual Medicine* and is on the editorial board for the *Journal of Sex Research* and the *International Journal of Psychology*. She conducts research on the sexual dysfunction, the development and evaluation of intervention programs to treat these sexual dysfunctions, body image, and the evaluation of treatment programs to address psychological problems among older people and those in palliative care.

DONALD R. MCCREARY is a senior research psychologist and leader of the Resilience Group at Defence Research and Development Canada in Toronto, Canada, as well as an adjunct professor of psychology at both York University (Toronto) and Brock University (St. Catharines).

BARBARA J. MCMORRIS is an associate professor at the University of Minnesota's School of Nursing. Her research focuses on risk and protective factors and youth development, including substance use, related violent or delinquent behaviors, and prosocial academic competency.

JANE MENDLE is an assistant professor of psychology at the University of Oregon. Her work particularly concentrates on pubertal development, and why it may hold more resonance and present more of a stumbling block for some children compared to others.

FAYE MISHNA is the dean of the Factor-Inwentash Faculty of Social Work, University of Toronto, and holds the Margaret and Wallace McCain Family Chair in Child and Family. Her research areas include bullying, cyber abuse/cyber bullying and cyber counseling, and school-based interventions for students with learning disabilities.

MICHELA MORLEO is the alcohol research manager of the Centre for Public Health at the Liverpool John Moores University in the UK.

ARMAND NICHOLI II is a clinical professor of psychiatry at Harvard Medical School and the Massachusetts General Hospital. His clinical work and research have focused on the impact of absent parents on the emotional development of children and young adults.

CHERYL K. OLSON is a public health and education researcher and practitioner. She is a former member of the psychiatry faculty of Harvard Medical School and teen issues columnist for *Parents* magazine. While at Massachusetts General Hospital, she co-founded the HMS Center for Mental Health and Media, an outreach, production, and research center devoted to mental health, behavioral health, and healthy child development. Her research on the effects of electronic games on preteens and teenagers led to a co-authored book, *Grand Theft Childhood: The Surprising Truth About Violent Video Games, and What Parents Can Do.*

CHARLOTTE J. PATTERSON is a professor in the University of Virginia's Department of Psychology and its Center for Children, Families, and the

Law. She is also the director of the interdisciplinary program Women, Gender, and Sexuality (WGS), and her research focuses on the psychology of sexual orientation, with an emphasis on sexual orientation, human development, and family lives.

PENELOPE A. PHILLIPS-HOWARD is a reader and the head of International Public Health Team at Liverpool John Moores University in the UK. Her current research is focused on the resolution of public health issues in the northwest, including alcohol, sexual health, obesity, and child well-being.

MARY JO PODGURSKI is the founder and president of the Academy for Adolescent Health, Inc. A nurse/educator/counselor by profession, she considers parenting her kids to be her first and most important career.

BRADFORD W. REYNS is an assistant professor in the Department of Criminal Justice at Weber State University and the book review editor for *Security Journal*. His research focuses on victims of crime, especially the intersection of technology and victimization, and opportunities for victimization.

LINA A. RICCIARDELLI is a senior researcher and associate professor of psychology at Deakin University. Her research interests include health psychology, developmental psychology, body image and disordered eating, substance use and abuse, and depression in young children.

MARGARET ROSARIO is an associate professor of psychology, Social Sciences Division, at the City College of New York. Her research includes psychosocial processes that influence health and adaptational functioning of populations at extreme risk for poor health.

IRENE M. ROSEN is the deputy chief of the Department of Family Medicine and Clinical Instructor at Madigan Army Medical Center, Fort Lewis, Washington.

CATHERINE M. SABISTON is an associate professor in the Faculty of Kinesiology and Physical Education at the McGill University, Montreal, Canada. Her areas of research interest are exercise and health psychology: psychosocial determinants of health behavior, body-related emotions, and physical self.

ERIC W. SCHRIMSHAW is an assistant professor of sociomedical sciences at Columbia University. His research interests focus on the role of interpersonal factors on health and well-being

LAUREN B. SHOMAKER is a postdoctoral research scientist and an adjunct assistant professor in the Department of Medical and Clinical Psychology, Uniformed Services University of the Health Sciences. Her research focuses on understanding eating behaviors in childhood and adolescence that promote the development of obesity and eating disorders.

SIECCAN (THE SEX INFORMATION AND EDUCATION COUNCIL OF CANADA) is a national registered charitable organization founded in 1964 to foster professional education and public knowledge about sexuality and sexual health. It publishes manuscripts from a variety of disciplines related to the study of human sexuality in a quarterly peer-reviewed journal, *The Canadian Journal of Human Sexuality*.

LINDA SMALLTHWAITE is principal of TSO/SAO of Warrington & Halton Trading Standards, a UK company that aims to create a fair, safe, and healthier trading environment for consumers and honest businesses through enforcement of a wide variety of consumer statutes and by offering a comprehensive advice service.

STEVEN SOLOMON is a school social worker for the Toronto District school board coordinating the Triangle Program, a human sexuality program.

JEREMY STAFF is an associate professor of sociology and crime, law, and justice at Pennsylvania State University. His research interests focus on criminology, life course studies, and stratification.

LAURENCE STEINBERG is the distinguished university professor and Laura H. Carnell professor of psychology at Temple University. He has authored over 300 articles and essays, and numerous books on growth and development during the teenage years. His research interests span adolescent brain, behavioral, and psychosocial development; parent–child relationships; developmental psychopathology; juvenile justice; and the implications of developmental research for legal and social policy. Steinberg has been the recipient of numerous honors, including lifetime achievement awards from the Society for Research on Adolescence and the American Psychological Association and teaching awards from the University of California, the University of Wisconsin, and Temple University.

CHARLES STEINFIELD is a professor in the Telecommunication, Information Studies, and Media Department at Michigan State University. His research interests include electronic commerce, online social networks, organizations, and information technology.

CHARLES D. STIMSON is a senior legal fellow at The Heritage Foundation. His expertise is in recognizing expert in national and homeland security, criminal law, military law, military commissions and detention policy, and crime control.

JOHN W. TOUMBOUROU is the associate dean in the Faculty of Health, and professor and chair in health psychology within the School of Psychology at Deakin University. His research covers healthy youth development, include drug abuse prevention, evaluation, and the role of community, family, and peer groups in adolescent health promotion.

ADIL VIRANI is an associate professor in pharmaceutical sciences at the University of British Columbia, and the director of Lower Mainland Pharmacy Services. He has authored several handbooks and papers related to psychopharmacology and the use of psychotropic drugs with children and adolescents.

DOROTHY WARNER is a clinical associate at Brookline Community Mental Health Center, a research associate at Judge Baker Children's Center, and an instructor in psychology at Harvard Medical School—Department of Psychiatry.

TAMAR D. WOHLFARTH is an epidemiologist and senior clinical assessor for the Medicines Evaluation Board of the Netherlands.

JENNIFER WOOLARD is an associate professor in the Department of Psychology at Georgetown University. She is also the co-director of Graduate Program in Developmental Science and Research Fellow, Center for Social Justice. She conducts action research on police interrogation, culpability, the attorney–client relationship, and the role of parents in adolescents' legal decision making and has published papers on the prevention of child abuse and neglect, policy regarding female delinquency, mental health needs of juvenile delinquents, and the overlap between child maltreatment and domestic violence.

ANASTASIA S. VOGT YUAN is an associate professor in the Department of Sociology at Virginia Polytechnic Institute and State University. Her research interests include mental and physical health, substance abuse, family, childhood, adolescence, and the life course.